International Financial Institutions and International Law

Kluwer Law International

International Financial Institutions and International Law

Edited By

Daniel D. Bradlow and David B. Hunter

Wolters Kluwer
Law & Business

AUSTIN BOSTON CHICAGO NEW YORK THE NETHERLANDS

Published by:
Kluwer Law International
PO Box 316
2400 AH Alphen aan den Rijn
The Netherlands
Website: www.kluwerlaw.com

Sold and distributed in North, Central and South America by:
Aspen Publishers, Inc.
7201 McKinney Circle
Frederick, MD 21704
United States of America
Email: customer.service@aspenpublishers.com

Sold and distributed in all other countries by:
Turpin Distribution Services Ltd.
Stratton Business Park
Pegasus Drive, Biggleswade
Bedfordshire SG18 8TQ
United Kingdom
Email: kluwerlaw@turpin-distribution.com

Printed on acid-free paper.

ISBN 978-90-411-2881-2

Printed in Great Britain.

Summary of Contents

Table of Contents

Acknowledgements

The editors would like to thank the various people who helped make this book possible. These include first, of course, the contributing authors who worked diligently and professionally to meet our deadlines and yet accepted with equanimity the inevitable delays that are part of the process of compiling an edited volume containing eleven separate contributions. We also would like to thank Dean Claudio Grossman for his support, both moral and material, of our research, and our colleagues at the American University Washington College of Law and the University of Pretoria who have created dynamic scholarly communities from which we have derived great support and stimulation as we laboured on this book. This book was also facilitated by the support of the Charles Stewart Mott Foundation, for which we are very thankful. Finally, and most importantly, this book would never have been completed without the tireless, enthusiastic, and professional work of Erika Lennon, the Program Coordinator of the American University Washington College of Law's Program on International and Comparative Environmental Law. She has, with good cheer and great commitment, been responsible for all of the hard work of ensuring accuracy, consistency, and clarity in this text.

Daniel D. Bradlow
David B. Hunter

List of Abbreviations

African Commission on Human and People's Rights	ACHPR
African Development Bank	AfDB
AfDB Independent Review Mechanism	IRM
Alien Tort Claims Act	ATCA
Articles on State Responsibility	ASR
Asian Development Bank	ADB
Association of Southeast Asian Nations	ASEAN
Board Inspection Committee (Asian Development Bank)	BIC
Bolivarian Alternative Plan for Latin America Bank	APLA
Bretton Woods Institutions	BWIs
Carbon Partnership Fund (World Bank)	CPF
Caribbean Basin Economic Recovery Act	CBERA
Caribbean Catastrophe Risk Insurance Facility	CCRIF
Civil Society Organization	CSO
Climate Investment Funds	CIFs
Climate Technology Fund	CTF
Committee on Economic Social and Cultural Rights	CESCR
Compliance Advisor/Ombudsman	CAO
Confederación General del Trabajo de la República Argentina	CGT
Consultative Group on International Agriculture and Research	CGIAR
Convention Against Torture	CAT
Convention for the Elimination of Discrimination Against Women	CEDAW
Convention on the Rights of the Child	CRC
Convention on the Rights of Persons with Disabilities	CRPD
Critical Ecosystem Partnership Fund	CEPF
Enhanced Structural Adjustment Facility	ESAF

Environmental and Social Impact Assessment	ESIA
Environmental Assessment	EA
European Bank for Reconstruction and Development	EBRD
EBRD Independent Recourse Mechanism	IRM
European Community	EC
European Convention on Human Rights	ECHR
European Court of Human Rights	ECtHR
European Investment Bank	EIB
Exogenous Shocks Facility	ESF
Export Credit and Insurance Agency	ECA
Federal Communications Commission (US)	FCC
Financial Stability Board	FSB
Food and Agriculture Organization of the United Nations	FAO
Foreign Direct Investment	FDI
Forest Investment Program	FIP
Forest Carbon Partnership Facility	FCPF
Foreign Sovereign Immunities Act	FSIA
Free, Prior and Informed Consent	FPIC
General Agreement on Tariffs and Trade	GATT
General Arrangement to Borrow	GAB
Global Environment Facility	GEF
Heavily Indebted Poor Countries	HIPC
Human Rights Accountability	HRA
Human Rights Impact Assessment	HRIA
Independent Evaluation Group	IEG
Inter-American Commission on Human Rights	IACHR
Inter-American Development Bank	IDB
IDB Independent Investigation Mechanism	IIM
IDIB Independent Consultation and Investigation Mechanism	ICIM
International Bank for Reconstruction and Development	IBRD
International Centre for Settlement of Investment Disputes	ICSID
International Convention on the Protection of the Rights of All Migrant Workers and Members of Their Families	MWC
International Court of Justice	ICJ
International Covenant on Civil and Political Rights	ICCPR
International Covenant on Economic, Social and Cultural Rights	ICESCR
International Development Association	IDA
International Environmental Law	IEL
International Finance Corporation	IFC
IFC's Environment and Social Review Procedure	ESRP
IFC's General Resources Account	GRA
International Financial Institution	IFI
International Fund for Agricultural Development	IFAD
International Law Association	ILA
International Law Commission	ILC

International Labour Organization	ILO
International Monetary Fund	IMF
IMF Extended Fund Facility	EFF
IMF General Resources Account	GRA
International Law Commission	ILC
International Organization	IO
International Organizations Immunities Act	IOIA
Islamic Development Bank	IsDB
Letter of Development Policy	LDP
Letter of Intent	LOI
Memorandum of Economic and Financial Policy	MEFP
Millennium Development Goal	MDG
Multilateral Development Bank	MDB
Multilateral Investment and Guarantee Agency	MIGA
New Arrangement to Borrow	NAB
Newly Industrializing Countries	NICs
New International Economic Order	NIEO
Non-Governmental Organizations	NGOs
Official Development Assistance	ODA
Operational Directive	OD
Operational Manual Policy	OMS
Operational Policy	OP
Organization for Economic Cooperation and Development	OECD
OECD Working Party on Aid Effectiveness	WP-EFF
OECD Development Assistance Committee	OECD DAC
Ozone Depleting Substances	ODS
Palestine Liberation Organization	PLO
Persistent Organic Pollutants	POPs
Pilot Program for Climate Resilience	PPCR
Policy Framework Paper	PFP
Policy Support Instrument	PSI
Poverty Reduction and Growth Facility	PRGF
Poverty Reduction Strategy Paper	PRSP
Prototype Carbon Fund	PCF
Reduce Emissions from Deforestation and Forest Degradation	REDD
Special Drawing Right	SDR
Stand-By Arrangement	SBA
Strategic Climate Fund	SCF
Structural Adjustment Credit	SAC
Structural Adjustment Facility	SAF
Structural Adjustment Loan	SAL
Structural Adjustment Participatory Review International Network	SAPRIN
Structural Adjustment Program	SAP
Third World Approach to International Law	TWAIL

Trade Promotion Authority	TPA
UK Department for International Development	DFID
United Nations	UN
United Nations Committee on the Elimination of Racial Discrimination	CERD
United Nations Declaration on the Rights of Indigenous Peoples	UNDRIP
United Nations Declaration on Human Rights	UNDHR
United Nations Development Programme	UNDP
United Nations Economic and Social Council	ECOSOC
United Nations Economic Commission on Latin America	ECLA
United Nations Educational, Scientific and Cultural Organization	UNESCO
United Nations Office of the High Commissioner for Human Rights	OHCHR
United Nations Permanent Forum on Indigenous Issues	PFII
United States Dollar ($)	USD
United States Executive Director	USED
Universal Declaration of Human Rights	UDHR
Western European Union	WEU
World Bank Group	WBG
World Bank Inspection Panel	WBIP
World Bank Office of Claims Resolution	OCR
World Development Report	WDR
World Health Organization	WHO
World Summit on Sustainable Development	WSSD
World Trade Organization	WTO

About the Authors

Co-editors

Daniel D. Bradlow

Daniel D. Bradlow is the SARCHI professor of International Development Law and African Economic Relations at the University of Pretoria in South Africa and Professor of Law at American University Washington College of Law. He is a member of the Roster of Experts for the Independent Review Mechanism at the African Development Bank. In addition, he is co-rapporteur of the International Law Association's study group on responsibility of international organizations, a member of the board of directors of ILEAP (International Lawyers and Economists against Poverty), and a member of the editorial advisory board of the Journal of Law, Social Justice, and Global Development. He served as a member of the International Law Association's Committee on Accountability of International Organizations and as an advisor to the Rethinking Bretton Woods Project. Professor Bradlow holds degrees from the University of Witwatersrand in South Africa, and Northeastern University and Georgetown University in the USA, and is a member of the New York and District of Columbia Bars.

David B. Hunter

David B. Hunter is an associate professor, director of the Program on International and Comparative Environmental Law and the Washington Summer Session on Environmental Law, and acting director of the International Legal Studies Program at American University Washington College of Law. He is the former executive director of the Center for International Environmental Law and was previously an associate with the law firm of Skadden, Arps, Slate, Meagher, and Flom. He currently serves on the boards of directors of the Environmental Law Alliance Worldwide-US, the Project on Government Oversight, the Bank Information Center, and Greenpeace-US. Additionally, Mr Hunter is a member scholar at the Center for Progressive Reform, a member of the Steering Committee of the IUCN Commission on Environmental Law, and a member of the Environmental Law

Expert's Group to the Organization of American States. Professor Hunter holds degrees from the University of Michigan and the Harvard Law School.

Author Contributors

Bhupinder S. Chimni

Dr B.S. Chimni is a professor of International Law and Chairperson of the Centre for International Legal Studies, at the School of International Studies, Jawaharlal Nehru University, New Delhi. He is the former vice chancellor of W.B. National University of Juridical Sciences, Kolkata. He has been a visiting professor at Brown and Tokyo Universities and a visiting scholar/fellow at Harvard, York (Canada), and Cambridge Universities. He has been teaching international economic law for the last twenty-five years and is the author of *International Commodity Agreements: A Legal Study*. He has also published a number of articles on different aspects of international economic law in leading journals. He self identifies as a member of a group of scholars engaged in articulating a critical third-world approach to international law. He is a general editor of the Asian Yearbook of International Law.

Charles E. Di Leva

Mr Di Leva is chief counsel of the Environmental and International Law Unit of the World Bank Legal Department. He has been a director of the IUCN Environmental Law Program. He has also been a trial attorney with the Department of Justice's Environmental Enforcement Section and senior programme officer in the United Nations' Environment Program Environmental Law Unit. He received a B.S. degree from the University of Rhode Island and his J.D. from Vermont Law School.

Steven Herz

Steven Herz is a lawyer and consultant based in Oakland, California. He advises global civil society organizations on international environmental and human rights law, and sustainable development policy. One focus of his work has been increasing public participation and accountability in the environmental decision-making of the World Bank and other international financial institutions. He is the author of a number of articles and reports on these subjects. He currently focuses on climate finance with Greenpeace International. He holds a B.A., M.A., and J.D. from the University of Virginia.

Jerome I. Levinson

Jerome Levinson is Distinguished Lawyer in Residence at American University Washington College of Law. He specializes in the legal aspects of foreign direct investment. Levinson is well known for his knowledge of international financial issues and workers' rights. He recently published *Who Makes United States Foreign Policy?*

Fergus Mackay

Fergus Mackay is a human rights lawyer and coordinator of the Human Rights and Legal Programme of the UK-based organization, the Forest Peoples Programme. He has worked as an attorney for indigenous people in Alaska and was legal advisor to the World Council of Indigenous Peoples for five years. He has litigated a number of cases before the Inter-American Court of Human Rights and the Inter-American Commission on Human Rights, and before the United Nations treaty bodies, including the 2007 *Saramaka People v. Suriname* case, decided by the Inter-American Court. He previously served as an expert advisor to the Organization of American States concerning its proposed American Declaration on the Rights of Indigenous Peoples and as a member of the advisory panel on the World Bank's Extractive Industries Review.

Siobhán McInerney-Lankford

Dr Siobhán McInerney-Lankford is counsel in the Environment and International Law Group of the World Bank LEGVPU. She works on human rights law and safeguard policies, advising on policy issues and coordinating research, analytic work, and consultations relevant to human rights. She leads the World Bank LEGVPU's research project on human rights and climate change, and supports the Nordic Trust Fund on human rights. Additionally, she is the World Bank's representative on the OECD Development Assistance Committee Human Rights Task Team, which she chaired for two years, and she represents the World Bank on the UN High-Level Task Force on the Right to Development. Dr McInerney-Lankford holds an LL.B. from Trinity College, Dublin, a B.C.L. from Oxford University, an LL.M. from Harvard Law School, and D.Phil. in EU human rights law from Oxford University.

August Reinisch

August Reinisch is a professor of international and European law at the University of Vienna and an adjunct professor at the Bologna Center of SAIS/Johns Hopkins University in Bologna, Italy. From 2004 to 2006, he was Dean for International Relations of the Law School of the University of Vienna. He currently serves as arbitrator on the In Rem Restitution Panel according to the Austrian General Settlement Fund Law 2001, dealing with Holocaust-related property claims; as president of an United Nations Commission on International Trade Law (UNCITRAL) investment arbitration tribunal; and as an arbitrator and expert in other investment cases. He has widely published in international law, with a recent focus on investment law and the law of international organizations. Additionally, he has served as an expert advisor in Austrian and foreign courts and as an international arbitrator. He holds Master's degrees in philosophy and in law as well as a doctorate in law from the University of Vienna and an LL.M. from NYU Law School.

Eisuke Suzuki

Eisuke Suzuki is professor of Policy Studies in the School of Policy Studies at Kwansei Gakuin University, Sanda-Kobe, Japan. In 2003, he was the principal architect of ADB's Accountability Mechanism and has held many leadership positions in the Asian Development Bank, including the Director General, Operations Evaluation, 2003–2005; Special Advisor to the President, 2003; and Deputy General Counsel, 1996–2003. He received his J.S.D. in 1974 from the Yale Law School, where he founded and served as editor-in-chief of *Yale Studies in World Public Order* from 1974 to 1978 (now *Yale Journal of International Law*).

Celine Tan

Celine Tan is a lecturer in Law at the Birmingham Law School at the University of Birmingham. Prior to this, she taught law at Warwick, was a consultant researcher with the Third World Network, and worked at a variety of international and non-governmental organizations relating to social and economic development and human rights. Dr Tan received her LL.B. from the University of London, and LL.M. and PhD from the University of Warwick.

Jakob Wurm

Jakob Wurm is a project assistant at the Department of European, International and Comparative Law at the Law School of the University of Vienna, in Vienna, Austria. He received an LL.M. from the University of Vienna, a European Master in Law and Economics from the Rotterdam Erasmus University, and was a visiting scholar at Boalt Hall, School of Law at the University of California, Berkeley. In addition to his position as an Austrian national reporter for the database, 'International Law in Domestic Courts' (ILDC), he is an ILDC associate editor. His research interests include International Economic Law (WTO dispute settlement), the Law of International Organizations (immunities and privileges of international organizations in Austria), Austrian judicial practice in international law, and European Law.

Introduction

Daniel D. Bradlow and David B. Hunter

Any discussion of the relationship of international law to the operations of international financial institutions (IFIs) must start with the international law applicable to all international organizations. The fundamental international legal issues relating to the status of international organizations, which are inter-governmental organizations created by treaties, are settled. Since the *Reparations* case in 1949, the international community has accepted that international organizations are subjects of international law.[1] It is also acknowledged that the international legal rights and obligations of international organizations are based on their constitutive treaties, any other treaties that the organizations may have signed, and applicable customary international legal principles.[2]

Beyond these general propositions, the international law pertaining to international organizations is less well established. This lack of clarity is attributable to a number of factors. First, the situation of international organizations as subjects of international law differs in important ways from the position of states. While states have general powers, rights, and responsibilities that they exercise relatively freely within their legally recognized geographical space, international organizations have defined powers and responsibilities determined by the organization's functions and purposes as spelled out in their constitutive treaties and as they are implemented in practice,[3] and not by geography. Following the *Reparations* case it is also accepted that, in addition to their explicitly conferred powers,

1. 'Reparation for Injuries Suffered in the Service of the United Nations', Advisory Opinion, I.C.J. Reports 1949, 174 (hereinafter *Reparations*).
2. *See* 'Interpretation of the Agreement of 25 March 1951 between the WHO and Egypt', ICJ Reports 1980, 73, para. 37.
3. *Reparations, supra* n. 1, 180.

international organizations have whatever additional implied powers may be necessary for them to perform their functions.[4]

Second, international organizations are created by states to perform functions that are of interest to their Member States. This means that, although international organizations clearly have a legal existence that is independent from their Member States, their governance, and thus their decision-making, is formally dominated by their Member States, or more accurately their most powerful Member States. This raises some issues relating to the functional independence of international organizations.[5] For example, the fact that the Member States play a role in the decisions taken by the organizations raises questions about the division of responsibility between the organization and the Member States for the consequences of these decisions.[6] In particular, it raises concerns about who is responsible for the decisions and actions of international organizations. In principle, there are three possibilities for assigning responsibility: the organizations are independently responsible for their decisions and actions; the organizations and their Member States are jointly responsible; or the international organization has primary responsibility and the Member States can be found to have a secondary responsibility for these decisions, at least in certain circumstances.[7] The legal independence of international organizations would suggest that the organization alone should be responsible for its own decisions and actions. However, this can be problematic if international organizations make decisions or undertake actions that the states themselves could not do – for example, decisions or actions that are not in compliance with treaties signed by the majority of their Member States but not signed by the organization. There are also issues relating to the legal implications arising from international organizations signing treaties separately from their Member States.[8] For example, would an international organization signing a treaty bind

4. *Ibid.*, 182.
5. *See generally*, Catherine Brölmann, *The Institutional Veil in Public International Law: International Organisations and the Law of Treaties* (Oxford & Portland, OR: Hart Publishing, 2007); José Alvarez, *International Organizations as Law-Makers* (Oxford & New York: Oxford University Press, 2005); Henry G. Schermers & Niels M. Blokker, *International Institutional Law*, 4th rev. edn (Boston, MA: Martinus Nijhoff Publishers, 2003).
6. *See* International Law Commission's work on the responsibility of international organizations. The reports of the International Law Commission's Special Rapporteur on Responsibility of International Organizations are available on the International Law Commission's website. International Law Commission, Search Page, <http://untreaty.un.org/ilc/dtSearch/Search_Forms/dtSearch.html> (hereinafter ILC Search Page). The Special Rapporteur issued his seventh report, on 27 Mar. 2009. Giorgio Gaja, ILC Special Rapporteur, 'Seventh Report on Responsibility of International Organizations', A/CN.4/610 (Geneva, 27 Mar. 2009). *See also*, International Law Association, 'Final Report of the Committee on Accountability of International Organizations' (2004) (hereinafter 'ILA Report').
7. *See, e.g.*, Rosalyn Higgins, 'The Legal Consequences for Member States of the Non-Fulfillment by International Organizations of Their Obligations Towards Third Parties', report for Insitut de Droit International (1995), in *Themes and Theories: Selected Essays, Speeches, and Writings in International Law*, ed. Rosalyn Higgins (Oxford & New York: Oxford University Press, 2009).
8. *See* Brölmann, *supra* n. 5. This concern with the implications of international organizations signing treaties not signed by all the Member States was one of the factors underlying the ILC's

only the organization, or does it also have international legal implications for their Member States, even if these Member States have not signed the treaties themselves?[9]

Third, the organization's relationship with its members, in principle, is conducted at the level of the state. This means that all interactions between the international organization and non-state actors in its Member States are expected to be indirect and involve the mediation of the state. Only the state has a direct relationship with the organization. This suggests that only the state should be able to hold the organization accountable for its decisions and actions that affect the state and its citizens. This in turn places emphasis on the role of each Member State in the governance of the international organization and on the existing mechanisms for Member States holding the organization accountable. This formal legal relationship is challenged by the functional reality of the active and direct engagement of many international organizations with non-state actors in their Member States, and of their ability to have significant impacts on the lives and activities of these non-state actors. Examples of the direct relationships that can exist between non-state actors and international organizations include, the work of the United Nations in refugee camps, the role that the United Nations played in the governance of Namibia and Timor-Leste during their transitions to independence, and the role of the World Bank and the International Monetary Fund (IMF) in many poor countries during their structural adjustment programmes.[10]

These direct non-contractual relations between international organizations and non-state actors raise two sets of important questions. The first relates to the actual ability of an individual Member State to hold the international organization accountable for the impact of its operations on the citizens of that Member State. This can be problematic because the state may be a partner with the organization in an operation that is of interest to the state, and so the state may have little incentive to raise the non-state actors' concerns with the international organization. In addition, the state may occupy a relatively weak position in the governance of the international organization and therefore may experience difficulty in having its concerns actually heard in the organization.

---

decision to treat treaties involving international organizations in a separate convention from the one dealing with international agreements only between states. *See* Vienna Convention on the Law of Treaties, 1155 U.N.T.S. 331 (1969, entered into force 27 Jan. 1980), *available at* <http://untreaty.un.org/ilc/texts/instruments/english/conventions/1_1_1969.pdf>; Vienna Convention on the Law of Treaties between States and International Organizations or between International Organizations (21 Mar. 1986) (this treaty is not yet in force because it has yet to be ratified by the requisite thirty-five states), *available at* <http://untreaty.un.org/ilc/texts/instruments/english/conventions/1_2_1986.pdf>.

9. *See* Brölmann, *supra* n. 5.
10. *See, e.g.*, Ralph Wilde, 'Enhancing Accountability at the International Level: The Tension between International Organization and Member State Responsibility and the Underlying Issues at Stake', *ILSA Journal of International and Comparative Law* 12 (2006): 395 & sources cited therein.

The second deals with the ability of adversely affected non-state actors themselves to hold the international organization accountable.[11] This ability can be constrained because to ensure that these international organizations can perform these functions effectively and freely, they are typically granted immunity from legal process in their Member States. This limit on the ability of non-state actors to ensure that the activities of international organizations do not negatively affect their lives has important implications for the organization's accountability for its actions.

In addition to the issues related to the international legal status of international organizations, there are many unresolved issues regarding both the international legal responsibilities of international organizations and the content of the international law applicable to their operations. Evidence of the former can be seen in the attention being paid to this topic by the International Law Commission (ILC) in its work on the responsibility of international organizations,[12] the International Court of Justice's rebuff of the World Health Organization's (WHO) efforts to provide advice on the legality of the use of nuclear weapons in armed conflict,[13] and the uncertainty surrounding the responsibilities of the United Nations (UN) for misconduct in its refugee camps and peace-keeping operations.[14] Evidence of the latter can be seen, for example, in the lack of clarity surrounding the human rights obligations of international organizations and in deciding exactly which international legal principles are applicable to the operations of the international organizations.[15]

The issue of which international legal principles are applicable to the operations of international organizations is further complicated by the number of international organizations, and the diversity in their functions and scope of operations. This suggests that, in addition to the general principles that are applicable to all international organizations, specific principles may apply to particular international organizations or groups of organizations and may lead to special legal outcomes. In this regard, it is important to note that, while legal scholars have written about many different international organizations, the organization that has received the greatest attention is the United Nations, and the subjects that have generated the most interest are its powers to deal with peace and security and its responsibilities in regard to these operations. This focus is understandable,

---

11. *See, e.g.*, 'ILA Report', *supra* n. 6.
12. ILC Search Page, *supra* n. 6; Gaja, 'Seventh Report on Responsibility of International Organizations', *supra* n. 6.
13. 'Legality of the Use by a State of Nuclear Weapons in Armed Conflict', Advisory Opinion, I.C.J. Reports 1996, 66.
14. *See* Wilde, *supra* n. 10; Frédéric Mégret & Florian Hoffmann, 'The UN as a Human Rights Violator? Some Reflections on the United Nations Changing Responsibilities', *Human Rights Quarterly* 25 (2003): 314–342, *available at* <http://muse.jhu.edu/journals/human_rights_quarterly/v025/25.2megret.pdf>; Alvarez, *supra* n. 5.
15. *See, e.g.*, Mac Darrow, *Between Light and Shadow: The World Bank, the International Monetary Fund and International Human Rights Law* (Oxford & Portland, OR: Hart Publishing, 2003); Sigrun Skogly, *The Human Rights Obligations of the World Bank and the International Monetary Fund* (London: Cavendish Publishing, 2001).

given that peace-keeping operations have been the most high-profile activities of the United Nations and that these operations are relatively novel and complex.

On the other hand, the developmental work of international organizations has received relatively less attention from international legal scholars. In fact, it is striking how little attention has been paid to the international legal issues relating to the operations of the IMF, the World Bank Group, and the regional development banks (collectively the IFIs).

This gap in the literature is somewhat surprising. The IFIs play important roles in global economic governance and are key actors in shaping the development trajectories in their developing Member States. Their operations can also have profound social and environmental impacts on their Member States, as well as on their economic policies. In addition, these institutions combine their public status as international legal subjects with financial operations that, by their nature, may be indistinguishable from private financial transactions. All of which suggests that the law applicable to their operations could involve both novel and important international legal issues. In addition, it suggests that a better understanding of these legal issues could help both the organizations and their Member States structure their transactions in ways that are more compatible with their developmental objectives and their international responsibilities. Consequently, the issue of what international legal principles are applicable to the operations of the IFIs is an important topic that would benefit from more rigorous study.

The purpose of this book is to address this deficiency in the treatment of international law and IFIs. It hopes to stimulate thought, debate, research and analysis, and action on the topic. It also hopes to contribute to the development of a clearer and better defined legal regime to govern the work of the IFIs. Towards this end it contains a set of contributions that address the various aspects of this topic from diverse perspectives in terms of experience, political viewpoint, and focus. Collectively, the contributions address a broad range of issues that we hope will help define the topic with greater clarity and depth.

The book is divided into two parts. The first part focuses on general issues related to the IFIs and international law. The purpose of this section is to set out the general principles of international law that are applicable to the IFIs and to consider how these are or should be evolving to produce IFIs that are respectful subjects of international law and accountable to all relevant stakeholders for their compliance with international law. The second part focuses on selected aspects of the IFIs' operations that both raise important and challenging international legal issues and that have substantial impacts on both the different stakeholders in the operations of the IFIs, and on the sustainability and success of the operations.

Part I: General Issues

The first chapter in this part provides a general overview of the international law applicable to the operations of the IFIs. In this chapter, the author, Daniel Bradlow, begins his analysis with a brief description of the two key universal IFIs – the IMF and the World Bank Group – and their operations. He then identifies the international legal principles applicable to IFI operations. His analysis shows that some customary international legal principles are applicable, or at least potentially applicable, to the social and environmental aspects of their operations, and to their contractual relations with their Member States. In the chapter, Bradlow also contends that the IFIs should not only be seen as passive recipients of international legal obligations and rights, but also as key players in the creation of international law through the formulation and implementation of their operational policies, the fact finding work of their independent accountability mechanisms, and their participation in certain international treaty regimes. This, he argues, underscores the importance of defining with more precision the scope of the IFIs' international legal obligations.

The second chapter, by B.S. Chimni, looks at the issue of IFIs and international law from a Third World perspective. He argues that the IFIs are not neutral subjects of international law and that their primary international function is to promote the international capitalist system. This mission is pursued in part by ensuring that IFIs remain subjects of international law that are not bound by international law. The ambiguities in their Articles, Chimni argues, allow them to interpret their mandates in ways that advance their real international function, while evading any obligations that they may have under international human rights law or as participants in the UN system. In addition, Chimni contends, their governance structures, with their weighted voting, restricted Board representation, and limited mechanisms of accountability, serve to constrain the role of the developing Member States and to keep them in a subaltern position. He concludes with a number of reforms that should be pressed by developing Member States and concerned social movements.

Chapter 3, by Eisuke Suzuki, explores the responsibility of the IFIs under international law. In the chapter, he looks at the ongoing work of the ILC's draft articles on the responsibility of international organizations and seeks to apply this work to the case of the IFIs. In particular, he focuses on the internal policies and directives of the IFIs, which he argues implement the mandates of these organizations and are independent of the municipal laws of the Member States. Suzuki argues that the function of the international policies raises a question about the practical and international legal consequences of an IFI's breach of these policies. He maintains that the ILC draft articles are troubling in that no international legal consequences seem to attach to an IFI's non-compliance with these internal policies. In Suzuki's view, the lack of consequences does not mean that they are not responsible for such acts of non-compliance. In fact, the independent accountability mechanisms in the various IFIs are designed, at least in part, to help address the issue of IFI responsibility for these acts of non-compliance. Suzuki ends the chapter with an interesting case study of the functioning of these independent accountability mechanisms and a proposal to extend the scope of the existing IFI administrative tribunals to serve as appellate bodies to review and make binding the decisions of existing accountability mechanisms.

The next two chapters address the accountability of IFIs from the perspective of national courts, particularly given the grant of immunity that accompanies IFIs' status as international organizations. Chapter 4, by August Reinisch and Jakob Wurm, examines how the IFIs have fared in cases in national courts. Although only a relatively small number of cases involve IFIs, they cover a broad range of issues, including IFI immunity, IFI capacity to sue in national courts, and the ability of various claimants, including creditors, employees, and non-contractual parties to sue IFIs in domestic courts. On the basis of their analysis of the cases, Reinisch and Wurm conclude that in general the IFIs are immune to suit in national courts unless they actually waive their immunity.

Chapter 5, written by Steven Herz, focuses more critically on the issue of IFI immunity. In this chapter, Herz evaluates the law relating to organizational immunity and builds the case for reducing the immunity of the IFIs. He notes the irony that, although initially international organizations were not supposed to have greater immunity than their Member States, over the past fifty years the immunity of states has shrunk while that of international organizations has grown. Particularly in the case of the IFIs, their immunity has expanded together with the widening scope of their activities. It is related, as Herz points out, to the fact that the rationale for international organizational immunity is connected to their need to perform freely the public functions for which they were originally created. In this chapter, Herz cogently argues that the current broad scope of the IFIs' immunity is untenable and needs to be reduced so that they can be held accountable for their actions. He bases his argument on a careful reading of both the functions of the IFIs and of the case law, particularly in the United States, regarding their immunity.

Part II: Selected Topics

The chapters in this section all focus on the international legal implications of specific aspects of IFI operations. The first chapter in this section addresses structural adjustment lending while the remaining chapters address human rights, the environment, and related issues regarding the rights and interests of third parties vis-à-vis the IFIs. While the authors tend to focus their analysis on the IMF and the World Bank Group, their conclusions can easily be extrapolated to other IFIs.

The first chapter in this section (Chapter 6), by Celine Tan, looks at the international law and policy relating to the IFIs' structural adjustment lending. She begins her analysis of this controversial topic with a review of the history and evolution of adjustment lending and the conditionalities attached thereto. She concludes that structural adjustment programmes serve a global economic governance function, particularly in regard to poor and weak states. However, it performs this function without the normal legal or institutional safeguards for states and affected communities that one would expect from well governed entities. Furthermore, Tan contends that through structural adjustment programmes, the IFIs have been able to expand their mandates and their authority over at least some of their Member States without any accompanying increase in their public accountability.

Chapter 7, by David Hunter, focuses on the development of the internal law of the IFIs – particularly the environmental and social policies adopted by the IFIs to address the rights and interests of third parties affected by IFI financing. He explains how the procedures for adopting policies at the IFIs are part of the emerging global administrative law and how, over time, they have developed into a robust set of procedures for providing non-state actors with access to information and opportunities to participate. These procedural rights in the formulation of policies are rooted in concepts of international human rights and good governance in the field of sustainable development. These procedures are both reflections of the IFIs' (and other international organizations') evolving international legal responsibilities in international policymaking and the IFIs' leading role in establishing new standards for the progressive development of customary law in this area. The chapter faults the IFIs for their ad hoc approach to these procedures and argues that minimum standards need to be codified to ensure no backsliding by the institutions and to meet the growing expectations and responsibilities for ensuring effective participation of non-state actors in international policymaking at the IFIs.

The third chapter in this part (Chapter 8), by Siobhán McInerney-Lankford, deals with the complex issue of the IFIs and international human rights. She begins her analysis by arguing that human rights law requires that the bearer of the human rights obligation be clearly identified, something she contends is only rarely done in regard to human rights in the development context. As a result, operationalizing human rights is difficult in the development context in general, and in regard to the IFIs in particular, especially given that the IFIs are not signatories to the international human rights conventions. She then notes that, pursuant to human rights conventions, the primary human rights obligations rest with states. McInerney-Lankford argues that states' obligations include seeking to protect, promote, and fulfil human rights in their actions in the IFIs. She maintains that the IFIs, as subjects of international law, have a responsibility to support Member States who are signatories to specific human rights conventions in their actions in these countries. In addition, and if appropriate, the IFIs have a responsibility to cooperate with the international bodies formally responsible for monitoring the implementation of human rights obligations.

The ninth chapter, by Fergus MacKay, looks at the impact of the IFIs on indigenous people. He argues that the international law relating to indigenous people has evolved to the point where important international legal documents, in the form of UN Declarations and International Labour Organization (ILO) Conventions, now clarify the international community's, including the IFIs', legal obligations towards indigenous people. In particular, he argues that indigenous people have a right to give their free, prior, and informed consent to IFI operations that affect them. He contends that this should be reflected in the applicable operational policies of the IFIs, and that they should be held accountable for their failure to comply with this obligation.

The tenth chapter, by Jerome Levinson, looks at the way in which the IFIs address the topic of respect for workers' rights, particularly the core workers' rights expressed in the ILO Conventions. The chapter looks at the history of the IFIs' treatment of workers' rights, particularly in the Latin American countries, and how this has evolved over time. He also looks at how the World Trade Organization

(WTO) has addressed this important topic. Levinson concludes that the IFIs have not always met their obligations in the labour context.

The final chapter in this part (Chapter 11), by Charles Di Leva, looks at how the IFIs have dealt with their obligations in regard to international environmental law. In this chapter, he focuses on the World Bank and its environmental activities. The chapter describes these activities in some detail. In addition, Di Leva discusses ways in which the Bank deals with some of the international environmental law issues that arise from these activities. The chapter helps underscore the important role the Bank is playing in regard to environmental affairs at both a global level, and in those developing Member States that use its services.

As the conclusion highlights, the chapters in this book collectively represent a detailed and critical overview of the IFIs and international law. Together, the book demonstrates that the IFIs have important responsibilities under international law and a powerful capacity to influence the development of international law in a number of areas. We hope that the book will both inform readers and stimulate them to undertake further research in this important area of international law. We also hope it will encourage more rigorous engagement between the IFIs and international lawyers on this topic, thereby leading to international law playing a more active role in the work of the IFIs.

Chapter 1

International Law and the Operations of the International Financial Institutions

Daniel D. Bradlow

I. INTRODUCTION

International financial institutions (IFIs) have a dual character. First, they are intergovernmental organizations that are created by states for a public purpose; and their authority and mandates are based on an international agreement to which all their Member States are party. As subjects of international law, their rights and obligations arise from the applicable public international law principles. Second, they engage in financial transactions, which, despite their public purpose, are, by nature, similar to market-based financial transactions. Legally the structure of these transactions share many characteristics with the private sector's financial contracts.[1] However, unlike these private transactions, the IFIs' transactions, because they involve agreements between international organizations and states, are also subject to those international legal principles applicable to international agreements. Unfortunately, there is not a well-developed public international

1. The International Monetary Fund claims that its stand-by agreements are not contractual and so are an exception to this general statement. For further discussion of this issue, *see* Joseph Gold, *The Stand-By Arrangements of the International Monetary Fund: A Commentary on Their Formal, Legal and Financial Aspects* (Washington, DC: International Monetary Fund, 1970).

Daniel D. Bradlow and David B. Hunter, *International Financial Institutions and International Law*, pp. 1–30.

financial law that addresses both the public purpose of IFI financial operations and the commercial nature of their transactions.

The combination of their dual character and the absence of well-defined international legal principles that are applicable to their operations has a number of consequences for the IFIs. First, it raises the issue of the IFIs' international legal obligations in planning, evaluating, and implementing the projects, activities, or policies they fund. Second, it confronts the IFIs with the issue of whether or not they have any specific international legal obligations with which they must comply in the structuring and drafting of their financial transactions. Third, there is the issue of the IFIs' obligations under international law to those who, whether or not they have a contractual relationship with the IFIs, might be affected by their operations. In resolving these issues, the IFIs must also deal with their role as actors in the international legal system. This last issue addresses whether the IFIs are merely passive recipients of international legal rights and responsibilities or if, through their operations, they actually play a role in the creation and interpretation of international law.

This chapter seeks to address these four issues in regard to the operations of the two universal and most prominent IFIs – the International Monetary Fund (IMF or the Fund) and the World Bank Group (World Bank).[2] It is divided into four sections. The first section describes the IMF and the World Bank Group and their operations. It provides readers with an overview of IFI operations and establishes the foundation on which to address the international legal issues raised in the previous paragraph. The second section explores the general sources of international law and the relevant principles derived therefrom that are applicable to IFI operations. The third section focuses on the role of IFIs in creating international law. The final section concludes that the IFIs' significant role in the world's globalizing economy makes them both critical subjects and creators of international law.

II. A BRIEF DESCRIPTION OF THE IFIs

The most prominent IFIs are two global organizations and a set of regional development banks. The two global organizations are the IMF and the World Bank Group,[3] each of which has 186 Member States. The most prominent regional

2. Given its focus, this chapter does not address the important topic of the international legal status of the IFIs. This topic is explored in Ch. 4 by Eisuke Suzuki.
3. For more information, *see* the World Bank, <www.worldbank.org>; the International Monetary Fund, <www.imf.org>; and their Articles of Agreements: International Bank for Reconstruction and Development, Articles of Agreement, 2 U.N.T.S. 13 (27 Dec. 1945) (hereinafter IBRD Articles of Agreement); International Development Association, Articles of Agreement, U.N.T.S. 439, 249 (24 Jan. 1960) (hereinafter IDA Articles of Agreement); International Monetary Fund, Articles of Agreement, 2 U.N.T.S. 39, Art. I (27 Dec. 1945) (hereinafter IMF Articles of Agreement). It should be noted that the Bank for International Settlements also seeks to perform a global financial role. However, its membership is composed of central banks and not

development banks are the African Development Bank (AfDB); the Asian Development Bank (ADB); the European Bank for Reconstruction and Development (EBRD); and the Inter-American Development Bank (IDB).[4] In addition, there are other multilateral development banks (MDBs) such as the Islamic Development Bank, the International Fund for Agricultural Development, and the European Investment Bank, each of which has a relatively limited membership, but operates in countries spread across a number of regions.[5]

While their specific mandates and responsibilities differ, each of these entities is an inter-governmental organization that is formed by an international agreement to which only their Member States are party. They all offer qualifying Member States a range of financial products, advisory services, and technical support services, all of which are designed to serve a public purpose, related to either macro-economic policy or to the general goals of development and poverty alleviation. Thus, while the nature of the transaction in which they engage may be similar to market-based financial institutions, the purpose of the transactions is different.[6]

The legal and governance structures and the purpose and functions of the major regional development banks are modelled on the most prominent entities in the World Bank Group. In addition, the international legal principles that are applicable to the World Bank are applicable to them. The IMF, which, because of its international monetary and macro-economic focus, is, in many ways, the most influential IFI, has a unique function,[7] but has a similar legal and governance structure to the International Bank for Reconstruction and Development (IBRD), the primary entity in the World Bank Group. Consequently, an understanding of the Fund and the World Bank Group provides a useful basis for understanding the international legal principles applicable to the operations of all the IFIs.

---

states. Consequently, it is not an inter-governmental institution in the strict sense and has been excluded from the scope of this chapter.

4. Collectively the regional development banks and the World Bank Group are frequently referred to as the multilateral development banks (MDBs). *See* the African Development Bank, <www.afdb.org>; the Asian Development Bank, <www.asdb.org>; the European Bank for Reconstruction and Development, <www.ebrd.org>; and the Inter-American Development Bank, <www.iadb.org>.
5. For more information on the Islamic Development Bank, *see* <www.isdb.org>; for more information on the International Fund for Agricultural Development, *see* <www.ifad.org/>; and for more information on the European Investment Bank, *see* <www.eib.org>.
6. It is important not to over-emphasize this distinction because many private lenders are involved in funding the infrastructure projects funded by the MDBs, and many non-governmental organizations and foundations fund the social sector projects that the MDBs also fund. However, it is less common, though not unprecedented, for private lenders to provide the general balance of payments support provided by the IMF.
7. It should be noted that the MDBs have begun, through their structural adjustment lending programmes, to provide similar general balance of payments support to that provided by the IMF. In addition, the IMF through some of its operations in low income countries is beginning to act a bit more like the MDBs.

A. International Monetary Fund[8]

According to Article I of its Articles of Agreement, the purpose of the IMF is to promote international monetary cooperation through consultation and collaboration; to promote orderly and stable exchange arrangements among members; to assist in the establishment of a multilateral system of payments for international trade; and to make the resources of the IMF 'temporarily available' to members 'under adequate safeguards' for the purpose of correcting their balance-of-payments problems 'without resorting to measures destructive of national or international prosperity', and to shorten the duration and lessen the severity of the disequilibria in the balance-of-payments of members.[9] The following sections describe how the IMF implements this mandate.

1. Membership and Voting

The IMF was established in 1944 at the Bretton Woods Conference as an international monetary institution to which all sovereign states could belong. In practice, this means that any state that is a member of the United Nations can join the IMF. It currently has 186 Member States, with the most prominent non-Member States being Cuba and North Korea.

Upon joining the IMF, each Member State is assigned a quota.[10] The quota that the new Member State receives takes into account the size of the country's economy and its contribution to the global economy. For historical reasons, the formula results, despite some relatively small recent adjustments, in a bias towards European states.

A Member State's quota is relevant to three aspects of membership in the IMF. First, voting in the IMF is based on the quotas. According to this system, each Member State receives 250 votes, known as the basic vote, plus one vote for each 100,000 SDR of its quota. This system, results, for example, in the United States, which has the largest quota, having 371,743 votes (about 17% of the total); Belgium having 46,302 votes (about 2% of the total); Brazil having 30,611 votes (about 1.4% of the total); Nigeria having 17,782 votes (about 0.8% of the total); and Palau, which has the smallest quota, having 281 votes (0.01%).

It should be noted that over time the share of the basic votes in the total votes has declined from about 11% to about 2%. In 2008, the IMF membership agreed to increase the share of basic votes in the total votes, which will primarily benefit

8. Additional information on the IMF can be found generally at its website. The website has a number of useful factsheets that briefly describe aspects of the IMF's structure and function. A list can be found at: <www.imf.org/external/np/exr/facts/eng/list.aspx>.
9. IMF Articles of Agreement, *supra* n. 3, Art. I.
10. *See* International Monetary Fund, IMF Quotas, *available at* <www.imf.org/external/np/exr/facts/quotas.htm> (31 Oct. 2009).

smaller and poorer countries.[11] As of July 2010, this measure had not yet been implemented.

Quotas also affect IMF financing. Each Member State is expected to make a contribution (known as a subscription) to the resources of the IMF, based on its quota. This contribution consists of 25% in special drawing rights (SDRs) or convertible foreign exchange and 75% in the Member State's local currency. The SDR or convertible currency portion, known as the reserve tranche, is relatively easily available to the Member State and can be treated as part of its foreign reserves.

Finally, quotas influence Member States' access to IMF financing. Each IMF financing facility offers members financing equal to a certain percentage of their quotas. For example, a facility might offer members access to financing equal to 100% of their quotas. Overall, members can gain access to financing worth significantly more than their quotas, although the IMF usually places a cap on how much financing any single Member State can receive from it, as well as from each individual financing facility.

2. Function

The IMF offers its Member States regulatory, financial, and technical support services. Its regulatory functions include conducting surveillance of all its Member States to ensure that they are following policies that are consistent with their membership obligations.[12] In accordance with Article IV(3)(b) of the IMF's Articles of Agreement, the IMF conducts regular, usually annual, consultations, with each Member State, regarding its economic and financial policies. These consultations typically culminate in the issuance of observations and recommendations by the IMF regarding each Member State's economic and financial policy performance and, if appropriate, comments on the regional and global implications of these policies. These surveillance exercises are expected to help the IMF oversee a stable system of exchange rates for the international community. The reports from these country surveillance missions are only intended to be advisory. Thus, in themselves they do not impose any obligations on the Member State. The reports are discussed by the IMF Board and are utilized by the IMF in preparing its World Economic Outlook Report and its other periodic reports to the international community on the state of the global monetary and financial system.

---

11. IMF Governance Structure, 'Directors Back Reforms to Overhaul IMF Quotas and Votes', IMF Survey (28 Mar. 2008), *available at* <http://www.imf.org/external/pubs/ft/survey/so/2008/new032808a.htm>.
12. IMF Articles of Agreement, *supra* n. 3, Art. IV(3)(a). *See* IMF, 'IMF Executive Board Adopts New Decision on Bilateral Surveillance over Members' Policies', Public Information Notice No. 07/69 (21 Jun. 2007), *available at* <www.imf.org/external/np/sec/pn/2007/pn0769.htm>. For an overview of criticisms of IMF surveillance, *see* John W. Head, 'Seven Deadly Sins: An Assessment of Criticisms Directed at the International Monetary Fund', *Kansas Law Review* 52 (2004): 521.

The IMF also offers financial support to those Member States that are experiencing balance-of-payments problems.[13] The amount of financing that the IMF will offer a Member State is a percentage – normally up to 300% – of its quota. In general, IMF financing is subject to IMF conditionality, which refers to the policy and other adjustment measures that the IMF expects the Member State to undertake to correct its monetary and economic problems in connection with its receipt of the IMF financing. The IMF oversees implementation of these conditionalities through frequent monitoring of economic and financial factors in those countries that have drawn on the financial services of the IMF.

With one exception, the IMF makes its financing available through a number of different facilities that are each subject to some form of conditionality. The IMF's financing facilities that involve conditionality include the Stand-By Arrangement, the Extended Fund Facility, the Supplemental Reserve Facility,[14] and the Poverty Reduction and Growth Facility (PRGF).[15] The one facility that is not subject to pre-disbursement conditionality is the Flexible Credit Line, which offers Member States that meet certain qualification criteria, quick and unconditional access to financing in case of a crisis.[16] It was established in 2009 and replaced the Contingent Credit Line facility.[17] It should also be noted that all Member States can access that portion of its quota, known as the 'reserve tranche', that the IMF holds in foreign exchange subject to a low level of conditionality. These funds are available whenever the Member State represents to the IMF that they need the funding to address a balance-of-payments need.

---

13. For more information on IMF financial operations, *see* IMF, 'About the IMF: Lending by the IMF', <www.imf.org/external/about/lending.htm>.
14. IMF, 'IMF Approves Supplemental Reserve Facility', Press Release No. 97/59 (17 Dec. 1997).
15. The Stand-By Arrangement was the first IMF Facility and is the basic means through which it provides financing to its Member States. *See* Joseph Gold, *The Stand-By Arrangements of the International Monetary Fund: A Commentary on Their Formal, Legal and Financial Aspects* (Washington, DC: International Monetary Fund, 1970). The Extended Fund Facility (dating from 1974) allows a member country to draw up to a specified amount over a longer term, usually three or four years. The Poverty Reduction and Growth Facility was introduced in 1999. It replaced the Enhanced Structural Adjustment Facility under which the IMF gives low-interest financing to help the poorest member countries facing protracted balance-of-payments problems, *see* IMF, 'IMF Quotas', *supra* n. 10.
16. IMF, 'IMF Overhauls Lending Framework', Press Release No. 09/85 (24 Mar. 2009), *available at* <www.imf.org/external/np/sec/pr/2009/pr0985.htm>.
17. IMF, 'IMF Tightens Defences against Financial Contagion by Establishing Contingent Credit Lines', Press Release No. 99/14 (25 Apr. 1999). The Supplemental Reserve Facility is financed with resources raised through past sales of IMF-owned gold and with loans and grants provided to the IMF for this purpose, mainly by wealthy countries – *see* James Raymond Vreeland, *The IMF and Economic Development* (Cambridge, England: Cambridge University Press, 2003), 10. The Supplemental Reserve Facility provides additional short-term financing to a member country experiencing exceptional balance-of-payments difficulty because of a sudden and disruptive loss of market confidence reflected in capital outflows. The Contingent Credit Line facility provided a precautionary line of defence. The idea was to enable a Member Country pursuing strong economic policies to obtain financing on a short-term basis when faced by a sudden and disruptive loss of market confidence because of contagion from difficulties in other countries.

The purpose of the conditionality[18] is to ensure that IMF resources are used by Member States to resolve their balance-of-payments problems consistent with their obligations under the IMF's Articles. The IMF expects its financing to provide Member States 'with an opportunity to correct maladjustments in their balance of payments without resorting to measures destructive of national or international prosperity' as stated in Article I(v) of the IMF's Articles of Agreement.[19] In an effort to promote compliance with the conditionality, the IMF disburses its funds in a series of tranches (rather than in a single lump sum), with the disbursement of each portion of the funding being subject to the Member State having to demonstrate compliance with the IMF's conditionalities.

The resources for all IMF financing facilities except the PRGF[20] are drawn from the IMF's general resources. The financing is provided in a sui generis form in that the IMF neither lends the Member State foreign exchange nor sells it, in the sense of a permanent transfer of ownership, to the Member State. Instead it transfers the funds to the Member State, based on a decision of its board of executive directors to support the adjustment policies of the Member State. The Member State is then expected to resell the funds back to the IMF, pursuant to its obligation, under the IMF's Articles of Agreement, to maintain its subscription arrangements with the IMF.[21] The IMF maintains that this unusual sale and repurchase arrangement, with each leg of the transaction having a different legal basis, consists of a set of parallel and not reciprocal promises. Consequently, the IMF argues, the arrangement does not include all the necessary elements of a contract and so should not be treated as a contractual arrangement. This hitherto untested claim allows the IMF to avoid many of the international legal consequences of entering into an international agreement with a Member State.[22]

The third function of the IMF is technical assistance.[23] The purpose of this activity is to help Member States design and implement the economic policies (both monetary and fiscal), and build the institutional capacity needed to comply with their obligations under the IMF's Articles of Agreement.[24] Examples of the

---

18. IMF Guidelines on Conditionality (25 Sep. 2002), *available at* <www.imf.org/External/np/pdr/cond/2002/eng/guid/092302.pdf>. Clause 11 of the Guidelines on Conditionality provides that the IMF will monitor the borrowing country's performance under agreements entered into with the IMF on the basis of prior actions, performance criteria, programme and other reviews, and other variables and measures established as structural benchmarks or indicative targets.
19. IMF Articles of Agreement, *supra* n. 3, Art. I(v).
20. The PRGF is funded through a special trust fund. Because it is not funded through the IMF's general resources, it can extend financing in the form it finds most useful for its purposes. Transactions with the PRGF are structured as loan agreements.
21. IMF Articles of Agreement, *supra* n. 3, Art. V(7).
22. For more information on the IMF's position, *see* Gold, *The Stand-By Arrangements of the International Monetary Fund: A Commentary on Their Formal, Legal and Financial Aspects*, *supra* n. 15.
23. For more information on technical assistance, *see* IMF, 'About the IMF: Technical Assistance', <www.imf.org/external/about/techasst.htm>.
24. IMF, Policy Statement on IMF Technical Assistance (1 Apr. 2001), *available at* <www.imf.org/external/pubs/ft/psta/index.htm>.

IMF's technical assistance activities are training programmes for officials from Member States on various aspects of monetary, fiscal, and financial affairs; advice on drafting monetary, fiscal, and financial legislation and regulations; and advice on creating effective financial and fiscal regulatory authorities.

3. Governance[25]

The highest governance body in the IMF is its Board of Governors. Each Member State is entitled to appoint one Governor and usually appoints either its Minister of Finance or the governor of its central bank to this position. The Board of Governors meets formally once a year at the IMF's annual meeting. It has delegated almost all its delegable powers to the twenty-four member Board of Executive Directors. However, certain decisions are reserved for the Board of Governors, such as decisions on admitting new members to the IMF, making quota adjustments, issuing SDRs, and amending the Articles of Agreement. Most decisions in the IMF can be made by simple majorities; others, such as adjustments in quotas, require an 85% majority. In such decisions, the United States, which has about 17% of the total vote, has an effective veto.

The twenty-four member Board of Executive Directors, which is chaired by the Managing Director of the Fund, oversees the work of the IMF. It is made up of:

- five members, each of whom is appointed by one of the Member States with the five biggest quotas: France, Germany, Japan, United Kingdom, and the United States;
- three members, called representatives of 'single member' constituencies, that are appointed by China, Russia, and Saudi Arabia; and
- sixteen members elected by constituencies of the remaining 178 Member States. The size of these constituencies range from seven to twenty-three Member States per constituency. The Executive Director representing a particular constituency has a vote equal to the total votes of all the members of the constituency and he/she must cast all the votes in a block. The votes of the constituencies vary from 113,969 votes (5.14% of the total) for a constituency that represents ten primarily European Member States to 29,855 votes (1.35% of the total) for a constituency representing twenty-three Sub-Saharan African Member States.[26]

The Executive Directors are based full-time at the IMF headquarters in Washington, DC. They each have an Alternate Executive Director and a small staff of advisors and support staff. They function as both officials of the IMF and representatives of their constituencies. The Board is responsible for overseeing the operations of the IMF. Thus its responsibilities include approving all IMF financing operations, reviewing all IMF country and thematic reports, and all IMF

---

25. *See generally* IMF, 'About the IMF: Governance', <www.imf.org/external/about/govern.htm>.
26. *See* IMF Executive Directors and Voting Power (last updated 8 Jan. 2010), *available at* <www.imf.org/external/np/sec/memdir/eds.htm>.

policies and internal organizational matters. Normally, the IMF Board operates by consensus, but, if necessary, it will make decisions by majority vote, with each Executive Director casting a vote equal to the total number of votes held by the Member States in the constituency he/she represents.

The work of the IMF is done by its management and staff, which is headed by the IMF Managing Director. In a formal sense, the staff and management are accountable to the Board. This means that the Board, in addition to its responsibilities in regard to the finances, human resources, and operational policies of the IMF, must also oversee the work of the management and staff. Given the diversity, scale, and complexity of the IMF's operations and the relatively limited resources available to each Executive Director, it is unclear how effectively the Board can fulfil its oversight responsibilities. This is particularly true for those Board members who represent constituencies that contain numerous countries that utilize IMF financing and technical support services.

B. The World Bank Group

The World Bank Group consists of five separate legal entities:[27] the International Bank for Reconstruction and Development (IBRD); the International Development Association (IDA); the International Finance Corporation (IFC); the Multilateral Investment Guarantee Agency (MIGA); and the International Centre for Settlement of Investment Disputes (ICSID). For current purposes, the two most relevant members of this group are the IBRD and the IDA (collectively referred to as 'the World Bank').

Pursuant to Article I of its Articles of Agreement,[28] the objectives of the IBRD are (i) assisting in the reconstruction and development of the territories of Member States by supporting the investment of capital for productive purposes; (ii) promoting private foreign investment by means of guarantees or participations in loans and other investments made by private investors; (iii) promoting the long-range balanced growth of international trade and the maintenance of equilibrium in balances of payments by encouraging international investment; (iv) arranging loans made or guaranteed by it for the more useful and urgent projects; and (v) conducting its operations with due regard to the effect of international investment on business conditions in the territories of Member States.[29] Based on these purposes, it is clear that the IBRD is expected primarily to fund development 'projects'.[30] Only in 'special circumstance'[31] is it supposed to provide funding for

27. *See generally* The World Bank, 'About Us', <http://web.worldbank.org/WBSITE/EXTERNAL/EXTABOUTUS/0,,pagePK:50004410~piPK:36602~theSitePK:29708,00.html>. The site has links to information on each entity.
28. IBRD Articles of Agreement, *supra* n. 3, Art. I.
29. *Ibid.*
30. *Ibid.*, Art. III(4)(vii).
31. *Ibid.*, Art. III.

non-project, policy-based purposes. In this regard, it is important to note that the IBRD's funding is not concessional funding, but is merely funding provided on more favourable terms than the terms its borrowers can obtain from commercial sources.

The IBRD raises its funds based on the capital provided by its Member States. Any state that is a member of the IMF can join the IBRD. Upon joining, each Member State is allocated a share of the Bank's capital, based on a formula that, because it is linked to the IMF quota formula, depends on such factors as its size and importance in the global economy. The Member State's votes in the organization are based on the number of shares it is allocated. The Member State pays a portion of the share price in cash and the balance in promissory notes. The IBRD relies on these pledges to raise funding in international financial markets.

The IBRD carries out its purposes principally through loan operations,[32] made either to a Member State of the Bank or to a public or private entity within the territory of a member. When the borrower is not a Member State, the loan must be fully guaranteed by the member government in whose territory the project to be financed is located. Consequently, every lending operation of the Bank leads to either a loan or guarantee agreement with a sovereign state.

The purposes of IDA compliment those of the IBRD.[33] They are to promote economic development, increase productivity, and thus raise the living standards in the poorest Member States by providing financing to meet their developmental requirements on terms which are more flexible, generous, and impact less heavily on the country's balance of payments than IBRD loans. IDA extends development credits to Member States with per capita incomes below about USD 1,855 per annum.[34] It provides these Member States with development credits for similar purposes and in similar form to IBRD financing but on significantly more attractive terms. In general its financing is provided interest-free, although subject to a service charge, for twenty to forty years with a ten-year grace period. IDA, because it provides funding on such generous terms, is not self-sustaining. Consequently, its capital is regularly replenished by its Member States.

Both IBRD loans and IDA credit agreements are treated by the World Bank as international agreements that are governed by international law.[35] As a result and

32. The Bank also renders important non-financial services to its members. *See* The World Bank, 'About Us: Operations', <http://go.worldbank.org/1YXPMBNDO0>; The World Bank, 'About Us: Challenge', <http://go.worldbank.org/DM4A38OWJ0>.
33. IDA Articles of Agreement, *supra* n. 3, Art. I.
34. In principle, states are eligible to borrow from IDA provided that their per capita income is below USD 1,855 per annum; in practice, however, IDA lends to states with a per capita income per annum of USD 1,135 (figures are in US dollars for IDA's FY 2010).
35. Aron Broches, 'International Legal Aspects of the Operations of the World Bank', *Recueil des Cours* 98 (1959): 297; John W. Head, 'Evolution of the Governing Law for Loan Agreements of the World Bank and Other Multilateral Development Banks', *American Journal of International Law* 90 (1996): 214. It should be noted that loan agreements with non-sovereign borrowers are always accompanied by guarantee agreements with the borrower's sovereign that

pursuant to Article 102 of the UN Charter, all these agreements are registered with the United Nations and are public. The agreements contain unusual governing law clauses. Specifically, the agreements provide that the rights and obligations of the Bank under such agreements shall be valid and enforceable in accordance with their terms notwithstanding the law of any state or political subdivision thereof to the contrary.[36] Thus, the agreements appear to have no governing law other than the agreements themselves. The agreements also provide for arbitration as the forum for settling disputes relating to the loan.[37]

The governance arrangements of the World Bank are similar to the IMF. They are based on weighted voting, a board of governors, a relatively small board of executive directors, and a management and staff headed by the bank president, who is also the chair of the board of directors.

III. GENERAL PRINCIPLES OF INTERNATIONAL LAW APPLICABLE TO IFIs

Pursuant to Article 38 of the statute of the International Court of Justice, the primary sources of international law are international treaties, customary international law, and general principles of law accepted by all nations.[38] This means that the international law applicable to the IFIs consists of their Articles of Agreements and any other treaties or international agreements to which they are party, any applicable customary international law, and applicable general principles of law accepted by all nations.[39]

---

are governed by international law. The loan agreements with state-owned entities are not governed by international law but nonetheless 'exclude' the operation of municipal law.

36. International Bank for Reconstruction and Development, 'General Conditions for Loans' (1 Jul. 2005), Art. VIII(8.01) (as amended through 12 Feb. 2008) (hereinafter IBRD General Conditions for Loans); International Development Association, 'General Conditions for Credits and Grants' (1 Jul. 2005), Art. VII(7.01) (as amended through 15 Oct. 2006) (hereinafter IDA General Conditions for Credits and Grants).
37. IBRD General Conditions for Loans, *supra* n. 36, Art. VIII(8.04); IDA General Conditions for Credits and Grants, *supra* n. 36, Art. VII(7.03).
38. Article 38 states that the sources of international law are: international conventions, whether general or particular, establishing rules expressly recognized by the contesting states; international custom, as evidence of a general practice accepted as law; the general principles of law recognized by civilized nations; and, subject to the provisions of Art. 59, judicial decisions and the teachings of the most highly qualified publicists of the various nations, as subsidiary means for the determination of rules of law. International Court of Justice, 'Statute of the Court', *available at* <www.icj-cij.org/documents/index.php?p1=4&p2=2&p3=0>.
39. *See Interpretation of the Agreement of 25 March 1951 between the WHO and Egypt*, ICJ Reports 1980, 73, para. 37; 'the International Law Commission's First Report on Responsibility of International Organizations', UN Doc. A/CN.4/532 (26 Mar. 2003), Art. 3; 'the International Law Commission's Third Report on Responsibility of International Organizations', UN Doc. A/CN.4/553 (13 May 2005), Art. 8.

A. Treaty Law

The most important treaty for the World Bank and the IMF is their founding document, their Articles of Agreement. Pursuant to these international agreements, the Bank and the IMF are generally expected to contribute to the long term growth and development of their Member States in ways that are consistent with the overall growth of international trade and that do not undermine the international monetary and financial system.[40] Exactly how each of them is expected to perform this task is set out in their Articles, which are written in broad general terms. For example, Article I of the IBRD states that it will assist in the 'reconstruction and development' of the territories of its Members States.[41] In addition, the IBRD is expected to fund 'projects';[42] only in 'special circumstance'[43] should it provide funding for non-project, policy-based purposes. Similarly, pursuant to Article I of its Articles of Agreement, the purposes of the IMF include promoting 'international monetary cooperation'; 'orderly and stable exchange arrangements'; and making the resources of the IMF 'temporarily available' to members 'under adequate safeguards' for the purpose of correcting their balance-of-payments problems 'without resorting to measures destructive of national or international prosperity'.[44] In neither case, are these exquisitely ambiguous terms or phrases defined. Pursuant to their articles, both the World Bank and the IMF are free to apply them as they deem appropriate in their operations. In fact, their articles specify that the authority to interpret the articles rests with the boards of executive directors, subject to an 'appeal' to their board of governors.[45]

The 1969 Vienna Convention on the Law of Treaties[46] (Vienna Convention) is the predominant guide to interpreting treaties, including the Articles of Agreement of the IFIs. Pursuant to this Convention, the Articles should be interpreted according to the ordinary meaning of their words in light of their purpose, and the context

40. The purposes of the IFIs are set out in the first articles of their Articles of Agreement. *See* IBRD Articles of Agreement, *supra* n. 3, Art. I; IDA Articles of Agreement, *supra* n. 3, Art. I; IMF Articles of Agreement, *supra* n. 3, Art. I. For information on the purposes of the other MDBs: Agreement Establishing the African Development Bank, U.N.T.S. 510 (4 Aug. 1963), 3, Arts I, II (hereinafter Agreement Establishing the AfDB); Agreement Establishing the Asian Development Bank, U.N.T.S. 571 (22 Aug. 1966), 123, Arts I, II (hereinafter Agreement Establishing the ADB); Agreement Establishing the European Bank for Reconstruction and Development, I.L.M. 29 (28 Mar. 1991), 1083, Arts I, II (hereinafter Agreement Establishing the EBRD); Agreement Establishing the Inter-American Development Bank, U.N.T.S. 389 (30 Dec. 1959), 69, Art. I (hereinafter Agreement Establishing the IDB).
41. IBRD Articles of Agreement, *supra* n. 3, Art. I.
42. *Ibid.*, Art. III(4)(vii).
43. *Ibid.*
44. *See* IMF Articles of Agreement, *supra* n. 3, Art. I; *see also* IMF, 'Factsheet: The IMF at a Glance' (10 Sep. 2009), *available at* <www.imf.org/external/np/exr/facts/glance.htm>.
45. *See* IMF Articles of Agreement, *supra* n. 3, Art. XXIX; IBRD Articles of Agreement, *supra* n. 3, Art. IX; IDA Articles of Agreement, *supra* n. 3, Art. X.
46. Vienna Convention on the Law of Treaties, U.N.T.S. 1155, 331 (23 May 1969), *available at* <http://untreaty.un.org/ilc/texts/instruments/english/conventions/1_1_1969.pdf> (hereinafter Vienna Convention).

in which they operate.[47] As stated above, the language of the IFIs' Articles of Agreement provides their management and Member States with substantial flexibility in how they choose to interpret key terms in their Articles. In fact, the lack of precision has both helped and challenged the IMF and the World Bank. Through creative interpretation of their Articles, they have been able to adapt to the changing conditions in which they have operated over the past sixty years. They have had to do so, however, while remaining true to the original vision of the drafters of the Articles and in compliance with international legal principles applicable to treaty interpretation, such as those set out in the Vienna Convention. The challenge this poses was succinctly summarized by Ibrahim Shihata, former General Counsel of the World Bank:[48]

> On the one hand, the Bank is expected at all times to adapt itself to the changing needs of the world, if only to ensure its continued relevance. On the other hand, it is extremely difficult to introduce changes through amendment of the Articles of Agreement. [...] How then can a counsel of that institution answer constant questions about the law governing Bank policies and operations which are, of course, subject to its Articles of Agreement? How does he or she identify the rules applicable to the Bank's varying transactions, which may be derived from international law or such domestic law as may be applicable, and cannot be inconsistent with the provisions of the Articles? This is perhaps the most challenging task performed by the office of the Bank's General Counsel.[49]

One response to this challenge has been to issue legal opinions that sought to establish, on the basis of the General Counsel's interpretation of the Articles, the conditions under which the Bank could undertake new types of operations. Because the Board of Executive Directors, which has the authority to interpret the Articles of Agreements, has endorsed the most important of these legal opinions, they have become the authoritative interpretations of the Articles, some of which have been published by the Bank's General Counsels.

The General Counsels at the IMF have adopted a similar approach.[50] Although in the case of the IMF, the Board of Executive Directors also publishes its most important decisions, most of which relate to operational matters but some of which are intended to explain its interpretation of the IMF's Articles of Agreement.[51]

In his opinions, Shihata used the ambiguity in the language of the Articles to help the Bank substantially expand the scope of its operations. For example, during

47. *Ibid.*, Art. 31.
48. Ibrahim F.I. Shihata, 'The Creative Role of the Lawyer – Example: The Office of the World Bank's General Counsel', *Catholic University Law Review* 48 (1999): 1041.
49. *Ibid.*, 1048.
50. *See also* Joseph Gold, 'Public International Law in the International Monetary System', *Southwestern Law Journal* 38 (1984): 7.
51. For the most recent volume (2009) of these selected decisions, *see* IMF, 'Selected Decisions and Selected Documents of the IMF, Thirty-Third Issue' (Jul. 2009), <www.imf.org/external/pubs/ft/sd/index.asp>.

the 1980s, the World Bank began to suggest that problems in its governance arrangements were a major cause of the developmental challenges, including problems in Bank-funded projects, in their Member States.[52] In response, the Bank's management indicated that the Bank could help these countries deal with their governance problems, by supporting activities such as legal and judicial reform, and reform of public sector administration. This meant that the Bank wanted to incorporate issues that are not obviously 'economic', into its operations. This posed a challenge for the Bank because both the IBRD and IDA's Articles explicitly prohibit these institutions from taking political considerations into account in their operations. For example, Article IV(10) of the IBRD Articles[53] is entitled 'Political Activity Prohibited' and states that the IBRD shall not interfere in the 'political affairs' of its Member States, nor shall it be influenced in its decisions by the 'political character' of the Member States and that only 'economic considerations' shall be relevant to its decisions. Thus, while this Article makes clear that the outer limit of the IBRD's mandate is determined by when it crosses the line from focusing on economic factors to becoming involved in 'political affairs', it does not define this limit with any precision.

In order to support the Bank's interest in assisting its Member States to deal with their governance challenges, while ensuring that the Bank operates within its mandate, the World Bank General Counsel took advantage of the Articles' lack of precision to expand the scope of the mandate and to define it as including certain matters that could be seen as 'political'. He opined that any activity that had a 'direct, preponderant and clear effect' on the country's economic development prospects could be treated as falling within its economic mandate as articulated in Article 1 of its Articles of Agreement even if it also had clear political dimensions.[54] Consequently, the Bank could support any good governance programmes that satisfied this test of what constituted 'economic' matters.

Intriguingly, the standard enunciated by the General Counsel is no more precise than the language used in the Articles. As a result, it has facilitated substantial expansion in the scope of the Bank's work so that today the Bank appears to be able to fund any activity – such as financing aspects of legal education, anti-corruption efforts, and demobilization of soldiers in post-conflict situations – that it is able to show to its own satisfaction has a 'direct, preponderant and clear' economic effect.

52. *See, e.g.*, World Bank, *Governance: The World Bank's Experience* (Washington, DC: The World Bank, 1994); World Bank, *Governance and Development* (Washington, DC: The World Bank, 1992).

53. The full text of Art. IV(10) is 'The Bank and its officers shall not interfere in the political affairs of any member; nor shall they be influenced in their decisions by the political character of the member or members concerned. Only economic considerations shall be relevant to their decisions, and these considerations shall be weighed impartially in order to achieve the purposes stated in Article I.' IBRD Articles of Agreement, *supra* n. 3, Art. IV(10).

54. *See* Ibrahim F.I. Shihata, 'The World Bank and "Governance" Issues in Its Borrowing Members', in *The World Bank in a Changing World*, ed. Ibrahim F.I. Shihata (Dordrect & Boston, MA: M. Nijhoff Publishers, 1991), 53. *See also* Ibrahim F.I. Shihata, *Prohibition of Political Activities in the Bank's Work: Legal Opinion by the Senior Vice President & General Counsel* (Washington, DC: World Bank, 12 Jul. 1995).

This expansion in the Bank's scope of operations has also complicated the work of the Bank. For example, it has made it difficult for the Bank to avoid the complex issue of its responsibilities in regard to human rights.[55]

The potential for the IMF to expand the scope of its operations is even greater than the Bank's because no obvious outer limit to its mandate exists, particularly in an era of relatively free choice in regard to exchange-rate and balance-of-payments policies. In fact, following the collapse of the par value system, the IMF began to treat any issue that can affect the foreign exchange and balance-of-payments of the Member State as a reasonable issue for inclusion in its surveillance activities and later in the conditionalities associated with its financial operations. As a result, the IMF can make a case to seek information and offer advice in connection with any issue in its Member States that takes its fancy.

In addition, the IMF's Articles do not have an explicit political prohibition. Instead, the Articles merely require the IMF to take the domestic social and political conditions in its Member States into account in its work in the country.[56] Interestingly, for many years the IMF's General Counsels interpreted this requirement as a strict political prohibition. However, they have subsequently loosened this interpretation so that the IMF can address governance issues in its Member States when it deems it necessary.[57]

The IFIs 'mission creep' has attracted criticisms.[58] These critics can be divided into two groups. First, there are those who criticize the Bank and the Fund

---

55. Starting in 1998, the Bank, issued public statements about the relationship between development and human rights. *See Development and Human Rights: The Role of the World Bank* (Washington, DC: World Bank, 1998); 'World Development Report 2006, Equity and Development' (2006). Roberto Dañino (Senior Vice-President and General Counsel), 'Legal Opinion on Human Rights and the Work of the World Bank' (27 Jan. 2006), *available at* <www.ifiwatchnet.org/sites/ifiwatchnet.org/files/DaninoLegalOpinion0106.pdf> (hereinafter Dañino Opinion) (indicating that human rights may constitute legitimate considerations for the Bank where they have economic ramifications or impacts, and it confirms the facilitative role the Bank may play in supporting its members to fulfil their human rights obligations). *See also* Siobhán McInerney-Lankford, 'International Financial Institutions and Human Rights: Select Perspectives on Legal Obligations', Ch. 8 herein; Mac Darrow, *Between Light and Shadow: The World Bank, the International Monetary Fund and International Human Rights Law* (Oxford & Portland, OR: Hart Publishing, 2003); Sigrun Skogly, *The Human Rights Obligations of the World Bank and the International Monetary Fund* (London: Cavendish Publishing, 2001).
56. IMF Articles of Agreement, *supra* n. 3, Art. IV(3)(b): 'These principles shall respect the domestic social and political policies of members, and in applying these principles the Fund shall pay due regard to the circumstances of members.'
57. *See* Robert Hockett, 'From Macro to Micro to "Mission Creep": Defending the IMF's Emerging Concern with the Infrastructural Prerequisites to Global Financial Stability', *Columbia Journal of Transnational Law* 41 (2002): 153, 177–178 (explaining (1) why it is appropriate for the IMF to adapt to changing circumstances in general; and (2) why the specific direction that the IMF has taken in expanding the scope of its attention is both legal and necessary. The IMF's charter vests in the IMF itself all power to interpret its own charter – a matter that raises 'a nearly irrebuttable presumption in favor of formal legality' of IMF action).
58. *See* John W. Head, 'Law and Policy in International Financial Institutions: The Changing Role of Law in the IMF and the Multilateral Development Banks', *Kansas Journal of Law & Public*

for the way they have gone about expanding their mission, rather than criticizing the fact that they have chosen to do so. This is a criticism about the direction and content of the mission creep. Some of these critics have contended mission creep feeds a tendency 'to politicize the two organizations in ways that . . . ultimately undermine their efficacy'.[59] Defenders of the World Bank and the IMF counter by stating that the mandates of these institutions are sufficiently flexible to accommodate, through well accepted means of treaty interpretation, the various types of operations they have undertaken.[60] For them, the exquisite ambiguity of the World Bank's and the IMF's Articles of Agreement provides the necessary support to their arguments. These defenders do not seem concerned that the IFIs either cannot or will not clearly articulate the outer limits of their mandates or explain how they should deal with the jurisdictional conflicts with other international organizations that are created by their mission creep.

The second group of mission creep critics focus on the content of the IFIs' operations rather than on the fact of its expanding mission.[61] These critics argue that the IFIs' operations raise questions about the obligations of the IFIs to respect international human rights and environmental law and their obligations to their Member States in this regard. While acknowledging that the IFIs are not signatories to the key international or regional treaties on these subjects, these critics maintain that, as subjects of international law, the IFIs at least have an obligation to ensure that their financing operations and the conditions attached thereto do not undermine their Member States' ability to comply with their own international legal commitments. These critics also suggest that customary international law may be a source of independent IFI obligations relating to the social and environmental impacts and consequences of their operations. On the other hand, some of these critics question the ability of the IFIs, given their specialized mandates, to assess these commitments adequately and ensure compliance with them. They, therefore, argue that the IFIs should respect the limits of their mandates and should defer on these important issues to other international organizations with greater authority and competence in these areas.

Policy 17 (2007): 194; Daniel Bradlow, 'Should the International Financial Institutions Play a Role in the Implementation and Enforcement of International Humanitarian Law?', *Kansas Law Review* 50 (2002): 695; Daniel Bradlow & Claudio Grossman, 'Limited Mandates and Intertwined Problems: A New Challenge for the World Bank and the IMF', *Human Rights Quarterly* 17 (1995): 411; Hockett, 'From Macro to Micro to "Mission Creep": Defending the IMF's Emerging Concern with the Infrastructural Prerequisites to Global Financial Stability', *supra* n. 57, 177–178.

59. Head, 'Law and Policy in International Financial Institutions: The Changing Role of Law in the IMF and the Multilateral Development Banks', *supra* n. 58.

60. *Ibid.* (citing Hockett, 'From Macro to Micro to "Mission Creep": Defending the IMF's Emerging Concern with the Infrastructural Prerequisites to Global Financial Stability', *supra* n. 57).

61. Head, 'Law and Policy in International Financial Institutions: The Changing Role of Law in the IMF and the Multilateral Development Banks', *supra* n. 58 (citing Mary C. Tsai, 'Globalisation and Conditionality: Two Sides of the Sovereignty Coin', *Law & Policy International Business* 31 (2000): 1317, 1318, 1329); Saladin Al-Jurf, 'Good Governance and Transparency: Their Impact on Development', *Transnational Law & Contemporary Problems* 9 (1999): 193, 206.

The IFIs are signatories to international agreements in addition to their Articles of Agreement. First, as specialized agencies of the United Nations, they each have signed a relationship agreement with the United Nations.[62] These agreements set out the terms of the relations between the United Nations and the IMF and the key entities in the World Bank Group. In substance, these agreements recognize that the IMF and the relevant World Bank Group entities have specialized mandates and expertise and that, while they should consult with and be respectful of the United Nations, they are not bound to comply with any instructions from the United Nations, with the exception of Article VII resolutions of the Security Council.[63] Second, they have concluded headquarters agreements with their host states and analogous agreements with other states in which they have offices. These agreements deal with the privileges and immunities of the IFI in the host states.[64] Their major relevance to the operations of the IFIs is that they seek to ensure that the IFIs are immune from suit in the courts of the host state. Finally, the IBRD and IDA and other IFIs enter into international agreements each time they conclude a loan or guarantee agreement with their Member States.[65] Since these three categories of agreements involve at least one international organization, they are not directly covered by the Vienna Convention. Instead, they are governed by customary international law and would be covered by the Vienna Convention on the Law of Treaties between States and International Organizations or between International Organizations, should it ever enter into effect.[66]

B. Customary International Law

It is difficult to identify many customary international law principles that are unambiguously applicable to the IFIs. In regard to the relations between the Member States and the IFIs, an important applicable customary international law principle is respect for the sovereignty of the Member States. This manifests itself

62. 'Agreements between the United Nations and the International Monetary Fund and the United Nations and the International Bank for Reconstruction and Development' 16 U.N.T.S. 328, 346 (1948) (hereinafter 'Relationship Agreement') (both came into force on 15 Nov. 1947); Agreement between the IDA and the United Nations, 394 U.N.T.S. 222 (27 Mar. 1961) (hereinafter UN-IDA Agreement).
63. *See* Relationship Agreement, *supra* n. 62.
64. *See, e.g.*, Headquarters Agreement between IMF and United States of America; Headquarters Agreement between IBRD and United States of America.
65. Broches, 'International Legal Aspects of the Operations of the World Bank', *supra* n. 35, 297; Head, 'Evolution of the Governing Law for Loan Agreements of the World Bank and Other Multilateral Development Banks', *supra* n. 35, 214.
66. The Vienna Convention on the Law of Treaties between States and International Organizations or between International Organizations, opened for signature on 21 Mar. 1986. The Convention has not yet obtained the requisite ratification of thirty-five states to enter into force. United Nations, 'Vienna Convention on the Law of Treaties between States and International Organizations or between International Organizations' (1986), *available at* <http://untreaty.un.org/ilc/texts/instruments/english/conventions/1_2_1986.pdf>.

in two ways. First, it means that the IFI in entering into an agreement, including a loan agreement, with one of its Member States must treat the agreement as an international agreement. This means that the IFIs should allow the State to subject the agreement to all the procedures for ratification that would be required for any international agreement. In addition, it should respect the requirements of Article 102 of the UN Charter and register the agreement with the United Nations.[67] In this regard, one important consequence of the IMF's contention that its stand-by arrangements are not contracts or agreements is that it does not feel compelled to comply with these international legal obligations.[68]

Second, respect for sovereignty means that the IFIs should refrain from interfering in those matters that fall within the 'domestic jurisdiction'[69] of their Member States. This obligation is becoming both easier and more complex. On the one hand, the scope of matters that are deemed by the United Nations to fall within a sovereign state's exclusive domestic jurisdiction has narrowed over time, so that currently, for example, states are required to report to international supervisory bodies on their compliance with specific international human rights agreements and there are some who contend that there is an international duty to protect groups and individuals from the most systematic and egregious human rights violations.[70] This suggests that the obligation to respect the domestic jurisdiction of their Member States does not set a particularly onerous limit on IFI operations.[71] On the other hand, the narrower scope of a sovereign's domestic jurisdiction imposes an obligation on the IFIs to deal responsibly with issues that were previously viewed as being within the Member State's exclusive jurisdiction and are now treated as being of international legal interest.

The challenges that this creates for IFIs can be seen most clearly in regard to the social and environmental consequences of their operations in their Member States. While it is clear that IFI operations can have profound social and environmental impacts – in fact, they are often specifically designed to have such impacts – it is less obvious that international law offers guidance to the IFIs in understanding their responsibilities in this regard. First, they are not signatories to any of the treaties that are applicable to these issues and so are not obliged to act in conformity

67. Broches, 'International Legal Aspects of the Operations of the World Bank', *supra* n. 35, 297 (It is important to note that the IFI that does not follow this requirement is the IMF because it does not view its stand-by arrangements as international agreements.).
68. Under its information disclosure policy, the IMF does make the stand-by decision of its Board public and does encourage its Member States to publicize their information memoranda. *See* IMF, 'IMF Executive Board Reviews Fund Transparency Policy', Public Information Notice No. 05/116 (15 Aug. 2005), *available at* <http://www.imf.org/external/np/sec/pn/2005/pn05116.htm>.
69. Charter of the United Nations, Art. 2(7) (24 Oct. 1945) (signed on 26 Jun. 1945), *available at* <www.un.org/en/documents/charter/intro.shtml>.
70. *See, e.g.*, José Alvarez, *International Organizations as Law-Makers* (Oxford & New York: Oxford University Press, 2005), 156–169, and sources cited therein.
71. It should be noted that over time and through the codification efforts of entities like the International Law Commission and the International Law Association the customary international legal obligations of international organizations are likely to evolve.

with their requirements. Second, not all their Member States may be signatories to these treaties, and so it is not clear that it would even be appropriate for the IFIs to insist that their Member States comply with these treaty requirements. Third, even if all Member States are parties to a particular treaty, it is not clear that the IFIs have the authority to impose their interpretation of that treaty on their Member States, particularly if the treaty is either open to differing interpretations or there is an entity charged with giving authoritative interpretations of the treaty and it has not yet decided a particular matter. Fourth, there is not general agreement on what constitutes the applicable customary international human rights and environmental law in regard to the IFIs.

Some commentators argue that the United Nations Declaration of Human Rights (UNDHR),[72] while not a binding treaty, is beginning to take on the characteristics of customary international law.[73] While this is an important issue, the challenge for the IFIs is that, even if this proposition is accepted, it is not clear what this functionally means. The provisions of the UNDHR are stated at the level of general principle, as it was always envisaged that they would be elaborated and eventually made binding through treaties. This would suggest that, at most, the UNDHR, as customary international law, would impose on the IFIs an obligation to respect, protect, and fulfil human rights. It can be seen from the chapter by Siobhán McInerney-Lankford in this book,[74] that the IFIs, if they wish, can take this general requirement quite far.[75] However, in the case of IFIs that are reluctant to assume this obligation, the lack of detail in the applicable customary international law provides them with an opportunity to argue that the obligation is difficult to operationalize. This can be seen in the case of the IMF, which has been more reluctant than the World Bank to address this issue.[76]

In regard to customary international environmental law, there are some that would argue that both the obligation to undertake impact assessments and the principle that one state should not cause environmental harm to a neighbouring state without its consent are assuming customary international law status.[77]

---

72. United Nations General Assembly Resolution, General Assembly Resolution 217 A (III) (Universal Declaration of Human Rights) (10 Dec. 1948), *available at* <www.ohchr.org/EN/UDHR/Pages/Introduction.aspx>.
73. For general discussion of this issue, *see* Darrow, *supra* n. 55, 129–133 and sources cited therein.
74. *See* Siobhán McInerney-Lankford, 'International Financial Institutions and Human Rights: Select Perspectives on Legal Obligations', Ch. 8 herein.
75. *See, e.g.*, Dañino Opinion, *supra* n. 55.
76. *See* François Gianviti, 'Economic, Social and Cultural Rights and the International Monetary Fund' (2002), *available at* <www.imf.org/external/np/leg/sem/2002/cdmfl/eng/gianv3.pdf>.
77. *See generally* David Hunter, James Salzman & Durwood Zaelke, *International Environmental Law and Policy*, 3rd edn (New York: Foundation Press, 2007). *See also* Legality of the Use by a State of Nuclear Weapons in Armed Conflict, Advisory Opinion, 1996 I.C.J. 66 (8 July); Trail Smelter Arbitration (1938/1941) 3 R.I.A.A. 1905; Stockholm Declaration of the United Nations Conference on the Human Environment, 11 I.L.M. 1416 (1972), *available at* <www.unep.org/Documents.Multilingual/Default.asp?DocumentID=97&ArticleID=1503>; Rio Declaration on Environment and Development, UN Doc. A/Conf.151/26 (vol. 1); 31 I.L.M. 874 (1992), *available at* <www.un.org/documents/ga/conf151/aconf15126-1annex1.htm>.

In regard to the IFIs, they are unlikely to find the requirement to undertake impact assessments particularly problematic. In fact, all the MDBs perform impact assessments before undertaking at least those projects that have a significant impact on their environment.[78] However, their motivation for doing so is not explicit and is therefore unclear. This means that we cannot be certain if they undertake these assessments because they believe they are obliged to do so or because they think it is prudent and best practice to do so. One indication that they view this as a binding obligation rather than merely as conforming to 'best practice' in their operations is that they all have relatively detailed public policies and procedures with which the impact assessments that they undertake should comply. While these policies are subject to change, developed internally, and only applicable to the relevant IFI itself, the fact that they may be approved by their Boards, are made publicly available, and that the IFIs can be held accountable for their compliance with these policies, suggest that they are viewed by the IFIs themselves as having an obligatory nature.

It is important to note that the IMF appears either not to accept that this is a binding principle of customary international law or does not believe that its operations have a substantial enough environmental impact to make this principle applicable to it. This can be deduced from the facts that it has not developed any publicly available policies or procedures on this subject and that it does not require impact assessments of any of its operations.

The World Bank's position on the case of the principle of not causing environmental harm to neighbouring states without prior consultation is less clear. On the one hand, the World Bank seems to recognize the principle in its policy on transboundary watercourses, in which it requires prior consultation and

78. *See, e.g.*, The World Bank, OP 4.01 – Environmental Assessment (January 1999) (requiring an environmental assessment of projects), *available at* <http://go.worldbank.org/RUEQVWD550>; IFC, 'International Finance Corporation's Performance Standards on Social & Environmental Sustainability' (30 Apr. 2006), PS 1 (laying out the criteria for the 'Social and Environmental Assessment and Management Systems' required for projects), *available at* <www.ifc.org/ifcext/sustainability.nsf/AttachmentsByTitle/pol_PerformanceStandards2006_full/$FILE/IFC+Performance+Standards.pdf>; Inter-American Development Bank, 'Environment and Safeguards Compliance Policy' (19 Jan. 2006), s. B.3, 4.17 (detailing the Bank procedure for 'Screening and Classification' including requiring an Environmental Impact Assessment for all projects 'likely to cause significant negative environmental and associated social impacts'), *available at* <http://idbdocs.iadb.org/wsdocs/getDocument.aspx?DOCNUM=665902>; European Bank for Reconstruction and Development, 'Environmental and Social Policy' (May 2008), PR1, *available at* <www.ebrd.com/about/policies/enviro/policy/2008policy.pdf>; African Development Bank, 'African Development Bank Group's Policy on the Environment' (February 2004), 6.6 (requiring an Environmental and Social Impact Assessment for Category 1 projects), *available at* <www.afdb.org/fileadmin/uploads/afdb/Documents/Policy-Documents/10000027-EN-BANK-GROUP-POLICY-ON-THE-ENVIRONMENT.PDF>; Asian Development Bank, 'Safeguard Policy Statement' (June 2009), para. 50 (projects with significant adverse environmental impacts must undergo an environmental impact assessment), *available at* <www.adb.org/Documents/Policies/Safeguards/Safeguard-Policy-Statement-June2009.pdf>.

agreement with potentially affected neighbouring states.[79] However, there is no clear indication that the Bank feels legally obliged to maintain this requirement. For example, it does not require similar consultations in regard to other forms of potential cross-border environmental impact. This would suggest that the Bank does not view itself as being legally obligated to comply with the more general principle.

A third more controversial example is the case of the precautionary principle. There are two aspects to the controversy. First, it is clear that not all IFI Member States accept that the precautionary principle has acquired the status of a principle of customary international law.[80] Some of the IFIs' largest Member States reject this position. Second, the IFIs, like most financial institutions, find the principle constricting and contend that, even if they were inclined to do so, it would not be easily applicable in their operations. Thus, they do not have any policies or procedures that explicitly require the application of the precautionary principle to their operations. Nevertheless, it can be argued that the World Bank's operational policies dealing with environmental issues are motivated in part by a precautionary impulse. However, the fact that this impulse is left implicit suggests that, to the extent the Bank acts in conformity with the precautionary principle, it is motivated more by its own operational choices than by a sense of legal obligation.

The above discussion indicates that the IFIs formulate in their operational policies and procedures their own approaches to potentially applicable principles of customary international law. In turn, these policies help educate the IFIs' borrowers about their requirements and help define their obligations to those directly affected by their operations. This suggests that the IFIs, in fact, may be playing some role in creating international law, a topic which we will discuss in more detail in the next section.

---

79. *See* The World Bank, Transboundary Waters, <http://web.worldbank.org/WBSITE/EXTERNAL/TOPICS/EXTWAT/0,,contentMDK:21633352~menuPK:4828556~pagePK:148956~piPK:216618~theSitePK:4602123,00.html>, 25 Feb. 2010 (providing information and links to policies and projects relating to how the World Bank addresses transboundary watercourses); The World Bank, OP 7.50 – Projects on International Waterways (June 2001), *available at* <http://web.worldbank.org/WBSITE/EXTERNAL/PROJECTS/EXTPOLICIES/EXTOPMANUAL/0,,contentMDK:20064667~menuPK:4564185~pagePK:64709096~piPK:64709108~theSitePK:502184,00.html>.

80. The European Union and the United States have long-debated the precautionary principle with the EU advocating for its use, and the US refusing to adopt it as a basis for assessing risk. *See, e.g.*, Jonathan B. Wiener & Michael D. Rogers, 'Comparing Precaution in the United States and Europe', *Journal of Risk Research* 5 (2002), *available at* <www.nicholas.duke.edu/solutions/documents/PP-EU-USpaperJRR2002final.pdf>; Bette Hileman, 'Precautionary Principle Debate', *Chemical & Engineering News (CENEAR)* 80(16) (22 Apr. 2002); Joel Tickner & Nancy Myers, 'Current Status and Implementation of the Precautionary Principle', Science & Environmental Health Network, <www.sehn.org/ppcurrentstatus.html>; Brian P. Rafferty, 'The Door Opens Slightly: Recent European Union Regulations on Genetically Modified Products and the Ongoing United States-European Union GM Product Dispute', *Georgetown International Environmental Law Review* (Winter 2004) (case note discussing the EU-US precautionary principle debate in the context of genetically modified products).

A second set of customary international law principles relate to the enforcement of any international agreements between the IFIs and the Member States. The Vienna Convention[81] codifies customary international law relating to international agreements. The most relevant of these is the principle of *pacta sunt servanda*, codified in Article 26,[82] which states that '[e]very treaty in force is binding upon the parties to it and must be performed by them in good faith'.[83]

This principle is tempered by the principle of *rebus sic stantibus*. Article 62 of the Vienna Convention codifies this principle, and states that a fundamental change of circumstances can, under some conditions, be a legal justification for failing to perform or suspending performance of treaty obligations.[84]

The principle of *rebus sic stantibus* is thus an exception to the rule of *pacta sunt servanda*. The Vienna Convention on the Law of Treaties between States and International Organizations or between International Organizations, although not yet in force, makes clear that the principles of *pacta sunt servanda* and *rebus sic stantibus* are also applicable to agreements involving the IFIs.[85]

An interesting example of how the IFIs have been taking both these principles into account, is how the IFIs have handled the sovereign debt crises of their Member States. At different times they have emphasized one or the other of these principles in the role that they have played during the debt crises of their Member States. They have emphasized *pacta sunt servanda* when they believe that their primary obligation is to help enforce debt obligations and uphold the sanctity of contract for the sake of the functioning of the international financial system. At other times they have been willing to champion a version of *rebus sic stantibus* (i.e., debt forgiveness and lending into arrears) when they have seen, as systemically more important, the debtor countries' need for substantial debt relief in order to meet their obligations to their own citizens.[86]

Jus cogens, which refers to those fundamental principles of international law from which no derogation is possible, constitutes a third category of customary international legal principles that are applicable to the IFIs. However, given the consequences that attach to *jus cogens* legal principles, they are limited to principles on which there is universal agreement, such as the prohibitions against torture, genocide, slavery, apartheid, use of force, and self-determination. Therefore,

81. Vienna Convention, *supra* n. 46, 331.
82. *Ibid.*, 339.
83. *Ibid.*, 340.
84. *Ibid.*, 347.
85. Vienna Convention on the Law of Treaties between States and International Organizations or between International Organizations, *supra* n. 66. *See also* Roberto Dañino Zapata, 'Why Treaties Matter', Opening Remarks – First Annual Conference 'Interpretation under the Vienna Convention on the Law of Treaties – 25 Years On' (London, 17 Jan. 2006), *available at* <http://siteresources.worldbank.org/INTLAWJUSTICE/214576-1139604306966/20817203/WhyTreatiesMatterLondon011706.pdf>.
86. For a more detailed discussion of this point, *see* Daniel Bradlow, 'Developing Country Debt Crises, International Financial Institutions, and International Law: Some Preliminary Thoughts', *German Yearbook of International Law* (13 Feb. 2009); American University, WCL Research Paper No. 09-01, *available at* SSRN: <http://ssrn.com/abstract=1342539>.

jus cogens principles are of limited application in the normal course of the IFI's operations. This should not, however, be interpreted to mean that *jus cogens* principles may not have some relevance in exceptional circumstances. For example, such principles could be relevant to an IFI that is funding a legal reform project in a country that routinely uses torture in its criminal justice system, or to an IFI in connection with its operations in a particularly difficult post-conflict situation.

C. General Principles Accepted by All Nations

In the best of circumstances, it is not easy to identify general principles of law that are accepted by all nations. It is even more difficult to identify general principles that are applicable to the operations of the IFIs. Arguably, the only general principles of law that are applicable to the IFIs are the principles of good faith[87] and non-discriminatory treatment. While these are easy to state, it is not clear exactly how useful they are in guiding the operations of the IFIs.

The principle of good faith can be interpreted, in addition to relating to performance of applicable treaty obligations, as a call to honesty in dealings between the IFIs and the stakeholders in their operations. This suggests that they should deal fairly and in a transparent manner with all these stakeholders. Exactly what constitutes fair dealing with these stakeholders is unclear. For example, when to consult with each of the stakeholders in a particular IFI operation, how much information to make available to the stakeholders, and how to handle complaints from the stakeholders may vary according to the identity of the stakeholders, their relationship to the IFI and, in some cases, the relevant Member State. Given these variables, and the fact that the meaning of good faith as a general principle is imprecise, the content of this obligation must be left to the discretion of each IFI.

Similarly, the principle of non-discrimination merely requires an international actor to treat all similarly situated parties in a like manner. Because the principle does not define 'similarly situated' with any clarity, it is left, in the first instance, to the IFIs to determine for themselves how to apply the principle of non-discrimination in their operations. While IFIs at times certainly have treated specific Member States in an overbearing or heavy-handed way, it is hard to show that this was discriminatory, that is that they would have treated any other Member State, had it been similarly situated, more favourably.

D. IFI Compliance with International Law

The introduction to this paper suggests that the compliance of IFI operations with international law should be evaluated in terms of three standards. First, they can be evaluated in terms of their observance of international law in regard to project

87. This can also be seen as merely a restatement of Art. 26 of the Vienna Convention, *supra* n. 46, which is the provision defining *pacta sunt servanda*.

planning, evaluation, and implementation. This involves testing their operational compliance with the terms of their Articles of Agreement. In the case of the World Bank and the IMF, the above indicates that their Articles place very loose limits on the kinds of activities they can fund and on the conditions they can attach to their financial transactions with their Member States. In addition, as indicated above, the IFIs' Articles of Agreement are interpreted by their general counsels and their boards of directors, who are free to interpret the Articles as they deem appropriate. Thus, it is difficult to clearly establish that an IFI is not complying with its Articles as interpreted and applied by it.

It also requires determining if they are complying with any customary international legal obligations and any general principles of law that may be applicable to their operations. As we can see, these sources of international law offer limited guidance to the IFIs in terms of how they should structure their operations. Based on the above discussion, it can be concluded that the IFIs do have some obligations in regard to international human rights and environmental matters, although the precise content of these obligations is unclear. At least the World Bank has acknowledged this obligation and does appear to be making some effort to incorporate these principles into the policies and procedures that are applicable to its operations and against which they can be held accountable. Since the IMF does not have as detailed and extensive operational policies and procedures as the Bank, it is harder to determine to what extent it feels bound by these aspects of customary international law. As was indicated above, however, the IMF's current operating practices suggest that it does not consider customary international environmental law as being applicable to it.

The second aspect of measuring IFI operational compliance with international law relates to the structuring of their financial agreements with their Member States. The only international legal principles applicable in this regard are *pacta sunt servanda* and *rebus sic stantibus*. The World Bank appears to be complying with both these principles in its financial transactions. Interestingly, the position in regard to the IMF is less clear because it is not willing to concede that all its transactions with its Member States are actually contractual. As a result, it does not accept that these principles are actually applicable to its transactions.

The third standard is the IFIs' relations with all the stakeholders in their operations. The applicable legal principles differ depending on the identity of the stakeholder and on the nature of their relationship. The legal relationships are more easily defined in regard to those stakeholders with whom the IFI has some form of contractual relationship. Thus, the general relationship between the IFIs and their Member States is governed primarily by their Articles of Agreement and the way in which those are interpreted. Their relationship with their borrowers and their suppliers is set out in their contractual arrangements and in any applicable provisions in their Articles of Agreement. Their relationship with the United Nations is governed by the applicable relationship agreement and how it is interpreted. The issue is most complex in regard to those stakeholders with whom the IFI does not have a direct contractual relationship, but who are nevertheless directly affected by its operations. These include those non-state actors who are often the intended beneficiaries of these operations or at least are directly affected by them. The above discussion indicates that the international law, stipulated in the applicable international agreements, customary international law, and general principles of law accepted by all nations, does not provide a clear answer regarding the law applicable to this relationship. This suggests, absent a significant step in the development of international law, that the IFIs have to resolve this issue for themselves. This, in turn, raises the issue of the IFIs' ability to shape the development of international law, which is the subject of the next section of this paper.

IV. IFIs AND THE DEVELOPMENT OF INTERNATIONAL LAW

The IFIs are not only subjects of international law who are passive recipients of the rights and obligations that the law grants or imposes on them, but they are also actors with the capacity to influence the development of international law. This can occur in three ways. The first is in regard to their policies and procedures. The second is through their efforts to make themselves more publicly accountable. Each of these is discussed below.

The third way is through the IFIs themselves signing and becoming parties to international agreements. As indicated above, all the IFIs are signatories to international treaties. To date, the IFIs have signed treaties that either deal with their relations with their Member States, like headquarter agreements or loan agreements, or with their relations with other international organizations, for example, relationship agreements. They have not signed international agreements that deal with substantive international legal issues, such as human rights or environmental issues. Given the relatively narrow scope of the treaties actually signed by the IFIs, this aspect of their capacity to help create international law is excluded from the following discussion.

A. Policies and Procedures

The MDBs, but not the IMF, each have a relatively detailed set of publicly available operational policies and procedures that are intended to guide both their staff and management in their work, and to help educate other stakeholders in MDB operations about how the MDBs go about doing their work. These policies address many aspects of their operations. They range from such technical issues as how funds are expected to be disbursed and then paid back to such issues as how they should address the social and environmental aspects of their projects.

The World Bank has adopted a set of 'safeguard policies' to ensure more effective treatment of social and environmental issues in its operations.[88] Other

88. World Bank, Operational Manual: Operational Policies and Procedures, *available at* <http://web.worldbank.org/WBSITE/EXTERNAL/PROJECTS/EXTPOLICIES/EXTOPMANUAL/0,,menuPK:64701637~pagePK:51628525~piPK:64857279~theSitePK:502184,00.html>.

MDBs have adopted similar sets of policies. The World Bank's safeguard policies address such issues as treatment of involuntarily resettled people; the IFIs responsibilities towards indigenous people; environmental impact assessments and environmental management plans; and the treatment of cultural physical property. All of these topics raise important and complex issues on which there are not generally agreed applicable international legal principles. Consequently, the positions that the IFIs incorporate into their operational policies and procedures and how they implement them have the potential to establish precedents that can influence other subjects of international law as they grapple with these issues and their international legal obligations in this regard. This means that as the IFIs implement and interpret their policies they will be both applying and shaping the applicable international law.

The impacts of the IFIs' decisions and actions, therefore, have a number of international legal implications. First, they suggest that the MDBs are creating at least a soft '*lex specialis*' to govern their own operations in regard to their Member States. As they implement this soft law, it has the potential to raise expectations among the stakeholders in these operations who begin to expect the MDBs to comply with this soft law in their operation and to anticipate that they can hold the MDBs to account if they fail to comply with them. In addition, the standards set by one MDB have the potential to influence the standards of other MDBs. In these ways, these soft law standards have the potential to 'harden' at least within the limited sphere of MDBs.

The standards established in the MDB policies and procedures also have the potential to influence other subjects of international law. Since the MDBs often operate in a broad range of countries and projects, the standards set out in their policies and procedures often tend to come to be seen as 'best practice' in particular areas. As a result, they have the potential to establish functional benchmarks that are then incorporated by other actors – private corporations and states – into their laws, policies, and procedures. The implementation of these MDB policies may thus shape state practice in certain areas. In this way, the MDB policies and procedures have the potential to influence the further development of international law.

Interestingly, as this process unfolds it has the potential to impact the policies and procedures of the IFIs themselves and to make it harder for them to justify changes in the principles and standards established in their own policies and procedures. This is particularly the case if the changes can be construed as lowering the standards set out in these policies and procedures.

Second, these practices create expectations in the intended beneficiaries of these policies. This in turn has implications for both lawmaking and accountability in the IFIs. In the case of lawmaking, the fact that the intended beneficiaries begin to develop an expectation of certain standards of treatment from the IFIs has the potential to create expectations about the policy-making process in the IFIs. In particular, it leads these beneficiaries and other stakeholders to expect that the drafting of these policies and procedures will not be a closed process and that they will have opportunities to participate in their formulation. This in turn means that the MDBs will have to establish certain procedures for drafting and adopting these policies and procedures. In other words, a form of international administrative law relating to rulemaking is beginning to emerge in regard to these policies and procedures.[89] It is to be expected that these rulemaking procedures will influence other IFIs and even other international organizations. In fact, it would appear that they have already begun to influence the IMF, which followed a particularly open process in adopting its new policies on conditionality.

Thus, through the formulation and implementation of their internal policies and procedures, the IFIs have the potential to play an active role in influencing aspects of international law, which are arguably outside their core mandates. They also have the potential to influence other international actors and their conduct. One interesting example in this regard is the way that the IFC's performance standards have influenced the conduct of international commercial banks.[90]

B. Accountability

The First Report of the ILA's Committee on Accountability of International Organizations states '[a]ccountability is not a notion which, for the sake of its operationality, is or has to be viewed as monolithic, calling for uniform and indiscriminate application. Such rigidity would not survive the complexities of international reality'.[91] Instead, accountability is multifaceted, with various degrees of consequences ranging from oversight, monitoring, and evaluation processes to censorship or other forms of sanctions to the attribution of legal liability for injuries, resulting in binding remedial action.[92]

The expansion of the mission of the IFIs has raised concerns about their accountability in two regards. First, given their increased engagement with the policy-making and governance structures of those Member States that use their services (consumer Member States), there is a concern about how relatively difficult it is for these Member States to raise their concerns directly in the boards of directors of the IFIs, on which they often do not have direct representation. Since this concern is a function of the weighted voting system and of the composition of the board, it has helped stimulate an ongoing debate over voting rights and board representation within the IFIs.[93] Given that resolving this issue requires some states to give up either some of their voting rights or their seats on the board, it

89. *See* David Hunter, 'International Law and Public Participation in Policy-Making at the International Financial Institutions', Ch. 7 herein, for a more detailed discussion of this issue.
90. *See* Equator Principles, *available at* <www.equator-principles.com/principles.shtml>.
91. Report of the International Law Association Committee on Accountability of International Organizations, *available at* <www.ila-hq.org/en/committees/index.cfm/cid/9> (the author was a member of the committee).
92. For critical view of this report, *see* Ige F. Dekker, 'Making Sense of Accountability in International Institutional Law', *Netherlands Yearbook of International Law* 36 (2005): 83.
93. Ariel Buira (ed.), *Challenges to the World Bank and the IMF: Developing Country Perspectives* (London & New York: Anthem Press, 2003), 55–90; Daniel Bradlow, 'The Governance of the

is unlikely that the issue will be resolved soon. In fact, the more likely short-term impact is to stimulate greater interest in alternative means of enhancing IFI accountability.

Second, a consequence of the expansion in the scope of IFI operations is that they have a broader impact in their Member States. In fact, de facto, they are often key actors in the policy-making processes of their Member States. This brings them into more direct contact with the citizens and other non-state actors in those Member States that use their services. However, there has historically only been indirect and limited ways in which these non-state actors and private citizens can seek to hold the IFIs accountable for their actions. Legally, the only route was for them to advocate to their governments to raise the issue either at the board of governors level or to the boards of directors of the IFIs. Few governments were ever willing to do this, particularly since they were usually partners in the operations about which the non-state actors were concerned. Consequently, historically the IFIs were effectively unaccountable to non-state actors for the adverse impacts of their operations. This changed in 1994 when the World Bank created the World Bank Inspection Panel (the Panel).[94] This example, subsequently followed in different forms in all regional development banks and the IFC, created a new mechanism through which private actors can hold IFIs accountable.[95] In particular, non-state actors, who believe that they have been harmed or threatened with harm because of the failure of the Bank to comply with its own policies and procedures in an operation in their country, can petition the Panel to investigate the project and make findings to the board of the Bank about the staff and management's compliance with the applicable policies. These mechanisms are relatively new and, at the time of writing, the oldest, the World Bank Inspection Panel, has only had

IMF: The Need for Comprehensive Reform' (prepared for G24 Technical Committee) (September 2006), *available at* <www.g24.org/brad0906.pdf>.

94. *See* IBRD Resolution 93–10 and IDA Resolution 93–6 (The World Bank Inspection Panel was adopted by the Bank's Board of Executive Directors on 22 Sep. 1993). For information on the creation of the Inspection Panel, *see* Ibrahim F.I. Shihata, *The World Bank Inspection Panel* (Oxford & New York: Oxford University Press, 1994); Daniel Bradlow, 'International Organizations and Private Complainants: The Case of the World Bank Inspection Panel', *Virginia Journal of International Law* 34 (1994): 553; Daniel Bradlow & Sabine Schlemmer-Schulte, 'The World Bank's New Inspection Panel: A Constructive Step in the Transformation of the International Legal Order', *Zeitschrift für Ausländisches Öffentliches Recht und Völkerrecht* 54 (1994): 392; Eisuke Suzuki & Suresh Nanwani, 'Responsibility of International Organizations: The Accountability Mechanisms of Multilateral Development Banks', *Michigan Journal of International Law* 27 (2005): 177.

95. For a comparative study of these mechanisms, *see* Daniel Bradlow, 'Private Complainants and International Organizations: A Comparative Study of the Independent Inspection Mechanisms in International Financial Institutions', *Georgetown Journal of International Law* 36 (2005): 403. *See also* Richard Bissell & Suresh Nanwani, 'Multilateral Development Bank Accountability Mechanisms: Developments and Challenges', *Manchester Journal of International Economic Law* 6, no. 1 (2009); David Hunter & Lori Udall, 'The World Bank Inspection Panel', *CIEL Issue Brief* No. 1 (April 1994) (reprinted in *Environment* (November 1994)).

fifty-eight requests for inspections.[96] Nevertheless, it would seem that these mechanisms, despite some concerns about their efficacy, have resulted in increased accountability for these institutions.[97]

The above suggests that the IFIs, or at least the MDBs, have made significant efforts to enhance their accountability to those non-state stakeholders who are directly affected by their operations, but who do not have a direct contractual relationship with them. It should be noted that the inspection panels are not able to review complaints raising international law issues unless these arise directly from the IFIs' operational policies. They are meeting their obligations both through the terms of their operational policies and procedures and through the independent accountability mechanisms that they have established. Thus, they are at least making progress towards satisfying the third standard in terms of which their operational compliance with international law can be evaluated. In addition, it is clear that, because of the reports and findings of the independent accountability mechanisms which necessarily have to interpret MDB policies, the IFIs are also becoming increasing relevant as creators of international law, at least in the sense of establishing precedents (or examples) that can be used by others in the development of international law.

V. CONCLUSION

The world today is very different from the one for which the World Bank and IMF were created. Powerful political, social, environmental, and economic forces are changing the way in which business is done in both developing and rich countries and are forcing all actors to adapt to this new reality.[98]

In such a complex environment, it is a challenge for the IFIs, as subjects of international law, to identify and determine how best to comply with all applicable international legal requirements. As we have seen the requirements that arise from customary international law and from general principles of law accepted by all nations are non-specific and are not easy to apply to the operations of the IFIs. In addition, all the IFIs have imprecise and flexibly drafted Articles of Agreement, which give them great discretion in interpreting and implementing their own Articles.

Nevertheless, the exquisite ambiguity of their Articles and the relative lack of precision in the applicable international legal principles mean that the IFIs have no

96. *See* The World Bank Inspection Panel, <www.worldbank.org/inspectionpanel> (providing information about all aspects of the Inspection Panel).
97. *See* Dana Clark, Jonathan Fox & Kay Treakle (eds), *Demanding Accountability: Civil Society Claims and the World Bank Inspection Panel* (Lanham, MD: Rowman & Littlefield Publishing, 2003); International Bank for Reconstruction and Development, 'Accountability at the World Bank – The Inspection Panel: 10 Years On' (2003), *available at* <http://siteresources.worldbank.org/EXTINSPECTIONPANEL/Resources/InspPanel_Front_matter.pdf>.
98. *See generally* Daniel Bradlow, 'Differing Conceptions of Development and the Content of International Development Law', *South African Journal of Human Rights* 21 (2005): 535.

choice other than to interpret these international legal requirements and decide how they apply to their operations. Since these principles relate to important, complex, and often unresolved international legal issues, it is to be expected that other international bodies will look to the IFIs to see how they resolve these issues. In this way, the IFIs become relevant and active creators of international law. This role is further enhanced by the work of the independent accountability mechanisms. Thus, it can be seen that the IFIs' operations are both guided by and influence the evolution of international law.

Given that the IFIs are facing complex and diverse economic, financial, political, social, and environmental issues, it can be seen that they are on the cutting edge of difficult and important international law issues. How they respond to these issues will set precedents that have the potential to influence other international actors and to guide their own further responses to these issues.

Chapter 2

International Financial Institutions and International Law: A Third World Perspective

B.S. Chimni

I. INTRODUCTION

In this essay, due to constraints of space, I explore *select aspects* of the following theses:

- The goal of international financial institutions (IFIs) is the defence and expansion of the global capitalist system.
- The different phases of the evolution of IFIs are a response to the changing needs, or crisis in, global capitalism.
- The IFIs derive their mandate and authority from international law, but are averse to observing the international rule of law.
- The ambiguities that characterize the mandates of IFIs allow them to be interpreted in a manner that helps realize the interests of advanced capitalist states.
- The IFIs assertion of being beyond politics allows them to ignore the purposes and principles of the UN system and international human rights law.
- The norms relating to the responsibility of international organizations in international law are underdeveloped allowing IFIs to evade accountability and legal responsibility for their policies and programmes.

Daniel D. Bradlow and David B. Hunter, *International Financial Institutions and International Law*, pp. 31–62.

- The deficiencies in the structure of management of IFIs and their weighted voting system contribute to the neglect of the concerns of third world countries.
- The IFIs will respond to the concerns of subaltern states and groups in the international system only if backed by global social movements.

I proceed in the following way. Section II identifies the key features of a third world approach to international law (TWAIL) that informs this essay. Section III briefly looks at the changing role of IFIs, and the interpretations advanced of their mandates and conditionalities, to contend among other things that IFIs are not beyond politics. Section IV looks at the relationship of IFIs with international human rights law and argues that, being subjects of international law, IFIs are bound by core international human rights conventions and obligations. Section V explores the question of accountability and responsibility of international organizations. Noting that international organizations are moral agents and therefore can be made responsible in international law, it briefly reviews the existing state of the law as reflected in the ongoing work of the International Law Commission (ILC). Section VI looks at the structure of management and decision-making in the IFIs to argue that their unique features reinforce the tendency to neglect subaltern states and groups. Section VII contains some final reflections.

II. THE TWAIL APPROACH TO INTERNATIONAL LAW AND INSTITUTIONS

A contemporary approach to international law and international institutions that seeks to examine the role of IFIs from the perspective of subaltern states and peoples is the Third World Approach to International Law (TWAIL).[1] The TWAIL approach has at its core at least five critical features or insights that help better understand the role of IFIs in the international system.

First, TWAIL suggests that international monetary law and institutions be viewed in the context of the character of contemporary international law (CIL) and institutions, which in the TWAIL view is imperial in character.[2] While

1. B.S. Chimni, 'Third World Approaches to International Law: A Manifesto', in *The Third World and International Order: Law, Politics and Globalization*, ed. Antony Anghie et al. (Leiden: Martinus Nijhoff, 2003), 47–75; B.S. Chimni 'A Just World Under Law: A View from the South', *American University International Law Review* 22 (2007): 199–220; Obiora Chinedu Okafor, 'Newness, Imperialism, and International Legal Reform in Our Time: TWAIL Matters', *Osgoode Hall Law Journal* 43 (2005): 171–190. *See also infra* n. 2.
2. Contemporary international law (CIL) may be defined as 'a system of principles and norms arrived at primarily between states, and secondarily through a network of non-state entities, embodying particular class interests, that are enforced by a range of means, increasingly international institutions that together signify the emergence of a nascent global state. CIL is today in transition from being bourgeois democratic in character to a bourgeois imperialist international law that increasingly codifies the interests of the emerging TCC [Transnational Capitalist Class] at the expense of interests of the subaltern classes and substantive global

developments in specialized branches of international law and institutions may not always coincide, there is a tendency for all branches to manifest similar trends, for these are shaped in the final analysis by the structure of the world economy and the distribution of global power.[3] The move to study IFIs in relation to the character of CIL and institutions has an important advantage. It allows a holistic perspective that evaluates the functioning and the impact of IFIs along with the role of other international laws and institutions (e.g., the World Trade Organization (WTO)). For instance, in considering the impact of IFI policies on third world peoples, the move to aggregate the role of IOs facilitates a more adequate response to questions of 'causality'. Thereby the rejoinder of critics that questions the causal relationship between IFI policies/programmes and serious violations of the human rights of peoples of borrowing states loses some of its edge. The growing empirical evidence of the impact of IFI policies and programmes only goes to strengthen the conclusion.

Second, TWAIL insists on a historical perspective in considering the role of CIL and institutions. It argues that CIL and institutions often have their basis in colonial ideas, categories, and practices. Anghie, for instance, has demonstrated how the IFIs perform essentially the same functions as the Mandate System of the League of Nations: civilizing the backward peoples of the world.[4] Mainstream international law scholarship has however ignored the historical continuity that marks the role of IFIs in framing policies that seek to bring economic stability, development, and good governance to former colonial countries.

---

democracy'. B.S. Chimni, 'An Outline of a Marxist Course on Public International Law', *Leiden Journal of International Law* 17 (2004): 9–10. The character of CIL, of course, is not shaped merely by the developments in the capitalist world economy. That assertion would represent crude economic determinism. 'CIL is shaped by a range of factors including: (i) the history and the internal logic and dynamics of international law; (ii) the cohesiveness and strength of the class that occupies center stage at the global level at a particular historical conjuncture; (iii) the nature of the states system (unipolar or multipolar) and its implications for the security of states; (iv) the role of non-state actors, including international institutions and civil society organizations; and (v) the strength of the opposition or dissent movements at the internal and international levels. Each of these factors may play a decisive role depending on the subject, arena, and political conjuncture of law making.' *Ibid.*, 9. On the character of CIL, *see also* Antony Anghie, *Imperialism, Sovereignty and the Making of International Law* (Cambridge: Cambridge University Press, 2004); B.S. Chimni, 'Marxism and International Law: A Contemporary Analysis', *Economic and Political Weekly* 34 (1999): 337–349. B.S. Chimni 'International Institutions Today: An Imperial Global State in the Making', *European Journal of International Law* 15 (2004): 1–39.

3. The ongoing fragmentation of international law, with different branches of international law emerging and developing without firm relation to others, simply reflects their inability to cohere in terms of the interests of subaltern states and groups as opposed to that of hegemonic states and classes. In other words, both unity and fragmentation are problematic depending on the perspective from which international law developments are approached. Unity is not necessarily a goal worth pursuing unless it is progressive unity.
4. Antony Anghie, 'Time Present and Time Past: Globalization, International Financial Institutions, and the Third World', *New York University Journal of International Law and Politics* 32 (2000): 243–290.

Third, TWAIL rejects the realist view that international organizations simply mirror the state of international politics and believes that international organizations possess a relative autonomy from the Member States. In the TWAIL view, the relative autonomy of contemporary international organizations is a function of the fact that they do not seek to advance the interests of one or another advanced capitalist state, but that of the global capitalist system in its different phases. A parallel is the role of the capitalist state whose key task is the construction and defence of capitalism rather than the interests of this or that capitalist.[5] This understanding also points to the limits of the possible reform of international organizations because international organizations that are crucial to sustaining the global capitalist system cannot be radically reformed to the advantage of subaltern states and groups in the international system.

Fourth, TWAIL contends that an important strategy through which the interests of global capital are realized in international law and institutions is what may be termed the interpretative strategy. A significant way of justifying and legitimizing the changing role of IFIs in response to developments in the global capitalist system is the reinterpretation of the constituent instruments or mandates of international organizations. These interpretations are advanced within a particular global knowledge-power constellation and therefore tend to be perceived as authoritative. To put it differently, the mandates of international organizations are framed in broad terms allowing expedient interpretations to be advanced by powerful states with relative ease to promote the interests of a global capitalist class.

Fifth, TWAIL proposes that acts of opposition and resistance to international laws and institutions by subaltern states and groups should be treated as an integral part of the discourse of international law.[6] However, in mainstream international law scholarship the protests against IFIs policies and programmes are not always seen as relevant from a legal and institutional standpoint. The acts of resistance therefore do not become part of an interpretive framework to give meaning to, and determine the legitimacy of, relevant legal texts and institutional practices, unless special institutional processes are created to take cognizance of them (e.g., World Bank's Inspection Panel). TWAIL, in contrast, suggests that international organization mandates be interpreted, and institutional practices be reformed, in the backdrop of the concerns of subaltern states and peoples that are the subject of international organization policies and programmes. This is especially necessary because the policies of international organizations today have come to have a crucial impact on the lives of ordinary citizens. While the IFIs have responded in a small way to criticisms emanating from global social movements, much more serious engagement is clearly necessary.[7]

5. Antonio Gramsci, *Prison Notebooks* (London: Lawrence & Wishart, 1971), 181–182.
6. Balakrishnan Rajagopal, *International Law from Below: Development, Social Movements and Resistance from Below* (Cambridge: Cambridge University Press, 2003); Chimni, 'Third World Approaches to International Law: A Manifesto', *supra* n. 1, 65 ff.
7. Robert O'Brien et al., *Contesting Global Governance: Multilateral Economic Institutions and Global Social Movements* (Cambridge: Cambridge University Press, 2000), 3.

III. CHANGING ROLE OF IFIs: INTERPRETATIONS OF MANDATES AND CONDITIONALITIES

The functions of IFIs are stated in their respective Articles of Agreement.[8] The International Monetary Fund (IMF) and the World Bank were designed to play distinct roles. The IMF was established *inter alia* to promote international monetary cooperation and to help Member States tide over temporary balance-of-payments problem, whereas the World Bank was created to promote private foreign investment and global capitalist development. Over the years, the roles of the two institutions have undergone change.[9] Indeed, some critics note that the IMF and World Bank have so departed from their original role that they have come to closely resemble each other. It has led to calls for the two institutions to go back to their original objectives.[10]

The different phases through which IFIs have evolved are the outcome of complex institutional and external factors, in particular the state of global capitalism. The international economic and political environment for capital accumulation has been, in particular, a critical variable in the evolution of IFIs. For example, until the global economic crisis that began in 2007, the Fund was faced with a relevance crisis resulting from the 'rapid reduction in credit outstanding to borrowing members', leading to the establishment of a High Level Committee ('Crockett' Committee) to consider how the Fund should manage its future expenditure.[11] In view of the problematic nature of conditionalities prescribed

8. *See* International Monetary Fund, 'Articles of Agreement of the International Monetary Fund' (27 Dec. 1945, amended 11 Nov. 1992), Art. I, *available at* <www.imf.org/external/pubs/ft/aa/index.htm> (hereinafter IMF Articles of Agreement); World Bank, IBRD Articles of Agreement (16 Feb. 1989), Art. I, *available at* <http://siteresources.worldbank.org/EXTABOUTUS/Resources/ibrd-articlesofagreement.pdf> (hereinafter IBRD Articles of Agreement). For a discussion of the purposes of the IMF and the World Bank, *see* Daniel D. Bradlow, 'International Law and the Operations of the International Financial Institutions', Ch. 1 herein.
9. Michael Barnett & Martha Finnemore, *Rules for the World: International Organizations in Global Politics* (Ithaca: Cornell University Press, 2004), 45–73; Michael Goldman, *Imperial Nature: The World Bank and Struggles for Social Justice in the Age of Globalization* (New Delhi: Orient Longman, 2006).
10. Conservative critics, for instance, demand that 'the World Bank and IMF return to their original mission, when the Bank, they believe, was small and effective and its loans were highly discriminating. Today, the "development has gone astray" analysts see the octopus-like Bank and arrogant IMF fuelling corruption and undermining these institutions' mandate for democracy by politicizing development. These observers assume that by becoming leaner and more discerning, the Bank and IMF can return to what they imagine these institutions once were: shrewd catalysts for economic development in the third world'. Goldman, *supra* n. 9, 17.
11. The Committee noted: 'The IMF's current financing model relies primarily on interest income derived from lending to fund the whole range of its activities. These include not only financial intermediation, but also multilateral and bilateral surveillance, crisis prevention, research and statistics, technical assistance and capacity building, and the accumulation of prudential reserves, among others. While this business model has served the Fund well over the years, fully covering running costs and allowing the build-up of strong financial reserves, its shortcomings are becoming apparent. A rapid reduction in credit outstanding to borrowing members

by IFIs (based on one-size-fits-all dogma), developing countries were hesitant to approach them for fresh loans and in a hurry to return previous loans. This was not the first time that the Fund had faced such a crisis. In the 1970s, the Fund had also had to deal with a 'crisis of clientele'.[12] Developing countries had even then, in the background of the call for establishing a new international economic order (NIEO), decided not to use Fund resources because of the nature of conditionalities that accompanied borrowings. The availability of alternative sources of financing, in particular lending from commercial banks and increased Official Development Assistance (ODA) facilitated this stance.[13] It caused the Fund to review the guidelines on conditionality culminating in new guidelines being adopted by the Executive Board in 1979. The key features of the new guidelines were the possibility of longer duration Stand-By Arrangements (SBAs) and the understanding that Structural Adjustment Programmes (SAPs) will 'pay due regard to the domestic social and political objectives, the economic priorities, and the circumstances of members including the causes of their balance of payments problems'.[14] But soon thereafter the situation changed with a sharp deterioration in the external economic environment of developing countries. There was a:

> shrinking of financing options for these nations. 1982 saw the explosion of the debt crisis, and the growing unwillingness of the commercial banks to lend to Third World nations. A significant, spontaneous source of alternative balance-of-payments financing for the creditworthy among them was therefore lost. Moreover, ODA from both the developed and OPEC countries, was on the decline in the recessionary circumstances of the early 1980s. A source of concessional financing for the poorer developing countries was thus also affected.[15]

The changed global environment forced the developing countries to approach the Fund for financing, which then tended to neglect the 1979 guidelines in prescribing conditionalities.[16] There was therefore a sense of déjà vu when the IMF revised its conditionality guidelines in 2002, this time recognizing that 'its programs have become unduly intrusive' and the consequent need to 'reduce the number of conditions to those that are essential to the achievement of the program's objectives'.[17]

---

has resulted in a drop in Fund income and a base-case projection that intermediation income will fall further. It is already the case that the income derived from lending is not sufficient to cover the Fund's projected operating expenses, unless the intermediation margin were to be raised to unsustainable levels.' IMF Committee to Study Sustainable Long-Term Financing of the IMF, Final Report (31 Jan. 2007), 4, *available at* <www.imf.org/External/np/oth/2007/013107.pdf>.

12. Tyrone Ferguson, *The Third World and Decision Making in the International Monetary Fund: The Quest for Full and Effective Participation* (London: Pinter Publishers, 1988), 200.
13. *Ibid.*, 211.
14. *Ibid.*
15. *Ibid.*, 214.
16. *Ibid.*, 216.
17. Daniel Bradlow, 'The Governance of the IMF: The Need for Comprehensive Reform', paper prepared for the Meeting of the G24 Technical Committee (Singapore, September 2006), 17, *available at* <www.g24.org/brad0906.pdf>.

The new guidelines were announced once again in the background of the reluctance of developing countries to approach the Fund. It would appear that the institution was biding its time, having internalized the historical lesson that the situation of the institution, including the lack of clientele, can change quickly creating new financial and operational opportunities, as has happened in the wake of global economic crisis. The IMF has received a new lease of life. It has been injected with fresh funds: its lending capacity has been tripled to USD 750 billion by G-20 countries.[18] To realize its operational objectives, old lending facilities have been made more flexible and new lending facilities created (e.g., the Flexible Credit Line).[19] It remains to be seen what the new conditionality guidelines mean in the new circumstances, even as the first signs are not encouraging.[20] A number of countries that have turned to the Fund for loans in the aftermath of the global economic crisis have had conditionalities prescribed that are no different from before.[21]

---

18. For details, *see* IMF Survey Magazine, 'G-20 Reaffirms IMF's Central Role in Combating Crisis' (3 Apr. 2009), <www.imf.org/external/pubs/ft/survey/so/2009/NEW040309A.htm>. For the official communique issued at the close of the G-20 London Summit held in April 2009, *see* The London Summit 2009, 'Global Plan for Recovery and Reform' (2 Apr. 2009), <www.londonsummit.gov.uk/resources/en/news/15766232/communique-020409>. For subsequent developments, *see* G-20 Publications Communiqués, <www.g20.org/pub_communiques.aspx>.
19. *See generally* International Montary Fund, 'Factsheet: IMF Lending' (9 Sep. 2009), *available at* <www.imf.org/external/np/exr/facts/howlend.htm>.
20. Bradlow notes that the 'new guidelines' 'are drafted in relatively non-specific terms and it is not clear how effective they will be in reducing the IMF's intrusion into its members domestic affairs.... It is important to note... that a reduction in quantity of conditions does not necessarily translate into a reduction in intrusiveness, particularly given that the new guidelines allow the IMF to continue engaging in institutional and governance reform in the monetary and financial area. In addition, the previous IMF guidelines on conditionality also attempted to impose limits on the scope of conditionality but these were largely ignored in practice'. Bradlow, 'The Governance of the IMF: The Need for Comprehensive Reform', *supra* n. 17, 17. Buira likewise notes that 'the guidelines on conditionality were disregarded in the past, so the proof of the pudding is in the eating'. Ariel Buira, 'An Analysis of IMF Conditionality', in *Challenge to the World Bank and IMF: Developing Country Perspectives*, ed. Ariel Buira (London: Anthem Press, 2003), 69.
21. Starting September 2008, the Fund negotiated Stand-By Arrangement (SBA) loans to nine countries by March 2009, Georgia, Ukraine, Hungary, Iceland, Latvia, Pakistan, Serbia, Belarus, and El Salvador. For conditionalities, the IMF's SBA loan of USD 532 million to Serbia for instance states that 'there is no scope now for countercyclical fiscal loosening. Anything less than a tight fiscal stance could also jeopardize the credibility of the program in the eyes of foreign investors and the Serbian public. Fiscal policy will in addition need to put a tight constraint on wage growth in government sectors and public enterprises'. IMF, 'Republic of Serbia: Request for Stand-By Arrangement' (23 Jan. 2009), *available at* <www.imf.org/external/pubs/cat/longres.cfm?sk=22640.0>. *See generally* Third World Network, 'The IMF's Financial Crisis Loans: No Change in Conditionalities', submission to The Commission of Experts of the President of the United Nations General Assembly on Reforms of the International Monetary and Financial System (11 Mar. 2009), *available at* <www.twnside.org.sg/title2/par/IMF.Crisis.Loans-Overview.TWN.March.2009.doc>.

On the other hand, third world countries have renewed their demand for greater policy flexibility in dealing with the ongoing global economic crisis. In this context, they have called for a clear development orientation of IFIs. The call is unlikely to be heeded as the IFIs are assigned by the developed world to promote the cause of global finance and industrial capital that requires that the policy space available to developing countries be limited. Indeed, now that the Fund, in coordination with new international bodies such as the Financial Stability Board (FSB), is called upon to play a more active role in the surveillance of national and global financial systems, it will enhance its ability to influence the policies of developing countries in directions suited to the interests of advanced capitalist countries.[22] A possible option before third world countries is to, *inter alia*, strengthen initiatives like the Chiang Mai plan and reproduce or support the newly created Bolivarian Alternative Plan for Latin America (ALBA) Bank.[23] But unfortunately key developing countries like China and India that could have taken the initiative in this regard appear to have been co-opted by the G-20 process by being given a seat at the high table.

The World Bank, like the IMF, has also gone through different phases since its creation. According to Goldman:

> Four distinct periods mark the history of the World Bank: the 'reluctant Banker' period of 1944–68; the Bank's 'rise to power' in the period of 1968–80 during which the calls for 'poverty alleviation' and meeting 'basic needs' for the 'absolute poor' reflected a new rhetorical turn in development; the 'debt and adjustment' period of 1980–89; and the 'green neoliberal' period from 1989 to the present.[24]

The Bank has also evolved in response to the changing international political and economic climate of global capitalism. For instance, the McNamara years (1968–1981) saw the World Bank embrace the language of poverty and development because of the changing international political situation:

> The late 1960s and early 1970s were [. . .] a period of street protests and revolutionary challenges to colonial and imperial orders around the world, the effects of which were to unsettle Northern political elites, economists, and McNamara himself. Even as secretary of defense, he began to borrow liberally from such enlightened policy makers as Barbara Ward, Mahbub ul Haq, and David Morse (head of the International Labor Organization).[25]

22. The bilateral surveillance system was updated in June 2007. *See* International Monetary Fund, 'IMF Surveillance – The 2007 Decision on Bilateral Surveillance', *available at* <www.imf.org/external/np/exr/facts/surv07.htm>.
23. On the creation of the ALBA Bank, *see* Kiraz Janicke, 'Summit of the Bolivarian Alternative (ALBA) Concludes in Venezuela: ALBA Bank Formed as Alternative to IMF and World Bank' (30 Jan. 2008), <www.globalresearch.ca/index.php?context=va&aid=7935>.
24. Goldman, *supra* n. 9, 50.
25. *Ibid.*, 73.

In recent years, the key change in the role of the World Bank is the increasing attention that has come to be given to the idea and objective of 'good governance' and the promotion of 'sustainable development'. In the latter context, there is of course a new focus on 'climate change' issues that has resulted in the adoption of a Clean Energy for Development Investment Framework and a Strategic Framework for Climate Change.[26] The Bank is likely to be assigned a central role in providing funds to developing countries to combat climate change. 'Good governance', 'sustainable development', and 'climate change' are thus key concepts used to redefine the role of the World Bank in the era of imperialist globalization, allowing intrusive social and economic conditionalities to be prescribed to borrowing states, even as it co-opts the critique of new social movements. These, and other changes in the operational strategy of the IFIs, have been legitimized through appropriate interpretations given to the respective mandates.

A. Interpreting the Mandates

Barnett and Finnemore note that 'mandates to IOs are often vague, broad or conflicting . . . Mandates [therefore] need to be interpreted'.[27] The point with regard to the indeterminacy that characterizes constituent instruments of IFIs may be elaborated with reference to the Articles of Agreement of the World Bank. These prohibit political considerations from influencing the decisions of the Bank requiring that only economic criteria be taken into account.[28] Article IV(10), for example, states:

> The Bank and its officers shall not interfere in the political affairs of any member; nor shall they be influenced in their decisions by the political

26. *See* The World Bank, 'Climate Change', <http://beta.worldbank.org/climatechange/>. *See also* Development Committee (Joint Ministerial Committee of the Boards of Governors of the Bank and Fund on the Transfer of Real Resources to Developing Countries), 'Clean Energy for Development Investment Framework: The World Bank Group Action Plan', DC 2007-0002 (28 Mar. 2007), *available at* <http://siteresources.worldbank.org/DEVCOMMINT/Documentation/21289621/DC2007-0002(E)-CleanEnergy.pdf>; The World Bank, 'Strategic Framework for Development and Climate Change', <http://beta.worldbank.org/overview/strategic-framework>; Global Environment Facility, <www.gefweb.org/>. Further, the 2010 *World Development Report* is on development and climate change, *see* The World Bank, *World Development Report 2010: Development and Climate Change* (Washington, DC: The World Bank, 2010), *available at* <http://econ.worldbank.org/wbsite/external/extdec/extresearch/extwdrs/extwdr2010/0,,contentMDK:21969137~menuPK:5287816~pagePK:64167689~piPK:64167673~theSitePK:5287741,00.html>. For a critique of World Bank's climate change finance policy, *see* Third World Network (Celine Tan), 'World Bank's Climate Funds Will Undermine Global Climate Action' (10 Apr. 2008), *available at* <www.twnside.org.sg/title2/finance/docs/Climate.Funds-Commentary.Revised.doc>; Gender Action (prepared by Anna Rooke), 'Doubling the Damage: World Bank Climate Investment Funds Undermine Climate and Gender Justice' (February 2009), *available at* <www.genderaction.org/images/2009.02_Doubling%20Damage_AR.pdf>.
27. Barnett & Finnemore, *supra* n. 9, 22.
28. Ibrahim F.I. Shihata, 'Democracy and Development', *The International and Comparative Law Quarterly* 46 (1997): 639.

> character of the member or members concerned. Only economic considerations shall be relevant to their decisions, and these considerations shall be weighed impartially in order to achieve the purposes stated in Article 1.[29]

The meaning given to such provisions by the Bank reveals how interpretations that are not convenient to the advanced capitalist states are excluded. The interpretative strategy is indeed an interesting one. To begin with, in order to justify new conditionalities, such as those that pertain to the world of 'good governance', the Bank concedes the need to embrace non-literal interpretations of the Articles of Agreement. Ibrahim Shihata, the former legal counsel to the Bank, has thus observed that 'the Bank has continuously developed its functions *beyond the literal provisions of its Articles of Agreement* while respecting *the overall purposes* stipulated in these Articles'.[30] This has allowed the Bank's operations, as Shihata remarks, to cover a range of diverse subjects such as population, education, health, women in development, social security, privatization, the environment, improving public sector management, and strengthening legal, regulatory, and judicial frameworks, 'none of which is mentioned by name in the Bank's Articles'.[31] However, in the same breath, Shihata notes that the provisions of the Articles of Agreement 'do not envisage a role for the World Bank in the political reform of its borrowing members'.[32] In his words, 'political reform of borrowing countries is not part of the Bank's purposes provided for in its Articles of Agreement'.[33] While Shihata is correct in rejecting an intrusive political role for the Bank, it is difficult to see how the agenda of 'good governance' is not political interference in the affairs of a member country.[34]

Through the different interpretative moves, the Bank's actions give meaning to the term 'political' in a way that serves the purpose of the powerful Member States. First, it defines 'political' in a manner that the 'non-economic' interests of advanced capitalist states are subsumed under the rubric of 'economic' decision-making. Second, the term 'political' is assigned a meaning that disregards the implications of the Bank agenda and the conditionalities prescribed for principles of sovereignty and non-intervention in the internal affairs of states. Third, the term

29. IBRD Articles of Agreement, *supra* n. 8, Art. IV(10).
30. Shihata, 'Democracy and Development', *supra* n. 28, 639–640 (emphasis added).
31. *Ibid.*
32. *Ibid.*
33. *Ibid.*, 640. According to Shihata 'drawing the Bank, which is an international institution of a predominantly financial character, directly into politically charged areas, with their typical vagaries and double standards, can only politicize its work and jeopardize its credibility, both in the financial markets where it borrows and in the member countries where it lends. In the final analysis, the purposes of the world community may be better served if *political* reform is pursued by political organizations, and *political* human rights are monitored by the relevant UN organizations, regional agencies, courts, commissions and the non-governmental organizations established for this purpose'. *Ibid.*, 642.
34. In the circumstances, why lament the fact that 'there is an increasing demand on the Bank and other multilateral financial institutions generally to be involved, in an open way, in the protection of political rights and the promotion of political reform'. *Ibid.*, 641.

'political' is interpreted to exclude from view the impact of Bank strategies and programmes on human rights of peoples of developing countries.[35] Bradlow makes the same larger point with regard to the IMF when he observes that, 'it is neither prudent nor principled for an organization that attaches conditions to its funding that relate to governance, corruption, budgetary allocations and privatization to pretend that it does not consider political and social factors in its operations'.[36]

Joseph Stiglitz writes that in this respect 'there was a certain irony in the stance of the IMF', for while 'it tried to pretend that it was above politics . . . it was clear that its lending program was, in part, driven by politics'.[37] In short, if the politicization of the IFIs is an issue then they are already immersed in politics.

B. The Interpretation of Conditionalities

The interpretations of the constituent instruments are advanced by powerful developed states in the matrix of a knowledge-power constellation that ensure that the interpretations proffered are perceived as authoritative. Knowledge production and dissemination is, to put it differently, a crucial function of IFIs. For instance, what the World Bank generates is a model of development that both creates demand for its resources and also legitimizes the conditionalities that accompany it. The role of knowledge production and dissemination thus is to propagate a development framework that allows IFIs to prescribe a certain set of conditionalities to borrowing states. As Goldman points out, the World Bank:

> depends on its capacity to generate the ideas of new global problems as well as on its own global expertise, new mechanisms for intervention as well as new reasons for countries to borrow, new development subjects and subjectivities as well as new forms of its own legitimation. The Bank works hard to create its own demand.[38]

On the legal plane, the legitimacy of conditionalities prescribed is reinforced by the contention that these are voluntarily accepted by the borrowing state.[39] The fiction is extended in the world of international law by the claim, in the context of IMF

35. 'The IMF has failed to define the limits of its mandate or to stipulate a principled basis on which it determines what issues it is willing to address and which issues are outside its mandate because of their inherently political or non-economic nature. This failure subjects the IMF to the charge that it is acting in an arbitrary and capricious fashion in interpreting its articles.' Bradlow, 'The Governance of the IMF: The Need for Comprehensive Reform', *supra* n. 17, 27.
36. *Ibid.*, 22.
37. Joseph Stiglitz, *Globalisation and Its Discontents* (New York: W.W. Norton, 2002), 47.
38. Goldman, *supra* n. 9, 34.
39. However, as Anders notes, '. . . the distinction between the international organization with its limited mandate and the sovereign nation-state is a fiction that provides a legitimization for neoliberal policies, rather than an explanation of the predicament of development'. Gerhard Anders, 'Good Governance as Technology: Towards an Ethnography of the Bretton Woods Institutions', in *The Aid Effect: Giving and Governing in International Development*, ed. David Mosse & David Lewis (London: Pluto Press, 2005), 40.

loans for instance, that the Letter of Intent and SBAs are not international agreements.[40] But as Anders notes, 'the splitting of the loan documents, their legal status and their sequencing are all aimed at reinforcing country ownership'.[41] But this image is in his view:

> undermined by the extent to which the consultants hired at the instigation of the Bretton Woods institutions ensure that the letters and documents . . . are 'acceptable' and meet the standards of the two institutions for project proposals. Hence the official presentation of ownership should be interpreted for what it is: a legitimizing strategy for a particular political ideology.[42]

Likewise, noting the 'expansion' and 'explosion' of conditionalities in the 1980s and 1990s, Hurrell observes:

> conditionality is an important aspect of institutionalized power in a globalizing system, not least because it usually has a consensual element and occupies the murky space between direct economic coercion and sanctions on the one hand, and freely entered-into contractual arrangements on the other.[43]

Gold admits as much when he writes that 'to bind governments by agreement to observe their objectives and policies, so that departures from them would be breaches of obligations, could exacerbate political tensions and increase the difficulties of negotiation'.[44]

Another significant legal question with respect to conditionalities is that while in principle authorized by IFI mandates, their content has nowhere been specified in the Articles of Agreement.[45] It is left to the executive bodies of IFIs to indicate

---

40. According to Gold, 'The two stand-by documents, the letter of intent and the stand-by arrangement, do not constitute an international agreement under which the member undertakes obligations to observe its objectives and policies.' Joseph Gold, *The Legal Character of the Fund's Stand-By Arrangements and Why It Matters* (Washington, DC: International Monetary Fund, 1980), 43.
41. Anders, *supra* n. 39, 55.
42. Anders also here talks about the normativity of numbers. 'Numbers may acquire normativity in two ways. First, the number itself can transform into a norm as a prior action, performance indicator or benchmark and, second, the collection of specific numbers using standardized methods can constitute a condition of the loan. Typical examples of the former are targets for economic growth, inflation and public expenditure. The second type of normativity of numbers exemplifies the neoliberal trend toward systems of self-control. The operation of the new systems of management and control depends on the collection of reliable and standardized data.' *Ibid.*, 53.
43. Andrew Hurrell, 'Power, Institutions, and the Production of Inequality', in *Power in Global Governance*, ed. Michael Barrett & Raymond Duvall (Cambridge: Cambridge University Press, 2005), 39.
44. Gold, *supra* n. 40, 37.
45. It may be recalled here that Keynes had argued for a automatic right to draw from the Fund because 'if countries are to be given sufficient confidence, they must be able to rely in all normal circumstances on drawing a substantial part of their quota without policing or unforeseen obstacles'. *Cited in*, Erik Denters, *Law and Policy of Conditionality* (The Hague: Kluwer Publishers, 1996), 72. For the legal basis of conditionality, *see ibid.*, 78 ff.

the same. But given the lack of guidance to the IFI management and staff and the weighted voting system (a matter addressed in a later section), it is virtually left to the dominant Member States to specify the conditionalities.[46] Once again the interpretive spaces in the mandates of IFIs are filled with hegemonic content (e.g., neo-liberal policies) that advances the interests of global capitalism. It is therefore not surprising that relative silence has met the question whether the IMF for instance is abiding by its objectives stated in Article I whose paragraph (v) requires that balance-of-payments support be provided under 'adequate safeguards... *without resorting to measures destructive of national and international prosperity*'.[47] The Fund 'has never clarified this point in a formal decision'.[48] It is also a matter of regret that developing countries have not made a request for a formal interpretation of Article I (v).[49] The 'obvious interpretation' request could be:

> is an adjustment programme which damages the socioeconomic position of vulnerable groups destructive of national prosperity? If so, is the Fund required, when laying down the conditionality, to allow the protection of government spending on vulnerable groups?[50]

Why the developing countries have not made such a request for interpretation under Article XXIX ('Interpretation') of the IMF Articles of Agreement is difficult to understand.[51] It is, however, a move still worth serious consideration.

IV. IFIs AND INTERNATIONAL HUMAN RIGHTS LAW

International human rights law is at the basis of much controversy and critique of IFI conditionality regimes.[52] But whether IFIs are bound by international human rights law and to what extent is a persistent question. Despite the perennial doubters, it can be persuasively shown that even though IFIs are not parties to international human rights instruments, they are bound to observe core international human rights obligations. First, as subjects of international law, IFIs are under an obligation to abide by norms of customary international law. This

46. Bradlow, 'The Governance of the IMF: The Need for Comprehensive Reform', *supra* n. 17, 25. According to Bradlow 'the IMF staff and management are effectively operating without any accountability... the IMF does not provide much guidance to the staff on how they should perform their responsibilities when they act in this policy-making capacity....' *Ibid.*
47. IMF Articles of Agreement, *supra* n. 8, Art. I(v) (note Articles were amended as of 1992) (emphasis added).
48. Denters, *supra* n. 45, 206.
49. *Ibid.*
50. *Ibid.*
51. *Ibid.*
52. Mac Darrow, *Between Light and Shadow: The World Bank, The International Monetary Fund and International Human Rights Law* (Oxford: Hart Publishing, 2003), 2. *See* Siobhán McInerney-Lankford, 'International Financial Institutions and Human Rights: Select Perspectives on Legal Obligations', Ch. 8 herein.

view was affirmed by the International Court of Justice (ICJ) in the *WHO* case: 'International organizations are subjects of international law and, as such, are bound by any obligations incumbent upon them under general rules of international law.'[53] Clapham surveying the relevant legal materials also concludes that 'the international financial institutions are bound by customary international law' including 'appropriate customary international law of human rights'.[54] Likewise, the International Law Association (ILA) notes: '[w]hen taking and implementing decisions such as designing SAPs and development projects, IOs should observe basic human rights obligations'.[55] The conclusion that international organizations are obligated to respect international human rights law is supported by the General Comments and resolutions of international human rights bodies and conferences respectively. Thus, for instance, the Committee on Economic Social and Cultural Rights (CESCR) has called upon the IFIs 'to pay enhanced attention in their activities to respect for economic, social and cultural rights'.[56] This does not mean, as Clapham explains, 'a new role for the UN Committee' nor will it lead to the 'assumption of "jurisdiction" over entities that are not formally bound by the treaty. Neither of these consequences flows from the assertion that the IMF is bound by human rights law'.[57] Such arguments are only deployed to deflect criticism from IFIs. While the detailed identification of rules in the different human rights conventions that have a bearing on IFI programmes can be debated, the basic idea that there are human rights obligations IFIs must meet is beyond question.

This view, secondly, is reinforced by the fact that as specialized agencies of the UN, IFIs are bound to respect the UN Charter. There are several provisions in the Charter, for instance, Articles 55–57, that suggest binding legal obligations on

---

53. *Interpretation of the Agreement of 25 March 1951 between the WHO and Egypt*, Advisory Opinion, I.C.J Reports 1980, 89–90; Eisuke Suzuki & Suresh Nanwani, 'Responsibility of International Organizations: The Accountability Mechanism of Multilateral Development Banks', *Michigan Journal of International Law* 27 (2005): 195; Andrew Clapham, *Human Rights Obligations of Non-state Actors* (Oxford: Oxford University Press, 2006), 144, 158.
54. Clapham, *supra* n. 53, 151. Clapham concludes from this chain of evidence that 'if the entity has sufficient legal capacity to be the bearer of international obligations, the relevant obligations include multiple aspects of the appropriate customary international law of human rights. The international financial institutions can therefore be said to have obligations, not only to respect human rights, but also to protect and even fulfil human rights in appropriate circumstances'. *Ibid.*, 147.
55. International Law Association (ILA), *Accountability of International Organizations Final Conference Report* (Berlin, 2004), 22–23, *available at* <www.ila-hq.org/en/committees/index.cfm/cid/9> (access by clicking on link to Final Conference Report Berlin (2004)). These include key provisions of the core international human rights treaties: the International Covenant on Civil and Political Rights (ICCPR), the International Covenant on Economic, Social, and Cultural Rights (ICESCR), the Convention on the Rights of the Child (CRC), the Convention against Torture (CAT), the Convention for the Elimination of Discrimination Against Women (CEDAW), and the Convention on the Elimination of Racial Discrimination (CERD) fit this description. Sigrun Skogly, *The Human Rights Obligations of the World Bank and the International Monetary Fund* (London: Cavendish, 2001).
56. Smita Narula, 'The Right to Food: Holding Global Actors Accountable Under International Law', *Columbia Journal of Transnational Law* 44 (2006): 745.
57. Clapham, *supra* n. 53, 147.

Member States and thereby on international institutions. Indeed, 'human rights are at the very core of the UN system's purposes' and, as specialized agencies, IFIs are expected to abide by them.[58] While the specialized agencies do possess a degree of autonomy in their functioning it does not extend to disregarding the provisions, purposes, and principles of the UN Charter. Unfortunately, the obligations of IFIs are seen as being confined to complying with the binding decisions of the UN Security Council.[59] But from a third world perspective, the duty extends to fulfilling the Charter commitment towards the promotion and protection of human rights. To ensure this, the relationship agreement of IFIs with the UN Economic and Social Council (ECOSOC) needs to be renegotiated *inter alia* to clarify the need to observe human rights obligations. It is somewhat absurd that IFIs seek to promote 'good governance' and the rule of law in Member States, and decline to do so where their policies and programmes are in issue.[60]

In discussing the human rights obligations of IFIs, a critical distinction, however, has to be made between taking cognizance of the human rights record of a Member State in deciding on the request for a loan and the concern with human rights violations as a result of adhering to policies and programmes prescribed by them. In the former case there is a legitimate worry on the part of third world countries that IFIs will 'become an enforcement arm for those governments wishing to impose their own vision of human rights on other governments'.[61] In so far as the impact of policies and programmes are concerned, a critical question remains as to whether the proposition that IFI policies and programmes violate human rights can be empirically demonstrated.[62] In this respect, reference may first be made to the fact that as a result of IFI lending and policies 'much more capital flows out of borrowing countries and to the World Bank, IMF, and Northern-based banks than in'.[63] Equally troubling is the allied fact that, as Stiglitz notes in the context of

58. Darrow, *supra* n. 52, 2; Skogly, *supra* n. 55.
59. In the words of Shihata, an '.... exceptional case is the Bank's duty to pay attention to the binding decisions of the UN Security Council taken under Articles 41 and 42 of the UN Charter which require the Bank not to deal with a certain country. The Bank is bound in this respect by virtue of its Relationship Agreement with the United Nation. In addition, all its members (except Switzerland) are also UN members and in that capacity are required by the UN Charter to implement Security Council decisions, an obligation of member States which under the UN Charter prevails over their other treaty obligations such as those under the Bank's Articles of Agreement'. Shihata, 'Democracy and Development', *supra* n. 28, 641.
60. International human rights have had a 'marginal influence on the research, policy and operational activities of both the Bank and the Fund'. Darrow, *supra* n. 52, 2.
61. Clapham, *supra* n. 53, 142.
62. It has been contended that given the fact that 'supporting evidence can be found on both sides of the debate', the focus of civil society organizations should be on economic, social, and cultural policies that 'can fairly be characterized as arbitrary or discriminatory', rather than on 'matters of pure distributive justice'. Kenneth Roth, 'Defending Economic, Social and Cultural Rights: Practical Issues Faced by an International Human Rights Organizations', *Human Rights Quarterly* 26 (2004): 69, 72.
63. Goldman, *supra* n. 9, xi, 90; Aziz Ali Mohammed, 'Who Pays for the IMF?', in *Challenge to the World Bank and IMF: Developing Country Perspectives*, ed. Ariel Buira (London: Anthem Press, 2003), 37–55.

the crisis of the world economy in the 1990s, the IFIs (in this case the IMF) 'seemed more often to focus on saving the Western creditors than on helping the countries in crisis and their people. There was money to bail out Western banks but not to support minimal food subsidies for those on the brink of starvation'.[64]

Second, there is considerable and growing evidence that conditionalities prescribed by IFIs lead to the violation of human rights of individuals and groups living in borrowing states.[65]

V. THE ACCOUNTABILITY AND RESPONSIBILITY OF IFIs IN INTERNATIONAL LAW

The violation of human rights, resulting from implementing IFI policies and programmes, should engage their accountability and responsibility. The principle of accountability is broader than the concept of responsibility in international law. Responsibility is incurred only when there is a breach of an international obligation. The principle of accountability goes further and demands that the IFIs be morally answerable to the peoples whose lives are impacted by loans and conditions advanced by them.[66] As the ILA has noted, accountability is *a multifaceted phenomenon* that 'is linked to the authority and power of an IO. Power entails accountability, that is the duty to account for its exercise'.[67] While arguably both

64. Joseph Stiglitz, *Making Globalisation Work* (London: Allen Lane, 2006), 18.
65. Dana L. Clark, 'The World Bank and Human Rights: The Need for Greater Accountability', *Harvard Human Rights Journal* 15 (2002): 206–207; Smita Narula, 'The Right to Food: Holding Global Actors Accountable under International Law', *Columbia Journal of Transnational Law* 44 (2006): 711 ff.; The Structural Adjustment Participatory Review International Network (SAPRIN), *Structural Adjustment: The SAPRI Report: The Policy Roots of Economic Crisis, Poverty and Inequality* (London: Zed Books, 2004); Rowan Abouharb & David Cingranelli, *Human Rights and Structural Adjustment* (Cambridge: Cambridge University Press, 2005); Anne Orford, 'Locating the International: Military and Monetary Interventions after the Cold War', *Harvard International Law Journal* 38 (1997): 443–485.
66. For 'the basic principles of good governance which the IMF advocates so eloquently to the governments of its member states should guide its own conduct towards those directly affected by its policy-making activities. After all, there is no obvious reason why the IMF, when it "descends" into the national policy-making process should be less accountable to those people directly affected by its decisions than other actors in this process'. Bradlow, 'The Governance of the IMF: The Need for Comprehensive Reform', *supra* n. 17, 17.
67. ILA, *Accountability of International Organizations Final Conference Report*, *supra* n. 55, 5. 'Accountability of IOs is *a multifaceted phenomenon*. The form under which accountability will eventually arise will be determined by the particular circumstances surrounding the acts or omissions of an IO, its [M]ember States or third parties. These forms may be legal, political, administrative or financial. A combination of the four forms provides the best chances of achieving the necessary degree of accountability.' *Ibid.* (emphasis added). For a brief review of different meanings of accountability with reference to international organizations *see* Suresh Nanwani, 'Holding Multilateral Development Banks to Account: Gateways and Barriers', *International Community Law Review* 10 (2008): 201–204. According to Nanwani, 'accountability' in the context of multilateral development banks 'should be treated as a multifaceted term according to the nature of the activity carried out and tested against the principles of transparency, participation, independence, credibility and effectiveness'. *Ibid.*, 203.

the principles of accountability and responsibility are involved when there is a violation of international human rights law the former calls for a response that goes beyond the world of law. To quote the ILA once again, 'the diversity of forms of accountability clearly rules out, from the start, any requirement that only legal interests may trigger accountability'.[68]

In determining the accountability and legal responsibility of IFIs, it may be pertinent to begin with two preliminary, albeit critical, questions. First, are international organizations moral agents? Second, can states act through international organizations in a manner that would incur responsibility if an individual or collective of states were to so act? The answer to the first question rests on the response to two further questions: 'whether moral agency is something that can be possessed by groups at all; and if, in theory, institutions can be moral agents, which specific entities in the international arena have the features to qualify them as such'.[69] It has been suggested that for institutions to be moral agents they 'must first be agents, they must possess a capacity for moral deliberation, and must also be able to act on the basis of this deliberation'.[70] From this standpoint IFIs are certainly moral agents. For IFIs are agents of states and however flawed the process of decision-making, there is always a deliberative component. The second question raises the issue of whether, by virtue of the independence of international organizations, violations of international laws can be tolerated? For the element of autonomy can tempt powerful states to use international organizations to realize interests that would not be possible for individual states without transgressing international laws. It stands to reason that Member States cannot be allowed to deploy international organizations to violate international laws when they cannot do so in their capacity as individual states. Brownlie has aptly pointed out that a:

> State cannot by delegation (even if this be genuine) avoid responsibility for breaches of its duties under international law.... This approach of public international law is not *ad hoc* but stems directly from the normal concepts of accountability and effectiveness.[71]

Likewise, the ILA has observed: 'States cannot evade their obligations under customary law and general principles of law by creating an IO that would not be bound by the legal limits imposed upon its Member States.'[72]

68. ILA, *Accountability of International Organizations Final Conference Report*, *supra* n. 55, 6.
69. Toni Erskine, 'Making Sense of "Responsibility" in International Relations: Key Questions and Concepts', in *Can Institutions Have Responsibilities? Collective Moral Agency and International Relations*, ed. Toni Erskine (Basingstoke: Palgrave Macmillan, 2003), 7.
70. Nicholas Rengger, 'On "Good Governance", Institutional Design, and the Practices of Moral Agency', in *Can Institutions Have Responsibilities? Collective Moral Agency and International Relations*, ed. Toni Erskine (Basingstoke: Palgrave Macmillan, 2003), 209.
71. Ian Brownlie, 'State Responsibility: The Problem of Delegation', in *Völkerrecht zwischen normativen Anspruch und politischer Realität*, ed. Konrad Ginther et al. (Berlin: Duncker & Humblot, 1994), 300–301.
72. ILA, *Accountability of International Organizations Final Conference Report*, *supra* n. 55, 18.

Crawford identifies five ways of dealing with the problem of accountability and responsibility of international organizations. First, there is moral criticism (incorporating the broader principle of accountability). Second, 'some form of internal auditing mechanism can be established'.[73] The World Bank Inspection Panel is such a mechanism. Third, 'the States which act on behalf of the organization remain responsible themselves for their own conduct'.[74] A fourth mode can be that 'the consequences of international action carried out on behalf of a State [is] to be internalized by the State itself'.[75] Fifth, 'the notion of secondary responsibility of States for the conduct of international organizations' can be generalized.[76] The modes of creating formal accountability mechanisms and international legal responsibility deserve particular attention.

A. Accountability of IFIs: The World Bank Inspection Panel

Accountability has 'various degrees of consequences ranging from oversight, monitoring, and evaluation processes to censorship or other forms of sanctions to the attribution of legal liability for injuries, resulting in binding remedial action'.[77] An important example of a formal accountability mechanism is the World Bank's Inspection Panel, which was established in 1993. Its mandate and functioning may be briefly considered to underline both its innovativeness and its lack of effectiveness. The objective of the Inspection Panel, as stated on the official website of the World Bank, is 'to address the concerns of the people who may be affected by Bank projects and to ensure that the Bank adheres to its operational policies and procedures during design, preparation and implementation phases of projects'.[78]

The Inspection Panel, consisting of three members appointed by the Executive Board of the Bank, provides private individuals with a forum to express their

73. James Crawford, 'Holding International Organizations and Their Members to Account', presented at the Fifth Steinkraus-Cohen International Law Lecture (London, March 2007), 7, *available at* <www.law.cam.ac.uk/faculty-resources/download/calling-international-organizations-anf-their-members-to-account/4135/pdf>.
74. *Ibid.*, 8.
75. *Ibid.*
76. *Ibid.*, 10.
77. Suzuki & Nanwani, 'Responsibility of International Organizations: The Accountability Mechanism of Multilateral Development Banks', *supra* n. 53, 180.
78. World Bank Inspection Panel, About Us, <http://web.worldbank.org/WBSITE/EXTERNAL/EXTINSPECTIONPANEL/0,,menuPK:64129249~pagePK:64132081~piPK:64132052~theSitePK:380794,00.html>. At a minimum, requesters must show in writing that they live in the project area (or represent people who do), and are likely to be affected adversely by project activities; they believe that actual or likely harm results from failure by the Bank to follow its policies and procedures; their concerns have been discussed with Bank management; and they are not satisfied with the outcome. World Bank Inspection Panel, Panel Process, <http://web.worldbank.org/WBSITE/EXTERNAL/EXTINSPECTIONPANEL/0,,contentMDK:20173251~menuPK:64129467~pagePK:64129751~piPK:64128378~theSitePK:380794,00.html>.

grievances. It functions essentially as a 'fact finding body'.[79] Since opening in September 1994, it has received more than sixty formal requests.[80] The Inspection Panel no doubt represents a progressive step. It has been described as 'an unprecedented act in the history of international financial institutions',[81] and as 'an extraordinary development' that has enhanced the transparency and accountability of IFIs.[82] According to Suzuki and Nanwani:

> Never before had any entity independent of the governing organs of an international organization existed to hear and investigate complaints filed by private individuals and groups affected by the organization. Although the Inspection Panel's mandate only includes the examination of the World Bank's compliance with its policies and procedures, it allows third parties to participate in the decision-making process of the organization for the first time. This development has fundamentally altered the relationship between international organizations on the one hand and private individuals and groups on the other.[83]

The nature of the mechanism is, however, carefully limited. The reviews by the Inspection Panel 'are not to be equated with the conduct of judicial proceedings'.[84] It is neither empowered 'to settle disputes between contractual parties', nor 'provide judicial-type remedies such as injunctions or damages for noncompliance with its policies and procedures'.[85] The result is:

> that the question of internal compliance or noncompliance has become the focus of the inspection process, and the real question of accountability toward people who are affected by MDBs' projects has become sidelined. Once the inspection function accepts the complainants' request for inspection and authorizes an inspection, the complainants themselves are left outside the system. The affected people who requested 'inspection' will eventually be

79. *See* The Inspection Panel, 'Annual Report 2006–2007' (Washington, DC: The International Bank for Reconstruction and Development/The World Bank, 2007), 13, *available at* <http://siteresources.worldbank.org/EXTINSPECTIONPANEL/Resources/InspP_2007_Annual_Report.pdf> (hereinafter Inspection Panel Annual Report 2006–2007).
80. The Inspection Panel, 'Accountability at the World Bank: The Inspection Panel at 15 Years' (Washington, DC: The International Bank for Reconstruction and Development/The World Bank, 2009), 24, *available at* <http://siteresources.worldbank.org/EXTINSPECTIONPANEL/Resources/380793-1254158345788/InspectionPanel2009.pdf>.
81. *See* Inspection Panel Annual Report 2006–2007, *supra* n. 79, 17.
82. Suzuki & Nanwani, 'Responsibility of International Organizations: The Accountability Mechanism of Multilateral Development Banks', *supra* n. 53, 187–188. *See also* David Hunter & Lori Udall, 'The World Bank's New Inspection Panel: Will It Increase the Bank's Accountability?' (1994), *available at* <www.ciel.org/Publications/issue1.html> (Hunter and Udall describe the Inspection Panel as a 'remarkable advancement in international law').
83. Hunter & Udall, *supra* n. 82.
84. Suzuki & Nanwani, 'Responsibility of International Organizations: The Accountability Mechanism of Multilateral Development Banks', *supra* n. 53, 206.
85. *Ibid.*

> informed of the outcome of the inspection process only *after* the process is completed, with the possibility that their problem will remain unresolved.[86]

There are also serious procedural hurdles that have been identified by Nanwani:[87] restrictions with regard to who can file a claim,[88] time bars on filing claims,[89] the costs involved in gathering information and presenting a claim,[90] the lack of opportunity to present views after the Inspection Panel issues a report,[91] and the absence of a process to monitor outcomes.[92] Finally, as Tan notes:

> At the time of its inception, there were high hopes that the Inspection Panel, along with the progressive development of the safeguard policies, would lead 'the upward harmonization of environmental and social standards globally' as well as 'influence the development of substantive areas of law applicable to the Bank's operations', including human rights law. The optimism has not been borne out in the decade since its inception, and although its safeguards have served as a template for other development agencies and commercial institutions, the Bank's compliance with its own safeguard policies has been disappointing.[93]

For the Bank has moved away from 'universal, mandatory norms in favour of discretionary standards'.[94] In short the Inspection Panel mechanism needs to be

86. *Ibid.*, 219. *See also* Nanwani, 'Holding Multilateral Development Banks to Account: Gateways and Barriers', *supra* n. 67, 205–206.
87. For a detailed review *see* Nanwani, 'Holding Multilateral Development Banks to Account: Gateways and Barriers', *supra* n. 67, 211 ff.
88. A claim by an individual is not permissible. Nanwani, 'Holding Multilateral Development Banks to Account: Gateways and Barriers', *supra* n. 67, 211.
89. '. . . the cut-off point for filing a claim when 95% or more of the loan (the 95% disbursement rule) has been disbursed has been considered to be "arbitrary" and effectively affects local communities who would not realize the project impacts till after the project is physically completed'. *Ibid.*, 213.
90. 'On the costs involved in gathering information and presenting the claim, it can take time for local communities to get the necessary information such as knowing who are the project financiers, how to approach them in getting the information and having matters redressed by the executing agencies and the bank's operations departments before brining the matter to the panel as is required before the panel can entertain the claim to determine eligibility.' *Ibid.*, 214.
91. 'When the World Bank Inspection Panel issues its report after completing its investigation, the claimants are not given an opportunity to present their views while the bank's management has an opportunity to provide its response.' *Ibid.*, 215.
92. Referring to the Yacyreta Hydroelectric Project claim filed in 1996 by Sobreviviencia – Friends of Earth Paraguay, Nanwani notes that 'notwithstanding the issuance of the reports by the World Bank Inspection Panel' there was no follow-up to solve the problem. New requests were later filed in 2002. For further details *see ibid.*, 218–219.
93. Celine Tan, 'Mandating Rights and Limiting Mission Creep: Holding the World Bank and the International Monetary Fund Accountable for Human Rights Violations', *Human Rights and International Legal Discourse* 2, no. 1 (2008): 97.
94. *Ibid.* Tan explains this conclusion as follows (readers will excuse a lengthy quote):

    > Coming on the heels of the Bank's switchover from its comprehensive Operation Directives (ODs) to the split Operational Policies (OPs) and Bank Procedures (BPs), separating

reviewed to make the Bank more accountable to third world states and peoples. The following desirable reforms flow from the critique. First, the social and environmental standards that are part of the existing safeguard regime should not be diluted. Second, the mandate of the Inspection Panel should be extended to provide 'reparations for harm done'.[95] Third, the principles of emerging global administrative law – transparency, participation, and accountability – must be brought to bear on the Inspection Panel to ensure that the subjects of its decisions are not left in the cold after a complaint has been made.[96] Fourth, other procedural hurdles to the effective use of the Inspection Panel (such as high costs to gather information) should be addressed.

> 'mandatory safeguard policy requirements' under OPs and 'best practice statements' under BPs, the Bank's piloting of its 'Country System Approach' (CSA) for project financing, introduced in 2004, will significantly limit the remit of institutional accountability for violations of social and environmental standards.
>
> Instead of mandating adherence to universal institutional safeguard policies in project design and implementation, the CSA approach will 'rely solely on a borrower government's social and environmental systems', including its 'relevant national, sub-national or sectoral implementing institutions and applicable laws'. Instead of Bank's policies, 'national systems will be evaluated against a simplified set of Bank safeguards, and if judged 'equivalent', will be used for project preparation and implementation.
>
> Consequently, interest groups and commentators are fearful that this pilot phase, which currently involves eight to 12 countries, may eventually be rolled out to replace existing safeguards. The CSA approach condenses 'some 65 pages of [bank] operational policies, procedures and annexes into a short 3-page table that by its very nature *drops numerous important safeguard provisions*' and it 'is against this weakened restatement of Bank safeguards that national systems will be judged not the bank's full policies'. According to CIEL, the new system, while strengthening 20 areas, is expected to weaken nearly 150 policy areas.
>
> ....
>
> Complaints to the Inspection Panel under the CSA approach will also no longer be based on the bank's operational policies but on the aforementioned synthesis of objectives and principles, a move that is expected to weaken the purview of the Panel and its recommendations. The bank may also establish alternative monitoring arrangements for overseeing project implementation although it retains the right to normal contractual remedies (such as suspension of disbursements) for failure of the client to comply with agreed procedures.

Ibid., 97–98 (emphasis in original).

95. *Ibid.*, 102. In this respect the following observation of the International Court of Justice in the Advisory Opinion on the *Difference Relating to Immunity from Legal Process of a Special Rapporteur of the Commission on Human Rights* may be noted, 'Finally, the Court wishes to point out that the question of immunity from legal process is distinct from the issue of compensation for any damages incurred as a result of acts performed by the United Nations or by its agents acting in their official capacity. The United Nations may be required to bear responsibility for the damage arising from such acts.' *Cited by* Nanwani, 'Holding Multilateral Development Banks to Account: Gateways and Barriers', *supra* n. 67, 225.
96. However, on the limits of global administrative law, *see* B.S.Chimni, 'Cooption and Resistance: Two faces of Global Administrative Law', *New York University Journal of Law and Politics* 37 (2005): 799–827. *See also* David Hunter, 'International Law and Public Participation in Policy-Making at the International Financial Institutions', Ch. 7 herein.

The other possibility is to devise an alternative mechanism to the Inspection Panel. Recently Carrasco and Guernsay have advanced a proposal that:

> envisions a two-stage process that first would require claimant communities to file a Request for Claim Resolution with a newly created Office of Claims Resolution ('OCR') at the World Bank. The Director of the OCR would appoint an independent Intermediator who would attempt to solve the problem created by the Bank's alleged noncompliance with its own policies and procedures.... If, however, the Intermediator failed to resolve the claim or if the Bank agreed to corrective measures but failed to abide by them, claimant communities would have the option to institute arbitration proceedings against the Bank.... The tribunal's decision would be public, final, and binding upon the parties. Its award could set forth corrective measures that the Bank would be required to take to bring it into compliance with its policies and procedures. The tribunal could also award damages to the claimant community.[97]

Whether this proposal will eliminate 'paternalistic, biased, and politically motivated approach[es] to resolving claims' cannot be assessed in this essay but is on the face of it worthy of consideration.[98]

B. ILC and Responsibility of International Organizations

In so far as the responsibility of international organizations in international law is concerned, reference may be made to the work of the ILC on the subject since 2002. As Crawford notes, however, there are presently serious problems related to implementation:

> The structural problem – the problem of implementation – remains both at the national and international level. At the national level, there is general immunity of international organizations before national courts. No comparable doctrine to restrictive state immunity has yet developed for international organizations, and even if it did it would not address the question of accountability for public as distinct from commercial acts. At the international level, systems for implementing responsibility (including the jurisdiction of international courts and tribunals) have been established almost exclusively by reference to States and not international organizations.[99]

---

97. Enrique R. Carrasco & Alison K. Guernsey, 'The World Bank's Inspection Panel: Promoting True Accountability through Arbitration' (2008), *available at* <http://works.bepress.com/cgi/viewcontent.cgi?article=1000&context=enrique_carrasco>, 5–6.
98. *Ibid.*, 72.
99. Crawford, 'Holding International Organizations and Their Members to Account', *supra* n. 73, 5. According to Suzuki and Nanwani, 'there are essentially five kinds of relationships that international organizations fashion in carrying out their respective functions at various levels of operations: the organization's relationship with (i) its member states; (ii) its staff; (iii) its non-member states and other international organizations; (iv) nonstate private entities under

But on the other hand, it is significant that 'the principle that IOs may be held internationally responsible for their acts is nowadays part of customary international law'.[100]

The ILC has adopted a set of articles that indicate the broad contours of the future law of responsibility of international organizations. The significant article for the present purposes is Article 28, which deserves to be cited in full:

> Article 28
>
> International responsibility in case of provision of competence to an international organization
>
> 1. A State member of an international organization incurs international responsibility if it circumvents one of its international obligations by providing the organization with competence in relation to that obligation, and the organization commits an act that, if committed by that State, would have constituted a breach of that obligation.
>
> 2. Paragraph 1 applies whether or not the act in question is internationally wrongful for the international organization.[101]

Even critics of the work of the ILC recognize the significance of Draft Article 28.[102] Alvarez writes of it:

> Draft article 28 is one of the few provisions in the ILC's current effort that I think is worth taking seriously and developing. It might indeed be desirable progressive development of the law to indicate that states are responsible should they 'circumvent' their international obligations by using an IO as article 28 states (assuming that we clarify a bit more what 'circumvent' means). Enforcing this principle when appropriate may create incentives for

---

contracts; and (v) other third parties, i.e., private individuals and groups. For each category of relationship, different sets of law will apply'. Suzuki & Nanwani, 'Responsibility of International Organizations: The Accountability Mechanism of Multilateral Development Banks', *supra* n. 53, 190. They 'focus on the development of access for third parties, particularly private individuals, to lodge claims against MDBs for noncompliance with their policies and procedures'. *Ibid.*, 181. There are some marginal mechanisms available in limited contexts such as employment contracts of international organizations with staff but nothing beyond.

100. ILA, *Accountability of International Organizations Final Conference Report*, *supra* n. 55, 25.
101. UN General Assembly Official Records Sixty-second session Supplement No.10 (A/62/10): Report of the International Law Commission Fifty-ninth session 7 May–5 Jun. and 9 Jul.–10 Aug. 2007), 194.
102. For a scathing critique of the work of ILC, *see* José E Alvarez, 'International Organizations: Accountability or Responsibility?', presented as the Luncheon Address at the Canadian Council of International Law, 35th Annual Conference on Responsibility of Individuals, States and Organizations (Ottawa, Ontario, Canada, 27 Oct. 2006), *available at* <www.temple.edu/law/ils/CCILspeech.pdf>. Alvarez writes of the ILC Draft Articles: '. . . unlike most of the rules of state responsibility, most of these articles appear to have emerged, fully formed, only from the heads of ILC members and not the real world'. *Ibid.*, 13.

> states to devise internal mechanisms that either prevent their IOs from acting wrongfully or that provide remedies when they do.[103]

Crawford likewise observes that such provisions 'seek to prevent a State from hiding behind an international organization to shield itself from responsibility for internationally wrongful conduct whether committed by the organization itself or by the State in aid or assistance to the organization'.[104] But the difficulties remain. Even when, for example, it is accepted that IFIs are expected to respect core international human rights norms the issue of responsibility is not an easy one. As Alvarez notes:

> Given the notorious disagreements among states with respect to the content of customary human rights, advocates of the human rights accountability of the UN rely on the human rights covenants or other human rights treaties but it is quite a leap to suggest that the UN, a third party to such treaties, can possibly be bound by agreements that not all of its members have ratified and that, even when they have, are subject to diverse (and sometimes quite extensive) reservations. And even if we were inclined for the sake of argument to say that, for example, the UN must be 'deemed' a party to all or some human rights treaties, it would involve considerable imaginative leaps to connect those enumerated state-centric rights to what IOs actually do. (Given the controversies that have emerged with respect to what is expected of governments, which have full control over their territories and branches of governments, in terms of 'respecting' and 'ensuring' the rights in the ICCPR, does anyone think that it is clear what it means to have the World Bank or the IMF or the Security Council be obligated 'to respect and ensure' such rights?).[105]

From a third world perspective, the issue is not simply one of the complexities in implementing the law relating to the responsibility of international organizations, real as it is, but also of global social movements alerting the international community to the possibility of making international organizations and their Member States responsible in international law. These movements alone can help open up imaginative and innovative spaces in law to defend the welfare of third world peoples (against the argument that law is ambiguous and practice is rare) even if it takes a while to realize.

Two examples of innovative doctrines advanced in the context of the responsibility of IFIs are the doctrines of 'odious debt' and 'illegitimate debt'. A recent trend is to focus on the accountability and responsibility of the lender as against the

103. *Ibid.*, 4–5.

104. Crawford, 'Holding International Organizations and Their Members to Account', *supra* n. 73, 14. Of course it is often contended that there is no existing law on the subject of the responsibility of international organizations but this view needs to be contested as the ILC has. *Ibid.*, 15.

105. Alvarez, *supra* n. 102, 15–16.

borrower.[106] Hanlon invokes, in favour of such a trend, the US call for the cancellation of Iraqi debts, several previous occasions when the US and other nations have made similar calls, and provisions of domestic laws. These initiatives rely on the doctrines of 'odious debt' and 'illegitimate debt', which invokes the liability of the lender (leading to debt cancellation) as against the borrower. 'Odious debts' include money lent to despotic or oppressive regimes, or with the knowledge that it would be misused.[107] 'Illegitimate debt' is a broader category, a more recent creation, that Hanlon functionally defines as consisting of loans 'which were improperly granted and are thus the liability of the lender and are not to be repaid'.[108] Hanlon sums up the doctrines of 'odious debt' and 'illegitimate debt' observing that:

> the issue here is one of moral hazard – unless lenders are punished for past misconduct, [. . .] they will not mend their ways. This is particularly true with the IMF, which is the bailiff that enforced international debt repayments and ensures that it is repaid first, and with the World Bank, which continues to lend to notorious dictators in the belief that it can enforce payment.[109]

There are two possibilities of arriving at a determination of illegitimate debt. The first is through international arbitration. The second, suggested by Hanlon, is 'a prior declaration of legitimacy'. In operational terms, 'a loan will be considered automatically legitimate if (1) it is approved by a parliament; and (2) that parliament has been elected in an internationally recognized election'.[110] There are complex legal issues involved here that will require careful consideration including those flowing from the principle of state sovereignty. But the basic thrust of making lender institutions accountable seems sensible and may be formulated as a general rule as part of its ongoing work on the responsibility of international organizations in international law.

VI. THIRD WORLD AND THE GOVERNANCE OF IFIs

In recent years, the IMF has accepted that as an 'institution of global governance' the 'quality and legitimacy of its own governance is central to its success in

106. *See* Joseph Hanlon, '"Illegitimate" Loans: Lenders, Not Borrowers, Are Responsible', *Third World Quarterly* 27 (2006): 211. *See also* Jeff A. King, 'The Doctrine of Odious Debt in International Law: A Restatement' (21 Jan. 2007), *available at* SSRN: <http://ssrn.com/abstract=1027682>; Max Mader & Andre Rothenbuhler (eds), *How to Challenge Illegtimate Debt: Theory and Legal Case Studies* (Basel: Aktion Finanzplatz Schweiz, November 2009), *available at* <www.aktionfinanzplatz.ch/pdf/Buch-d.pdf>. *But see* Albert H. Choi & Eric A. Posner, 'A Critique of the Odious Debt Doctrine', *University of Chicago Law & Economics, Olin Working Paper No. 323*, *available at* SSRN: <http://ssrn.com/abstract=957346>.
107. Hanlon, '"Illegitimate" Loans: Lenders Not Borrowers, Are Responsible', *supra* n. 106, 214.
108. *Ibid.*, 220.
109. *Ibid.*, 223.
110. *Ibid.*, 222.

carrying out its mission to promote maximum global growth and international financial stability'.[111] Indeed, few today dispute that IMF governance is 'a central issue in IMF reform'.[112] Bradlow has identified some of the key elements of IMF governance that call for reform: 'non-responsiveness to the concerns of key stakeholders in the IMF, lack of accountability, non-representative decision-making, lack of transparency, and poorly defined relations with other international organizations'.[113] It is no different in the case of the World Bank. The need to reform the organizational structure and working of IFIs acquired greater urgency after the global financial crisis as it further undermined the credibility and legitimacy of IFIs. Therefore, the G-20 summits convened to address the crisis considered the relevant issues and made recommendations that are to be implemented in the near future. These are considered below in the context of the reform of central elements of the governance structure of IFIs.

A key concern of the developing countries for long has been the structure of weighted voting in decision-making in IFIs. The IFIs embody a voting structure under which a certain number of basic votes are granted to all Member States on the basis of the principle of sovereign equality of states and further votes are allocated in accordance with the financial contribution (or quotas) of a Member State. The quotas are reviewed every five years. Over the years, the basic votes (250 votes to each Member State) as a proportion of the total votes, at a peak of 14% in 1955, have plummeted to around 3%.[114] Along with the quota system it has led to many anomalies in the governance structure of IFIs. For example, it has been noted:

> that the combined votes on the IMF Executive Board of Brazil, China, and India are 19 percent less than the combined votes of Belgium, Italy, and the Netherlands at the same time (2000–2001) that their combined GDPs at market exchange rates are 23 percent higher, their GDPs at purchasing power parity (2000 PPP estimates) are four times higher, and their populations are 29 times higher.[115]

Clearly the voting structure of IFIs called for pressing review.[116] Truman has noted several possible ways for bringing this reform about.[117] These range from redefining the economic variables used for calculating quotas to increasing basic votes to

111. Edwin M. Truman (ed.), *Reforming the IMF for the 21st Century* (Washington, DC: Institute for International Economics, 2006), 13; John Glenn, 'Global Governance and the Democracy Deficit: Stifling the Voice of the South', *Third World Quarterly* 29, no. 2 (2008): 217–238.
112. Truman, *supra* n. 111, 17.
113. Bradlow, 'The Governance of the IMF: The Need for Comprehensive Reform', *supra* n. 17, 1.
114. Ngaire Woods, 'Making the IMF and the World Bank More Accountable', *International Affairs* 77 (2001): 87.
115. Truman, *supra* n. 111, 73.
116. Stiglitz, *Making Globalisation Work*, *supra* n. 64, 281–282; Richard Gerster, 'Proposals for Voting Reform within the International Monetary Fund', *Journal of World Trade* 3 (1993): 121–135.
117. Truman notes the following: the Cooper proposal that 'recommended a simplified formula based on two variables: GDP (the potential ability to contribute to the Fund) and the variability

taking population into account as one relevant variable. The essential issue is whether developing states, the only subjects of IFI policies and programmes, can have a substantial voice in the decision-making process without compromising the revolving nature of IFIs. The Charter of Economic Rights and Duties adopted in 1974, at the height of the call for a NIEO, stated in Article 10:

> All states are juridically equal and, as equal members of the international community, have the right to participate fully and effectively in the international decision-making process in the solution of world economic, financial and monetary problems, *inter alia*, through the appropriate international organizations in accordance with their existing and evolving rules, and to share equitably in the benefits resulting therefrom.[118]

The third world states, it can be seen, did not demand a one state-one vote formula even as a part of ushering in a NIEO, but focused on the need for full and effective participation in the work of international economic institutions. It offers a flexible formula for reviewing the voting structure of IFIs.

In the wake of the global economic crisis, the G-20 countries have undertaken to reform the IFIs to give 'greater voice and representation' to emerging and developing economies.[119] In the case of the IMF, the G-20 countries have recommended a shift in quota share 'of at least 5% from over-represented countries to under-represented countries using the current quota formula as the basis to work from'.[120] While this is a welcome step it is unlikely to allow the developing and emerging economies an effective say in the working of IMF. Although decisions in IFIs are taken on the basis of a simple weighted majority, nearly all crucial decisions requiring 70% or 85% majorities (e.g., the amendment of IMF Articles of Agreement). Buira notes the most important of these:

> Among the issues that the IMF Executive Board must resolve by qualified majority are: decisions on quota size, rates of charge, exchange-rate

---

of current receipts and net long-term capital flows (an alternative measure of the potential need to borrow from the Fund), with the coefficient on the former twice that on the latter composite'; the Kelkar et al. proposal that suggests 'replacing GDP at market prices and current exchange rates with GDP on a PPP basis, which ceteris paribus would tend to boost the quota shares of developing countries'; the Bryant proposal that includes population in the formula along with GDP increasing the voting power of developing countries; a proposal of small developing countries that the basic votes be adjusted (requiring an amendment to the IMF Articles of Agreement); the Wood and Lombardi proposal involving quota redistribution and 'expanding the double-majority approach, in which certain decisions require various weighted majority plus various majorities of members'; or 'both the United States and the European Union could agree to reduce their voting power below 15 percent as part of a grand bargain on IMF reform freeing up a large share of quotas and votes for reallocation'. Truman, *supra* n. 111, 73–76.

118. Charter of Economic Rights and Duties of States, GA Res. 3281 (xxix) (1974), Art. 10, *available at* <www.vilp.de/Enpdf/e162.pdf>.
119. *See* The London Summit 2009, 'Global Plan for Recovery and Reform', *supra* n. 18, para. 20.
120. *See* 'Leaders' Statement: The Pittsburgh Summit' (24–25 Sep. 2009), para. 20, *available at* <www.pittsburghsummit.gov/mediacenter/129639.htm>.

> arrangements, matters related to special drawing rights (SDRs), policies on access to IMF resources, payments to the IMF, use of IMF's gold holdings and reserves, management of the IMF's investment accounts, publication of reports, remuneration of creditor positions and temporary suspension of IMF operations. Thus, all significant decisions – those related to the size of the IMF and the use of its resources, to SDRs, gold and the international monetary system – are subject to the will of one or a few countries.[121]

Indeed, decisions requiring an 85% majority allow one state alone (the United States) to have a veto over important decisions in an institution established to promote *international* monetary cooperation.[122] This is unlikely to change as the United States will in all likelihood retain its veto power over decisions requiring an 85% qualified majority vote and together with other developed countries have the same power over decisions calling for a 70% qualified majority vote. Any serious reform of the decision-making process of the Fund should at least ensure that one country alone does not possess a veto over critical decisions of the Fund. In the instance of the World Bank, the G-20 countries 'stressed the importance of adopting a dynamic formula' which 'primarily reflects countries' evolving economic weight and the World Bank's development mission, and that generates an increase of at least 3% voting power for developing and transition countries [DTC], to the benefit of under-represented countries'.[123] A recent report of the World Bank explains the first phase of this reform:

> Phase 1 reforms will increase DTC voting power in the International Bank for Reconstruction and Development (IBRD) from 42.6 percent to 44.1 percent by increasing Basic Votes to 5.55% of total votes, and allocating IBRD shares to sixteen DTCs whose voting power would be reduced by the proposed increase in Basic Votes.[124]

---

121. Ariel Buira, 'The Governance of the IMF in a Global Economy', in *Challenge to the World Bank and IMF: Developing Country Perspectives*, ed. Ariel Buira (London: Anthem Press, 2003), 18.
122. *Ibid.*
123. 'Leaders' Statement: The Pittsburgh Summit', *supra* n. 120, para. 21 of the preamble and para. 21 of the text, respectively.
124. Development Committee (Joint Ministerial Committee of the Boards of Governors of the Bank and Fund on the Transfer of Real Resources to Developing Countries, 'Enhancing Voice and Participation of Developing and Transition Countries in the World Bank Group: Update and Proposals for Discussion', DC 2009-0011 (29 Sep. 2009), para. 2, *available at* <http://siteresources.worldbank.org/DEVCOMMINT/Documentation/22335196/DC2009-0011(E)Voice. pdf> (hereinafter IMF-World Bank Development Committee, 'Enhancing Voice and Participation of Developing and Transition Countries in the World Bank Group: Update and Proposals for Discussion'). The document also reports on the present status of the required amendments: 'The proposed amendment of the IBRD Articles of Agreement to increase Basic Votes has been approved by the Board of Governors and has been transmitted to all members for acceptance. Currently, acceptances have been received from two-thirds of members representing over 50% of total voting power. While this meets the required three-fifths of members, more acceptances are needed to reach the 85% of the total voting power that is required for the amendment to be effective. Subscription to the unallocated shares can

It remains to be seen whether these reforms will secure the developing countries a more effective voice in the decision-making.

A second significant issue with respect to the reform of the governance structure of IFIs relates to the structure of management. Even prior to the global economic crisis there was growing consensus that it *inter alia* meant putting into place an open and legitimate process of appointment for the heads of the institutions; a stronger role for the executive boards in overseeing the work of the institutions; a structure of representation that better reflects the stakes of all Member States; and measures which assisted in enhancing the accountability of Executive Directors to their governments and voters.[125] The G-20 countries have agreed that besides adjusting quota shares in the IMF a number of other critical issues will need to be addressed, including:

> the size and composition of the Executive Board; ways of enhancing the Board's effectiveness; and the Fund Governors' involvement in the strategic oversight of the IMF. Staff diversity should be enhanced.... the heads and senior leadership of all international institutions should be appointed through an open, transparent and merit-based process.[126]

In the case of the World Bank, it has been proposed to add, in Phase 1 of reforms, an elected Executive Director for Sub-Saharan Africa (SSA) on the World Bank Group's Boards of Director. There has also been agreement on 'strengthening Board effectiveness and internal governance; deepening responsiveness to DTC [developing and transitioning country] views on development; and a merit-based and transparent selection process of the Bank's President'.[127] But the precise details of some of the proposed reforms have not been spelt out. There are various views that have been aired earlier. For example, in relation to the IMF, Bradlow recommends a Member State's governor to the IMF or his/her representative be allowed to participate in any discussion in the Executive Board on the Member State.[128] Buira adds that 'representation on the Board could be regulated so that an increase in the number of Directors representing developing countries is matched by a corresponding reduction in the number of Directors from industrial countries'.[129]

---

begin after this amendment has become effective. For the third SSA executive director, discussions among SSA Governors on the realignment of the two current SSA constituencies are well advanced'. *Ibid.*, para. 3.

125. Woods, *supra* n. 114, 100.
126. *See* 'Leaders' Statement: The Pittsburgh Summit', *supra* n. 120, para. 21.
127. IMF-World Bank Development Committee, 'Enhancing Voice and Participation of Developing and Transition Countries in the World Bank Group: Update and Proposals for Discussion', *supra* n. 124, para. 29 ff. (for Phase II reforms).
128. Bradlow, 'The Governance of the IMF: The Need for Comprehensive Reform', *supra* n. 17, para. 29.
129. Buira, 'The Governance of the IMF in a Global Economy', *supra* n. 121, 24. Buira notes that the ideal candidate for reduction is Europe as it has 'the greatest number of representatives on the Board'. *Ibid.* He also suggests that 'no Executive Director should represent more than, say, 10 countries'. *Ibid.*, 25.

Such measures, along with positive steps towards independent evaluation and inspection would doubtless improve the accountability of the IMF.[130]

A third issue has been the lack of transparency in IFI functioning. Thus, while the IMF complains of the lack of good governance in the borrowing countries 'it lacked ... basic rules of democratic institutions: namely, transparency, so that citizens could see what issues were on the table and have the time to react, and also so they could see how officials had voted, so that they could be held accountable'.[131] Transparency, in other words, is necessary if the civil society is to play a watchdog role. In so far as the World Bank is concerned, a step towards enhancing transparency was taken on 17 November 2009 when its executive board adopted a new access-to-information policy under which the Bank will disclose any information in its possession that is not on a list of exceptions.[132] This is a welcome step. It does not, however, exclude the need for a comprehensive global right to information convention, for unless concerned civil society organizations can access in a timely fashion all necessary information, it is impossible for them to inform the institutional process of the concerns and anxieties of subaltern and marginal groups. In short, there is an urgent need to adopt a Global Right to Information Convention.[133]

VII. FINAL REMARKS

Six points may be made by way of conclusion. First, much of mainstream international law literature on IFIs fails to locate these organizations within the larger global economic and political environment. The result is a relative inability to appreciate and characterize the role of IFIs in relation to different phases of global capitalism; being sanguine about IFIs promoting sustainable and equitable growth in the world economy; and believing that the knowledge production functions of IFIs are employed to this end. From a critical third world or TWAIL perspective the role and character of IFIs is essentially a function of the changing needs of global capitalism and the power of advanced capitalist states.[134] This

130. Bradlow, 'The Governance of the IMF: The Need for Comprehensive Reform', *supra* n. 17, 29.

131. Stiglitz, *Making Globalization Work*, *supra* n. 64, 19.

132. *See* The World Bank, 'World Bank Reform', <www.worldbank.org/html/extdr/worldbankreform/>. This is a significant and positive move to making the Bank more transparent, but it remains to be seen how the policy works in practice, especially how the exceptions are interpreted.

133. Chimni, 'Cooption and Resistance: Two Faces of Global Administrative Law', *supra* n. 96, 811, 827. Access to information in the IFI context is discussed further in, David Hunter, 'International Law and Public Participation in Policy-Making at the International Financial Institutions', Ch. 7 herein.

134. As one writer notes, 'to fruitfully engage questions concerning the responsibilities of either individuals or institutions, we must assess the justice of the social arrangements within which they operate'. Christian Barry, 'Global Justice: Aims, Arrangements, and Responsibilities', in *Can Institutions Have Responsibilities? Collective Moral Agency and International Relations*, ed. Toni Erskine (Basingstoke: Palgrave Macmillan, 2003), 233.

understanding is validated by the response of developed states to the ongoing global economic crisis. The reform of IFIs has essentially been undertaken to shore up the credibility and legitimacy of IFIs and the global capitalist system and not to meet the concerns of developing countries, in particular subaltern groups and classes seriously affected by the economic crisis. The legitimacy outcome is to be achieved through introducing marginal reforms in the IFIs' decision-making and lending structures. But the crisis has equally been used to enhance their lending power and accompanying supervision over economies and polities of the developing world. There has been, for instance, no discernible change in the nature of conditionalities being prescribed to borrowing states.

Second, third world countries, in the wake of the global economic crisis, have missed the opportunity to advance an alternative vision of the role of IFIs and/or call for the creation of new institutions that are more responsive to their needs. The present failure to do so contrasts with efforts in the early 1970s, when in the backdrop of recession, key areas of reform in the working of IFIs were identified as an integral part of a call for establishing a NIEO. The failure to articulate alternative thinking has meant that there has been no systematic reflection on options like the Chiang Mai initiative or creation of institutions like the ALBA Bank. Another consequence is the absence of a separate and progressive conceptual vocabulary in the matrix of which the interpretation of IFI mandates by developed countries and management can be contested. A primary reason for this failure to advance a distinct third world outlook is the growing coincidence of interests of the ruling elite in the developed world and key developing countries.[135]

Third, the vigorously affirmed fragmentation of international law by IFIs makes it difficult to bring the language of international human rights law to bear on their functioning. Once again, key developing countries failed to draw the attention of the international community (especially when having the opportunity to do so in recent G-20 meetings) to the imperative of requiring IFIs to comply with international human rights law. Unfortunately, the global civil society also did not actively canvass this position in the context of G-20 meetings. This should not, however, discourage critics of IFIs, for an inclusive global capitalism, in so far as it is possible, is a goal worth pursuing. It may be useful in the context of making IFIs adhere to core international human rights obligations that their relationship agreements with ECOSOC be renegotiated.

Fourth, there is an urgent need to adopt an effective set of international law rules regulating the responsibility of international organizations. The ILC draft formulations on the subject are a step in this direction. These however need to be more robust in their orientation if they are to help tackle issues like 'odious' or 'illegitimate' debt and human rights violations. Meanwhile particular accountability mechanisms like the World Bank Inspection Panel need to be strengthened.

Fifth, a pitch should be made for adopting a Global Right to Information Convention as it can greatly help concerned NGOs/global social movements to

135. *See generally* Chimni, 'International Institutions Today: An Imperial Global State in the Making', *supra* n. 2, 4–5.

access relevant information from IFIs in a timely manner. While some of the steps that IFIs, in particular the World Bank, have recently taken towards improving the transparency of these organizations is welcome; they do not go far enough.

Sixth, at a fundamental level the third world critique of IFIs is about being spoken down to and being treated as objects of rational policies devised by the advanced capitalist countries.[136] While the global economic crisis has compelled these countries to undertake some reform of IFIs, and these reforms should not be scoffed at, it remains to be seen if these will help turn developing countries from being the objects of international law and institutions into active and effective participants.

136. Himadeep Muppidi, 'Colonial and Postcolonial Global Governance', in *Power in Global Governance*, ed. Michael Barnett & Raymond Duvall (Cambridge: Cambridge University Press, 2005), 273–294.

Chapter 3

Responsibility of International Financial Institutions under International Law

Eisuke Suzuki

I. INTRODUCTION

In *Reparation for Injuries suffered in the service of the United Nations*,[1] the International Court of Justice (ICJ) ruled in 1949 that '[the United Nations Organization] is a subject of international law and capable of possessing international rights and duties, and that it has capacity to maintain its rights by bringing international claims'.[2] The ICJ thus cleared the way for international organizations to hold states responsible whether or not any state is a member of the organization concerned.[3]

It is a corollary that if international organizations, as international legal personality, can bring claims for injuries done to their interests, then they should

1. Reparation for Injuries Suffered in the Service of the United Nations, Advisory Opinion, 1949 I.C.J. 174 (11 April) (hereinafter 'Reparation for Injuries').
2. *Ibid.*, 179.
3. *Ibid.*, 184–185. Israel was not a member of the United Nations when the Secretary-General's envoy, Count Bernadotte, was assassinated in 1948. The organization is 'an entity possessing objective international personality, and not merely personality recognized by [the Member States]'. *Ibid.*, 185.

Daniel D. Bradlow and David B. Hunter, *International Financial Institutions and International Law*, pp. 63–101.

be equally subject to claims against them for their conduct.[4] In the words of the Secretary-General of the United Nations, 'the international responsibility of the United Nations for the activities of United Nations forces is an attribute of its international legal personality and its capacity to bear international rights and obligations'.[5] The principle of reciprocity and the mutuality of obligations demand that the legal personality of international organizations entails responsibility for their conduct. The ICJ reaffirmed its position when it stated that 'international organizations are subjects of international law and, as such, are bound by any obligations incumbent upon them under general rules of international law, under their constitutions or under international agreements to which they are parties'.[6] But what are the obligations of international organizations under international law?

This article primarily focuses on the responsibility of international financial institutions (IFIs), which are organized on the basis of capital subscription by members, and where the voting power of each member is determined by share holding in the IFI concerned.[7] In Part II, the article analyses the implications of some of the International Law Commission's (ILC) draft articles on the responsibility of international organizations that help to clarify the special aspects of IFIs and examine the fundamental problems of immunity that underlie the establishment of responsibility of international organizations. Part III reviews the relationship between the internal law of IFIs and international responsibility. Part IV appraises the development and usefulness of accountability mechanisms established by IFIs and includes analysis of a case brought against the Asian Development Bank due to its financing of a wastewater treatment plant in Thailand. Finally in Part V, the article proposes changes that can be made to improve the ability of people to challenge IFI-financed projects, including the expansion of the jurisdictional competence of each administrative tribunal of the IFIs to deal with

4. *See* C.F. Amerasinghe, *Principles of the Institutional Law of International Organizations*, 2nd edn (Cambridge: Cambridge University Press, 2005), 399; Jan Klabbers, *An Introduction to International Institutional Law* (Cambridge: Cambridge University Press, 2002), 306; Philip Sands & Pierre Klein, *Bowett's Law of International Institutions*, 5th edn (London: Sweet & Maxwell, 2001), 513; James Crawford, *The International Law Commission's Articles on State Responsibility: Introduction, Text and Commentaries* (Cambridge: Cambridge University Press, 2002), 80 (stating 'It may be that the notion of responsibility for wrongful conduct is a basic element in the possession of international legal personality').
5. 'Report of the Secretary-General on the Administrative and Budgetary Aspects of the Financing of United Nations Peacekeeping Operations', U.N. Doc. A/51/389 (20 Sep. 1996), para. 6.
6. Interpretation of the Agreement of 25 Mar. 1951 between the WHO and Egypt, Advisory Opinion, 1980 I.C.J. 73 (30 December).
7. *See generally*, Edward S. Mason & Robert Asher, *The World Bank since Bretton Woods* (Washington, DC: Brookings Institution, 1973); Kenneth W. Dam, *The Rules of the Game: Reform and Evolution in the International Monetary System* (Chicago: University of Chicago Press, 1982), 71–114; Joseph Gold, *Legal and Institutional Aspects of the International Monetary System: Selected Essays* (Washington, DC: International Monetary Fund, 1979), 292. *See also* Dennis Leech & Robert Leech, 'Voting Power in the Bretton Woods Institutions', in *The IMF, World Bank and Policy Reform*, ed. Alberto Paloni & Maurizio Zanardi (London: Routledge, 2006), 29–48.

third-party claims from private individuals and groups rather than being a tribunal solely devoted to solving internal employment disputes.

II. THE INCONGRUITY OF STATE RESPONSIBILITY, THE RESPONSIBILITY OF INTERNATIONAL ORGANIZATIONS, AND THE WALL OF IMMUNITY OF INTERNATIONAL ORGANIZATIONS

At its fifty-second session in 2000, the ILC decided that it would work on the issue of international responsibility of international organizations as part of its long-term programme.[8] As it was completing its state responsibility project in 2001, the topic was chosen as 'a sequel' to the draft Articles on State Responsibility (ASR).[9] Unhappily, despite its own good counsel that 'the responsibility of international organizations is governed by rules which are not necessarily the same as those governing the responsibility of States',[10] the ILC's work appears to have been too closely aligned with the ASR for the sake of conformity to the text and organization of the ASR. Considerable state practice and ample case law address state responsibility, as the ASR confirms.[11] Such rich real-world experiences of state responsibility prompted one commentator to say that 'the ASR have a legitimate claim to being a mere codification of what actually existed, with progressive development occurring as always, but only on the margins'.[12] That is not the case in regards to the responsibility of international organizations. Nonetheless, the ILC followed the basic approach set out in the ASR and, as the chairman of the drafting committee clarified, 'to the extent that any particular article, in the new topic, is expressing the same legal principle or statement as in an article in State Responsibility, the language should remain in order to avoid any confusion and ambiguity'.[13] For example, the ILC's draft Article 3, 'General Principles', provides:

> 1. Every internationally wrongful act of an international organization entails the international responsibility of the international organization.

---

8. 'Report of the International Law Commission', fifty-second session, Supp. No. 10, U.N. Doc. A/55/10 (2000), 292.
9. Giorgio Gaja, 'First Report on Responsibility of International Organizations', U.N. Doc. A/CN.4/532 (26 Mar. 2003), para. 20 (written by Special Rapporteur).
10. *Yearbook of the International Law Commission*, vol. II (1975), 89–90.
11. *See* Crawford, *The International Law Commission's Articles on State Responsibility: Introduction, Text and Commentaries*, *supra* n. 4.
12. José E. Alvarez, 'International Organizations: Accountability or Responsibility', luncheon address given at Canadian Council of International Law, 35th Annual Conference on Responsibility of Individuals, States and Organizations (Ottawa, 27 Oct. 2006), 12.
13. 'Statement of the Chairman of the Drafting Committee', given at the 55th session of the ILC, UN Doc. A/CN.4/L.632 (Geneva, 2003). *Cf.* James Crawford, 'Holding International Organizations and Their Members to Account', paper given at Fifth Steinkraus-Cohen International Law Lecture at the University of London, School of Oriental and African Studies (London, 15 Mar. 2007), 34 (noting '[t]here is lots of customary law on State responsibility, and the action of international organizations is by definition linked to the actions or omissions of States').

2. There is an internationally wrongful act of an international organization when conduct consisting of an action or omission:
(a) Is attributed to the international organization under international law; and
(b) Constitutes a breach of an international obligation of that international organization.[14]

Article 3 mirrors Articles 1 and 2 of the ASR.[15] But what are international obligations of international organizations when international law typically does not address international organizations as subjects? Rarely are international organizations parties to international treaties in which international obligations arise, which creates profound uncertainty about the content of the professed principles of responsibility of international organizations under international law. If they are not bound by most treaties, then the applicable law regulating their conduct is limited to customary international law, their constituent treaties, internal laws, and headquarters agreements. In addition, international organizations will have those obligations, if any, that they have voluntarily assumed under international treaty law.[16] Instances of applicability of customary international law to international organizations are understandably ambiguous.[17] For example, the Universal Declaration of Human Rights,[18] which is now considered customary international law and thus binding upon international organizations,[19] is primarily concerned about safeguarding against the abuses of State power.

Even if the laws governing the conduct of international organizations are clear, two fundamental issues still impede the creation of a legal framework for responsibility of international organizations.[20] One is that a huge difference exists

14. International Law Commission, 'Responsibility of International Organizations', A/CN.4/L.632 (4 Jun. 2003), Art. 3, *available at* <http://untreaty.un.org/ilc/documentation/english/a_cn4_l632.pdf>.
15. *Ibid.*
16. Eisuke Suzuki & Suresh Nanwani, 'Responsibility of International Organizations: The Accountability Mechanisms of Multilateral Development Banks', *Michigan Journal of International Law* 27 (2005): 212–213. Responsibility of international organizations is one of the areas of international law where 'customary international law as being generally applicable will govern', *see* Amerasinghe, *Principles of the Institutional Law of International Organizations*, 2nd edn, *supra* n. 4, 19. On the question of the voluntary assumption of obligations, *see* Günther Handl, 'The Legal Mandate of Multilateral Development Banks as Agents for Change toward Sustainable Development', *American Journal of International Law* 92 (1998): 642, *reprinted in* Günther Handl, *Multilateral Development Banking: Environmental Principles and Concepts Reflecting General International Law and Public Policy* (Boston: Kluwer Law International, 2001), 26. *See also* W.M. Reisman & Mahnoush H. Arsanjani, 'The Question of Unilateral Governmental Statement as Applicable Law in Investment Disputes', in *Common Values in International Law: Essays in Honor of Christian Tomuschat*, ed. Pierre-Mari Dupuy et al. (Kehl, Germany: N.P. Engel Verlag, 2006), 409.
17. Alvarez, 'International Organizations: Accountability or Responsibility', *supra* n. 12, 14–15.
18. Universal Declaration of Human Rights, GA Res. 217(III), UN Doc. A/810 (1948), 71.
19. W.M. Reisman, 'Sovereignty and Human Rights in Contemporary International Law', in *Democratic Governance and International Law*, ed. G.H. Fox & B.R. Roth (Cambridge: Cambridge University Press, 2000), 239.
20. In this chapter, we refer to 'international organization' as defined in Art. 2(1)(i) of the Vienna Convention on the Law of Treaties, 1155 U.N.T.S. 331; 8 I.L.M. 679 (1980), and Art. 2(1)(i) of

in power, function, and purpose among international organizations, which are not equal before the law. Besides, reciprocity and threats of retaliation, which govern the conduct of states on the basis of sovereign equality, do not apply to international organizations. The other is the immunity of international organizations from national jurisdiction.[21] The Committee on Accountability of International Organizations of the International Law Association mentioned that '[a] case-law development of a comprehensive responsibility/liability regime for IO's is not feasible as in most of them a system of judicial review of acts of the Organization is absent'.[22]

Firstly, international organizations differ widely, in terms of the domain of membership and scope of mandate, 'from regional [organizations] to those that aspire to universal membership, to those charged with international peace and security to those restricted to ensuring health, protecting international civil aviation, labor standards, or foiling trade protectionism',[23] and their powers and obligations are subject to the 'principle of speciality'.[24] The principle of speciality ordains that international organizations are not equal *inter se*, because they have only those rights and duties that can be ascribed to them by their respective charters and internal rules, along with those rights and duties that have been developed in practice. Accordingly, there is no semblance, even in legal fiction, of the equality of international organizations, equivalent notionally to the equality of sovereign states. The legal personality of international organizations, thus, cannot be treated uniformly.[25]

Secondly, the immunity accorded to international organizations also undermines the establishment of the legal responsibility of international organizations.[26]

---

the Vienna Convention on the Law of Treaties between States and International Organizations or between International Organizations, 25 I.L.M. 543 (1986).

21. *See* a Belgian claim against the *United Nations, M. v. Organisation des Nations Unies et l'État Belge*, *International Law Reports* 45 (1972): 446. The Civil Tribunal of Brussels dismissed the plaintiff's claim by stating, 'one cannot see where the U.N. could be sued, nor how, nor on what legal basis... so long as it shelters behind its immunity from jurisdiction'. *Ibid.*, 455. *See also* August Reinisch, *International Organizations before National Courts* (Cambridge: Cambridge University Press, 2000); August Reinisch & Jakob Wurm, 'International Financial Institutions before National Courts', Ch. 4 herein; Steven Herz, 'Rethinking International Financial Institution Immunity', Ch. 5 herein.
22. ILA Committee on Accountability of International Organizations, 'Third Report' (New Delhi Conference, 2002), 793.
23. Alvarez, 'International Organizations: Accountability or Responsibility', *supra* n. 12, 26.
24. Legality of the Use by a State of Nuclear Weapons in Armed Conflict, Advisory Opinion, 1996 I.C.J. 66, 79, para. 25 (8 July) (hereinafter 'Nuclear Weapons').
25. Alvarez, 'International Organizations: Accountability or Responsibility', *supra* n. 12, 25–26.
26. Klabbers, *An Introduction to International Institutional Law*, *supra* n. 4, 152 (noting that '[The idea of functional necessity] is almost by definition biased in favour of international organizations, to the possible detriment of others.'). *See also* Steven Herz, 'Rethinking International Financial Institution Immunity', Ch. 5 herein; P.H.F. Bekker, *The Legal Position of Intergovernmental Organizations: A Functional Necessity Analysis of Their Legal Status and Immunities* (Boston: Martinus Nijhoff, 1994); Reinisch, *International Organizations before National Courts*, *supra* n. 21; Gerhard Thallinger, 'Piercing Jurisdictional Immunity: The

The ICJ tentatively opened the liability door in its advisory opinion on a case concerning immunity:[27]

> [T]he Court wishes to point out that the question of immunity from legal process is distinct from the issue of compensation for any damages incurred as a result of acts performed by the United Nations or by its agents in their official capacity. The United Nations may be required to bear responsibility for the damage arising from such acts.[28]

The Opinion quickly qualified the principle:

> However, as is clear from Article VIII, Section 29, of the General Convention, any such claims against the United Nations shall not be dealt with by national courts but shall be settled in accordance with the appropriate modes of settlement that '[t]he United Nations shall make provisions for' pursuant to Section 29.[29]

But Article VIII of the Convention on the Privileges and Immunities of the United Nations[30] 'only says that the UN should provide some procedure for dispute settlement, with no reference to specific methods'.[31] Plus, disputes are limited to 'disputes arising out of contracts or other disputes of a private law character to which the United Nations is a party',[32] and 'disputes involving any official of the United Nations who by reason of his official position enjoys immunity, if immunity has not been waived by the Secretary-General'.[33] It is clear that no recourse to national courts will be available unless international organizations waive their immunity or the United Nations is under an obligation to provide 'appropriate modes of settlement' with respect to the non-contractual activities of the United Nations.[34] No doctrine comparable to restrictive state immunity applies to

---

Possible Role of Domestic Courts in Enhancing World Bank Accountability', 2, no. 1, <www.icl-journal.com>, 1 Mar. 2008, 4; Michael Singer, 'Jurisdictional Immunity of International Organizations: Human Rights and Functional Necessity Concerns', *Virginia Journal of International Law* 36 (1995): 53. For a discussion on the need to restrict the scope of immunity of an international organization, *see* Emmanuel Gaillard & Isabelle Pingel-Lenuzza, 'International Organizations and Immunity from Jurisdiction: To restrict or to Bypass', *International & Comparative Law Quarterly* 51 (2002): 1.

27. Difference Relating to Immunity from Legal Process of a Special Rapporteur of the Commission on Human Rights, Advisory Opinion, 1999 I.C.J. 62 (29 April).
28. *Ibid.*, 88–89 (para. 66).
29. *Ibid.*
30. Convention on the Privileges and Immunities of the United Nations, U.N.T.S. 15 (13 Feb. 1946).
31. Mahnoush H. Arsanjani, 'Claims against International Organizations: Quis Custodiet Ipsos Custodies', *Yale Journal of World Public Order* 7 (1981): 131, 142.
32. Convention on the Privileges and Immunities of the United Nations, *supra* n. 30, Art. VIII(29)(a).
33. *Ibid.*, Art. VIII(29)(b).
34. Suzuki & Nanwani, 'Responsibility of International Organizations: The Accountability Mechanisms of Multilateral Development Banks', *supra* n. 16, 202; Karel Wellens, *Remedies Against International Organizations* (Cambridge: Cambridge University Press, 2002), 114–132.

international organizations, and even if such doctrine were available, it would be of no use to public acts of a non-commercial nature because immunity restrictions are applicable only to state commercial activities.[35] Besides, the ICJ has already clarified that the arguments based on the states' sovereignty in favour of a restrictive interpretation of the provisions governing the jurisdiction of a tribunal adjudicating between states are not applicable to international organizations.[36] In any event, to organize some form of dispute settlement mechanism requires not only agreement by the parties to a dispute, but more fundamentally, the political will and support of the government as 'the arbitral system itself is created and sustained by state institutions'.[37]

III. INTERNATIONAL FINANCIAL INSTITUTIONS AND INTERNATIONAL LAW

All IFIs are treaty organizations with their own international legal personality.[38]

35. Crawford, 'Holding International Organizations and Their Members to Account', *supra* n. 13, para. 11.
36. Judgments of the Administrative Tribunal of the ILO Upon Complaints Made against the UNESCO, Advisory Opinion, 1956 I.C.J. 77, 97 (23 October).
37. W.M. Reisman, 'International Arbitration and Sovereignty', *Arbitration International* 18 (2002): 235.
38. International Financial Institutions (IFIs), here, refer principally to the International Monetary Fund (the IMF) and the International Bank for Reconstruction and Development (the World Bank), both created at the Bretton Woods conference in 1944. *See* United Nations Monetary and Financial Conference, 'Articles of Agreement of the International Monetary Fund' (Bretton Woods, NH, 22 Jul. 1944), *available at* <www.imf.org/external/pubs/ft/aa/index.htm>; 'Articles of Agreement of the International Bank for Reconstruction and Development', 2 U.N.T.S. 134 (Bretton Woods, NH, 22 Jul. 1944), *available at* <http://avalon.law.yale.edu/20th_century/decad047.asp>. *See also* Stephen D. Krasner, *Sovereignty: Organized Hypocrisy* (Princeton: Princeton University Press, 1999), 143–151. Additionally, IFIs include the regional development banks, such as the Inter-American Development Bank (IDB) established in 1959; the African Development Bank (AfDB) in 1964; the Asian Development Bank (ADB) in 1966; and the European Bank for Reconstruction and Development (EBRD) in 1991. *See* Eisuke Suzuki, *Regional Development Banks*, in *Max Planck Encyclopedia of Public International Law*, ed. Rüdiger Wolfrum, <www.mpepil.com>, 29 Feb. 2009. The Inter-American Development Bank (IDB) set up by the 'Agreement Establishing the Inter-American Development Bank' (January 1996), <www.iadb.org/leg/Documents/Pdf/Convenio-Eng.Pdf> (hereinafter 'IDB Charter'); the African Development Bank set up by the 'Agreement Establishing the African Development Bank', <www.afdb.org/fileadmin/uploads/afdb/Documents/Legal-Documents/30718627-EN-AGREEMENT-ESTABLISHING-THE-AFRICAN-DEVELOPMENT-BANK-6TH-EDITION.PDF>, July 2002 (hereinafter 'AfDB Charter'); the Asian Development Bank set up by the 'Agreement Establishing the Asian Development Bank', <http://adb.org/Documents/Reports/Charter/charter.pdf> (hereinafter 'ADB Charter'); and the European Bank for Reconstruction and Development set up by the 'Agreement Establishing the European Bank for Reconstruction and Development', <www.ebrd.com/pubs/insti/basics.pdf> (hereinafter 'EBRD Charter'). Later the Member States in the IBRD created other entities: the International Development Association (IDA), the International Finance Corporation (IFC), and the Multilateral Investment and Guarantee Agency (MIGA). Articles of Agreement of the International

A. International Financial Institutions and the U.N. System

The International Monetary Fund (IMF) and the World Bank became specialized agencies under Articles 57 and 63 of the United Nations Charter.[39] Subsequently, International Development Association (IDA), International Finance Corporation (IFC), and MIGA became specialized agencies as members of the World Bank Group, whereas all other regional multilateral development banks (MDBs) are not specialized agencies. This has created two groups of IFIs in regards to their responsibilities under international law. First, Article 58 of the United Nations Charter applies to the relationship between the World Bank Group and the IMF, and the United Nations. The ICJ recently commented on the overall effect of Article 58 of the United Nations as follows:

> [T]he Charter of the United Nations laid the basis of a 'system' designed to organize international co-operation in a coherent fashion by bringing the United Nations, invested with powers of general scope, into relationship with various autonomous and complementary organizations, invested with sectorial powers. The exercise of these powers by the organizations belonging to the 'United Nations system' is co-ordinated, notably, by the relationship agreements concluded between the United Nations and each of the specialized agencies.[40]

Pressure for coordination under Article 58 of the United Nations Charter has inevitably increased even though the World Bank and the IMF had managed to carve out more leeway for autonomy and independence through their respective agreements with the United Nations, which recognizes that 'by reason of the nature of its international responsibilities and the terms of its Articles of Agreement, the Bank [the IMF] is, and is required to function as, an independent international organization'.[41]

Development Association, 11 U.N.T.S. 2284 (1960) (hereinafter IDA Articles of Agreement); Articles of Agreement of the International Finance Corporation, 264 U.N.T.S. 117 (1955) (hereinafter IFC Articles of Agreement); Convention Establishing the Multilateral Investment Guarantee Agency, 1508 U.N.T.S. 99 (1985), *available at* <www.miga.org/quickref/index_sv.cfm?stid=1583> (hereinafter MIGA Convention).

39. Agreements between the United Nations and the International Monetary Fund and the United Nations and the International Bank for Reconstruction and Development, 16 U.N.T.S. 328, 346 (1948), respectively (hereinafter 'Relationship Agreement'). Both agreements came into force on 15 Nov. 1947.
40. Nuclear Weapons, *supra* n. 24, para. 26.
41. Relationship Agreement, *supra* n. 39, Art. I, para. 2. 'At that time, though, when the two BWIs [Bretton Woods Institutions] and UN signed the agreements and it was approved by the General Assembly, at the instance of the United States, the two BWIs virtually got away with murder in terms of their escaping even remote accountability to the UN that the Charter requires.' Chakravarthi Raghavan, 'WTO-UN Relationship Issue Becomes Muddied' in *Suns-South-North Development Monitor*, <www.sunsonline.org/trade/process/towards/10120094.htm>, 12 Oct. 1994.

The General Counsel of the IMF opined:

> [t]hus the relationship established by the 1947 Agreement is not one of 'agency' but one of 'sovereign equals'. It follows that the Fund's relationship agreement with the United Nations does not require it to give effect to resolutions of the United Nations, such as the resolutions under which the members of the General Assembly adopted the Universal Declaration or the [International] Covenant [on Economic, Social and Cultural Rights], or to international agreements, such as the Covenant, entered into by the members of the United Nations.[42]

Whether such a position is still tenable is contingent upon the development of certain obligations *erga omnes*.[43] The ICJ stated in its *Advisory Opinion on the Legality of the Threat or Use of Nuclear Weapons* that 'a great many rules of humanitarian law' are 'to be observed by all States whether or not they have ratified the conventions that contain them, because they constitute intransgressible principles of international customary law'.[44] The ICJ reiterated its view that 'these rules incorporate obligations which are essentially of an *erga omnes* character'.[45]

Additionally, the ICJ reminds us that 'customary international law continues to exist and to apply, separately from international treaty law, even where the two categories of law have an identical content'.[46] This means that international organizations are bound by such customary international law even though they are not parties to the corresponding treaties. Further, the commentary to Article 12 of the ASR notes that, '[i]nternational obligations may be established by a customary rule of international law, by a treaty or by a general principle applicable within the international legal order'.[47]

---

42. Francois Gianviti, 'Economic, Social and Cultural Human Rights and the International Monetary Fund', U.N. Doc. E/C.12/2001/WP.5 (7 May 2001), para.16.
43. Barcelona Traction, Light and Power Company, Limited, Second Phase, Judgment, 1970 I.C.J. 3, 32, para. 33 (5 February): 'In view of the importance of the rights involved, all States can be held to have a legal interest in their protection; they are obligations *erga omnes*.' *See* Mahnoush H. Arsanjani & W. Michael Reisman, 'The Quest for an International Liability Regime for the Protection of the Global Commons', in *International Law: Theory and Practice*, ed. Karel Wellens (The Hague: Martinus Nijhoff, 1998), 469, 482–485.
44. Advisory Opinion, 1996 I.C.J. 226, 257, para. 79 (8 July). In any event, the IMF relies on Art. 24 of the Covenant which provides: 'Nothing in the present Covenant shall be interpreted as impairing the provisions of the Charter of the United Nations and of the constitutions of the specialized agencies which define the respective responsibilities of the various organs of the United Nations and of the specialized agencies in regard to the matters dealt with in the present Covenant.' G.A. Res. 2200A (XXI) of 16 Dec. 1966. In the words of the General Counsel of the IMF, 'the Covenant is not a treaty that is binding on the Fund, and thus it has no direct effect on the Fund'. Gianviti, *supra* n. 42, para. 23.
45. Legal Consequences of the Construction of a Wall in the Occupied Palestinian Territory, Advisory Opinion, 2004 I.C.J. 136, 199, para. 157 (9 July).
46. Military and Paramilitary Activities (*Nicar. v. U.S.*), 1986 I.C.J. 14, 96, para. 179 (27 June).
47. Crawford, *The International Law Commission's Articles on State Responsibility: Introduction, Text and Commentaries*, *supra* n. 4, 126, para. 3. Note that, the ILC only changed the wording of Art. 12 of the ASR by replacing 'state' with 'international organization' when it wrote draft Art. 8 to address breaches of international obligations by international organizations.

Article 48 of the UN Charter requires 'all the members of the United Nations or by some of them, as the Security Council may determine', to take the action necessary 'to carry out the decisions of the Security Council for the maintenance of international peace and security . . . directly or through their action in the appropriate international agencies of which they are members'.[48] Under the Relationship Agreement, the World Bank and the IMF each:

> takes note of the obligation assumed, under paragraph 2 of Article 48 of the United Nations Charter, by such of its members as are also Members of the United Nations, to carry out the decisions of the Security Council through their actions in the appropriate agencies of which they are members, and will, in the conduct of its activities, have due regard for decisions of the Security Council under Articles 41 and 42 of the United Nations Charter.[49]

These provisions in reality undermine the notion that the World Bank is an 'independent international organization'[50] and the understanding 'that the action to be taken by the Bank on any loan is a matter to be determined by the independent exercise of the Bank's own judgment in accordance with the Bank's Articles of Agreement'.[51] A binding decision under Chapter VII of the UN Charter will desiccate any operative meaning of the Relationship Agreement in light of the explicit provision in Article 103 of the UN Charter of the supremacy of the obligations under the Charter over obligations under any other international agreement. That was the consequence of Security Council Resolution 757 of 30 May 1992, which established an embargo on products, commodities, and financial and economic contact from, and imposed a freeze on payment of funds to, the Federal Republic of Yugoslavia (Serbia and Montenegro).[52] Moreover, it contained the following provision:

> [The Security Council] calls upon all states, including states not members of the United Nations, and *all international organizations*, to act strictly in accordance with the provision of the present resolution, not withstanding the existence of any rights or obligations conferred or imposed by any international agreement or any contract entered into or any license or permit granted prior to the date of the present resolution (emphasis added).[53]

Ibrahim F. I. Shihata, then-Senior Vice President and General Counsel of the World Bank, conceded that 'the Bank cannot reasonably place its members in a situation where they would be violating their obligations under the UN Charter if

48. Charter of the United Nations, Art. 48 (26 Jun. 1945), *available at* <www.un.org/en/documents/charter/index.shtml> (hereinafter UN Charter).
49. Relationship Agreement, *supra* n. 39, Art. VI.
50. *Ibid.*, Art. I, para. 2.
51. *Ibid.*, Art. IV, para. 3. It further provides: 'The United Nations recognizes, therefore, that it would be sound policy to refrain from making recommendations to the Bank with respect to particular loans or with respect to terms or conditions of financing by the Bank.' *Ibid.*
52. Security Council Resolution 757 (30 May 1992).
53. *Ibid.*

they agree with a proposed action by the Bank' and that the Bank cannot propose a new loan to a country which is subject to a comprehensive mandatory embargo imposed by the Security Council.[54] The World Bank's *Guidelines for Procurement* stipulate:

> Firms of a country or goods manufactured in a country may be excluded if, . . . (ii) by an act of compliance with a decision of the United Nations Security Council taken under Chapter VII of the Charter of the United Nations, the Borrower's country prohibits any import of goods from or payments to, a particular country, person, or entity. Where the Borrower's country prohibits payments to a particular firm or for particular goods by such an act of compliance, that firm may be excluded.[55]

With respect to disbursement under ongoing loans, the Bank's action is subject to the provisions of the Loan Agreement and the General Conditions; and Management may suspend the loan in accordance with the provisions specifying when events are liable for suspension because they would make it improbable that the project could be carried out, or that the Borrower or the Guarantor will be able to perform its obligations under the Loan or Guarantee Agreement.[56]

Consider Judge Ammoun's plea in his separate opinion in the *Namibia* case:

> The specialized agencies in which the voting is based on the democratic rule of one State, one vote, have all decided to refrain from any support to South Africa: for example, UNESCO, ILO, FAO and WHO. The recalcitrant attitude of the IBRD and the IMF is to be explained by the multiple voting system on a capitalist basis which operates therein, by which the financial Great Powers have a number of votes calculated according to the size of their share in the capital of these two institutions. These Powers are primarily the States which the General Assembly has described as commercial partners of South Africa. In future, States ought to take it as a matter of course that *they should bring their attitude in these institutions into line with decisions of the United Nations* (emphasis original).[57]

This opinion highlights the difficulty of having the World Bank follow all of the United Nations' provisions.

Of late, the group of seventy-seven is moving steadily to restructure the United Nations' activities in economic and related areas. In Resolution 45/264, adopted in 1990, the General Assembly sought to enable the UN Economic and Social Council (ECOSOC) to 'discharge the responsibilities entrusted to it by the Charter by

54. Ibrahim F. I. Shihata, *The World Bank Legal Papers* (The Hague: Martinus Nijhoff, 2000), 809.
55. 'World Bank Guidelines for Procurement', para. 1.8, <http://go.worldbank.org/1KKD1KNT40>, May 2004.
56. *Ibid.*, 810.
57. Legal Consequences for States of the Continued Presence of South Africa in Namibia (South West Africa) Notwithstanding Security Council Resolution 276 (1970); Advisory Opinion, 1971 I.C.J. 16, 95, fn. 2 (21 June) (separate opinion of Vice President Ammoun).

enhancing its role as a central forum for major economic, social and related issues and policies and its coordinating functions relating to the United Nations system in the economic, social and related fields'.[58] The effect of this resolution can be seen by the work of the Ad Hoc Working Group on 'Enhancing International Cooperation for Development: The Role of the United Nations System'.[59]

The centripetal forces of the ECOSOC in organizing high level forums in connection with the Millennium Declaration[60] are so powerful that regional organizations that are not part of the United Nations system are drawn into the ECOSOC's policy agenda and implementation programmes. The High Level Forum on Harmonization[61] is one example of the movement toward global harmonization and integration. Of course, the real underlying power that is driving such policy agenda and implementation programmes is that of Member States participating in this global decision process.[62] Given the decision-making structure of international organizations, the notion of autonomy and independence of international organizations is, in reality, far more circumscribed than their rhetoric would otherwise suggest.

Apart from administrative obligations within the purview of the head of an international organization, obligations of an international organization cannot be created without the participation of Member States in decision-making.[63] As James

58. U.N. Doc. A/RES/45/264, 13 May 1991, Annex, para. 4(a).
59. *See generally*, Joachim Müller (ed.), *Reforming the United Nations: New Initiatives and Past Efforts* (The Hague: Kluwer Law International, 1997).
60. U.N. Doc. A/RES/55/2 (8 Sep. 2000).
61. *See, e.g.*, 'Information Paper on the High Level Forum on Harmonization, presented at Rome, Italy, 24–25 February 2003', <www.adb.org/Documents/Conference/Harmonization/Forum_on_Harmonization.pdf>. *See also* the second High Level Forum's 'Paris Declaration on Aid Effectiveness', adopted at Paris, France, 28 Feb. – 2 Mar. 2005, <www.oecd.org/dataoecd/11/41/34428351.pdf>; the Third High Level Forum's 'Accra Agenda for Action', adopted at Accra, Ghana, 2–4 Sep. 2008, <www.oecd.org/dataoecd/58/16/41202012.pdf>. These High Level meetings have been organized by the OECD-led Working Party on Aid Effectiveness (WP-EFF) rather than by the ECOSOC. *See* OECD, Working Party on Aid Effectiveness – Overview, <www.oecd.org/document/4/0,3343,en_2649_3236398_43414212_1_1_1_1,00.html> (explaining what the OECD Working Party on Aid Effectiveness is and what it does) (hereinafter OECD, WP-EFF).
62. *See* Myres S. McDougal, Harold D. Lasswell & W. Michael Reisman, 'The World Constitutive Process of Authoritative Decision', in *International Law Essays: A Supplement to International Law in Contemporary Perspective*, ed. Myres S. McDougal & W. Michael Reisman (Mineola, NY: Foundation Press, 1981), 191.
63. Given this decision process, it is common knowledge, contrary to Judge Rosalyn Higgins's suggestion, that regardless of whether members know 'that they are potentially liable for contractual damages or tortious harm caused by the acts of an international organization, they will necessarily intervene in virtually all decision-making by international organizations'. Rosalyn Higgins, 'The Legal Consequences for Member States of Non-fulfillment by International Organizations of Their Obligations towards Third Parties: Provisional Report', in *Annuaire de L'institut de Droit International* 66-I (1995): 373, 419. Member States intervene at their will even in matters over which the head of an international organization is solely responsible, for example, personnel appointments.

Crawford mentioned, 'the action of international organizations is by definition linked to the actions or omissions of States'.[64] Thus, the significance of Article 57 of the ASR cannot be overstated. It is a saving clause: 'These articles are without prejudice to any question of the responsibility under international law of an international organization, or of any State for the conduct of an international organization.'[65]

Additionally, specialized agencies may enjoy the benefits of advisory opinions given by the ICJ, 'the principal judicial organ of the United Nations'.[66] Article 96, paragraph 2, of the United Nations Charter provides in relevant part that 'specialized agencies, which may at any time be so authorized by the General Assembly, may also request advisory opinions of the Court on legal questions arising within the scope of their activities'.[67] Under the Relationship Agreement, the General Assembly of the United Nations:

> authorizes the [World] Bank to request advisory opinions of the International Court of Justice on *any legal questions arising within the scope of the Bank's activities* other than questions relating to the relationship between the Bank and the United Nations or any specialized agency (emphasis added).[68]

None of the regional multilateral development banks have the authority to solicit such opinions.[69]

For the purpose of establishing the responsibility of IFIs, access to the ICJ for Advisory Opinions, which may be accepted as binding decisions by agreement between the parties to a dispute, may provide a convenient forum. But 'whether a mechanism of accountability will be dependable if it can only be initiated by the very actor that it is hoped to hold to account'[70] is another matter. Of course states can also seek advisory opinions from the ICJ, but this may add little to the political accountability states have as members of the IFIs.

---

64. Crawford, 'Holding International Organizations and Their Members to Account', *supra* n. 13, para. 34.
65. Crawford, *The International Law Commission's Articles on State Responsibility: Introduction, Text and Commentaries*, *supra* n. 4, 310. It excludes from the scope of the ASR, according to the commentary, 'those cases where the international organization is the actor and the State is said to be responsible by virtue of its involvement in the conduct of the organization or by virtue of its membership of the organization'. The question of secondary or concurrent liability of Member States has become one of the most difficult issues under consideration of the ILC. *See* Giorgio Gaja (ILC), 'Second Report on Responsibility of International Organizations', U.N. Doc. A/CN.4/541 (2 Apr. 2004) (hereinafter 'Special Rapporteur's Second Report').
66. Statute of the International Court of Justice, Art. 1, <www.icj-cij.org/docments/index.php?p1=4&p2=2&p3=0>.
67. UN Charter, *supra* n. 48, Art. 96.2.
68. Relationship Agreement, *supra* n. 39, Art. VIII.
69. *See* Eisuke Suzuki, 'The Review and Repudiation of Judgments of International Administrative Tribunals', *Asian Yearbook of International Law* 7 (1997): 175, 205–206.
70. Crawford, 'Holding International Organizations and Their Members to Account', *supra* n. 13, para. 14.

B. IFIs and the Liability of Member States

Unlike the United Nations and most other international organizations incorporated into the United Nations system, the IFIs are based on capital subscription and weighted voting powers rather than on sovereign equality and one vote per Member State. In the UN system organization, each organization is financed by the annual contributions of Member States according to the agreed assessment table. The amount of annual contributions may influence the quota allocation of staff and the distribution of preferred senior staff positions not previously taken by the Security Council's permanent Member States as their preserved positions,[71] but in terms of voting, each Member State's vote is of equal value to that of any other Member State, irrespective of financial contributions (except in the proceedings of the Security Council, which require the consent of all permanent members). That means the number of Member States equals the number of votes. However, the situation is quite different in the case of the IFIs. The World Bank Group and the IMF obtained a concession from the United Nations as part of their relationship as specialized agencies:

> The United Nations agrees that, in the interpretation of paragraph 3 of Article 17 of the United Nations Charter it will take into consideration that the Bank [and the IMF] does not rely for its annual budget upon contributions from its members, and that the appropriate authorities of the Bank [and the IMF] enjoy full autonomy in deciding the form and content of such budget.[72]

Each IFI is capitalized like a corporation. A member government subscribes to shares of the capital stock of an organization like an investor. The organizers of a corporation determine the distribution of the initial number of shares to be subscribed to by original shareholders. The share allocation determines the contours of control of the organization. Indeed, the IFIs are 'functional extensions' of Member States[73] in a more pronounced manner than any of the UN system organizations. The larger the share holding of a Member State, the larger the stake and power of that Member State, although its liability is limited to the extent of shareholding. For example, the Agreement Establishing the Asian Development Bank[74] (the ADB Charter) stipulates, '[t]he liability of the members on shares shall be limited to the unpaid portion of their issue price'.[75] However, payment under the callable capital stock of the Bank may be called 'only as and when required by the Bank to meet its obligations' incurred in connection with borrowings of funds or guarantees for the purposes of its operations.[76] For each IFI, the question of members' liability

71. *See* Theodor Meron, *The United Nations Secretariat: The Rules and the Practice* (Lexington, MA: Lexington Books, 1977).
72. Relationship Agreement, *supra* n. 39, Art. X, para. 3
73. Romana Sadurska & C.M. Chinkin, 'The Collapse of the International Tin Council: A Case of State Responsibility', *Virginia Journal of International Law* 30 (1990): 845, 854.
74. ADB Charter, *supra* n. 38.
75. *Ibid.*, Art. 5, para. 6.
76. *Ibid.*, Art. 6.5.

on shares arises only in those two instances to the exclusion of any other obligations. For example, Article 5, paragraph 7 of the ADB Charter states that '[n]o member shall be liable, by reason of its membership, for obligations of the Bank',[77] and thus makes it abundantly clear that Member States will not be liable for the Bank's acts. This provision irrevocably precludes the question of Member States' liability to third parties in connection with the acts of the Bank.[78] Of the IFIs, only the ADB and the EBRD have this provision expressly precluding the liability of Member States to third parties.[79] For all other IFIs, the question of liability of Member States to third parties remains unsettled.[80]

As for the question of responsibility of IFIs in connection with the borrowing and guarantee obligations mentioned above, they do not enjoy the privileges and immunity otherwise available to them. For example, Article 50(1) of the ADB Charter excludes 'cases arising out of or in connection with the exercise of its powers to borrow money, to guarantee obligations, or to buy and sell or underwrite the sale of securities'[81] from the enjoyment of immunity from every form of legal process. This means that borrowing or guarantee agreements to which an IFI is a party are governed by the domestic law of choice and subject to the jurisdiction of a court 'in the territory of a country in which the Bank has its principal or a branch office, or has appointed an agent for the purpose of accepting service or notice of process or has issued or guaranteed securities'.[82] Thus, lenders,

77. *Ibid.*, Art. 5.7.
78. ILC's draft Art. 29, para. 1, provides, 'Without prejudice to draft articles 25 to 28, a State member of an international organization is responsible for an internationally wrongful act of that organization if: (a) It has accepted responsibility for that act; or (b) It has led the injured party to rely on its responsibility.' The commentary on this draft states, 'membership does not as such entail for Member States international responsibility when the organization commits an internationally wrongful act'. 'ILC Report on the work of its fifty-eighth session' (1 May to 9 Jun. 2006 and 3 Jul. to 11 Aug. 2006), Supplement No. 10 (A/61/10), 287, para. (2), *available at* <http://daccess-dds-ny.un.org/doc/UNDOC/GEN/G06/636/20/PDF/G0663620.pdf?OpenElement> (containing the ILC Draft Articles on Responsibility of International Organizations) (hereinafter ILC, 'Draft Articles on Responsibility of International Organizations'). *See* Andrew Stumer, 'Liability of Member States for Acts of International Organizations: Reconsidering the Policy Objections', *Harvard International Law Journal* 48 (2007): 553.
79. EBRD Charter, *supra* n. 38, Art. 5, para. 7 (stating 'The liability of the members on shares shall be limited to the unpaid portion of their issue price. No member shall be liable, by reason of its membership, for obligations of the Bank.'). *Cf.* Stumer, *supra* n. 78, 565, n. 72.
80. *See Westland Helicopters Ltd v. the Arab Organization for Industrialization (AOI), International Law Reports* 80 (Interim award of 5 Apr. 1984): 600, 613 ('In default by the four States of formal exclusion of their liability, third parties which have contracted with the AOI could legitimately count on their liability. This rule flows from general principles of law and from good faith.'). However, the Court of Justice of Geneva set aside the award. *Ibid.*, 622. *See* Ignaz Seidl-Hohenveldern, 'Liability of Member States for Acts or Omissions of an International Organization', in *Liber Amicorum Ibrahim F.I. Shihata: International Finance and Development Law*, ed. Sabine Schemmer-Schulte & Ku-Yang Tung (The Hague: Kluwer Law International, 2001), 727, 739.
81. ADB Charter, *supra* n. 38, Art. 50, para. 1.
82. *Ibid.*

underwriters, and guarantors to the Bank enjoy an exception to the Bank's immunity not afforded to other parties, for example, states or communities affected by Bank lending.

C. Internal Rules of IFIs and International Responsibility

Article 27 of the 1969 Vienna Convention on the Law of Treaties[83] provides that a party may not invoke the provisions of its internal law as justification for its failure to perform a treaty, and Article 3 of the ASR thus provides:

> [t]he characterization of an act of a State as internationally wrongful is governed by international law. Such characterization is not affected by the characterization of the same act as lawful by internal law.[84]

Article 3 reflects the principle of customary international law that 'the characterization of a given act as internationally wrongful is independent of its characterization as lawful under the internal law of the State concerned'.[85] The Special Rapporteur, Giorgio Gaja, overstated his assumption that this customary principle will equally apply to international organizations when he questioned 'whether it [was] really necessary to restate this principle in the draft articles on responsibility of international organizations'.[86] The internal law of a state is not international law, whereas rules of international organizations, as defined in the draft articles on responsibility of international organizations, are the law internal to an international organization and therefore part of international law, including the 'established practice of the organization'.[87]

Nonetheless, the question remains, to what extent decisions and instruments adopted in accordance with the authority and procedures laid down by the constituent documents of an international organization should be considered part of 'international law' proper. Are staff regulations and other administrative rules of an international organization part of international law?[88] Surely, they are not subject to local jurisdiction, and the basis of authority for that exemption only derives from the provisions of the headquarters agreement with the host state. Article III, section 7(b) of the headquarters agreement between the United Nations and the United States, which is the genesis of most headquarters agreements for

83. Vienna Convention on the Law of Treaties, *supra* n. 20.
84. Crawford, *The International Law Commission's Articles on State Responsibility: Introduction, Text and Commentaries*, *supra* n. 4, 86.
85. *Ibid.*, para. (1) of the Commentary to the article.
86. Giorgio Gaja, 'First Report on Responsibility of International Organizations', Doc. A/CN.4/532 (26 Mar. 2003), para. 37 (prepared by Special Rapporteur).
87. ILC, 'Draft Articles on Responsibility of International Organizations', *supra* n. 78, draft Art. 4, para. 4.
88. *See* C.F. Amerasinghe, *The Law of the International Civil Service as Applied by International Administrative Tribunals* (Oxford: Clarendon Press, 1988), 22–25.

international organizations, illustrates the relationship of international organizations with local law.[89] It states:

> *Except as otherwise provided in this agreement or in the General Convention,* the federal, state and local law of the United States shall apply within the headquarters district (emphasis added).[90]

This provision must, in turn, be read in conjunction with both the Charter of the United Nations and the Convention on Privileges and Immunities of the United Nations, which safeguard the full and independent exercise of the organization's operations, administration, and performance of its functions by recognizing a rulemaking or regulatory competence within the headquarters seat.[91] Article III, section 8 stipulates, '[t]he United Nations shall have the power to make regulations, operative within the headquarters district, for the purpose of establishing therein conditions in all respects necessary for the full execution of its functions'.[92] The United Nations 'has never recognized Article III, section 7(b) of the Headquarters Agreement as imposing local law upon contracts concluded at the Headquarters'.[93]

The question of responsibility of an IFI primarily arises in areas where its relationship with Member States intersects with its relationship with private individuals and groups of individuals within Member States, who may be affected by IFI-financed projects. The qualifying phrase, '[e]xcept as otherwise provided in this agreement or in the General Convention', of Article III, section 7(b) of the UN Headquarters Agreement delineates the contours of areas of activities which are not subject to either local jurisdiction or to local law. Accordingly, the United Nations took steps to limit its tort liability concerning activities in its headquarters district.[94]

89. UN Secretariat, Office of Legal Affairs, 'Law Applicable to Contracts Concluded by the United Nations with Private Parties – Procedures for Settling Disputes Arising out of such Contracts – Relevant Rules and Practice', *1976 U.N. Juridical Yearbook*, 159, 160–161 (hereinafter UN Legal Opinion).
90. 'Agreement Regarding the Headquarters of the United Nations', 1 U.N.T.S. 16 (26 Jun. 1947).
91. UN Legal Opinion, *supra* n. 89, 160.
92. Section 26 of the United Nations Headquarters Agreement provides:

> The provisions of this agreement shall be complementary to the provisions of the General Convention. In so far as any provision of this agreement and any provisions of the General Convention relate to the same subject matter, the two provisions shall, wherever possible, be treated as complementary so that both provisions shall be applicable and neither shall narrow the effect of the other; but in any case of absolute conflict the provisions of this agreement shall prevail.

Section 27 of the same agreement further states: 'This agreement shall be construed in the light of its primary purpose to enable the United Nations at its headquarters in the United States, fully and efficiently, to discharge its responsibilities and fulfill its purposes.'

93. UN Legal Opinion, *supra* n. 89, 161. *See* Suzuki & Nanwani, 'Responsibility of International Organizations: The Accountability Mechanisms of Multilateral Development Banks', *supra* n. 16, 192, n. 68.
94. G.A. Res. 41/210, para. 1, U.N. Doc. A/RES/41.210 (11 Dec. 1986). *See* Paul Szasz, 'The United Nations Legislates to Limit Its Liability', *American Journal of International Law* 81 (1987): 739.

According to one knowledgeable insider, 'this is not an exercise that relies on the Organization's immunity from suits in American and other national courts; rather, it is an exercise in legislation, establishing a particular tort regime for the only territory within the United States over which the United Nations has – albeit limited – jurisdiction'.[95] But it is the Organization's immunity that gives it the power of legislation.

Similarly, IFIs' policy directives and instructions relating to their respective operations are to carry out each IFI's mandate and functions entrusted to it by its constituent document, including implied powers. IFIs operate in borrowing Member States to pursue their respective mandates and functions. They adopt policy directives and implementation guidelines that are independent of the internal law of any State members. According to draft Article 8 of the ILC:

> 1. There is a breach of an international obligation when an act of that international organization is not in conformity with what is required of it by that obligation, regardless of its origin and character.
> 2. The preceding paragraph also applies in principle to the breach of an obligation set by a rule of the organization.[96]

The Commentary to draft Article 8 states, '[f]or an international organization most obligations are likely to arise from the rules of the organization'[97] and 'obligations arising from the constituent instruments or binding acts that are based on those instruments are indeed international obligations'.[98] Moreover, the wording in paragraph 2 dispels any doubt that breaches of obligations created by the rules of the organization are also covered by the present draft.[99] In short, the Commentary is unambiguous in stating that obligations created by the rules of an international organization are subject to international law.

IV. THE RULES OF THE IFIs REGARDING THEIR ACCOUNTABILITY UNDER INTERNATIONAL LAW

A. Accountability or Responsibility?

In contrast to the concept of 'responsibility' adopted by the ILC in reference to the consequences under international law of internationally wrongful acts,[100] the

95. Szasz, *supra* n. 94, 744.
96. ILC, 'Draft Articles on Responsibility of International Organizations', *supra* n. 78, draft Art. 8. para. 1 of draft Art. 8 is identical to Art. 12 of ASR except for the replacement of the word 'State' with 'international organization'.
97. United Nations International Law Commission, Official Records of the General Assembly, Sixtieth Session, Supplement No. 10 (A/60/10), the commentary to draft Art. 8, para. (4), at 88.
98. *Ibid.*
99. *Ibid.*
100. The ILC refers to 'responsibility which international organizations incur for their wrongful acts'. ILC Report A/57/10 (2002), Ch. VIII, para. 465.

International Law Association (ILA) adopted a much broader concept of accountability[101] as the starting point. The ILA explained that 'accountability is linked to the authority and power of an [international organization] IO. Power entails accountability, that is the duty to account for its exercise'.[102] The ILA defined accountability of international organizations as 'a multifaceted phenomenon',[103] consisting of the following three interrelated and mutually supportive levels:

> *First Level* – the extent to which international organizations, in the fulfillment of their functions as established in their constituent instruments, are and should be subject to, or should exercise, forms of internal and external scrutiny and monitoring, irrespective of potential and subsequent liability and/or responsibility;
>
> *Second Level* – tortious liability for injurious consequences arising out of acts or omissions not involving a breach of any rule of international and/or institutional law (e.g. environmental damage as a result of lawful nuclear or space activities); and
>
> *Third Level* – responsibility arising out of acts or omissions which do constitute a breach of a rule of international and/or institutional law (e.g. violations of human rights or humanitarian law, breach of contract, gross negligence, or as far as institutional law is concerned acts of organs which are ultra vires or violate the law of employment relations).[104]

The ILA concluded, '[t]he diversity of forms of accountability clearly rules out, from the start, any requirement that only legal interests may trigger accountability'.[105]

All of the established accountability mechanisms that IFIs have adopted, in effect, have a similar operative notion of accountability.[106] Because each accountability mechanism is designed to improve the administrative efficiency and operational effectiveness of the organization's internal processes, it encompasses the entire spectrum of operational policy directives and their implementation procedures. The World Bank's Inspection Panel, for example, is concerned with acts or

---

101. Gerhard Hafner, 'Accountability of International Organizations', *American Society of International Law Proceedings* 97 (2003): 236, 239.
102. 'Final Report of the International Law Association Committee on Accountability of International Organizations 71st ILA Conference' (Berlin: 2004), 5 (hereinafter 'ILA Final Report').
103. *Ibid.*
104. *Ibid.* For detailed discussions on different forms and levels of accountability, *see* the 'Report of the Sixty-eighth ILA Conference' (Taipei: 1998), 15–17.
105. 'ILA Final Report', *supra* n. 102, 6.
106. *See* Maartie van Putten, *Policing the World: Accountability Mechanisms for Multilateral Financial Institutions and Private Financial Institutions* (Netherlands & Montreal, Canada: Tilburg University, 2006), 12–20.

omissions of the Bank in following its own operational policies and procedures.[107] The mechanism does not purport to be a judicial system. Ibrahim F. I. Shihata, then-senior vice president and general counsel of the World Bank, underscored the following two points:

> (i) violation by the Bank of its policy, even if established by the Panel, is not necessarily a violation of *applicable law that entails liability* for ensuing damages (emphasis added); and (ii) since the Panel is not a court of law, its findings on Bank violations cannot be taken *ipso facto* as a conclusive evidence against the Bank in judicial proceedings.[108]

The statement in point (i) above that says, in effect, that a violation of an internal rule of an IFI is not necessarily a breach of an international obligation, is unsettling, in that the ILC Commentary provides that 'an obligation arising from the rules of the organization has to be regarded as an obligation under international law'.[109] The question is whether the rules of the organization may preclude or limit the applicability of the responsibility regime. Surely such self-serving 'legislation' would be in conflict with the provisions of draft Articles 8 and 35 of the ILC. As noted above draft Article 8 clearly states that internal rules are a source of international obligations.[110] Draft Article 35 states:

> Unless the rules of the organization otherwise provide for the relations between an international organization and its member States and organizations, the responsible organization may not rely on the provisions of its pertinent rules as justification for failure to comply with the obligations under this Part.[111]

Whatever limitations the accountability mechanisms of IFIs may have, private individuals and groups affected by IFIs have now won access to forums independent of the governing organs of the IFIs in which to file a complaint

107. 'Resolutions Establishing the Inspection Panel', No. IBRD 93-10/No. IDA 93-6, para. 12. By 'operational policies and procedures' are meant to be 'the Bank's Operational Policies, Bank Procedures and Operational Directives, and similar documents issued before these series were started', but they do not include 'Guidelines and Best Practices and similar documents or statements.' *Ibid.* For a detailed analysis of the accountability mechanisms of the IFIs, *see* van Putten, *supra* n. 106; Daniel D. Bradlow, 'Private Complaints and International Organizations: A Comparative Study of the Independent Inspection Mechanisms in International Financial Institutions', *Georgetown Journal of International Law* 36 (2005): 403; Suzuki & Nanwani, 'Responsibility of International Organizations: The Accountability Mechanisms of Multilateral Development Banks', *supra* n. 16.
108. Ibrahim F.I. Shihata, *The World Bank Inspection Panel: In Practice*, 2nd edn (Washington, DC: A World Bank Publication, 2001), 234.
109. ILC Report, Sixtieth Session, Supplement No. 10 (A/60/10) (2008), 89, para. (6).
110. *See supra* n. 96 and discussion around it. *See also* Giorgio Gaja, 'Third Report on Responsibility of International Organizations', UNGA Doc. A/CN.4/533 (13 May 2005) (prepared by the Special Rapporteur during the ILC 57th Session).
111. Giorgio Gaja, 'Fifth Report on Responsibility of International Organizations', UNGA Doc. A/CN.4/583 (2 May 2007) (prepared by the Special Rapporteur).

against them. The accountability mechanisms allow private individuals to participate in the decision-making process of the IFIs for the first time. The ILA's final report states, '[t]he principle that IO-s may be held internationally responsible for their acts is nowadays part of customary international law'.[112]

B. Analysis of Possible Claims against IFIs for their Failure to Comply with Internal Policies and Procedures

The requirements for filing claims against the World Bank in connection with its operational activities are laid out by the World Bank Inspection Panel:

> The affected party must demonstrate that its rights or interests have been or are likely to be directly affected by an action or omission of the Bank as a result of a failure of the Bank to follow its operational policies and procedures with respect to the design, appraisal and/or implementation of a project financed by the Bank (including situations where the Bank is alleged to have failed in its follow-up on the borrower's obligations under loan agreements with respect to such policies and procedures) provided in all cases that such failure has had, or threatens to have, a material adverse effect.[113]

All other IFIs have adopted essentially the same admissibility requirements, in that, all of the IFI's accountability mechanisms focus on the failure of the IFI concerned to comply with its own policies and procedures throughout all the stages of the project cycle. Such failure refers to the IFI's action or omission in the project preparation, fact-finding, pre-appraisal, and appraisal stages. Likewise, the failure in terms of project 'implementation' means not only the IFI's failure to conform to its own policies and procedures during implementation, but also its failure to monitor and follow up on the borrowers/executing agencies' contractual obligations under the IFI's loan/project or guarantee agreements relating to projects concerned.

The IFI's contractual obligations are, first and foremost, with the government or entity concerned as the borrower/guarantor. The IFI's financing of any undertaking in a Member State cannot be made without the consent and cooperation of the government of that Member State.[114] Furthermore, none of the IFIs control the

---

112. 'ILA Final Report', *supra* n. 102, 26. The ILA reminds us of one of the fundamental problems in the establishment of a responsibility regime for international organizations: '[I]f a universal responsibility regime for IO's is not developed in the near future, the injured third parties or Member States are likely to engage in "forum shopping", that is seeking a national law that provides the most favourable solution to the claimant.' *Ibid.*
113. 'Resolutions Establishing the Inspection Panel', *supra* n. 107, para. 12. For an analysis of major features of accountability mechanisms, *see* Suzuki & Nanwani, 'Responsibility of International Organizations: The Accountability Mechanisms of Multilateral Development Banks', *supra* n. 16, 206–218.
114. Article 14 (iii) of the ADB Charter, for example, stipulates: 'The bank shall not finance any undertaking in the territory of a member if that member objects to such financing.' ADB

implementation, operation, and administration of the project facilities. In this respect, the IFI and the borrower share concurrent responsibility for project performance. The IFI is responsible for its portfolio management as the lender, while the borrower is responsible for its project management as the owner of the project. However, none of the accountability mechanisms of the IFIs has the power to investigate the borrower's accountability, that is, how the borrower discharges its responsibility; how it conducts the process of implementation; and how it manages project performance as the 'owner' of the project. Limiting the review to only the failure of the IFI is consistent with the principle of non-interference with the domestic affairs of other states.[115] Nevertheless, given the mechanisms' competence to investigate the IFIs' failure to follow up on the borrower's obligations under the loan agreement, the scope of what constitutes such failure is an essentially relative question: it depends on the relations between the IFI and the borrower concerned, and it may necessarily address the performance of the borrower, at least to some extent.[116]

Charter, *supra* n. 38. Art. III, s. 7 (b) of the IDB Charter, and Art. 13 (iii) of the EBRD Charter, contain exactly the same provision. IDB Charter, *supra* n. 38; EBRD Charter, *supra* n. 38. Art. 17.1.b of the AfDB Charter provides, 'The Bank shall not provide for the financing of a project in the territory of a member if that member objects thereto.' AfDB Charter, *supra* n. 38.

115. Elsewhere I have maintained that 'in a global state of interdependence and simultaneity, a traditional proscription of "foreign intervention" in internal events has become obsolete'. Eisuke Suzuki, 'Extraconstitutional Change and World Public Order: A Prologue to Decision-Making', *Houston Law Review* 15 (1977): 23, 78. 'In fact, external actors are decision-makers that influence the course of events by modulating their behavior and symbolic communications toward contending groups in the contestation of power.' *Ibid.* In this respect, *see* Mark Malan, 'The Principle of Non-interference and the Future of Multilateral Intervention in Africa', *African Security Review* 6, no. 3 (1997), *available at* <www.iss.co.Za/ASR/6No3/Malan.html>. For a classic statement, *see* Myres S. McDougal & W. Michael Reisman, 'Rhodesia and the United Nations: The Lawfulness of International Concern', *American Journal of International Law* 62 (1968): 1. For a useful summary of the principle of non-interference in contemporary international law, *see* a summary of the Chatham House International Law discussion group meeting held on 28 Feb. 2007, 'The Principle of Non-intervention in Contemporary International Law: Non-interference in a State's Internal Affairs Used to be a Rule of International Law: Is It Still?' As Michael Reisman succinctly stated, 'In modern international law, what counts is the sovereignty of the people and not a metaphysical abstraction called the state.' W. Michael Reisman, 'Haiti and the Validity of International Action', *American Journal of International Law* 89 (1995): 82–83. The accountability mechanism is to hold officials to account for their action or omission. 'By shifting the fulcrum of the system from the protection of sovereigns to the protection of people, it works qualitative changes in virtually every component.' W. Michael Reisman, 'Sovereignty and Human Rights in Contemporary International Law', *American Journal of International Law* 84 (1990): 866–867.

116. *See* Tunis-Morocco Nationality Decrees, Advisory Opinion, 1923 P.C.I.J. (ser. B) No. 4, 24 (7 February): 'The question whether a certain matter is or is not solely within the jurisdiction of a State is an essentially relative question; it depends upon the development of international relations.' Consider in this connection the development of IFIs' competence to examine and take into account 'governance issues' in spite of the formal prohibition on interference 'in the political affairs of any member' and the formal requirement of only 'economic considerations'. In the analysis of accountability, any argument against political considerations 'now has

There is an additional requirement unique to the IFIs' accountability mechanisms: the alleged failure of the IFI concerned must have had, or be likely to have a *direct and material adverse effect* on the claimants' rights and interests.[117] If such a failure is confirmed and the direct nexus is established between the failure and the materially adverse effect on the claimants' rights and interests, proper remedies should be demanded to deal not only with correcting the project to conform to the IFI's own policies and procedures, but also with compensating the claimants for the infringement of their rights and interests directly affected by the IFI's failure. However, this is dependant on whether the IFI's failure is deemed a violation of applicable law.[118]

Such a finding would normally trigger an obligation in customary international law relating to 'the duty of reparation',[119] the essential forms of which were laid down by the Permanent Court of International Justice as follows:

> The essential principle contained in the actual notion of an illegal act – a principle which seems to be established by international practice and in particular by the decisions of arbitral tribunals – is that reparation must, as far as possible, wipe out all the consequences of the illegal act and reestablish the situation which would, in all probability, have existed if that act had not been committed. Restitution in kind, or, if this is not possible, payment of a sum corresponding to the value which a restitution in kind would bear; the award, if need be, of damages for loss sustained which would not be covered by restitution in kind or payment in place of it – such are the principles which should serve to determine the amount of compensation due for an act contrary to international law.[120]

much less force, not least because of those institutions' own commitments to good governance, sustainable development, and poverty reduction'. Christine Chinkin, 'The United Nations Decade for the elimination of Poverty: What Role for International Law?', *Current Legal Problems* 54 (2001): 553, 559. *See* Handl, 'The Legal Mandate of Multilateral Development Banks as Agents for Change toward Sustainable Development', *supra* n. 16, 643; Krasner, *supra* n. 38, 144; Shihata, *The World Bank Legal Papers*, *supra* n. 54, 245–282.

117. *See* International Bank for Reconstruction and Development & International Development Association, 'The World Bank Inspection Panel', Resolution No. IBRD 93-10, Resolution No. IDA 93-6 (22 Sep. 1993), *available at* <http://siteresources.worldbank.org/EXTINSPECTIONPANEL/Resources/ResolutionMarch2005.pdf>.
118. It should be noted that none of the IFI accountability mechanisms are empowered to explicitly make findings about possible violations of applicable law – although, this may be implicit in their findings of non-compliance with the internal policies and guidelines of the IFIs. For further discussion, *see infra* nn. 122–130 and accompanying text below.
119. In the *Rainbow Warrior* arbitration, the Tribunal said, 'any violation by a State of any obligation, of whatever origin, gives rise to State responsibility and consequently, to the duty of reparation'. Rainbow Warrior (New Zealand/France), XX R.I.A.A., 217, 251, para. 75 (Decision of 30 Apr. 1990) (hereinafter 'Rainbow Warrior').
120. Factory at Chorzów, Merits, Judgment No. 13, 1928, P.C.I.J., Series A, No. 17, 47, *quoted in* Legal Consequences of the Construction of a Wall in the Occupied Palestinian Territory, Advisory Opinion, 2004 I.C.J. para.152 (9 July).

The *Rainbow Warrior* Tribunal underscored that 'in the international law field, there is no distinction between contractual and tortuous responsibility'.[121]

That no situation should arise in which an international organization would not be accountable to some authority for an act that might be deemed illegal is an accepted proposition.[122] In the IFI context, however, access to effective remedies is largely absent due to the IFIs' immunity from local jurisdiction. Indeed, this is the essential reason for the establishment of the accountability mechanisms, but they still remain *internal* mechanisms independent of local jurisdiction from which the IFI will remain immune.[123] It is not intended to be one of 'the appropriate modes of settlement', as contemplated in Article VIII, section 29 of the General Convention on the Privileges and Immunities of the United Nations,[124] so as to enable the IFI 'to bear responsibility for the damages arising from such acts' since 'the question of immunity from legal process is distinct from the issue of compensation for any damages . . . '.[125] None of the IFIs' accountability mechanisms are designed to be judicial or quasi-judicial bodies like administrative tribunals of IFIs. The accountability mechanism is not a court of law, and has no power to interpret definitively the IFI's charter, loan or guarantee agreements, or other instruments between the IFI concerned and its borrowers. Nor is it empowered to adjudicate the rights and obligations between the IFI concerned and private individuals or groups.

In the *Effect of Awards of Compensation Made by the United Nations Administrative Tribunal*,[126] the ICJ held that the General Assembly had the power to create an independent tribunal competent to make decisions binding on the General Assembly, at least in the areas of staff relations as 'the General Assembly is given by the Charter a power to regulate staff relations'.[127] Likewise, as the board of directors of each IFI has the power to take decisions on all aspects of its operations, it has competence to create an accountability mechanism in the form of a special tribunal capable of making binding decisions on the IFI. However, none of the IFIs has chosen to do so because, I suspect, powerful Member States would rather retain the present state of ambiguity.

For any IFI to be legally liable for its act or omission in undertaking its operations there must be applicable law that could establish a breach of obligations under domestic or international law. It is a common understanding, however, that IFIs' operational policies and procedures do not by themselves form part of such applicable law, either domestic or international. The obligations imposed on an

121. Rainbow Warrior, *supra* n. 119, 75.
122. Interpretation of the Agreement of 25 Mar. 1951 between the WHO and Egypt, Advisory Opinion, 1980 I.C.J. 73 (30 December).
123. Suzuki & Nanwani, 'Responsibility of International Organizations: The Accountability Mechanisms of Multilateral Development Banks', *supra* n. 16, 206.
124. Convention on the Privileges and Immunities of the United Nations, *supra* n. 30, Art. VIII, s. 29, *available at* <www1.umn.edu/humanrts/instree/p&i-convention.htm>.
125. Nuclear Weapons, *supra* n. 24, 88–89, para. 66.
126. Advisory Opinion, 1954 I.C.J. 47 (13 July).
127. *Ibid.*, 59–61.

IFI under its operational policies and procedures do not create the corresponding rights on the part of local private individuals and groups. Although the World Bank's Inspection Panel, the first of the IFIs' accountability mechanisms, was hailed as 'an unprecedented means for increasing the transparency and accountability of the Bank's operations',[128] international law does not extend a direct means of remedies to private individuals and groups. Normally, private individuals' or groups' claims must be pursued through the government of their nationality against the other party to the dispute. In order to bring a claim in respect to the breach of an international obligation, a state must first establish its right to do so, as required by the following rules: 'The first is that the defendant State has broken an obligation towards the national State in respect of its nationals. The second is that only the party to whom an international obligation is due can bring a claim in respect of its breach.'[129] However in the case of the IFI, the government is the borrower and the owner of the project that is the source of the complaint. The government controls the process of arbitration from the beginning to the end.[130]

The proper method for dispute settlement between the IFI concerned and its borrowers, when the dispute is not resolved by negotiations, is arbitration as provided for in the applicable loan regulations if such disputes arise in connection with the performance of the loan or guarantee agreement.[131] Moreover, Article 52.2 of the ADB Charter provides that 'no action shall be brought against the Bank by any member, or by any entity or person directly or indirectly acting for or deriving claims from a member or from any agency or instrumentality of a member'.[132] Instead, the same Article specifically directs how disputes between ADB and its members should be settled: 'Members shall have recourse to such special procedures for the settlement of controversies between the Bank and its members as may be prescribed in this Agreement, in the by-laws and regulations of the Bank, or in contracts entered into with the Bank'.[133] Needless to say, accountability mechanisms are not 'special procedures for the settlement of controversies' contemplated under Article 50.2 of the ADB Charter or its equivalent of the other IFIs' charters.

---

128. James Wolfensohn, 'Foreword', in *The World Bank Inspection Panel, The First Four Years (1994–1998)*, ed. Alvaro Umaña (Washington, DC: World Bank Publications, 1998).
129. Reparation for Injuries, *supra* n. 1, 181–182.
130. Suzuki & Nanwani, 'The Legal Mandate of Multilateral Development Banks as Agents for Change toward Sustainable Development', *supra* n. 16, 200–201. The basic framework is given by the ICJ in Case Concerning the Barcelona Traction, Light and Power Co., Ltd, *supra* n. 43, 44, para. 79: 'The State must be viewed as the sole judge to decide whether its protection will be granted, to what extent it is granted, and when it will cease. It retains in this respect a discretionary power the exercise of which may be determined by considerations of a political or other nature, unrelated to the particular case. Since the claim of the State is not identical with that of the individual or corporate person whose cause is espoused, the State enjoys complete freedom of action.'
131. *E.g.*, s. 11.04 of ADB's Ordinary Operations Loan Regulations dated 1 Jul. 2001.
132. ADB Charter, *supra* n. 38, Art. 50.2. Additionally, Art. XI, s. 3, second paragraph, of the IDB Charter, Art. 52.1 of the AfDB Charter, and Art. 46 of the EBRD Charter contain similar provisions.
133. ADB Charter, *supra* n. 38, Art. 50.2.

C. The Case Study: The Samut Prakarn Wastewater Management Project

Judge Higgins said, '[i]f members were liable for the defaults of the organization, its independent personality would be likely to become increasingly a sham'.[134] But when the organization is protected by immunity and none of 'the appropriate modes of settlement'[135] are available in either contractual or tortious liability cases, it would be a sham to argue that the organization has an independent personality when powerful Member States make real decisions. The accountability of international organizations is therefore in a Catch-22 situation because constituent Member States cannot be held liable for acts done by international organizations that enjoy a separate legal personality under international law.[136] There is no effective recourse for either staff members of these international organizations who are subject to the virtually unfettered rule of administration[137] or contractors

134. Institute of International Law, 'The Legal Consequences for Member States of the Non-fulfilment by International Organizations of Their Obligations towards Third Parties', *Yearbook Institute of International Law* 66-I (1995): 249. *See also* C. F. Amerasinghe, 'Liability in Third Parties of Member States of International Organizations: Practice, Principle and Judicial Precedent', *American Journal of International Law* 85 (1991): 278. For comment, *see* Stumer, *supra* n. 78, 565–569.

135. *See* Convention on the Privileges and Immunities of the United Nations, *supra* n. 30, Art. VIII, s. 29.

136. *Maclaine Watson & Co. Ltd v. Department of Trade and Industry*, 80 I.L.R. 39 (Judgment of 29 Jul. 1987); *J. H. Rayner (Mincing Lane) Ltd v. Department of Trade and Industry and Others*, 80 I.L.R. 47 (Judgment of 27 Apr. 1988); *Australia & New Zealand Banking Group Ltd and Others v. Commonwealth of Australia and 23 Others*; *Amalgamated Metal Trading Ltd and Others v. Department of Trade and Industry and Others*; *Maclaine Watson & Co. Ltd v. Department of Trade and Industry*; *Maclaine Watson & Co. Ltd v. International Tin Council*, Judgment of 26 Oct. 1989, International Legal Material 29 (1980): 671. *See also* Giorgio Gaja, 'Fourth Report on Responsibility of International Organizations', U.N. Doc. A/CN.4/564/Add.2 (20 Apr. 2006) (prepared by special rapporteur). For comment, *see* Sadurska & Chinkin, *supra* n. 73.

137. International organizations have fashioned the exhaustion of internal remedies as a condition of admissibility to an administrative tribunal in order 'to facilitate the settlement of disputes by informal means before they are subjected to the more rigorous test of judicial scrutiny'. Amerasinghe, *The Law of the International Civil Service as Applied by International Administrative Tribunals*, *supra* n. 88, 232. Some elaborate conditions would defeat the purpose of the exhaustion of internal remedies, however, ADB's internal grievance procedures, for example, require 'compulsory reconciliation' as the first step of the administrative review process. Administrative Order No. 2.06, para. 3.2. If the compulsory conciliation is not successful, the second step is for the staff member to make a request for administrative review to the head of the personnel department. *Ibid.*, para. 3.8. The staff member then has to file an appeal to the Appeals Committee before he/she can file an application to the Administrative Tribunal. *Ibid.*, para. 7.1. Such conditions of admissibility would make it extremely time consuming and onerous to exhaust internal remedies. On top of that, Art. X, para. 6 of the Statute of ADB Administrative Tribunal stipulates:

> The Tribunal may order that reasonable compensation be made by the applicant to the Bank for all or part of the cost of defending the case, if it finds that:

whose contracts are not governed by domestic legislation.[138] Needless to say, there are also no effective remedies for third parties.[139]

To further examine the effectiveness of accountability mechanisms to fill this accountability gap, this paper will examine the Samut Prakarn Wastewater Management Project, which was funded by the ADB. The Samut Prakarn Wastewater Management Project encompassed the building of wastewater treatment facilities in a village outside of Bangkok. Though initially conceived as a way to improve the quality of life for the Thai people, the end result is that this project is a dramatic demonstration of the difficulty of holding IFIs accountable and a stark reminder of how an accountability mechanism could fail 'to deliver the level of accountability and justice demanded by affected communities'.[140]

Since 1986, the ADB has provided three technical assistance grants amounting to USD 1.2 million for feasibility studies for wastewater treatment facilities. From these studies, the Thai government secured from the ADB two successive loans, USD 150 million in 1995 and USD 80 million in 1998 for the planning, design, and construction of two wastewater treatment facilities in the province of Samut Prakarn, 'the most heavily industrialized and rapidly urbanizing of the five provinces of the Bangkok Metropolitan Region'.[141]

(a) the application was manifestly without foundation either in fact or under existing law, unless the applicant demonstrates that the application was based on a good faith argument for an extension, modification, or reversal of existing law; or
(b) the applicant intended to delay the resolution of the case or to harass the Bank or any of its officers or employees.

Admittedly, this provision follows the provisions of Art. XV of the Statute of the IMF Administrative Tribunal, but this explicit provision of the possible imposition of costs against the applicant is contrary to the basic policy that 'the Tribunal should be open and accessible to international civil servants without the dissuasive and chilling effect of possible adverse awards of costs'. ILO Administrative Tribunal, Judgment No. 1884, in re Vollering (No. 15) (1999), para. III. That the tribunal has the inherent power to impose a costs penalty on either an applicant or the respondent as part of the necessary power to control its own process is understandable, but in the proceedings before the Administrative Tribunal the respondent and the applicant are not equal; the proceedings of the Tribunal begin only by the application of the staff member. The employer is always the respondent and the employee is always the applicant. Costs awarded as part of the judgment on the merit of the case against the respondent are not the same as a costs penalty imposed on the applicant on its conduct of the Tribunal proceedings.

138. 'In the case of commercial contracts, express reference has rarely been made to a given system of municipal law. The standard practice is for the contract to contain no choice of law clause as such; provision is made, however, for the settlement of disputes by means of arbitration when agreement cannot be reached by direct negotiations.' UN Legal Opinion, *supra* n. 89, 162.

139. *See generally* Moshe Hirsch, *The Responsibility of International Organizations toward Third Parties: Some Basic Principles* (Boston: Martinus Nijhoff, 1995); Wellens, *Remedies Against International Organizations*, *supra* n. 34.

140. Probe International Canada, 'An Assessment of the Asian Development Bank's Inspection of Thailand's Samut Prakarn Wastewater Treatment Project', <www.adb.org/inspection/comments_probe.pdf>, 2 Dec. 2007.

141. 'Final Report of Inspection Panel on Samut Prakarn Wastewater Management Project' (14 Dec. 2001), para. 1, *available at* <www.adb.org/Projects/SamutPrakarn/RRIC/report_bob.pdf>, 2 Dec. 2007 (hereinafter the 'Inspection Panel's Final Report').

At appraisal and at the time of submission of the project for board approval, the total cost was estimated at USD 507 million for the design, construction, and operation for three years of the two treatment plants. The use of turnkey packaging was selected for implementation of the Project.[142] Contrary to the usual situation in which the government would be responsible for the acquisition of land, it became part of the responsibility of the turnkey contractor because that was what the government requested.

In the course of selecting the turnkey contractor, the Pollution Control Department and the Executing Agency allowed bids for a single plant site. The final bid selected proposed combining the two treatment facilities into a single treatment plant located at the Klong Dan site and proposed a change in the treatment process as well. At the time of signing of the turnkey contract on 20 August 1997, the project cost had escalated to USD 948 million due to all the design changes.

In the meantime by mid-1997, it was evident that Thailand was facing a financial crisis as seen in the decline in the baht's value from THB 25 to THB 41 to the US dollar. While the devalued baht reduced the cost of the project to USD 687 million equivalent, the change in technology increased the direct foreign exchange costs by USD 80 million compared to the appraisal cost estimates. With the worsening of the crisis in 1997, the government eventually approached the ADB for a supplementary loan, which the Board approved on 3 December 1998.[143]

The ADB's Project Profiles on Samut Prakarn Wastewater Management (Supplementary) included the following remarks:

> Some NGOs have raised concerns regarding the Samut Prakarn Wastewater Management Project in the Bangkok metropolitan region during the ADB's 33rd annual meeting held in Chiang Mai, Thailand, from May 6 to 8, 2000. The ADB responded to specific questions and said it would further consult the affected community of Klong Dan. Subsequently, the ADB undertook a review of the Project from June 19 to 28, 2000. The Mission, comprising a senior project engineer, a social development specialist, and ADB's resident advisor in Thailand, met with representatives of the Klong Dan community, NGO groups, the media, government agencies, the turnkey consortium and the project management team. Their aim was to clarify issues surrounding the

---

142. Turnkey Packaging refers to a situation in which the company contracted with initially controls all parts of the project, including the design, building, and running the project; and in return for being all-in-one, the turnkey contractor gets a portion of the revenue. Here, it referred to a single company receiving a contract allowing them to control every step of the process, which included acquiring the land, as well as design, construction, and operation of the wastewater treatment plant. Additionally, the turnkey contractor was responsible for conducting the EIA. Turnkey contracts can result in a conflict of interest because one company is responsible for all aspects including studies, mitigation costs, etc. This turnkey contract was the largest single turnkey contract in ADB's history. For the specifics on this turnkey contract *see* 'Inspection Panel's Final Report', *supra* n. 141, 14.

143. *Ibid.*, 4.

> Project and encourage a dialogue between the community, NGO groups and government officials....[144]

On 27 November 2000, the President of the Bank received an initial letter of complaint from Narong Khomklom, mayor of Klong Dan, and Chalao Timthong and Dawan Chanterahassadee, both Klong Dan villagers, writing on behalf of the communities of Klong Dan and Song Klong. They asked for a halt to disbursements to the project and for their concerns to be investigated.

Not satisfied with ADB's management response, Samut Prakarn's affected groups filed an official request for inspection with the board inspection committee on 5 April 2001.[145] The Board authorized an inspection 'to determine whether ADB has complied with its operational policies or procedures in processing or implementing the Samut Prakarn Wastewater Management Project in Thailand', and if the Inspection Panel (the Panel) determined that the ADB had not complied with its policies, the Board further asked the Panel 'to determine whether this noncompliance has had, or is likely to have, a direct and material adverse effect on the rights and interests of the group making the request (the Requesters)'.[146]

From the outset, the Panel ran into a serious obstacle in securing a 'no objection' from the Government of Thailand to allow the Panel's proposed fact-finding visit to the project site.[147] The Government attached a number of conditions to be

---

144. ADB Project Profiles, Samut Prakarn Wastewater Management (Supplementary) (Loan: THA 26227-02), <www.adb.org/Documents/Profiles/LOAN/26227023.asp>, 2 Dec. 2007.
145. This request was filed under the then existing ADB independent inspection mechanism. It is important to note that, partly as a result of this case, the ADB initiated a review of the mechanism, which resulted in the creation of a new and substantially reformed mechanism in 2003. For more information on the new mechanism established in 2009, *see* Suzuki & Nanwani, 'Responsibility of International Organizations: The Accountability Mechanisms of Multilateral Development Banks', *supra* n. 16, 203–248; Review of the Inspection Function: Establishment of a New ADB Accountability Mechanism, ADB Doc. R-79-03 (2003), available at <www.adb.org/Documents/Policies/ADB_Accountability_Mechanism/ADB_accountability_mechanism.pdf>. *See also* Independent Evaluation, <www.adb.org/Evaluation/>.
146. 'Inspection Panel's Final Report', *supra* n. 141, para. 13.
147. Paragraph 52 of the Inspection Procedures provided as follows:

    > As part of an inspection, a Panel may also visit the project area and meet with the requester, other local communities, organizations and groups, project managers and government officials in the country where the project is located (or in an adjacent member country, if relevant to the inspection). However, before the Panel or any of its consultants undertakes such activities, the committee must confirm with the director representing the relevant country that the government of the country has no objection. If the government objects to any such activities, the Panel will modify its work plan accordingly and carry out its review on the basis of reports and other information available to the Panel and the Bank.

    Asian Development Bank, *ADB's Inspection Policy: A Guidebook* (1996), 11, 25. For a discussion on the issues involved in a site visit, *see* Suzuki & Nanwani, 'Responsibility of International Organizations: The Accountability Mechanisms of Multilateral Development Banks', *supra* n. 16, 214–215.

met for a one-time visit of two days. The conditions referred to possible law-and-order issues, and financial liability issues for any costs as a result of the inspection visit. Because the Government did not change its original position on the conditions for a project site visit, the Panel had no choice but to revise its work plan. Eventually, despite difficulties associated with implementing a new mechanism for the first time, the Panel managed to submit its report to the Board on 14 December 2001.

The Panel found six cases of non-compliance by the ADB with its policies and procedures in processing and implementing the project: (i) Supplementary Financing of Cost Overruns; (ii) Bank's Operational Missions; (iii) Environmental Considerations in Bank Operations; (iv) Involuntary Resettlement; (v) Incorporation of Social Dimensions in Bank Operations; and (vi) Governance.

The Panel concluded that 'in not carrying out a reappraisal of the entire project for the supplementary loan proposal there was non-compliance by the Bank of OM [Operational Manual] 13/BP/OP, December 12, 1995. This omission became a crucial factor from which other consequences followed'.[148] From the perspective of the requesters, the central question was whether the ADB had met the requirements for the appraisal of the supplementary loan as stated in the relevant operational policies. The management adopted a very narrow interpretation of the OM saying that the limited coverage of the appraisal was appropriate, because it had met the requirements set forth in the format prescribed in the ADB's board paper 'Simplification of Board Documentation for Supplementary Loans' (Doc. Sec. M48-89, 12 September 1989). But this argument must have been a *post facto* justification of omissions on the part of the ADB management and staff. As the Panel observed, '[w]ith the issuance of new OMs and the cumulative changes occurred in the Project since 1995, it is imperative for the Bank staff and Management to review all important issues'.[149] The Board Inspection Committee suggested that 'if there were to be any inconsistencies between an underlying policy paper and the resulting OM this would be very unfortunate and would represent a failure of Management in itself'.[150]

At the time of the ADB's annual meeting in 2000 at Chang Mai, Thailand, Samut Prakarn had become a cause célèbre symbolizing innocent villagers as victims at the hand of intransigent and corrupt government officials and the ADB. For the ADB, it was the first serious case brought for inspection and, as the Board Inspection Committee noted, 'there is no precedent in ADB's experience to guide Management'.[151] The Committee performed a balancing role between the two 'contending' parties, management and the Panel, and even provided counsel to management, for future references, on the form and content of management's

148. 'Inspection Panel's Final Report', *supra* n. 141, para. 75.
149. *Ibid.*, 18, para. 61(g), 1998 Supplementary Loan.
150. 'Report and Recommendation of the Inspection Committee to the Board of Directors on Inspection Request: Samut Prakarn Wastewater Management Project' (28 Feb. 2002), 5, para. 27 (hereinafter 'Board Inspection Committee Report'), *available at* <www.adb.org/Projects/SamutPrakarn/RRIC/r50_02.pdf>.
151. *Ibid.*, 13, para. 66.

response.[152] The Committee managed to produce its own version of recommendations.[153] The board of directors *noted* the Committee's Report, and approved three recommendations made by the Committee with one clarification bearing on the first recommendation that 'should be understood in the context of paragraphs 57, 58, and 81 of the [Committee's] Report'.[154]

---

152. *Ibid.*, 12–15, paras 66–76.
153. The Committee recommends:

> (i) That the Board confirm ADB's commitment to being an active participant in both the discussions with the Klong Dan community and all other efforts mentioned in paragraph 166 of the Panel's Report;
> (ii) That the Board instruct Management to continue to monitor resettlement effects and to ensure that all legitimate concerns with respect to consultation with an participation by affected people are met. To this end the Committee recommends that the Board instruct Management to provide semi-annual reports on the status of implementation of the resettlement plan including payment of compensation; and
> (iii) That the Board note paragraph 56 of Management's Response, in which it is stated that data and mechanisms for monitoring the social and environmental impacts have either already developed and incorporated in the EMP or are being developed as recommended in the EMP, and that the Board instruct Management to provide semi-annual reports on:
>
> – the system for monitoring of socio-economic impacts, based on baseline data;
> – the progress in community involvement; and
> – problems associated with odor and effluent (if any), together with a description of measures taken.

Ibid., 16, para. 83.

154. Board of Directors' Decision on Inspection Request-Samut Prakarn Wastewater Management Project (Loan Nos. 1410-THA and 1646-THA), para. 2.1(i), *available at* <www.adb.org/Projects/Samutprakarn/bod_decision.pdf>. Stating:

> 57. Paragraph 166(i) [of the Panel's Final Report] proposes that negotiations should be instituted to establish the extent of damages and 'appropriate and adequate compensation' for those affected. Management's Response has correctly pointed out (in paragraph 54) that 'an inspection is not a judicial process and its purpose is not to adjudicate awards for damages or make suggestions for the settlement of possible damages'. The Committee also agrees with paragraph 55 of Management's Response, which notes that the Government of Thailand is obliged (as a matter of Thai law and, by virtue of the loan documents for the project and ADB's resettlement policy) to make appropriate compensation to those affected by the Project and that it is ADB's job to ensure that ADB's resettlement policy is complied with.
> 58. The Committee notes however that the Panel's Report does not include any purported award of damages or any suggestion that the Panel regards it as part of the Panel's job to make one. Rather the Committee's interpretation of the Panel's recommendation is that ADB should be an active participant in the process of facilitating the proper assessment of damages by the Thai government and where relevant the award of appropriate compensation.
> 81. With respect to the recommendations in paragraph 166 [of the Panel's Final Report], Management acknowledged the merits of improving community participation. In this context Management noted that the Pollution Control Department [of the Government of Thailand] is currently working on a compensation mechanism, in line with ADB's resettlement policy. Management will review progress on this matter every six months.

Speaking as Chairman of the Board of Directors, the ADB President was able to say:

> While the recommendations approved today did not specifically mention the question of compliance with ADB's operational policies and procedures, views on that key question were divided. We all know the views expressed in the Panel's Report, Management's response, and the [Committee] report; and I do not need to mention them here. Let me emphasize, however, that I respect their respective views and professional judgments.[155]

The Board Inspection Committee unequivocally concluded that 'the Panel's finding that ADB's policy on supplementary financing of cost overruns has not been complied with, and that a reappraisal of the entire Project would indeed have been required, is correct'.[156] It is a clever *démarche*, nonetheless, to leave the opinions expressed by the committee in the main body of its report as those of the committee alone. The committee did not ask the Board to adopt those conclusions as the judgment of the Board as well. The end result was no judgment by the Board of Directors on the accountability of management and staff and, therefore, no consequences, except instructing management to report semi-annually to the Board on the progress of the implementation of the committee's recommendations approved by the Board. In the words of Kenji Fukuda of Mekong Watch, an NGO in Tokyo:

> The ADB continued to disburse the loan for the project while substantially ignoring the major issues local people raised. Thus, the accountability of the ADB to the people affected by its project was not fulfilled even though the Panel's findings made clear that the ADB had violated its own policies and procedures in the Samut Prakarn Project.[157]

> Management further indicated that as an integral part of the EMP [Environment Management Plan] for the Samut Prakarn wastewater treatment plant, community liaison groups will be established to foster greater community involvement in the management and operation of the treatment plant. Management indicated that work on establishing baseline data for socioeconomic parameters; a mechanism for meaningful community involvement in the risk assessment of future problems; and a mechanism for timely public notifications is already under way. Management confirmed that while strictly speaking it will not be a partner in any negotiations, it is keen to be an active participant in these efforts.

155. Chairman's Concluding Statement: Board of Directors' Decision on Inspection Request-Samut Prakarn Wastewater Management Project (Loan Nos 1410-THA and 1646-THA), presented at Board of Directors Meeting (25 Mar. 2002), para. 3, *available at* <www.adb.org/projects/samutprakarn/chairman_statement.asp>.
156. 'Board Inspection Committee Report', *supra* n. 150, 15, para. 79.
157. Kenji Fukuda, 'Will We Finally See Accountability at the ADB? Critical Analysis of the New Accountability Mechanism of the Asian Development Bank', in *A Handbook on the Asian Development Bank: the ADB and Its Operations in Asia and the Pacific Region*, ed. Dorothy Guerrero (Essen: Asienhaus, 2003), *available at* <www.mekongwatch.org/policy/adb-accountability/analysis.html> (this book is part of the *Focus Asian* series and is No. 16).

The first semi-annual report to the Board of Directors covering the period from 26 March 2002 to 25 September 2002 concluded that all measures were 'being developed' or 'being put in place'.[158] Prime Minister Thaksin Shinawatra visited Klong Dan and met with the community in April 2002, which led to a series of environmental studies by the Ministry of Environment. The Government announced the suspension of the construction of the project in February 2003. The second semi-annual report, covering 26 September 2002 to 25 March 2003, noted that 'ongoing investigations into the Project by the Government had resulted in the main turnkey contract being declared null and void. It is unclear at this stage what steps the Government will take next, or what form the Project may take as a result of the investigations'.[159] It also warned that '[t]he future of the Project is uncertain given the recent developments concerning the turnkey contract'.[160]

The third semi-annual report, covering the period between 26 March 2003 and 25 September 2004, provided a detailed explanation about the main turnkey contract being declared null and void.[161] The report summarized the status of the project as follows:

> Since submission of the second semiannual report, all project-related activities have ceased, as a result of the turnkey contract being declared null and void. Accordingly, no actions or decisions have been taken on (i) approval of the compensation plan, (ii) monitoring of project impacts, (iii) community involvement initiatives, or (iv) odor and effluent management. There is much uncertainty in Thailand about the future form of the Project, as well as the timing of any further developments. . . .[162]

The fourth semi-annual report explains the status of the project: the physical progress remains unchanged since February 2003 at about 95% complete. At the end of November 2003, the loan period under the principal loan expired and the loan account was closed in December 2003. With respect to the supplementary loan, the utilization period of which was open until 30 June 2004, ADB and the Thai Ministry of Finance agreed to close this loan account at the same time. In monetary terms, almost USD 130 million of the principal loan of USD 150 million was used, and the total amount of the supplementary loan, USD 80 million, was spent. The report concluded:

> Following loan closure, and after more than 1 year of investigations, the Project remains incomplete and suspended. No further action or progress has

158. 'First Semiannual Report to the Board of Directors on Implementation of the Recommendations of the Board Inspection Committee as Adopted on March 25, 2002' (September 2002), 7–8, para. 30, <www.adb.org/Documents/Reports/Samut_Prakarn/IN251-02.pdf>, 4 Dec. 2007.
159. 'Second Semiannual Report' (March 2003), 1, para. 2, <www.adb.org/Documents/Samut_Prakarn/in6703.pdf>, 4 Dec. 2007.
160. *Ibid.*, 4, para. 20.
161. 'Third Semiannual Report' (October 2003), 1, paras 3–8, <www.adb.org/Documents/Reports/Samut_Prakarn/IN253-03.pdf>, 4 Dec. 2007.
162. *Ibid.*, 3, para. 13.

> occurred on the compensation plan, monitoring activities, community involvement initiatives or odor and effluent management. There is no clear indication of what the Government's next steps will be with regard to the future of the Project and when they will be taken.[163]

The fifth semi-annual report reiterated the same dormant status of the project that remains incomplete and all project-related activities remain suspended.[164] In the end, the ADB made the following conclusion and recommendation in June 2005:

> In view of the static status of the Project in all the key monitoring aspects, it is recommended that submission of semiannual reports be discontinued as of this report. The staff will continue to monitor the Project and report the new development, if any.[165]

The unfinished wastewater treatment plant stands without any use. The Thai government continues to repay debts to ADB.

For the affected people concerned, they at least won the suspension of the project. However, the Board of Directors failed to establish the accountability of ADB even though the Panel and the Board Inspection Committee agreed on the consequence of ADB's non-compliance. The Committee report states in plain terms: '[t]he Panel has concluded on the basis of the information available to it that a relevant group has suffered direct and material harm as a result of ADB's non-compliance with operational policies and procedures. The Committee accepts this conclusion'.[166] Who is ultimately responsible for this wholesale failure of accountability? The president is the legal representative of ADB, but it is the Board of Directors that failed to establish the accountability of ADB, and it is a sham when nobody is accountable.[167]

V. RECOMMENDATIONS

The ILC once acknowledged that 'the responsibility of international organizations is governed by rules which are not necessarily the same as those governing the responsibility of States'.[168] Each international organization's functions and purposes are delineated by the 'principle of speciality'; Member States give the

---

163. 'Fourth Semiannual Report' (April 2004), 2, para. 11, <www.adb.org/inspection/samut_prakarn-4thsemirep.pdf>, 4 Dec. 2007.
164. 'Fifth Semiannual Report' (February 2005), <www.adb.org/Documents/Reports/Samut_Prakarn/IN47-05.pdf>, 31 Dec. 2007.
165. 'Sixth Semiannual Report' (June 2005), para. 9, <www.adb.org/Documents/Reports/Samut_Prakarn/R151-05.pdf>, 31 Dec. 2007.
166. 'Board Inspection Committee Report', *supra* n. 150, 10, para. 51.
167. *See* Eisuke Suzuki, 'How to Lift Tattered Morale at the ADB', *Financial Times*, 1 Feb. 2008, Letters to the Editor, *available at* <www.ft.com/cms/s/0/cdae656c-d067-11dc-9309-0000779fd2ac.html>. ADB policy on Good Governance, ADB Doc. R151-95 (17 Aug. 1995), <www.adb.org/Documents/Policies/Governance/govpolicy.pdf>, 25 Dec. 2007.
168. *Yearbook of the International Law Commission*, vol. II, Part Two (1975), *supra* n. 10, 89–90.

international organizations they create certain powers, 'the limits of which are a function of their common interests whose promotion those States entrust to them'.[169] As subjects of international law and ascribed with international legal personalities, international organizations are subject to an international responsibility regime suitably adopted with appropriate variations from the principles of state responsibility. As the ILA stated, the focus should be on 'the variations needed'.[170] The principle of speciality supports organizational effectiveness, and the need for organizational effectiveness should determine the scope of how an IFI discharges its responsibility and provides remedies in the settlement of private claims.[171]

A. Clarification of Policies

The right to a remedy is so well established that it is now considered customary international law.[172] Article 10 of the Universal Declaration of Human Rights sums up the basic policy for an institutional framework for ensuring remedies: '[e]veryone is entitled in full equality to a fair and public hearing by an independent and impartial tribunal in the determination of his rights and obligation and of any criminal charge against him'.[173] This entitlement to 'a fair and public hearing' must comprise both 'the substantive right to a remedy' and 'the procedural right of effective access'.[174] These are the operative policies for the establishment of a tribunal in which third-party private individuals and groups may file claims for the settlement of their disputes with IFIs.[175] These operative policies must be designed to support the protection of the individual's rights, which are directly and materially affected by the allegedly wrongful actions or omissions of the IFI concerned.

---

169. Nuclear Weapons, *supra* n. 24, 78, para. 25.
170. 'Report of the International Committee on the Accountability of International Organizations, Final Report' (Berlin Conference, 2004), 27.
171. The ILA's Committee's First Report pointed out that the rules of the accountability regime 'will have to keep the balance between preserving the necessary autonomy in decision-making of International Organizations and guaranteeing that the International Organizations will not be able to avoid accountability'. *Ibid.*, 27.
172. Wellens, *Remedies Against International Organizations*, *supra* n. 34, 17. *See also* Dinah Shelton, *Remedies in International Human Rights Law* (Oxford: Oxford University Press, 1999), 182.
173. Universal Declaration of Human Rights, *supra* n. 18.
174. Shelton, *supra* n. 172, 14–15; Wellens, *Remedies against International Organizations*, *supra* n. 34, 17.
175. *See* Myres S. McDougal, Harold D. Lasswell & Lung-chu Chen, *Human Rights and World Public Order* (New Haven, CT: Yale University Press, 1980), 192–198. For an extensive exposition of a policy-oriented jurisprudence, *see generally* Harold D. Lasswell & Myres S. McDougal, *Jurisprudence for a Free Society: Studies in Law, Science, and Policy* (New Haven, CT: New Haven Press, 1992). *See also* W. Michael Reisman, 'The View from the New Haven School of International Law', *American Society of International Law Proceedings* 86 (1992): 118; Eisuke Suzuki, 'The New Haven School of International Law: An Invitation to a Policy-Oriented Jurisprudence', *Yale Studies in World Public Order* 1 (1974): 1.

The protection of individual rights in the context of the IFI's operations is to help maintain minimum public order without which development is impossible.[176] Article 28 of the Universal Declaration of Human Rights underscores the necessity of minimum order: 'Everyone is entitled to a social and international order in which the rights and freedoms set forth in this Declaration can be fully realized.'[177]

In 1986, the United Nations General Assembly resolved that 'the right to development is an inalienable right' and 'states have the duty to take steps individually and collectively, to formulate international development policies with a view to facilitating the full realization of the right to development'.[178] The right to development complements Article 25(1) of the Universal Declaration of Human Rights:

> Everyone has the right to a standard of living adequate for the health and well being of himself and of his family, including food, clothing, housing and medical care and necessary social services, and the right to security in the event of unemployment, sickness, disability, widowhood, old age or other lack of livelihood in circumstances beyond his control.[179]

These universal rights can be used to help clarify an individual IFI's policies in regards to its accountability mechanism. I recommend that these policies and guaranteed rights should be used in fashioning a tribunal to protect individuals' rights in regards to IFIs' operations.[180]

---

176. *See* Myres S. McDougal & Siegfried Wiessner, 'Law and Minimum World Public Order', in *The International Law of War: Transnational Coercion and World Public Order*, ed. Myres S. McDougal & Florentino P. Feliciano (New Haven, CT: New Haven Press, 1994), xxviii.
177. Universal Declaration of Human Rights, *supra* n. 18, Art. 28.
178. Declaration on the Right to Development, G.A. Res. 41/128, Annex 4, 41 U.N. GAOP, 97th plen.mtg., Supp. No. 53 at 186, U.N. Doc. A/41/53 (4 Dec. 1986). The UN Secretary-General urged the IFIs to gradually 'incorporate human rights criteria in [their] work at all stages, including in project and policy lending, preparation of guidelines, as well as in project and policy appraisal, monitoring and assessment'. The Secretary-General, 'Report of the Secretary-General in Pursuance of Resolution 1994/37 on The Realization of Economic, Social and Cultural Rights', U.N. Doc. E/CN.4/Sub.2/1995/10 (4 Jul. 1995), para. 248.
179. Universal Declaration of Human Rights, *supra* n. 18.
180. It is not rules that make a decision, which is a culminating choice among policy options, but the individual person that decides or makes choices. In the words of Harold D. Lasswell and Myres S. McDougal:

> Just as there can be no neutral or autonomous theories of law, in the sense of rules devoid of policy content, so also there can be no indifferent theories about law, in the sense of knowledge or ignorance, without policy consequences. In the context of these exigencies, it is the unique opportunity of observers specialized to inquiry about law not merely to relate law to its past policy content, but rather, and further, to clarify and promote change toward policies better designed to serve the particular kind of public order for which they are willing to commit themselves with their fellow community members. It is only by the deliberate clarification of, and explicit commitment to, basic community goals – at all levels of abstraction and from both short-term and long-term time perspectives – that dependable, creative, and economic guidance can be given to the examination of past trends, the allocation of effort to the assessment of factors affecting decision, and the evaluation of future probabilities and alternatives.

B. Reconfiguration of Authority and Control

As can be seen in the analysis of the Samut Prakarn Waste Management project above, affected peoples often find themselves with inadequate redress when challenging an IFI funded project. To provide this redress and ensure that someone is held accountable for actions that negatively affect people, the IFIs need to look at their internal procedures and create a more effective mechanism for addressing citizen complaints.[181] Institutionally, as has been mentioned elsewhere,[182] we could make better use of the administrative tribunal that each IFI has established for the settlement of employment disputes. Administrative tribunals are judicial bodies within the IFIs that hear cases involving employment disputes within the IFI itself. Thus, if an employee of the ADB has an employment issue, he or she may bring this issue to the administrative tribunal. However, administrative tribunals, which have the authority to make judicial decisions and practice in doing so, are

---

Lasswell & McDougal, *Jurisprudence for a Free Society: Studies in Law, Science, and Policy*, *supra* n. 175, 19–20. *See*, in this connection, Roberto Daniño, 'Legal Opinion on Human Rights and the Work of the World Bank' (27 Jan. 2006), <www.ifiwatchnet.org/sites/ifiwatchnet.org/files/DaninoLegalOpinion0106.pdf>, 18 Jan. 2008: 'The interpretation espoused here is a purposive one, guided by a broad view of the objectives of the Articles [of the World Bank] and examined against the backdrop of the current international legal regime and the evolving understanding of development. This interpretative approach remains governed by the principles of "effectiveness (*effet utile*), reasonableness, good faith and the common interests of the organization and its members as a whole".' *Ibid.*, para. 6 (internal citations omitted). *In accord with* the WTO Appellate Body's decision in the *Shrimp/Turtle* case. Appellate Body Report, United States – – Import Prohibition of Certain Shrimp and Shrimp Products, WTO Doc. WT/DS58/AB/R (12 Oct. 1998), which interpreted 'exhaustible natural resources' of Art. XX(g) of the GATT 1994 to include 'living or non-living' natural resources consistent with 'the objective of sustainable development'. *Ibid.*, paras 127–131. The Appellate Body invoked the principle of effectiveness in treaty interpretation. *Ibid.*, para. 131. *See* Myres S. McDougal, Harold D. Lasswell & James C. Miller, *The Interpretation of International Agreements and World Public Order: Principles of Content and Procedure*, 2nd edn (Boston, MA: Martinus Nijhoff Publishers, 1994), 184. *See also* Philip Alston & Mary Robinson (eds), *Human Rights and Development: Toward Mutual Reinforcement* (Oxford: Oxford University Press, 2005); Chinkin, 'The United Nations Decade for the elimination of Poverty: What Role for International Law?', *supra* n. 116.

181. ADB established its new Accountability Mechanism in 2003 replacing its 1995 Inspection Function under which the Samut Prakarn case was considered. The new Accountability Mechanism has introduced a separate, but complementary 'Consultation Phase' in addition to the 'Compliance Phase'. Complainants will normally go through the Consultation Phase first where the Special Project Facilitator will respond to specific problems of locally affected people in ADB-financed projects through a range of informal and flexible methods. For details, *see* ADB, Review of the Inspection Function: Establishment of a New Accountability Mechanism, *supra* n. 145.

182. Suzuki & Nanwani, 'Responsibility of International Organizations: The Accountability Mechanisms of Multilateral Development Banks', *supra* n. 16, 224. For a proposal in favour of a separate arbitration mechanism, *see* Enrique R. Carraso & Alison K. Guernsey, 'The World Bank's Inspection Panel: Promoting True Accountability Through Arbitration', *Cornell International Law Journal* 41 (2008): 577, *available at* <www.uniowa.edu/ifdebook/nzciel/Carraso_Guernsey.doc>.

not authorized to hear cases from third parties. For an administrative tribunal to be transformed into a tribunal of broader jurisdiction in order to deal with private third-party claimants, it needs to expand its jurisdictional competence. As it is organized today, the statute mandating the creation of an administrative tribunal gives it the limited capacity to hear and pass judgment on the alleged breach of the contract of employment. To enable an IFI to be responsible for its project-affected people, the statute must be amended to give the administrative tribunals the ability to decide non-contractual disputes, including tortious liability claims of those individuals and groups who suffer 'a material adverse effect' as a result of the IFI's breach of obligations. With a receptive basis of authority provided by the revised statute of a tribunal, these affected people will be in a position to participate in the process of global decision-making.[183]

When the rights and interests of private individuals and groups conflict with those of international organizations through claims lodged with an administrative tribunal of expanded jurisdiction, a reconfiguration of authority and control over decisions of IFIs inevitably occurs.[184] The substantive and procedural goals as contained in the Universal Declaration of Human Rights that will guide the process of reconfiguration of authority and control have been indicated above. To ensure that private claimants before a reorganized tribunal can be effective, we need to clarify eligibility or admissibility conditions relating to the exhaustion of internal remedies available within the relevant IFI. For third-party private claimants, the exhaustion of internal remedies must be linked only to the exhaustion of the internal process of the accountability mechanism each IFI has established. Additionally, the eligibility conditions must remain the same as the accountability mechanism's competence: *ratione personae* (concerning the standing of the complainant), *ratione materiae* (concerning the merits of the complaint, that is, the alleged harm and violation), and *ratione temporis* (the timing of the complaint in relation to the project cycle).[185] Also recommended is that each IFI amend the resolution establishing its accountability mechanism to reorganize procedural requirements with respect to fact-finding, so that a panel could function as a fact-finding body whose finding can be used by a new administrative tribunal of expanded jurisdiction.

For the purposes of harmonization and efficient use of administrative tribunals of all IFIs, each IFI's administrative tribunal should be reorganized to be a tribunal

183. W. Michael Reisman, 'The Democratization of Contemporary International Law-Making Processes and the Differentiation of Their Application', in *Developments of International Law in Treaty Making*, ed. Rüdigger Wolfrum & Volker Röben (Berlin: Springer, 2005), 15, 21 (noting that people can 'enhance their influence by finding niches in critical decision functions which would allow them to shape prescriptions incorporating their preferred policies'.)

184. *See generally* W. Michael Reisman, *Nullity and Revision: The Review and Enforcement of International Judgments and Awards* (New Haven, CT: Yale University Press, 1971), 13.

185. *See* Ibrahim Shihata, *Role of the Inspection Panel in the Preliminary Assessment of whether to Recommend Inspection*, in *The World Bank Inspection Panel: In Practice*, 2nd edn, ed. Ibrahim Shihata (Washington, DC: A World Bank Publication, 2001), Annex I-4.

of first instance as its own 'district court', so to speak, from which legal issues should be raised on appeal to the World Bank Tribunal which should act as 'a Court of Appeal' for each IFI representing a functional region.[186] Needless to say, the Statute of the World Bank Administrative Tribunal must be amended to allow it to act as a Court of Appeal for all other IFIs. Since all major shareholders are the same major shareholders of all IFIs, it is a matter of political will and good faith determination to make these major changes through the board of directors of each IFI. Eventually, the hope is that out of this 'Court of Appeals' will emerge further appeals to the ICJ at the apex of this judicial hierarchy as 'the principal judicial organ of the United Nations'.[187]

VI. CONCLUSION

The role that international law plays in governing IFIs remains complicated and unclear. However, IFIs have taken steps toward assuming greater responsibility by creating accountability mechanisms to allow citizens to bring claims against the IFI when the projects being funded are interfering with their basic human rights. Although these accountability mechanisms are not perfect, citizens' claims against IFIs animate the reconfiguration of authority and control over the decision-making process of IFIs.[188] IFIs still need to create a legal regime in which people can bring claims, appeal decisions, and seek effective redress against IFIs. By expanding the role of existing administrative tribunals to serve as appellate bodies that make binding decisions regarding third-party claims, IFIs can ensure that they are serving the best interests of the people who live in the countries in which their projects are based, and can assure the public that someone, or the IFI itself, will be held accountable for the negative effects of IFI funded projects. In so doing, the IFI can be at the forefront of the development of the international law of human rights, which 'depend[s] in no small measure upon the ability of individuals and private groups to challenge unlawful deprivations'.[189]

---

186. For detailed analysis of necessary institutional arrangements, *see* Eisuke Suzuki, 'The Review and Repudiation of Judgments of International Administrative Tribunals', *Asian Yearbook of International Law* 7 (1997): 175, 204–207.
187. *Ibid.*, 207. IFIs are unique, in that every IFI has its own administrative tribunal. For the purpose of administrative tribunals, the World Bank Group (IBRD, IDA, IFC, and MIGA) is treated as one IFI. The question is not so much the proliferation of administrative tribunals as the fairness of judgment by endogamous bodies of a smaller regional domain. There is no appeal from any of these administrative tribunals. Each tribunal's decision is final. *Ibid.*, 179–183.
188. Reisman, 'The Democratization of Contemporary International Law-Making Processes and the Differentiation of Their Application', *supra* n. 183, 21.
189. McDougal, Lasswell & Chen, *Human Rights and World Public Order*, *supra* n. 175, 279.

Chapter 4

International Financial Institutions before National Courts

August Reinisch and Jakob Wurm

I. INTRODUCTION

International financial institutions (IFIs)[1] usually operate on the international level, by engaging in lending operations with states or regulating their monetary policies. Because some credit operations also involve contacts with private actors, IFIs must be endowed with legal personality under national law in order to enter into contracts and be able to pursue their rights before national courts. Of course, such private law lending operations may also result in claims being brought against IFIs. These practical needs are usually addressed by specific rules concerning domestic legal personality and by limiting the immunity from legal process normally enjoyed by international organizations.

Nevertheless, IFIs are, in general, fairly rare 'clients' before national courts. This chapter will look at the case law involving IFIs before national courts, as far as it is available, and will try to structure it according to typical kinds of cases. Before doing so, it is necessary to briefly analyse the applicable legal provisions conferring personality and immunity on IFIs.

1. The present analysis refers to IFIs as international organizations that address financial and monetary issues such as development banks and monetary institutions.

Daniel D. Bradlow and David B. Hunter, *International Financial Institutions and International Law*, pp. 103–135.

II. APPLICABLE LEGAL PERSONALITY AND IMMUNITY PROVISIONS

Like for most other international organizations, the constituent instruments of IFIs usually expressly provide for their domestic legal personality, enabling them to enter into private law relationships for their procurement needs, settle delictual claims, and appear in courts. A typical provision of such domestic legal personality can be found in the Articles of Agreement of the International Monetary Fund (IMF) and the World Bank: International Bank for Reconstruction and Development (IBRD) which both provide:

> The Fund/Bank shall possess full juridical personality and, in particular, the capacity: (i) to contract; (ii) to acquire and dispose of immovable and movable property; and (iii) to institute legal proceedings.[2]

Similar provisions are included in most other IFI constituent instruments[3] and can also be found in headquarters agreements as well as in other treaties addressing the status of IFIs.[4]

In contrast to the immunity provisions of most other international organizations, international development banks, such as the World Bank and others, usually do not enjoy 'full' functional immunity or other broad grants of immunity from legal process before national courts.[5] Instead, the typical 'indirect' immunity clause for such IFIs reaffirms the possibility to sue these organizations before

2. Articles of Agreement of the International Monetary Fund, 2 U.N.T.A. 40 (27 Dec. 1945), Art. IX(2) (hereinafter IMF Articles of Agreement); Articles of Agreement of the International Bank for Reconstruction and Development, 2 U.N.T.S. 134 (27 Dec. 1945), Art. VII(2) (hereinafter IBRD Articles of Agreement).
3. *See* Articles of Agreement of the International Development Association, 439 U.N.T.S. 249 (26 Jan. 1960), Art. VIII(2) (date is the day Executive Directors of IBRD approved it for submission to the governments) (hereinafter IDA Articles of Agreement); Agreement Establishing the Inter-American Development Bank, 389 U.N.T.S. 69 (8 Apr. 1959), Art. XI(2) (hereinafter IDB Articles of Agreement); Agreement Establishing the European Bank for Reconstruction and Development, 1646 U.N.T.S. 97 (29 May 1990), Art. 45 (hereinafter EBRD Articles of Agreement); Agreement Establishing the Asian Development Bank, 571 U.N.T.S. 123 (22 Aug. 1966), Art. 49 (hereinafter ADB Articles of Agreement); Agreement Establishing the African Development Bank, 1276 U.N.T.S. 3 (7 May 1982), Art. 50 (hereinafter AfDB Articles of Agreement); Convention establishing the Multilateral Investment Guarantee Agency, 24 I.L.M. 1605 (11 Oct. 1985), Art. 1(b) (hereinafter MIGA Convention); Articles of Agreement of the International Finance Corporation, 264 U.N.T.S. 118 (25 May 1955), Art. VI(2) (hereinafter IFC Articles of Agreement).
4. *See, e.g.*, Headquarters Agreement between the Government of the United Kingdom of Great Britain and Northern Ireland and the European Bank for Reconstruction and Development, 1656 U.N.T.S. 264 (15 Apr. 1991), Art. 3 (hereinafter EBRD Headquarters Agreement); Agreement between the Republic of Austria and the OPEC Fund for International Development Regarding the Headquarters of the Fund, Austrian Federal Law Gazette No. (BGBl. Nr.) 248/1982, 1291 U.N.T.S. 210 (21 Apr. 1981), Art. 7.
5. *See, e.g.*, IBRD Articles of Agreement, *supra* n. 2, Art. VII(3). For further discussion, *see* Steve Herz, 'Rethinking International Financial Institution Immunity', Ch. 5 herein.

national courts. The reason for this limitation is evident: International development banks finance their lending operations substantially through borrowing operations on the financial markets. In order to attract lender confidence, they have to ensure that private parties have access to the courts. Thus, international development banks are usually amenable to suit before the national courts of Member States. The archetypical example is Article VII, section 3 of the IBRD Articles of Agreement, which provides:

> Actions may be brought against the Bank only in a court of competent jurisdiction in the territories of a member in which the Bank has an office, has appointed an agent for the purpose of accepting service or notice of process, or has issued or guaranteed securities. No actions shall, however, be brought by members or persons acting for or deriving claims from members. The property and assets of the Bank shall, wheresoever located and by whomsoever held, be immune from all forms of seizure, attachment or execution before the delivery of final judgment against the Bank.[6]

A less restrictive immunity can be found in more recent instruments, such as the Articles of Agreement of the African Development Bank (AfDB) or of the Asian Development Bank (ADB). For example, Article 52 of the AfDB Articles of Agreement provides:

> 1. The Bank shall enjoy immunity from every form of legal process except in cases arising out of the exercise of its borrowing powers when it may be sued only in a court of competent jurisdiction in the territory of a member in which the Bank has its principal office, or in the territory of a member or non-member State where it has appointed an agent for the purpose of accepting service or notice of process, or has issued or guaranteed securities. No actions shall, however, be brought by members or persons acting for or deriving claims from members.
>
> 2. The property and assets of the Bank shall, wherever located and by whomsoever held, be immune from all forms of seizure, attachment or execution before the delivery of final judgment against the Bank.[7]

Similarly, Article 50(1) of the ADB Articles of Agreement provides:

> The Bank shall enjoy immunity from every form of legal process, except in cases arising out of or in connection with the exercise of its powers to borrow money, to guarantee obligations, or to buy and sell or underwrite the sale of securities, in which cases actions may be brought against the Bank in a court of competent jurisdiction in the territory of a country in which the Bank has its

6. IBRD Articles of Agreement, *supra* n. 2, Art. VII(3); similarly EBRD Articles of Agreement, *supra* n. 3, Art. 46; MIGA Convention, *supra* n. 3, Art. 44; IFC Articles of Agreement, *supra* n. 3, Art. VI(3).
7. AfDB Articles of Agreement, *supra* n. 3, Art. 52.

> principal or a branch office, or has appointed an agent for the purpose of accepting service or notice of process, or has issued or guaranteed securities.[8]

These general immunity clauses contained in the constituent documents of IFIs are sometimes reproduced or made more precise in headquarters agreements.[9] For example, the Headquarters Agreement for the European Bank for Reconstruction and Development (EBRD) qualifies the limited immunity of the Bank in the following terms:

> Within the scope of its official activities the Bank shall enjoy immunity from jurisdiction, except that the immunity of the Bank shall not apply:
>
> (a) to the extent that the Bank shall have expressly waived any such immunity in any particular case or in any written document;
> (b) in respect of civil action arising out of the exercise of its powers to borrow money, to guarantee obligations and to buy or sell or underwrite the sale of any securities;
> (c) in respect of a civil action by a third party for damage arising from a road traffic accident caused by an Officer or an Employee of the Bank acting on behalf of the Bank;
> (d) in respect of a civil action relating to death or personal injury caused by an act or omission in the United Kingdom;
> (e) in respect of the enforcement of an arbitration award made against the Bank as a result of an express submission to arbitration by or on behalf of the Bank; or
> (f) in respect of any counter-claim directly connected with court proceedings initiated by the Bank.[10]

As opposed to the international development banks, other IFIs like the IMF enjoy the 'usual' functional immunity. The rationale for the broad immunity usually enjoyed by international organizations is the 'functional necessity' of protecting the independent functioning of international organizations. This requirement is usually seen as necessitating an exemption from the jurisdiction and possible interference of national courts in the affairs of international organizations.[11]

---

8. ADB Articles of Agreement, *supra* n. 3, Art. 50(1).
9. In the case of the ADB, Art. III, s. 5 of the Agreement Between the Asian Development Bank and the government of the republic of the Philippines Regarding the headquarters of the Asian Development Bank provides as follows: 'The Bank shall enjoy immunity from every form of legal process, except in cases arising out of or in connection with the exercise of its powers to borrow money, to guarantee obligations, or to buy and sell or underwrite the sale of securities, in which cases actions may be brought against the Bank in a court of competent jurisdiction in the Republic of the Philippines.' Agreement between the Asian Development Bank and the government of the republic of the Philippines regarding the headquarters of the Asian Development Bank, 615 U.N.T.S. 375 (22 Dec. 1966), Art. III(5) (hereinafter ADB Headquarters Agreement).
10. EBRD Headquarters Agreement, *supra* n. 4, Art. 4(1).
11. *See* C.F. Amerasinghe, *Principles of the Institutional Law of International Organizations*, 2nd edn (Cambridge: Cambridge University Press, 2005), 316; Jan Klabbers, *International Organizations* (Aldershot, England & Burlington, VT: Ashgate & Dartmouth, 2005), 351;

Thus, the majority of the constituent instruments of international organizations provide for functional immunity, that is the immunity necessary for the fulfilment of their purposes.[12] Often this immunity is made more precise in general privileges and immunities treaties or headquarters agreements providing for an unqualified, hence absolute, immunity from suit.[13] In the case of the IMF, a provision that corresponds to the broad immunity clauses applicable to many international organizations states:

> The Fund, its property and its assets, wherever located and by whomsoever held, shall enjoy immunity from every form of judicial process except to the extent that it expressly waives its immunity for the purpose of any proceedings or by the terms of any contract.[14]

What is remarkable is the fact that this clear difference in the applicable immunity provisions has played a less important role than one might expect. However, before addressing such immunity issues, it is interesting to see that the (logically preceding) issue of legal personality has led to rather extensive litigation before national courts.

III. THE STANDING OF IFIS TO PURSUE THEIR RIGHTS IN NATIONAL COURTS – THE *HASHIM v. AMF* SAGA

The domestic legal personality of IFIs is usually provided for in the constituent instruments of such organizations and often reaffirmed in headquarters agreements.[15] Thus, in practice, it rarely poses any problems in Member States or in the headquarters state. The recognition of the legal personality of an IFI may, however, become an issue in third countries where the organization is also active. In these situations, the legal personality of an IFI, usually based on a clear treaty provision providing for the 'juridical personality and, in particular, the capacity:

Frederic Kirgis, *International Organizations in their Legal Setting*, 2nd edn (St Paul, Minnesota: West Publishing Co., 1993), 26; August Reinisch, *International Organizations before National Courts* (Cambridge: Cambridge University Press, 2000), 234; Philippe Sands & Pierre Klein, *Bowett's Law of International Institutions*, 5th edn (London: Sweet & Maxwell, 2001), 486; Henry Schermers & Niels Blokker, *International Institutional Law: Unity within Diversity*, 4th edn (Boston: Martinus Nijhoff Publishers, 2003), 252, 1020.

12. *E.g.*, Charter of the United Nations, 1 U.N.T.S. 993 (26 Jun. 1945), Art. 105(1) ('The Organization shall enjoy in the territory of each of its Members such privileges and immunities as are necessary for the fulfilment of its purposes.') (hereinafter UN Charter).
13. *Cf.* Convention on the Privileges and Immunities of the United Nations, 1 U.N.T.S. 15 (13 Feb. 1946), Art. II(2) ('The United Nations, its property and assets wherever located and by whomsoever held, shall enjoy immunity from every form of legal process except insofar as in any particular case it has expressly waived its immunity. It is, however, understood that no waiver of immunity shall extend to any measure of execution.').
14. IMF Articles of Agreement, *supra* n. 2, Art. IX(3).
15. *See* discussion in s. II, *supra* nn. 2–10.

(i) to contract; (ii) to acquire and dispose of immovable and movable property; and (iii) to institute legal proceedings',[16] may be doubtful.

The international cause célèbre in which the (alleged lack of) domestic legal personality of an IFI was in issue is the UK case of *Arab Monetary Fund v. Hashim (No. 3)*.[17] The Arab Monetary Fund (AMF), headquartered in Abu Dhabi, United Arab Emirates, was created in 1976 by an international agreement between twenty Arab states and the Palestine Liberation Organization (PLO).[18] According to Article 2 of the 1976 Agreement, 'the Fund shall have an independent juridical personality and shall have, in particular, the right to own, contract and litigate'.[19]

This was given effect in the domestic legal systems of the Member States. When AMF instituted legal proceedings before English courts in order to recover sums allegedly embezzled by its former director-general, the defendant sought the dismissal of the action on the ground that the Fund 'did not exist in English law and therefore could not sue [him]'.[20] Thus the central issue in this litigation was the domestic legal personality of an IFI of which the forum state was not a member. The controversial nature of this issue is reflected in the different outcomes at three levels of English courts. The Court of First Instance, Chancery Division, held that:

> [w]here [an] international organisation had been accorded legal personality under a foreign system of domestic law of a contracting state [*i.e.*, to the treaty establishing the international organization] it was to be regarded as being constituted under that law as a separate persona ficta and as such was entitled to recognition under English conflict of laws rules as an ordinary foreign juridical entity.[21]

The Court of Appeal[22] reversed and found that it was prevented from applying the conflict of laws approach adopted by the lower court since the Fund was created by public international law and not by the law of the United Arab Emirates:

> An international organisation constituted under international law by a treaty between foreign sovereign states to which the United Kingdom was not a party

16. *See* IBRD Articles of Agreement, *supra* n. 2, Art. VII(2).
17. *Arab Monetary Fund v. Hashim (No. 3)*, Chancery Division, 9–12 Oct., 14 Nov. 1989 [1990] 1 All E.R. 685; [1990] 3 W.L.R. 139, Hoffmann J; Court of Appeal, 26, 27 Mar., 9 Apr. 1990, [1990] 2 All E.R. 769; [1990] 3 W.L.R. 139; House of Lords, 26, 27, 28 Nov. 1990, 21 Feb. 1991, [1991] 1 All E.R. 871; [1991] 2 W.L.R. 729; *see also* the case notes by Ilona Cheyne, 'Status of International Organisations in English Law', *International & Comparative Law Quarterly* 40 (1991): 981; Jonathan Hill, 'International Corporations in the English Courts [AMF v. Hashim]', *Oxford Journal of Legal Studies* 12 (1992): 135; Edmund M. A. Kwaw, 'International Organizations as Foreign Entities: *AMF v. Hashim (No. 3)*', *Banking and Finance Law Review* 7 (1992): 453; F.A. Mann, 'International Organisations as National Corporations', *The Law Quarterly Review* 107 (1991): 357.
18. Articles of Agreement of the Arab Monetary Fund, 85 I.L.R. 671 (27 Apr. 1976) (hereinafter AMF Articles of Agreement).
19. *Ibid.*, Art. 2.
20. [1990] 1 All E.R. at 685.
21. [1990] 1 All E.R. at 686.
22. [1990] 1 All E.R. at 769; [1990] 3 W.L.R. at 139, C. A.

> and which was not the subject of any United Kingdom legislation would not be recognised as a foreign juridical person with the capacity to bring proceedings in the English courts, even though it had been accorded independent juridical personality as a persona ficta by one of the signatory states in line with its obligations under international law to give direct effect to the treaty as part of its own municipal law, since, as a matter of English private international law, the legislation conferring personality under the law of the signatory state was to be regarded as purely territorial in scope, its purpose being solely to give effect to the treaty within that state's own territory and not to create a separate entity capable of recognition abroad. Accordingly the plaintiff was not entitled to recognition as a foreign municipal juridical person with the capacity to bring proceedings in the English courts. The appeals would therefore be allowed and the plaintiff's action struck out.[23]

The House of Lords again reversed and held that there was no rule under English law that would prevent the courts from recognizing an international organization without the legislative authority of the International Organisations Act 1968[24] or any other enactment.[25] While the 1976 AMF Articles of Agreement as such were not sufficient to create personality under English law, the foreign incorporation led to the application of the normal conflicts rule that English courts recognize legal persons created under the law of foreign states. The House of Lords held that:

> [a]lthough when sovereign states entered into an agreement by treaty to confer legal personality on an international organisation the treaty did not create a corporate body with capacity to sue and be sued in English courts, the registration of that treaty in one of the sovereign states conferred legal personality on the international organisation and thus created a corporate body which the English courts could and should recognise, since by comity the courts of the United Kingdom recognised corporate bodies created by the law of a foreign state recognised by the Crown.[26]

The outcome of this case was dependent on a number of peculiar features of English law. On the one hand, under a 'dualist' legal system requiring domestic 'incorporation' of international law, English courts were not in a position to directly 'enforce' international agreements.[27] Pursuant to English law, '[t]he making of a treaty is an act of the executive, not of the legislature, and it is therefore a fundamental principle of [the] constitution that the terms of a treaty do not by virtue

23. [1990] 1 All E.R. at 769.
24. 'International Organisations Act 1968 (c. 48)', Halsbury's Statutes of England, 4th edn, vol. 10, Constitutional Law (1968), Pt. 5.
25. [1991] 1 All E.R. at 871; [1991] 2 W.L.R. at 729, H.L.
26. [1991] 1 All E.R. at 871–872.
27. Robert Jennings & Arthur Watts (eds), *Oppenheim's International Law*, 9th edn (London: Longmans, 1992), 58 et seq.

of the treaty alone, have the force of law in the United Kingdom'.[28] On the other hand, *Arab Monetary Fund v. Hashim (No. 3)* was largely decided on English private international law principles governing the recognition of 'foreign' corporate entities.[29] The issue was further complicated by a decision handed down by the House of Lords in the course of the *Tin Council* litigation[30] while *Arab Monetary Fund v. Hashim (No. 3)* was pending. That precedent was understood to establish the principle that an IO created under international law could not be treated as having legal personality in English law without statutory authorization.[31] The final decision of the House of Lords in the *AMF* case, based on a private international law-recognition of a 'foreign' international organization, was a pragmatic solution to a problem that may have otherwise lead to a rather surprising result, that is that the AMF, while engaged in a number of actual operations, did not legally 'exist' in the English legal order. In spite of the ultimate 'common sense' resolution of the personality issue by the House of Lords, the *AMF* case demonstrates an inherent risk posed to the practical operation of IFIs in non-member countries: the danger that national courts may abstain from adjudicating disputes involving international organizations because they do not recognize the legal personality of such a 'foreign' international organization under domestic law.

The well-known English *AMF* case should be contrasted with the less known 1995 US decision *In Re Jawad Mahmoud Hashim et al.*[32] This case was in many respects a continuance of the English *Arab Monetary Fund v. Hashim (No. 3)* litigation. After the English courts had entered judgment in favour of the AMF in 1993 and 1994, Dr Hashim and his family left England and finally settled in Arizona where they voluntarily filed for bankruptcy protection before the AMF could bring suit to enforce the English judgment. They listed the Fund as a creditor whose claims they disputed and – relying on arguments similar to those brought

28. *In re International Tin Council*, High Court, Chancery Division, 22 Jan. 1987; 77 ILR 18 (1988), at 26.
29. *Cf.* James Fawcett & Peter North, *Cheshire & North: Private International Law*, 11th edn (London: Butterworths, 1987), 173, 901 et seq.
30. *See* Ilona Cheyne, 'The International Tin Council', *International & Comparative Law Quarterly* 38 (1989): 417; Ilona Cheyne & Colin Warbrick, 'The International Tin Council', *International & Comparative Law Quarterly* 36 (1987): 931; Carsten Thomas Ebenroth, 'Shareholders' Liability in International Organizations – The Settlement of the International Tin Council Case', *Leiden Journal of International Law* 4 (1991): 171; Christopher Greenwood, 'Put Not Your Trust in Princes: The Tin Council Appeals', *Cambridge Law Journal* 48 (1989): 46; Christopher Greenwood, 'The Tin Council Litigation in the House of Lords', *Cambridge Law Journal* 49 (1990): 8; Romana Sadurska & Christine M. Chinkin, 'The Collapse of the International Tin Council: A Case of State Responsibility?', *Virginia Journal of International Law* 30 (1990): 845; Ignaz Seidl-Hohenveldern, 'Failure of Controls in the Sixth International Tin Agreement', in *Towards More Effective Supervision by International Organizations. Essays in Honour of Henry G. Schermers*, ed. Niels Blokker & Sam Mueller (Dordrecht: Martinus Nijhoff, 1994), 255.
31. *J H Rayner (Mincing Lane) Ltd v. Department of Trade and Industry*, House of Lords, 26 Oct. 1989, [1990] 3 W.L.R. 969, 81 ILR (1990), 670.
32. *In Re Jawad Mahmoud Hashim et al.*, 188 Bankr. 633 (D. Arizona 1995); 27 Bankr. Ct. Dec. 1161 (D. Arizona 1995); 107 ILR (1997), 405.

forward in the English proceedings – they specifically contended that the AMF lacked capacity to sue in the United States and that it could not participate in any way in the debtors' bankruptcy cases. In a special order concerning 'standing and capacity of Arab Monetary Fund', a US bankruptcy judge rejected the Hashims' arguments. The American judge basically followed the reasoning of the House of Lords and combined a private international law and a customary personality concept. It was clear that the AMF, as a regional international organization – in which the US did not participate and which was not specifically designated under the International Organizations Immunities Act (IOIA)[33] – could not derive its legal status from domestic legislation. The court held, however, that 'the AMF is a juridical person (a corporation, a persona ficta, an entity capable of legal battle) under U.A.E. law [. . .] Once this has been decided, capacity follows under American law as a matter of "customary law" '.[34]

This precedent suggests it is unlikely that judicial de-recognition might threaten a 'foreign' IFI in the United States. In fact, the 'recognition' of international organizations as entities possessing domestic legal personality, even in non-Member States usually does not encounter serious difficulties. Many legal systems also appear ready to accept the domestic legal personality of such 'foreign' international organizations.

IV. IFIs AND THEIR 'IMPLICIT' IMMUNITY IN EMPLOYMENT DISPUTES

Based on the fact that IFIs regularly enjoy legal personality, including the right to institute legal proceedings, they may be parties to lawsuits in domestic courts. Their rather exceptional 'immunity clauses'[35] have led to a rich jurisprudence concerning employment-related disputes brought against IFIs. The normal 'functional' or 'absolute' immunity of international organizations usually implies that staff members cannot bring an action against their employer organization. Instead, they have to pursue such claims before internal mechanisms, usually ending before administrative tribunals. This exclusion of employment disputes from domestic courts is, however, less clear in the case of IFIs, which do not enjoy such broad immunity. Thus, in a number of cases, domestic courts had to address the issue to what extent such immunity from employment-related actions must be presumed or read into the governing texts. More recently, the tendency to accord immunity in

33. International Organizations Immunities Act (IOIA), 59 Stat. 669, 22 U.S.C.A. §§ 288 et seq. (1945) (hereinafter IOIA 1945). IOIA, Title I, s. 1 provides: 'For the purposes of this title, the term "international organization" means a public international organization in which the United States participates pursuant to any treaty or under the authority of any Act of Congress authorizing such participation or making an appropriation for such participation, and which shall have been designated by the President through appropriate Executive Order as being entitled to enjoy the privileges, exemptions, and immunities herein provided.'
34. *In Re Jawad Mahmoud Hashim et al.*, 188 Bankr. at 649.
35. *See* s. II of this chapter and associated footnotes.

employment cases has met a countertendency stressing the need of access to justice that may sometimes override immunity considerations.

The development before American courts aptly demonstrates the problem of a general possibility to sue IFIs, on the one hand, and the need to shield them from employment disputes in order to ensure their independent functioning, on the other. The leading case that limited the broad possibility to sue IFIs according to their constituent instruments and excluded 'internal' administrative disputes from the jurisdiction of US courts is *Mendaro v. The World Bank.*[36] In this case, the D.C. Court of Appeals interpreted Article VII, section 3 of the IBRD Articles of Agreement[37] to permit lawsuits only in respect of external affairs of the Bank. Thus, it held the Bank immune from suits in employment disputes.

The case was instituted by a former employee of the World Bank whose employment as a researcher had come to an end in 1979. She alleged that she had been the victim of sexual discrimination and harassment and filed a complaint with the US Equal Employment Opportunity Commission alleging that her rights under Title VII of the US Civil Rights Act of 1964 had been violated. The Commission dismissed for lack of jurisdiction. The D.C. District Court and, on appeal, the D.C. Court of Appeals affirmed the dismissal.

The appellate court addressed this issue primarily from the point of view of the applicable US immunity legislation concerning international organizations, the IOIA. This statute, with regard to immunity, provides that:

> [i]nternational organizations, their property and their assets, wherever located, and by whomsoever held, shall enjoy the same immunity from suit and every form of judicial process as is enjoyed by foreign governments, except to the extent that such organizations may expressly waive their immunity for the purpose of any proceedings or by the terms of any contract.[38]

For the court the crucial issue was whether Article VII, section 3 of the IBRD Articles of Agreement,[39] which can be regarded as a 'functional waiver', encompassed employment-related disputes or not. The court refused to read this provision as a blanket 'waiver of immunity' from every type of suit not expressly prohibited by Article VII, section 3. According to a systematic reading of this provision and taking into account the 'functions of the Bank' and the 'underlying purposes of

---

36. *Mendaro v. The World Bank*, 717 F.2d 610 (D.C.Cir. 1983); case notes by Norman G. Abrahamson, 'International Organizations – International Organizations Immunity Act – Waiver of Immunity for World Bank denied, *Mendaro v. The World Bank*, 717 F.2d 610 (D.C.Cir. 1983)', *Suffolk Transnational Law Journal* 8 (1984): 413; Frances W. Henderson, 'How Much Immunity for International Organizations?: *Mendaro v. World Bank*', *North Carolina Journal of International Law & Commercial Regulation* 10 (1985): 487; Monroe Leigh, 'Immunity of International Organizations – Waiver of Immunity – International Organizations Immunities Act, Mendaro v. World Bank, 717 F.2d 610. U.S. Court of Appeals, D.C. Cir., Sept. 27, 1983', *American Journal of International Law* 78 (1984): 221.
37. *See* IBRD Articles of Agreement, *supra* n. 2.
38. IOIA 1945, *supra* n. 33, Title I, s. 2(b).
39. *See* IBRD Articles of Agreement, *supra* n. 2, Art. VII(3).

international immunities', it was evident, in the court's opinion, that the Bank's members only intended to waive the organization's immunity from suit by its:

> debtors, creditors, bondholders, and those other potential plaintiffs to whom the Bank would have subject itself to suit in order to achieve its chartered objectives. Since a waiver of immunity from employees' suits arising out of internal administrative grievances is not necessary for the Bank to perform its functions, this immunity is preserved by the members' failure expressly to waive it.[40]

The *Mendaro* court heavily relied upon policy arguments concerning the jurisdictional immunity of international organizations as they had already been formulated in its *Broadbent v. OAS* decision.[41] With regard to staff disputes it stated in particular that, 'the purpose of immunity from employee actions is rooted in the need to protect international organizations from unilateral control by a member nation over the activities of the international organization within its territory'.[42]

The court found that this immunity had already become 'an accepted doctrine of customary international law'.[43] Against this background it concluded that:

> the Bank's articles waive the Bank's immunity from actions arising out of the Bank's *external* relations with its debtors and creditors. However, a waiver of immunity to suits arising out of the Bank's *internal* operations, such as its relationship with its own employees, would contravene the express language of Article VII section 1.[44]

While one may doubt whether this distinction was indeed that clear as a matter of the Bank's constituent agreement, it was cogently reasoned as a matter of policy and has been followed by US courts since.

In *Chiriboga v. IBRD*,[45] a US district court expressly followed the *Mendaro* and *Broadbent* precedents. The case arose from the death of a World Bank employee in an aircraft accident while on home leave. A personal representative of the deceased and beneficiaries of her World Bank employees' benefits plan brought proceedings against the Bank and her insurer to recover under her travel accident policy. Without any in-depth analysis, the court qualified this dispute as

40. *Mendaro*, 717 F.2d at 615.
41. *Broadbent v. OAS*, 628 F.2d 27, 35 (D.C.Cir. 1980) ('An attempt by the courts of one nation to adjudicate the personnel claims of international civil servants would entangle those courts in the internal administration of those organizations. Denial of immunity opens the door to divided decisions of the courts of different member states passing judgment on the rules, regulations, and decisions of the international bodies. Undercutting uniformity in the application of staff rules or regulations would undermine the ability or the organization to function effectively.').
42. *Mendaro*, 717 F.2d at 615.
43. *Ibid.*
44. *Ibid.*, 618. Art. VII, s. 1 of the IBRD Articles of Agreements provides: 'To enable the Bank to fulfill the functions with which it is entrusted, the status, immunities and privileges provided in this Article shall be accorded to the Bank in the territories of each member.'
45. *Chiriboga v. IBRD*, 616 F. Supp. 963 (D.D.C. 1985).

an employment dispute in which the Bank enjoyed immunity: '[t]he dispute focuses on what the Bank did or did not contract to provide to its employees. It is difficult to imagine a suit that touches more closely on the internal operations of an international organization'.[46] It thus dismissed the action.

Further, a law suit brought by a World Bank employee alleging age discrimination led to the same result. The court in *Novak v. World Bank*[47] relied on *Mendaro* and upheld the Bank's immunity.

The immunity-friendly approach of US courts towards IFIs was even expanded in *Morgan v. IBRD*[48] in which a US court held that the 'employment-related immunity' of the Bank also extended to persons working at the Bank on placement from a temporary employment agency. In the court's view, 'employee relations of any kind cannot be the subject of litigation against the Bank'.[49] The case was no ordinary staff dispute. Rather, it was a tort action claiming intentional infliction of emotional distress, false imprisonment, libel, and slander. The plaintiff, who was an employee of a temporary employment agency and had been placed in a position at the World Bank, alleged that he had been forcibly detained by security guards of the Bank, accused of stealing money, and exposed to subsequent acts of harassment. His action was dismissed because the court found that '[p]ursuant to applicable provisions [of the IOIA] and principles of international law, international organizations such as the World Bank are, absent waiver, absolutely immune from suits arising out [of] their internal operations'.[50] While the *Morgan* case is certainly atypical, it is clear that US case law generally recognizes the immunity of IFIs in staff disputes.

However, not all courts have consistently followed this approach. In *Margot Rendall-Speranza v. Edward A. Nassim and the International Finance Corp.*,[51] a sexual harassment law suit by an International Finance Corporation (IFC) staff member against her supervisor as well as against the employer organization, a D.C. district court denied the IFC's claim to immunity. The court based its reasoning only on the wording of the applicable statutory law, the IOIA. In a first decision, distinguishing *Morgan v. IBRD*,[52] the court held that the acts complained of did not involve a policy judgment on the part of the IFC which would confer immunity from suit under the Foreign Sovereign Immunities Act (FSIA) discretionary function exception to the tort exemption from immunity.[53] In a second decision the same court even more specifically addressed the nature of the IFC's immunity

46. *Chiriboga*, 616 F. Supp. at 967.
47. *Novak v. World Bank*, 703 F.2d 1305 (1983).
48. *Morgan v. IBRD*, 752 F. Supp. 492 (D.D.C. 1990); case note by Daniel Hammerschlag, 'Morgan v. International Bank for Reconstruction and Development', *Maryland Journal of International Law and Trade* 16 (1992): 279.
49. *Morgan*, 752 F. Supp. at 494.
50. *Ibid.*, 493.
51. *Rendell-Speranza v. Nassim & the IFC (Rendell-Speranza I)*, 942 F. Supp. 621 (D.D.C. 1996); *Rendell-Speranza v. Nassim & the IFC (Rendell-Speranza II)*, 932 F. Supp. 19 (D.D.C. 1996).
52. *See generally Morgan*, 752 F. Supp. 492.
53. *Rendell-Speranza I*, 942 F. Supp. at 627.

from suit under US law. The court noted that the issue of whether 'the IOIA incorporates the subsequently enacted FSIA [. . .] is an unsettled question', and went on to hold that it had to 'adhere to the plain language of the IOIA, which affords to international organizations only the immunity of foreign governments'.[54] Consequently, the Court of First Instance denied the IFC's immunity from suit. On appeal, however, this result was reversed, although the DC Circuit Court managed to avoid deciding the 'delicate issue', whether the enactment of the FSIA in 1976 also implied that the immunity provided for international organizations in the IOIA had to be regarded as restrictive immunity.[55] The appellate court held that the claim against the IFC was time-barred and thus dismissed the case.

The 'delicate issue' alluded to in the *Rendall-Speranza* case stems from the wording of the IOIA which clearly indicates that state immunity principles should be relevant for deciding on the jurisdictional immunity of international organizations.[56] US courts had difficulties in determining whether the reference to state immunity – made at a time when absolute immunity for foreign states was the accepted principle – was 'frozen' in time and thus implied absolute immunity for international organizations, or was dynamic and thus referred to the principles of state immunity at the time proceedings are brought. Since the acceptance of a restrictive immunity doctrine by the US judiciary[57] and the adoption of the FSIA,[58] restrictive state immunity has been firmly established in US law. This would imply that international organizations should also enjoy only restrictive immunity.[59]

Only in 1998, after a number of cases had managed to avoid this crucial issue by holding that even under a restrictive state immunity standard a particular action would be inadmissible against an international organization,[60] did the US Court of Appeals for the District of Columbia Circuit clarify the matter.

54. *Rendell-Speranza II*, 932 F. Supp. at 24.
55. *Rendall-Speranza v. Nassim & the IFC (Rendell-Speranza III)*, 107 F.3d 913 (D.C. Cir. 1997) ('[. . .] the issues raised by the IFC's various claims of immunity, and particularly the issue of the effect (if any) that the FSIA has upon the IOIA, are both difficult and, because of their implications for the foreign relations of the United States, delicate. If they can be avoided merely by advancing the time at which the court reaches its decision upon the statute of limitation defense, then they should be.').
56. *See* discussion of Title I, s. 2(b) of IOIA 1945, *supra* n. 33, which is discussed at n. 38.
57. *Cf.* US State Department, 'Tate Letter', 26 Dep't State Bull. (1952), 984; *see also Alfred Dunhill of London v. Republic of Cuba*, 425 U.S. 682 (1976).
58. US Foreign Sovereign Immunities Act 1975, 90 Stat. 2891, 28 U.S.C.A. §§ 1330 et seq. (1976), 15 I.L.M. 1388.
59. One of the rare older cases leading to this result is *Dupree Associates, Inc. v. Organization of American States and the General Secretariat of the Organization of American States*, 63 I.L.R. 92 (1977).
60. *Morgan*, 752 F. Supp. 492; *De Luca v. United Nations Organization, Perez de Cuellar, Gomez, Duque, Annan, et al.*, 841 F. Supp. 531 (S.D.N.Y. 1994); *Tuck v. Pan American Health Organization (Tuck I)*, 668 F.2d 547 (D.D.C. 1980); *Tuck v. Pan American Health Organization (Tuck II)*, 668 F.2d 547 (D.C.Cir. 1981), UNJYB (1981), 177. *See also* Reinisch, *International Organizations before National Courts*, *supra* n. 11, 197 et seq.

In *Atkinson v. Inter-American Development Bank*,[61] an ex-wife of an employee of the Inter-American Development Bank (IDB) instituted garnishment proceedings against the IDB after her ex-husband had defaulted on a judgment on alimony and child support. The IDB invoked immunity. In its analysis, the court turned to statutory provisions for the determination of the bank's exemption from domestic jurisdiction and specifically addressed the question of whether the immunity of the IDB was absolute by virtue of the IOIA's reference to 'the same immunity from suit and from every form of judicial process as is enjoyed by foreign governments'.[62]

It rejected the view that a correct interpretation of the IOIA had to take into account the recent developments in the field of immunities of international organizations, and should be interpreted to restrict rather than to broaden the immunity granted to IFIs:

> In light of this text [of the IOIA] and legislative history, we think that despite the lack of a clear instruction as to whether Congress meant to incorporate in the IOIA subsequent changes to the law of immunity of foreign sovereigns, Congress' intent was to adopt that body of law only as it existed in 1945 – when immunity of foreign sovereigns was absolute.[63]

In line with the court's support of an absolute immunity protection, it rejected the view that the enactment of the 1976 FSIA altered the immunity understanding of the IOIA. It did not accept the interpretation that Congress had been aware of the impact of the restrictive immunity doctrine on the IOIA, and that choosing not to revise it also demonstrated Congress's intent to apply a restrictive immunity understanding to the IOIA. Rather, the IOIA did not incorporate post-1945 changes because 'the Congress does not express its intent by a failure to legislate and even if it did, the will of a later Congress as to the meaning of a law enacted by an earlier Congress is of little weight'.[64] Thus, the *Atkinson* case was the first that clearly stressed that an international organization's immunity under the IOIA was absolute and corresponded to the absolute immunity accorded to foreign states in 1945.

The necessary flexibility to respond to changes required of the immunity of international organizations is ensured by a different approach in the US context. The IOIA provides for 'executive orders' by the US President, which allow the executive branch 'to modify, condition, limit and even revoke the otherwise absolute immunity of a designated organization'.[65] For this reason, IFIs claiming immunity before US courts usually refer not only to the *Atkinson* interpretation of the IOIA (which is typically combined with a reference to the FSIA), but also

61. *Atkinson v. Inter-American Development Bank*, 156 F 3d. 1335 (D.C.Cir. 1998).
62. *See* IOIA 1945, *supra* n. 33, Title I, s. 2(b) (a discussion of which correlates to n. 37).
63. In the footnote to this paragraph, the court 'accordingly disapprove[s] of the contrary holding in Rendall-Speranza v Nassim'. *See Atkinson*, 156 F 3d. at 1341.
64. *Ibid.*, 1342.
65. *See* IOIA 1945, *supra* n. 33; *Atkinson*, 156 F.3d at 1341.

invoke the appropriate presidential executive order that recognizes the IFI in question as an 'international organization' under the IOIA.

For an additional reason, the *Atkinson* case is remarkable. It advanced the so-called *Mendaro*-test concerning the scope of a waiver of immunity of IFIs. Referring to the rationale of 'functional immunity', the *Mendaro* court had pointed out that:

> [s]ince the purpose of the immunities accorded international organizations is to enable the organizations to fulfil their functions, applying the same rationale in reverse, it is likely that most organizations would be unwilling to relinquish their immunity without receiving a corresponding benefit which would further the organization's goal.[66]

This test could imply that a Bank's immunity should be considered waived unless it would impair the bank's objectives. However, the *Atkinson* case clarified that, on the contrary, 'the Bank's immunity should be construed as not waived unless a particular type of suit would further the Bank's objectives'.[67] It referred to this understanding as an 'opposite default rule'.[68] This test puts the Bank's objectives into the centre of the examination as they become decisive in determining whether the immunity of an IFI can be lifted. Because they are of crucial importance, it is clear why courts seek additional elements for their determination and apply a cost-benefit assessment. In *Atkinson*, the relevant part of this test was worded as follows:

> Here, waiver of immunity from garnishment proceedings, unlike waiver of immunity from employment suits, provides no conceivable benefit in attracting talented employees; in fact, garnishment of an employee's wages makes the (prospective) employee worse off [. . .]. This clear lack of benefit – indeed disadvantage – of a waiver of immunity from garnishment proceedings compels the conclusion that Section 3 of the agreement should not be construed to waive the Bank's immunity in this case.[69]

The 'corresponding benefit' test[70] clarified that the waiver was to be read narrowly. This approach is now regularly applied by US courts.[71]

Also in the employment context, the *Dujardin v. IBRD*[72] case illustrates that US courts regularly refer to this 'functional purpose' approach when they examine the waiver of immunity. In this instance, a defamation suit was brought by a former

66. *Mendaro*, 717 F.2d at 617 (cited at *Atkinson*, 156 F.3d at 1338).
67. *Atkinson*, 156 F.3d at 1338.
68. *Ibid.*, 1338.
69. *Atkinson*, 156 F.3d at 1339.
70. One of the recent US court decisions that explicitly uses this term is *Bro Tech v. EBRD*, 2000 U.S. Dist. LEXIS 17049 (E.D. Pa. 2000), *see infra* n. 158.
71. Cases applying the *Atkinson* test in the field of financial activities of IFIs are, for instance, *Ashford v. World Bank Group et al.*, *infra* n. 119; *Atlantic Tele-Network v. Inter-American Development Bank*, *infra* n. 123 and the recent case of *Salah Osseiran v. IFC*, *infra* n. 129.
72. *Dujardin v. IBRD*, 9 Fed. Appx. 19, 2001 U.S. App. LEXIS 13893 (D.C. Cir. 2001).

employee of the IBRD whom the Bank allegedly recruited to work for the borrower. The court found that this particular type of suit did not further the bank's objectives, nor did it enhance IBRD's ability to participate in commercial transactions. Therefore, immunity of the IBRD was upheld.

In *Weinstock v. Asian Development Bank*,[73] an ADB employee advanced numerous vague allegations. They included not only violations of his constitutional rights because other ADB employees had allegedly assisted in his arrest on the occasion of a child-custody dispute in Manila, but also stressed that he had been denied a promotion by the ADB subsequent to these incidents. He had unsuccessfully filed an appeal with the ADB's Administrative Tribunal regarding the denial of the promotion and instituted proceedings before the US district court. The US court unsurprisingly denied a waiver because this dispute did not fit into the limited category of exceptions to the immunity of the ADB.[74] It specifically stressed that the 'dissatisfaction with the efficacy of the administrative remedy [offered by the ADB] is insufficient to dissolve [the] Defendant's immunity as an international organization or [to] create an exception through which the Court can retain jurisdiction'.[75]

Sometimes staff members try to avoid the immunity of IFIs by instituting legal proceedings not directly against their employer organization, but rather against other staff members who are their superiors. For instance, in *Kissi v. De Larosiere*,[76] a US national brought an employment discrimination suit against the managing director of the IMF alleging that he had been unlawfully denied a position within IMF. Noting the functional immunity of IMF officials with respect to acts performed in their official capacity, the DC District Court dismissed the action because the 'law could not be clearer as to the defendant's immunity from this suit, which undeniably involves action by defendant, in rejecting plaintiff's employment applications, in his official capacity'.[77]

English courts also generally accord immunity to IFIs in employment suits. In *Mukoro v. European Bank for Reconstruction and Development and Another*,[78] an English labour court affirmed the EBRD's immunity from suit brought by a potential employee who had alleged that the rejection of his job application resulted from unlawful racial discrimination. According to the applicable immunity regime laid down in the headquarters agreement, the EBRD was to enjoy 'functional' immunity for 'official acts'.[79] The court held that the activity relevant to be qualified as 'official' was the selection of staff for employment and not the alleged unlawful discrimination which concerned only 'the mode of performance of the activities and the consequences of performance'. This precedent was

73. *Weinstock v. Asian Development Bank*, 2005 U.S. Dist. LEXIS 16870 (D.D.C. 2005).
74. *See* ADB Articles of Agreement, *supra* n. 3, Art. 50(1).
75. *Weinstock*, 2005 U.S. Dist. LEXIS 16870 at 13.
76. *Kissi v. De Larosiere*, No. 82-1267 (D.D.C. 1985) (unpublished opinion from 23 Jun. 1982).
77. *Ibid.*
78. Employment Appeal Tribunal, 19 May 1994, [1994] ICR 897; 107 ILR 604.
79. EBRD Headquarters Agreement, *supra* n. 4, Art. 4(1) ('Within the scope of its official activities the Bank shall enjoy immunity from jurisdiction [. . .].').

followed in *Bertolucci v. European Bank for Reconstruction and Development and Others*,[80] a sexual discrimination claim dismissed because of the EBRD's immunity from suit. The court expressly held that:

> staff management falls within the acts performed by managers in their official capacity, whether or not it was performed in a discriminatory manner, and the employment of staff and management of staff relations falls within the official activities of the Bank.[81]

A similar result was reached in the Nigerian case of *African Reinsurance Corporation v. Abate Fantaye*.[82] The African Reinsurance Corporation is an international organization set up between the Member States of the Organization of African Union and the AfDB headquartered in Nigeria. The applicable immunity provision stated that '[l]egal actions may be brought against the Corporation in a court of competent jurisdiction in the territory of a country in which the Corporation has its Headquarters, or has appointed an agent for the purpose of accepting service of process, or has otherwise agreed to be sued'.[83] In a lawsuit by a former employee of the Bank who claimed damages for wrongful termination of his employment contract, the defendant organization's plea of immunity was initially rejected both by the High Court of Lagos and the appellate court. The Supreme Court, however, reversed and held that the Nigerian Government had conferred upon the corporation the status of a recognized international organization and that as such it enjoyed diplomatic immunity and had immunity from suit and legal process. Although the treaty establishing the corporation did not contain an express immunity from suit, Nigerian domestic legislation provided for its immunity from suit and legal process. It further stated that the immunity provision in question was no waiver of immunity that – according to domestic legislation – had to be express and positive.

The result that IFIs generally enjoy immunity in employment disputes can be found in other jurisdictions as well. Good examples are the Argentine cases of *Araya v. Institute for Latin-American Integration/Inter-American Development Bank*[84] and *Ezcurra de Mann v. Inter-American Development Bank*[85] in which the

80. Employment Appeal Tribunal, 19 Aug. 1997, EAT/276/97 (Transcript) Lexis file.
81. *Ibid.*
82. Supreme Court, 20 Jun. 1986, [1986] 3 *Nigerian Weekly Law Reports* 811; 86 ILR 655.
83. *See* Ch. IX on 'Status, Immunities, Exemptions and Privileges', Art. 48 of the Agreement Establishing the African Reinsurance Corporation, 1197 U.N.T.S. 76 (24 Feb. 1976). The Agreement was concluded between the African States' members of the Organization of African Unity and the African Development Bank.
84. Argentina, Labor Court, 1974, *cited in* Andrew N. Vorkink & Marilou C. Hakuta, *Lawsuits against International Organizations: Cases in National Courts Involving Staff and Employment*, World Bank Legal Department (Washington, DC: IBRD, 1 Jul. 1985), 25 (hereinafter Vorkink & Hakuta, 'Argentina Labor Court 1974').
85. Argentina, Labor Court, 15 Aug. 1978, Court of Appeals, 11 Jun. 1979, *cited in* Andrew N. Vorkink & Marilou C. Hakuta, *Lawsuits against International Organizations: Cases in National Courts Involving Staff and Employment*, World Bank Legal Department (Washington, DC: IBRD, 1 Jul. 1985), 36.

deciding courts interpreted the restricted immunity of an international lending institution broadly. In the latter case the appellate court decided that it lacked jurisdiction because the Bank enjoyed 'diplomatic immunity', which could only be waived by express consent. It found that Article XI, section 3 of the IDB Articles of Agreement[86] did not constitute a 'waiver of immunity',[87] but rather that the Bank 'may or may not accept such service or notice'.[88] The court then affirmed the lower court's decision holding that the appointment of an agent alone would not suffice to subject the Bank to the jurisdiction of Argentine courts but rather that such agent 'is empowered to accept service or notification of process or, conversely, not to accept same'.[89]

In a few cases, national courts have refused to accord immunity from suit to IFIs. Such refusal may be based on very formalistic reasons, as was evident in the Philippines case of *Velasquez v. Asian Development Bank.*[90] In this employment dispute, a domestic labour arbitrator upheld jurisdiction because the defendant IFI had failed to show that the Bank's constituent treaty and headquarters agreement had been ratified by the Philippines. On the basis of such law, he ordered reinstatement of the Bank's employee and the payment of back wages. Only after diplomatic representations made by the ADB did the Philippine Foreign Ministry advise the Ministry of Labor that the latter had no jurisdiction to decide on the matter.

More recently, another strand of national case law has developed which sometimes leads to a denial of immunity of IFIs in employment disputes. This is based less on formal than on substantive reasons in the interest of the right of access to court of employees, and reflects a general tendency of many national courts, in particular in Europe, to restrict the immunity of international organizations where such immunity would lead to a denial of justice.[91] This trend has its roots in the jurisprudence of the European Court of Human Rights, which held in *Waite and Kennedy*[92] that 'a material factor in determining whether granting [. . .]

86. *See* IDB Articles of Agreement, *supra* n. 3.
87. *Cf.* the US waiver of immunity cases *Lutcher*, *infra* n. 105; *Mendaro*, *supra* n. 36.
88. Vorkink & Hakuta, 'Argentina Labor Court 1974', *supra* n. 84, 36.
89. *Ibid.*
90. Philippines, Ministry of Labor, Region IV, Manila, 25 Nov. 1979 Case No. RB-IV-AB-1841-79, *cited in* Andrew N. Vorkink & Marilou C. Hakuta, *Lawsuits against International Organizations: Cases in National Courts Involving Staff and Employment*, World Bank Legal Department (Washington, DC: IBRD, 1 Jul. 1985), 38.
91. *See* Nicolas Angelet & Alexandra Weerts, 'Les immunités des organisations internationales face à l'article 6 de la Convention européenne des droits de l'homme', *Journal du droit international* 134 (2007): 3; August Reinisch & Ulf Andreas Weber, 'The Jurisdictional Immunity of International Organizations, the Individual's Right of Access to the Courts and Administrative Tribunals as Alternative Means of Dispute Settlement', *International Organizations Law Review* 1 (2004): 59.
92. *Waite and Kennedy*, Application No. 26083/94, European Court of Human Rights, 18 Feb. 1999, [1999] ECHR 13, 116 ILR 121, 134; case note by August Reinisch, '*Case of Waite and Kennedy v. Germany*, Application No. 26083/94; *Case of Beer and Regan v. Germany*, Application No. 28934/95, European Court of Human Rights, 18 February 1999', *American Journal of International Law* 93 (1999): 933.

immunity from [. . .] jurisdiction is permissible is whether the applicants had available to them reasonable alternative means to protect effectively their rights under the Convention'.[93] The case involved the European Space Agency and led to the acceptance of the organization's immunity from suit before German courts because an internal staff dispute mechanism was available.

Subsequent national cases have come to different conclusions. For instance, in *Siedler v. Western European Union*,[94] a Belgian appellate court found that the internal procedure for the settlement of employment disputes within the Western European Union (WEU) did not offer the guarantees inherent to a fair trial. Thus, it denied the organization's claim to immunity because such limitation of the access to the normal courts was incompatible with Article 6(1) of the European Convention on Human Rights (ECHR).[95]

In a similar way, French courts are increasingly questioning the appropriateness of a general immunity of international organizations in employment matters in which no alternative remedy is available and have applied this scepticism to IFIs. The French Supreme Court decision in *Banque africaine de développement v. M.A. Degboe*[96] illustrates this well. It arose from a claim brought by a former employee of the AfDB who could not access the organization's administrative tribunal because it was set up after his dismissal and thus lacked jurisdiction over his claim. The Cour de Cassation held that the impossibility of access to justice constituted a denial of justice. Therefore, the defendant organization was not entitled to immunity from suit.[97] In this case, the French court relied less upon ECHR Article 6(1)

93. *Waite and Kennedy*, *supra* n. 92, para. 68.
94. *Siedler v. Western European Union*, Brussels Labour Court of Appeal (4th chamber), 17 Sep. 2003, *Journal des Tribunaux* 2004, 617, ILDC 53 (BE 2003); case notes by Eric David, 'L'immunité de juridiction des organisations internationales', *Journal des Tribunaux* (2004): 619; Jan Wouters & Maarten Vidal, 'Internationaal recht voor de Belgische rechter: een bloemlezing uit de recente rechtspraak', in *Internationaal en Europees Recht, Themis Cahier no 31*, ed. Koen Lenaerts & Jan Wouters (Brussels: Die Keure, 2005), 55.
95. Article 6(1) of the European Convention on Human Rights provides: 'In the determination of his civil rights and obligations or of any criminal charge against him, everyone is entitled to a fair and public hearing within a reasonable time by an independent and impartial tribunal established by law.' European Convention for the Protection of Human Rights and Fundamental Freedoms, 213 U.N.T.S. 221 (1953), Art. 6(1) (adopted 4 Nov. 1950, entered into force 3 Sep. 1953).
96. *Banque africaine de développement v. M.A. Degboe*, Cour de Cassation, Chambre sociale, 25 janvier 2005, 04-41012, 132 *Journal du droit international* (2005) 1142; case note by Isabelle Pingel-Lenuzza, *Rev. crit. dr. int. pr.* (2005), 477.
97. *Banque africaine de développement v. M.A. Degboe*, Cour de Cassation, Chambre sociale, 25 janvier 2005, 04-41012, 132 *Journal du droit international* (2005): 1142 ('Mais attendu que la Banque africaine de développement ne peut se prévaloir de l'immunité de juridiction dans le litige l'opposant au salarié qu'elle a licencié dès lors qu'à l'époque des faits elle n'avait pas institué en son sein un tribunal ayant compétence pour statuer sur des litiges de cette nature, l'impossibilité pour une partie d'accéder au juge chargé de se prononcer sur sa prétention et d'exercer un droit qui relève de l'ordre public international constituant un déni de justice fondant la compétence de la juridiction française lorsqu'il existe un rattachement avec la France [. . .]'). In the follow up to this litigation, the Cour de Cassation reaffirmed its earlier decision that '[. . .] l'absence de toute juridiction du travail au sein de la banque [. . .] mettait

than on the concept of 'ordre public international' encompassing the prohibition of a 'déni de justice', or 'denial of justice'. This approach demonstrates that the idea of a 'forfeiture' of immunity in case no alternative remedy is provided for is not limited to cases in which the right of access to justice is derived from the ECHR. Rather, it indicates that the notion of a 'conditional' immunity may be 'transferable' to other jurisdictions where it may be based on due process or the prohibition of denial of justice, which could be regarded as elements of an 'ordre public international' or equally of customary international law.[98]

In fact, this concern had already been voiced in connection with the leading American case of *Mendaro v. The World Bank*.[99] Critics of the immunity decision concluded that in the particular case, the US court should have exercised jurisdiction 'especially since Mendaro had nowhere else to turn due to the World Bank's lack of an internal dispute settlement mechanism at the time'.[100] Moreover, in 1985, the then newly established World Bank Administrative Tribunal[101] rejected Mendaro's complaint as inadmissible because most events giving rise to applicant's complaint had occurred before the entry into force of the Tribunal's Statute and because, to the extent they arose subsequently, the complaint was filed three years after the time-limit had expired.[102]

It is too early to state with any reasonable certainty whether the trend evident in cases like *Banque africaine de développement v. M.A. Degboe* and *Siedler v. Western European Union* will develop into a dominant jurisprudence.[103] But it is

le salarié dans l'impossibilité d'exercer son droit à un tribunal pour connaître sa cause [. . .]'. *M.X v. Banque africaine de développement*, Cour de Cassation, Chambre sociale, 11 janvier 2007, 05-40157.

98. *Cf.* American Law Institute, *Restatement (Third) Foreign Relations Law of the United States* (St Paul, Minnesota: American Law Institute, 1987), s. 711 Reporters' note 2.B; Jan Paulsson, *Denial of Justice in International Law* (Cambridge: Cambridge University Press, 2005), 134 et seq.
99. *Mendaro, supra* n. 36.
100. Abrahamson, *supra* n. 36, 422.
101. The World Bank Administrative Tribunal was established by a resolution adopted by the Boards of Governors of the IBRD, IDA, and IFC on 30 Apr. 1980.
102. *Mendaro v. IBRD*, World Bank Administrative Tribunal, 4 Sep. 1985, World Bank Administrative Tribunal Reports [1985], Decision No. 26.
103. Obviously inherent to this development is the requirement not only for the availability, but also for the de facto effectiveness of the alternative remedy provided by an international organization. The *Yacyretá* case is an illustrative example. The overly time-consuming construction of the Yacyretá Hydroelectric Project financed by the IDB and World Bank on the border between Argentina and Paraguay raised considerable protest in the mid-1990s by the local population affected by the non-enforcement of the banks' own environmental and resettlement policies. Complaints were brought before the newly established Independent Investigation Mechanism (IIM) of the Inter-American Development Bank and the World Bank Inspection Panel, which, in May 1997, urged the Board of the Inter-American Development Bank to even allow a parallel investigation before these tribunals in order to address the allegation of inadequate remedies. *Cf.* Richard Bissell, 'Current Development: Recent Practice of the Inspection Panel of the World Bank', *American Journal of International Law* 91 (1997): 742.

obvious that there are valid arguments in favour of a restriction of immunity where such immunity may lead to a denial of justice.

V. IFIs AND THEIR LACK OF IMMUNITY IN BORROWING AND LENDING OPERATIONS

As outlined above, most IFIs do not enjoy the same broad jurisdictional immunity as other international organizations. According to their constituent agreements most international development banks can be sued before domestic courts by private parties, but not by Member States.[104] The rationale of this provision is obvious: it would have a negative effect on the creditworthiness of a financial institution if its creditors had no access to court in order to recover their claims. This justification has been aptly addressed in *Lutcher v. Inter-American Development Bank*[105] in which a US appellate court remarked:

> Just as it is necessary for the Bank to be subject to suit by bondholders in order to raise its lending capital, it may be that responsible borrowers committing large sums and plans on the strength of the Bank's agreement to lend would be reluctant to enter into borrowing contracts if thereafter they were at the mercy of the Bank's good will, devoid of means of enforcement.[106]

Interestingly, only a limited number of reported cases involve straightforward creditor claims against IFIs. This may, of course, result from the fact that the lack of immunity is so clear that the immunity issue is regularly not litigated. It may also stem from the fact that IFIs manage to avoid disputes from reaching a litigious phase. All this is speculation, and it is thus from the few available cases that one has to draw conclusions.

One of the rare court cases concerning lending operations of IFIs is the US decision in *Lutcher S.A. Celulose e Papel v. Inter-American Development Bank*[107] in which the DC Circuit Court, in principle, permitted a borrower to bring suit against the IDB. The case was not a simple contract claim involving loans given by the defendant IFI, but rather, it involved an alleged breach of an implicit agreement combined with a tort action. Lutcher, a Brazilian corporation sought damages and an injunction against the IDB, arguing that loans made or about to be made to its competitors violated an 'implied obligation' of its own loan agreement with the Bank to act prudently in considering loan applications from competitors. The federal appellate court affirmation of the district court's dismissal for failure to state a claim ended the dispute. What is interesting, however, is the fact that the Court of Appeals disagreed with the lower court's alternative reasoning that the

104. *See* IBRD Articles of Agreement, *supra* n. 2, Art. VII(3).
105. *Lutcher S.A. Celulose e Papel v. Inter-American Development Bank*, 382 F.2d 454 (D.C.Cir. 1967), 28 Mar. 1966; 42 ILR (1967): 183, 337.
106. *Lutcher*, 382 F.2d at 459.
107. *Ibid.*, 454.

Bank enjoyed immunity from suit. The applicable immunity provision of the IDB, Article XI, section 3 of the Bank's Articles of Agreement, was identical to Article VII, section 3 of the IBRD Articles of Agreement.[108] The Bank had argued that this provision, allowing suit in competent courts of the Member States, permitted only actions brought by 'bondholders, creditors, and beneficiaries of its guarantees' because only this exception from immunity would contribute to the effectiveness of the Bank's operation.[109] The Court of Appeals, however, stressed the precise wording of Article XI, section 3 that contemplated suits brought in 'the territories of a member in which the Bank has an office' and which excluded only suits by Member States or persons acting for or deriving claims from members.[110] In the court's view, '[p]rovision for suit in *any* member country where the bank has an office must have been designed to facilitate suit for some class other than creditors and bondholders, *i.e.* borrowers'.[111]

As a result, the court affirmed that IFIs with 'immunity clauses' like the IDB do not enjoy broad immunity from suit in domestic courts. One can only speculate whether national courts would uphold this reasoning in similar cases brought against IFIs like the ADB or the AfDB. Because their constituent instruments provide for jurisdictional immunity except for actions involving the banks as 'borrower', the banks as lenders could still be regarded as immune from suits of the type in issues in the *Lutcher* case.

There is some support for such a restrictive interpretation of the 'borrowing exception' to the immunity of the AfDB in the Belgian case of *Scimet v. African Development Bank.*[112] The case was instituted by a Belgian company that had provided services to an AfDB-financed rainwater purification project in Chad. The court held the case inadmissible as a result of the Bank's immunity from jurisdiction. The claimant had tried to rely upon Article 52 of the AfDB Agreement which provided for 'immunity from every form of legal process except in cases arising out of the exercise of its borrowing powers'.[113] According to the Belgian court:

> the only exception to the immunity of the African Development Bank provided for in Article 52 of the Agreement concerns cases where the Bank obtains its own finance on the international capital markets in the Member States in question or elsewhere [. . .]. This exception has absolutely nothing to do with the present dispute. The broad interpretation of Article 52 proposed by the claimant cannot be accepted.[114]

---

108. *See* IDB Articles of Agreement, *supra* n. 3, Art. XI(3); IBRD Articles of Agreement, *supra* n. 2, Art. VII(3).
109. *Lutcher*, 382 F.2d at 456.
110. *Ibid.*, 458.
111. *Ibid.*
112. *Scimet v. African Development Bank*, Court of First Instance of Brussels, 14 Feb. 1997, 128 I.L.R. 582.
113. AfDB Articles of Agreement, *supra* n. 3, Art. 52 (*see* related text).
114. *Scimet*, 128 ILR at 585.

The *Scimet* case is also interesting because it discussed another possible restriction of the immunity of international organizations. The claimant argued that the Bank's immunity was in fact functionally limited and that because it had acted outside the performance of its functions it should not enjoy immunity. The claimant tried to derive the functional limitation of the Bank's jurisdictional immunity from a provision in the Bank's Agreement that referred to the functional rationale of its immunity. Article 50 of the AfDB Agreement provides:

> To enable it to fulfil its purpose and the functions with which it is entrusted, the Bank shall possess full international personality. To those ends, it may enter into agreements with members, non-member States and other international organizations. To the same ends, the status, immunities, exemptions and privileges set forth in this chapter shall be accorded to the Bank in the territory of each member.[115]

The Belgian court, however, held that:

> the text of Article 50 clearly indicates that the immunities conferred on the African Development Bank are intended to enable it to achieve its purpose and perform its functions but that the drafters of this provision thereby merely indicated the reason for granting the immunities in question, without intending to restrict their scope.[116]

Thereby it refused to read a functional limitation of immunity into the text of the AfDB Agreement, which speaks of a clearly unqualified immunity (with the exception of the Bank's borrowing powers), and merely linked it to the policy reason of why the bank should enjoy immunity in the first place. In addition, the court rejected the ultra vires argument as a matter of substance; it found that:

> by participating in a project with the object of furthering the economic and social development of Chad (purification of rainwater in the city of N'Djamena), and by cooperating with the African Development Fund, the defendant acted within the limits of its objects and functions.[117]

Also, the more recent US case law hints at a restrictive approach regarding the determination of the scope of the immunity waiver. As in the case of employment-related disputes, disputes relating to the core financial activities of IFIs raise the question whether a 'waiver of immunity' should be assumed in order to further the IFI's objectives as stated in the constituent agreements.[118]

---

115. AfDB Articles of Agreement, *supra* n. 3, Art. 50 (*see* related text).
116. *Scimet*, 128 ILR at 584.
117. *Ibid.*
118. *See* IMF Articles of Agreement, *supra* n. 2; IBRD Articles of Agreement, *supra* n. 2; IDA Articles of Agreement, *supra* n. 3; IDB Articles of Agreement, *supra* n. 3; EBRD Articles of Agreement, *supra* n. 3; ADB Articles of Agreement, *supra* n. 3; AfDB Articles of Agreement, *supra* n. 3; MIGA Convention, *supra* n. 3; IFC Articles of Agreement, *supra* n. 3.

For instance, in *Ashford v. World Bank Group et al.*[119] attention was paid to the benefits connected to a possible 'waiver of immunity' of the IBRD and the IDA, as members of the World Bank Group, and the IDB. The case related to the exercise of control over loan receiving nations during a bidding process. The international company Ashford was active in the field of information technology and participated in the bidding on contracts offered by nations that received loans from the IBRD, the IDA, and the IDB. Ashford alleged to have been disqualified despite having submitted the lowest bids and, therefore, accused the banks of having neglected their duty to monitor and oversee the bids, resulting in their liability for its disqualification.

Before the US court dismissed the action due to Ashford's failure to state an actionable claim, it elaborated on the scope of immunity to conclude that it was 'unlikely that the [banks] waived their immunity to suit'.[120] The analysis of the existence of an implicit waiver of immunity resulted in the rejection of the plaintiff's argument that this 'suit furthers [the banks'] stated objectives by holding [the banks] to their prescribed methods of overseeing the bid selection process'.[121] Rather, the court concluded that it 'seems more probable that it would not further each of the Bank's objectives to subject its internal policies relating to the selection process to oversight by the courts of one of its members'.[122]

The rather extraordinary *Atlantic Tele-Network v. Inter-American Development Bank*[123] case shares similarities to the *Lutcher* decision.[124] A telecommunications company, Atlantic, contested a loan agreement between the IDB and the Republic of Guyana. The case concerned the financing of a telecommunications system in addition to an already operating system built by Atlantic. The company feared that it would be deprived of recovering sums linked to the exclusive operation of the system in place since it was granted a fixed percentage on the return on capital investment of the exclusively operating local Guyanese telecom operating company. Accordingly, Atlantic sued the Republic of Guyana, the IDB, and two officials exercising control over the IDB lending activities for breach of contract. Although Atlantic acknowledged that the IDB enjoyed absolute immunity according to the IOIA,[125] it invoked a 'lending exception', that is a limited waiver of IDB's immunity according to Article XI, section 3 of the IDB Agreement.[126]

The court, however, rejected Atlantic's argument that 'this suit will aid the IDB in attracting responsible borrowers as well as encouraging American investment in developing nations generally'.[127] Rather, in the course of the

119. *Ashford v. The World Bank Group et al.*, 2006 U.S. Dist. LEXIS 17286 at 10 (N.D.Ga. 2006).
120. *Ibid.*
121. *Ibid.*, 11.
122. *Ibid.*
123. *Atlantic Tele-Network v. Inter-American Development Bank*, 251 F. Supp. 2d 126 (D.D.C. 2003).
124. *See Lutcher*, 382 F.2d 454.
125. *See* IOIA 1945, *supra* n. 33, Title I, s. 2(b).
126. This provision corresponds to IBRD Articles of Agreement, *supra* n. 2, Art. VII(3).
127. *Atlantic Tele-Network*, 251 F. Supp. 2d at 133.

assessment of costs and benefits of subjecting IDB to jurisdiction, it supported IDB's view that 'were this suit to be allowed, virtually any U.S. citizen with a commercial grievance against a debtor nation could challenge an IDB loan to that nation without any "corresponding benefit" accruing thereby to the IDB whatsoever'.[128]

One of the few cases where a US court ruled in favour of a waiver of immunity was the recent *Salah Osseiran v. IFC*[129] decision. A private investor alleged that the IFC was in breach of an agreement on the purchase of shares since it postponed its execution and finally entered into a stock-selling agreement with a third party. As a result, the investor alleged that this impeded his ability to gain the controlling shares in a merchant banking and investment company. Because the IFC had not explicitly waived its immunity, the court referred to Article VI, section 3, of the IFC Articles of Agreement[130] for its analysis of a possible implicit waiver. It examined the connection between the IFC's negotiations to obtain capital from a sale of stock and the IFC's overall purpose to 'contribute to the development of its member countries by making investments', to bring 'together investment opportunities, domestic and foreign private capital, and experienced management', and 'to stimulate, and to help create conditions conducive to, the flow of private capital, domestic and foreign, into the productive investment of member countries'.[131]

The court found that in accordance with *Atkinson*,[132] a '[w]aiver of immunity for litigation arising from transactions involving a sale of stock to a private investor provides a clear benefit in attracting additional investors willing to engage in financial transactions with IFC which would further development objectives'.[133] Thus, due to the 'innumerable benefits' which 'furthered [IFC's] objectives'[134] linked to the negotiation and consummation of sales of stock, the IFC immunity was regarded as waived. The material claim for the breach of a sales contract was rejected, as no binding sales agreement had been entered into by the parties. Yet, the court ruled in favour of the additional claims for the breach of the confidentiality agreement and for promissory estoppel.

Finally, an extraordinary decision by a US District Court directly addressed lending operations of an IFI. *Concesionaria DHM v. IFC*[135] supports the argument that immunity is not invoked in cases in which the lack of immunity is too obvious. In a dispute on the (unsubstantiated) failure to further disburse according to a loan agreement for a toll road construction project in Ecuador, the defendant, IFC, and the other lender, the Corporación Andina de Fomento, in fact, focused on possibilities other than immunity as the means by which to argue for dismissal of

128. *Ibid.*
129. *Salah Osseiran v. IFC*, 498 F.Supp. 2d 139 (D.D.C. 2007).
130. *See* IFC Articles of Agreement, *supra* n. 3, Art. VI(3).
131. The court explicitly referred to the IFC objectives as stated in Art. I of the IFC Articles of Agreement. *Osseiran*, 498 F.Supp. 2d at 144.
132. *See Atkinson*, 156 F 3d. 1335.
133. *Osseiran*, 498 F.Supp. 2d at 145.
134. *Ibid.*
135. *Concesionaria DHM v. IFC*, 307 F.Supp. 2d 553 (S.D.N.Y. 2004).

the claim. Yet, neither their improper venue contention nor the closely related forum non conveniens argument led to the dismissal of the breach of contract suit by the borrower *Concesionaria*, an Ecuadorian special purpose company.

VI. SPECIFIC CIRCUMSTANCES INVOLVING IFIs BEFORE NATIONAL COURTS

Obviously, the special status of IFIs may also be relevant in cases that neither fall into the category of employment disputes nor of typical 'core' financial activities of IFIs.

The early US case *International Bank for Reconstruction and Development and International Monetary Fund v. All America Cables & Radio, Inc. and Other Cable Companies*[136] defined the functional scope of an IFI and thus, implicitly, its breadth of immunity protection in the specific field of the determination of telecommunication rates payable by these organizations. The IMF and IBRD argued that privileges and immunities granted to international organizations served 'to protect the operation of these organizations from unreasonable interference (including protection against unreasonably high rates)'.[137] The defendant replied that 'there has been no showing that the Bank and the Fund need lower-than-commercial-rates to carry out their functions'.[138] While the US Federal Communications Commission (FCC) materially accepted the complaint by the IFIs and allowed them to continue to pay lower rates, it avoided a thorough discussion of the underlying functional immunity arguments.[139]

The IMF's absolute immunity from suit was implicitly recognized for instance in *Loughran, et al. v. United States.*[140] There, the owners of real property expropriated by the United States to allow construction of additional buildings for the IMF challenged this taking. In order to decide an interlocutory appeal, the DC Court of Appeals had to pass on the finality of the district court's taking judgment. It held that the intended immediate transfer of title to the IMF after the United States had validly acquired title as a result of the district court's judgment made this judgment a final one which was not appealable because the IMF was 'an entity which [was] immune from all judicial process of the United States'.[141]

In *Gruslin v. IBRD*,[142] a party dissatisfied with the outcome of an International Centre for Settlement of Investment Disputes (ICSID) arbitration challenged the result by claiming damages from the responsible IFI. However, the suit was bound

136. *Int'l Bank for Reconstruction & Development & International Monetary Fund v. All America Cables & Radio, Inc., et al.*, 22 I.L.R. 705 (1953).
137. 22 ILR at 709.
138. *Ibid.*
139. *Ibid.*, 711 et seq.
140. *Loughran, et al. v. United States*, 317 F.2d 896 (D.C. Cir. 1963).
141. *Ibid.*, 898.
142. *Philippe Gruslin v. La Banque Internationale pour la Reconstruction et le Développement*, Tribunal de première instance de Bruxelles, 72ème Chambre, 19 Aug. 2005 (not published).

to fail because the plaintiff selected the wrong organization: instead of suing ICSID, which is an independent international organization in itself, he chose to institute legal proceedings against the World Bank.[143] Despite close legal ties between the ICSID and the World Bank,[144] the Centre is an autonomous international organization, enjoying its own international legal personality.[145] Thus, lawsuits against the World Bank that concern arbitration or conciliation activities conducted under the auspices of the ICSID are directed against the wrong defendant. However, because of the ICSID's broad immunity from legal process actions against it are unlikely to succeed.[146]

In a few instances, IFIs are subject to regular tort claims, such as in *Robert A. Mitishen v. Otis Elevator Company and IBRD.*[147] There, an employee of the IBRD successfully filed a suit after an elevator accident had happened on the premises of the World Bank. The holding of the court confirmed the general restrictive immunity approach for IFIs as provided for in the applicable agreements, and therefore rejected the employee's claim for damages. The court specified that the plaintiff could only claim workers' compensation benefits, which were exclusive and replaced all liability of the employer in relation to the employee.[148]

VII. IFIs' INVOLVEMENT IN BANKRUPTCY PROCEEDINGS

Typically, parties try to argue that the immunity of IFIs should be waived because of their qualified involvement in the activities of their 'clients' subsequent to the initial agreement.[149] This argument has particular importance in bankruptcy proceedings where bankruptcy creditors are faced with the risk of being ultimately unable to recover assets.

A good example is provided by the bankruptcy proceedings before US courts in the *Kaiser*[150] case. It concerned the involvement of the IFC subsequent to the

143. *Gruslin v. Malaysia*, ICSID Case No. ARB/99/3; Award, 27 Nov. 2000, *available at* <http://ita.law.uvic.ca/documents/Philippe_Gruslin_v_Malaysia.pdf>.
144. *See* Christoph Schreuer, *The ICSID Convention: A Commentary* (Cambridge: Cambridge University Press, 2001), Comment 5 to Art. 2.
145. Pursuant to Art. 18 of the ICSID Convention, '[t]he Centre shall have full international legal personality'. Convention on the Settlement of Investment Disputes between States and Nationals of Other States, 575 U.N.T.S. 159; 4 ILM 532 (1965), Art. 18 (hereinafter ICSID Convention).
146. According to Art. 20 of the ICSID Convention, '[t]he Centre, its property and assets shall enjoy immunity from all legal process, except when the Centre waives this immunity'. *Ibid.*, Art. 20.
147. *Mitishen v. Otis Elevator Co. & IBRD*, 1990 U.S. Dist. LEXIS 12465 (D.D.C. 1990).
148. *Ibid.*, at 4.
149. An illustrative example is the previously discussed case *Ashford v. World Bank Group* (2006 U.S. Dist. LEXIS 17286), *see supra* n. 119.
150. In re: *Kaiser Group International, Inc., IFC v. Kaiser Group International, Inc. (Kaiser I)*, 302 B.R. 814 (D. Del. 2003), 2003 U.S. Dist. LEXIS 23852; In re: *Kaiser Group International, Inc., IFC v. Kaiser Group International, Inc. (Kaiser II)*, 308 B.R. 666 (D. Del. 2004), 2004

grant of a loan for a project relating to the construction of a steel mill in the Czech Republic. A construction agreement had been entered into by a subsidiary of Kaiser Group International Corporation (Kaiser) with the Czech company Nova Hut. The IFC had agreed to grant a secured loan to Nova Hut and had been accordingly assigned Nova Hut's rights and title to the steel mill. In the bankruptcy proceedings initiated by Kaiser, the IFC was accused of having allowed Nova Hut's improper draws on its letter of credit, and thus to have been actively involved in the financial collapse of the project.

Interestingly, the IFC did not straightforwardly invoke immunity, but filed a proof of claim because it sought recovery from Kaiser based on an assignment it had received from Nova Hut. However, the IFC stressed that in doing so, it did not consent to the jurisdiction of the claim with respect to Kaiser's accusations for the improper draw of the letter of credit. For this reason, the IFC filed a motion to dismiss the initial order of the US bankruptcy court.[151] While the Delaware District Court found that it needed supplementary information before it could ultimately decide on the matter, it emphasized that the IFC had waived its immunity because it had actively participated in the bankruptcy proceedings through the filing of the proof of claim.[152]

The dispute continued before the same court a few months later[153] and again the court relied on procedural aspects specific to the United States to rule that Kaiser's counterclaims were not covered by the waiver of IFC's immunity. On appeal by Kaiser, the US Court of Appeals for the Third Circuit[154] reversed the District Court's judgment and remanded the case to the Delaware bankruptcy court for a decision on the merits.[155]

U.S. Dist. LEXIS 3098; In re: *Kaiser Group International, Inc., IFC v. Kaiser Group International, Inc. (Kaiser III)*, 399 F.3d 588 (3rd Cir. 2005); 2005 U.S. App. LEXIS 3288; 60 Fed. R. Serv. 3d (Callaghan) 1153; Bankr.L.Rep (CCH) P80, 244; 44 Bankr. Ct. Dec. 89.

151. *Kaiser I*, 302 B.R. 814.
152. This waiver of immunity is explicitly provided for in US bankruptcy law. Section 106(b) of the US Bankruptcy Code stipulates that when in bankruptcy proceedings a 'governmental unit' has filed a proof of claim, a waiver of its 'sovereign immunity' is to be assumed in relation to a claim 'that is the property of the estate' and 'that arose out of the same transaction or occurrence out of which the claim of such governmental unit arose'. Therefore, the subsequent bankruptcy proceedings focussed precisely on these two elements, that is the 'property of the estate' and the 'same transaction or occurrence requirement'.
153. *Kaiser II*, 308 B.R. 666.
154. *Kaiser III*, 399 F.3d 588.
155. While no evidence of the Delaware bankruptcy court's holding in relation to the IFC in this context is retrievable, the developments relating to Nova Hut before the Delaware court are remarkable and are influenced by the resort to arbitration by Kaiser. On 2 Jan. 2004, the Kaiser subsidiary Kaiser Netherlands filed a request for arbitration with the International Chamber of Commerce, which ultimately resulted in an Arbitration Award of 26 Apr. 2006. Therefore, in in re: *Kaiser Group International, Kaiser Group International, Inc. v. Nova Hut* (307 B.R. 449 (D. Del. 2004)) the advisory proceedings initiated by Kaiser were stayed. However, the role of the legal counsel and the allegation of its improper influence on the outcome of the arbitration was again subject matter before the Delaware District Court (In re: *Kaiser Group International, Kaiser Group International, Inc. v. Nova Hut*, 2007 Bankr. LEXIS 2256

The IFC was also involved as a bankruptcy creditor in one of the most publicly discussed bankruptcy cases in the United States at the turn of the century, the collapse of the American energy company Enron Corporation (Enron) in 2001. This case related to Enron's attempt to recover certain initially made transfers. Enron had instituted adversary proceedings against the IFC which had acquired securities as a 'mediate transferee'. The first decision, *Enron Corp v. IFC*,[156] rejected the recovery attempt directed against the IFC because it did not address the annulment of the initial transfers. Unsurprisingly, this result was confirmed in the appeal before the US District Court of the Southern District of Delaware.[157] Even though the *Enron v. IFC* decisions did not particularly consider questions of immunity of an IFI, they nonetheless serve as an example for the breadth of the involvement of IFIs in domestic (bankruptcy) proceedings.

While not a bankruptcy case *stricto sensu*, the determination of the scope of the waiver of the EBRD was subject matter in the *Bro Tech v. EBRD* case.[158] The EBRD had agreed to invest in a Romanian joint venture for the production of ion exchange materials, which led to the creation of Virolite, a joint stock company according to Romanian law. The EBRD's involvement was in accordance with its purpose to promote private and entrepreneurial initiatives in the countries of Central and Eastern Europe.[159]

At the brink of Virolite's insolvency, the other parties involved in the venture – entrepreneurs of US origin – were faced with EBRD's refusal to re-finance. EBRD, together with another private investment corporation, initiated insolvency procedures against Virolite in Romania. At the same time, the suit before the US court directed against the EBRD claimed breach of loyalty vis-à-vis the other joint venturers, such as the breach of the joint venturer's fiduciary duty, tortuous interference, and conspiracy.

The US court first referred to Article 46 of the EBRD Agreement[160] in order to analyse the requirements of a waiver of the EBRD's immunity. The court relied on the *Atkinson* rationale for the determination of a waiver of immunity and accordingly found that the 'corresponding benefit' to allow a waiver was to enable the

---

(D. Del. 2007)). Yet, the court found that the legal counsels did not violate their obligations. The most recent decision of the Delaware bankruptcy court (in re: *Kaiser Group International, Kaiser Group International, Inc. v. Nova Hut*, 2007 Bankr. LEXIS 3035 (D. Del. 2007)) addressed the specific issue of the parties' motions for summary judgment in the light of the allegation that Kaiser tried to enforce only parts of the Arbitration Award. The court still did not finally decide on the matter, but found that there were genuine issues of material fact left to be decided.

156. *Enron Corp. v. IFC*, 2006 Bankr. LEXIS 800 (S.D.N.Y. 2006).
157. *Enron Corp. v. IFC*, U.S. Dist. LEXIS 75626 (S.D.N.Y. 2007).
158. *Bro Tech v. EBRD*, 2000 U.S. Dist. LEXIS 17049 (E.D. Pa. 2000).
159. *Cf.* EBRD Agreement, *supra* n. 3. It states in its first Article that '[i]n contributing to economic progress and reconstruction, the purpose of the Bank shall be to foster the transition towards open market-oriented economies and to promote private and entrepreneurial initiative in Central and Eastern European countries committed to and applying the principles of multi-party democracy, pluralism and market economics'.
160. *See* EBRD Agreement, *supra* n. 3, Art. 46.

EBRD to 'function on the international, commercial marketplace'.[161] Therefore, an immunity waiver was, in principle, conceivable.

Curiously, the court then turned to an arbitration agreement concluded between the parties[162] in order to determine the scope of the waiver of immunity. In its relevant clause, the agreement stated that any 'dispute, controversy, or claim arising out of, or relating to, this Agreement, or the breach, termination or invalidity thereof, shall be referred to and finally resolved in' arbitration. Therefore, the court found in a rather misleading formulation that the 'EBRD's waiver is limited, and that the EBRD had only waived its immunity with respect to the resolution of disputes through arbitration'.[163] The court then found that '[b]ecause all of the claims are controlled by the arbitration clauses',[164] subject matter jurisdiction was denied.

The wording does not reveal whether the court's approach could be viewed as giving the arbitration agreement a *lex specialis* character in relation to the immunity waiver provisions contained in the EBRD Articles of Agreement. The reference to an arbitration clause as an 'interpretative tool' in order to determine the scope of the waiver of immunity was certainly atypical and the conclusion that the court had no jurisdiction is hard to reconcile with its assertion that the Bank had waived its immunity in the limited field in issue.

Different approaches can be identified with regard to the general relationship between an arbitration clause and the scope of immunity of a (financial) organization. While in a few instances, express references to immunity rules exist,[165] it is disputed whether in the absence of such provisions, an arbitration clause, as such, amounts to an implicit waiver of immunity. Even if this view is accepted, the extent of immunity granted to the organization is controversial. It is thus in most cases necessary to identify whether the arbitral agreement entered into by an organization can be interpreted as a waiver of immunity, either in relation to the usual legal supervision of such arbitral proceedings and/or for the enforcement of the final award.

Some scholars link the existence of an implicit immunity waiver to a specific constellation. Domestic jurisdiction is said to exist only if a choice of law rule is included that provides that the arbitration procedure itself should be governed by a particular domestic law.[166] This view is primarily based on the French case,

161. *Bro Tech*, 2000 U.S. Dist. LEXIS 17049 at 16.

162. EBRD invoked two agreements, the 'Amended and Restated Cooperation Agreement for Virolite Functional Polymers S.A.' (Amended Agreement), and the Transformation Contract for the Transformation of Purolite International Polimeri Functional SRL into a Joint Stock Company Called Virolite Functional Polymers S.A. (Transformation Contract).

163. *Bro Tech*, 2000 U.S. Dist. LEXIS 17049 at 23.

164. *Ibid.*, 24.

165. Such a rare example is, for example, Art. 6(1) of the International Tin Council Order 1972 (Privileges and Immunities), which provides for the International Tin Council's immunity from suit and legal process 'except: (a) to the extent that [the ITC] shall have expressly waived such immunity in a particular case [. . .] and (c) in respect of the enforcement of an arbitration award'.

166. *See* for instance, Christian Dominicé, 'L'arbitrage et les immunités des organisations internationales', in *Etudes de droit international en l'honneur de Pierre Lalive*, ed. Christian

Beaudice v. ASCENA,[167] in which an appellate court held that rules on the choice of law were also decisive for the exercise of judicial control over the arbitration.[168] Thus, the cautious approach on the qualification of the impact of the arbitration award on the EBRD immunity by the US court in the *Bro-Tech* case corresponds with the more prudent interpretation exemplified by the *ASCENA* case.[169]

Finally, in *Banco de Seguros v. IFC*[170] the collapse of a Uruguayan bank (Banco Montevideo SA) raised the question of whether third parties could involve an IFI in disputes before national courts based on the specific relationship of an IFI to their contracting party. In this case, Banco Montevideo was involved in irregular banking transactions, notably the allowance of improper loans to insiders. The breach of banking procedures through wilful and intentional activities of

---

Dominicé, Robert Patry & Claude Raymond (Basel, Switzerland, Frankfurt am Main: Helbing & Lichtenhahn, 1993), 492. Support of this view can be inferred from case law which links the explicit choice of a specific domestic law with the establishment of domestic jurisdiction of an international organization. For instance, in *Standard Chartered Bank v. ITC and Other*, 77 I.L.R. 8 (1986), the ITC agreed to English law and jurisdiction of English courts by means of a facility later in relation to a loan agreement. Others reject that the choice of domestic law rule relating to arbitral proceedings should be interpreted as an implicit waiver of immunity for international organizations, for example, *see* Loquin, *Journal du droit international* 106 (Clunet, 1979): 135.

167. Cour d'Appel de Paris, 25 Nov. 1977. In this case, an employment dispute between a technician and the Agency for the safety of air navigation in Africa and Madagascar (Agence pour la sécurité de la navigation aérienne en Afrique et Madagascar, ASCENA) was brought before the President of the Administrative Tribunal of Paris as an arbitrator. On appeal against the arbitral decision, the French court upheld jurisdiction. It thus decided that the rule of the ASCENA employment contract on the nomination for an arbitrator permitted French law to govern the arbitral procedure and that therefore the recourse to domestic courts was admitted.

168. There are only a limited number of cases that relate to the choice of law rules contained in arbitral agreements and its interpretation as an implicit waiver of immunity for international organizations. This conclusion can for instance be inferred *e contrario* from the *UNRWA v. General Trading and Transport Co.* (the *Rice)* case, an Arbitration Award of 1958 (*cf. Yearbook of the International Law Commission*, vol. II (New York: United Nations, 1967), 208), in which the arbitrator excluded domestic jurisdiction because the arbitration clause between the United Nations Relief and Work Agency for Palestine in the Near East (UNWRA) and a private party was based in, and thus governed by, international law and not a national system of law. Accordingly, the recourse to a domestic judge to adjudicate the subject matter was barred. In the *Centre pour le développement industriel (CDI) v. X* case of 13 Mar. 1992, the Tribunal Civil de Bruxelles held that the CDI had waived its immunity from jurisdiction by agreeing to arbitration. Therefore, the lower court's *exequatur* order was valid, which resulted in the enforcement of an arbitral award against the organization. Similarly, in *ITC v. Amalgamet Inc.*, 80 I.L.R. 31 (N.Y. 1988), the New York Supreme Court qualified the entering into an arbitration agreement on the subject matter of the dispute as a waiver of immunity of the ITC.

169. Interestingly, only a relatively small number of arbitral decisions involve international organizations, which is even more surprising as arbitration clauses are frequently included in contracts of international organizations with mostly private third parties. *Cf.* August Reinisch, *International Organizations before National Courts*, *supra* n. 11, 266.

170. *Banco de Seguros del Estado v. IFC*, U.S. Dist. LEXIS 69741 (S.D.N.Y. 2007).

directors and shareholders reached a severe criminal level and resulted in the bank's liquidation being ordered by the Uruguayan Central Bank.

One of the creditors of the bank, Banco de Seguros, filed a suit against the IFC. It argued that the IFC owned shares of the Banco Montevideo and was entitled to participation through the appointment of a director on the board of directors. Thus, liability of the IFC was invoked as it had 'failed to supervise the functioning of the bank and neglected to appoint a director as its investment agreement authorized it to do'.[171] The US District Court for the Southern District of New York rejected this reasoning and referred to functionality considerations to emphasize the immunity of the IFC. Because Banco de Seguros did not belong to 'the types of persons, and their claims are not the types of claims for which IFC has waived immunity in Article VI Section 3 of its Articles of Agreement',[172] the IFC had to remain immune from suit. While it is difficult to draw further conclusions from this decision, it nevertheless underlines the unwillingness of this domestic court to extend the restricted scope of a waiver of immunity to third parties, notably if they claim to be related to an IFI by means of the IFI's liability.

VIII. CONCLUSION

Domestic cases involving IFIs help to highlight problems relating to their specific legal position, which is decisively shaped by their financial activities. As the UK decisions in *Hashim v. AMF* aptly demonstrated, IFIs' domestic legal personality can be central to a dispute if the forum state is not a member of the IFI in question.

The definition of the exact scope of immunity is particularly critical in the context of employment disputes brought against IFIs. Usually, staff members of an international organization are impeded to bring actions against their employer organization in domestic courts and have to bring their claims before administrative tribunals. The restricted scope of the immunity of IFIs in this context necessitates a differentiated approach by national courts. Traditionally, policy considerations have led to the recognition of immunity in staff disputes.

The analysis of domestic cases involving IFIs provides evidence for the typical balancing act a national judge is faced with when dealing with IFIs. Because their scope of immunity is less wide when compared to other international organizations, domestic courts tend to interpret the remaining immunity broadly in order to abstain from adjudicating such disputes. This analysis is subject to subsequent modifications which take into account the existence of 'internal' administrative disputes settlement systems, as evidenced by the leading *Mendaro* case.

---

171. *Ibid.*, 9.
172. *Ibid.*, 23. The text of Art. VI, s. 3 of the IFC Articles of Agreement is identical to the wording of Art. VII, s. 3 of the IBRD Articles of Agreement. *See* IBRD Articles of Agreement, *supra* n. 2, Art. VII(3).

Sometimes, arguments in favour of a waiver of immunity relate to the purpose of IFIs and stress the duty of an IFI to supervise the activities of their contractual partners following the initial agreement. This line of reasoning can notably be retraced in US cases, such as *Ashford* and the *Kaiser* bankruptcy proceedings.

Starting with the 1998 *Atkinson* case, a recent strand of US case law particularly emphasizes functional aspects in determining the restricted immunity of IFIs. These cases typically allude to the purpose of the activity of an IFI as stated in its governing instruments and regularly stress that the IFI's immunity 'should be construed as *not waived* unless the particular type of suit would further its objectives'.[173] Accordingly, US courts have fine-tuned the assessment of objectives as a decisive factor for the determination of the immunity of IFIs. Clearly, their constituent treaties provide the key benchmarks. Yet, the development of this field is illustrated by the fact that the analysis regularly does not merely include a simple reference to the Articles of Agreement or the Headquarters Agreement. Rather, the courts typically apply a cost-benefit assessment of whether the burden of allowing the suit in a particular circumstance is outweighed by an additional benefit that furthers the development of the bank's objectives.

In Europe, following the *Waite and Kennedy* jurisprudence of the European Court of Human Rights, the link between immunity and denial of justice considerations has been emphasized by some national courts. According to this reasoning, immunity should be denied when no other 'reasonable alternative means' to pursue claims exist. While the Belgian appellate court ruling in *Siedler v. Western European Union* relied on denial of justice considerations in accordance with ECHR, Article 6(1), the French Supreme Court decision in *Banque africaine de développement v. M.A. Degboe*, referred to denial of justice as an element of an '*ordre public international*'.

The assessment of the case law does not allow a definite answer on the further development of the immunity of IFIs. US courts seem to broaden their immunity by adding further restrictive criteria for the assessment of a 'waiver' or 'implicit waiver' derived from their constituent instruments. Courts in Europe start to follow the *Waite and Kennedy* jurisprudence and to support an exemption from immunity when otherwise a severe interference of the rights of the party is at stake. According to the most pronounced view, the level of the infringement must amount to a violation of the '*ordre public international*'.

173. *Atkinson*, 156 F.3d at 1338.

Chapter 5

Rethinking International Financial Institution Immunity

Steven Herz

At this point, it is pretty much taken for granted that International Financial Institutions (IFIs) enjoy broad immunity from suit in national courts. In theory at least, this immunity is limited to what is 'functionally necessary' for IFIs to discharge their delegated responsibilities effectively and to achieve the agreed upon objectives of their Member States. The 'functional necessity' standard could provide a useful framework in which to balance the operational requirements of IFIs against other competing social values, such as fairness to private litigants and accountability under the rule of law. In practice, however, IFIs – including those whose charters clearly contemplate that they will be sued in national courts – have insisted that only absolute or near-absolute immunity can sufficiently protect them from the burdens of judicial scrutiny. And courts have tended to honour these assertions without fully considering their theoretical justifications or weighing competing normative or policy considerations.[1] As a result, courts in many countries have conflated 'functional necessity' with a presumption of absolute immunity, and have refused to exercise jurisdiction in cases in which the organization has not waived its immunity.

---

1. For a thorough review of litigation against IFIs in national courts, *see* August Reinisch & Jakob Wurm, 'International Financial Institutions before National Courts', Ch. 4 herein.

Daniel D. Bradlow and David B. Hunter, *International Financial Institutions and International Law*, pp. 137–165.

As the 'functional necessity' standard suggests, however, jurisdictional immunity is just a tool to help IFIs fulfil their organizational objectives – it is not an end in itself. It is therefore worth considering whether expansive protections from national jurisdiction are consistent with other legal norms, policy priorities, and public expectations that may dictate narrower immunity. In my view, absolute or near-absolute immunity cannot be reconciled with basic principles regarding the legal obligations and public accountability of international organizations. These include that: (1) IFIs have obligations to individuals under international law and should be responsible when they violate them; (2) sovereigns, and entities that derive their authority from sovereigns, are not above the rule of law and therefore generally are not afforded absolute immunity; (3) individuals are entitled to minimum standards of procedural fairness, including access to justice, in resolving claims against public entities; and (4) IFIs derive their legitimacy in part by providing meaningful opportunities for citizens to directly hold them to account. In order to give these principles their appropriate effect, IFIs should not be swaddled in broader jurisdictional immunity than is provided for in their charters or is strictly necessary for them to achieve their organizational objectives, and should only receive immunity when alternative avenues of redress are available that can adequately serve these principles.

Unfortunately, no such alternative mechanisms currently exist. Although most IFIs have created quasi-independent compliance and/or dispute resolution mechanisms to address citizen complaints, they lack some of the basic hallmarks of a fair judicial process.[2] They do not have the mandate to address violations of international or domestic law, and can only consider whether the institution has complied with its internal operational policies and procedures. Moreover, they have no remedial powers of any kind – they cannot award monetary damages or provide injunctive relief. As such, they are incapable of providing the kind of access to justice under the rule of law that would qualify them to be considered an equivalent, alternative mechanism of redress.

The combination of expansive immunity and the absence of an alternative mechanism of recourse enables IFIs to operate largely outside of the strictures of legal obligation and direct citizen accountability. This gap should be rectified in one of two ways – either IFIs should strengthen their existing accountability mechanisms to allow them to hear legal claims and to provide appropriate remedies, or they should be required to submit to the jurisdiction of local courts to resolve these claims.

Concerns that less expansive immunity would open the door to a flood of litigation that could cripple IFIs' ability to achieve their public purposes can be discounted for three reasons. First, while IFIs would lose the presumption of near-absolute immunity, they would retain the immunities they actually need to achieve their organizational objectives. An IFI would not be subject to jurisdiction where it can show that its organizational objectives would be compromised if it were

2. For further discussion of IFI accountability mechanisms, *see* Eisuke Suzuki, 'Responsibility of International Financial Institutions under International Law', Ch. 3 herein.

required to defend itself in court. Second, an IFI could still avoid jurisdiction by creating (or submitting to) an effective, alternative mechanism to hear complaints and provide redress. Jurisdiction would only be imposed where adequate alternative mechanisms are not in place. Finally, it is important to remember that immunity is only a threshold question that enables a court to hear a claim at issue. Applying a more restrictive understanding of IFI immunity would not lessen any of the other procedural or substantive hurdles that a plaintiff must overcome to prove a cause of action and win a judgment. In many cases, these are likely to be daunting. For example, IFIs traditionally act by providing financial or technical assistance to governments or private-sector actors. When one of these third parties has caused the harm at issue, the plaintiff may have to offer a persuasive theory why the IFI should be responsible, notwithstanding the traditional presumption against lender liability. Such procedural and substantive hurdles will not only deter spurious claims, but provide courts with ample tools to dismiss non-meritorious claims at early stages of litigation.

I. THE PUBLIC ACCOUNTABILITY OF IFIs

Traditionally, public accountability of international organizations was entirely political and narrowly circumscribed. International organizations were thought to be accountable only to their Member States, who could assert their interests through the formal governance mechanisms of the organization. In the absence of an express relationship with the organization – such as membership or privity of contract – individuals and other non-state actors could not directly hold an institution accountable without the institution's consent.[3] Rather, they could only influence policy or practice, or seek redress by petitioning their government representatives to act on their behalf.[4]

Under this traditional approach, accountability to non-state actors was virtually non-existent. Although international organizations were understood to be creatures of international law and to enjoy international legal personality, their obligations under international law were narrowly circumscribed. The prevailing view, promulgated largely by the organizations themselves, was that their obligations were limited to those specifically provided for in their charters, or in other treaties and conventions to which they had formally acceded.[5] In particular, they

3. Daniel D. Bradlow, remarks in 'The Accountability of International Organizations to Non-state Actors', *American Society of International Law Proceedings* 92 (1–4 Apr. 1998): 359.
4. *Ibid.*
5. Francois Gianviti, 'Economic, Social, and Cultural Human Rights and the International Monetary Fund', in *Non-state Actors and Human Rights*, ed. Philip Alston (Oxford: Oxford University Press, 2005), 113–138. Gianviti is ambiguous as to the IMF's obligations under customary or general international law. Gianviti, 'Economic, Social, and Cultural Human Rights and the International Monetary Fund', 122. The views of the former General Counsel of the World Bank can be found at Ibrahim Shihata, 'The World Bank and Human Rights', presented at the International Commission of Jurists Conference on Economic, Social, and Cultural Rights

denied any obligations under treaties and conventions to which the IFIs are not parties, including those that protect individual interests, including human rights conventions.[6]

The traditional understanding of international organization accountability was largely a function of a particular approach to international law that was ascendant in the middle of the twentieth century, when the most important international organizations were created and flourished. Under this view, international law was concerned only with the rights and remedies of sovereign states in their interactions with each other.[7] States were seen as the sole source and repository of legitimate authority. Sovereignty was inviolable within a state's territory, and constrained by international law only by consent.[8] Individuals and other non-state actors were beyond the ken of international law.[9] Because states were the only legitimate subjects of international law, and therefore the exclusive representative of their citizens' interests on the international stage, it was up to the state to press any international law claims on behalf of its aggrieved citizens.[10]

Ironically, the edifice of an exclusively state-centred international law was already starting to crumble in the immediate aftermath of World War II, when the most important international organizations were being created. As Harold Koh has explained, the war crimes tribunals in Nuremberg and Tokyo began the recovery of a lost tradition in international law in which rights of individuals and the responsibilities of public officials were legitimate foci of attention.[11] In so doing, they 'pierced the veil of state sovereignty and dispelled the myth that international law is for states only . . . . Thereafter, private citizens, government officials, nongovernmental organizations and multinational enterprises could all be rightsholders and

---

(Abidjan, 1998), 145; Ibrahim F. I. Shihata, 'Human Rights, Development, and International Financial Institutions', *American University Journal of International Law & Policy* 8 (1992): 28 (arguing that the World Bank's Articles of Agreement preclude the Bank from applying certain human rights norms in its operations).

6. Gianviti, 'Economic, Social, and Cultural Human Rights and the International Monetary Fund', *supra* n. 5, 113–138 (denying that the International Covenant on Economic, Social, and Cultural has any legal effect on the IMF).
7. Lea Brilmayer, 'International Law in American Courts: A Modest Proposal', *Yale Law Journal* 100 (1991): 2292; Philip Jessup, *A Modern Law of Nations* (New York: Macmillan Co., 1952), 2, 8, 15.
8. Louis Henkin, 'Human Rights and State "Sovereignty"', *Georgia Journal of International and Comparative Law* 25 (1995/96): 31–32.
9. Brilmayer, *supra* n. 7, 2292.
10. *Banco Nacional de Cuba v. Sabbatino*, 376 U.S. 398, 422–423 (1964) ('Because of [international law's] peculiar nation-to-nation character the usual method for an individual to seek relief is to exhaust local remedies and then repair to the executive authorities of his own state to persuade them to champion his claim in diplomacy or before an international tribunal.').
11. Koh notes, for example, that the 'law of nations' had long included bodies of maritime and merchant law, and had recognized piracy and slave trading as international crimes, even though they were committed by individuals against other individuals. Harold Hongju Koh, 'Transnational Public Law Litigation', *Yale Law Journal* 100 (1991): 2351–2354, 2358–2359, fn. 66.

responsible actors under international law . . . '.[12] At the same time, the newly ratified United Nations Charter – with its recognition of the importance of human rights and its express commitments by Member States to cooperate in promoting respect for those rights – further reinforced the idea that the treatment of individuals was a matter of international concern.[13] Since then, it has become generally accepted that international law affords legal rights to individuals, including claims by citizens against their own governments.[14]

The expanded recognition of the individual as a rightsholder and legitimate object of concern under international law came with a concomitant reduction in the inviolability of state sovereignty. Thus, the post-war era saw a marked decline in the sanctity of sovereignty as the central organizing principle of international law and relations.[15] This decline has manifested itself in a number of ways,[16] of which four are particularly relevant to the accountability and jurisdictional immunity of IFIs. First, as we have seen, a state's autonomy within its territorial borders is no longer absolute. At least in principle (if not always in practice), state action is now circumscribed by the recognition that international human rights law can legitimately address the manner in which a government treats its own citizens.[17] Similarly, state action is also increasingly subject to an emerging body of international development law, which defines the rights and obligations of states and non-state

12. *Ibid.*, 2358–2359; *see also* Henkin, *supra* n. 8, 31; Mark Janis, *An Introduction to International Law* (Boston, MA: Little, Brown, 1988), 174.
13. Charter of the United Nations, Arts 1, 55, 56 (26 Jun. 1945), *available at* <www.un.org/en/documents/charter/index.shtml> (hereinafter UN Charter); Henkin, supra n. 8, 34. *See also* Universal Declaration of Human Rights, G.A. Res. 217 A (III) (10 Dec. 1948), *available at* <www.un.org/en/documents/udhr/>; Convention on the Prevention and Punishment of the Crime of Genocide, Approved and proposed for signature and ratification or accession by G.A. Res. 260 A (III) of 9 Dec. 1948 (entry into force 12 Jan. 1951).
14. *Restatement (Third) of Foreign Relations Law of the United States* (Philadelphia: American Law Institute, 1987), Pt II, introductory note Pt VII, introductory note, § 1 comment a, § 703(3), § 906; August Reinisch, 'The Changing International Legal Framework for Dealing with Non-state Actors', in *Non-state Actors and Human Rights*, ed. Philip Alston (Oxford: Oxford University Press, 2005), 38; Brilmayer, *supra* n. 7, 2287, 2295.
15. As Jessica Mathews has explained, '[t]he absolutes of the Westphalian system – territorially fixed states where everything of value lies within some state's borders; a single, secular authority governing each territory and representing it outside its borders; and no authority above states – are all dissolving'. Jessica Mathews, 'Power Shift', *Foreign Affairs* 76 (1997): 50. *See also* Reinisch, 'The Changing International Legal Framework for Dealing with Non-state Actors', *supra* n. 14, 74 (describing 'a major structural change in the international legal order: the decrease and partial disappearance of the state as a mediating institution between the international law level and the rights and duties of non-state actors'.); Henkin, *supra* n. 8, 32–33.
16. There is a rich, multidisciplinary literature concerning the decline of the power and authority of states. *See, e.g.*, Reinisch, 'The Changing International Legal Framework for Dealing with Non-state Actors', *supra* n. 14, 74, fn. 190 (citing a range of representative work); *see also* Oscar Schacter, 'The Decline of the Nation-State and its Implications for International Law', *Columbia Journal of Transnational Law* 36 (1997): 7 (including sources cited therein).
17. Henkin, *supra* n. 8, 32–33.

actors in the development process by reference to international trade, human rights, and environmental law principles.[18]

Second, states are no longer thought to have unfettered discretion in how they organize their governmental processes. As fundamental civil and political rights have become increasingly well-established, a normative expectation (if not yet a clear legal requirement) has emerged that the exercise of sovereign power must be legitimized by the consent of the governed through democratic processes.[19] Democratic governance, in all of its forms, has accordingly become the benchmark of political legitimacy – there are no longer any widely-accepted alternatives.[20]

Third, states' traditional role as the sole legitimate representatives of their people in international relations has been challenged by the emergence of transnational civil society.[21] Although states continue to lead in articulating and representing their national interests, citizens are increasingly bypassing their government representatives and asserting their interests in international fora through non-governmental organizations and social movements that they believe more reliably or effectively articulate their interests.[22] As a result, states must now share the stage with a variety of non-state actors, many of whom may have markedly different priorities or conceptions of the public good.

Finally, the expansive deference states once enjoyed in the courts of other countries has been substantially curtailed. As Michael Singer has explained, courts

---

18. Daniel D. Bradlow, 'Development Decision-Making and the Content of International Development Law', *Boston College International and Comparative Law Review* 27 (2004): 195; Gunther Handl, 'The Legal Mandate of Multilateral Development Banks as Agents for Change Toward Sustainable Development', *American Journal of International Law* 92 (1998): 662 ('It cannot be denied, first, that there exists today a growing and ever more specific body of norms of international law bearing on "sustainable development;" and second, that a large number of these concepts clearly represent affirmative duties incumbent upon states and international institutions . . . ').
19. Thomas Franck, 'The Emerging Right to Democratic Governance', *American Journal of International Law* 86 (1992): 46. For a discussion of the norm of democratic governance in international law, including some skeptical perspectives, *see* Greg H. Fox & Brad R. Roth (eds), *Democratic Governance and International Law* (Cambridge: Cambridge University Press, 2000).
20. Freedom House, 'Democracy's Century: A Survey of Global Political Change in the 20th Century', <www.freedomhouse.org/reports/century.pdf>, 1999; United Nations Development Program (UNDP), 'Human Development Report 2002: Deepening Democracy in a Fragmented World' (2002), 1; Fareed Zakaria, 'The Rise of Illiberal Democracy', *Foreign Affairs* (November/December 1997).
21. Mathews, *supra* n. 15, 50; United Nations Commission on Global Governance, 'Our Global Neighborhood' (1995), 6; Myres S. McDougal et al., *Human Rights and World Public Order: The Basic Policies of an International Law of Human Dignity* (Connecticut: Yale University Press, 1980). Robert O'Brien et al., *Contesting Global Governance: Multilateral Economic Institutions and Global Social Movements* (Cambridge: Cambridge University Press, 2000), 3.
22. *E.g.*, civil society organizations have been instrumental in placing issues of pressing concern on the global agenda – including climate change, human rights, gender equity, AIDS, and debt relief – and have effectively mobilized public opinion to demand that they are adequately addressed. United Nations Panel of Eminent Persons on United Nations – Civil Society Relations, 'We the Peoples: Civil Society, the United Nations and Global Governance' (June 2004), 26.

no longer treat sovereigns 'as if they had emerged from the pages of Shakespeare crowned, robed and preceded by trumpets'.[23] Rather, increased concern with fairness to private litigants,[24] and a growing discomfort with broadly exempting governments from the rule of law and from popular moral judgment, has led to a more restrictive understanding of the proper scope of sovereign immunity.[25] As a result, there has been a considerable expansion of the use of 'transnational public law litigation', in which individuals seek to obtain compensation and redress, vindicate public rights, and facilitate the development of international legal norms through judicial findings of international law violations.[26] Perhaps the most important manifestation of this trend is the *Filártiga* line of cases under the Alien Tort Claims Act (ATCA), in which foreign nationals have used US courts to bring human rights cases against corporations and foreign government officials.[27]

As these developments have displaced the state-centred approach to international law, they have also largely discredited the traditional understanding of international organization accountability. IFIs can no longer claim public legitimacy or accountability exclusively through the participation of Member States in their formal governance structures.[28] First, as democracy has become the litmus

---

23. Michael Singer, 'Jurisdictional Immunity of International Organizations: Human Rights and Functional Necessity Concerns', *Virginia Journal of International Law* 36 (1995): 141.
24. *E.g.*, the Universal Declaration of Human Rights, *supra* n. 13, Art. 10; the International Covenant on Civil and Political Rights, G.A. Res. 2200A (XXI), U.N. Doc. A/6316 (1966), 999 U.N.T.S. 171 (23 Mar. 1976), Art. 14(1), *available at* <www1.umn.edu/humanrts/instree/b3ccpr.htm>; Council of Europe, The European Convention on Human Rights (Rome, 4 Nov. 1950), Art. 6(1), *available at* <www.hri.org/docs/ECHR50.html#Convention>. Each provide for a right to access to a court for the determination of rights and obligations. *See* August Reinisch, *International Organizations before National Courts* (Cambridge: Cambridge University Press, 2000), 281–282 (discussing the contradiction between the international law-based human right to access to courts and the restriction of such access through expansive grants of immunity).
25. *National City Bank v. Republic of China*, 348 U.S. 356, 359 (1955) (sovereign immunity 'has increasingly been found to be in conflict with the growing subjection of governmental action to the moral judgement'); Reinisch, *International Organizations before National Courts*, *supra* n. 24, 287 (discussing a 'growing consensus that measures aimed at . . . immunizing certain persons from their accountability or responsibility [have] become less and less acceptable under current human rights standards'.). Michael H. Cardozo, 'Sovereign Immunity: The Plaintiff Deserves a Day in Court', *Harvard Law Review* 67 (1954): 608 (arguing that concern with the rights of private litigants should inform the Court's approach to sovereign immunity); Hersch Lauterpacht, 'The Problem of Jurisdictional Immunities of Foreign States', *British Yearbook of International Law* 28 (1951): 22.
26. Koh, 'Transnational Public Law Litigation', *supra* n. 11, 2349, 2368.
27. *Filártiga v. Peña-Irala*, 630 F.2d 876 (2d Cir. 1980). For an analysis of current ATCA jurisprudence, *see* Beth Stephens, 'Sosa v. Alvarez-Machain: "The Door Is Still Ajar" for Human Rights Litigation in U.S. Courts', *Brooklyn Law Review* 70 (2005): 533.
28. Benedict Kingsbury, Nico Krisch & Richard Stewart, 'The Emergence of Global Administrative Law', *Law & Contemporary Problems* 68 (Summer/Autumn 2005): 26 ('In our view, international lawyers can no longer credibly argue that there are no real democracy or legitimacy deficits in global administrative governance because global regulatory bodies answer to states, and the governments of those states answer to their voters and courts.'). Menno T. Kamminga, 'The Evolving Status of NGOs under International Law: A Threat to the

test of acceptable governance at the national level, it has also become a guiding principle of the governance of international institutions.[29] Citizens who evaluate the legitimacy of their own governments against democratic standards of representation, transparency, participation, and accountability are increasingly insisting on the same qualities of governance from their international institutions.[30] Towards this end, they are demanding more inclusive and responsive mechanisms of participation and accountability.

These claims have been only partially satisfied by IFIs. Since the mid-1990s, there has been sustained public pressure on IFIs to improve transparency, open new avenues of accountability, and increase the political space for non-state actors to influence decision-making. As a result, most IFIs have expanded their public consultations, revised their information disclosure policies to allow for more informed public input, and created formal grievance mechanisms to enable project-affected peoples to raise complaints with management or the board of

---

Inter-State System?', in *Non-state Actors and Human Rights*, ed. Philip Alston (Oxford: Oxford University Press, 2005), 110 ('By contributing the views of civil society, [NGOs] confer badly needed legitimacy on the international system'); Daniel C. Esty, 'Good Governance at the Supranational Scale: Globalizing Administrative Law', *Yale Law Journal* 115 (2006): 1530 ('Openness and some opportunity for public participation have thus emerged as nearly universal principles of good governance.'). Even under a state representation model of legitimacy, the lines of accountability between individuals and their nominal representatives are often so attenuated that representation is more notional than real. *See* Steven Herz & Alnoor Ebrahim, 'A Call for Participatory Decision-Making: Discussion Paper on World Bank-Civil Society Engagement', <www.civicus.org/new/media/World_Bank_Civil_Society_Discussion_Paper_FINAL_VERSION.pdf#search=%22herz%22>, 2005, 22–27.

29. Boutros Boutros-Ghali, 'Democracy: A Newly Recognized Imperative', *Global Governance* (1995).
30. This is not to say that international organizations must adopt the governance mechanisms of a Madisonian or Continental democracy to achieve democratic legitimacy. Much of the political infrastructure that supports democratic governance at the state level – direct election of representatives, 'one-person, one-vote' apportionment of the franchise, political parties, etc. – does not yet exist at the international level, and is unlikely to develop any time soon. Rather, the most pressing legitimacy challenge for international organizations is to democratize decision-making within these existing structural constraints by improving transparency, accountability, representativeness, and public participation. Boutros-Ghali, 'Democracy: A Newly Recognized Imperative', *supra* n. 29; United Nations, Panel of Eminent Persons on United Nations – Civil Society Relations, 'We the Peoples: Civil Society, the United Nations and Global Governance' (2004), 8; Joseph Nye, Jr., 'Globalization's Democratic Deficit: How to Make International Institutions More Accountable', *Foreign Affairs* 80, no. 4 (2001): 1, 3; Ruth Grant & Robert Keohane, 'Accountability and Abuses of Power, in World Politics', *International Law and Justice Working Paper* 2004/7 (New York University School of Law: Institute for International Law and Justice, 2004); Devesh Kapur, 'The Changing Anatomy of Governance of the World Bank', in *Reinventing the World Bank*, ed. J.R. Pincus & J.A. Winters (Ithaca, NY: Cornell University Press, 2002): 75. The absence of these mechanisms, and the prodigious challenge of developing them, have led some observers to conclude that international institutions like the Bank are unlikely to ever be much more than venues for bureaucratic bargaining between elites. Robert A. Dahl, 'Can International Organizations be Democratic? A Skeptic's View', in *Democracy's Edges*, ed. Ian Shapiro & Casiano Hacker-Cordon (Cambridge: Cambridge University Press, 1999), 19.

executive directors.[31] Yet substantial 'democracy deficits' remain.[32] IFIs generally still lack consistently effective mechanisms for public participation in policy development and project planning,[33] have inadequate mechanisms of accountability, and cannot credibly claim to derive their legitimacy from the consent of affected populations.[34] Public confidence in these institutions has suffered accordingly. As the United Nations Development Programme has observed, '[l]arge parts of the public no longer believe that their interests are represented in institutions such as the IMF [and] World Bank... or that the institutions are adequately accountable for what they do'.[35]

Second, an IFI's fidelity to its internal governance procedures – regardless of their democratic bona fides – is no longer sufficient to confer legitimacy. Now, international organizations are also expected to adhere to the applicable principles of international law. There is an emerging consensus that international organizations are subjects of international law and must therefore adhere to general principles and customary norms of international law, including certain human rights norms.[36] This idea has a distinguished legal pedigree. In 1980, the International

31. *See* David Hunter, 'International Law and Public Participation in Policy-Making at the International Financial Institutions', Ch. 7 herein.
32. *See generally*, Joseph S. Nye et al., *The Democracy Deficit in the Global Economy: Enhancing the Legitimacy and Accountability of Global Institutions* (Washington, DC: Trilateral Commission, 2003); Herz & Ebrahim, 'A Call for Participatory Decision-Making: Discussion Paper on World Bank-Civil Society Engagement', *supra* n. 28, 22–27.
33. For a discussion of the World Bank's experience, *see* Herz & Ebrahim, 'A Call for Participatory Decision-Making: Discussion Paper on World Bank-Civil Society Engagement', *supra* n. 28, 22–27; World Bank, 'Issues and Options for Improving Engagement between the World Bank and Civil Society Organizations', External Affairs, Communications and United Nations Affairs, Environmentally and Socially Sustainable Development Network, Operations Policy and Country Services Network (March 2005), *available at* <www-wds.worldbank.org/external/default/WDSContentServer/WDSP/IB/2005/11/08/000160016_20051108153720/Rendered/INDEX/341600ENGLISH01and1Options01PUBLIC1.txt>.
34. Jan Aart Scholte, 'Civil Society and Democracy in Global Governance', *Global Governance* 8 (2002): 281; Gerald K Helleiner, 'Markets, Politics and Globalization: Can the Global Economy be Civilized?' presented at the Palais des Nations: 10th Raúl Prebisch Lecture (Geneva, Switzerland, 11 Dec. 2000); Ngaire Woods, 'Unelected Government: Making the IMF and World Bank More Accountable', *Brookings Review* 21 (March 2003): 9–12.
35. United Nations Development Programme, 'Human Development Report 2002: Deepening Democracy in a Fragmented World' (2002), 112.
36. Reinisch, 'The Changing International Legal Framework for Dealing with Non-state Actors', *supra* n. 14, 46 ('The underlying tenor of recent developments appears to be that international organizations, as a result of their international personality, are considered to be bound by general international law, including any human rights norms, that can be viewed as customary law or general principles of law.'); Henry Schermers & Niels Blokker, *International Institutional Law: Unity Within Diversity*, 3rd edn (The Hague: Kluwer Law International, 1995), 822 ('... as [international organizations] have been established under international law, these rules apply directly as part of the legal order of the organization in question ... '); Phillipe Sands & Pierre Klein, *Bowett's Law of International Institutions*, 5th edn (London: Street & Maxwell, 2001), 458–459 ('This view [that [international organizations] are bound by the generally accepted standards of the world community] appears unimpeachable.... '); C.F. Amerasinghe, *Principles of the Institutional Law of International Organizations* (Cambridge: Cambridge

Court of Justice (ICJ) observed that 'International Organisations are subjects of international law and, as such, are bound by any obligations incumbent upon them under general rules of international law, under their constitutions or under international agreements to which they are a party.'[37] More recently, this conclusion has been affirmed in the jurisprudence of the European Court of Justice[38] and the International Criminal Tribunal for the Former Yugoslavia,[39] and in the pronouncements of the United Nations' International Law Commission,[40] Special Rapporteurs of the United Nations Commission on Human Rights,[41] the International Law Association,[42] and the vast majority of academic commentators and practitioners that have expressed a view on the subject.[43]

University Press 1996), 240 ('. . . there can be no doubt that under customary International law . . . international organisations can also have international obligations towards other international persons . . . '). *See also* Daniel D. Bradlow, 'International Law and the Operations of the International Financial Institutions', Ch. 1 herein; Eisuke Suzuki, 'Responsibility of International Financial Institutions under International Law', Ch. 3 herein; B.S. Chimni, 'International Financial Institutions and International Law: A Third World Perspective', Ch. 2 herein.

37. Interpretation of the Agreement of 25 Mar. 1951 between the WHO and Egypt, Advisory Opinion, 1980 I.C.J. 73 (December 20) (hereinafter ICJ, WHO-Egypt Advisory Opinion), 89–90; *see* Reparation for Injuries Suffered in the Service of the United Nations, Advisory Opinion, 1949 I.C.J. 174 (11 April) (concluding that the United Nations is 'a subject of international law and capable of possessing international rights and duties . . . ') (hereinafter ICJ, *Reparation* case).
38. Advisory opinion of 28 Mar. 1996 of the European Court of Justice on Accession by the Community to the European Convention for the Protection of Human Rights and Fundamental Freedoms, Opinion 2/94, 1996 E.C.R. I-1759 (concluding that although the European Community (EC) cannot accede to the European Convention on Human Rights (ECHR), 'respect for human rights is a condition of the lawfulness of Community acts', because human rights, including the provisions of the ECHR, are given effect as general principles of EC law) (hereinafter European Court of Justice Opinion).
39. *Prosecutor v. Simic et al.*, Case IT-95-9-PT, Decision on motion for judicial assistance to be provided by SFOR and others, 18 Oct. 2000, para. 46 (concluding that the Statute of the Tribunal applies to 'collective enterprises undertaken by States, in the framework of international organizations' such as the NATO-led Stabilisation Force (SFOR)) (hereinafter *Simic* case).
40. United Nations International Law Commission (UN ILC), 'First Report on Responsibility of International Organizations' (March 2003).
41. Joseph Oloka-Onyango & Deepika Udagama, 'Globalization and Its Impact on the Full Enjoyment of Human Rights', progress report submitted to the United Nations Commission on Human Rights, E/CN.4/Sub.2/2001/10, 25–27 (2 Aug. 2001) (arguing that intergovernmental organizations are creatures of the international legal system, and are therefore bound by fundamental principles of international law such as the obligation to respect universal human rights norms).
42. Report of the Seventy-First Conference, 'Final Report of the International Law Association Committee on Accountability of International Organizations' (Berlin, 16–21 Aug. 2004), 26.
43. *See, e.g.*, Reinisch, 'The Changing International Legal Framework for Dealing with Non-state Actors', *supra* n. 14, 46; Eisuke Suzuki & Suresh Nanwani, 'Responsibility of International Organizations: The Accountability Mechanisms Of Multilateral Development Banks', *Michigan Journal of International Law* 27 (2006); 177, 179 (arguing that it is now clear that the legal personality of international organizations entails a responsibility for their conduct to non-state actors.); Mahnoush H. Arsanjani, 'Claims Against International Organizations: Quis Custodiet Ipsos Custodies', *Yale Journal of World Public Order* 7 (1981): 133–134. Thomas Buergenthal,

Nevertheless, some prominent IFIs such as the World Bank and the International Monetary Fund (IMF) traditionally have refused to recognize any international legal obligations beyond their charter and treaty obligations to their members, *jus cogens* requirements, and Chapter VII Security Council resolutions.[44] The General Counsel of the World Bank cogently summarized this position in 1998, when he complained that it 'demeaned' his institution to suggest that the Bank had responsibilities that were not specified in its Articles of Agreement.[45]

This unwillingness to recognize international law obligations has begun to erode, at least at the Bank. While the IMF has shown no sign of reconsidering its claim to independence from most of international law,[46] the World Bank has become markedly more circumspect in its rhetoric, and no longer seems to take umbrage at the suggestion that it is subject to the rule of international law.[47]

'The World Bank and Human Rights', in *The World Bank, International Financial Institutions and the Development of International Law*, ed. Edith Brown Weiss, Andrés Rigo Sureda & Laurence Boisson de Chazournes (Washington, DC: American Society of International Law, 1999); Sigrun Skogly, *The Human Rights Obligations of the World Bank and the International Monetary Fund* (London: Cavendish Publishing, 2001); Daniel D. Bradlow, 'The World Bank, the IMF and Human Rights', *Transnational Law & Contemporary Problems* (Spring 1996); Andrew Clapham, *Human Rights Obligations of Non-state Actors* (Oxford: Oxford University Press, 2006), 137–159; Mac Darrow, *Between Light and Shadow: The World Bank, the International Monetary Fund, and International Human Rights Law* (Oxford: Hart Publishing, 2003); Fergus MacKay, 'Universal Rights or a Universe unto Itself? Indigenous Peoples' Human Rights and the World Bank's Draft Operational Policy 4.10 on Indigenous Peoples', *American University International Law Review* 17 (2001): 527; Adam McBeth, 'Breaching the Vacuum: A Consideration of the Role of International Human Rights Law in the Operations of the International Financial Institutions', *International Journal of Human Rights* 10 (2006): 385. For a dissenting view, *see* Robert McCorquodale, 'Overlegalizing Silences: Human Rights and Nonstate Actors', *American Society for International Law Proceedings* (2002): 384 ('The international human rights law system is a statebased system. . . . It ignores actions by nonstate actors, such as the United Nations and other intergovernmental organizations. . . . ').

44. For the IMF's perspective, *see* François Gianviti, *Economic, Social and Cultural Human Rights and the International Monetary Fund: Working Paper Submitted by the General Counsel of the International Monetary Fund to United Nations Economic and Social Council* (7 May 2001); Gianviti, 'Economic, Social, and Cultural Human Rights and the International Monetary Fund', *supra* n. 5, 113–138. The views of the former General Counsel of the World Bank can be found at Shihata, 'The World Bank and Human Rights', *supra* n. 5, 145; Shihata, 'Human Rights, Development, and International Financial Institutions', *supra* n. 5, 28 (arguing that the World Bank's Articles of Agreement preclude the Bank from applying certain human rights norms in its operations). The United Nations, by contrast, has been far more willing to interpret the provisions of its Charter in accordance with the basic norms of international law. *See* Ian Brownlie, *Principles of Public International Law* (Oxford: Clarendon Press, 1973), 294; United Nations, General Assembly, 'Vienna Declaration and Programme of Action', U.N. Doc. A/Conf.157/23 (1993), para. 4 (recognizing the promotion and protection of human rights as a priority objective of the United Nations [despite the UN Charter's prohibition on involvement in the domestic jurisdiction of any state]).
45. Shihata, 'The World Bank and Human Rights', *supra* n. 5, 145.
46. Gianviti, 'Economic, Social, and Cultural Human Rights and the International Monetary Fund', *supra* n. 5, 113–138.
47. Ana Palacio, 'The Way Forward: Human Rights and the World Bank', *Development Outreach* (October 2006).

Thus, the Bank has become much more willing to discuss the human rights implications of its work, and has even suggested in a general way that it may have responsibilities to respect those rights.[48] For example, in January 2006, the World Bank's General Counsel concluded that its Articles of Agreement 'permit, and in some cases require the Bank to recognize the human rights dimensions of its development policies and activities'.[49]

Despite this important shift in its rhetoric, the Bank still vigorously resists the suggestion that international law may impose limits on how it designs or implements its programmes, except those limits that are embedded in its charter or operational policies. Consider, for example, the Bank's response to the Inspection Panel claim arising out of the IDA-supported 'Land Administration Project' in Honduras.[50] In that claim, an indigenous community argued that by supporting the project, the Bank had violated its Indigenous Peoples policy and facilitated the Honduran Government's violation of its commitments under International Labour Organization (ILO) Convention No. 169.[51] The Panel, mindful that its mandate extends only to alleged violations of the Bank's operational policies, found that ILO Convention No. 169 was applicable to the Bank through its policy on project appraisal (OMS 2.20), which requires it to ensure that financed activities are consistent with international agreements regarding a country's environment and the health and well-being of its citizens.[52] In response, the Bank's General Counsel objected that the policy should be read only to apply to international obligations that are 'essentially of an environmental nature' – a position that provoked the 'serious concern' of the Panel.[53] By taking this position, the Bank not only declined to accept the Panel's suggestion that it may have obligations under ILO conventions, but also sought to narrowly interpret its policies to limit its responsibility to respect the international commitments of its borrowers.

The objections of certain IFIs notwithstanding, the broader recognition that IFIs have obligations under international law leads naturally to the conclusion that they, like other legal entities, may be responsible when they violate those obligations. As Mahnoush Arsanjani has observed, there is no convincing reason to exempt international organizations from the general principle that a legal entity is responsible for the harms that it may cause.[54] Accordingly, in the 1999 case concerning the *Difference Relating to Immunity from Legal Process of a Special Rapporteur of the Commission on Human Rights*, the ICJ concluded that the United Nations may be required to pay compensation for damages caused by its actions or

48. *Ibid.*
49. World Bank, Senior Vice President and General Counsel, 'Legal Opinion on Human Rights and the Work of the World Bank' (27 Jan. 2006), 9.
50. World Bank Inspection Panel, *Investigation Report: Honduras: Land Administration Project (IDA Credit 3858-HO)* (2007).
51. *Ibid.*, para. 243.
52. *Ibid.*, paras 253, 255 (*citing* World Bank, Operational Manual Statement (OMS) 2.20 (Project Appraisal)).
53. *Ibid.*, para. 254.
54. Arsanjani, *supra* n. 43, 132.

those of its agents acting in their official capacity.[55] Indeed, the principle that international organizations may be internationally responsible for their tortious acts is now so well-accepted that it is considered to be part of customary international law.[56]

Customary international law provides for two distinct types of remedies for violations of international law: the responsible party may be required to stop any ongoing violations[57] and to make reparations for the damages it has caused.[58] In its recent opinion regarding the *Legal Consequences of the Construction of a Wall in the Occupied Palestinian Territory*, the ICJ explained that to meet customary law standards, reparations 'must, so far as possible, wipe out all the consequences of the illegal act and reestablish the situation which would, in all probability, have existed if that act had not been committed'.[59] When such restitution is not available, equivalent monetary damages must be provided.[60]

Third, consensus is emerging that under international human rights law one has a fundamental right to have their legal claims adjudicated by an independent and impartial court or tribunal.[61] The right to a fair and impartial proceeding is specifically recognized in the Universal Declaration of Human Rights,[62] the International Covenant on Civil and Political Rights,[63] and the European Convention on Human Rights.[64] For its part, the European Court of Human Rights

55. 'Difference Relating to Immunity from Legal Process of a Special Rapporteur of the Commission on Human Rights', 1999 I.C.J. 62, 88–89, para. 66 (29 April). The Court went on to observe that under the specific provisions of the Convention on the Privileges and Immunities of the United Nations, such claims could not be raised in domestic courts.
56. Report of the Seventy-First Conference, 'Final Report of the International Law Association Committee on Accountability of International Organizations', *supra* n. 42, 26; *But cf.* Ian Brownlie, *Principles of Public International Law*, 6th edn (Oxford: Oxford University Press, 2003), 655 (questioning the legal responsibility of the United Nations for the tortious acts of its peacekeepers).
57. Legal Consequences of the Construction of a Wall in the Occupied Palestinian Territory, Advisory Opinion, 2004 I.C.J. para. 150; Military and Paramilitary Activities in and against Nicaragua (*Nicar. v. U.S.*), Merits, Judgment, I.C.J. Reports 1986, 149; United States Diplomatic and Consular Staff in Tehran, Judgment, I.C.J. Reports 1980, 44, para. 95; Haya de la Torre, Judgment, I.C.J. Reports 1951, 82.
58. Legal Consequences of the Construction of a Wall in the Occupied Palestinian Territory, Advisory Opinion, 2004 I.C.J. para. 152.
59. *Ibid.* (quoting Factory at Chorzów, Merits, Judgment No. 13, 1928 P.C.I.J. (ser. A), No. 17, at 47).
60. Legal Consequences of the Construction of a Wall in the Occupied Palestinian Territory, *supra* n. 58, para. 152.
61. Reinisch, *International Organizations before National Courts*, *supra* n. 24, 281–282.
62. Universal Declaration of Human Rights, *supra* n. 13, Art. 10. (providing that 'Everyone is entitled in full equality to a fair and public hearing by an independent and impartial tribunal, in the determination of his rights and obligations and of any criminal charge against him.')
63. International Covenant on Civil and Political Rights, *supra* n. 24, Art. 14(1) (providing that '[a]ll persons are equal before the courts and tribunals. In the determination of any criminal charge against him, or of his rights and obligations in a suit at law, everyone shall be entitled to a fair and public hearing by a competent, independent, and impartial tribunal established by law').
64. European Convention on Human Rights, *supra* n. 24, Art. 6(1) (providing that '[i]n the determination of his civil rights and obligations or of any criminal charge against him, everyone is

(ECtHR) has consistently interpreted this right in the European Convention to include the right of access to court.[65] Again, there is no clear reason why these basic due process requirements should not apply when an IFI is the subject of the complaint. As the International Law Association's Committee on Accountability of International Organizations has concluded, '[n]o situation should arise where an [international organization] would not be accountable to some authority for an act that might be deemed illegal'.[66]

An aggrieved party's right to fair process does not necessarily imply a right to have one's claims heard in any specific court or tribunal, but it does require that some fair and adequate remedial procedure be available. Thus, in its opinion on the *Effect of Awards of Compensation Made by the United Nations Administrative Tribunal*, the ICJ suggested that the grant of jurisdictional immunity in the United Nations Charter necessarily entailed an obligation for the United Nations to create an alternative judicial or arbitral mechanism for United Nations staff to resolve employment disputes.[67] Similarly, in *Waite and Kennedy v. Germany*, the ECtHR held that a critical factor in determining whether a forum state could grant an international organization broad immunity in domestic courts was 'whether the applicants had available to them reasonable alternative means to protect effectively their rights under the Convention'.[68] In the United States, the DC Circuit has also used the existence of an administrative grievance mechanism as a partial justification for upholding jurisdictional immunity.[69] And, in *Bosphorus Hava Yollary Turizm ve Ticaret Anonim Sirketi v. Ireland*, the ECtHR noted that Member States of international organizations also have an obligation to ensure that claimants have access to fair remedial processes. Thus, the Court concluded that in order for a state to fulfil its human rights obligations when it acts through an international organization, the state must ensure that the organization not only protects the basic substantive guarantees, but also that the organization provides a procedural

entitled to a fair and public hearing within a reasonable time by an independent and impartial tribunal established by law').

65. *See Richard Waite & Terry Kennedy v. Germany*, European Commission of Human Rights, Application No. 26083/94, para. 63 (24 Feb. 1997); *Golder*, European Court of Human Rights, 21 Feb. 1975, Series A, No. 18, para. 36; Reinisch, *International Organizations before National Courts*, *supra* n. 24, 281; August Reinisch & Ulf Andreas Weber, 'In the Shadow of Waite and Kennedy: The Jurisdictional Immunity of International Organizations, the Individual's Right of Access to the Courts and Administrative Tribunals as Alternative Means of Dispute Settlement', *International Organizations Law Review* 1 (2004): 59.
66. Report of the Seventy-First Conference, 'Final Report of the International Law Association Committee on Accountability of International Organizations', *supra* n. 42, 26.
67. I.C.J., 'Effect of Awards of Compensation Made by the United Nations Administrative Tribunal', I.C.J. Reports 47 (1954), 57 ('It would, in the opinion of the Court, hardly be consistent with the expressed aim of the Charter to promote freedom and justice for individuals and with the constant preoccupation of the United Nations Organization to promote this aim that it should afford no judicial or arbitral remedy to its own staff for the settlement of any disputes which may arise between it and them.').
68. *Waite & Kennedy v. Germany*, *supra* n. 65, para. 68.
69. *Mendaro v. World Bank*, 717 F.2d 610, 616 (D.C. Cir. 1983).

mechanism for controlling their observance that is at least equivalent to that which is required under the Convention.[70]

In practice, a number of headquarters agreements and international conventions protect the right to fair process by requiring organizations that enjoy certain immunities from domestic jurisdiction to create alternative mechanisms for resolving disputes.[71] For example, both the *Convention on Privileges and Immunities of the United Nations* and the *Convention on Privileges and Immunities of Specialized Agencies* require the organizations to 'make provision for appropriate modes of settlement' of any private law disputes to which they are a party.[72]

Most IFIs have acted to protect the due process rights of their employees by creating an administrative procedure in which to resolve employment disputes.[73] Indeed, this practice is so common that some commentators have argued that IFIs and other international organizations now have a customary obligation to establish a mechanism of redress for their employees.[74] At least some IFIs agree that they have a legal obligation to create an administrative remedy.[75] The President of the World Bank, for example, explained the creation of the World Bank's Administrative Tribunal by referencing the fair hearing and due process principles included in many domestic legal systems and the Universal Declaration of Human Rights.[76]

No similar mechanisms currently exist for other aggrieved parties to seek redress from an IFI that has caused them harm. To their credit, most IFIs have at least implicitly recognized an obligation to provide a forum for non-employees to resolve grievances. Beginning in the early 1990s with the World Bank's Inspection Panel, most IFIs have created mechanisms in which citizens who are adversely affected by bank-financed operations can file a complaint before a

---

70. *Bosphorus Hava Yollary Turizm ve Ticaret Anonim Sirketi v. Ireland*, Judgment of 30 Jun. 2005, para. 155.
71. *See* International Law Commission, Leonardo Díaz-González (Special Rapporteur), 'Fourth report on relations between States and international organizations (second part of the topic)', A/CN.4/424 and Corr.1 (1989), 160–161.
72. *Convention on Privileges and Immunities of the United Nations*, adopted by the General Assembly of the United Nations (13 Feb. 1946), *available at* <www.onug.ch/80256EDD006B8954/%28httpAssets%29/C8297DB1DE8566F2C1256F2600348A73/$file/Convention%20P%20&%20I%20%281946%29%20-%20E.pdf>; *Convention on Privileges and Immunities of Specialized Agencies*, G.A. Res. 179(11) (21 Nov. 1947), *available at* <www.uia.org/legal/app51.php>.
73. Reinsich, *International Organizations before National Courts*, *supra* n. 24, 271–273.
74. Suzanne Bastid, 'Have the UN Administrative Tribunals Contributed to the Development of International Law?', in *Transnational Law in a Changing Society: Essays in Honor of Philip C. Jessup*, ed. Wolfgang Friedman, Louis Henkin & Oliver Lissitzyn (New York: Columbia University Press, 1972), 298, 309.
75. Reinisch & Weber, 'In the Shadow of Waite and Kennedy: The Jurisdictional Immunity of International Organizations, the Individual's Right of Access to the Courts and Administrative Tribunals as Alternative Means of Dispute Settlement', *supra* n. 65, 70. For further discussion on administrative law and the IFIs, *see* David Hunter, 'International Law and Public Participation in Policy-Making at the International Financial Institutions', Ch. 7 herein.
76. Memorandum to the Executive Directors from the President of the World Bank, Doc. R80-8 (14 Jan. 1980), 1 et seq.

quasi-independent panel.[77] Some of these mechanisms, such as the World Bank's Inspection Panel, have a mandate that is limited to reviewing the Bank's compliance with its internal policy directives. Their primary purpose is to improve accountability by enhancing the ability of the member governments to supervise management's implementation of internal policy directives.[78] Others, such as the International Finance Corporation's (IFC's) Compliance Advisor/Ombudsman (CAO), play mostly a 'problem-solving' role, in which they facilitate mediation and other forms of negotiated dispute resolution between the claimants and the IFI and its clients.

Although these mechanisms undoubtedly have improved the accountability of IFIs to the people who are adversely affected by their projects,[79] they are not (and were not intended to be) equivalent alternatives to the legal process. For one thing, they generally lack the explicit authority to determine whether violations of international or domestic law have occurred.[80] Instead, they may only assess whether the institution has complied with its internal operational policies and procedures.[81] For another, even if these mechanisms could address whether Bank

---

77. For an overview of these mechanisms, *see* Daniel D. Bradlow, 'Private Complainants and International Organizations: A Comparative Study of the Independent Inspection Mechanisms in International Financial Institutions', *Georgetown Journal of International Law* 36 (2005): 403.
78. Sabine Schlemmer-Schulte, 'The World Bank Inspection Panel: A Record of the First International Accountability Mechanism and Its Role for Human Rights', *Human Rights Brief* 6, no. 2 (1999).
79. Dana Clark, Jonathan Fox & Kay Treakle (eds), *Demanding Accountability: Civil Society Claims and the World Bank Inspection Panel* (Lanham, MD: Rowman & Littlefield Publishing, 2003).
80. The CAO is a limited exception. The CAO's Operational Guidelines preclude it from supporting negotiated outcomes that violate international law, and authorize it to consider violations of international law as part of the compliance function. Compliance Advisor/Ombudsman, 'Operational Guidelines' (2006), 18, *available at* <http://www.cao-ombudsman.org/howwework/filecomplaint/documents/EnglishCAOGuidelines06.08.07Web.pdf>.
81. In a few cases, the World Bank Inspection Panel has considered international law violations within the context of its narrow mandate to assess alleged violations of internal policy. World Bank Inspection Panel, Inspection Report: China: Western Poverty Reduction Project (Credit No. 3255-CHA and Loan No. 4501-CHA) (2000), xii (The Bank must interpret its Indigenous Peoples policy in accordance with the policy's human rights objective.). Inspection Panel, Investigation Report Chad: Petroleum Development and Pipeline Project, Management of the Petroleum Economy Project, and Petroleum Sector Management Capacity Building Project (2002) (The Bank must assess whether human rights issues impede compliance with its policies). World Bank Inspection Panel, Investigation Report: Honduras: Land Administration Project (IDA Credit 3858-HO) (2007) (The Bank must ensure that its projects do not contravene the borrower's international human rights commitments, and must take into account human rights protections enshrined in national constitutions or other sources of domestic law.). For a discussion of these claims, *see* Steven Herz & Anne Perrault, 'Bringing Human Rights Claims to the World Bank Inspection Panel' (October 2009), *available at* <www.accountabilityproject.org/downloads/Inspection%20Panel%20and%20Human%20Rights%20Oct09.pdf>. These reports suggest that Günther Handl's expectation that inspection procedures would serve an important declarative function by 'call[ing] attention also to the very existence of international obligations incumbent upon the [multilateral development bank] concerned and to the degree to which these obligations are reflected in the institution's by-laws and policies in the first place' may yet come to pass. Günther Handl, 'The Legal Mandate of Multilateral Development Banks as Agents for Change toward Sustainable Development', *American Journal of International Law* 92 (1998): 642.

actions were lawful, they lack the power to impose any of the remedies that are available under customary international law. They have no authority to enjoin ongoing operations or to award money damages. At the end of the day, their powers are entirely declarative and precatory. The most that a claimant can reasonably expect to achieve from filing a compliance complaint is that the IFI's accountability mechanism will produce favourable findings of fact and recommendations that the claimant can use to gain political leverage to achieve a more acceptable outcome.[82] That may be quite significant to poor and politically disempowered claimants, but it should not be equated with a proper adjudication of legal rights and interests.

To summarize, the decline of state sovereignty as the overriding principle in international law and politics has transformed legal norms and public expectations regarding the governance and accountability of international organizations. As a result, IFIs can no longer plausibly claim that their obligations are defined *exclusively* by their founding agreements and the expressed preferences of their Member States acting through their formal governance structures. Rather, they now must adhere to the rule of international law, including the internationally recognized rights of individuals, and meet public expectations regarding democratic legitimacy. To do this, they must provide meaningful opportunities for members of the public to directly assert their rights and express their interests; and to hold the organization to account if those rights and interests are violated. However, despite some noteworthy advances, IFIs still largely fail to meet these norms and expectations. Their governance structures remain plagued by substantial democracy deficits and formal lines of accountability continue to run almost exclusively to member governments. Although the IFIs' quasi-independent inspection mechanisms have improved the IFIs' legitimacy and accountability by expanding the opportunities for the public to directly engage decision-makers, they do not provide mechanisms for aggrieved individuals to obtain the customary forms of legal redress for internationally wrongful acts. As a result, vindication of third-party interests remains essentially a political matter.

II. IMMUNITY AND ACCOUNTABILITY

A. THE PREVAILING VIEW: 'FUNCTIONAL NECESSITY' AS ABSOLUTE IMMUNITY

Despite the profound shifts in our understanding of the accountability of IFIs, one central element of the traditional approach has proven stubbornly resistant to reconsideration – the presumption that IFIs enjoy broad immunity from suit in domestic courts. Even as the immunities of sovereigns have been drastically

82. Jonathan Fox & Kay Treakle, 'Concluding Propositions', in *Demanding Accountability: Civil Society Claims and the World Bank Inspection Panel*, ed. Dana Clark, Jonathan Fox & Kay Treakle (Lanham, MD: Rowman & Littlefield Publishing, 2003), 285–286.

curtailed, IFIs continue to confidently insist that they must be afforded expansive jurisdictional immunities to ensure their independence and effectiveness. And courts typically honour these assertions as a matter of course, without fully considering their legal or theoretical justifications or weighing competing policy considerations.[83] As with the other elements of the traditional approach to accountability, however, expansive jurisdictional immunity is fundamentally at odds with contemporary notions of individual rights, due process, and the legal responsibility of international organizations.

The scope of the jurisdictional immunities enjoyed by an IFI is a function of the interplay between the domestic law and international legal obligations of the forum state. As an initial matter, every nation has the discretion to determine the jurisdiction of its own courts, including the nature of the available immunities from that jurisdiction.[84] Accordingly, the immunity enjoyed by an IFI in a domestic court is first and foremost a question of domestic law. Nevertheless, domestic legal sources alone do not settle the matter because a state may have international law obligations to provide an IFI with immunity. These obligations may arise under the constituent agreement of the organization, other multilateral or bilateral treaties conferring immunity, a bilateral 'headquarters' agreement between the organization and the host country, or customary international law. How these obligations affect the jurisdictional rules of domestic courts will depend on the nature of the domestic legal regime. In 'monist' countries, where international legal obligations are automatically incorporated into domestic law, any immunity provided for under international law will apply directly in domestic courts. On the other hand, in 'dualist' countries, where international obligations do not take domestic effect until they are implemented by appropriate legislative, executive, or administrative action, the nature of the immunity will be defined by the implementing law.[85] If a dualist country fails to implement its obligations in domestic law, the international obligation continues to be in effect, and the country is considered to be in default.[86]

Most states ostensibly determine the scope of the immunity that they afford to international organizations by reference to the 'functional necessity' of the organizations. Under this approach, international organizations are given the immunities they need to effectively discharge their delegated functions and to achieve their organizational objectives.[87] These immunities are primarily intended to insulate

83. Singer, 'Jurisdictional Immunity of International Organizations: Human Rights and Functional Necessity Concerns', *supra* n. 23, 56; Reinisch, *International Organizations before National Courts, supra* n. 24, 234–235.
84. *See, e.g., The Schooner Exchange v. McFaddon*, 7 Cranch 116 (1812).
85. Reinisch, *International Organizations before National Courts, supra* n. 24, 178–179.
86. *Restatement (Third) of Foreign Relations Law of the United States* (Philadelphia: American Law Institute, 1987), Pt I, § 111, n. 5, § 115, comment b.
87. Josef L. Kunz, 'Privileges and Immunities of International Organizations', *American Journal of International Law* 41 (1947): 836. Reinisch, *International Organizations before National Courts, supra* n. 24, 234–235; Singer, 'Jurisdictional Immunity of International Organizations: Human Rights and Functional Necessity Concerns', *supra* n. 23, 56.

IFIs from undue external interference and the potential burdens of divergent or politically motivated judgments.[88] As a result, it is generally agreed that functional necessity concerns are strongest with respect to internal administrative matters.[89] Courts therefore have been loath to consider employment-related cases, in which they might be required to scrutinize the internal administration of an organization and to impose onerous administrative costs by subjecting an organization to a patchwork of potentially conflicting national employment laws.[90]

The 'functional necessity' standard of immunity is widely accepted and is not particularly controversial.[91] Few commentators dispute that international organizations need some measure of immunity to effectively discharge their responsibilities.[92] Moreover, the doctrine of 'functional necessity' appears to offer an approach that is flexible enough to accommodate competing concerns about fairness to private litigants. After all, the concept of necessity is inherently restrictive, and by definition should exclude those immunities that are merely desirable or convenient.[93] Most observers therefore agree that an international organization should be entitled to no more immunity than is 'strictly necessary' to fulfil its functions.[94] Read in this way, the 'functional necessity' approach would allow many claimants to have their day in court. For example, it is difficult to see why international organizations would ever need immunity from liability for knowingly violating clearly established human rights norms, even in an effort to achieve their legitimate objectives.[95]

This need to limit the immunity of IFIs in domestic courts is reflected in the foundational agreements of most IFIs. Only the IMF's charter provides for absolute

88. Reinisch, *International Organizations before National Courts*, *supra* n. 24, 234–235; Peter H.F. Bekker, *The Legal Position of Intergovernmental Organizations* (Boston: Martinus Njihoff, 1994), 48.
89. Singer, 'Jurisdictional Immunity of International Organizations: Human Rights and Functional Necessity Concerns', *supra* n. 23, 99.
90. *Mendaro v. World Bank*, 717 F.2d 610, 619 (D.C. Cir. 1983); *Broadbent v. Organization of American States*, 628 F.2d 27, 34–35 (D.C. Cir. 1980); Singer, 'Jurisdictional Immunity of International Organizations: Human Rights and Functional Necessity Concerns', *supra* n. 23, 99.
91. Reinisch, *International Organizations before National Courts*, *supra* n. 24, 253; *Waite & Kennedy v. Germany*, *supra* n. 65, at para. 63; International Law Commission, Díaz-González, 'Fourth report on relations between States and international organizations (second part of the topic)', *supra* n. 71, para. 24.
92. Reinisch, *International Organizations before National Courts*, *supra* n. 24, 235 (describing the view that international organizations require some jurisdictional immunity to protect their independent functioning as an 'almost universally shared opinion').
93. *Ibid.*, 253.
94. General Assembly Resolution of 13 Feb. 1946, A/Res/22A (1) (2000), s. D; Singer, 'Jurisdictional Immunity of International Organizations: Human Rights and Functional Necessity Concerns', *supra* n. 23, 101. Bekker, *The Legal Position of Intergovernmental Organizations*, *supra* n. 88, 39.
95. Singer, 'Jurisdictional Immunity of International Organizations: Human Rights and Functional Necessity Concerns', *supra* n. 23, 93–94; Arsanjani, *supra* n. 43, 175.

immunity.[96] The Asian Development Bank's (ADB's) Articles of Agreement commits its Member States to provide broad immunities, except in specifically enumerated circumstances:

> The Bank shall enjoy immunity from every form of legal process, except in cases arising out of or in connection with the exercise of its powers to borrow money, to guarantee obligations, or to buy and sell or underwrite the sale of securities. . . .[97]

The charters of all other IFIs contemplate amenability to suit in the domestic courts of their members. Thus, the Articles of Agreement of the key financing institutions of the World Bank – International Bank for Reconstruction and Development (IBRD), International Development Association (IDA), and IFC – each provide:

> Actions may be brought against the Bank only in a court of competent jurisdiction in the territories of a member in which the Bank has an office, has appointed an agent for the purpose of accepting service or notice of process, or has issued or guaranteed securities. No actions shall, however, be brought by members or persons acting for or deriving claims from members.[98]

The foundational agreements of the Inter-American Development Bank (IDB) and the European Bank for Reconstruction and Development (EBRD) define the circumstances in which they agree to be sued in nearly identical terms.[99] Similarly, the Statute of the European Investment Bank (EIB) allows for all legal disputes to proceed in domestic courts, except certain specified categories of cases that are

---

96. Section IX of the Articles of Agreement provides:

> The Fund, its property and its assets, wherever located and by whomsoever held, shall enjoy immunity from every form of judicial process except to the extent that it expressly waives its immunity for the purpose of any proceedings or by the terms of any contract.

'Articles of Agreement for the International Monetary Fund' (Bretton Woods, NH, 22 Jul. 1944), Art. IX(3), *available at* <www.imf.org/external/pubs/ft/aa/index.htm> (hereinafter IMF Articles of Agreement).

97. Asian Development Bank, 'Agreement Establishing the Asian Development Bank' (1966), Art. 50, *available at* <http://adb.org/Documents/Reports/Charter/charter.pdf>.
98. 'Articles of Agreement of the International Bank for Reconstruction and Development', 2. U.N.T.S. 134 (Bretton Woods, NH, 22 Jul. 1944, amended 16 Feb. 1989), Art. VII(3), *available at* <http://siteresources.worldbank.org/EXTABOUTUS/Resources/ibrd-articlesofagreement.pdf> (hereinafter IBRD Articles of Agreement); International Development Association, 'Articles of Agreement', 11 U.N.T.S. 2284 (1960), Art. VII(3), *available at* <http://siteresources.worldbank.org/IDA/Resources/ida-articlesofagreement.pdf>; International Finance Corporation, 'Articles of Agreement' (as amended 28 Apr. 1993), Art. VI(3), *available at* <www.ifc.org/ifcext/about.nsf/Content/ArticlesofAgreement>.
99. Inter-American Development Bank, 'Agreement Establishing the Inter-American Development Bank' (1959), Art. XI(3), *available at* <www.iadb.org/leg/Documents/Pdf/Convenio-Eng.Pdf>; European Bank for Reconstruction and Development, 'Agreement Establishing the European Bank for Reconstruction and Development' (1990), Arts 44, 46, *available at* <www.ebrd.com/pubs/insti/basics.pdf>.

referred to the European Court of Justice.[100] Unlike other IFIs, the EIB apparently has not tried to assert broader immunities than its charter provides.

In many countries, however, the scope of 'functional necessity' immunity has been extended far beyond what the members of most IFIs committed to provide, or what the plain meaning of the term should allow. Even international organizations whose charters clearly contemplate that they will be sued in national courts have insisted that, unless they explicitly waive their immunity, only expansive or absolute immunity will allow them to achieve their objectives.[101] Courts generally have been unwilling to closely scrutinize these claims, and have often extended jurisdictional immunity to all activities within the organizations' competence. In so doing, they have conflated 'functional necessity' with a presumption of absolute immunity, and refused to exert jurisdiction in cases in which the organization has not waived its immunity. To cite one example, in *Mendaro v. World Bank*, the US Court of Appeals for the D.C. Circuit stood the presumption against necessity on its head by interpreting the functional necessity doctrine to require immunity unless the organization needed to be vulnerable to suit to achieve its institutional objectives.[102]

B. Objections to the Prevailing View

This overly-expansive understanding of 'functional necessity' – which fully vindicates an IFI's interest in decision-making discretion at the expense of a potential claimant's interests in a fair and accessible judicial process, and the public's interest in respect for the rule of law and the accountability of public institutions – is firmly rooted in the traditional view that international organizations were generally only accountable to their Member States.[103] Although it is rarely challenged, it is best understood as an anachronism that should be subjected to the same fundamental reassessment as the other discredited assumptions of the

100. Statute of the European Investment Bank (2004), *available at* <www.eib.org/Attachments/general/statute/eib_statute_en.pdf>. The European Court of Justice has jurisdiction over disputes that (a) arise between the Bank and its Member States; (b) raise the issue of the legality of the decisions taken by the Board of Governors or Board of Directors; (c) arise between the Bank and a borrower or lender where the parties have contractually agreed to submit to the Court's jurisdiction; and (d) arise between the EIB and its staff.

101. Singer, 'Jurisdictional Immunity of International Organizations: Human Rights and Functional Necessity Concerns', *supra* n. 23, 66–67.

102. The D.C. Circuit concluded that the Bank had broad immunities, and its members 'could only have intended to waive the Bank's immunity from suits by its debtors, creditors, bondholders, and those other potential plaintiffs to whom the Bank would have to subject itself to suit in order to achieve its chartered objectives'. *Mendaro v. World Bank*, 717 F.2d 610, 614–615 (D.C. Cir. 1983). *See also Atkinson v. Inter-American Development Bank*, 156 F.3d 1335 (D.C. Cir. 1998). For a critique of how international organization immunity has been interpreted in US courts, *see* Steven Herz, 'International Organizations in U.S. Courts: Reconsidering the Anachronism of Absolute Immunity', *Suffolk Transnational Law Review* 31 (2008): 471.

103. *See* s. I *supra*.

traditional approach. After all, in light of the persistent shortcomings in the practice of international organization accountability – particularly the lack of any mechanisms of redress for international law violations – the need for alternative avenues of direct accountability should be apparent. A more restrictive approach to international organization immunity could potentially provide the same kinds of accountability benefits as the restrictive approach to sovereign immunity – increased deterrence of official wrongdoing and expanded opportunities for aggrieved citizens to obtain redress, vindicate their public rights, and contribute to the development of international legal norms.[104]

Equally, the repudiation of the traditional understanding of international organization accountability has overturned most of the doctrinal impediments to a more restrictive approach to jurisdictional immunities. First, as we have seen, international organizations traditionally answered only to their Member States acting through their formal governance structures. Accountability, therefore, was entirely political and essentially unconstrained by legal norms, as there were few limits on how the Member States could exercise their governance prerogatives.[105] In that context, jurisdictional immunities served to reinforce the state monopoly on institutional governance by foreclosing alternative avenues of redress.[106] With nowhere else to turn, aggrieved individuals were forced to petition their government representatives to take action on their behalf. More importantly, Member States that were unhappy with how their interests were being served by the institution were also precluded from circumventing the governance processes by asking a court to intervene. Indeed, it was this latter concern that was uppermost in the minds of the World Bank's founders. Although the Articles of Agreement allow the Bank to be sued in certain circumstances, they expressly prohibit Member States from ever bringing suit against the Bank.[107]

Today, however, the standard-less, state-centered approach to institutional governance and accountability no longer meets normative expectations of accountability. International organizations are expected to adhere to the rule of international law,[108] and there is a widely recognized need for legal mechanisms through which individuals can seek redress when their international rights have been violated. Under these circumstances, expanded tort liability should no longer be seen as an existential threat to institutional governance structures.

Second, given that it is now well-established that IFIs have obligations under international law, actions that violate those obligations should be considered ultra

104. Koh, 'Transnational Public Law Litigation', *supra* n. 11, 2349, 2368.
105. Brilmayer, *supra* n. 7, 2307.
106. *Waite & Kennedy v. Germany*, *supra* n. 65, para. 70; Reinisch, *International Organizations before National Courts*, *supra* n. 24, 239–240.
107. IBRD Articles of Agreement, *supra* n. 98, Art. VII(3) (providing, in part: 'No actions shall, however, be brought by members or persons acting for or deriving claims from members.').
108. *See supra* n. 36–43. *See also* Herz & Perrault, 'Bringing Human Rights Claims to the World Bank Inspection Panel', *supra* n. 81; Handl, 'The Legal Mandate of Multilateral Development Banks as Agents for Change toward Sustainable Development', *supra* n. 81.

vires and unworthy of immunity.[109] IFIs' obligations under international law arise from their international legal personality. Moreover, they are creatures of limited mandates and may only exercise powers that have been delegated to them by their Member States, and Member States may not authorize an IFI to violate international law.[110] As such, there is no legal basis – let alone a functional need – for an IFI to enjoy immunity from international law-based claims.[111]

Third and relatedly, before it was established that IFIs had a duty of care to respect the international rights of non-state actors, there was no reason to be concerned with how that duty of care would be enforced. Now that those obligations are no longer in doubt, and there is much greater recognition of the rights of aggrieved parties to due process and effective redress, the question of where citizens can go to obtain an adequate remedy naturally emerges. As we have seen, currently no mechanisms are in place that can serve this function. Even the citizen-driven accountability mechanisms that most IFIs have created are not well-structured to address international law claims and lack the authority to award appropriate relief. In the absence of any alternative mechanisms, then, tort liability in domestic courts seems increasingly appropriate.[112]

Fourth, the repudiation of absolute sovereign immunity for states has considerably undermined the case for extending such immunity to international organizations. Since judicial scrutiny of the conduct of states has been expanded in both domestic and foreign courts, it is not obvious why the activities of international organizations should be broadly and presumptively exempted from similar review. For one thing, international organization immunity has traditionally been justified, at least in part, by analogy to state sovereign immunity.[113] In the United States, for example, the law of international organization immunity is explicitly tethered to that of state sovereign immunity.[114] For another, there is no compelling jurisprudential or policy reason why a collection of states acting through an international organization should be entitled to substantially broader immunity than the Member States enjoy when they act alone. Because it is well-accepted that states may not evade their international obligations by acting through international organizations,[115] granting an IFI much broader immunities than their Member

109. Nigel White, *The Law of International Organisations*, 2nd edn (Manchester, UK: Manchester University Press, 2005), 190.

110. ICJ, WHO-Egypt Advisory Opinion, *supra* n. 37, 104 (Judge Gros separate opinion: 'A decision of the WHO which is contrary to international law does not become lawful because a majority of States has voted in favour of it . . . Numbers cannot cure a lack of constitutional competence.').

111. Arsanjani, *supra* n. 43, 153.

112. Reinisch, *International Organizations before National Courts*, *supra* n. 24, 263.

113. *Ibid.*, 258 et seq.

114. International Organization Immunity Act, 22 U.S.C. § 288.

115. *Matthews v. United Kingdom*, Application No. 24833/94, Judgment of 18 Feb. 1999, para. 32 (European Convention on Human Rights does not exclude the transfer of competences to international organizations provided that states continue to 'secure' Convention rights.). *See also* Ian Brownlie, 'State Responsibility: The Problem of Delegation', in *Völkerrecht zwischen normativen Anspruch und politischer Realität*, ed.

States may create perverse incentives for countries to try to use them to circumvent their own international law obligations.[116]

In addition, the case for absolute immunity as a practical imperative overlooks the current size, stature, and influence of many of these institutions. Expansive jurisdictional immunity arguably may have been a functional requirement when these international organizations were fledgling, under-resourced, and politically precarious, but this is hardly the case today. The most prominent IFIs are now well-funded and firmly established in the international system, and have considerable legal and political resources at their disposal to defend their independence and organizational prerogatives. In fact, the power and influence of the more prominent IFIs have expanded to the point where they are largely insulated from overreaching by most of their Member States. Countries that have come to depend on these institutions for budgetary support, debt forgiveness, technical assistance, or private-sector development are unlikely to jeopardize their relationship with an IFI (or its donors) by abusing their judicial processes to gain leverage in any particular case.[117] On the other hand, the countries that do have the wherewithal to take on an IFI – the large donor countries and major borrowers – already wield such disproportionate influence within formal governance structures that they have little need to circumvent them to advance their national interests. Thus, while these institutions may still find it desirable or convenient to retain the full measure of their current immunities, it is increasingly difficult for them to maintain that it is a necessary prerequisite of their effective operation.

Indeed, the argument that absolute immunity is a functional necessity of IFIs is belied by the practice of the EIB, the European Union's main financing institution, which submits to legal process as a matter of course. According to its charter, most disputes between the Bank and 'creditors, debtors or any other person', are to be decided by national courts in the Member States where the dispute arises. In other

---

Konrad Ginther et al. (Berlin: Duncker & Humblot, 1994), 300–301 ([A] 'State cannot by delegation (even if this be genuine) avoid responsibility for breaches of its duties under international law . . . ').

116. Lest one think that this is merely a hypothetical concern, consider the analogous case of *Mohammed v. Harvey* (2006 U.S. Dist. LEXIS 75717), in which a United States District Court declined to hear the habeas corpus petition of an American citizen detained by the Multinational Force in Iraq (MNF-I). Although the petitioner was physically being held by American soldiers, the Court concluded that he could not invoke the Court's jurisdiction because he was in the nominal custody of the Multinational Forces 'who derive their ultimate authority from the United Nations and the MNF-I member nations acting jointly, not from the United States acting alone'. The US Supreme Court ultimately rejected this reasoning in *Munaf v. Geren*, holding that the habeas corpus statute 'extends to American citizens who are held overseas by American forces operating subject to an American chain of command, even when those forces are acting as part of a multinational coalition'. 553 U.S. ______, 128 S. Ct. 2207 (2008), *available at* <http://scholar.google.com/scholar_case?case=3716427826682805560&q=munaf+v.+geren&hl=en&as_sdt=80000000000002>.

117. Indeed, in many cases, IFIs have the bargaining power to require borrowing countries to agree to assume responsibility for any third-party claims against the bank as a condition of financing. *See* Suzuki & Nanwani, *supra* n. 43, 194, fn. 79; Arsanjani, *supra* n. 43, 140, fn. 26–27.

specified circumstances, jurisdiction is conferred on the European Court of Justice or the European Ombudsman.[118]

C. Human Rights and Other International Law-based Claims

The case for a thorough reappraisal of the scope of IFI immunity in light of contemporary norms of accountability is strongest where human rights are at issue. As a general rule, the Member States of an IFI cannot invest it with legal authority that the states themselves do not have. Accordingly, states cannot evade their human rights obligations by delegating the authority to commit violations to an IFI.[119] Thus, it cannot be argued that an IFI's amenability to suit for claims based on international human rights law would impede it from achieving its legitimate objectives, because those legitimate objectives cannot include violations of basic human rights norms.[120] Put another way, the contrary conclusion – that judicial accountability to human rights law would impede an international organization's ability to achieve its organizational purposes – necessarily depends upon the untenable assumption that the organization's Member States intended to create an organization with the power to violate obligations the Member States were assuming.[121]

Moreover, human rights claims do not implicate any of the specific concerns that animate the 'functional necessity' analysis. First, an individual's suit to vindicate her human rights is an extremely unlikely vehicle for a host government to use to attempt to exert undue influence over an international organization. Indeed, since most human rights violations require state action, the host government is likely to be complicit in the violations, or even a co-defendant in the case. It would therefore be surprising to find a government ginning up human rights litigation to

118. *See* 'Statute of the European Investment Bank', *supra* n. 100 (conferring jurisdiction on the European Court of Justice). *See also* European Investment Bank, 'European Ombudsman', <www.eib.org/about/cr/governance/complaints/ombudsman/index.htm?lang=-en> (explaining the relationship of the European Ombudsman to the EIB and the authority of the European Ombudsman); 'Memorandum of Understanding between the European Ombudsman and the European Investment Bank concerning information on the Bank's policies and procedures and the handling of complaints, including complaints from non-citizens and non-residents of the European Union' (Luxembourg, 9 Jul. 2008), *available at* <www.eib.org/attachments/strategies/complaints_mou_eo_eib_en.pdf>.

119. *See Waite & Kennedy v. Germany*, *supra* n. 65, para. 67; Report of the Seventy-First Conference, 'Final Report of the International Law Association Committee on Accountability of International Organizations', *supra* n. 42, 18; Brownlie, 'State responsibility: the problem of delegation', *supra* n. 115, 300–301 ('. . . [A] State cannot by delegation (even if this be genuine) avoid responsibility for breaches of its duties under international law . . .').

120. For a more in depth discussion of human rights and the IFIs, *see* Siobhán McInerney-Lankford, 'International Financial Institutions and Human Rights: Select Perspectives on Legal Obligations', Ch. 8 herein.

121. Arsanjani, *supra* n. 43, 132.

gain a strategic advantage over an IFI. Second and relatedly, human rights cases do not appear to be fertile ground for prejudicial judgments against international organizations. Given that the forum state is likely to be complicit in the alleged violations and that the victims are often politically marginalized, the risks of judicial overreaching in favour of human rights claimants is small.[122] If anything, the risks of prejudice run strongly in favour of the IFI.[123] Finally, the concern that amenability to suit will expose an IFI to divergent or contradictory judgments in various jurisdictions has little merit with respect to human rights claims, which by definition are based on a universal body of substantive law.

Perhaps the most compelling reason to reassess international organization immunity in human rights cases, however, is to give due consideration to contemporary norms of accountability for human rights violations. There is an emerging consensus that insulating those who perpetrate or are complicit in human rights violations from accountability is inconsistent with contemporary human rights standards.[124] Just as human rights considerations may limit the immunity of sovereigns and their executive officials, so should they restrict the immunity of international organizations.[125] A court, therefore, should consider an IFI's immunity claims in light of the forum state's customary or treaty-based obligations to prevent or punish human rights abuses and to provide an adequate means of redress.[126] Where the norm at issue is considered to be *jus cogens* or is enshrined in the UN Charter, the human rights principle is indisputably a higher order obligation than the commitment to provide immunity and should prevail.[127] Even when the human rights principle is not clearly of a superior status, it is not obvious why human rights concerns should be reflexively subordinated to an IFI's purported interest in avoiding judicial scrutiny.[128] As Michael Singer has argued,

---

122. Suzuki & Nanwani, *supra* n. 43, 200 ('[t]he disposition of private third parties' claims against an international organization over its activities in the territory of a member state must necessarily be contingent upon the support of state institutions').
123. *E.g.*, the United States government has repeatedly intervened to impede access to justice for human rights victims in ATCA cases brought in the United States. *See* Richard Herz, 'The Liberalizing Effects of Tort: How Corporate Complicity Liability Under the Alien Tort Statute Advances Constructive Engagement', *Harvard Human Rights Journal* 21 (2008): 207.
124. Reinisch, *International Organizations before National Courts*, *supra* n. 24, 287.
125. *Ibid.*, 288.
126. Singer, 'Jurisdictional Immunity of International Organizations: Human Rights and Functional Necessity Concerns', *supra* n. 23, 96; Reinisch, *International Organizations before National Courts*, *supra* n. 24, 287; Report of the Seventy-First Conference, 'Final Report of the International Law Association Committee on Accountability of International Organizations', *supra* n. 42, 34.
127. The United Nations Charter provides: 'In the event of a conflict between the obligations of the Members of the United Nations under the present Charter and their obligations under any other international agreement, their obligations under the present Charter shall prevail.' UN Charter, *supra* n. 13, Art. 103. The Universal Declaration of Human Rights is considered to be the authoritative elaboration of the human rights obligations contained in the UN Charter. Singer, 'Jurisdictional Immunity of International Organizations: Human Rights and Functional Necessity Concerns', *supra* n. 23, 96–97.
128. Reinisch, *International Organizations before National Courts*, *supra* n. 24, 287.

courts should resolve this tension by declining to apply the 'functional necessity' analysis where a clear norm of international human rights law is at issue, because an IFI can never have the functional need (or the authority) to transgress these guarantees.[129] Thus, for Singer, courts should assert jurisdiction over such cases unless the international organization has established its own adequate mechanisms for redress.[130]

Similar considerations support a withdrawal of immunity for claims that arise under other customary norms and general principles of international law. As with human rights claims, there is no reason why an IFI should find it necessary to transgress these norms and principles to achieve its chartered objectives. Even if they did find such actions to be expedient, they would exceed the legitimate mandate of the organization and therefore should not be eligible for immunity. Moreover, like human rights claims, claims that arise under other types of customary international law are not particularly likely to be manipulated by overreaching host governments or otherwise pose a significant threat to the operations of the organization. They will often involve state complicity and are unlikely to be abused by the forum state to gain undue influence or to impose prejudicial judgments. Also like human rights claims, such claims are unlikely to subject the institution to the spectre of divergent legal obligations in different jurisdictions, since they would be based on a universal body of international law.

III. THE WAY FORWARD: ALTERNATIVE MECHANISMS AS A PREREQUISITE FOR IMMUNITY

As the previous sections have shown, absolute or near-absolute IFI immunity is largely an artefact of a discredited approach to international law and international organization accountability that emphasized the rights and remedies of sovereign states above all other considerations. As the rights of individuals have gradually been recognized as a proper subject of international law, the normative case for aggrieved individuals to have greater access to mechanisms of accountability and redress has solidified, while the IFI's interests in being insulated from such claims have diminished. Nevertheless, the jurisprudence of IFI immunity has not evolved in accordance with these developments. By and large, IFIs continue to enjoy much broader immunities than their members agreed to provide them in their charters, or than they actually need to fulfil their mandates. The limitations on immunity inherent in the doctrine of functional necessity are honoured mostly in the breach. Further, claimants who are denied access to national courts by expansive immunity have no alternative judicial or arbitral mechanisms in which to seek redress. As a result, there is a pressing need to strike a more appropriate balance between

129. Singer, 'Jurisdictional Immunity of International Organizations: Human Rights and Functional Necessity Concerns', *supra* n. 23, 94, 151.
130. *Ibid.*, 100.

protecting IFI autonomy and effectiveness, and ensuring that they will not be able to evade accountability for violating their legal obligations.[131]

Such a rebalancing should follow three basic principles. First, countries should ensure that the jurisdictional immunities that they provide to IFIs are consistent with *all* of their international law commitments, not just those they have made to other IFI members in the charter agreements. Presently, many states choose to over-enforce their charter commitments to provide immunity at the expense of human rights commitments that may require them to vindicate certain rights or provide an appropriate forum to hear certain claims. Even where the organizational charter appears to require Member States to grant broad or blanket jurisdictional immunities, states should interpret those commitments in light of their other international obligations. This is particularly the case when those commitments may be of a higher order than their agreements to provide immunity.

Second, when the charters contemplate that the institution will submit to domestic jurisdiction (as most IFI charters do), immunity should be determined by reference to the plain meaning of the term 'functional necessity'. Accordingly, there should be a presumption in favour of jurisdiction, and IFIs should only claim (and receive) those immunities that are strictly necessary for them to fulfil their organizational purposes. Indeed, this was clearly the expectation that animated the General Assembly's original efforts to define the immunities of the United Nations and its Specialized Agencies. Recognizing that the United Nations Charter afforded it immunities necessary to fulfil its purposes, the General Assembly resolved that:

> The privileges and immunities of the United Nations should be regarded, as a general rule, as a maximum within which the various specialized agencies should enjoy such privileges and immunities as the appropriate fulfillment of their respective functions may require, and that no privileges and immunities which are not really necessary should be asked for.[132]

Third, even when an IFI can demonstrate a functional need to be exempted from the jurisdiction of local courts, it should only receive immunity when there is an alternative mechanism in place that is fair and impartial, and can provide customary remedies for legal violations.[133] This is essential to ensure that the forum state does not allow the operational interests of an IFI to override a potential litigant's rights to fair process and appropriate remedies.[134] Indeed, under the jurisprudence

131. Report of the Seventy-First Conference, 'Final Report of the International Law Association Committee on Accountability of International Organizations', *supra* n. 42, 33.

132. General Assembly Resolution of 13 Feb. 1946, A/Res/22A (I), s. D.

133. Reinisch & Weber, 'In the Shadow of Waite and Kennedy: The Jurisdictional Immunity of International Organizations, the Individual's Right of Access to the Courts and Administrative Tribunals as Alternative Means of Dispute Settlement', *supra* n. 65; Singer, 'Jurisdictional Immunity of International Organizations: Human Rights and Functional Necessity Concerns', *supra* n. 23, 53.

134. Reinisch & Weber, 'In the Shadow of Waite and Kennedy: The Jurisdictional Immunity of International Organizations, the Individual's Right of Access to the Courts and Administrative Tribunals as Alternative Means of Dispute Settlement', *supra* n. 65, 68.

of the ECtHR, the immunity of IFIs and other international organizations is contingent upon the existence of an alternative mechanism of redress.[135] Moreover, as with the strict interpretation of immunity, requiring a fair alternative procedure simply restores the essential quid pro quo enshrined in the grants of immunity in such foundational immunity agreements as the *Convention on Privileges and Immunities of the United Nations* and the *Convention on Privileges and Immunities of Specialized Agencies.*

In their current form, the citizen-driven accountability mechanisms that most IFIs have created cannot provide the kinds of redress that might be achieved through domestic litigation. They have the substantive jurisdiction only to consider violations of internal policies, and cannot award compensatory or injunctive relief. Given the limited mandate and lack of remedial powers of these accountability mechanisms, they cannot be considered adequate alternatives to domestic courts. Therefore, unless they are strengthened to allow them to consider the lawfulness of the IFIs' conduct and to impose appropriate remedies, they are insufficient to justify immunity from the jurisdiction of domestic courts.[136]

IV. CONCLUSION

The traditional 'functional necessity' standard of IFI immunity has generally been interpreted to create a presumption of expansive immunity that is out of step with contemporary notions of due process and human rights, sovereign immunity, and the accountability of international organizations. IFI immunity, therefore, should be narrowed to better accommodate these competing interests. Towards this end, countries should limit jurisdictional immunities to reflect their international law commitments, including those that require them to safeguard substantive rights or provide a fair and adequate forum to hear certain claims. 'Functional necessity' should be interpreted with a presumption in favour of jurisdiction, and IFIs should only be granted those immunities that are strictly necessary for them to fulfil their organizational mandates. Even when such necessity can be shown, immunity should only be available where an adequate alternative mechanism for redress is available. Such a rebalancing of IFI immunity would afford them sufficient protection to achieve their institutional objectives, while filling significant gaps in public accountability and legal redress.

135. *Waite & Kennedy v. Germany*, *supra* n. 65, para. 68.

136. *See* Eisuke Suzuki, 'Responsibility of International Financial Institutions under International Law', Ch. 3 herein (discussing the possibility of expanded jurisdiction for administrative tribunals).

Chapter 6

Regulation and Resource Dependency: The Legal and Political Aspects of Structural Adjustment Programmes

*Celine Tan**

I. INTRODUCTION

Structural Adjustment Programmes (SAPs) represent one of the most controversial aspects of the operations of the Bretton Woods institutions, the International Monetary Fund (IMF or Fund) and the World Bank. Originally conceived as a substitute for collateral for short-term financing from the IMF, SAPs have evolved to serve as the objects for financing in themselves. The macroeconomic and structural reforms attached to these programmes and aimed at transforming countries' social, economic, and, often, political structures have developed into the basis for financial support from the IMF and World Bank. Additionally, these reforms have become preconditions for other sources of funding, such as debt relief. This evolution of SAPs from a modality for regulating compliance with financing agreements to a mechanism for embedding policy and regulatory reforms has had significant impacts on international law and global economic governance.

* The author thanks Daniel Bradlow and David Hunter for their constructive comments on the chapter and Erika Lennon for her editorial assistance.

Daniel D. Bradlow and David B. Hunter, *International Financial Institutions and International Law*, pp. 167–197.

This chapter examines the legal aspects of IMF and World Bank SAPs, tracing the historical development of these arrangements and situating them within the geo-political and global economic context in which they evolved. It will demonstrate that the differences in the legal characteristics of SAPs reflect the diversity of the financing instruments to which they are attached and the circumstances in which such funding is sought. Thus, the nature of states' obligations are contingent not only upon the type of financing arrangements entered into with the international financial institutions (IFIs), but also the political and economic clout of these states and the conditions of the global political economy at the time of entry into such agreements.

The chapter further argues that the evolution of SAPs must be located within a corresponding discussion of the progressive entrenchment of policy conditionality as a default regulatory instrument governing the relationships between the IFIs and their client states. SAPs have extended and refined the doctrine of conditionality, which has become pivotal in determining how many countries around the world engage with domestic constituents and external actors. Through its use in SAPs, conditionality has evolved not only to alter the relationships between the Bank and IMF and their borrowing members, but also to reshape these members' engagement with the global economy. This, in turn, has significant implications in international law, both in terms of IFI governance as well as on international financial law and policy.

The rest of the chapter will be organized into four parts. First, it will trace the historical roots of SAPs and their development within the Bretton Woods system. Second, the chapter will explore the contemporary policy and practice relating to SAPs, considering their legal and non-legal normative impacts. The third section of the chapter will chart the link between SAPs and the emergence of policy conditionality as an instrument of law and policy in the context of international law and global economic governance. Finally, and by way of conclusion, the chapter will examine the future of SAPs in light of the changes in the international financial architecture resulting from the global financial crisis of the late 2000s.

II. STRUCTURAL ADJUSTMENT FROM STABILIZATION TO DEBT RELIEF

The origins of SAPs can be traced back to the early years of the Bretton Woods institutions. Even at their infancy, the concept of conditional lending, which forms the premise for SAPs, generated much controversy and debate about the scope and mandate of the newly created IFIs. Over the years, various permutations of SAPs have been developed in response to the bureaucratic and geo-political needs of the IMF, the World Bank, and their Member States, and developments in the international political economy. The doctrine of conditionality[1] underpinning the

1. The term 'conditionality' must be distinguished from 'conditions of financing'. 'Conditionality' refers to the conditions that regulate the aspect of the economic programme or specific

SAP framework has correspondingly evolved in tandem with the changing circumstances of the IMF and World Bank and the institutional and international environment in which they operate.

A. From Automaticity to Conditionality

Established in the latter stages of the Second World War, the IMF and the International Bank for Reconstruction and Development (IBRD) were formed as two international economic organizations endowed with clearly demarcated mandates: the IMF was to oversee international monetary cooperation and the IBRD[2] was to facilitate international investment. Central to meeting these objectives is the provision of multilateral financing: the provision of liquidity to maintain international monetary stability and prevent deflationary adjustments in countries facing balance-of-payments problems (IMF), and the facilitation of capital for reconstruction and development (IBRD).[3]

The modalities for the provision of financing were, however, the subject of much contestation and debate during the Bretton Woods negotiations, particularly with regard to the IMF. The idea that a Member State seeking financial assistance from the cooperative monetary union of the IMF would be subjected to conditions requiring domestic policy and regulatory reforms engendered much discord among its founding members. While the United Kingdom, concerned that conditional financing would not only jeopardize access to resources, but also impede upon national sovereignty, sought unconditional access to IMF reserves subject to quota

institutional or structural reforms that are being financed by the IMF or World Bank, while 'conditions of financing' comprise the financial terms of the legal agreement between the institutions and the financed state, such as conditions pertaining to repayment periods, loan charges, interest rates, procedures for loan withdrawals, and dispute settlement provisions. *See* Vinod Agarwal, 'Legal Aspects of Debt Negotiations', in *Negotiation of Specific Clauses of Loan Agreements, Document 10*, United Nations Institute for Training & Research (UNITAR) (Geneva: UNITAR, 2000), 1–9; Celine Tan, 'Responsible Financing or Unwarrented Interventions: Fiduciary Obligations in Loan and Aid Contracts Between Donors, Client States and Citizens', Briefing Paper for the European Network on Debt and Development (Eurodad) (2006), 18.

2. The IBRD was subsequently joined by four other institutions to make up the World Bank Group: The International Finance Corporation (IFC) established in 1956 to finance private companies seeking to invest in IBRD Member States; the International Development Association (IDA), the World Bank's concessional lending facility created in 1960; the International Centre for the Settlement of Investment Disputes (ICSID) established in 1966 as a forum for the settlement of members' investment disputes; and the Multilateral Investment Guarantee Agency (MIGA) created in 1988 to provide insurance and guarantees to private investors. The IBRD and IDA share the same management (though the others have separate structures) and are the institutions commonly referred to as the 'World Bank'.
3. Yilmaz Akyüz, 'Rectifying Capital Market Imperfections: The Continuing Rationales for Multilateral Lending', in *The New Public Finance: Responding to Global Challenges*, ed. Inge Kaul & Pedro Conceição (New York & Oxford: Oxford University Press, 2006), 486–492.

limitations;[4] the United States (as the IMF's largest shareholder) rejected the idea of automatic financing and insisted that conditions be applied to drawings to safeguard the institution's resources.[5]

The result was an ambiguous compromise in the IMF's Articles of Agreement which provided that each Member State could draw on the resources of the Fund when it needed to because of balance of payments or reserve problems.[6] However, this was subject to the member demonstrating to the Fund that such drawings were both necessary and consistent with the provisions of the Articles of Agreement.[7] In 1947, the IMF's executive board authorized the institution to challenge representations by Member States if there were reason to believe that such drawings were not needed or because the payments would be inconsistent with the Articles of Agreement.[8]

Consequently, despite the initial rejection of explicit conditional financing, 'the process of legitimizing and ratcheting conditionality' began soon after the conclusion of the Bretton Woods conference, leading to an erosion of the concept of automaticity in Fund drawings.[9] The executive board officially adopted the

---

4. IMF members are allocated a quota on the basis of their relative economic strength (although quota calculations have always been highly politicized), with quotas serving as the basis for determining each Member State's financial contributions to the Fund, voting power, and access to financing. On the latter, quotas determine how much Member States can borrow from the IMF, with access limits ranging from the traditional 100% of quotas to exceptional limits of up to 600%. *See* International Monetary Fund (IMF), 'IMF Quotas: A Factsheet', <www.imf.org/external/np/exr/facts/quotas.htm>, 3 Apr. 2009. However, in 2009, the IMF approved the establishment of an unlimited access facility, the Flexible Credit Line (FCL) aimed mainly at emerging markets in the context of the global financial crisis. *See* IMF, 'IMF Implements Major Lending Policy Improvements' (24 Mar. 2009), *available at* <www.imf.org/external/np/pdr/fac/2009/pdf/032409.pdf>.
5. Akyüz, 'Rectifying Capital Market Imperfections: The Continuing Rationales for Multilateral Lending', *supra* n. 3, 490; Ngaire Woods, *The Globalizers: The IMF, the World Bank and Their Borrowers* (Ithaca & London: Cornell University Press, 2006), 25; James Raymond Vreeland, *The International Monetary Fund: Politics of Conditional Lending* (Abington & New York: Routledge, 2007), 21–22.
6. *See* Articles of Agreement of the International Monetary Fund (27 Dec. 1945, as amended 10 Aug. 2009), Art. V(3), *available at* <www.imf.org/external/pubs/ft/aa/> (hereinafter IMF Articles of Agreement). *See also* Akyüz, 'Rectifying Capital Market Imperfections: The Continuing Rationales for Multilateral Lending', *supra* n. 3, 491; Yilmaz Akyüz, 'The Rationale for Multilateral Lending: A Critical Assessment', draft paper for discussion (5 Jul. 2004), 13; Andreas F. Lowenfeld, *International Economic Law*, 2nd edn (Oxford: Oxford University Press, 2008), 611.
7. IMF Articles of Agreement, *supra* n. 6; Akyüz, 'Rectifying Capital Market Imperfections: The Continuing Rationales for Multilateral Lending', *supra* n. 3; Akyüz, 'The Rationale for Multilateral Lending: A Critical Assessment', *supra* n. 6; Lowenfeld, *International Economic Law*, 2nd edn, *supra* n. 6.
8. Akyüz, 'Rectifying Capital Market Imperfections: The Continuing Rationales for Multilateral Lending', *supra* n. 3, 492; IMF, *Selected Decisions and Selected Documents of the International Monetary Fund*, 28th issue (Washington, DC: IMF, 2003), 209–210 (referencing 'IMF, 1948').
9. Akyüz, 'The Rationale for Multilateral Lending: A Critical Assessment', *supra* n. 6, 19.

principle of conditionality in a decision on 13 February 1952,[10] the provisions of which were extended and codified by the First Amendment to its Articles of Agreement in 1969 to allow the Fund to 'adopt policies' and 'establish adequate safeguards' for the use of its general resources.[11]

The same 1952 decision established Stand-By Arrangements (SBAs) as the operational modality for drawings from the Fund's General Resources Account (GRA). A line of credit extended by the IMF to a member facing balance-of-payments problems, a SBA assures a requesting member that it will be able to draw from the GRA in accordance with agreed terms.[12] As discussed further below, these instruments were created to avoid any legal connotations or language of credit (e.g., repayment and interest) in the construction of Fund agreements out of some deference to the founding rationale of the Fund as a credit union. SBAs were introduced so that a programme of economic adjustment could be designed prior to the disbursement of resources in order to regulate the means by which IMF funds were disbursed and utilized by its members.

Countries wishing to borrow from the Fund beyond their reserve tranche[13] would have to submit a Letter of Intent (LOI) and/or a Memorandum of Economic and Financial Policy (MEFP) stipulating the policy measures that country authorities will undertake in return for financial assistance.[14] Once approved by the executive board, this programme of economic adjustment then constitutes the basis for considering the country's eligibility to draw from the Fund, with the measures contained in the programme serving as the conditions for the financial assistance. The introduction of phased drawings in 1956 and the use of performance criteria, policy actions that must be implemented before each tranche of financial package is released, further cemented the move away from automatic

---

10. Here, the IMF's Executive Board, while reiterating that financial resources should not be denied to members in need, stated for the first time that in disbursing its resources, 'the Fund should pay attention to a member's *general creditworthiness*, particularly *its record with the Fund*'. IMF, 'Executive Board Decision No. 10-(51/11)' (13 Feb. 1952) (emphasis added).
11. IMF Articles of Agreement, *supra* n. 6, Art. V(3).
12. *Ibid.*, Art. XXX(b).
13. The reserve tranche refers to funds equivalent to 25% of a country's quota at the IMF. Countries wishing to draw beyond this or in the upper credit tranches can do so only via a stand-by arrangement. Access by members to resources in the credit tranches are subjected to annual and cumulative limits that are subject to review by the IMF's executive board. Until 2009, countries could normally draw up to 100% of their quotas annually or 300% cumulatively, but with the possibility that access above these limits (sometimes up to 600% of quota) would be approved by the executive board under exceptional circumstances. *See* IMF, 'Review of the Fund's Financing Role in Member Countries' (28 Aug. 2008): 17–18. In March 2009, the executive board approved a doubling to these limits to 200% annually and 600% cumulatively for non-concessional drawings. *See* IMF, 'IMF Overhauls Nonconcessional Lending: Facilities and Conditionality', Public Information Notice (PIN) No. 09/40 (3 Apr. 2009). The same decision also introduced FCL, the first IMF facility with no hard cap on the amount to be drawn by countries. IMF, 'IMF Implements Major Lending Policy Improvements', *supra* n. 4, 2.
14. *See* IMF, 'Guidelines on Conditionality', Executive Board Decision No. 12864 (02/102) (Washington, DC: IMF, 25 Sep. 2002), para. 10.

drawings and effectively kept 'the requesting members on a short-leash' vis-à-vis the Fund.[15]

The SBA model of financial assistance, which is based on a pre-approved programme of economic reforms and policy actions, and enforced through the phasing of disbursements ('tranching') and implementation of programme conditions, remains the template for IMF financing. It has formed the basis for the development of new lending facilities by the Fund over the years, including the facilities which gave birth to the SAPs. It also influenced the design of the World Bank's own SAPs implemented through the policy-based lending facilities introduced in the late 1970s at both the IBRD and its concessional lending counterpart, the International Development Association (IDA).

B. A New Landscape for Development Financing

The 1970s marked a turning point in international financial law and policy, both in terms of international financial governance and multilateral lending. By 1974 the fixed exchange rate regime under the original Bretton Woods agreements collapsed, leading the IMF to adopt the pivotal Second Amendment to its Articles of Agreement in 1979, which allowed states to adopt flexible exchange rate policies. Meanwhile, operational changes at both the IMF and the World Bank led to the development of new forms of international public finance, including those underpinned by SAPs.

In addition to abolishing the par value system and providing for a new regime to supervise countries' exchange rate policies, the constitutional reforms of the Second Amendment codified lending practices of the institution, which had broadened its financing beyond the standard drawings from the GRA under SBAs. In particular, it cemented the IMF's foray into development financing, expanded its role from a short-term lender of last resort to a funder of longer-term economic development, and reinforced the role of conditionality in Fund financing.

The significance of the latter reforms cannot be overstated. The IMF's new lending instruments became the new means of international financial regulation under the amended articles. Without explicit authority to enforce fixed exchange rate policies at the supranational level, the IMF and its Member States turned to monitoring domestic policies as a means of policing international financial flows and ensuring global financial stability. Although the revised Article IV enabled IMF Member States to choose their own exchange rate arrangements as opposed to adherence to a multilateral standard,[16] it also obligated Member States to undertake domestic economic and financial policies that would not produce disruptions in the global economy.[17] The revised Article IV further conferred upon the IMF a

15. Akyüz, 'The Rationale for Multilateral Lending: A Critical Assessment', *supra* n. 6, 19–20.
16. IMF Articles of Agreement, *supra* n. 6, Art. IV(2)(b).
17. *Ibid.*, Art. IV(1).

corresponding authority to exercise 'surveillance' over the international monetary system, including members' exchange rate policies, both bilaterally and multilaterally.[18]

Under the new regulatory regime, threats to the international financial system were perceived as stemming from errant domestic policies undertaken by countries rather than from inherent systemic problems with the governance of the global economy or from the destructive policies of other Member States. International financial regulation was no longer premised on supervision by a multilateral institution, but rather was based on creating the appropriate domestic framework within countries to prevent international financial crisis.[19] Financing from the Fund therefore became increasingly conditional upon members' willingness to undertake 'appropriate' domestic policies to redress economic instability, and a key instrument for enforcing these policies in Member States was to impose them as conditions of lending. Thus, structural adjustment emerged as the mechanism through which such discipline could be enforced.

In 1974, the IMF established the Extended Fund Facility (EFF), the first international financial facility explicitly to support structural adjustment in borrowing Member States. Like SBAs, Extended Arrangements are based on a programme of policy and regulatory reform and policed by the application of conditionality. However, the *content* of EFF conditionality signalled a departure from the institution's traditional business. Structural conditionality under EFF programmes, unlike the circumscribed and temporary nature of fiscal and monetary conditions, was aimed at fundamentally altering underlying institutions of the economy, such as trade policy or domestic production.[20]

In the late 1970s, structural adjustment lending was extended to low-income countries with the introduction of concessional financing via trust funds, established first under the IMF's implied powers and, after the Second Amendment, through express powers provided for under revised Article V of the IMF's Articles of Agreement. Again, this represented an expansion of the IMF's conventional portfolio, enabling the IMF to disburse funds to Member States from resources generated outside the GRA, such as through gold sales or bilateral contributions from other members. Under this authority, in 1976, the IMF established a Trust Fund, which was succeeded by the Structural Adjustment Facility (SAF) in 1986;

18. IMF Articles of Agreement, *supra* n. 6, Art. IV(3).
19. *See* Martin Khor, 'A Critique of the IMF's Role and Policy Conditionality', *TWN Global Economy Series* No. 4 (Penang: Third World Network, 2001): 4–5; Sundhya Pahuja, 'Technologies of Empire: IMF Conditionality and the Reinscription of the North/South Divide', *Leiden Journal of International Law* 13 (2000): 778–779.
20. Sarah Babb & Ariel Buira, 'Mission Creep, Mission Push in Sociological Perspective: The Case of IMF Conditionality', paper presented at the XVIII G24 Technical Group Meeting (Geneva, 8–9 Mar. 2004), 9; Akyüz, 'Rectifying Capital Market Imperfections: The Continuing Rationales for Multilateral Lending', *supra* n. 3, 493; IMF, 'Conditionality in Fund-Supported Programs: Policy Issues' (Washington, DC: IMF, 16 Feb. 2001), 42.

the Enhanced Structural Adjustment Facility (ESAF) in 1987; and most recently, the Poverty Reduction and Growth Facility (PRGF) in 1999.[21]

At the same time, the IMF's sister institution, the World Bank, was broadening its own activities, and moving away from its traditional focus on project lending towards financing policy and regulatory reforms in client states and providing technical assistance on a range of social and economic areas. The appointment of former US Defense Secretary Robert McNamara as World Bank president in 1968 led to a rapid expansion of the Bank's work programme, both in terms of its lending portfolio and its research infrastructure.[22]

Where previously the Bank had financed mainly discrete infrastructure projects, such as the construction of power plants and transportation networks, the McNamara presidency shifted the institution's attention to economies as a whole. Not only did the range of project financing expand into areas such as agriculture and industrial services to become more complex and multi-faceted, but the Bank also began targeting the policy framework and institutions in their client states by offering funding for policy and regulatory reforms in areas the institution indentified as needing restructuring.[23]

In the early 1980s, the IBRD and IDA introduced structural adjustment loans and credits (SALs/SACs), respectively, to support such 'policy-based' financing.[24] Approval for financing for these loans hinged on two preconditions: (1) the country was anticipating or experiencing a balance-of-payments problem, necessitating 'rapidly disbursing' external financing; and (2) the country's government was agreeable to a programme of policy reform or 'adjustment' in return for financing.[25]

Like the IMF's adjustment lending, a Bank borrower's compliance with the programme of economic reform would be regulated by the use of conditionality.[26] However, unlike IMF adjustment lending, the *basis* of financial support for World Bank adjustment loans was the programme of economic reform rather than the need for external financing for which the programme served as conditions. In other words, the Bank's loans are aimed at supporting the implementation of economic

21. The Trust fund was established under an implied power, while the SAF, ESAF, and PRGF were established under express powers conferred under the revised Art. V. For further discussion of this topic, *see* s. III.B *infra*.
22. Woods, *supra* n. 5, 44–45.
23. *Ibid.*, 44–45; Susan George & Fabrizio Sabelli, *Faith and Credit: The World Bank's Secular Empire* (Boulder, CO: Westview Press, 1994), 43–44.
24. SALs and SACs have been supplemented over the years by a plethora of other adjustment instruments, including sectoral adjustment loans/credits (SECALs/SECACs), subnational adjustment loans (SNALs), and programmatic adjustment loans and credits (PSALs/PSACs). World Bank, *Adjustment Lending Retrospective: Final Report* (Washington, DC: World Bank, 2001), 1.
25. Ibrahim Shihata, *The World Bank Legal Papers* (The Hague: Kluwer Law International, 2000), 377; World Bank, 'Review of World Bank Conditionality: Legal Aspects of Conditionality in Policy-Based Lending' (Washington, DC: World Bank, 29 Jun. 2005), 2.
26. World Bank, 'Review of World Bank Conditionality: Legal Aspects of Conditionality in Policy Based Lending', *supra* n. 25, 7–8.

reforms under the adjustment programme, while at the IMF economic reforms are imposed *in exchange* for external financing aimed at redressing the country's balance-of-payments problems. This difference in rationale behind the IMF's and Bank's adjustment lending is significant when considering the legal dimensions of these programmes and the role of conditionality.[27]

C. The Debt Crisis and the Entrenchment of Structural Adjustment

The expansion in IFI structural adjustment lending in the 1970s was further driven and reinforced by a number of other internal and external factors in the 1980s. Firstly, the changes in the form and content of multilateral lending reflected the changing clientele of the IMF and World Bank coupled with their inherent institutional governance asymmetries. Since the collapse of the Bretton Woods system, the majority of Member States seeking financial assistance from the Fund shifted from industrialized countries to post-colonial and other developing states. In the context of the governance structures of these two institutions,[28] this has meant that the states holding the decision-making power within the IMF and World Bank are not the same states subject to their operational (and other regulatory) policies.

The effects of this asymmetry have been twofold. First, the conditions of financing no longer needed to reflect the economic priorities of their economically powerful Member States as these states do not still borrow from the Bank or Fund, nor have they borrowed from the Bank since before the collapse of the Bretton Woods system. Second, it resulted in the de facto cartelization of multilateral financing by the IMF and World Bank as creditor/donor countries opt to channel finance through the institutions over which they have the greater influence.

Therefore, it was unsurprising that the World Bank and IMF's SAPs became the key instruments for responding to the debt crisis of the 1980s and to the vulnerability of indebted developing countries in accordance with the geo-political and economic concerns of the major institutional shareholders. While the IMF provided stabilization loans to developing countries to service their external debt to foreign private creditors, the World Bank stepped in to provide the financing buffer for states to undertake the economic reforms necessary to meet this debt

27. *See* s. III *infra*.
28. Both the IMF and World Bank have a weighted decision-making structure in which countries with the largest quotas (IMF) or capital subscriptions (IBRD) are apportioned a larger share of votes and representation on the respective executive boards, resulting in five G7 countries, the US, Japan, Germany, France, and the UK, possessing the largest share of votes at the institutions. *See* Woods, *supra* n. 5, 22–24. The advent of bilateral concessional facilities, such as the IDA and the IMF's ESAF/PRGF, has further compounded this asymmetry by submitting the institutions to operational and other policy demands of major contributors during periodic replenishment processes of the concessional facilities.

servicing and to prevent the crisis from providing fodder for ideological ferment during the Cold War.[29]

Correspondingly, the proliferation of SAPs was also driven by the emergence of the IMF and, to a lesser extent, the World Bank as gatekeepers to other sources of development financing. As conditionality developed beyond an instrument for regulating the relationship between parties in financing to a mechanism of regulatory reform in its own right,[30] SAPs began to assume a new signalling role in international development finance. In other words, access to sources of private and official financing, especially for low-income developing countries, soon became largely contingent on countries' adoption of and adherence to an IMF programme of reform.

The IMF terms this the 'catalytic role' of its economic reform programmes, serving to 'unlock other financing'.[31] According to the Fund, conditionality in a member's programme serves as a signal or 'stamp of approval' to 'help reinforce policy credibility' and 'increase investors' confidence in the direction of economic policies' irrespective of the size of the Fund's financial contribution.[32] SAPs soon became *de rigeur* for countries seeking external financing in crisis and non-crisis circumstances, with many countries embarking on an IMF programme without necessarily requiring financial resources from the IMF itself. Commercial creditors, often, have tied loan agreements to performance clauses of an IMF arrangement for the purposes of 'piggy-backing' on the Fund's relationship with borrowing Member States and its supervision of their economic policies.[33]

The signalling role of SAPs was enhanced further by its use in official debt rescheduling processes throughout the 1980s and 1990s. In particular, debtor countries wishing to restructure their debt with Paris Club creditors needed to demonstrate, *inter alia*, that they had an IMF adjustment programme in place.[34] For countries eligible for bilateral and multilateral debt relief under the Heavily Indebted Poor Countries (HIPC) initiative, which was introduced in 1986, or enhanced HIPC initiative, which was introduced in 1999, successful implementation of a SAP – under an IMF or IDA supported instrument – is a prerequisite for achieving the landmark 'decision' or 'completion' points for debt relief.[35] In 2005,

29. Structural Adjustment Participatory Review International Network (SAPRIN), *Structural Adjustment: The SAPRI Report – The Policy Roots of Economic Crisis, Poverty and Inequality* (London & New York, Penang, Manila & Bangalore: Zed books, Third World Network, Ibon Foundation, and Books for Change, 2004), 1–4 (hereinafter SAPRRIN); Woods, *supra* n. 5, 47–51.
30. For more discussion, *see* s. III *infra*.
31. IMF, 'Review of the Fund's Financing Role in Member Countries', *supra* n. 13, 7.
32. *Ibid.*
33. Richard W. Edwards, 'Is an IMF Stand-by Arrangement a "Seal of Approval" on Which Other Creditors Can Rely', *Journal of International Law & Politics* 17, no. 3 (1984): 592.
34. Juan Carlos Villanova & Matthew Martin, 'The Paris Club', Publication 3 (London: Debt Relief International, 2001), 2.
35. IMF, 'Heavily Indebted Poor Countries (HIPC) Initiative and Multilateral Debt Relief Initiative (MDRI): Status of Implementation' (12 Sep. 2008), 4; IMF, 'Instrument to Establish a Trust for Special PRGF Operations for the Heavily Indebted Poor Countries and Interim PRGF Subsidy Operations' (February 1997), s. III, para. 2(c).

the IMF introduced a purely catalytic SAP in the form of a Policy Support Instrument (PSI), a non-disbursing Fund-monitored programme, which served primarily as a signalling instrument for low-income countries graduating from the PRGF.[36]

In 2004, following the introduction of the Poverty Reduction Strategy Papers (PRSPs) to replace the Policy Framework Papers (PFPs) as preconditions for concessional lending from the IMF and the World Bank, the World Bank overhauled its adjustment lending framework by replacing the term 'adjustment lending' with 'development policy lending'. More than a change in nomenclature, reform of the Bank's policy-based operations included a restructuring of design, fiduciary arrangements, and policies for dissemination and disclosure; and the unification of all previous structural and sectoral adjustment instruments under a single umbrella.[37]

Aside from marking a shift in the purpose of such loans from short-term macroeconomic adjustment to 'longer-term developmental and institutional' support, the new terminology was also aimed at signalling the Bank's adoption of new approaches to development policy financing and conditionality, including the focus on 'country ownership' and participation by stakeholders,[38] capturing the general 'mood shift' in global economic policymaking. This includes a commitment by the Bank to facilitate greater government involvement in the determination of economic reform policies and dialogue between borrowing governments and their citizens in this process. For example, the PRSP, serving as a centrepiece for this new approach, is supposed to refocus national economic policymaking on developmental objectives such as poverty reduction, and must be developed nationally through a participatory process involving a cross-section of stakeholders.[39]

---

36. IMF, 'The Policy Support Instrument: A Factsheet', <www.imf.org/external/np/exr/facts/psi.htm>, November 2008.
37. World Bank, 'Development Policy Lending Replaces Adjustment Lending: The World Bank Overhauls Its Guidelines for Policy-Based Lending to Reflect 20 Years of Experience' (10 Aug. 2004), *available at* <http://web.worldbank.org/WBSITE/EXTERNAL/NEWS/0,,contentMDK:20237378~menuPK:34457~pagePK:64003015~piPK:64003012~theSitePK:4607,00.html>; World Bank, 'From Adjustment Lending to Development Policy Support Lending: Key Issues in the Update of World Bank Policy' (6 Jun. 2002), paras 11, 15.
38. World Bank, 'Development Policy Lending Replaces Adjustment Lending: The World Bank Overhauls Its Guidelines for Policy-Based Lending to Reflect 20 Years of Experience', *supra* n. 37; World Bank 'From Adjustment Lending to Development Policy Support Lending: Key Issues in the Update of World Bank Policy', *supra* n. 37.
39. There is naturally a gap between the reality and the rhetoric of this new approach as experience since the reforms have indicated that such ownership and participation remains lacking in many cases. *See*, *e.g.*, Jeremy Gould, *The New Conditionality: Poverty Reduction Strategies: Aid and Domestic Policies* (London: Zed Books, 2005).

III. LEGAL DIVERSITY, POLITICAL MULTIPLICITIES: THE NORMATIVE CHARACTER OF STRUCTURAL ADJUSTMENT

SAPs provide the framework through which the legal and political relationships between the IMF and the World Bank and their clients are defined, monitored, and enforced under particular financing circumstances. However, the precise legal character of these programmes depends on the financing arrangements to which they are attached. In particular, there are significant differences in the legal nature of Fund- and Bank-supported adjustment lending, and between concessional and non-concessional lending facilities. Importantly, these differences reflect the normative realities of states' obligations to these institutions, which are contingent not only on the types of financial instruments involved, but also on the economic and political clout of states and conditions of the global economy at their time of entry into such arrangements.

A. IMF Arrangements as Collateral Substitutes

For the IMF, the Stand-By Arrangement (SBA) and Extended Arrangement (under the EFF and SAF) remain the 'workhorse[s]' for countries seeking to draw from its GRA,[40] and are the principal instruments through which funds are made available.[41] Although these arrangements are carefully negotiated between the IMF and the Member State drawing from the GRA, the Fund, traditionally, has refused to characterize them as conventional contracts or international agreements.[42]

This reluctance stems from the deference to and recognition of both the source of such financing and the Fund's original design as a credit union, as well as the institution's constitutional obligation under Article I(v) of its Articles of Agreement to assist members facing financial difficulties.[43] Funds in the GRA are drawn from a repository of members' currencies, which lodge with the Fund through quota subscriptions or via stand-by credit arrangements with members' central banks.[44]

40. IMF, 'Review of the Fund's Financing Role in Member Countries, *supra* n. 13, 2.
41. Joseph Gold, *Interpretation: The IMF and International Law* (London, The Hague & Boston, MA: Kluwer Law International, 1996): 347; Lowenfeld, *International Economic Law*, 2nd edn, *supra* n. 6, 615.
42. Lowenfeld, *International Economic Law*, 2nd edn, *supra* n. 6, 616–617; Edwards, *supra* n. 33, 585.
43. *See* IMF Articles of Agreement, *supra* n. 6, Art. I(v); IMF, 'Financial Organization and Operations of the IMF', pamphlet series no. 45, 6th edn (Washington, DC: IMF, 2001), 8, 19–21.
44. Resources in the GRA are supplemented by the IMF borrowing funds from official lenders under both the General Arrangements to Borrow (GAB) and New Arrangements to Borrow (NAB), which are agreements with a group of eleven industrialized and twenty-five industrialized and emerging market economies, respectively. IMF, 'Financial Organization and Operations of the IMF', *supra* n. 43, 72–73; *see also* Woods, *supra* n. 5, 30–32.

As such, members seeking these resources can be described as asserting their *right* to draw upon funds to which they contributed under the terms of the IMF's constitutional charter. Therefore, the 'language of credit' is absent in the construction of IMF arrangements as a result of the founding ethos of the institution to treat this automaticity of financing as a right.[45]

The revised 2002 Guidelines on Conditionality, thus, reaffirmed the decision made in the original 1979 Guidelines on the Use of the IMF's General Resources and SBAs, in stating that:

> A Fund arrangement is a *decision of the Executive Board* by which a member is assured that it will be able to make purchases or receive disbursements from the Fund in accordance with the terms of the decision during a specified period and up to a specified amount. Fund arrangements are *not international agreements* and therefore language having contractual connotation will be avoided in arrangements and in program documents (emphasis added).[46]

Accordingly, a member's use of Fund resources is deemed to be governed by the provisions of its constitution so as to represent its obligations to the membership of states that the institution represents, rather than by contractual terms entered into between the drawing member and the institution as a bureaucracy. In other words, when a member draws on IMF resources, it does so as a matter of right under the IMF's Articles of Agreement and its legal relationship is one primarily with the other members who have contributed the resources to make this drawing possible. Hence, failures to comply with the terms and conditions of the drawings are classified as failures to comply with the respective provisions governing such drawings under the Fund's constitution. However, as suggested by former IMF General Counsel, Joseph Gold, it is the difficulty with defining breaches and administering penalties for breaches of the Fund's Articles of Agreement that has led to the creation of facilities such as SBAs in order to regulate the behaviour of members and meet the institution's fiduciary obligations under the charter without recourse to contractual terminology.[47]

Although the IMF's Articles of Agreement enable the IMF to limit or suspend members' access to its general resources under Article V, section 5,[48] Article VI, section 1,[49] or Article XXVI, section 2(a),[50] ambiguity exists as to the interpretation of these provisions. Here, the difficulty in prescribing uniform criteria for

45. Akyüz, 'The Rationale for Multilateral Lending: A Critical Assessment', *supra* n. 6, 13; Edwards, *supra* n. 33, 585.
46. IMF, 'Guidelines on Conditionality', Executive Board Decision No. 12864 (02/102) (Washington, DC: IMF, 25 Sep. 2002), para. 9.
47. Gold, *Interpretation: The IMF and International Law*, *supra* n. 41, 343–355.
48. IMF Articles of Agreement, *supra* n. 6, Art. V(5) (specifying that limiting access to resources can happen for using funds 'in a manner contrary to the purposes of the Fund').
49. *Ibid.*, Art. VI(1) (specifying that limiting access to resources can happen for using funds to meet a large or sustained outflow of capital).
50. *Ibid.*, Art. XXVI(2)(a) (specifying that limiting access to resources can happen for failure to fulfil any obligations in the charter).

establishing what measures are adequate to constitute a fulfilment of a member's obligations under the respective provisions – such as what constitutes appropriate use under Article V, section 5 – has led to the reluctance on the part of Fund members to consider failure to comply with financing conditions as a breach of a member's constitutional obligations.[51]

Regulation of a member's use of Fund resources turned to a less legalistic regime – the adoption of a supervised economic reform programme policed by the use of conditionality – as a fiduciary safeguard. These fiduciary instruments have to ensure that resources from the Fund are utilized in accordance with its mandate, but without the penalty of a constitutional violation should such obligations not be fulfilled. An SBA or Extended Arrangement, therefore, is treated, according to Edwards, as 'a unilateral statement of intention by the member country to pursue stated policies, and a unilateral decision of the IMF to provide a specified amount of resources from the [GRA] upon call to support those policies'.[52]

A Member State's failure to observe the policies outlined in a Fund-supported programme, therefore, would not constitute a breach of a legal obligation.[53] Instead, non-compliance could result in the interruption of disbursements under the phased financing arrangements of the relevant facilities.[54] Monitoring of the programme is executed through the application of conditionality, including prior actions, programme reviews, and, until March 2009, structural performance criteria.[55] According to the Fund, the application of conditionality in this manner 'helps reduce risks to the Fund by linking financial exposure to the member's actions to solve its balance of payments problem and strengthen its position to repay the Fund'.[56]

In their consideration of this aspect of conditionality, Mosley, Toye, and Harrington conceive of it as 'a side condition designed to ensure the execution

---

51. Gold, *Interpretation: The IMF and International Law*, *supra* n. 41, 345.
52. Edwards, *supra* n. 33, 586; *see also* Ross Leckow, 'Conditionality in the International Monetary Fund', paper by the Assistant General Counsel of the IMF (Washington, DC: IMF, 2002): 2.
53. Edwards, *supra* n. 33, 586; Gold, *Interpretation: The IMF and International Law*, *supra* n. 41, 354; Leckow, 'Conditionality in the International Monetary Fund', *supra* n. 52, 2.
54. *See* Edwards, *supra* n. 33, 586.
55. In a decision on 24 Mar. 2009, the IMF executive board discontinued the use of structural performance criteria in all Fund arrangements, including its concessional lending facilities. Although structural conditionalities will remain 'integral' to Fund programmes, monitoring of countries' compliance with these reforms will be implemented through other forms of conditionality, notably programme reviews. This means that failure to comply with a specific structural criterion will not result in an automatic suspension of disbursements, but will be assessed in the context of a wider review of the adjustment programme. *See* IMF, 'IMF Overhauls Nonconcessional Lending: Facilities and Conditionality', *supra* n. 13; IMF, 'IMF Implements Major Lending Policy Improvements', *supra* n. 4. For broader information, *see* IMF, 'Conditionality in Fund-Supported Programmes: Purposes, Modalities and Options for Reform' (29 Jul. 2009), para. 9.
56. IMF, 'Conditionality in Fund-Supported Programmes: Purposes, Modalities and Options for Reform', *supra* n. 55, para. 9.

of a *contract*' in international financial agreements.[57] The authors contend that without collateral, financial institutions involved in lending to sovereign states do not have much in the way of a guarantee in the event of debt default. Conditionality, therefore, serves as 'a substitute for collateral' by 'increasing the likelihood of loan repayment' through policy reform and monitoring of compliance with such reforms, thereby 'giving the lender an early warning of potential repayment difficulties'.[58]

Consequently, the exercise of conditionality governs the execution of the adjustment programme as detailed in the relevant Letters of Intent and Memoranda of Economic and Financial Policy,[59] and in the Executive Board decisions approving the programme of financial assistance. The practice of conditionality has eroded the automaticity of Fund financing over time, leading commentators to suggest that the extensive use of conditionality in Fund programmes has curtailed any real sense of *entitlement* an IMF Member State may have to draw beyond its reserve tranche.[60] Additionally, this commentary has become increasingly focused on shifting progressively towards the *content* of conditionality policies, rather than on the *role* of conditionality. As Kalderimis notes, 'most of the debate now centres on the meaning of "adequate safeguards" in Article 1(v)/Article V(3)(a)', reserving the right for the IMF to require conditions for use of its credit and to determine what those conditions should be.[61]

B. Trust Fund Arrangements and Concessional Lending

The evolution from automatic to conditional financing at the IMF was reinforced by the introduction of concessional financing via trust funds in the late 1970s.[62] The Second Amendment of the IMF Articles of Agreement in 1979 conferred upon the Fund the power to grant concessional loans to low-income countries under Article V, section 2(b). This authorized the IMF to 'perform financial and technical services, including the administration of resources contributed by members' if so requested and if consistent with the purposes of the Fund.[63]

A significant distinction between financing from the GRA and financing under the concessional lending trusts is the IMF's treatment of the legal status of the

57. Paul Mosley, John Toye & Jane Harrigan, *Aid and Power: The World Bank and Policy-Based Lending*, vol. 2 (London: Routledge, 1991), 66.
58. *Ibid.*
59. For a more detailed discussion, *see* s. II.A *supra*.
60. Daniel Kalderimis, 'IMF Conditionality as Investment Regulation: A Theoretical Analysis', *Social and Legal Studies* 12, no. 1 (2004): 115; *see also* Akyüz, 'The Rationale for Multilateral Lending: A Critical Assessment', *supra* n. 6, 19–21.
61. Kalderimis, *supra* n. 60, 115.
62. For an extended discussion, *see* s. II.B *supra*.
63. IMF Articles of Agreement, *supra* n. 6, Art. V(2)(b); *see also* Gold, *Interpretation: The IMF and International Law*, *supra* n. 41, 368–369.

financing agreement between the parties to the financing. Unlike SBAs and other arrangements to draw from general resources, financing from the trust funds – such as from the PRGF Trust (formerly the ESAF Trust) or from the Exogenous Shocks Facility (ESF) – is clearly defined as 'loans'. Section I(1) of the Instrument to Establish the PRGF Trust states clearly that: 'The Trust shall assist in fulfilling the purposes of the Fund by providing *loans* on concessional terms . . . to low-income developing members that qualify for assistance' (emphasis added).[64]

The language of credit in these financing instruments again has roots in the nature and source of such financing. Unlike financing from the GRA, financing from the PRGF or the ESF involves drawing on funds that have not been contributed by the borrowers themselves, but rather are 'loans' from other sources with interest rates subsidized by the PRGF or PRGF-ESF Trusts.[65] The language of constitutional obligation and cooperative purpose that characterize the SBAs do not seem to apply to PRGF financing. Funds from the PRGF are earmarked for countries who meet the eligibility criteria for assistance from better-off members, disbursement of which is contingent upon compliance with Fund conditionalities. Accordingly, as former IMF General Counsel, the late Joseph Gold has remarked, the 'day-to-day parlance' of the Fund 'has long since abandoned these niceties of law and diplomacy and instead has used the rougher tongue that reflects the economic view that a member receives credit from the Fund'.[66]

In spite of this, Gold was of the opinion that regardless of its classification, nothing in the trust instruments for concessional financing suggest that policies prescribed within a member's programme supported by Fund financing has contractual force 'so that no inference could be drawn that a departure from them was a breach of [a contractual] obligation'.[67] This view appears to be supported by the executive board decision on the 2002 Guidelines on Conditionality.[68] While reaffirming that no Fund arrangements can be considered to have contractual force, the statement does not refer specifically to general resources and, therefore, can be assumed to encompass all forms of IMF financing, including concessional lending under the PRGF.

Nonetheless, as trustee, the IMF is under a fiduciary duty to ensure that the terms and conditions of the trust instruments are complied with. In this regard, the

64. IMF, 'Instrument to Establish the Poverty Reduction and Growth Facility Trust', Decision 12087-(99/118) (21 Oct. 1999), s. I(1).
65. The PRGF Trust borrows from a number of sources to lend to PRGF-eligible countries and repays the loans with market rate interest to the lenders. The difference between the rate of interest paid to lenders and the concessional interest rate of 0.5% paid to the Trust by PRGF borrowers is subsidized by contributions from bilateral donors and from earnings from the IMF. *Ibid.*, s. IV. The PRGF-ESF Trusts operate on the same basis. IMF, 'Instrument to Establish a Trust for Special PRGF Operations for the Heavily Indebted Poor Countries and Interim PRGF Subsidy Operations', *supra* n. 35.
66. Gold, *Interpretation: The IMF and International Law*, *supra* n. 41, 368.
67. *Ibid.*, 369.
68. IMF, 'Guidelines on Conditionality', *supra* n. 46, para. 9 (entire paragraph reproduce in prior s. III(A)).

Fund is generally accorded wide powers of discretion to determine the terms of eligibility and conditions for financial assistance to eligible members. For example, sections II(1)(b) and (bb) of the Instrument to Establish the PRGF Trust provide that assistance should be given to a qualifying member upon approval by the Fund of a three-year macroeconomic and SAP with disbursements contingent upon reviews of the country's performance under the programme, including compliance with key structural reform policies.[69]

However, the trust instrument is silent on the content of the SAP to be undertaken and on the criteria for determining compliance with the conditions for policy reform in the borrowing Member State. Under the PRGF Trust Instrument, it is left to the Trustee (the IMF) to determine the phasing of loan disbursements and the conditions attached to such disbursements 'in the context of a review of the program with the member'.[70] This gives the IMF broad discretionary authority to determine the content of loan conditions and when, and if, those conditions are met by borrowers. As discussed earlier, the Fund is reluctant to declare members ineligible under Article V, section 5 for failure to comply with the conditions of their loans. Similarly here, conditionality offers a less punitive mechanism for disciplining errant borrowers, and one that still allows the Fund to link policy compliance with the disbursement of resources.

Consequently, it may be argued that the difference between financing from the GRA and from specially-administered accounts, such as those under the PRGF and PRGF-HIPC Trusts, does not substantially alter the nature of the adjustment programmes and conditionality with respect to individual IMF facilities. Conditionality remains the primary regulator of the relationship between the Fund and its members. The preference for such 'soft law' stems from a reluctance to both confer on or hold members accountable to obligations under formal IMF law, that is, the laws originating from its Articles of Agreement or its formal trust instruments.

Conditionality also regulates the policies of low-income IMF borrowers who undertake a voluntary SAP in the form of a PSI.[71] Aimed at countries graduating from the PRGF, the PSI acts primarily as a signalling device for official and private creditors and donors, and can serve as a means of rapid access to the IMF's ESF in cases of sudden economic shocks.[72] Policy reforms carry the same discipline as that of a standard financing arrangement and programme reviews are scheduled in a similar manner as that of a regular SAP.[73] This new IMF facility further highlights the evolution of SAP from a substitute for collateral to a policy and regulatory tool in its own right.

69. IMF, 'Instrument to Establish the Poverty Reduction and Growth Facility Trust', *supra* n. 64.
70. *Ibid.*, s. II(1)(bb).
71. For more discussion, *see* s. II.C *supra*.
72. IMF, 'The Policy Support Instrument: A Factsheet', *supra* n. 36.
73. *Ibid.*

C. THE WORLD BANK'S POLICY-BASED LENDING

The introduction of structural adjustment lending at the World Bank has had significant constitutional and operational implications for the institution. Like the IMF, the Bank's foray into policy-based financing has led to an expansion not only of its traditional lending portfolio, but also of its mandate under its Articles of Agreement. Also like the Fund, the economic reform programmes attached to structural adjustment loans are monitored and enforced through the use of policy conditionality. In fact, for the World Bank, conditionality is synonymous with policy-based lending as it is through this form of financing that conditionality was first introduced at the institution.[74]

For the Bank, however, the rationale for its SAPs differs from that of the IMF although their effect is similar. While IMF adjustment programmes aim at restoring a country's balance-of-payments equilibrium and ensuring the institution is repaid, the objective of the Bank's programmes is the economic restructuring itself. The Bank's memorandum introducing structural adjustment lending stated that such lending 'must be conceived as an association with a borrower in a program of structural change . . . which will require financial support and technical cooperation [during the period of the loan]'.[75] This distinction is also reflected in the difference in legal construction of the Bank's lending versus the Fund's.

The World Bank's financing instruments are clearly regarded as loans and give rise to contractual obligations.[76] Further, these agreements are classified as international treaties between the borrowing Member State and the World Bank, and are registered as such with the UN Secretary-General pursuant to Article 102 of the United Nations Charter.[77] In project or investment operations, loan agreements 'describe the project objectives and components', but in policy-based loans the agreements refer to the borrower's programme that the loan supports.[78] The object of the former is the infrastructure or other project itself, while the object of the latter is the policy and institutional actions that the borrower undertakes in return for the financial assistance.

Therefore, unlike the Fund where the relationship between the organization and its members is defined, primarily, by the institution's constituent treaty, the Bank operates very much like a financial institution in which the principal legal instrument that regulates the relationship between itself and a borrower is that of a

74. *See* World Bank, 'Review of World Bank Conditionality: Legal Aspects of Conditionality in Policy-Based Lending', *supra* n. 25, 2, para. 5.
75. Shihata, *The World Bank Legal Papers*, *supra* n. 25, 163 (quoting from the World Bank's 1980 memorandum).
76. World Bank, 'Operational Policy 7.00 – Lending Operations: Choice of Borrower and Contractual Agreements' (Washington, DC: World Bank, February 2001, revised August 2004), paras 8–9, *available at* <http://go.worldbank.org/7C4C4JE8S0> (hereinafter OP 7.00).
77. United Nations, 'Charter of the United Nations' (24 Oct. 1945), Art. 102, *available at* <www.un.org/en/documents/charter/index.shtml> (hereinafter UN Charter).
78. World Bank, 'OP 7.00', *supra* n. 76, paras 12, 16; World Bank, 'Review of World Bank Conditionality: Legal Aspects Conditionality in Policy-Based Lending', *supra* n. 25, para. 35.

contractual agreement for financing. A borrower taking out a policy-based loan from either the IBRD or IDA is required to submit a Letter of Development Policy (LDP), the Bank's equivalent of the IMF's letter of intent, to their executive board.[79] This LDP summarizes the 'salient elements' of the adjustment programme supported by the loan and contains a declaration of the borrower's commitment to execute the programme.[80]

The loan agreement incorporates the LDP by reference,[81] but unlike a borrower's legal obligation to carry out a project in investment loans, a borrower's commitment to execute the adjustment programme under a policy-based loan is *not* regarded as 'contractually enforceable' by the Bank.[82] Bank general counsels, accordingly, have advised Bank staff that while there should be explicit and precise documentation of disbursement conditions in loan agreements, such agreements have to be structured *to avoid covenanted legal obligations*.[83] This lack of contractual enforceability stems primarily from two concerns: (1) the possibility of intervening in the sovereign prerogative to determine critical policy and institutional reforms necessitated by the lending agreement; and, more importantly, (2) the potential financial repercussions of declaring a country in breach of their contractual obligations to the Bank, including donor support and the borrower's standing in international financial markets.[84]

Further, as suggested by a former Bank general counsel, the 'mere adoption of new policies cannot in itself be a legally acceptable reason for making Bank loans' under the Bank's Articles of Agreement.[85] Technically speaking, the Bank is financing the *costs* associated with the policy and institutional changes proposed under the adjustment programme and not the reforms per se.[86] It follows that the policies of the economic adjustment programme itself cannot be regarded as contractual terms of the loan agreement, but rather as means of complying with the object of the loan, which is the removal of structural and other barriers to economic and other developmental objectives considered part of the IBRD and IDA's respective mandates.

Consequently, like the IMF, World Bank supervision of the terms of the loan agreement turned to the instrument of conditionality as a means of monitoring borrower compliance with the programme supported by the loan. The introduction of conditionality as a regulatory instrument in Bank policy-based lending – in spite of these loans' differing legal status from IMF financing – was also driven primarily by this reluctance to impose full contractual force on policy conditions in

79. For more discussion *see* s. II.A *supra*.
80. World Bank, 'Review of the World Bank Conditionality: Legal Aspects of Conditionality in Policy-Based Lending', *supra* n. 25, para. 27; World Bank, 'OP 7.00', *supra* n. 76, para. 16.
81. World Bank, 'OP 7.00', *supra* n. 76, para. 16.
82. World Bank, 'Review of the World Bank Conditionality: Legal Aspects of Conditionality in Policy-Based Lending', *supra* n. 25, para. 38.
83. Shihata, *The World Bank Legal Papers*, *supra* n. 25, 382–383.
84. World Bank, 'Review of the World Bank Conditionality: Legal Aspects of Conditionality in Policy-Based Lending', *supra* n. 25, para. 39.
85. Shihata, *The World Bank Legal Papers*, *supra* n. 25, 166.
86. *Ibid.*

light of the potential legal and financial ramifications of doing so. At the same time, the Bank is bound by its fiduciary and due diligence duties, including meeting its institutional purposes under the Articles of Agreements of the IBRD and IDA. Thus, the Bank maintains that conditioning the release of loan funds is necessary for meeting such requirements, with conditionality providing 'assurances that its limited resources are used effectively and responsibly, helping borrowing countries to grow and reduce poverty'.[87]

Mosley, Toye, and Harrigan distinguish World Bank conditionality from the IMF's rationale for conditionality on this basis. The authors argue that unlike the IMF's basis for administering conditionality – serving as a collateral substitute – the purpose of conditionality in the Bank's policy-based lending is not to increase the likelihood of loan repayment, but rather as a way of administering reforms to remove 'policy-induced obstacles' to wider developmental objectives, notably economic growth, that are considered part of the Bank's mandate.[88] Although this objective has been revised in the switchover from adjustment lending to development policy support lending to encompass goals such as 'poverty reduction', the core focus of policy-based loans remains the same: to influence government policy to support policy aims under a programme of lending.

This is reflected in the Bank's current operational policy on policy-based loans. The new Operational Policy on Development Lending (OP 8.60) restated the provisions in the substituted Operational Directive on Adjustment Lending (OD 8.60) enabling the Bank to specify the 'policy and institutional actions' it deems as critical for implementation of the programme supported by the loan.[89] The OP 8.60, which governs all Bank policy-based loans, states that loan disbursements are contingent upon: the 'maintenance of an adequate macroeconomic policy framework, implementation of the overall program in a manner satisfactory to the Bank, and compliance' with critical policy and institutional actions.[90] The Bank's legal department has adopted these three requirements as 'essential conditions' for loan disbursements that are 'appropriately reflected in the legal agreement for these operations'.[91]

In this manner, conditionality serves to trigger financial disbursements from the Bank, the non-compliance of which will halt such transfers. In single-tranche loans, funds are made available when the borrower complies with all the necessary conditions for disbursement, while in multi-tranche operations, disbursements are

87. World Bank, 'Review of World Bank Conditionality: Modalities of Conditionality' (Washington, DC: World Bank, 30 Jun. 2005), para. 5.
88. Mosley, Toye & Harrigan, *supra* n. 57, 66–67.
89. World Bank, 'Review of the World Bank Conditionality: Legal Aspects of Conditionality in Policy-Based Lending', *supra* n. 25, para. 15; World Bank, 'Operational Policy 8.60 – Development Policy Lending' (Washington, DC: The World Bank, August 2004), *available at* <http://go.worldbank.org/N3Y839UBH0> (hereinafter OP 8.60).
90. World Bank, OP 8.60, *supra* n. 89, para. 13 (on 'Conditions'); World Bank, 'Review of the World Bank Conditionality: Legal Aspects of Conditionality in Policy-Based Lending', *supra* n. 25, para. 9.
91. World Bank, 'Review of the World Bank Conditionality: Legal Aspects of Conditionality in Policy-Based Lending', *supra* n. 25, para. 9.

made in stages 'as successive program conditions are met'.[92] At the same time, although non-compliance with programme conditions may not constitute a breach of a contractual obligation, the General Conditions for IBRD and IDA lending stipulate that the Bank may suspend financial transfers under the loan agreement if the borrower fails to perform its debt service or *any other obligation* under the agreement.[93]

Specific conditions attached to individual agreements also enable the Bank to suspend disbursements if, *inter alia*, the borrower's macroeconomic policy framework becomes inconsistent with the programme's objectives or if it takes an action or reversed an action 'in a manner that would, in the opinion of the Bank, adversely affect the achievement of the objectives' of the programme.[94] The borrower is also under an obligation to consult the Bank 'on any proposed action' that would have the effect of 'materially reversing' the programme's objectives or 'any actions taken under it', including tranche release conditions, both during and after disbursements.[95]

This means that although failure to comply with a condition of a World Bank programme will not necessarily mean a breach of a legal covenant, it may be considered evidence of a violation of the terms of the lending agreement if the Bank deems it fundamental to the agreement. Therefore, countries may risk being in breach of their financing agreement if they fail to implement the policies contained in the agreed programme in a manner acceptable to the Bank. Determination of this rests, as we shall see further below, largely with the Bank staff, management, and executive board, and involves reviews of critical policy and institutional decisions of their clients. Structural adjustment lending, therefore, has shifted the World Bank's fiduciary role from a purely technical focus – adherence to the technical obligations of traditional development financing (project documentation) – to that of an increasingly political role of monitoring policy reform as a means of monitoring compliance with the terms of the lending.

IV. STRUCTURAL ADJUSTMENT, CONDITIONALITY, AND THE BRETTON WOODS INSTITUTIONS

The entrenchment of conditionality as a default instrument for regulating the relationship between the World Bank and the IMF and their client states has led

92. *Ibid.*, paras 11–13.
93. IBRD, 'General Conditions for Loans' (1 Jul. 2005, amended through 12 Feb. 2008), s. 7.02; IDA 'General Conditions for Credits and Grants' (1 Jul. 2005), s. 6.02.
94. *See, e.g.*, Republic of Guatemala, 'Loan Agreement (Third Broad-Based Growth Development Policy Loan) between the Republic of Guatemala and the IBRD', Loan Number: 7482-GU (22 May 2008), s. 4.01; Republic of Peru, 'Loan Agreement (Results and Accountability (REACT) Development Policy Loan) between the Republic of Peru and the IBRD', Loan Number: 7455-PE (20 Aug. 2008), s. 4.01.
95. World Bank, 'Review of World Bank Conditionality: Legal Aspects of Conditionality in Policy-Based Lending', *supra* n. 25, paras 41, 46.

to the progressive intensification of this instrument as a mechanism of economic governance and a corresponding expansion of its regulatory scope. Although technically few legal penalties exist for non-adherence to conditions under SAPs, the high financial and political costs of non-compliance render the instrument of conditionality one of the most powerful forms of international economic regulation for countries subject to their jurisdiction. This, in turn, has raised crucial legal questions about the mandates of the Bank and Fund and their respective roles in the global economy and in international economic law.

A. Conditionality and Policy Regulation

Although conditionality is primarily a means of regulating the behaviour of the party in receipt of financing through the terms of credit disbursement, the bulk of its content is not concerned with the technical exercise of due diligence, but instead is focused on changes in government policy and institutional reform. Typically, conditionalities under SAPs have involved reforms of fiscal and monetary policies, including exchange rate policy; changes in trade policy; financial and agricultural sector reforms; and, increasingly, reform of public sector governance and institutions.[96]

The combination of the policy reform content of conditionality and the link between such policy prescriptions and financial transfers has lead Kalderimis to conclude that the practice of conditionality is a form of 'regulation by appropriation'[97] whereby regulatory norms are inserted into a jurisdiction through the terms of credit disbursement and, thus, outside conventional arenas of lawmaking or norm-creation.[98] This form of 'soft' regulation enables the entity with greater bargaining power to influence the behaviour of other entities through financial leverage, including that of formulating legislative and other regulatory changes desired by the former.[99] Although the World Bank is not legally authorized to do so,[100] it has acknowledged that conditionality can serve as a means of purchasing policy reform in client states by compensating the government 'for the expected costs of reform and the implementation of the policy', including social and political costs of economic reforms.[101]

96. *See* Khor, *supra* n. 19; *see also* SAPRIN, *supra* n. 29; World Bank, 'Review of World Bank Conditionality: The Theory and Practice of Conditionality: A Literature Review' (Washington, DC: World Bank, 6 Jul. 2005).
97. Kalderimis, *supra* n. 60, 105.
98. Note that although compliance with conditionality entails regulatory reform, the borrowing state still needs to implement these reforms domestically via its regular legislative or administrative procedures.
99. Kalderimis, *supra* n. 60, 105.
100. *See* Shihata, *The World Bank Legal Papers*, *supra* n. 25, 166.
101. World Bank, 'Review of World Bank Conditionality: Legal Aspects of Conditionality in Policy-Based Lending', *supra* n. 25, 3, paras 9–11.

It is this wide regulatory impact – the impact of conditions of lending outside the subject of the loans – that not only differentiates the doctrine of conditionality from conventional contractual principles, but which also represents the source of opposition to the principle of conditionality and, by extension, to SAPs generally. Over the past three decades, the application and effect of SAP conditionalities have come under significant criticism from governments, civil society groups, and academics. Aside from the inappropriateness of the policy prescriptions and the human and ecological costs associated with the application of such policies,[102] critics of SAPs, additionally, have questioned the legitimacy of policymaking under the rubric of conditionality.

A serious concern is that the Bank and the Fund are not adequately accountable to those who are affected by their conditionality policies. This gap in accountability is compounded by the increasing porousness of Bank and Fund operations due to the influence of external financiers, in addition to pressure from their major shareholders. For the IMF, the growing reliance on sources of financing outside its GRA to fund its operations – including through the General and New Arrangements to Borrow[103] (GAB and NAB, respectively) – and the introduction of concessional financing trust funds have rendered the institution highly susceptible to the interests of these external creditors and donors.

Gould's study of the influence of supplementary financiers, 'private and official financiers who supplement the Fund's loans to borrowers', and IMF conditionality reveal that these financiers have been significantly instrumental in expanding the scope and content of IMF programme conditions.[104] In particular, the study found that the evolution from the broad macroeconomic targets in the 1950s and 1960s to today's 'micro-conditionality' – specifying policy reforms, such as governance and enterprise reform, in detail – can be attributed to the 'mutually dependent relationship' between the IMF and these external financiers.[105]

---

102. A five-year, cross-continental study undertaken by the Structural Adjustment Participatory Review Network (SAPRIN), a civil society initiative, for example, concluded that 'the economic policies that comprise the core of structural adjustment programmes have failed to engender the healthy economies promised by their architects'. The study found that 'the overall impact of adjustment policies has included the generation of increased current-account and trade deficits and debt; disappointing levels of economic growth, efficiency and competitiveness; the misallocation of financial and other productive resources; the "disarticulation" of national economies; the destruction of national productive capacity; and extensive environmental damage' in the countries profiled. SAPRIN, *supra* n. 29, 218.
103. General and New Arrangements to borrow are credit arrangements between the IMF and a number of countries and central banks to provide supplementary resources to the IMF to cope with financial crises and other threats to the international financial system. IMF, 'Financial Organization and Operations of the IMF', *supra* n. 43, 72–74.
104. *See* Erica R. Gould, 'Money Talks: Supplementary Financiers and International Monetary Fund Conditionality', *International Organization* 57 (2003).
105. *Ibid.*, 551–555.

Similarly, at the World Bank, the operational framework of IDA, coupled with the proliferation of other discrete donor-led trust funds, has led to a distortion of the Bank's own governance structure and disproportionately influenced the content of conditionality in adjustment programmes. IDA replenishment is undertaken every three years, during which IDA policies are reviewed. Over the years, the nature of the replenishment process – with its periodicity and burden-sharing characteristics – has 'rendered it extremely susceptible' to the influence of the major shareholders.[106] Donors have taken the opportunity during replenishment rounds to impose conditions on IDA financing in return for contributions, a situation which former Bank General Counsel, the late Ibrahim Shihata has denounced as raising 'serious questions regarding the legal governance of the Bank'.[107]

The design of both structural and sectoral adjustment programmes at the Bank, in many cases, has reflected the interests of these concessional creditors and donors. In particular, pressure from major IDA contributors over the past few replenishment rounds has resulted in a disproportionate focus on domestic governance and public expenditure conditions in policy-based loan arrangements. Public sector governance conditions, such as reforms of public financial management systems, fiscal governance, and other public sector institutions, now account for the largest share of conditionalities in policy-based loans.[108] Meanwhile, domestic governance frameworks and the 'quality' of a country's policies and institutions constitute two pivotal aspects of the allocation criteria for IDA clients, which include determining how much and under what conditions financing is made available to IDA borrowers.[109]

B. Discretionary Control

The questionable regulatory nature of structural adjustment conditionality is compounded by the discretionary nature of these arrangements. The use of conditionality to police Bank and Fund financial transactions in lieu of formal legal arrangements has accorded the Bank and the Fund significant autonomy and wide discretionary powers vis-à-vis the nature and substance of their financial and policy interactions with their borrowing Member States.

The IMF's membership, for example, has interpreted the 'safeguards' provision under Article V of its Articles of Agreement as one delegating authority to the institution to implement its own policies, such as through the issuance of its Guidelines on Conditionality, to ensure that funds are disbursed in accordance with

106. Devesh Kapur, 'Do As I Say Not As I Do: A Critique of the G-7 Proposals on Reforming the Multilateral Development Banks', G-24 Discussion Paper Series No. 4 (February 2003), 2–3; *see also* Shihata, *The World Bank Legal Papers*, *supra* n. 25, 5645–5668.
107. *Shihata, The World Bank Legal Papers*, *supra* n. 25, 567.
108. World Bank, 'Review of World Bank Conditionality: Legal Aspects of Conditionality in Policy-Based Lending', *supra* n. 25, para. 22.
109. IDA, 'How IDA Resources Are Allocated' (June 2009), Annex 1, *available at* <http://go.worldbank.org/F5531ZQHT0>.

their fiduciary obligations under its constituting treaty.[110] At the same time, the provisions of its trust instruments also accord the Fund significant discretion in determining the conditions of financing from its special disbursement windows, such as the PRGF. Similarly, the World Bank is authorized by its membership to establish its operational procedures, including the OP 8.60, to govern its engagement with its borrowers. Further, IDA borrowers must also comply with requirements specific to the concessional facility, notably the conditions established by donors in successive replenishment rounds.[111]

The consequence of these developments has been the construction of a highly discretionary regime of financing that relies on the supervision of client states by an army of expert staff within the IMF and World Bank, which have correspondingly few either fixed rules of guidance or constitutional limitations on the decision-making powers conferred on Bank and Fund bureaucrats.[112] For Woods, this situation not only gave the United States, as the major shareholder, significant influence over the financing policies of the institution, but 'it also cast a large role' for the technocrats at the institutions, who de facto have the discretion to make decisions and to provide advice to the executive boards in determining how and what conditions to impose on borrowing countries[113] without the necessary checks and balances.

The significant powers of discretion accorded to the World Bank and IMF under the practice of conditionality have enabled them to extract a wide range of policy commitments from borrowing states. Conditionality enabled them to implement more intrusive reforms without either the corresponding sanction of Member States' challenges to the system due to a breach of the constitutional norms governing the institutions or subjecting the institutions to wider international law. As Gold notes, whatever consequences a breach of IMF's 'soft law' may entail, they fall short of such constitutional penalties such as the 'ineligibility to use the general resources of the IMF, suspension of the right to use SDRs, suspension of voting rights, or compulsory withdrawal from the organization'.[114]

---

110. *See* IMF Articles of Agreement, *supra* n. 6, Art. V(3)(a) (stating 'The Fund shall adopt policies on the use of its general resources, including policies on stand-by or similar arrangements, and may adopt special policies for special balance of payments problems, that will assist members to solve their balance of payments problems in a manner consistent with the provisions of this Agreement and that will establish adequate safeguards for the temporary use of the general resources of the Fund.').
111. Replenishment of the IDA is undertaken every three years, during which IDA policies are reviewed. Over the years, the replenishment process has 'rendered it extremely susceptible' to the influence of the major shareholders. *See* Kapur, *supra* n. 106, 2–3; *see also* Shihata, *The World Bank Legal Papers*, *supra* n. 25, 564–568. Donors have taken the opportunity during replenishment rounds to impose conditions on IDA financing in return for contributions, a situation which Ibrahim Shihata, the former World Bank General Counsel, has denounced as raising 'serious questions regarding the legal governance of the Bank'. Shihata, *The World Bank Legal Papers*, *supra* n. 25, 567.
112. Woods, *supra* n. 5, 25–26.
113. *Ibid.*, 27.
114. Gold, *Interpretation: The IMF and International Law*, *supra* n. 41, 302.

Moreover, the IMF and World Bank, traditionally, have resisted external justiciability of their operations, preferring instead to rely on internal administrative processes as opposed to external adjudication of disputes arising between them and Member States and/or other stakeholders. For example, the institutions have always reserved for themselves the right to interpret their own constitutions and by-laws. Also, while both institutions have agreements with the United Nations enabling them to seek advisory opinions from the International Court of Justice (ICJ) on matters of interpretation and legal issues arising from their operations, this procedure has never been utilized.[115]

The doctrine of conditionality, therefore, operates within the framework of self-adjudication in which the executive boards (and to a certain extent, the Management) of the Bank and the Fund operate as both rule-maker and enforcer. The practice of conditionality allows the Executive Directors to set preconditions for access to development financing, determine which conditions should apply to countries, and establish if a condition has been met and which penalties should be meted out to a non-compliant Member State.

At the same time, the IMF's and World Bank's internal procedures provide limited mechanisms for review of their operations. The World Bank's Inspection Panel[116] provides a forum for redress for stakeholders affected by the operations of the IBRD and IDA, but its mandate remains limited to considering if the design, appraisal, or implementation of projects and programmes meet the Bank's own operating policies and procedures. The ring-fenced remit of the Inspection Panel means that it is primarily an investigatory mechanism and can only relay its findings to the board of executive directors, which then decides on the appropriate course of action to take in the event of substantiated allegations.[117] It also means that any revision of IBRD or IDA policies and procedures could lead to a downgrading of standards, if not the threshold, for compliance.[118] And given the broad language of OP 8.60, there will be difficulty in defining what constitutes the Bank's failure to adhere to its operational policy for adjustment lending.[119] The IMF does not have a corresponding mechanism for reviewing its operations in this regard.

Another area of contention with stakeholders stems from the ambiguous legal nature of SAPs. As the programmes of economic reform, outlined in countries'

---

115. Ibrahim Shihata, 'The Dynamic Evolution of International Organizations: The Case of the World Bank', *Journal of the History of International Law* 2 (2000): 222.
116. The Panel was established in 1993 and consists of three members, independent of Bank staff and management, who are appointed by and report directly to the executive directors. The Panel has the power to consider complaints received from any group of individuals who allege that its rights or interests have been or are likely to be directly affected by an action or omission of the Bank as a result of a failure of the Bank to follow its operational policies and procedures. World Bank, 'The World Bank Inspection Panel', IBRD Resolution No. 93-10/ IDA Resolution No. 93-6 (22 Sep. 1993), paras 2–12.
117. *See* World Bank, 'The World Bank Inspection Panel', *supra* n. 116.
118. Celine Tan, 'Mandating Rights and Limiting Mission Creep: Holding the World Bank and the International Monetary Fund Accountable for Human Rights Violations', *Human Rights and Legal Discourse Journal* 2, no. 1 (2008): 96–97.
119. *See* World Bank, OP 8.60, *supra* n. 89.

Letters of Intent (IMF) or Letters of Development Policy (World Bank), are not considered legal agreements between the IMF and World Bank and their clients, much of the negotiations on their content take place between the financial institutions and the executive arm of the client state, notably the treasuries, central banks, and/or ministries of finance. In many cases, authorization from national legislatures is not required prior to executive commitment to financing arrangements, especially from the IMF, as they are not considered international treaties.[120]

In spite of the operational shifts towards widening country 'ownership' and public 'participation' in formulating adjustment programmes at the IMF and World Bank and the inception of the PRSP framework premised on the notion of participatory decision-making, discussion of the policy content of SAPs remains very much a closed door exercise between IMF and World Bank staff and civil servants from respective government departments in the countries concerned. This effectively means that elected representatives and citizens in SAP countries have very little voice in determining the outcomes of policy negotiations that have a significant impact not only on national legislation, but also social and economic welfare.

C. Mission Creep

The intensification of the regulatory role of conditionality has been facilitated and accompanied by the World Bank's and IMF's progressive encroachment into areas outside their original mandates. Section II highlighted how the advent of structural adjustment lending changed not only the operational framework of financing from the Bretton Woods institutions, but also, importantly, expanded their roles in the international financial architecture. Conditionalities under SAPs have enabled the Bank and Fund to circumvent limitations on their constitutional role and enabled them to expand the scope of their operations beyond what their initial founders envisaged when the institutions were established.

Firstly, for the IMF, the inception of adjustment lending altered the role of the Fund from that of an organization for multilateral financial discipline focused on short-term, counter-cyclical lending to that of a development agency engaged in long-term economic rehabilitation. In doing so, the mandate of the Fund and, correspondingly, the remit of conditionality were expanded to encompass broader

120. *E.g.*, a 2004 joint report by the African Network on Debt and Development (Afrodad) and Christian Aid concluded that the formal loan cycle of the Bank or the Fund allows little scope for the active participation of parliament or civil society in the content of development financing agreements between the state and the IFIs in sub-Saharan Africa. Afrodad & Christian Aid, 'Owning the Loan: Poor Countries and the MDGs' (28 Apr. 2004): 2, 24. Two of the five countries surveyed – Mozambique and Tanzania – have no provision, constitutionally or otherwise, for parliamentary approval of a loan agreement or for enactment of the conditions thereof. *Ibid.*, Table 5, Figure 5. The other three countries – Malawi, Uganda, and Zambia – require parliamentary approval to authorize and ratify loan agreements made between the executive and the financing institution, but the legislatures generally do not have much control over the details of the loans or the extent to which the countries are exposed to external debt.

structural economic reforms in client countries. Unlike previous conditionality focused on short-term variables on a nation's balance of payments, which were reversible upon expiry of an IMF arrangement, structural conditionality is 'aimed at the fundamental transformation of the underlying institutions governing national economies'.[121]

These developments further marked the shift away from the IMF's original function as an institution for global financial governance. IMF financing no longer is viewed solely as a means of ensuring international financial stability, but also as an end in itself. This, in turn, has resulted in asymmetries in the way in which the Fund carries out its regulatory responsibilities. SAPs allowed the IMF to intervene in the domestic policies of members borrowing from the Fund, but did not enable the Fund to regulate the activities of those members who do not, even when those members' economies pose a greater threat to international financial stability. Instead, conditionality has emerged as a key mechanism for organizing, harmonizing, and enforcing regulatory norms across different jurisdictions in the developing world where it is applied routinely.

In particular, given the shift in the clientele of the IMF and World Bank since the 1970s – from the industrialized countries to developing countries – the implementation of structural adjustment conditionality has become primarily a north-south debate. When one set of members are subject to IMF surveillance and policy supervision resulting from resource dependency while another set of members are not, the character of international financial oversight acquires a radically different agenda. As Akyüz points out, the failure of IMF surveillance arrangements in preventing international financial crises 'reflects the unbalanced nature of the procedures', which focus inordinately on disciplining the domestic economies of debtor developing countries, but 'give too little recognition to shortcomings in the institutions and policies in major industrial countries with large impact on global economic conditions'.[122] Conditionality, working as what Pahuja terms 'an enforcement mechanism with selective effect', thus enhanced the asymmetrical obligations of the north and south 'as subjects of IMF law'[123] by demarcating the *rule-makers* and the *rule-takers* within the IMF membership.

Meanwhile, unlike the IMF, the World Bank was not established as a regulatory body. It was not endowed with a governance mandate such as that established under the IMF's Articles of Agreement with regard to multilateral financial discipline. However, since the introduction of policy-based loans, the combination of financing and policy reform has led to a progressive embedding of a governance function in which regulatory norms across jurisdictions are harmonized through the Bank's credit process. In other words, the Bank has, through its SAPs, introduced reforms, such as the adoption of banking sector codes and standards, which

121. Babb & Buira, *supra* n. 20, 9.
122. Yilmaz Akyüz, 'Back to the Drawing Board', *TWN Global Economy Series* no. 7 (Penang: Third World Network, 2006): 48–49.
123. Pahuja, *supra* n. 19, 780.

are not only standardized across borrowing countries, but which also commit countries to international regulatory norms they otherwise may not have adopted.

This expanding regulatory role sits uncomfortably with the Bank's Articles of Agreements, particularly in light of the constitutional questions the proliferation of policy-based lending raises for the institution. Article III, section 4(vii) of the IBRD's Articles of Agreement states: 'Loans made or guaranteed by the Bank shall, except in *special circumstances*, be for the purpose of specific projects of reconstruction or development' (emphasis added).[124] A corresponding provision in the Article V, section 1(b) of the IDA's Articles of Agreement provides that its financing 'shall be for purposes . . . of high developmental priority . . . and, except in *special circumstances*, shall be for specific projects' (emphasis added).[125]

Traditionally, the Bank has relied upon this 'special circumstances' exception to justify their disbursement of policy-based loans, and the old Operational Directive on Adjustment Lending Policy (OD 8.60) set a guideline ceiling stating that the share of adjustment lending should not normally exceed 25% of the total IBRD and IDA commitments over three years.[126] However, with the exception increasingly becoming the norm over the years, combined IBRD and IDA policy-based lending, including structural and sectoral adjustment loans, have exceeded one-third of all lending since 1998.[127] The Bank, increasingly, has disregarded this legal constraint and reinterpreted the constitutional provision to suit the evolving circumstances. The new OP 8.60 dispenses with the quota on such lending, providing instead that the volume or share of development policy lending for a borrower be established on a case-by-case basis by the executive directors, taking into account factors such as the country's overall financing requirements and debt sustainability.[128]

V. CONCLUSION

Developments within the IFIs in the 1970s resulted in a massive growth in the scope and scale of multilateral financing, with SAPs emerging as a key instrument for international development financing. The introduction of SAPs also led to the emergence of the Bretton Woods institutions as key players in the policymaking process of their Member States, as well as in the international regulatory arena. Over the years, structural adjustment conditionalities have evolved into important

124. International Bank for Reconstruction and Development, Articles of Agreement (May 1945, amended 16 Feb. 1989), Art. III(4)(vii), *available at* <http://siteresources.worldbank.org/EXTABOUTUS/Resources/ibrd-articlesofagreement.pdf>.
125. International Development Association, Articles of Agreement (24 Sep. 1960), Art. V(1)(b), *available at* <http://siteresources.worldbank.org/IDA/Resources/ida-articlesofagreement.pdf>.
126. World Bank, 'From Adjustment Lending to Development Policy Support Lending: Key Issues in the Update of World Bank Policy', *supra* n. 37, para. 17.
127. World Bank, *World Bank Report 2009* (Washington, DC: World Bank, 2009), i; World Bank, 'From Adjustment Lending to Development Policy Support Lending: Key Issues in the Update of World Bank Policy', *supra* n. 37, para. 17.
128. World Bank, OP 8.60, *supra* n. 89, paras 4, 8.

means of facilitating the roles of the Bank and Fund as intermediaries between third world states and the exterior, governing not just the relationship between the IMF and World Bank and their borrowers, but also borrowers' engagement with the global economy.

Thus, SAPs have emerged as an important means of global economic governance, without necessarily the accompanying legal or institutional safeguards for states and communities affected by their application. There is clearly a disjuncture between the broadening of the IMF's and the World Bank's mandates in this respect and their accountability in the face of such an expansion. This, once again, reflects the IMF and the World Bank's governance structures and the geo-political realities of the international environment in which the Bank and the Fund operate. Serving as the only ostensibly 'multilateral' financing institutions, the IMF and the World Bank offer their major shareholders convenient vehicles through which funding for certain global public goods, including financing to ensure international financial stability, may be channelled. SAPs enable such financing to be disbursed in accordance with the priorities and interests of key players in the international economy by providing the requisite supervisory mechanisms to ensure compliance. The disciplinary force of SAPs, therefore, reverberates beyond the terms of the individual financing arrangement to which they are attached.

The need to debate the operational framework of SAPs, including their legal implications, has resurged with the onset of the global financial crisis in 2007–2008. While both the IMF and the World Bank faced increasing marginalization from their middle-income borrowers in the few years preceding the financial crisis, these institutions have regained relevance in the wake of the crisis. The IMF has seen an unprecedented increase in the requests for drawings from its GRA, and countries which have previously graduated from the PRGF have begun to seek concessional assistance from other facilities, such as the ESF.[129] With the G-20 agreeing to treble the resources available to the GRA to the tune of USD 750 billion and the IMF executive board approving to double the resources to the IMF's concessional lending facilities,[130] it is clear that the IMF has regained its role as the preferred international lender of last resort.

129. The IMF's lending has increased dramatically since 2008 with commitments reaching a record level of USD 157 billion in May 2009. IMF, 'A Changing IMF: Responding to the Crisis', A Factsheet (May 2009), *available at* <www.imf.org/external/np/exr/facts/changing.htm>. This includes sharp rises in concessional lending as well as credits totalling USD 78 billion to Colombia, Mexico, and Poland under the new FCL. *Ibid.* In 2008, Iceland became the first industrialized country to seek IMF financial assistance since the 1970s; and in April, Tanzania, which had previously graduated from Fund financing post-HIPC, sought funding from the ESF.

130. Peter Chowla, 'IMF: Bigger but Not Much Nicer', *Bretton Woods Update* 65 (London: Bretton Woods Project, March/April 2009): 7; IMF, 'IMF Overhauls Nonconcessional Lending: Facilities and Conditionality', *supra* n. 13; IMF, 'IMF Implements Major Lending Policy Improvements', *supra* n. 4.

At the same time, the World Bank is planning to expand its lending portfolio dramatically. The IBRD aims to triple its lending in 2009,[131] with much of the additional lending delivered through policy-based loans, while the IDA established a fast track facility in 2008 to front load USD 2 billion to low-income countries to mitigate effects of the financial crisis.[132] The Bank, also, has called on industrialized countries to commit 0.7% of their financial packages to a Bank-administered vulnerability financing fund to expedite financing for social safety nets and food security programmes, including access to World Bank lending instruments.[133]

As the bulk of the crisis-related financing from the IMF and World Bank will take the form of instruments involving SAPs, the re-emergence of these institutions as pivotal players in international public financing will mean a greater role for the IMF and World Bank in the regulatory oversight of Member States. Given the problematic nature of conditionality and the constitutional questions arising from the expanded mandates of the Bank and Fund under SAPs, the imperative to establish parallel mechanisms to ensure accountability, transparency, and effective operational review within and outside the institutions is more pressing than ever before. It remains to be seen if this will take place, or if the IMF and World Bank will continue 'business as usual'.

---

131. The Bank expects to raise its lending from USD 13 billion to USD 35 billion in 2009; and as of early March 2009, committed or planned crisis-related policy loans stood at a total of USD 2 billion. World Bank, 'World Bank Group Response to the Financial Crisis' (4 Mar. 2009), para. 4, *available at* <www.worldbank.org/html/extdr/financialcrisis/pdf/WBGResponse-VFF.pdf>.
132. *Ibid.*, para. 4.
133. *Ibid.*, paras 7–13.

Chapter 7

International Law and Public Participation in Policy-Making at the International Financial Institutions

David B. Hunter

I. INTRODUCTION

Beginning in the late 1980s, environmental, human rights, and other civil society organizations (CSO) began to confront the World Bank Group[1] and other international financial institutions (IFIs) about the negative environmental and social impact of their projects and the deficiencies in their policies and operations that led to such impacts. These efforts influenced the World Bank Group and other IFIs to adopt an array of environmental and social 'sustainability' policies. These sustainability policies arguably provide a minimal normative framework for the achievement of sustainable development in international development finance.[2]

1. The World Bank Group is comprised of the International Bank for Reconstruction and Development (IBRD), the International Development Association (together sometimes referred to as the 'World Bank'), the International Finance Corporation, the Multilateral Investment Guarantee Agency, and the International Centre for the Settlement of Investment Disputes.
2. *See, e.g.*, The World Bank, *Operational Manual: Operational Policies: Environmental Assessment*, World Bank OP 4.01 (January 1999), *available at* <http://siteresources.worldbank.org/INTFORESTS/Resources/OP401.pdf> (hereinafter World Bank Environmental Assessment Policy); International Finance Corporation, *Performance Standards on Social & Environmental*

Daniel D. Bradlow and David B. Hunter, *International Financial Institutions and International Law*, pp. 199–238.

Although the international legal status of these sustainability policies and the substantive issues inherent in them are interesting and worthy of debate,[3] less explored has been the process by which the IFIs have adopted this sustainable development framework.[4] Engaging civil society, including affected communities, in the policy-making process presented significant new challenges to the IFIs. These stakeholders challenged the state-centred view of international organizations as being accountable primarily, if not solely, to their Member States. These civil society stakeholders were also not interested in being borrowers, bondholders, or employees whose relationship with the IFIs was shaped by contracts and private law. These civil society stakeholders were drawn to the IFIs by their impact and some notion of the broader public interest, and little precedent in either law or practice shaped such a relationship between the 'public' and the IFIs.

This chapter describes the methods, practice, and procedures by which the IFIs engaged civil society in policy development over time – in other words the administrative procedural norms that have emerged at these institutions in developing policies of general applicability to their operations.[5] The chapter focuses particularly on the public's rights to participate effectively in these administrative processes.

Although the development and use of procedural norms is occurring in many areas of IFI operations, this chapter focuses primarily on the process leading to the development of the IFIs' environmental and social policies. These provide a particularly good lens through which to view the development of policy-making procedures at the IFIs, because the adoption of environmental and social policies has repeatedly set new precedents in the IFIs' evolving administrative procedures. Outside pressure on the IFIs has often been the most acute in the development of environmental and social policies, as international networks of environmental and

---

Sustainability (30 Apr. 2006), *available at* <www.ifc.org/ifcext/sustainability.nsf/AttachmentsByTitle/pol_PerformanceStandards2006_full/$FILE/IFC+Performance+Standards.pdf> (hereinafter IFC Environmental Policy & Performance Standards) (for links to the IFC's *Policy on Social and Environmental Sustainability*, as well as the Performance Standards, and the Guidance notes to the Performance Standards, *see* IFC, 'Environmental and Social Standards', <www.ifc.org/ifcext/sustainability.nsf/Content/EnvSocStandards>).

3. Some commentators, for example, argue that IFIs acting in this context are undertaking a form of transnational 'regulatory standard-setting'. Kenneth Abbott & Duncan Snidal, 'The Governance Triangle: Regulatory Standards Institutions and the Shadow of the State', in *The Politics of Global Regulation*, ed. Walter Mattli & Ngaire Woods (Princeton, NJ: Princeton University Press, 2009).
4. For an early treatment of the process surrounding the development of the World Bank's water policy, *see* Deborah Moore & Leonard Sklar, 'Reforming the World Bank's Lending for Water: The Process and Outcome of Developing a Water Resources Management Policy', in *The Struggle for Accountability; the World Bank, NGOs and Grassroots Movements*, ed. Jonathan Fox & L. David Brown (Cambridge, MA: MIT Press, 1998).
5. This can be contrasted to their rules for access to information and consultation with respect to specific projects or country assessment strategies, which can be found in the environmental assessment or other policies of the respective IFIs. *See, e.g.*, World Bank, Bank Procedure 2.11 – Country Assistance Strategies, para. 7 (June 2005) (requiring that Bank staff work with governments to allow public consultations in the preparation of country assessment strategies).

human rights organizations champion stronger policies through the policy-making process.[6] Moreover, the IFIs' environmental and social policies are aimed at protecting local communities and vulnerable groups such as indigenous peoples; such policies have limited legitimacy if those stakeholders are not allowed to participate fully in policy development.

One result of the relatively strong civic interest in engaging in policy development on environmental and social issues is that the procedures used to develop the policies draw a lot of attention. Over time, virtually every feature of a robust administrative policy-making procedure has been an element at some point in the environmental and social policy-making processes of the IFIs. Thus, for example, the IFIs have adopted notice-and-comment rule-making procedures through the Internet; required disclosure of first drafts, interim drafts, and final drafts of policies before final decisions are made; held public consultations both at the IFI headquarters and in the regions in which they operate; provided formal responses to all the comments received; and arranged for stakeholders to brief top decision-makers. The IFIs have even established accountability mechanisms that could be readily adopted to ensure compliance with administrative procedures in policy making. In fact, and rather ironically, because of the close scrutiny IFIs have faced from civil society, IFIs arguably now have the most well-developed practice of public-oriented administrative procedures of any group of international organizations.

What is missing, however, is any effort to systematize the administrative practice by codifying minimum standards for public involvement and engagement in these policy-making processes. The IFIs have generally failed to release any written procedural standards or guidelines establishing what process will normally be followed in the development or modification of their policies. Rather, the process for civic engagement has been, and continues to be, largely ad hoc, with virtually every announcement of plans for establishing or modifying an IFI policy being met with an immediate demand by CSOs for stronger administrative procedural rights.

Despite the lack of codification, this chapter argues that a consistent practice has emerged at the IFIs to engage civil society in policy-making that reflects emerging norms and standards of international law. After describing the environmental and social policy context at the IFIs and the importance of minimum policy-making procedures, the chapter turns to an analysis of the policy-making procedures followed at the IFIs. These procedures are consistent with emerging international procedural rights and norms found in international human rights and international environmental law. The chapter suggests that the emerging practice

6. For a discussion of the way in which civil society networks are organized to participate in World Bank reform, *see* David Hunter, 'Civil Society Networks and the Development of Environmental Standards at International Financial Institutions', *Chicago Journal of International Law* 8 (2008): 437; David A. Wirth, 'Partnership Advocacy in World Bank Environmental Reform', in *The Struggle for Accountability; the World Bank, NGOs and Grassroots Movements*, ed. Jonathan Fox & L. David Brown (Cambridge, MA: MIT Press, 1998).

of IFIs in developing participatory frameworks constitute an emerging customary law for IFIs that obligates the IFIs to continue this practice in future policy making.[7] The chapter then argues for codifying this practice further in an 'administrative procedures policy' at each of the IFIs as an important and beneficial step to protect all concerned stakeholders and their participation. Such a policy should reflect the current practice of the IFIs and related international norms of transparency, inclusivity, and accountability.

II. THE FOCUS OF THE POLICY-MAKING PROCESS: CONFLICT OVER THE IFIs' ENVIRONMENTAL AND SOCIAL STANDARDS

A. Pressure from the Outside: Managing Conflicts with Civil Society

Much of the pressure to develop administrative policy-making procedures has emanated outside the IFIs, primarily through demands for broader participation from civil society representatives who seek to strengthen the IFIs operating policies. Demands for greater transparency and participation at the IFIs began in the early 1990s, as the recognition of the impact of IFI lending on affected communities became better known.[8] Partly this reflected the expansion of IFI operations, but it is also reflected the spread of globalized communications and the growth of a truly global civil society. An informal, international network of non-governmental organizations formed to advance the rights and interests of people and communities affected adversely by IFI-financed projects.[9] Empowered by the Internet and global communications, civil society can demonstrate the impacts, both negative and positive, of IFI-financed operations in ways not possible a generation ago. Now, project-affected communities are more likely to know that IFI financing is involved in a project and be connected to international advocacy organizations that will help them champion community concerns.

Part of the resulting global civic dialogue between IFIs and the public led to a professionalization of advocacy around the IFIs. Opposition to IFI-financed projects was increasingly expressed in relation to the need for a stronger environmental and social policy framework. Rather than (or perhaps in addition to) taking to the streets, civil society opponents to IFI operations sought changes in the policy framework and raised their concerns with bank management, the executive

7. For more on the development of common customary law at international organizations, *see* Finn Seyerstad, *Common Law of International Organizations* (Leiden & Boston: Martinus Nijhoff, 2008).
8. *See, e.g.*, Bruce Rich, *Mortgaging the Earth: The World Bank, Environmental Impoverishment, and the Crisis of Development* (Boston: Beacon Press, 1994).
9. This international network includes the Bank Information Center, the Center for International Environmental Law, Friends of the Earth, Environmental Defense, Urgewald, IFI-Watch, The Corner House, Halifax Initiative, and FoE-Japan, amongst others.

directors, or the media. Community-based concerns over specific project impacts were translated by international CSOs into demands for changes in the IFIs' environmental and social policies and the need for access to formal mechanisms to raise their concerns.[10]

As part of their engagement in the policy-making process, these vertical networks of CSOs increasingly demand effective and fair minimum procedures in the development of the policies.[11] Typically, the first conflict in the resulting policy dialogues is the scope and sufficiency of the participatory process: when will draft policies be made available?; in what languages?; will there be public consultations?; how many and in what locations?; will second drafts be released?; and will public comments be taken into account? These demands frequently raise concerns of 'fairness' and 'due process', and invoke the rights to access information and to participate.

The IFIs' response to this increasingly engaged civil society has been mixed. The IFIs repeatedly and instinctively revert back to an internally focused, top-down approach that emphasizes their own technical expertise while underestimating the importance of public participation. For example, in 1991, during one of the early policy dialogues, CSOs led by the Environmental Defense Fund and the International Rivers Network, sought to have an expanded consultative process with the World Bank over proposed revisions to its water management policy.[12] After initially meeting with organizations, the World Bank staff decided against releasing any draft policies or engaging in any further consultation with civil society. One senior Bank staff person explained 'NGOs don't have anything useful to offer, water resources management is a highly technical issue.'[13] It is also highly political, and the CSOs flooded the Bank with fifty letters from thirty-five countries. The Bank ultimately agreed to further consultations and release of further draft policies. These commitments would also not be honoured, however, as the Bank struggled internally with what information to disclose and how best to consult with civil society. It would take a full two years amid continual struggles over both substance and process, before the Bank issued its final policy in 1993. The IFIs should not be seen as a monolith in such discussions, but in general, IFI interests in streamlining processes for experts to make their decisions clash

10. For a discussion of these vertical civil society networks, *see* Hunter, 'Civil Society Networks and the Development of Environmental Standards at International Financial Institutions', *supra* n. 6.
11. For a discussion of various controversial projects and the reform campaigns that emerged around them, *see* Jonathan A. Fox & L. David Brown (eds), *The Struggle for Accountability: The World Bank, NGOs, and Grassroots Movements* (Cambridge, MA: MIT Press, 1998); Catherine Caufield, *Masters of Illusion: The World Bank and the Poverty of Nations* (New York: Henry Holt, 1997); Rich, *Mortgaging the Earth: The World Bank, Environmental Impoverishment, and the Crisis of Development*, *supra* n. 8; Raymond F. Mikesell & Larry Williams (eds), *International Banks and the Environment: From Growth to Sustainability, an Unfinished Agenda* (San Francisco, CA: Sierra Club Books, 1992).
12. The dialogue over the water management policy is described in detail in Moore & Sklar, *supra* n. 4, 345.
13. *Ibid.*, 360 (quoting a 'senior bank staff').

with civil society interests in opening the processes to greater public involvement and a wider range of perspectives.[14]

In the resulting conflicts over procedure, civil society often has the expertise, legitimacy, and moral high ground that advantage them in these debates. It is, after all, hard to argue for the exclusion of stakeholders from processes meant ultimately to benefit them, or to argue that civil society does not have expertise in the issue of how best to engage civil society. Moreover, civil society has substantial allies with IFI senior management, executive directors, and donor governments that can translate into significant political pressure to ensure fair and open dialogue. Finally, procedural concessions are often easier than substantive changes. Through concessions on process issues, the IFIs can show good faith in dealing with civil society, channel dissent into professionalized and managed forms of dialogue, and build legitimacy for their ultimate decisions – without necessarily changing substantive outcomes.

As a result, many examples now exist of comprehensive administrative practice in the development of policies at the IFIs. The net result of creating administrative procedure in response to conflict over specific policy reform efforts, however, is that the administrative procedure has developed without any coherent strategy or overall commitment by the institutions. The IFIs understandably view administrative procedure as a field of conflict with civil society, instead of an area where they can justifiably promote their status as leaders in the field. Although many examples now exist of IFIs and civil society cooperatively developing the consultation plan in advance, the IFIs have yet to codify their practices into more broadly applicable administrative procedures for policy making.

B. The Outcome of the Policy Dialogue: The IFIs' Environmental and Social Policies

As a result of the past two decades of policy dialogue, environmental and social policies have been developed and revised over time at the World Bank Group[15] and other multilateral development banks (MDBs),[16] as well as at export credit and

14. *See, e.g.*, Protest Letter Concerning World Bank and Mangroves to Ronald D. Zweig, Senior Aquaculturalist, The World Bank (11 May 2005) (complaining about the failure to include local communities in the development of a World Bank code of conduct for mangrove management). This bi-polar view of the dialogue on public processes is admittedly simplistic as the IFIs have many fierce advocates for greater procedural rights inside their institutions. *See, e.g.*, Galit A. Sarfaty, 'The World Bank and the Internalization of Indigenous Rights Norms', *Yale Law Journal* 114 (2005) (discussing the role of internal supporters in the development and internalization of the World Bank's norms on indigenous rights).
15. *See, e.g.*, World Bank Environmental Assessment Policy, *supra* n. 2; IFC Environmental Policy & Performance Standards, *supra* n. 2.
16. *See, e.g.*, Inter-American Development Bank, 'Environment and Safeguards Compliance Policy' (19 Jan. 2006), *available at* <http://idbdocs.iadb.org/wsdocs/getDocument.aspx?DOCNUM=665902>; European Bank for Reconstruction and Development, 'Environmental and Social Policy' (May 2008), *available at* <www.ebrd.com/about/policies/enviro/policy/2008policy.pdf>;

insurance agencies (ECAs),[17] and even many private commercial banks.[18] Although the environmental and social standards vary somewhat across the financial institutions, the World Bank Group's environmental and social standards are emulated by many of the other financial institutions. Public financial institutions largely use the International Bank for Reconstruction and Development's (IBRD's) environmental and social policies, collectively known as the World Bank 'safeguard policies',[19] as a model, while lenders to the private sector largely follow the International Finance Corporation's (IFC's) environmental and social 'performance standards'. In both cases, the policies establish minimum standards for, among other things, the preparation of environmental and social impact assessments (ESIAs),[20] the treatment of indigenous peoples,[21] and the compensation for people involuntarily resettled in favour of IFI-financed projects.[22]

African Development Bank, 'African Development Bank Group's Policy on the Environment' (February 2004), *available at* <www.afdb.org/fileadmin/uploads/afdb/Documents/Policy-Documents/10000027-EN-BANK-GROUP-POLICY-ON-THE-ENVIRONMENT.PDF>; Asian Development Bank, 'Safeguard Policy Statement' (June 2009), *available at* <www.adb.org/Documents/Policies/Safeguards/Safeguard-Policy-Statement-June2009.pdf>.

17. Organization for Economic Co-operation and Development (OECD), *Revised Council Recommendation on Common Approaches on the Environment and Officially Supported Export Credits*, OECD Doc. TAD/ECG(2007)9 (12 Jun. 2007) (hereinafter *2007 OECD Common Approaches*).
18. *The 'Equator Principles': A Financial Industry Benchmark for Determining, Assessing and Managing Social & Environmental Risk in Project Financing* (6 Jul. 2006), *available at* <www.equator-principles.com/documents/Equator_Principles.pdf> (hereinafter *The Equator Principles*).
19. *See, e.g.*, Sarfaty, *supra* n. 14, 1791.
20. World Bank Environmental Assessment Policy, *supra* n. 2.
21. *See, e.g.*, The World Bank, *Operational Manual: Operational Policies: Indigenous Peoples*, World Bank OP 4.10 (July 2005), *available at* <http://go.worldbank.org/TE769PDWN0> (hereinafter World Bank Indigenous Peoples Policy). For a discussion of the evolution of the World Bank's indigenous peoples policy, *see* Andrew Gray, 'Development Policy, Development Protest: The World Bank, Indigenous Peoples, and NGOs', in *The Struggle for Accountability: The World Bank, NGOs, and Grassroots Movements*, ed. Jonathan A. Fox & L. David Brown (Cambridge, MA: MIT Press, 1998), 267. *See also* Fergus MacKay, 'Universal Rights or a Universe unto Itself? Indigenous Peoples' Human Rights and the World Bank's Draft Operational Policy 4.10 on Indigenous Peoples', *American University International Law Review* 17 (2002): 527; Marcus Colchester & Tebtebba Foundation, Inc. & Forest Peoples Programme (eds), *Extracting Promises: Indigenous Peoples, Extractive Industries & the World Bank* (Baguio City, Philippines: Tebtebba Foundation & Forest Peoples Programme, 2003); Benedict Kingsbury, 'Operational Policies of International Institutions as Part of the Law-Making Process: The World Bank and Indigenous Peoples', in *The Reality of International Law: Essays in Honor of Ian Brownlie*, ed. Guy S. Goodwin-Gill & Stefan Talmon (Oxford: Clarendon Press, 1999), 323. *See also* Fergus MacKay, 'Indigenous Peoples and International Financial Institutions', Ch. 9 herein.
22. *See, e.g.*, The World Bank, *Operational Manual: Operational Policies: Involuntary Resettlement*, World Bank OP 4.12 (December 2001), *available at* <http://siteresources.worldbank.org/INTFORESTS/Resources/OP412.pdf> (hereinafter World Bank Resettlement Policy). *See also* Robert Picciotto, Warren van Wicklin & Edward Rice, *Involuntary Resettlement: Comparative Perspectives* (New Brunswick, NJ: Transaction Publishers, 2001) (discussing experiences in implementing the World Bank resettlement policy); Jonathan A. Fox, 'When Does Reform Policy Influence Practice? Lessons from the Bankwide Resettlement Review', in *The Struggle*

The environmental and social standards of the IFIs are frequently recognized as part of emerging global administrative law.[23] To some extent these standards are simply *internal* regulations, aimed primarily at setting the norms that constrain how the IFI operates. The World Bank's safeguard policies and the IFC's Environmental and Social Policy, for example, elaborate how the institutions' respective employees should conduct their due diligence in evaluating and reviewing the environmental and social impacts of proposed projects.[24] Similarly, the World Bank Inspection Panel and other comparable accountability mechanisms are authorized to investigate only the institution's own acts of non-compliance; they are not authorized to judge the compliance of borrowers or host countries, for example.[25]

Focusing solely on the internal aspects of the IFI environmental and social standards, however, risks missing their significant *external* impact.[26] The IFIs' environmental and social standards are designed to change the behaviour of their borrowers. The IFC's eight 'Performance Standards' are meant, for example, to establish normative conditions on the private sector lenders from the IFC, and not just on the IFC itself.[27] Depending on the type and scale of the project, private sector borrowers may be required *inter alia* to conduct environmental and social impact assessments, consult with the communities regarding the project, create an environmental management plan, allow employees to bargain collectively, or create a community-based grievance mechanism.

Borrowing governments, too, are subject to conditions found in the IFIs' environmental and social policies. They must, for example, ensure minimal levels of compensation for people involuntarily resettled to accommodate IFI-financed projects, and such projects must comply with minimum requirements for public consultation. State sovereignty concerns are avoided as these requirements are included as conditions of the final loan agreements. Consent to the loan agreements is seen as consent to the environmental and social conditionalities attached. In this

---

for Accountability: The World Bank, NGOs, and Grassroots Movements, ed. Jonathan A. Fox & L. David Brown (Cambridge, MA: MIT Press, 1998), 303. On the safeguard policies generally, *see* Bank Information Center, 'Environmental and Social Policies: Background', *available at* <www.bicusa.org//en/Issue.Background.4.aspx>, 17 Nov. 2007.

23. On the emergence of global administrative law generally, *see, e.g.*, Daniel Esty, 'Good Governance at the Supranational Scale: Globalizing Administrative Law', *Yale Law Journal* 115 (2006): 1490; Benedict Kingsbury, Nico Krisch & Richard Stewart, 'The Emergence of Global Administrative Law', *Law & Contemporary Problems* 68 (2005): 15.
24. IFC Environmental Policy & Performance Standards, *supra* n. 2.
25. *See* International Bank for Reconstruction and Development (IBRD) and International Development Association (IDA), World Bank Inspection Panel, Resolution No. IBRD 93-10/IDA 93-6, para. 12 (22 Sep. 1993), *reprinted in* 34 I.L.M. 520 (1995) (hereinafter Resolution Establishing the World Bank Inspection Panel).
26. *See* Laurence Boisson de Chazournes, 'Policy Guidance and Compliance: The World Bank Operational Standards', in *Commitment and Compliance: The Role of Non-binding Norms in the International Legal System*, ed. Dinah Shelton (Oxford & New York: Oxford University Press, 2000), 281.
27. *See* IFC, 'Environmental and Social Standards', *supra* n. 2 (describing IFC's Performance Standards as defining the 'clients' roles and responsibilities in managing their projects').

way, the environmental and social policies set mandatory requirements on states, enforceable at least theoretically through the remedies set forth in the underlying loan agreements. Given that project loan agreements between the MDBs, such as the World Bank, and states are treaties in international law, the conditions found in the underlying environmental and social policies may contribute to the development of international law over time.

The IFI environmental and social policies go further than impacting the borrowers, however, as they also are intended to establish or protect the rights and interests of third-party individuals who are affected by proposed projects. For example, the environmental and social impact assessment procedures require that affected people receive information about potential impacts and opportunities to participate;[28] involuntarily resettled people receive compensation, including offers of land;[29] and indigenous peoples are consulted and share in the benefits of projects on their traditional lands.[30]

As noted above, the standards adopted by the World Bank Group have also profoundly influenced the development of similar standards at other international organizations, including other MDBs, bilateral ECAs, private commercial lenders, and many multinational corporations. As the largest multilateral lender, the World Bank Group's general size and economic significance spill over to influence environmental and social standards at other IFIs. Interestingly, the harmonization of environmental and social standards across a variety of IFIs has been facilitated by civil society engagement. Interconnected civil society networks frequently seek similar substantive standards at all institutions providing international project finance.[31] Private sector borrowers also prefer to face one set of harmonized standards rather than a multiplicity of different standards; corporations and their trade associations are becoming more frequent participants in the global policy-making dialogue over IFI policies.

Notwithstanding the significant internal and external reach of these environmental and social standards, their status in international law is not clear. Having been generated by an international organization, the environmental and social standards do not immediately fit into the paradigmatic sources of international law – treaties, custom, general principles, or learned writings[32] – but they can

---

28. World Bank Environmental Assessment Policy, *supra* n. 2. *See also* Robert J.A. Goodland, 'The World Bank's Environmental Assessment Policy', *Hastings International & Comparative Law Review* 14 (1992): 811; Diane M. Kohn, 'Environmental Impact Assessment Policies of Multilateral Development Banks and Export Credit Agencies', *Environmental Law* 9 (September 2002): 281.
29. World Bank Resettlement Policy, *supra* n. 22.
30. World Bank Indigenous Peoples Policy, *supra* n. 21.
31. For a discussion of the process of harmonizing the environmental and social standards across IFIs, *see* Hunter, 'Civil Society Networks and the Development of Environmental Standards at International Financial Institutions', *supra* n. 6.
32. United Nations, Statute of the International Court of Justice, Art. 38 (26 Jun. 1945) (citing treaties, custom, general principles, and learned writings as the sources of international organizations), *available at* <www.icj-cij.org/documents/?p1=4&p2=2&p3=0>. *See generally*, José E. Alvarez, *International Organizations as Law-Makers* (Oxford & New York: Oxford

be related to those sources. The policies are, for example, frequently adopted by the boards of executive directors (representing the Member States). Moreover, as noted above applicable policies are often included by reference into IFI project loan agreements, which have the status of an international treaty. Given the uniformity of the standards across various IFIs and the widespread state membership in these IFIs, particularly the World Bank, the decision to support such standards and to be bound in various loan agreements to the standards could also be evidence of state practice. They thus arguably (although not without controversy) can be offered as evidence of customary law, reflecting the practice of the states that are parties to the various IFIs. Others have discussed such norms emerging from UN agencies as part of a 'universal' international law,[33] have cited them as evidence of general principles of law,[34] or argue that they contribute to a 'common law' of international organizations.[35]

Trying to fit the IFIs' environmental and social standards into the state-centric, Article 38 box of public international law sources, however, does not fully reflect either the process by which these standards were developed nor the role that they play among multiple non-state actors.[36] To be sure, they have substantially influenced the development and implementation of environmental and social norms in both the international and domestic context of the IFIs' Member States, but they have also contributed to the practice of private commercial banks and non-commercial corporations. These policies form part of 'global environmental law', which cannot easily be catalogued as either international or national law.[37]

Just as important for our purposes, a state-centric perspective misses the critical role that civic engagement has played in developing these environmental and social standards, and as a result the equally critical role of the administrative procedures that have shaped that civic engagement. Indeed the source of the legal authority of these policies may emanate formally from the approval by the IFIs' executive directors, but their legitimacy and informal authority comes less from state consent than from the fact that they are the product of substantial public

---

University Press, 2005), 235–241 (discussing the legal status of the IFIs' environmental and social guidelines).

33. *See* Jonathan Charney, 'Universal International Law', *American Journal of International Law* 87 (1993): 543–548.
34. *See* Case Concerning the Gabcikovo-Nagymaros Project (*Hung v. Slov*), 1997 I.C.J. 92 n4 (25 September) (separate opinion of Vice-President Weeramantry) (citing the World Bank's and other financial institutions' support for the principle of sustainable development as partial support for arguing that it is accepted as a general principle of international law).
35. *See* Seyerstad, *supra* n. 7.
36. *See* discussion of the IFI environmental and social standards in Alvarez, *International Organizations as Law-makers*, *supra* n. 32, 235–241.
37. *See* Tseming Yang & Robert Percival, 'The Emergence of Global Environmental Law', *Ecology Law Quarterly* 36 (2009): 615; *see also* Global Environmental Law, <www.globalenvironmentallaw.com/>. The authors have set up the aforementioned website to support their forthcoming casebook.

engagement.[38] Although a state-centered view of international law does not recognize the binding nature of policies emerging from a dialogue with non-state actors, that dialogue is arguably just as important to the effective application of those policies in the short term and the 'hardening' of those policies into customary law over the longer term.

III. THE IMPORTANCE OF ADMINISTRATIVE PROCEDURES IN THE IFI CONTEXT

The IFIs' environmental and social policies are thus properly understood as the product of an ongoing policy dialogue between civil society and IFIs. This dialogue catalysed the growth of administrative procedures for policy making at the IFIs, exactly at the time that broader trends were challenging the state-centred view of international law and expanding the procedural rights of non-state actors. This part looks at some of the broader factors driving the growth of administrative procedures for policy making at the IFIs.

A. The Growing Linkage between Process Rights and Development Effectiveness

The IFIs' struggles over the environmental and social policies were part of a broader shift toward sustainable development that occurred in the early 1990s.[39] As part of the international embrace of sustainable development, international organizations recognized that anti-democratic operations can also be anti-development. Increasingly, enhanced participation and a rights-based approach to development were seen as critical components to improving development effectiveness.[40] Parties at the 2002 World Summit on Sustainable Development (WSSD), for example, concluded that achieving the goals of sustainable development required 'more effective, democratic and accountable international and multilateral institutions'.[41]

---

38. In this regard, *see* B.S. Chimni, 'International Financial Institutions and International Law: A Third World Perspective', Ch. 2 herein (describing the role of social movements in international law making).
39. *See* David Hunter, James Salzman & Durwood Zaelke, *International Environmental Law & Policy*, 3rd edn (New York: Foundation Press, 2007), 162–218.
40. Steve Herz & Alnoor Ebrahim, 'A Call for Participatory Decision-Making: Discussion Paper on World Bank-Civil Society Engagement', paper commissioned by the Civil Society Members of World Bank-Civil Society Joint Facilitation Committee (15 Jun. 2005), 19–21; World Commission on Dams, 'Dams and Development: A New Framework for Decision-Making', final report (World Commission on Dams, November 2000).
41. World Summit on Sustainable Development, 'Johannesburg Declaration on Sustainable Development' (Johannesburg, South Africa, 2–4 Sep. 2002), para. 31, *available at* <www.un.org/esa/sustdev/documents/WSSD_POI_PD/English/POI_PD.htm> (political declaration adopted at the summit and recommended to the UN General Assembly for adoption).

In recent years, the World Bank has frequently acknowledged this linkage between process rights and its development mandate. The World Bank General Counsel, for example, has noted that '[d]evelopment is no longer confined to economic development narrowly defined, but encompasses broad areas of human development, social development, education, governance and institutions, as well as issues such as inclusion and cohesion, participation, accountability and equity'.[42] The World Bank's 2009 Access to Information Policy further recognizes the linkage with development effectiveness in the following way:

> The World Bank recognizes that transparency and accountability are fundamentally important to the development process and central to achieving the Bank's mission to alleviate poverty. . . . Openness promotes engagement with stakeholders, which, in turn, improves the design and implementation of projects and policies, strengthening development outcomes. It facilitates public oversight of Bank-supported operations, which not only assists in exposing potential wrongdoing and corruption, but also enhances the possibility that problems will be identified and addressed early on.[43]

IFIs, thus, have recognized administrative process rights as a necessary path to the fulfilment of their development mission, particularly in the context of specific development projects having significant environmental or social impacts. Indeed, central tenets of the IFIs' environmental and social policies discussed above are requirements ensuring full disclosure of environmental and social impacts and allowing public consultation during the project-design phase.[44] The IFIs could not reconcile the importance of transparency and participatory processes at the project-design level with denials of similar processes in the design of policies that shape those projects. If the rights of participation are intended to protect the rights and interests of those affected by decisions, it should matter not whether the decision is about a project or a policy.

Similarly, the World Bank and other IFIs have demonstrated the link between good governance at the domestic level and development effectiveness.[45] The IFIs are now placing certain 'good governance' conditionalities, including requirements for transparency in revenue flows and in open government, on their borrowers as prerequisites for financial support. More generally, public participation,

---

42. Roberto Dañino, Senior Vice-President and General Counsel of the World Bank, 'Legal Opinion on Bank Activities in the Criminal Justice Sector' (31 Jan. 2006), para. 9; Roberto Dañino, Senior Vice President and General Counsel, 'Legal Opinion on Human Rights and the Work of the World Bank' (27 Jan. 2006), para. 7.
43. World Bank, Operations Policy and Country Services, 'Toward Greater Transparency through Access to Information: The World Bank's Disclosure Policy' (16 Oct. 2009), para. 1, *available at* <http://siteresources.worldbank.org/INFODISCLOSURE/Resources/5033530-1236640024078/AccesstoInformationPolicy_Oct16.pdf> (hereinafter World Bank Information Disclosure Policy).
44. *See, e.g.*, World Bank Environmental Assessment Policy, *supra* n. 2.
45. *See generally* World Bank, *Governance and Development* (Washington, DC: The World Bank, 1992).

transparency, and accountability are hallmarks of good governance for public administration.[46] This applies equally to the governance of international organizations.[47] For the World Bank and other IFIs to require such transparency in the governance of their borrowers, but to deny the same set of rights in their own activities, is hypocritical and undermines the IFI good-governance message.[48] Anti-democratic operations at the international level can infect efforts to improve governance at the state level. While strong transparent, inclusive, and accountable practices at the international level, on the other hand, may be mirrored at the state level.

B. Procedural Fairness as a Source of Legitimacy

The civil society-IFI dialogue regarding environmental and social policies has also taken place as recognition of the importance of procedural fairness in international governance is expanding. Procedural fairness, or at least the perception of fairness, to all stakeholders lends legitimacy to the resulting policies of international organizations, just as it does at the national level. As Thomas Franck wrote in explaining the importance of both distributive (substantive) fairness and discursive (procedural) fairness in the international context:

> [People] expect that decisions about distributive and other entitlements will be made by those duly authorized, in accordance with procedures which protect against corrupt, arbitrary, or idiosyncratic decision-making or decision-executing. The fairness of international law, as of any other legal system, will be judged, first by the degree to which the rules satisfy the participants' expectations of justifiable distribution of costs and benefits, and secondly by the extent to which the rules are made and applied in accordance with what the participants perceive as right process.[49]

46. *See, e.g.*, World Bank, *Governance: The Bank's Experience* (Washington, DC: The World Bank, 1994), Preface, iv (describing good governance to include 'predictable, enlightened and open policy-processes, bureaucracy with a professional ethos, a government accountable for its actions, a strong civil society participating actively in public affairs, and all under the rule of law'). For more on the relationship between governance, human rights, and development, *see* Hans-Otto Sano & Gudmundur Alfredsson, *Human Rights and Good Governance: Building Bridges* (The Hague: Martinus Nijhoff, 2002).
47. The International Law Association, for example, has found that the 'principle of good governance . . . provides the necessary guidance as to the institutional and operational activities of an [international organization]'. International Law Association, 'Accountability of International Organisations, Berlin Conference Final Report' (Berlin, Germany, 2004), 8 (hereinafter ILA, Accountability of International Organisations).
48. *See, e.g.*, B.S. Chimni, 'Cooption and Resistance: Two Faces of Global Administrative Law', *New York University Journal of Law and Politics* 37 (2005).
49. Thomas Franck, *Fairness in International Law and Institutions* (New York: Oxford University Press, 1995), 7.

The transformation that is occurring in international law is that, until recently, procedural fairness was considered primarily in the context of fairness to states, as the primary subjects of international law. Regardless of whether individuals have become formally the subjects of international law, the growing scope and potential impact of international organizations on the lives of individuals in a globalized economy has meant that individuals increasingly feel as if they are de facto, if not de jure, subjects of international law. Particularly in the context of concerns about potentially negative human rights and environmental impacts of international organizations, questions of fairness and legitimacy in international law increasingly embrace the rights of individuals to obtain information or participate. As Susan Marks has put it:

> The contradiction has to be confronted between 'structures of power that seem to be increasingly internationalised, globalized, in some sense universalised and processes of participation, representation, accountability and legitimation that remain rooted in the institutionalised apparatuses of states'.... The central implication of this analysis is that the nation-state cannot remain democracy's container.[50]

This was exactly the structural gap faced by IFIs. The processes recognized under the traditional state-centric view of international organizations were inadequate to allow a meaningful dialogue with civil society – which could claim with some legitimacy that they should be stakeholders in the policy-making process. States remained important, but civil society demanded the right to be heard directly regarding policies and impacts that directly impacted them. Policies designed to afford communities access to specific information, rights to participate, or access to a grievance mechanism are not going to be considered legitimate if developed through a process that denies those same rights of transparency, inclusivity, and accountability.[51]

In the beginning, the IFIs and civil society were left with little international law or experience to guide this civic dialogue. In practice, they naturally resorted to processes (such as notice and consultation) that drew from the analogous process of rule making found at the national level, at least in western democracies. Over-time, however, international law relating to the administrative process rights of the public has been emerging, particularly in the context of sustainable development.

C. Administrative Procedural Rights in International Law

Procedural rights of the public are increasingly viewed as part of the emerging principles of international law in the field of sustainable development. Rooted in

50. Susan Marks, 'Democracy and International Governance', in *The Legitimacy of International Organizations*, ed. Jean-Marc Coicaud & Veijo Heiskanen (Tokyo & New York: United Nations University Press), 11–12.
51. Abbott & Snidal, *supra* n. 3, 64 (noting that multi-stakeholder participation is critical for the legitimacy of transnational regulation).

both international human rights and the treaties and practice of international environmental law, these procedural rights in the context of sustainable development are generally divided into three specific rights: (1) the right to access information; (2) the right to participate in decisions that affect your life and livelihood; and (3) the right of access to justice in some form. Notwithstanding their legal status in other contexts, these three 'access' rights or norms (also sometimes referred to as transparency, inclusivity, and accountability) are viewed as fundamental pillars of both environmental democracy and good governance.[52] Over time, they are emerging as critical international law principles, backed up by substantial state practice, in the context of sustainable development.

Principle 10 of the 1992 Rio Declaration on Environment and Development (endorsed by virtually all countries of the world) first recognized the importance of these three principles to sustainable development decision-making:

> Environmental issues are best handled with the participation of all concerned citizens, at the relevant level. At the national level, each individual shall have appropriate access to information concerning the environment that is held by public authorities, including information on hazardous materials and activities in their communities, and the opportunity to participate in decision-making processes. States shall facilitate and encourage public awareness and participation by making information widely available. Effective access to judicial and administrative proceedings, including redress and remedy, shall be provided.[53]

The Rio Declaration confirmed the importance of participation to sustainable development at the *relevant* level, which at least on its face would presumably cover the decision-making of international institutions such as the IFIs. On the other hand, Principle 10 clearly and deliberately limits the right of access to information to *national* level decision-making. The last sentence's endorsement of the right of access to judicial and administrative proceedings is unclear textually, but in context would appear also to apply only to states and national level decision-making.

Since 1992, Principle 10 has been endorsed and developed further in a number of different international contexts and instruments. Most notably, the UN Economic Commission for Europe implemented Principle 10 through the Convention on Access to Information, Public Participation in Decision-Making, and Access to

---

52. *See, e.g.*, ILA, Accountability of International Organisations, *supra* n. 47, 8 (defining good governance with respect to international organizations as including 'the following elements: transparency in both the decision-making process and the implementation of the ensuing institutional and operational decisions; a large degree of democracy in the decision-making process; access to information open to all potentially concerned and/or affected by the decisions at stake; the well-functioning of the international civil service; sound financial management; and appropriate reporting and evaluation mechanisms').
53. Rio Declaration on Environment and Development, UN Doc. A/Conf.151/26 (vol. 1); 31 I.L.M. 874 (1992), Principle 10, *available at* <www.un.org/documents/ga/conf151/aconf15126-1annex1.htm>.

Justice in Environmental Matters.[54] The so-called 'Aarhus Convention', named after the Danish town in which the Convention was signed, sets forth minimum standards for national decision-making in the same broad categories as Principle 10: transparency, inclusivity, and accountability. Although open for signature from any country, the Aarhus Convention was primarily aimed at the integration of the former Soviet bloc countries into the European Union and other western alliances. As of December 2009, forty-four countries had ratified the Aarhus Convention.

The Aarhus Convention provides substantial detail on how the three pillars of environmental democracy should be implemented, but it is almost entirely aimed at national level decision-making. The Convention's sole exception is Article 3.7, which specifically addresses the Parties' participation in international organizations. In Article 3.7, the Parties agree to 'promote the application of the principles of this Convention in international environmental decision-making processes and within the framework of international organizations in matters relating to the environment'.[55] The Aarhus Parties thereby confirmed an intent, if not an obligation, to apply the Aarhus principles to the decisions of international organizations. The Aarhus Parties would further explicate Article 3.7 and the applicability of procedural rights in international governance in the 2005 Almaty Guidelines on Promoting the Application of the Principles of the Aarhus Convention in International Forums.[56]

---

54. United Nations Economic Commission for Europe, Convention on Access to Information, Public Participation in Decision-Making and Access to Justice in Environmental Matters, UN Doc. ECE/CEP/43 (Aarhus, Denmark, 25 Jun. 1998), *available at* <www.unece.org/env/pp/documents/cep43e.pdf> (hereinafter Aarhus Convention). On the Aarhus Convention in general, *see* Veit Koester, 'The Convention on Access to Information, Public Participation in Decision-Making and Access to Justice in Environmental Matters (Aarhus Convention)', in *Making Treaties Work: Human Rights, Environment and Arms Control*, ed. Gèir Ulfstein et al. (Cambridge & New York: Cambridge University Press, 2007), 179–217; Marc Pallemaertz, 'The Aarhus Convention: A Model for Engaging the Disenfranchised in Decision-Making through the Institutionalization of Procedural Rights?', in *The Politics of Participation in Sustainable Development Governance*, ed. Jessica F. Green & W. Bradnee Chambers (Tokyo: UN University Press, 2006).
55. Aarhus Convention, *supra* n. 54, Art. 3.7. For a thorough discussion of the development and implementation of Art. 3.7 as well as the Almaty Guidelines discussed below, *see* Eric Dannenmaier, 'Europe's Commitment to Environmental Citizenship: Aarhus Article 3.7 and Public Participation in International Forums', *2007 Yearbook of International Environmental Law* 18 (2008): 32.
56. United Nations Economic Commission for Europe, Meeting of the Parties to the Convention on Access to Information, Public Participation in Decision-Making and Access to Justice in Environmental Matters, Report of the Second Meeting of the Parties, Addendum, Decision II/4, 'Promoting the Application of the Principles of the Aarhus Convention in International Forums', UN Doc. ECE/MP/PP/2005/2/Add.5 (Almaty, Kazakhstan, 25–27 May 2005) (adopted at the second meeting of the parties) (hereinafter 'Decision II/4'); UNECE, Meeting of the Parties to the Convention on Access to Information, Public Participation in Decision-Making and Access to Justice in Environmental Matters, Annex, 'Almaty Guidelines on Promoting the Application of the Principles of the Aarhus Convention in International Forums', UN Doc. ECE/MP/PP/2005/2/Add.5 (20 Jun. 2005) (hereinafter 'Almaty Guidelines'), *both available at* <www.unece.org/env/documents/2005/pp/ece/ece.mp.pp.2005.2.add.5.e.pdf>.

The Almaty Guidelines 'provide general guidance to Parties on promoting the application of the principles of the Convention in international forums in matters relating to the environment'.[57] Notwithstanding their non-binding status, the Guidelines do reflect the growing recognition that the access rights found in the Aarhus Convention should apply to international organizations. They confirm the importance of these procedural rights as 'fundamental elements of good governance at all levels and essential for sustainability'.[58] The Guidelines then set out principles or approaches for ensuring that access rights are promoted within international forums, including the IFIs.[59]

Other regions have not followed the Aarhus model of a binding regional convention, for promoting the access rights confirmed in the Rio Declaration. The Organization of American States, for example, has chosen to implement Principle 10 through a non-binding action programme.[60] At the national level, many countries have addressed access rights through their constitutions or in domestic law.[61] Notwithstanding the aggregation of these three access rights in Principle 10 and the Aarhus Convention, the international legal context for each category of process rights – access to information, public participation, and access to justice – differ and each is discussed further below.

1. Access to Information and Transparency

The right to access publicly held information regarding decisions that affect your life or well-being is rooted in Article 19 of the International Covenant on Civil and Political Rights (ICCPR): '[e]veryone shall have the right to freedom of expression; this right shall include freedom to seek, receive and impart information and ideas of all kinds . . . '.[62] The UN Special Rapporteur on Freedom of Opinion and

---

57. Almaty Guidelines, *supra* n. 56, para. 1.
58. *Ibid.*, para. 11.
59. *Ibid.*, para. 4 (explaining that the Guidelines cover Aarhus Parties' roles in '[i]nternational environmental and development policy forums; and [d]ecision-making processes within the framework of other international organizations in matters relating to the environment'); *see also ibid.*, para. 9 (defining international forum).
60. *See* Organization of American States, Unit for Sustainable Development and Environment, *Inter-American Strategy for the Promotion of Public Participation in Decision-Making for Sustainable Development* (Washington, DC: Organization of American States, 2001), *available at* <www.oas.org/dsd/PDF_files/ispenglish.pdf>.
61. *See, e.g.*, Carl Bruch, *Constitutional Environmental Law: Giving Force to Fundamental Rights in Africa*, 2nd edn (Washington, DC: Environmental Law Institute, 2007), 51–80 (describing the procedural rights in African Constitutions); *see also* Joseph Foti, *Voice and Choice: Opening the Door to Environmental Democracy* (Washington, DC: World Resources Institute, 2008) (describing progress on access rights in various parts of the world), *available at* <http://pdf.wri.org/voice_and_choice.pdf>.
62. United Nations, International Covenant on Civil and Political Rights, 999 U.N.T.S. 171 (23 Mar. 1976), Art. 19, *available at* <www1.umn.edu/humanrts/instree/b3ccpr.htm>; *see generally* Art. 19: Global Campaign for Free Expression, <www.article19.org>. For a thorough comparative survey of the right to access information, *see* Toby Mendel, *Freedom of Information: A Comparative Legal Survey* (New Delhi, India: UNESCO, 2003), *available at*

Expression has subsequently affirmed that Article 19 includes the right to access information held by the state.[63] The right of access to information has also been recognized by the Inter-American Court of Human Rights,[64] the Inter-American Commission on Human Rights,[65] the Council of Europe,[66] and the African Commission on Human and Peoples' Rights.[67] According to a recent survey, freedom of information is now guaranteed in constitutions or laws in at least sixty-nine countries,[68] and the right is increasingly upheld and enforced in domestic courts.

The right to access information is particularly recognized in the sustainable development context. The Aarhus Convention sets forth minimal elements necessary for ensuring access to information in the environmental context, including a general requirement that public authorities provide information within at least one month of any request from the public.[69] The Almaty Guidelines have explained how these access-to-information rights should be applied in international forums:

> Environmental information contained in all official documents developed and produced within each international forum should be made available to the public through the Internet, or through other appropriate means, in a timely manner. . . . Environmental information should be provided proactively, in a meaningful, accessible form, including, as appropriate, in the official languages of the concerned international forum, so that access to information may translate into an increase in knowledge and understanding. . . . [A]ny member of the public should have access to environmental information developed and held in any international forum upon request, without having to state

---

<http://portal.unesco.org/ci/en/file_download.php/fa422efc11c9f9b15f9374a5eac31c7efreedom_info_laws.pdf>.

63. Report of the Special Rapporteur, 'Promotion and Protection of the Right to Freedom of Opinion and Expression', UN Doc. E/CN.4/1998/40 (28 Jan. 1998), para. 14. The International Law Association has also recommended that international organizations should provide the public non-confidential information held by them. *See* ILA, Accountability of International Organisations, *supra* n. 47, at 9.
64. *See* Inter-American Court of Human Rights, *Compulsory Membership in an Association Prescribed by Law for the Practise of Journalism*, Advisory Opinion OC-5/85 (13 Nov. 1985), para. 30, *available at* <www1.umn.edu/humanrts/iachr/b_11_4e.htm>.
65. Inter-American Commission on Human Rights, 'Inter-American Declaration of Principles on Freedom of Expression' (19 Oct. 2000), para. 3 (adopted at the 108th Regular Session), *available at* <www.cidh.oas.org/declaration.htm>.
66. Council of Europe, 'Recommendation No. R(81)19 on Access to Information Held by Public Authorities' (25 Nov. 1981), 2 (adopted by the Committee of Ministers at the 340th Meeting of the Ministers' Deputies), *available at* <www.coe.int/t/e/legal_affairs/legal_co-operation/administrative_law_and_justice/Texts_&_Documents/Conv_Rec_Res/Recommendation%2881%2919.asp>.
67. African Commission on Human and Peoples' Rights, 'Declaration of Principles on Freedom of Expression in Africa' (Banjul, Gambia, 17–23 Oct. 2002), Part IV (adopted at 32nd session), *available at* <www1.umn.edu/humanrts/achpr/expressionfreedomdec.html>.
68. Foti, *Voice and Choice: Opening the Door to Environmental Democracy*, *supra* n. 61, x.
69. Aarhus Convention, *supra* n. 54, Art. 4; *see also* European Parliament, 'Directive 2003/4/EC of the European Parliament and of the Council on Public Access to Environmental Information' (2003).

an interest. 'When environmental information is requested by a member of the public, it should be provided as soon as possible following the request, and subject to an appropriate time limit, recalling that the time limit under the Convention is one month.'[70]

The importance of access-to-information policies in the context of sustainable development has been reflected in the practice of the IFIs; all of the IFIs have passed access-to-information policies.[71] By contrast, within the United Nations system only the UN Development Programme has adopted an information disclosure policy – but that policy is not well known and has been used sparingly.[72]

2. Public Participation

The right of individuals to participate in decisions that affect their lives is an aspect of individuals' civil and political rights. Increasingly, international human rights law is seen as including certain minimum 'due process' rights that must be met in the administration of the rule of law at the state level.[73] Article 25 of the ICCPR states that '[e]very citizen shall have the right and the opportunity . . . to take part in the conduct of public affairs, directly or through freely chosen representatives'.[74] Although on its face directed at national administration, the Human Rights Committee has stated that Article 25 'covers all aspects of public administration, and the formulation of policy at international, national, regional and local levels'.[75]

70. Almaty Guidelines, *supra* n. 56, paras 20–24.
71. *See e.g.*, World Bank Information Disclosure Policy, *supra* n. 43; IFC, 'International Finance Corporation's Policy on Disclosure of Information' (30 Apr. 2006), *available at* <www.ifc.org/ifcext/enviro.nsf/AttachmentsByTitle/pol_Disclosure2006/$FILE/Disclosure2006.pdf> (hereinafter IFC Disclosure Policy); Inter-American Development Bank, 'Disclosure of Information Policy' (7 Aug. 2006), *available at* <http://idbdocs.iadb.org/wsdocs/getdocument.aspx?docnum=784916>; European Bank for Reconstruction and Development, 'Public Information Policy' (September 2008), *available at* <www.ebrd.com/about/policies/pip/pip.pdf>; African Development Bank, 'The African Development Bank Group Policy on Disclosure of Information' (October 2005), *available at* <www.afdb.org/fileadmin/uploads/afdb/Documents/Policy-Documents/10000004-EN-THE-AFRICAN-DEVELOPMENT-BANK-GROUP-POLICY-ON-DISCLOSURE-OF-INFORMATION.PDF> (hereinafter AfDB Disclosure Policy); Asian Development Bank, 'The Public Communications Policy of the Asian Development Bank: Disclosure and Exchange of Information' (March 2005), *available at* <www.adb.org/Documents/Policies/PCP/PCP-R-Paper.pdf> (hereinafter ADB Disclosure Policy).
72. UN Development Programme, Public Information Disclosure Policy (1997) (the updated version of UNDP's Information Disclosure Policy (2008) is available at <www.undp.org/idp/>; *see also* Mendel, *supra* n. 62, 112 (discussing UNDP's information disclosure policy).
73. *See generally* Carol Harlow, 'Global Administrative Law: The Quest for Principles and Values', *The European Journal of International Law* 17 (2006): 187–214.
74. International Covenant on Civil and Political Rights, *supra* n. 62, Art. 25.
75. Gregory H. Fox & Brad R. Roth (eds), *Democratic Governance and International Law* (Cambridge, UK & New York: Cambridge Press, 2000), 55 (citing 'Annotation of Secretary-General of the Draft International Covenants on Human Rights', UN GAOR, 10th Sess., Supp. No. 19 (1955), 173).

Rights to participate are viewed as an integral part of good governance and a cornerstone of administrative law, at least in western democracies. Thus, for example, the European Code of Good Administrative Behavior, states that '[e]very member of the public shall have the right, in cases where a decision affecting his rights or interests has to be taken, to submit written comments and, when needed, to present oral observations before the decision is taken'.[76] The US Administrative Procedure Act similarly requires that interested persons be given 'notice' and 'an opportunity to participate' in rule makings by the federal government.[77]

As noted above, rights to participate are also central to the Aarhus Convention. ?Parties to the Aarhus Convention clarified their responsibilities to promote public participation in international forums through the Almaty Guidelines:

> Participation of the public concerned in the meetings of international forums, including their subsidiary bodies and other groups established by the forums to contribute to the decision-making, in matters relating to the environment should be allowed at all relevant stages of the decision-making process, unless there is a reasonable basis to exclude such participation according to transparent and clearly stated standards that are made available, if possible, in advance. . . .
>
> Effective participation of the public concerned may be ensured through a variety of forms, depending on different factors, such as the type of international forum concerned and the nature and phase of the decision-making process. Such forms could include, at meetings in international forums, observer status, advisory committees open to relevant stakeholders, forums and dialogues open to members of the public and webcasting of events, as well as general calls for comments.[78]

The rights of local communities to participate in the development of programmes to combat desertification are required in the 1996 United Nations Convention to Combat Desertification.[79] International rights to participate have been further recognized in the context of citizens and communities affected by transboundary environmental impacts. Since the 1970s, the Organisation for Economic Co-operation and Development (OECD), for example, has promoted equivalent treatment for persons suffering from transfrontier pollution who live in the neighbouring state, including 'the right to take part in, or have resort to, all administrative and

76. The European Ombudsman, *European Code of Good Administrative Behavior* (Luxembourg: Office for the Official Publications of the European Communities, 2005), Art. 16.
77. 5 U.S.C., s. 553.
78. Almaty Guidelines, *supra* n. 56, paras 29, 33.
79. United Nations Convention to Combat Desertification, 3 U.N.T.S. 1954; UN Doc. A/AC.241/27 (entry into force 26 Dec. 1996), Art. 3 (requiring Parties to 'ensure that decisions on the design and implementation of programmes to combat desertification and/or mitigate the effects of drought are taken with the participation of populations and local communities . . . .'), *available at* <www.unccd.int/convention/text/pdf/conv-eng.pdf>.

judicial procedures existing within the Country of origin' relating to the transfrontier pollution.[80]

The right of the public to participate is particularly relevant to the sustainable development context. As the Inter-American Development Bank (IDB) concluded in its Strategy for Civil Society Participation:

> There is a wealth of empirical evidence attesting to the merits of carefully designed and conducted participatory processes in development projects, in the form of efficiency, effectiveness, equity, and sustainability gains. From a broader perspective, the Organization for Economic Cooperation and Development has affirmed that 'strengthening relations with citizens is a sound investment in better policy making and a core element of good governance. It allows governments to tap new sources of policy-relevant ideas, information and resources when making decisions. Equally important, it contributes to building public trust in government, raising the quality of democracy and strengthening civic capacity'.[81]

The World Bank's General Counsel has also recognized the link between international human rights and the public participation and consultation requirements in the World Bank's policies.[82]

3. Access to Justice and Accountability

A third pillar of access rights relates to access to justice or to some form of mechanism that can hold public institutions – in our case, IFIs – accountable for their actions. Article 10 of the 1948 Universal Declaration of Human Rights provides: 'Everyone is entitled in full equality to a fair and public hearing by an independent and impartial tribunal, in the determination of his rights and obligations and of any criminal charge against him.'[83] This right to due process has been

---

80. OECD, Recommendation of the Council for the Implementation of a Regime of Equal Right of Access and Non-Discrimination in Relation to Transfrontier Pollution, C(77)28/Final (17 May 1977), para. 4, *available at* <http://webdomino1.oecd.org/horizontal/oecdacts.nsf/linkto/C%2877%2928>; *see also Restatement (3rd) of the U.S. Foreign Relations Law* (St Paul, MN: American Law Institute Publishers, 1987), s. 602(2) ('Where pollution originating in a state has caused significant injury to persons outside that state, or has created a significant risk of such injury, the state of origin is obligated to accord to the person injured or exposed to such risk access to the same judicial or administrative remedies as are available in similar circumstances to persons within the state'); *Bier v. Mines de Potasse d'Alsace*, 1976 Eur. Comm. Ct.J.Rep. 1735 (holding that within the European Community the victim of transfrontier pollution may sue either in his or her own or in the polluter's country).
81. Inter-American Development Bank (IDB), 'Strategy for Promoting Citizen Participation in Bank Activities' (19 May 2004), para. 2.1 (quoting OECD, Public Management Policy Brief No. 10), *available at* <http://idbdocs.iadb.org/wsdocs/getdocument.aspx?docnum=483088> (hereinafter IDB Citizen Participation Strategy).
82. Dañino, Legal Opinion on Human Rights and the Work of the World Bank, *supra* n. 42, para. 21.
83. United Nations, Universal Declaration of Human Rights, UN G.A. Res. 217 A(III) (10 Dec. 1948), Art. 10, *available at* <www.un.org/en/documents/udhr/>.

extended to civil matters that affect an individual's rights and responsibilities by the European Convention on Human Rights[84] and numerous national constitutions.[85] The EU Charter of Fundamental Freedoms, for example, upholds the 'right of every person to be heard, before any individual measure which would affect him or her adversely is taken' and the 'right to have his or her affairs handled impartially, fairly and within a reasonable time'.[86]

Although accountability can come in many forms,[87] we are concerned here primarily with the relationship of the public institution to external stakeholders, particularly those affected by the agency's actions. In the state-centric context of IFIs, a variety of obstacles impede such an individual's access to justice. Access to national courts is impeded by IFI claims of broad immunity;[88] and access to international forums is impeded by the general rule that individuals are not subjects of international law and cannot bring claims in international tribunals.

Barring significant shifts in these rules, access to justice with respect to IFIs necessarily implicates broader, alternative concepts of accountability. Even if access to judicial review in the traditional sense is not available, the right requires alternative means of providing affected individuals with access to an impartial review of decisions that affect their lives with a reasonable potential to obtain a remedy. According to the International Law Association (ILA) in its review of the accountability of international organizations, such organizations 'should establish the institutional framework to respect and to guarantee the right to a remedy for . . . non-state parties who are affected in their interests or rights by actions or omissions of an [international organization] . . . or one of its agents'.[89]

In the IFI context, access to an independent review is fulfilled at least partially by the independent accountability mechanisms, such as the World Bank Inspection

84. Council of Europe, Convention for the Protection of Human Rights and Fundamental Freedoms (Rome, 4 Nov. 1950; entry into force 3 Sep. 1953), Art. 6(1), *available at* <http://conventions.coe.int/Treaty/en/Treaties/Html/005.htm> (hereinafter European Convention on Human Rights).
85. *See, e.g.*, U.S. Constitution, Amendment V ('No person shall . . . be deprived of life, liberty or property without due process of law').
86. Charter of Fundamental Rights of the European Union, 2000/C 364/1 (18 Dec. 2000), Art. 41, *available at* <www.europarl.europa.eu/charter/pdf/text_en.pdf> (hereinafter EU Charter of Fundamental Freedoms).
87. *See, e.g.*, ILA, Accountability of International Organisations, *supra* n. 47 (discussing both internal and external accountability). For a more conceptual discussion of accountability, *see* Ruth W. Grant & Robert O. Keohane, 'Accountability and Abuses of Power in World Politics', *American Political Science Review* 99, no. 1 (February 2005): 1, 9, *available at* <www.princeton.edu/~rkeohane/publications/apsr_abuses.pdf>. Thus, although IFIs may be accountable through their Board of Executive Directors to the Member States of the institution, such accountability is related to affected communities only indirectly through their respective governments, if at all.
88. For discussions of IFI claims to immunity from national jurisdiction, *see* Steven Herz, 'Rethinking International Financial Institution Immunity', Ch. 5 herein; August Reinisch & Jakob Wurm, 'International Financial Institutions before National Courts', Ch. 4 herein.
89. ILA, Accountability of International Organisations, *supra* n. 47, 33.

Panel and the IFC's Compliance Advisor/Ombudsman.[90] These mechanisms allow citizens to file claims to a relatively independent entity that, depending on the mechanism, will either provide an opportunity to mediate the dispute or investigate the IFIs' compliance with its own policies and procedures, or both. In either case, affected parties are thus provided a limited opportunity to be heard and the potential for a remedy to harm they may have suffered. However, because the IFIs have not yet developed any formal policies codifying administrative procedures at the IFIs, these accountability mechanisms are not yet available as a means for enforcing administrative process rights in the policy-making context.

IV. THE EMERGING ADMINISTRATIVE PRACTICE OF IFIs

Given the broader trends relating to administrative law in international governance and the specific requirements for civic engagement the IFIs faced in the environmental and social context over the past two decades, it is probably not surprising that the IFIs have instituted a diverse range of administrative procedures aimed at incorporating non-state stakeholders into policy making. The IFIs' practices are described below first by summarizing the recent process for developing one policy – the World Bank's new information disclosure policy – and subsequently by looking in more detail at different stages of the process.

A. A Brief Illustration: Revising the World Bank Information Policy

The World Bank formally announced its procedures for revising its information policy by releasing a Consultation Plan in February 2009.[91] This plan set forth the

---

90. For general information on the World Bank Inspection Panel, *see* Daniel Bradlow, 'International Organizations and Private Complainants: The Case of the World Bank Inspection Panel', *Virginia Journal of International Law* 34 (1994): 553–554; David Hunter, 'Perspective: Using the World Bank Inspection Panel to Defend the Interests of Project-Affected People', *Chicago Journal of International Law* 4 (Spring 2003): 201–211; Dana Clark, Jonathan Fox & Kay Treakle (eds), *Demanding Accountability: Civil Society Claims and the World Bank Inspection Panel* (Lanham, MD: Rowman & Littlefield Publishing, 2003); Ibrahim Shihata, *The World Bank Inspection Panel: In Practice*, 2nd edn (Oxford: Oxford University Press, 2000); Lori Udall, *The World Bank Inspection Panel: A Three Year Review* (Washington, DC: Bank Information Center, 1997); Gudmundur Alfredsson & Rolf Ring (eds), *The Inspection Panel of the World Bank: A Different Complaints Procedure* (The Hague & Boston: Martinus Nijhoff, 2001); The Inspection Panel, *Accountability at the World Bank: The Inspection Panel Ten Years On* (Washington, DC: The World Bank, 2003), *available at* <http://siteresources.worldbank.org/EXTINSPECTIONPANEL/Resources/TenYear8_07.pdf>. These inspection panels have also been endorsed by the International Law Association. *See* ILA, Accountability of International Organisations, *supra* n. 47, 45.
91. IBRD, 'Toward Greater Transparency: Rethinking the Bank's Disclosure Policy: Consultation Plan' (February 2009), *available at* <http://siteresources.worldbank.org/INFODISCLOSURE/

process the Bank would use to engage civil society in the review and development of the information policy. As set forth in the Plan:

> The public consultations would allow stakeholders to provide inputs through the cycle of policy development, from the early stages of drafting through consideration by the Board. The consultation process would comprise the following main steps: (a) notification, (b) electronic comments and live consultations, (c) feedback to stakeholders, and (d) a period to review the revised draft.[92]

This public consultation phase would be preceded by consultation with Member States to ensure that they were informed of the Bank's intentions to make significant changes in its information disclosure policy.

One month later, on 12 March 2009, the Bank launched its public review of the information disclosure policy by releasing an 'approach paper' on the Internet that set forth guiding principles and key elements of the proposed revised policy.[93] The Bank also committed to ensuring widespread notification of its intent to revise the policy by issuing notifications through the Internet, Bank country offices, civil society networks, and local media. As set forth in its initial consultation plan, the Bank created a website dedicated to the process which hosted the approach paper in the six UN languages, and allowed the public to submit comments, receive updates, or otherwise communicate with the Bank.

In addition to accepting online comments, the Bank held public consultations in thirty-three Member Countries. It also posted a survey of specific questions on which it was particularly interested in receiving comments and input. The Bank worked closely with several CSOs, including the Bank Information Center, to identify CSOs that should be invited to the meetings. After each consultation, the Bank posted lists of the participants and summaries of each consultation (prepared by the attending CSOs) on a dedicated website.[94] The Bank also posted a summary of all electronic comments and survey submissions it received on the proposed

Resources/5033530-1236640024078/ConsultationPlan_March12.pdf> (hereinafter World Bank Consultation Plan).

92. *Ibid.*, para. 3.

93. World Bank, Operations Policy and Country Services, 'Toward Greater Transparency: Rethinking the World Bank's Disclosure Policy, Approach Paper' (29 Jan. 2009), *available at* http://siteresources.worldbank.org/INFODISCLOSURE/Resources/5033530-1236640024078/English_full.pdf (hereinafter World Bank's Disclosure Policy Approach Paper); *see also* The World Bank, *World Bank – Civil Society Engagement: Review of Fiscal Years 2007 to 2009* (Washington, DC: the International Bank for Reconstruction and Development, 2009), 16 (summarizing the process for developing the new information policy), *available at* <http://siteresources.worldbank.org/CSO/Resources/CivilSocietyBook2009final.pdf>.

94. World Bank, Information Disclosure Policy, Summaries of the Consultations, <http://web.worldbank.org/WBSITE/EXTERNAL/PROJECTANDOPERATIONS/EXTINFODISCLOSURE/0,,contentMDK:22168765~menuPK:5904357~pagePK:64865365~piPK:64864641~theSitePK:5033734,00.html>.

revisions.[95] Based on the comments and consultations, the Bank issued a revised draft disclosure policy on 21 October 2009, which was designed to go to the Board of Directors for final adoption.[96] The document was made available to the public, which allowed CSOs time to evaluate the draft and engage their representatives in the Board of Directors before they voted on the policy. The final policy was officially adopted by the Board of Directors on 10 December 2009.[97]

B. THE STAGES OF THE IFI POLICY-MAKING PROCESS

The process employed by the World Bank in revising its information policy is admittedly more extensive than what is typically seen at the World Bank, let alone other IFIs, but it is nonetheless illustrative of the range and extent of administrative procedures used at the IFIs. Even at IFIs with less capacity or political will to engage civil society than the World Bank,[98] some of these same components have been used at times in the policy-making process. As a result, although the World Bank is the leader in this regard, many of the IFIs' policy review processes routinely include one or more of the following stages: (1) notification; (2) consultation planning; (3) problem definition and scoping; (4) disclosure of the draft policy and one or more public comment and consultation periods; (5) the IFIs' public response to the comments; (6) release of a second or additional drafts (if need be) before final decisions are made; (7) documentation of the decision; and (8) access to an independent review of the policy development procedure. Together these stages could form the basis for a strong administrative procedures policy at the IFIs. Moreover, although inconsistencies exist in the implementation of these different stages, multiple examples exist across multiple institutions of effective implementation of best practices in each of these stages.

1. Notice of Process

Although often overlooked, the important first phase is the public announcement of the IFI's intention to establish a new policy or modify an old one. Clear initial notification is important regarding the overall process for allowing the public to

95. World Bank, Disclosure Policy Review & Global Consultations, Record of Online and E-mail Comments, *available at* <http://siteresources.worldbank.org/INFODISCLOSURE/Resources/5033530-1236640024078/online_comments4.pdf>.
96. IBRD, 'Toward Greater Transparency through Access to Information: The World Bank Disclosure Policy (Revised Draft)' (2 Oct. 2009), *available at* <http://siteresources.worldbank.org/INFODISCLOSURE/Resources/5033530-1236640024078/AccesstoInformationPolicy_Oct5.pdf>.
97. World Bank Information Disclosure Policy, *supra* n. 43.
98. For a comparison of the IMF's relative lack of operational policies as compared to the World Bank, *see* Daniel D. Bradlow, 'Operational Policies and Procedures and an Ombudsman', in *Accountability of the International Monetary Fund*, ed. Barry Carin & Angela Wood (Ottawa: International Development Research Centre & Burlington, VT: Ashgate Publishing Company, 2005).

prepare to participate effectively, but attention to notification is also important throughout the process. In particular, the IFIs struggle with ensuring that notifications of public consultation processes, including meetings, are well known among all of the diverse IFI stakeholders. Also, an important part of notification is ensuring that key documents are made available and translated in advance of any consultation process.[99]

Today, most IFIs use the Internet as the primary outlet for notification, with dedicated Internet sites, use of listserves, and dedicated e-mail accounts. The IDB even recently used a YouTube video to provide information on the consultation process for revising the IDB's accountability mechanism.[100] Given that many affected countries do not have large Internet capacity, however, the IFIs will often use other means, including distribution through their country offices, deliberate actions to access of civil society networks, and use of local media outlets. Despite such advances, significant challenges still exist in ensuring that a wider range of the public is aware of the IFIs' proposed activities. Most problematic has been ensuring that notifications and proposed policies are translated in a timely fashion into languages other than English. The IFIs complain that translation slows the process and is expensive, and only rarely are draft policies made available in more than one or two languages other than English.

Often the initial notification is released in conjunction with the consultation plan (stage 2) or the results of an evaluation of the status quo (stage 3).

2. Release of Consultation Plan

Part of adequate notification is the establishment of a consultation plan that lays out the steps in the policy-making process from beginning to end. A recent example is illustrated by the IFC's planned review of its 2006 'Sustainability Framework', which is comprised of a policy on social and environmental sustainability, and accompanying performance standards. When it originally adopted the Sustainability Framework, the IFC announced it would review the framework's effectiveness after three years. True to its word, in August 2009, the IFC announced its consultation plan for the review of the Sustainability Framework, with plans for three phases of public consultation.[101]

99. World Bank, *World Bank-Civil Society Engagement: Review of Fiscal Years 2007–2009*, *supra* n. 93, 15 (noting that the draft Strategic Framework for Climate Change was made available on a dedicated website in eight languages).

100. Inter-American Development Bank, Proposal to Create the Independent Consultation and Investigation Mechanism (10 Nov. 2009), 19 (hereinafter IDB Proposal to Create the ICIM). The YouTube video received 1,450 views.

101. IFC, Policy and Performance Standards and Disclosure Policy Update and Review Process Timeline, <www.ifc.org/ifcext/policyreview.nsf/Content/Timeline>, last visited 10 Jan. 2010; *see also, e.g.*, Asian Development Bank, Consultations with CSOs, <www.adb.org/NGOs/consultation.asp> (providing an overview of the consultations the ADB conducts with civil society including review of the Asian Development Bank's Accountability Mechanism).

The consultation plan envisioned using a multitude of tools to solicit input from the public:

> IFC will solicit feedback through a combination of web-based consultations, face-to-face consultations in Washington, D.C. and in different regions. Some meetings will be 'by invitation only' while others will be open to anyone. We will also consult with project-affected communities in addition to organizing a limited number of thematic face-to-face meetings to examine the most pressing challenges related to sustainability framework implementation. IFC will also use available electronic tools to organize live e-discussion meetings open to a broad spectrum of stakeholders. Information on specific dates and venues will be provided in the bulletin board on this website.[102]

The plan also elaborated the multiple phases of the proposed consultation process. The first phase would include a sixty-day public comment period intended to identify potential key issues and challenges regarding the implementation of the framework. Based in part on these comments and on internal evaluations of the framework's effectiveness, the IFC would release an initial draft of the revised policies. That initial draft will be subject to a second sixty-day consultation period that will allow both online comments and in-person consultations. After reviewing those comments, the IFC will revise text for a shortened thirty-day comment period before submitting the text to the Board for adoption.

The release of such a clear and comprehensive consultation plan allows both the IFIs and civil society to benefit from a predictable process. From the IFIs' perspective, the consultation plan allows for staff to create a work plan and for management to ensure that sufficient funds will be allocated for the dialogue. Consultation plans also help to structure the initial discussion over the process by presenting civil society with an early opportunity to argue for greater access to information, more consultations, or more time to deliberate over draft documents. Consensus over the consultation plan can build good will, facilitating a more constructive dialogue over the substance of the policy. From civil society's perspective, consultation plans allow networks and organizations to prepare for their participation – to research the issue, build consensus among themselves, and organize their input – into the policy-making process.

3. Problem Definition and Initial Scoping

Part of the recurring criticism of the policy-making process at the IFIs has been that the draft policies emerge fully fledged, with little opportunity for civil society to provide input into the fundamental direction or goals of the policy. In recent years, however, a number of IFI policy-making processes have been preceded by either an evaluation of the effectiveness, strengths, and weaknesses of the existing policies;

---

102. IFC, 'Consultation and Engagement Process', <www.ifc.org/ifcext/policyreview.nsf/Content/Process>, last visited 10 Jan. 2010.

or a scoping paper intended to identify and solicit public feedback on the major issues or approaches that should be considered in developing the new or revised policy. As noted above, the IFC's review of its performance standards began with an initial comment period aimed at identifying major issues for the review. In another example, in 2001 the Asian Development Bank (ADB) announced its intention to review its existing accountability mechanism. The ADB had been embroiled in a controversial project that had left both internal and external stakeholders dissatisfied with the existing mechanism.[103] The widespread dissatisfaction offered an opportunity to revisit and significantly revise the ADB accountability mechanism, but the ADB recognized it would need to engage civil society in an open and comprehensive dialogue over the new proposal. The ADB launched the process by releasing an issues paper to prompt a dialogue for identifying the major issues prior to releasing any new draft policy.[104] Similar practices were followed in revisions to the accountability mechanisms at the other regional development banks.[105]

Expanding civil society dialogue at this problem definition or scoping phase allows for a consensus to emerge over what the major issues are. In this way, fewer surprises will emerge later in the process. The IFIs will be better able to anticipate what the most contentious issues will be in their policy development, and work from the outset towards compromise or at least towards cabining off the controversies. From civil society's perspective, participating in this scoping phase is

---

103. For a detailed discussion of the controversy over this project (the Samut Prakarn wastewater treatment project), *see* Eisuke Suzuki, 'Responsibility of International Financial Institutions under International Law', Ch. 3 herein. In the interest of full disclosure, David Hunter, the author of this chapter, served as a consultant to the Asian Development Bank in the preparation of its revised accountability mechanism.

104. Asian Development Bank, 'External Consultations to Review the Inspection Function' (April 2002), *available at* <www.adb.org/Documents/Guidelines/Inspection_Function_Review/In8802.pdf>.

105. *See, e.g.*, African Development Bank (AfDB), Ongoing Review of the Independent Review Mechanism (8 Oct. 2009), *available at* <www.afdb.org/en/news-events/article/afdb-ongoing-review-of-the-independent-review-mechanism-5164/> (explaining the review process for the AfDB Independent Review Mechanism (IRM) including the initial review of the IRM by a consultant, who wrote a Draft Review Report. Michelo Hansungule, 'Review of the IRM, Findings and Recommendations' (26 Sep. 2009), *available at* <www.afdb.org/fileadmin/uploads/afdb/Documents/Compliance-Review/Draft%20Review%20Report%20by%20Prof.%20Hansungule%20%2826%20September%202009%29.pdf>); European Bank for Reconstruction and Development (EBRD), '2008 Review of the Independent Recourse Mechanism', <www.ebrd.com/about/integrity/irm/review.htm> (providing an overview of the EBRD's review process for its IRM); Inter-American Development Bank (IDB), Independent Consultation and Investigation Mechanism (ICIM), <www.iadb.org/PublicConsultation/MICI/index.cfm?id=5603&lang=en> (providing links to the documents related to the Public Consultation, including the Public Consultation Plan, <www.iadb.org/PublicConsultation/MICI/index.cfm?id=5606&lang=en> and the Invitation to Comment: Public Consultation Process for the Proposed Independent Consultation and Investigation Mechanism of the Inter-American Development Bank (6 May 2009), <http://idbdocs.iadb.org/wsdocs/getdocument.aspx?docnum=2045735> (which contains overviews of the consultation process and a summary of the proposed ICIM)).

critical because it provides an opportunity to shape the priorities of the policy development before the positions of the IFI staff responsible for developing the policy harden.

4. Soliciting Comments on Draft Policies

IFIs have used many different techniques to solicit comments on draft policies. More recently, reliance on the Internet has allowed for greater information exchange and ongoing dialogue between the IFIs and interested civil society stakeholders during the policy-making process. The mechanisms have included the use of dedicated websites and e-mails to provide information and receive comments, webinars to explain draft policies, and listserves created solely to facilitate communication during a specific policy-making process.[106] Expanding use of the Internet has allowed for one centralized location to house all relevant documents, and to be accessible to a relatively wide (though not universal) set of stakeholders. Such a one-stop shop for information eases civil society's efforts to follow the consultation process, to keep informed of its progress, and to participate effectively.

However, expanding reliance on the Internet does not replace the need for face-to-face consultations. One important IFI category of stakeholders – local communities affected by IFI operations – are the ones most likely to be disadvantaged by consultations limited to written comments over the Internet.[107] These communities may have low literacy rates and even lower Internet connectivity rates. Moreover, the urgency and passion felt by some stakeholders cannot be readily conveyed through the antiseptic nature of Internet comments. Face-to-face consultations are thus necessary to expand the range of potential stakeholders engaged in the dialogue.

As a result, public consultations remain a critical element of most IFI consultation plans and some of them can be quite extensive. The World Bank's consultations over its 2006 draft Governance and Anticorruption (GAC) Strategy, for example, were among the largest global consultations ever. According to the Bank,

---

106. *See, e.g.*, World Bank, Energy Strategy Consultations, <http://web.worldbank.org/WBSITE/EXTERNAL/TOPICS/EXTENERGY2/EXTESC/0,,menuPK:6297620~pagePK:64168427~piPK:64168435~theSitePK:6297515,00.html> (providing a link to the 'Online Consultation' form and links to the overall process for consultation); IFC, Policy Review, Frequently Asked Questions, <www.ifc.org/ifcext/policyreview.nsf/Content/FAQ#Q4> (offering an overview of how the public can participate, including through e-mail, the website, document editing, a blog, live web chats, mail, and in-person consultations); IDB, Public Consultations, Independent Consultation and Investigation Mechanism, <www.iadb.org/PublicConsultation/MICI/index.cfm?id=5606&lang=en> (explaining the consultation process for the establishment of the ICIM including links to the 'Proposed Independent Consultation and Investigation Mechanism' and documents explaining how to participate through the website and in person). The IDB ultimately received 270 comments online, over 85 of which were from non-governmental organizations. *See* IDB Proposal to Create the ICIM, *supra* n. 100, 18 (describing changes made in the policy in light of public consultation).
107. *See* Chi Carmody, 'Beyond the Proposals: Public Participation in International Economic Law', *American University International Law Review* 15 (2000): 1321.

'[m]ore than 3,200 representatives from government, parliaments, civil society, media, the private sector, and other stakeholders participated in consultation meetings held in 48 countries. There were also four global dialogue meetings (connected through a video link), as well as electronic feedback via the Bank's website'.[108] Similarly, the World Bank's consultations over its climate strategy involved seventy-one consultation meetings and more than 1,800 participants.[109] More typical are the IDB's 2009 consultations over proposed revisions to their accountability mechanism, which were attended by 226 participants in twelve countries.[110] Although the scale of a consultation neither equates with its quality nor means that the most vulnerable or affected populations are being effectively consulted, it does indicate the seriousness that the IFIs attach to consultation and the willingness to put significant staff and financial resources toward the process.

In most cases, public consultations are coordinated by the IFI's technical staff people who are responsible for the development of the policy. They are also responsible for collecting, analyzing, and responding to the diverse comments that may be submitted. If the timing works out, consultations are sometimes held in conjunction with the annual meetings or semi-annual meetings of the respective IFIs. More than three hundred civil society representatives attended the World Bank's 2009 spring meetings, which is over twice as many as a few years before.[111] Civil society may also be the catalyst for such meetings, by co-hosting sessions with the Bank or requesting to meet with top decision-makers on specific policy decisions. Although perhaps not part of the formal consultation plan, such consultations made in response to specific requests by civil society have become an important part of the policy-making dialogue at IFIs.

Slightly less common have been occasional 'technical briefings' typically hosted by one or more executive directors' offices or top IFI management. These meetings are designed to allow outside stakeholders to brief interested executive directors or managers on a specific policy or project issue, as most consultations between IFIs and civil society do not involve top IFI management. Rarer still is the opportunity for public consultation to be a formal agenda item of the full board of directors of an IFI. Only once has the World Bank Board of Executive Directors, itself, held a public hearing, which was co-chaired by the dean of the Board (at the time, the Russian executive director) and the executive director of the Bank Information Center. The meeting, which was part of a comprehensive review of the early experience with the World Bank Inspection Panel, was attended by virtually all the executive directors or their alternates and led to a critical clarification of the Inspection Panel's procedures.[112]

---

108. World Bank, *World Bank-Civil Society Engagement: Review of Fiscal Years 2007–2009*, *supra* n. 93, 13.
109. *Ibid.*, 15.
110. IDB Proposal to Create the ICIM, *supra* n. 100, 16.
111. *Ibid.*, 2.
112. For further description of this meeting, *see* Daniel Bradlow, 'Lessons from the NGO Campaign against the Second Review of the World Bank Inspection Panel: A Participant's Perspective', *ILSA Journal of International and Comparative Law* 7 (2001): 247.

5. Response to Comments

For several years, even after adopting the practice of allowing public comment, the IFIs generally refused to provide any substantive response to the comments they received. Participants to the process understandably raised concerns that they had no way of knowing whether their concerns had even been considered, particularly when little seemed to change from the initial draft to the final document.

As early as the 1992 review of the World Bank's water policy, the IFIs began to provide at least brief summaries of the comments received during the consultations.[113] More recently, the IFIs have occasionally provided summaries of comments received as well as the institutions' reaction to the comments. During the ADB's review of its inspection function, for example, the Bank provided a detailed chart summarizing and grouping all comments received during the consultation, and providing the institution's response to each comment (including an explanation for why the comment was not reflected in the final policy).[114] In this way, the consultation becomes a more rich dialogue with the institution.

Civil society activists often view the commenting period as an important step in their overall advocacy, but they are largely sceptical over how often consultation results in significant changes. But public comments often do make a difference in subsequent policies.[115] And public comments can strengthen the position of the IFI staff people who are fighting inside the institutions for stronger policies. Close alliances sometimes emerge during policy dialogues between environmental and social specialists inside the IFIs and civil society representatives who are seeking essentially the same outcome. By participating in the comment period, civil society also learns the arguments of IFIs in response to their comments, providing them an opportunity to strengthen their arguments as they raise their agenda to the executive directors or top IFI management.

6. Release of Final Draft Recommendation before Decision

In some instances, IFIs have recognized the need for additional public comment periods after submitting the initial comments on a draft policy. Particularly in

113. Moore & Sklar, *supra* n. 4, 367 (noting that the World Bank provided both a three-page memo on the lessons learned from the consultation and an edited transcript of the consultation).

114. Asian Development Bank, Review of the Inspection Function, Second Draft of Working Paper (22 Jul. 2002), Annex 7 ('Summary of Comments from the First Round of Consultations and Initial Response').

115. *See, e.g.*, Moore & Sklar, *supra* n. 4, 368 (noting that NGOs 'were pleased to find that many of their ideas had, in fact, been incorporated in the document'.). As another example, the opening statement of the purpose of the World Bank's new information disclosure policy is taken verbatim from a model policy provided by the Bank Information Center. *See* World Bank Information Disclosure Policy, *supra* n. 43, 1; Bank Information Center, 'GTI Submits a Model Disclosure Policy to the World Bank' (27 May 2009), *available at* <www.bicusa.org/en/Article.11213.aspx> (providing a link to the Model Disclosure Policy). *See also* IDB Proposal to Create the ICIM, *supra* n. 100 (describing changes made in the policy in light of public consultation).

situations in which extensive public consultation has revealed substantial criticisms of the initial drafts, the IFIs have agreed to release subsequent versions of the drafts for public review and comment. IFIs now regularly anticipate the need for more than one consultation phase and frequently include this in their initial consultation plan.[116]

The most problematic issue in the public consultation procedures is how to move from drafts that are open for public discussion to the final drafts that will be voted on by the IFI board of directors or other decision-maker. Generally speaking, decision documents for the board are not supposed to be released publicly prior to the IFI directors' vote. This conflicts with civil society's demands that they be provided an opportunity to review the final draft *before* a final decision is made, for the explicit purpose of trying to influence the board of directors to improve the policy. This conflict in fundamental goals was frequently reconciled in the past through the informal release (i.e., leaks) of board documents.

More recently, some IFIs have conducted multiple phases of consultations on iterative draft policies, including an additional, sometimes shortened, comment period to allow for the release of a near-final document before it goes to the board. Thus, for example, the IFC's consultation plan for its Sustainability Framework included two sixty-day consultations followed by a thirty-day consultation on the second draft immediately before it headed to the Board for decision.[117] Similarly, for its review of the inspection function, the ADB held public consultations for both first and second drafts of the proposed policy. The third draft of the revised policy was submitted, after the consultations, to the Board where it was approved after further modifications.[118]

7. Documentation of Decision

The ultimate decision regarding policies at the IFIs will of course eventually become known to the public as the IFI begins to implement its new policy, but this process has not always been formal or publically known. In the past, some IFIs even deliberately obfuscated what policies applied at what time, in this way ensuring maximum 'flexibility' and a lack of accountability in their operations. Thus, through the early 1990s, the IFC proclaimed to environmental groups that they were following World Bank safeguard policies, while at the same time they were

116. *See, e.g.*, IFC, 'Consultation and Engagement Process', *supra* n. 102 (setting forth three phases).
117. *See ibid.*
118. *See, e.g.*, Eisuke Suzuki & Suresh Nanwani, 'Responsibility of International Organizations: the Accountability Mechanisms of Multilateral Development Banks', *Michigan Journal of International Law* 27 (Fall 2005): 206. This can be contrasted with the more recent experience at the IDB, which did not release its second draft of the policy despite substantial changes made in light of public consultations. *See* IDB Proposal to Create the ICIM, *supra* n. 100 (this is the document that went to the Board, but was never released officially to the public; a copy is available from the author).

apparently not informing their borrowers that these policies were mandatory.[119] The spread of the Internet and the increasing use of IFI websites to disclose their policies have alleviated this problem considerably as most existing policies are now available for both the public and the borrowers to see.

The need to document a final decision goes beyond ensuring clarity over whether and when a new policy goes into effect. The International Law Association has recommended that international organizations should publicly explain the reasons for a decision, including the factual and legal reasons on which the decision is based.[120] This can contribute to fair and objective decision-making; reduce the opportunities for the misuse of power; and allow for more effective supervision and monitoring of the policy's implementation.

Also of interest to civil society is who supported or opposed the decision, whether any conditions were placed on the policy, or whether any specific interpretations of the policy were made by the board. For this reason, civil society is seeking greater transparency in the board deliberations over certain policies, and this has sparked continued debate over opening IFI board deliberations to the public, releasing minutes of the board meetings, or releasing the statements of individual board members. Thus far, IFIs have resisted opening up their board meetings to the public, but the World Bank has decided to now disclose the minutes of board meetings and related documents.[121] Also, board statements made by individual board members can be released at the discretion of the Member State on whose behalf the statement was made, and some countries now routinely make their statements publicly available.

8. Access to Independent Review

As noted above, individuals affected by IFI activities – but who are not in a contractual relationship with the IFI – have virtually no access to any remedy for

---

119. *See* Jay Hair, 'Pangue Hydroelectric Project: An Independent Review of the International Finance Corporation's Compliance with Applicable World Bank Group Environmental and Social Requirements' (4 Apr. 1997) (a redacted version is available from the author); *see also* David Hunter, Cristian Opaso & Marcos Orellana, 'The Biobio's Legacy: Institutional Reforms and Unfulfilled Promises at the International Finance Corporation', in *Demanding Accountability: Civil Society Claims and the World Bank Inspection Panel*, ed. Dana Clark, Jonathan Fox & Kay Treakle (Lanham, MD: Rowman & Littlefield Publishing, 2003), 115, 128–131 (discussing the conclusions of the Independent Review). More recently, the Overseas Private Investment Corporation (OPIC), a bilateral financial institution, behaved similarly, apparently using its discretion in generally waiving the applicability of the environmental and social policies on specific projects. *See* OPIC Office of Accountability, 'Office of Accountability Compliance Review of OPIC's Social Due Diligence of the Coeur d'Alene Mines/San Bartolome Project: Final Report' (February 2009), 6, 9, *available at* <www.opic.gov/sites/default/files/docs/coeur_d_alene_mines_san_bartolome_compliance_review_report.pdf>.

120. ILA, Accountability of International Organisations, *supra* n. 47, 13.

121. *See* World Bank Information Disclosure Policy, *supra* n. 43, 6–7 (noting that the Bank will now disclose the following records: 'Board minutes, Minutes of Board Committee meetings, Summings-up of Board meetings and Committee of the Whole meetings, Summaries of Discussion, . . . and Annual Reports of Board Committees').

harm caused by the IFI. The combination of immunity from national judicial proceedings and the state-centric perspective of international law means that citizens harmed by the IFIs have no recourse to traditional methods for reviewing a public agency's actions. This accountability gap has given rise to the creation of a variety of IFI accountability mechanisms, beginning with the 1993 creation of the World Bank Inspection Panel. Today, citizens enjoy accountability mechanisms at seven multilateral financial institutions[122] and three bilateral financial institutions[123] where they can seek to enforce the environmental and social policies of the institutions. Each of these mechanisms differs to some degree, but they share one common attribute: they all provide local people with an opportunity to seek oversight of the institution's compliance with applicable environmental and social policies.

These mechanisms apply to violations of the underlying environmental and social policy framework as it is applied to a specific project. Thus, for example, the failure of the World Bank to categorize a project correctly under its environmental assessment policies could give rise to an Inspection Panel claim. Because none of the IFIs have codified a normative procedural framework for the development of policies, however, none of the mechanisms can yet be used to police the adequacy of the administrative process of policy development.

V. NEXT STEPS: TOWARD CODIFICATION OF ADMINISTRATIVE PROCEDURES AT IFIs

As the above survey of recent administrative practice at the IFIs suggests, the IFIs have developed a robust and diverse set of procedures for engaging civil society in policy development. But the practice is inconsistent and in many cases the IFIs still use inadequate procedures that unnecessarily cause conflict with civil society and delegitimize the IFIs' actions. Given that the IFIs frequently embrace the concept of broader public participation and access rights in the context of specific policy-making processes, they should take the next step and set minimum procedural benchmarks that they commit to following in every case, thus guaranteeing minimum rights of transparency, participation, and accountability.

---

122. The seven citizen enforcement mechanisms include: (1) the World Bank Inspection Panel; (2) the International Finance Corporation's Compliance Advisor/Ombudsman; (3) the Asian Development Bank's Accountability Mechanism; (4) the Inter-American Development Bank's Independent Consultation and Investigation Mechanism; (5) the European Bank for Reconstruction and Development's Compliance Office; (6) the African Development Bank's Independent Review Mechanism; and (7) the European Investment Bank's Complaint Mechanism.

123. The three bilateral financial institutions are (1) the Japan Bank for Investment Cooperation's Compliance Examiners; (2) the Environment Development Canada's Compliance Officer; and (3) the US Overseas Private Investment Corporation's Office of Accountability.

A. The Authority to Codify Administrative Procedures

The international law context for establishing procedural rights at the IFIs is also strengthening. As international organizations, the World Bank and other IFIs are subjects of international law, and thus have rights and obligations under international law.[124] Although nowhere in their Articles of Agreement or constituent documents do IFIs have the explicit authority to issue a policy on administrative procedures, such capacity can be justified as part of the functions necessary to carry out the IFIs' underlying missions and purposes.[125] The International Court of Justice (ICJ) has stated that under international law, international organizations 'must be deemed to have those powers which, though not expressly provided in the Charter, are conferred upon it by necessary implication as being essential to the performance of its duties'.[126]

In line with this ICJ opinion, the IFIs have long endorsed a 'purposive' interpretation of their mission that recognizes the multidimensional nature of development and allows for broad interpretation informed by the principles of 'effectiveness, reasonableness, good faith and the common interests of the organization and its members as a whole'.[127] Indeed, it is the same purposive approach that allowed the IFIs to develop and implement environmental and social standards in the first place. Except for the EBRD, no IFI has 'sustainable development' in its mandate; the rest of the IFIs have developed their environmental and social safeguard policies under authorities implied, and not precluded, by their Articles of Agreement. IFIs thus have the legal capacity or authority to issue administrative

---

124. *See* Interpretation of the Agreement of 25 Mar. 1951 between the WHO and Egypt, I.C.J. Reports 1980, 73, 89–90, para. 37, *available at* <www.icj-cij.org/docket/files/65/6303.pdf> ('International organizations are bound by any obligations incumbent on them under international law.'); Sigrun I. Skogly, *The Human Rights Obligations of the World Bank and the International Monetary Fund* (London: Cavendish Publishing, 2001), 63–73. *See also* Eisuke Suzuki, 'Responsibility of International Financial Institutions under International Law', Ch. 3 herein, Siobhán McInerney-Lankford, 'International Financial Institutions and Human Rights: Select Perspectives on Legal Obligations', Ch. 8 herein; B.S. Chimni, 'International Financial Institutions and International Law: A Third World Perspective', Ch. 2 herein; Daniel D. Bradlow, 'International Law and the Operations of the International Financial Institutions', Ch. 1 herein.
125. *See* Skogly, *supra* n. 124, 71–76.
126. *Reparation for Injuries Suffered in the Service of the United Nations, Advisory Opinion*, I.C.J. Reports 1949 (11 April), 178, 183, *available at* <www.icj-cij.org/docket/files/4/1835.pdf?PHPSESSID=c2ca077aae4031563ed544a97d5e516f> (determining that the UN possessed international personality, and thus the ability to file a claim against a State under international law, when the answer 'is not settled by the actual terms of the Charter') (hereinafter *Reparation Advisory Opinion*); *see also* José E. Alvarez, 'Constitutional Interpretation in International Organizations', in *The Legitimacy of International Organizations*, ed. Jean-Marc Coicaud & Veijo Heiskanen (New York: United Nations University Press, 2001), 104, 121–122.
127. Dañino, 'Legal Opinion on Human Rights and the Work of the World Bank', *supra* n. 42, para. 6 (quoting Ibrahim Shihata, 'Interpretation as Practiced at the World Bank', in *The World Bank Legal Papers*, ed. Ibrahim F.I. Shihata (Boston: Martinus Nijhoff, 2000), XLIV).

procedures for the development of their own policies and standards. More complicated is whether international law *requires* them to do so.

The customary practice of international organizations, including IFIs, may provide evidence for the subsequent interpretation of the organization's charter.[128] In this way, the customary practice of the IFIs in adopting democratic administrative procedures to the extent they are seen as interpreting the respective IFI charters would become part of the normative framework constraining the organization. According to Article 31 of the Vienna Convention on the Law of Treaties, treaties (including IFI Charters) can be interpreted by reference to 'subsequent practice'.[129] Typically this provision refers to the subsequent practice of states, but in the context of international organizations, the subsequent practice of the international organization can also be used to interpret its organic charter.

Thus, recognizing the current customary practice of the IFIs in adopting democratic administrative procedures could inform any future dispute over, for example, whether the use of administrative procedures extends beyond an IFI's mission. To the extent arguments against democratic administrative procedures create conflict over the interpretation of the role and mission of IFIs, the customary practice that has built up over time can be used to interpret the original charter and to justify the perpetuation of such principles. The IFIs are thus not only authorized to codify their current customary practice in a set of administrative procedures, but also such procedures would have to meet the minimum standards set by the customary practice of IFIs to date. In other words, no backsliding from contemporary practice should be allowed in the codification of the IFIs' administrative procedures.

The need for a more formal and predictable administrative process for policy making is not a new point of discussion at the IFIs. The World Bank-Civil Society Joint Facilitation Committee recommended that the World Bank adopt a fixed administrative procedure for developing and revising Bank operational policies and strategies.[130] While the IDB, for example, has adopted a broad strategy for civic engagement in part 'to move from the body of experience amassed to a set of procedures that will systematically provide for public participation in the Bank's operational activities'.[131]

---

128. *See* Alvarez, 'Constitutional Interpretation in International Organizations', *supra* n. 126, 117–121 (discussing the role of customary practice in interpreting the charters of international organizations).
129. Vienna Convention on the Law of Treaties, 1155 U.N.T.S. 331 (23 May 1969), *available at* <http://untreaty.un.org/ilc/texts/instruments/english/conventions/1_1_1969.pdf>.
130. Herz & Ebrahim, 'A Call for Participatory Decision-Making: Discussion Paper on World Bank-Civil Society Engagement', *supra* n. 40.
131. IDB Citizen Participation Strategy, *supra* n. 81. Although recognizing the value of systematizing public participation, the IDB (like the other banks) focuses almost exclusively on the participation in specific projects, ignoring the need for systematic procedures in the institution's policy making. Moreover, the IDB has done little to operationalize its civil society engagement strategy.

B. THE ADVANTAGES OF CODIFICATION

Although the IFIs have in practice adopted a fairly robust de facto administrative procedure, they have for the most part refused to codify it in a set of clear and predictable standards. In part, this can be explained by a desire to maintain flexibility, for example, to design each process according to the specific needs of the situation. It may also reflect reluctance on the part of the institutions to recognize any general responsibility to conduct open and transparent, multi-stakeholder processes for their policies.

Codifying existing best practices into an Administrative Rule-making Policy, however, would have several positive effects. First, by guaranteeing certain minimum procedural benchmarks, the IFIs will facilitate richer, more predictable, and more transparent policy engagement with civil society.[132] Policy-making at the IFIs would become more efficient because every process would not first have to go through a contentious debate about the appropriate amount of public participation that is required. These debates draw out the policy-making process, exhaust participants on both sides, and almost always result in civil society gaining additional procedural steps that the IFIs should have offered in the first place. In addition, conflicts over procedure can obscure both differences and agreements over the substance, making it more difficult to achieve consensus or at least narrow the substantive policy differences.

Second, a set of objective procedures, implemented consistently across all operations would enhance the chances for administrative due process and help the IFIs fulfil their obligation not to discriminate.[133] As the ILA has recognized, 'procedural regularity' in the operations of international organizations can 'prevent abuse of discretionary powers; avoid errors of fact or law; and ensure respect for due process and fair treatment'.[134] A codified general process can ensure greater harmonization, more objectivity in policy making, and less risk of discrimination against politically less powerful or more controversial groups. With a minimum set of standards identified in advance of any particular policy context, the IFIs will be less tempted to shape a particular process to avoid uncomfortable consultations or exclude particularly strong critics.

Third, establishing an administrative procedure would create a policy framework necessary to allow the institutions to build internal expertise around the administrative process. Just as the processes have been ad hoc, so too have the staffing and expertise applied to these policy processes. Little internal capacity has been developed at the IFIs for designing and implementing effective public participation plans. Outside of the World Bank, the processes frequently rely on

132. Although much of this chapter's discussion is focused on the World Bank and MDBs, many of the same arguments can be applied to the IMF. *See* Bradlow, 'Operational Policies and Procedures and an Ombudsman', *supra* n. 98 (arguing that the IMF 'needs to establish a transparent and predictable rule-making procedure that will govern how the IMF develops all its operational policies and procedures').
133. International Covenant on Civil and Political Rights, *supra* n. 62, Art. 2.
134. ILA, Accountability of International Organisations, *supra* n. 47, 14.

outside consultants who may know little about the IFIs' institutional or policy context, or the target constituents for the policy dialogue. Even competent consultants leave little institutional capacity behind, requiring the IFIs to re-create and re-staff the process every time. To be sure, some of the smaller regional development banks face chronic staffing and capacity problems on a variety of issues, but the codification of administrative procedures would raise the profile of these issues in the institution, illuminate the demand for such capacity, and help to build the case for increasing the institution's staffing.

Fourth, a codified administrative procedure would also introduce the possibility for a form of 'judicial review' when the policy is violated. The World Bank Inspection Panel and similar mechanisms could be accessible by individuals who believed that their procedural rights in the development of IFI policies have been violated. In addition to adopting a clear policy on administrative procedures, some of the complaint mechanisms' operational policies may have to be amended to empower them to review compliance in the policy-making context as opposed to only reviewing compliance in the specific project context.[135]

Fifth, codifying the administrative policy-making processes would continue the current trend of redefining who legitimate stakeholders in IFI operations are. The current administrative process has been born from pressure brought by civil society that has been affected by IFI operations. They have demanded to be recognized as legitimate voices in the policy dialogue with IFIs even if they are neither states nor in contractual relationships with the IFI. Indeed, most IFIs, even those with development missions, inherently tend to think of their borrowers as their sole client, too often ignoring the community most directly affected by their projects. The broader policy dialogue around environmental and social standards, including the associated engagement with civil society, forces IFIs to embrace a broader definition of stakeholder – one that includes, most critically, those local communities affected by the projects they finance. Formally expanding the processes by which those communities, and CSOs that champion their rights, can participate in policy-making inherently confirms these sectors as legitimate stakeholders of the organization.

Finally, codifying the administrative practice at the IFIs will add to the progressive development of administrative law in the international context. The IFIs would set a precedent for how international institutions orient themselves to the public. In some ways, the IFIs are further along in developing administrative procedures than are many other international institutions. By codifying their existing practice and struggling with some of the difficult balancing issues inherent in establishing effective, efficient, and fair procedures, the IFIs would advance the role of administrative procedures and the rights of the public in international

135. *See, e.g.*, World Bank, 'Inspection Panel Operating Procedure', <http://web.worldbank.org/WBSITE/EXTERNAL/EXTINSPECTIONPANEL/0,,contentMDK:20175161~menuPK:64129254~pagePK:64129751~piPK:64128378~theSitePK:380794,00.html>, last visited 10 Jan. 2010 (providing that only people living in the country where the *project* is located can bring a claim).

policy-making more generally. Eventually, such efforts at codifying administrative procedures at the IFIs and other institutions could lead to a broader discussion about the need for an international instrument that codifies minimum administrative procedure for all international organizations.[136] Regardless of whether such an international instrument is negotiated, the administrative practice of the IFIs is creating the international analogue to state practice, and thereby can be viewed as furthering the customary law of international organizations.

C. Conclusion

Regardless of whether administrative procedural rights are part of universal human rights of due process, such rights are clearly critical in the development context and thus are particularly important for the operations of development institutions like the World Bank and other IFIs. The IFIs already regularly include minimum administrative procedures in their policy-making processes. As demonstrated above, the IFIs' participatory approach has included the full range of procedural mechanisms from providing early notice of proposed policy making, to the public release of a reasoned final decision by the IFI. What is missing is any consistency or predictability to the procedures implemented by the IFIs. Each policy-making process triggers the design and implementation of a new procedure, *sua sponte*.

Having been drawn reluctantly into a public-oriented approach to policy making, the IFIs have been disinclined to acknowledge it or legitimate it by proactively setting forth a set of minimum standards. The ad hoc nature of the policy-making process reflects the failure of the institutions to make a policy decision that they do in fact endorse open, transparent, and multi-stakeholder processes for their own policies. At the policy level, the institutions have not explicitly recognized that they are developing an administrative practice and have not committed to developing a consistent and comprehensive approach to it.

The net result is inefficiency in the policy-making process as well as a system that ensures greater procedural rights only in those processes where civil society (mostly from donor countries) has generated sufficient political pressure to expand the IFIs' procedural approach. The ad hoc approach to a participatory process obscures the significant advances the IFIs have made in implementing administrative procedures. The hidden nature of these advances means that few in the

136. Some commentators have begun arguing that minimum standards for public participation should be developed at the international level, perhaps in the form of an administrative procedures treaty. *See, e.g.*, James Speth, *Red Sky at Morning: America and the Crisis of the Global Environment* (New Haven, CT: Yale University Press, 2004); 'The World Bank's New Inspection Panel and the Need to Create an International Framework Agreement for Administrative Procedures', Testimony of Durwood Zaelke and David Hunter before the Subcommittee on International Development, Finance, Trade and Monetary Policy (21 Jun. 1994); David Hunter, 'Global Environmental Protection in the Twenty-First Century', in *Global Focus: US Foreign Policy at the Turn of the Millennium*, ed. Martha Honey & Tom Barry (New York: St. Martin's Press, 2000), 136–137.

institutions know or take pride in the open and transparent processes the IFIs run. As a result, the institutions have not internalized or mainstreamed their innovative approaches and are seen as being mostly reflexive to civil society pressures instead of proactive leaders. In short, the current approach engenders conflict over the procedure, creating a confrontational atmosphere where none is necessary. The IFIs are put on the defensive and have yet to take advantage of greater legitimacy, efficiency, and public support by more proactively embracing the processes they have already been following. By taking steps to codify the best practice in their administrative procedures, the IFIs could illuminate their ongoing leadership in this area, secure equal and effective participatory rights for all civil society, and advance the further development of public rights in international administrative law.

Chapter 8

International Financial Institutions and Human Rights: Select Perspectives on Legal Obligations

*Siobhán McInerney-Lankford**

I. INTRODUCTION

Human rights and development interact in a variety of ways. They may be seen to converge, through the apparent compatibility of their aims and the proximity of their activities. Their relationship at the level of obligations is one of the most important yet least explored aspects of public international law. This chapter considers the various sources of public international law, and the unsettled area of human rights obligations of international organizations, to examine human rights obligations that may have relevance to development institutions and international financial institutions (IFIs). Given the broad reach of development policies and activities, the discussion explores viable means to uphold accountability in development, and posits obligations under human rights treaties

* The findings, interpretations, and conclusions expressed herein are those of the author and do not necessarily reflect the views of the executive directors of the International Bank for Reconstruction and Development, the World Bank or the governments they represent. The author is indebted to Charles Di Leva, Nathan Lankford, and Kenneth Mwenda for comments on earlier drafts of this chapter: responsibility for any errors or omissions remains the author's own. This work is dedicated to Chloé Basse.

Daniel D. Bradlow and David B. Hunter, *International Financial Institutions and International Law*, pp. 239–285.

as one effective way of addressing the accountability gaps in relation to human rights.[1]

A particular focus is placed on the World Bank[2] as emblematic of a development institution historically accused of human rights violations and accountability-related harms, as well as claims that it is subject to international human rights obligations. As a prominent IFI and a UN specialized agency within the meaning of Article 57 of the UN Charter,[3] the World Bank epitomizes the challenges of accountability and the limits of the law as it stands.

This chapter revisits the question of human rights obligations and IFIs to 'reflect the complexity of the situation or reveal the layers of legal obligation'.[4] The intrinsic value of human rights is widely recognized[5] and broadly transposed into international legal frameworks, and yet human rights accountability (HRA) in development remains imperfect.[6] There is a need to reorient the focus on positive obligations of states under treaties and exploit the unused potential extant in international law before exploring non-treaty based sources, despite the obvious appeal these may have in identifying the obligations of non-state actors.[7] This is an area of growing interest due to an exponential increase in the power and activities of non-state actors. The law, however, has not kept up with this expansion in

---

1. For a positivist approach to public international law, *see* Lassa Oppenheim, 'The Science of International Law: Its Task and Method', *American Journal of International Law* 2 (1908): 313.
2. For the purposes of this discussion, the term international financial institutions (hereinafter IFI) shall be taken to cover the World Bank (IBRD and IDA), IFC, MIGA, the IMF, and regional development banks.
3. On the IBRD as a specialized agency and subject of international law, *see generally*, Aron Broches, 'International Legal Aspects of the Operations of the World Bank', *Hague Academie de droit international: Receuil des cours* (1959): 301.
4. Andrew Clapham, *Human Rights Obligations of Non-state Actors* (Oxford: Oxford University Press, 2006), 138.
5. Thomas Buergenthal, 'The Normative and Institutional Evolution of International Human Rights', *Human Rights Quarterly* 19, no. 4 (1997): 703–723; Manfred Nowak, *Introduction to the International Human Rights Regime* (Leiden: Brill Academic Publishers, 2003); Maurice Cranston, *What are Human Rights?* (New York: Taplinger Publishing Co., 1973); Jack Donnelly, *The Concept of Human Rights* (London: Croom Helm, 1985); Jack Donnelly, *Universal Human Rights in Theory and Practice*, 2nd edn (Ithaca, NY: Cornell University Press, 2003). *See further*, Christian Tomuschat, *Human Rights: Between Idealism and Realism* (Oxford: Oxford University Press, 2003); Paul Sieghart, *The Lawful Rights of Mankind* (Oxford: Oxford University Press, 1986); Richard Falk, 'Theoretical Foundations of Human Rights', in *Human Rights in the World Community*, ed. Richard Pierre Claude & Burns H. Weston, 2nd edn (Philadelphia: University of Pennsylvania Press, 1992), 31–40; Philip Alston, *Human Rights Law* (Aldershot: Dartmouth Publishing, 1996). Philip Alston, Henry Steiner & Ryan Goodman, *International Human Rights in Context: Law, Politics, Morals*, 3rd edn (Oxford: Oxford University Press, 2007); Oscar Schachter, 'Human Dignity as a Normative Concept', *American Journal of International Law* 77 (1983): 848.
6. Arguing for an 'integrated approach' to the international law of sustainable development, drawing on human rights, *see* Dominic McGoldrick, 'Sustainable Development and Human Rights', *International and Comparative Law Quarterly* 45 (1996): 796.
7. Philip Alston (ed.), *Non-state Actors and Human Rights* (Oxford: Oxford University Press, 2005).

practice, resulting in the need for new legal norms, or the revisiting of traditional sources. This work focuses on the latter. It recognizes the existence of HRA lacunae,[8] but recalls that states bear the primary responsibility for human rights under international law.[9] Traditional notions of state sovereignty in international law have transformed, but not eliminated states' obligations, which are still the principal means of tackling HRA in development.

II. ESTABLISHING THE CONTEXT: HUMAN RIGHTS AND DEVELOPMENT AS INTERRELATED SPHERES

Development and human rights have evolved towards similar goals,[10] albeit along parallel tracks.[11] This section addresses the overlap of these two spheres, highlighting their commonalities and mutually reinforcing features,[12] as well as the divergences and tensions that persist between them. The connections between human rights and development can be identified at distinct 'levels'.[13] Specifically, one can view their relationship as a tripartite framework: practice, principles, and obligations.[14] Thus, while some substantial 'rapprochement', including concerted efforts to promote the mutual reinforcement of human rights and development

---

8. In this work, the term 'human rights accountability' is used as shorthand to describe legal responsibility for the respect, protection, promotion, and fulfilment of human rights, or their realization broadly understood, in development policies and projects.
9. Frances Butler (ed.), *Human Rights Protection: Methods and Effectiveness* (London: Kluwer Law International, 2002). Hurst Hannum, *Guide to International Human Rights Practice*, 2nd edn (Philadelphia: University of Pennsylvania Press, 1992); Philip Alston, *The United Nations and Human Rights: A Critical Appraisal* (Oxford: Clarendon Press, 1992).
10. An early linkage between development and human rights can be found in the 1969 Tehran Declaration's proclamation of the right to development and the Declaration on the Right to Development. Resolution 41/117/128 (4 Dec. 1986), which was reaffirmed in several later resolutions and in the 2000 Millennium Declaration, <www.un.org/millennium/declaration/ares552e.htm>. *See* Roland Y. Rich, 'The Right to Development as an emerging Human Right', *Virginia Journal of International Law* 23 (1983): 287; and the recent work of the UN High Level Task Force on the Right to Development, of which the World Bank is a member, <www2.ohchr.org/english/issues/development/right/index.htm>.
11. Peter Uvin, *Human Rights and Development* (Sterling, VA: Kumarian Press, 2004), 47.
12. Mary Robinson & Philip Alston, 'The Challenges of Ensuring the Mutuality of Human Rights and Development Endeavours', in *Human Rights and Development: Towards Mutual Reinforcement*, ed. Mary Robinson & Philip Alston (Oxford: Oxford University Press, 2005), Ch. 1, 11–18.
13. Ernst-Ulrich Petersmann, 'Human Rights and International Economic Law in the 21st Century: The Need to Clarify Their Interrelationships', *Journal of International Economic Law* 4, no. 1 (2001): 3–39.
14. Siobhán McInerney-Lankford, 'Human Rights and Development: Some Institutional Perspectives', *Netherlands Quarterly of Human Rights* 25, no. 3 (2007): 459. *See* 'Human Rights in Development Cooperation – Report from the Informal Experts' Workshop jointly organized by the OECD Development Centre and CIDA' (Paris, 5–6 Feb. 1996), printed in *Human Rights in Development Cooperation* (SIM Special Number 22, edited by Henny Helmich & Elena Borghese, Utrecht: OECD Development Centre (December 1998)), 10.

is evident,[15] it is more apparent at the level of activities and principles than at the level of obligations. A key concern here is that the expanse of this overlap increases the need for greater accountability, and despite the advances that have been made to integrate human rights and development, obligations remain weakly transposed in this area.

A. Human Rights Related Practice

A broad substantive overlap exists between the expanding range of functions, responsibilities, and activities of development institutions, and the material provisions of core human rights treaties.[16] In respect of the World Bank, some identify 'a steady expansion into "human rights territory" and *de facto* adoption of certain human rights conditionalities in its operations'.[17] Others note that '[. . .] human rights issues are implicitly part of the development mandate of the World Bank and central to the success of poverty alleviation programs of the Bank and the IMF'.[18] Still others observe that 'the World Bank has been paying more and more attention to basic rights in the course of its existence; its policies have become increasingly enwrapped in "fundamental rights of everyone" '.[19]

---

15. UNDP, *Integrating Human Rights with Sustainable Development: A UNDP Policy Document* (New York: UNDP, 1998); UNDP, *Human Development Report 2000: Human Rights and Human Development* (New York: UNDP, 2000) (arguing that human rights formed an intrinsic part of development and that development should be viewed as a means to realizing human rights). *See also*, UNDP, *A Human Rights-Based Approach to Development Programming in UNDP – Adding the Missing Link* (New York: UNDP, 2001); UNDP, *Human Rights and Development Practice Note* (New York: UNDP, 2003); Amparo Tomas (UNDP), *A Human Rights Approach to Development – Primer for Development Practitioners* (New York: UNDP, August 2003). Endorsement of the critical links between human rights and development has come also from the UN High Commissioner for Human Rights, 'Statement by Ms. Louise Arbour, High Commissioner for Human Rights to the Open-Ended Working Group established by the Commission on Human Rights to consider options regarding the elaboration of an optional protocol to the International Covenant on Economic, Social and Cultural Rights' (2004), *available at* <www.unhchr.ch/huricane/huricane.nsf/view01/ECAE2629449C1EBCC1256F8C0035047D?opendocument>.
16. *See* McInerney-Lankford, 'Human Rights and Development: Some Institutional Perspectives', *supra* n. 14, 463–467. *See, e.g.*, Daniel Bradlow & Claudio Grossman, 'Limited Mandates and Intertwined Problems: A New Challenge for the World Bank and the IMF', *Human Rights Quarterly* 17 (1995): 411–442. *See* Gernot Brodnig, 'The World Bank and Human Rights: Mission Impossible?', Carr Center for Human Rights Policy Working Paper T-01-05 (2001) (arguing that human rights have become part of the Bank's mandate, based on practice as a central organizing principle for the interpretation of its Articles of Agreement).
17. Brodnig, 'The World Bank and Human Rights: Mission Impossible?', *supra* n. 16, 3.
18. Manisuli Ssenyonjo, 'Non-state Actors and Economic, Social and Cultural Rights', in *Economic, Social and Cultural Rights in Action*, ed. Mashood A. Baderin & Robert McCoquodale (Oxford: Oxford University Press, 2007), 131.
19. Godefridus van Hoof & B.G. Tahzib, 'Supervision with respect to the Right to Food and the Role of the World Bank', in *International Law and Development*, ed. Paul de Waart, Paul Peters & Eric Denters (Dordrecht: Martinus Nijhoff, 1988), 334.

Development has evolved substantially to include a broad range of poverty reduction activities,[20] the promotion of human development[21] and social development,[22] and the empowerment of poor and marginalized groups.[23] In terms of modality,[24] it now includes policy-based interventions in addition to investment lending operations.[25] These expanses have led some to argue that development now includes the fulfilment of human rights, at least indirectly.[26]

The impacts of development activities are therefore expansive, but not always positive.[27] These impacts are rarely confined to particular projects or interventions,

---

20. *See, e.g.*, Operational Policy O.P. 1.00 on *Poverty Reduction*, which reflects the current framework of the World Bank's poverty reduction mandate and business procedures. *See also* Ravi Kanbur & Nora Lustig (World Bank), *WDR 2000/01 Attacking Poverty* (Oxford: Oxford University Press; Washington, DC: World Bank, 2000). On Poverty Reduction Strategies, *see* World Bank, *PRS Sourcebook* (2004), *available at* <http://web.worldbank.org/WBSITE/EXTERNAL/TOPICS/EXTPOVERTY/EXTPRS/0,,contentMDK:20175742~pagePK:210058~piPK:210062~theSitePK:384201,00.html>.
21. World Bank, *WDR 1980* (1980); *WDR 1996 From Plan to Market* (1996); 'World Bank Annual Report 1997' (all supporting the connection between investing in human development and achieving economic progress).
22. World Bank, Social Development, <http://go.worldbank.org/8WWCZQW5Q0>.
23. Deepa Narayan, *Voices of the Poor, Can Anyone Hear Us?*, vol. I (Washington, DC: World Bank, 2000); Deepa Narayan et al., *Voices of the Poor: Crying Out for Change*, vol. II (Washington, DC: World Bank, 2000); Deepa Narayan & Patti Petesch (eds), *Voices of the Poor: From Many Lands*, vol. III (New York: World Bank & Oxford University Press, January 2001); Deepa Narayan, *Empowerment and Poverty Reduction: A Sourcebook* (Washington, DC: World Bank, 2002). *See, e.g.*, World Bank *Comprehensive Development Framework*, which emphasized an integral approach and the 'two dimensions of development': The CDF confirmed 'without the protection of human and property rights, and a comprehensive framework of laws, no equitable development is possible'. *See also* Inter-American Development Bank, Articles of Agreement (30 Dec. 1959, as amended 31 Jan. 1995), Art. I(1), <www.iadb.org/leg/Documents/Pdf/Convenio-Eng.Pdf>; Asian Development Bank proclamation of poverty reduction as its primary goal, <www.adb.org/Poverty/default.asp>; Joseph Stiglitz, 'Towards A New Paradigm for Development Strategies, Policies and Processes', Prebrisch Lecture given at UNCTAD (Geneva, 19 Oct. 1998).
24. Ibrahim Shihata, commenting on expansive scope of operations of the Bank 'beyond anything envisaged at the time of its establishment'. Ibrahim Shihata, 'The Dynamic Evolution of International Organizations: The Case of the World Bank', *Journal of the History of International Law* 2 (2000): 247.
25. Bradlow & Grossman, 'Limited Mandates and Intertwined Problems: A New Challenge for the World Bank and the IMF', *supra* n. 16, 421. Structural Adjustment Lending has been replaced with Development Policy Lending O.P. 8.60, *see* 'Development Policy Lending Replaces Adjustment Lending: The World Bank Overhauls its Guidelines for Policy-Based Lending to Reflect 20 years of Experience' (10 Aug. 2004), *available at* <http://go.worldbank.org/QQ9078Z4K0>.
26. *See contra*, Robert Kneller, 'Human Rights, Politics and the Multilateral Development Banks', *Yale Studies in World Public Order* 6 (1979–1980): 361, 405–409.
27. Mac Darrow, *Between Light and Shadow: The World Bank, the International Monetary Fund and International Human Rights Law* (Portland, OR: Hart Publishing, 2003), 53–64; Arne Tostensen, 'The Bretton Woods Institutions: Human Rights and PRSPs', in *Casting the Net Wider: Human Rights, Development and New Duty-Bearers*, ed. Margot Salomon, Arne Tostensen & Wouter Vandenhole (Antwerp & Oxford: Intersentia, 2008), 185–209; M. Rodwan Abouharb & David Cingranelli, *Human Rights and Structural Adjustment* (Cambridge & New York: Cambridge University Press, 2007).

often spanning broad structural changes and macro-economic policies affecting institutions and governance.[28] As the 2006 World Development Report: *Equity and Development* recognized, all categories of macro and micro economic policy have effects on both efficiency (and growth) and equity (and distribution), and criticisms that assign responsibility for human rights violations to World Bank-financed projects are well known.[29] For example:

> [T]he World Bank is also funding world-wide projects that have a direct impact on human rights across the globe. These projects range from giving Pakistan and Somalia loans in order to create work opportunities to refugees, to provide loans in order to promote the equal treatment of women in third-world countries.[30]

The potential human rights impacts are therefore vast, and potentially negative. The Committee on Economic, Social and Cultural Rights has remarked:

> development cooperation activities do not automatically contribute to the promotion of respect of economic, social and cultural rights. Many activities undertaken in the name of 'development' have subsequently been recognized as ill-conceived and even counter-productive in human rights terms. In order to reduce the incidence of such problems, the whole range of issues dealt with in the covenant should, wherever possible and appropriate, be given specific and careful consideration.[31]

World Bank activities in these areas of overlap *relate to and may impact* human rights,[32] but are not properly characterized as human rights-based, or as automatically contributing to the realization of human rights. These activities do not typically recognize rights as such, and while these activities may be valid in development terms, they are neither conceived nor evaluated in human rights

---

28. World Bank, 'Implementation Plan for Strengthening World Bank Group Engagement on Governance and Anticorruption' (28 Sep. 2007), *available at* <http://go.worldbank.org/6HHK3NDGL0>.
29. *See, e.g.*, Daniel Bradlow, 'The World Bank, the IMF, and Human Rights', *Transnational Law and Contemporary Problems* 6 (1996): 47, 59–64; Thomas Hutchins, 'Using the International Court of Justice to Check Human Rights Abuses in World Bank Projects', *Columbia Human Rights Law Review* 23 (1991): 487.
30. Halim Moris, 'The World Bank and Human Rights: Indispensable Partnership or Mismatched Alliance?' *ISLA Journal of International & Comparative Law* 4 (1997): 173, 199 (reviewing the case for and against 'using the World Bank to enforce and/or monitor human rights').
31. OHCHR, Committee on Economic, Social, and Cultural Rights, 'General Comment 2: International Technical Assistance Measures' (1990), para. 7, *available at* <www.unhchr.ch/tbs/doc.nsf/(symbol)/CESCR+General+comment+2.En?OpenDocument> (hereinafter General Comment No. 2).
32. *See* Bradlow, 'The World Bank, the IMF and Human Rights', *supra* n. 29, 50–51 (discussing 'the operational human rights issue', which refers to the 'human rights impacts of the IFIs' operations in their Member States'. It focuses on the IFIs' responsibility to promote and protect human rights when designing and implementing their programmes).

terms, remaining disconnected from human rights obligations.[33] Clapham has noted that:

> It is quite clear that the objectives of an institution such as the World Bank include, in a general way, the realization of human rights. However, the aim of these institutions are rarely expressed in human rights terms, or organized with serious attention being paid the actual rights concerned.[34]

B. Human Rights Principles

Arguably developed as a means of mitigating the negative impacts of the overlap identified in relation to practice, a convergence is discernible in relation to principles that are increasingly incorporated into mainstream development policies.[35] This evolution is not always fully or evenly transposed in practice[36] and appears sometimes to occur 'alongside' it, rather than defining of it.

In some ways, these principles define the evolving objectives of development,[37] and reflect a more deliberate attempt to shape the process and orientation of development in normative terms that evidence a deeper affinity with human rights. The ultimate aims of development are now defined more by notions of sustainability, the enhancement of the human condition and the eradication of poverty, with economic development rarely understood as an end in itself. Poverty is no longer understood as material deprivation alone, but critically in terms of

---

33. Sigrun Skogly, 'The Position of the World Bank and the IMF in the Human and Human Rights Field', in *Introduction to the International Protection of Human Rights: A Textbook*, ed. Raija Hanski & Markku Suksi, 2nd rev. edn (Turku/Åbo: Institute for Human Rights, Åbo Akademi University, 1999), 195–196.
34. Clapham, *Human Rights Obligations of Non-state Actors*, *supra* n. 4, 138.
35. World Bank, *Comprehensive Development Framework* (1999). Earlier, *see* President Robert McNamara, Address to the Meeting of the Board of Governors (Copenhagen, Denmark, 21 Sep. 1970), quoted in *The World Bank Since Bretton Woods*, Edward Mason & Robert Asher (Washington, DC: Brookings Institution, 1973), 475. ('[We] believe that economic progress remains precarious and sterile without corresponding social improvement. Fully human development demands attention to both. We intend, in the Bank, to give attention to both.')
36. Mac Darrow describes this as 'euphemism creep' in describing the consistency of human rights principles with instrumental development rationales. Darrow, *supra* n. 27, 154–156.
37. Philip Alston, 'Ships Passing in the Night: The Current State of the Human Rights and Development Debate Seen through the Lens of the Millennium Development Goals', *Human Rights Quarterly* 27, no. 3 (2005): 755–829; Robinson & Alston, *Human Rights and Development: Towards Mutual Reinforcement*, *supra* n. 12, especially *Introduction*, Ch. 1: 'The Challenges of Ensuring the Mutuality of Human Rights and Development', 1–18; Mac Darrow & Amparo Tomas, 'Power, Capture, and Conflict: A Call for Human Rights Accountability in Development Cooperation', *Human Rights Quarterly* 27, no. 2 (2005): 471–538; Klaus Decker, Siobhán McInerney-Lankford, & Caroline Sage, 'Human Rights and Equitable Development: "Ideals", Issues and Implications', background paper to the 'World Development Report 2006: Equity and Development' (2005), *available at* <http://econ.worldbank.org/WBSITE/EXTERNAL/EXTDEC/EXTRESEARCH/EXTWDRS/EXTWDR2006/0,,contentMDK:20232899~menuPK:477651~pagePK:64167689~piPK:64167673~theSitePK:477642,00.html>.

exclusion and disempowerment and the absence of substantive freedoms and capabilities. Human rights target structural inequalities and 'unfreedoms',[38] and give voice to the very poorest, most marginalized, and most 'unfree', illustrating a compatibility between the current definition of human rights and development goals. In this connection, the relevance of human rights to the Millennium Development Goals (MDGs) is apposite too, particularly in relation to accountability.[39] Beyond substantive overlaps,[40] there are direct links between them in the principles of empowerment, participation, equality, and inclusion,[41] as well as 'do no harm'.[42]

Human rights principles can now be said to pervade development policies of various sorts. Participation, for example, is now understood to be central to sustainable development policies.[43] Participation emerges as a key component of many development actors' policies,[44] and is supported in their policies' consultation requirements,[45] or even through their disclosure policies.[46] The importance of participation as a fundamental aspect of good development practice is evident in its

38. Amartya Sen, *Development as Freedom* (New York: Knopf, 1999), *Introduction*, 3–4 (describing the range of determinants or factors that can violate freedoms, from economic poverty, to lack of public facilities and social care to denials of political and civil liberties).
39. UN Millennium Development Goals, <www.un.org/millenniumgoals/>. *See, e.g.*, UN Millennium Project, 'Investing in Development: A Practical Plan to Achieve the Millennium Development Goals' (London: Earthscan, 2005), *available at* <www.unmillenniumproject.org/reports/fullreport.htm> (noting on page 108 that: 'Another strategy is to use national and international human rights accountability mechanisms. This can complement the efforts of national economic and finance ministries to monitor progress toward the Goals.') (hereinafter UN Millennium Project Report).
40. Ashwani Saith, 'From Universal Values to Millennium Development Goals: Lost in Translation', *Development and Change* 37, no. 6 (2006): 1167–1199.
41. UN Millennium Project Report states: 'To ensure the Goals are applied in a manner consistent with human rights, governments need to recognize the relevance of their human rights obligations, encourage community participation, and develop human rights-based accountability mechanisms.' UN Millennium Project Report, *supra* n. 39, 118.
42. UN Office of the High Commissioner for Human Rights (OHCHR), *Claiming the Millennium Development Goals: A Human Rights Approach* (Geneva: United Nations, 2008), 13, 46 (box 42).
43. Daniel Bradlow, 'Development Decision-Making and the Content of International Development Law', *Boston College International & Comparative Law Review* 27 (2004): 208.
44. *E.g.*, World Bank, O.P. 4.10: Indigenous Peoples (July 2005), *available at* <http://go.worldbank.org/TE769PDWN0>.
45. *Ibid.*; O.P. 4.01: Environmental Assessment (January 1999), *available at* <http://go.worldbank.org/RUEQVWD550>; O.P./BP 4.04: Natural Habitats (June 2001), *available at* <http://go.worldbank.org/WZQM56JT30>; O.P. 4.09: Pest Management (December 1998), *available at* <http://go.worldbank.org/Q5C205JR50>; O.P./B.P. 4.12: Involuntary Resettlement (December 2001), *available at* <http://go.worldbank.org/96LQB2JT50>; O.P./B.P. 4.36: Forests (November 2002), *available at* <http://go.worldbank.org/6NQDXLHG10>; O.P.N. 11.03: Cultural Property (September 1986), *available at* <http://info.worldbank.org/etools/docs/library/38147/OP4.11CulturalProperty.pdf>.
46. *See* World Bank Disclosure of Information Policy (1993), <www1.worldbank.org/operations/disclosure/>. The Bank's board of executive directors approved revisions to the policy in 2005.

centrality to Poverty Reduction Strategies,[47] and to their effectiveness and credibility generally.[48] Equality and non-discrimination provide other strong examples of where human rights principles have found strong analogues in development policy, even if not a perfect or comprehensive transposition. They are strongly manifest in the MDGs concerning gender equality and evident also in the prominence of principles like equity; the 2006 World Development Report endorsed the idea that inequities are relevant to development for both intrinsic and instrumental reasons.

Despite the clear convergence around principles, the development equivalents have their weaknesses: the lack of a normative baseline, prescriptive quality, and enforceable, specific obligations making the principles binding. This convergence could be usefully complemented by anchorage in binding instruments which bring with them enforceability, specificity, and a more comprehensive 'frame' of analysis for the systematic inclusion of the claims and interests of the most vulnerable. Critically, the broader based accountability frameworks of human rights identify duties and a strong normative structure, and establish a legal baseline for the activities and policies reviewed above.

C. Human Rights

Can one go further than practice or principle and identify a convergence around human rights? The answer is a qualified 'yes'. One can identify some convergence around rights, but far less around obligations. Thus, while a positive convergence can be identified at distinct levels of practice and principle, there is no systematic incorporation of human rights per se in development. This is clear also in the lack of emphasis on duty-bearers and human rights *obligations*.

A range of approaches exists on the integration of human rights in development, from explicit rights-based approaches to the mainstreaming of human rights principles in programs or sectors,[49] or from specific human rights projects to the

---

47. *See* World Bank, 'Participation in Poverty Reduction Strategy Papers: A Retrospective Study' (January 2002), *available at* <http://siteresources.worldbank.org/INTPCENG/1143251-1116505087139/20509213/PRSPretro.pdf>. *See also* World Bank, 'PRSP Sourcebook', <http://go.worldbank.org/3I8LYLXO80>.
48. 'Participation is the process by which stakeholders influence and share control over priority setting, policymaking, resource allocations, and/or program implementation. [...] Participatory processes in Poverty Reduction Strategy Papers (PRSPs), including information dissemination, dialogue, collaboration in implementing programs, and participatory monitoring and evaluation, are most effective when they are designed to be outcome-oriented. The ultimate outcome of a PRSP is not the paper but public and community actions to reduce poverty. Therefore, in planning a participatory process, it is important to keep in mind that outcome-based approaches that are initiated and the institutional arrangements that support them can have an enduring influence over policymaking and implementation.' World Bank, Poverty Net: Participation, <http://web.worldbank.org/WBSITE/EXTERNAL/TOPICS/EXTPOVERTY/EXTPRS/0,,contentMDK:20177433~pagePK:148956~piPK:216618~theSitePK:384201,00.html>.
49. Clarence Dias, 'Mainstreaming Human Rights in Development Assistance: Moving from Projects to Strategies', in *Human Rights in Development Cooperation* (SIM Special Number 22,

implicit incorporation of human rights considerations.[50] Some actors see human rights as a discreet area of activity, while others see them integrated in governance,[51] justice, or gender activities, while others still integrate human rights at the level of political dialogue or political conditionality. The range of approaches to human rights in development is thus extremely broad and influenced by a widely divergent set of factors.[52]

The rise in prominence of human rights in development discourse is evident in a range of UN initiatives including the 2003 UN Common Understanding on a Human Rights-Based Approach to Development Cooperation,[53] and the 2005 UN Millennium Project Report.[54] It has also been endorsed in 'Action 2'[55] and again in the UN Secretary General's 2005 Report, *In Larger Freedom*, which underscored the interrelationship of security, development, and human rights.[56] Recognition of the role of various types of UN agencies in respect of this connection emanate from the United Nations Development Programme (UNDP),[57] as well as the UN Office of the High Commissioner for Human Rights (OHCHR), which has worked on developing positive linkages between human rights and development,[58] including a 'rights-based approach to the MDGs'.[59] The result is that a rights-based

---

edited by Henny Helmich and Elena Borghese, Utrecht: OECD Development Centre (December 1998)), 73–94.

50. OECD-DAC Govnet, *Integrating Human Rights Into Development, Donor Approaches, Experiences and Challenges* (Paris: OECD, 2006), 25–36.
51. *See ibid.*, 40–43, 61–62.
52. *See Human Rights in Development Cooperation*, *supra* n. 14, 10–20. *See also* Simia Ahmadi, 'Key Issues in Donor Practices: Human Rights and Development Assistance', in *Human Rights in Development Cooperation* (SIM Special Number 22, edited by Henny Helmich and Elena Borghese, Utretcht: OECD Development Centre (December 1998)), 23–52. For a summary of DAC Members Bilateral Activities on Development Co-operation for the Promotion of Human Rights, *see Human Rights in Development Cooperation*, *supra* n. 14, Annex 1, 109–178.
53. UNDG Programme Group, 'Statement on a Common Understanding on a Human Rights Based Approach to Development Cooperation' (2003), *available at* <http://portal.unesco.org/shs/en/ev.php-URL_ID=7733&URL_DO=DO_TOPIC&URL_SECTION=201.html>.
54. Sachs Report, <www.unmillenniumproject.org/> (hereinafter 'the Sachs Report').
55. UN Secretary-General, 'Strengthening of the United Nations: an agenda for further change', A/57/387 (9 Sep. 2002) (report from which the strengthening and mainstreaming of human rights in the UN has come to be known as 'Action 2'). 'Action 2' related to Strengthening UN Support for the Promotion and Protection of Human Rights Worldwide. *See* 'Action 2', <www.un.org/events/action2/>. *See further Action 2 Interagency Plan of Action – Strengthening Human Rights-Related UN Action at Country Level* (2003), adopted by UNDG, ECHA, and OHCHR in 2003 pursuant to the Secretary-General's report.
56. Secretary-General Kofi Annan, 'In Larger Freedom: Towards Development, Security and Human Rights for All' (2005), report *reproduced in*, *Law and Practice of the United Nations: Documents and Commentary*, ed. Simon Chesterman, Thomas Franck & David Malone (Oxford: Oxford University Press, 2008), *available at* <www.un.org/largerfreedom/>.
57. *E.g.*, UNDP, *Human Rights in UNDP Practice Note* (New York: UNDP, April 2005).
58. OHCHR, *Frequently Asked Questions on a Rights-Based Approach to Development* (New York: United Nations, 2006), *available at* <www.ohchr.org/Documents/Publications/FAQen.pdf>.
59. OHCHR, *Claiming the Millennium Development Goals: A Human Rights Approach* (Geneva: United Nations, 2008).

approach is mandated as integral to the approach and content of the UN's development policy.[60]

More recently, the OECD Development Assistance Committee (OECD DAC) approved an *Action-Oriented Policy Paper on Human Rights and Development* that concluded:

> The importance of human rights for development is widely recognized. Human rights and equitable, sustainable development are mutually reinforcing. Human rights have intrinsic value, and achieving them is seen as an objective in its own right.[61] But human rights are also a critical factor for the long term sustainability of development.[62]

The World Bank's public pronouncements echo a similar, albeit bounded acknowledgement of the connection, highlighting the complementarities between the goals of human rights and development.[63] 'The world now accepts that sustainable development is impossible without human rights, what has been missing is the recognition that the advancement of an interconnected set of human rights is impossible without development.'[64] Successive general counsels have opined on the relationship between human rights and development as it relates to the Bank: '[i]n terms of individual human progress, the concepts of development and human rights are so intertwined that they cannot in my view be meaningfully addressed as separate issues'.[65] More often, the analysis has centered on the limitations on the Bank's mandate and emphasized how the Bank contributes to that realization of

---

60. 'All UNCTs [United Nations Country Teams] must use a human rights-based approach (HRBA) to support country analysis, advocate for priorities in the national development framework, and prepare an UNDAF that demonstrates a strategic use of UNCT resources and expertise. A HRBA leads to better and more sustainable outcomes by analyzing and addressing the inequalities, discriminatory practices and unjust power relations which are often at the heart of development problems. It puts the international human rights entitlements and claims of the people and the corresponding obligations of the State in the centre of the national development debate, and it clarifies the purpose of capacity development.', United Nations Development Group, 'Human Rights-based Approach to Development Programming', <www.undg.org/index.cfm?P=221>.
61. Henry Steiner, 'Social Rights and Economic Development: Converging Discourses?', *Buffalo Human Rights Law Review* 4 (1998): 40.
62. OECD DAC, 'DAC Action-Oriented Policy Paper on Human Rights and Development' (23 Feb. 2007), *available at* <www.oecd.org/dataoecd/50/7/39350774.pdf>. The paper drew on the work of the DAC Governance Network's Task Team on Human Rights and Development during 2005–2006. The World Bank is a member of the Task Team since 2005 and its co-chair from 2007–2008.
63. On 'rhetorical incorporation', *see* Uvin, *supra* n. 11, 50.
64. *Development and Human Rights: The Role of the World Bank* (Washington, DC: IBRD, 1998), 2.
65. Ibrahim Shihata, 'The World Bank and Human Rights', in *The World Bank in a Changing World Selected Essays and Lectures*, vol. II, ed. Ibrahim Shihata (Dordrecht: Martinus Nijhoff, 1991), 567; similarly, *see* Ibrahim Shihata, 'Human Rights and International Financial Institutions', in *The World Bank in a Changing World Selected Essays and Lectures*, vol. II, ed. Ibrahim Shihata (Dordrecht: Martinus Nijhoff, 1991), 553.

human rights.[66] None articulates the nature and extent of that contribution to human rights *as the subject of legal obligation*, and few address the question of what relevance human rights obligations of Member States might have for the World Bank.[67] Thus, in 1988 the then-General Counsel opined:

> While there are limits on the possible extent to which the World Bank can become involved with human rights, especially those of civil and political nature, the Bank certainly can play, and has played, within the limits of its mandate, a very significant role in promoting various economic and social rights.[68]

According to this view, the Bank promotes human rights either directly or indirectly through its development activities;[69] that view even extended to civil and political rights, albeit indirectly.[70]

More recent writings of the Bank's General Counsel evidence an evolution in the position, and a greater openness to considering human rights *qua* rights. A more nuanced conception emerged of 'political' in relation to the Articles of Agreement's proscriptions on political activities.[71] It evinced a view of human rights as

66. Shihata, 'The World Bank and Human Rights', *supra* n. 65, Ch. 3, 97 (describing 'Human Rights promoted by the Bank's Operations' from 109–132).
67. 'My purpose today is to highlight the contribution of the World Bank to the promotion of human rights, to emphasize the complementarity of the respect for human rights and human development in general, and to indicate briefly the limitation placed on the Bank's activities with respect to political matters.' Then General Counsel, Ibrahim Shihata, 'The World Bank and Human Rights – A Presentation before the 1993 UN World Conference on Human Rights', in *World Bank Legal Papers* (The Hague: Martinus Nijhoff, 2000), 817.
68. Ibrahim Shihata, 'The World Bank and Human Rights: An Analysis of the Legal Issues and a Record of Achievements', *Denver Journal of International Law & Policy* 17, no. 1 (1988): 48. The analysis goes on to discuss the Bank's role in relation to the right to development, freedom from poverty, education, the right to health, 'women in development', refugees, environment and involuntary resettlement, and concludes with a discussion of 'other human rights'. *See also* Shihata, 'The World Bank and Human Rights', *supra* n. 65, 567, 568–572.
69. 'By joining hands with developing countries and other international agencies in the alleviation of poverty, in combating diseases, malnutrition, illiteracy, and fighting for the preservation of the environment, the Bank is not only promoting economic and social human rights, but is no doubt playing a catalytic role in creating conditions in which all basic rights can develop and flourish.' Shihata, 'The World Bank and Human Rights: An Analysis of the Legal Issues and a Record of Achievements', *supra* n. 68, 65.
70. 'In fact, the Bank's work has promoted a broad array of economic, social and cultural human rights. At present, its proclaimed overriding objective is to enable its borrowing countries to enjoy freedom from poverty, a basic freedom which many find to be required for the full enjoyment of human rights.' And after listing relevant Bank activities concludes: 'Clearly, these activities have a direct effect on the amelioration of non-political human rights. They may even pave the way for greater awareness and protection of political rights in the borrowing countries.' Ibrahim Shihata, 'Political Activity Prohibited', in *World Bank Legal Papers* (The Hague: Martinus Nijhoff, 2000), 233–234.
71. International Bank for Reconstruction and Development Articles of Agreement (amended 16 Feb. 1989), Art. IV(10), *available at* <http://siteresources.worldbank.org/EXTABOUTUS/Resources/ibrd-articlesofagreement.pdf> (hereinafter IBRD Articles of Agreement).

relevant both positively – due to the current breadth of the concept of development, and negatively – because of the economic consequences or relevance of human rights violations or their indicative significance for risk assessments for specific operations.[72] Writing about the Articles' political limitations in 2005, former General Counsel, Roberto Dañino concluded '[...] neither of these limitations would prevent the Bank from considering political issues that have economic consequences or implications – so long as this is done in a non-partisan, non-ideological and neutral manner'.[73] Thus, these prohibitions do not bar all political considerations, since not all such considerations amount to interference in the political affairs of a member, or relate to the political character of a member.[74] Dañino went further, however, anchoring the shift in position beyond an 'economic impacts' rationale. 'Just as the prevailing understanding of what can constitute economic considerations has evolved over the past sixty years, it is clear that the concept of interference in the sovereign affairs of a country has undergone a similar process.'[75] He went on to conclude: '[i]nternational law now recognizes that there are issues which traverse national boundaries'.[76]

This evolution was endorsed in a 2006 article by then World Bank Group General Counsel, Ana Palacio. In it, she outlined a permissive legal interpretation of the Bank's Articles of Agreement that would allow, but not mandate action on the part of the Bank in relation to human rights. The Bank's Articles of Agreement, she held, must be interpreted 'according to the demands and values of our times'.[77] Palacio confirmed the standing of human rights as the subjects of binding legal obligations under treaties. She states:

> Human rights now constitute defined legal standards of the international constitutional order. Seven core international human rights treaties have been ratified by the majority of the world's countries. A significant body of international legal obligations and jurisprudence now exists with respect to a core of civil and political as well as economic, social and cultural rights. How this body of law and principle relates to the World Bank is an issue ripe

72. *See* Kneller, *supra* n. 26, 405–423.
73. Roberto Dañino, 'Legal Aspects of the World Bank's Work on Human Rights: Some Preliminary Thoughts', in *Human Rights and Development: Towards Mutual Reinforcement*, ed. Mary Robinson & Philip Alston (Oxford: Oxford University Press, 2005), 518.
74. *See* Yozo Yokata, 'Non-political Character of the World Bank', *Japanese Annual of International Law* 20 (1976): 39.
75. Dañino, 'Legal Aspects of the World Bank's Work on Human Rights: Some Preliminary Thoughts', *supra* n. 73, 518 (citing Henry Steiner, 'The Youth of Rights', *Harvard Law Review* 104 (1991): 929).
76. Dañino, 'Legal Aspects of the World Bank's Work on Human Rights: Some Preliminary Thoughts', *supra* n. 73, 519. For an excellent analysis of the legal basis for linking Official Development Assistance (ODA) and human rights which raise some of the same questions of international law, Kaoru Okuizumi, 'Implementing the ODA Charter: Prospects for Linking Japanese Economic Assistance and Human Rights', *New York University Journal of International Law and Politics* 27 (1994–95): 370–377.
77. Ana Palacio, 'The Way Forward: Human Rights and the World Bank', in *Development Outreach Human Rights*, ed. Sunetra Puri (Washington, DC: World Bank, October 2006): 35–36.

for analysis, in light of the evolving connection between human rights and development in the international context, in international law, and in the World Bank.[78]

The World Bank's approach had once been confined to general acknowledgement of the intrinsic worth of human rights, or assertions that the Bank fulfils a broadly positive role in regard to human rights[79] or indirectly promotes rights through growth and development.[80] There are now signs that the Bank recognizes the significance of human rights for development as the subject of binding legal obligations, and indications of receptivity to a role in supporting its members in fulfilling those obligations.

III. HUMAN RIGHTS OBLIGATIONS UNDER INTERNATIONAL LAW

A. Introduction: Human Rights Obligations – The Neglected Dimension

Perhaps the most important but neglected aspect of human rights in the context of development is that of obligations or duties.[81] As a conceptual matter, human rights are distinctive in implying duties.[82] 'Rights require correlative duties.'[83]

78. Palacio, *supra* n. 77, 35.
79. *See, e.g.*, 'The Bank contributes directly to the fulfillment of many human rights articulated in the Universal Declaration. Through its support of primary education, health care and nutrition, sanitation, housing and the environment, the Bank has helped hundreds of millions of people attain crucial economic and social rights. In other areas, the Bank's contributions are necessarily less direct, but perhaps equally significant. By helping to fight corruption, improve transparency and accountability in governance, strengthening judicial systems and modernize financial sectors, the Bank contributes to building environments in which people are better able to pursue a broader range of human rights.' World Bank, *Development and Human Rights: The Role of the World Bank* (Washington, DC: The World Bank, 1998), 3. Shihata's concession on this point is worthy of note: 'The Bank's record in meeting the requirements of economic and social entitlements of the populations of its developing member countries is impressive, in spite of some possible adverse effects on the poor in certain cases.' Shihata, 'The World Bank and Human Rights: An Analysis of the Legal Issues and a Record of Achievements', *supra* n. 68, 66.
80. Ruth Alsop & Andrew Norton, *Power, Rights and Poverty: Concepts and Connections* (Washington, DC: World Bank, 2004), 7.
81. Herbert Morais, 'The Globalization of Human Rights Law and the Role of International Financial Institutions in Promoting Human Rights', *George Washington International Law Review* 33 (2000): 71; Victoria Marmorstein, 'World Bank Power to Consider Human Rights Factors in Loan Decisions', *Journal of International Law and Economics* 13 (1977): 113; Ernst-Ulrich Petersmann, 'Time for Integrating Human Rights into the Law of Worldwide Organizations: Lessons from European Integration Law for Global Integration Law', *Jean Monnet Working Paper* 7/01 (New York: New York University School of Law, 2001).
82. Jeremy Waldron (ed.), *Theories of Rights* (Oxford: Oxford University Press, 1984).
83. Asbjørn Eide, 'Economic, Social and Cultural Rights as Human Rights', in *Economic, Social and Cultural Rights: A Textbook*, ed. Asbjørn Eide, Catarina Krause & Allan Rosas (Dordrecht: Martinus Njihoff, 2001), 22.

Thus, without duty there is no right.[84] In the context of development, obligations define a critical aspect of what human rights can contribute – the very essence of their 'value-added'.

Rights promote accountability, and through this secure perhaps the single most important contribution that human rights can make to improve development.[85] Rights offer a means of individual and personal empowerment through providing specific modalities for holding government and others to account through the duties that correlate with rights. Rights offer the means to enforce that duty, and thus ensure accountability.

Accountability emerges with increasing prominence in development discourse. It arises in legal and fiduciary terms in development institutions' obligation to use funds for productive purposes and their intended uses,[86] in social accountability[87] and social guarantees,[88] and in relation to corporate social responsibility,[89] policies on social and environmental sustainability,[90] and human rights impact assessment tools.[91] Mutual accountability is a core principle of the

84. On the relationship between rights and duties or duty-bearers and right-bearers, *see* 'choice' theory of rights (e.g., Hart) and 'benefit' or 'interest' theories of rights which focus on duty (e.g., Bentham, Raz, Lyons, McCormick). On the 'correlativity of rights and duties', Bernard Mayo, 'What are Human Rights?', in *Political Theory and the Rights of Man*, ed. D.D. Raphael (Bloomington, IN: Indiana University Press, 1967), 68, 72.
85. McInerney-Lankford, 'Human Rights and Development: Some Institutional Perspectives, *supra* n. 14, 476.
86. Ibrahim Shihata, '"Issues of Governance" in Borrowing Members: The Extent of Their Relevance under the Bank's Articles of Agreement', in *World Bank Legal Papers*, ed. Ibrahim Shihata (The Hague & Boston, MA: Martinus Nijhoff, 2000), 245.
87. *E.g.*, John Ackerman, *Social Accountability in the Public Sector: A Conceptual Discussion*, Social Development Paper No. 82 (2005), *available at* <http://siteresources.worldbank.org/INTPCENG/214574-1116506074750/20542263/FINALAckerman.pdf>.
88. World Bank: Social Development Department, 'Realizing Rights through Social Guarantees', Report 40047-GBL (2007).
89. *E.g.*, Antonio Vives, 'The Role of Multilateral Development Institutions in Fostering Corporate Social Responsibility', *Development* 47, no. 3 (Washington, DC: Inter-American Development Bank, 2004): 45–52. For the IFC, *see generally*, IFC, Accountability, <www.ifc.org/ifcext/sustainability.nsf/Content/Accountability>.
90. IFC, Corporate Social Responsibility, <www.ifc.org/ifcext/economics.nsf/Content/CSR-IntroPage>. IFC's 2006 Policy on Social and Environmental Sustainability provides 'the roles and responsibility of the private sector in respecting human rights are emerging as an important aspect of corporate social responsibility. The performance standards developed by IFC to help private sector clients address environmental and social risks and opportunities are consistent with these emerging roles and responsibilities', *available at* IFC, Environmental & Social Standards (2006), *available at* <www.ifc.org/ifcext/enviro.nsf/Content/EnvSocStandards> (hereinafter IFC's 2006 Policy on Social & Environmental Sustainability).
91. IFC's 2006 Policy on Social & Environmental Sustainability, *supra* n. 90, provides 'the roles and responsibility of the private sector in respecting human rights are emerging as an important aspect of corporate social responsibility. The performance standards developed by IFC to help private sector clients address environmental and social risks and opportunities are consistent with these emerging roles and responsibilities'. *See also* IFC, *Guide to Human Rights Impact Assessment and Management Tool*, Road-Testing Draft (June 2007), *available at* <www.ifc.org/ifcext/enviro.nsf/AttachmentsByTitle/p_SocialResponsibility_HRIARoadTesting/$FILE/Final+HRIA+road-testing+draft.pdf>.

Paris Declaration,[92] defining horizontal and vertical accountability as a pillar of the current political framework for international cooperation on aid effectiveness. Accountability is manifest also in IFIs' accountability mechanisms,[93] with the recourse they provide being consistent with, if not exhaustive of, HRA in that context.[94]

Yet despite an increasing emphasis on accountability, there is little or no concomitant emphasis on obligations, much less legal obligations.[95] Human rights obligations require a clear and unequivocal locating of the duty-bearer. This is something generally lacking in development policy, which tends to address human rights in terms of principle, rather than obligations.[96] In order to address that weakness, and the 'accountability lacunae' that exist as a result, including in respect of IFIs, this chapter argues for locating those obligations with states, at least initially.

Here, obligations are understood in terms of substantive legal duties under the UN Charter, human rights treaties, custom, or general principles of law. The failure to establish international obligations for human rights in development calls for a reorientation of the focus towards states' responsibilities as a way of addressing the accountability lacunae. Without discounting the possible existence of human rights obligations for IFIs under non-treaty sources of law,[97] a pragmatic approach

---

92. The full text of the 'Paris Declaration on Aid Effectiveness' (2005), *available at* <www.oecd.org/dataoecd/11/41/34428351.pdf>. On the links between human rights and mutual accountability or other Paris Declaration Principles, *see* OECD DAC, Human Rights and Aid Effectiveness, DAC Update, <www.oecd.org/dac/governance/humanrights>, April 2007. OECD DAC Human Rights Task Team, *Human Rights and Aid Effectiveness: Key Actions to Improve Inter-linkages* (2008).
93. World Bank Safeguard Policies, <http://go.worldbank.org/WTA1ODE7T0>.
94. Ibrahim Shihata, *The World Bank Inspection Panel* (Oxford: Oxford University Press, 1994). Ibrahim Shihata, *The World Bank Inspection Panel: In Practice*, 2nd edn (Oxford: Oxford University Press, 2000). A distinct body fulfils an analogous function for the IFC and MIGA (Compliance Advisor/Ombudsman) and similar bodies exist in other MDBs. For a review of independent inspection mechanisms in IFIs, *see* Daniel Bradlow, 'Private Complainants and International Organizations: A Comparative Study of the Independent Inspection Mechanisms in International Financial Institutions', *Georgetown Journal of International Law* 36, no. 2 (2005): 403.
95. This is true even in the policies and pronouncements of actors that promote a rights-based approach to development, *see, e.g.*, Laure-Hélène Piron & Francis Watkins, *DFID Human Rights Review: A Review of How DFID Has Integrated Human Rights into Its Work* (London: Overseas Development Institute, July 2004), 11, *available at* <www.odi.org.uk/rights/publications/DFIDRightsReview07.04.pdf>.
96. On divergent discourses of human rights and development, and the benefits of 'a human rights approach', in terms of benchmarks, explicit recognition of the rights involved and accountability, *see* Philip Alston, 'What's in a Name: Does It Really Matter if Development Policies Refer to Goals, Ideals or Human Rights', in *Human Rights in Development Co-operation* (SIM Special Number 22, edited by Henny Helmich and Elena Borghese, Utrecht: OECD Development Centre (December 1998)), 95 et seq.
97. Henry G. Schermers & Niels M. Blokker, *International Institutional Law*, 3rd edn (Dordrecht: Martinus Nijhoff, 1995), 984 (citing *Interpretation of the Agreement of 25 March 1951 between WHO and Egypt*, Advisory Opinion, 1990 I.C.J. Reports, at 90). C.F. Amerasinghe, *Principles*

favours exploiting the positive potential extant in the human rights framework for development in order to address the gaps in concrete and enforceable ways. Focus on the putative obligations of IFIs has deflected attention away from states' obligations,[98] and compounded rather than mitigated the accountability deficit by leaving the discussion at too high a level of generality, failing to ground the ostensible obligations firmly enough and ignoring the potential in treaty obligations of states. This is at least partly due to the source of those putative obligations being in non-treaty sources, which come with significant limitations as the following sections reveal.

B. Non-treaty Sources

This section will briefly review non-treaty based sources of human rights obligations, highlighting their limitations with respect to meeting the accountability lacunae for IFIs.[99]

Custom: International custom is a recognized source of international law under Article 38(1) of the Statute of the International Court of Justice (ICJ). Custom is also a source of human rights obligations,[100] but a number of elements render it unsuitable for responding to the HRA lacunae in development.[101] These include the complexity and indeterminacy[102] of its core elements,[103] the challenges human rights present to sovereignty which is central to custom,[104] and the difficulties of

---

of Institutional Law of International Organizations (Cambridge: Cambridge University Press, 1996), 241; Gunther Handl, 'The Legal Mandate of Multilateral Development Banks as Agents for Change Toward Sustainable Development', *American Journal of International Law* 92 (1998): 654–655.

98. Sigrun I. Skogly, 'The Human Rights Obligations of the World Bank and the IMF', in *World Bank, IMF and Human Rights*, ed. Willem van Genugten, Paul Hunt & Susan Mathews (Nijmegen, the Netherlands: Wolf Legal Publishers, 2003), 45.
99. For further discussion of IFIs and non-treaty sources of international law, *see* Daniel D. Bradlow, 'International Law and the Operations of the International Financial Institutions', Ch. 1 herein.
100. Statute of the International Court of Justice (26 Jun. 1945), Art. 38(1)(b), *available at* <www.icj-cij.org/documents/index.php?p1=4&p2=2&p3=0>. Art. 38 refers to 'international custom, as evidence of general practice accepted as law'.
101. 'Symposium on Human Rights in Customary International Law', *Georgia Journal of Comparative and International Law* 25 (1995–96); Isabelle Gunning, 'Modernizing Customary International Law: The Challenge of Human Rights', *Virginia Journal of International Law* 31 (1991).
102. For an exposition of these contradictions, Martti Koskenniemi, *From Apology to Utopia: The Structure of International Legal Argument* (Helsinki: Finnish Lawyers' Publishing Co., 1989), 342–421.
103. Karol Wolfke, 'Some Persistent Controversies Regarding Customary International Law', *Netherlands Yearbook of International Law* 24 (1993).
104. Gunning, 'Modernizing Customary International Law: The Challenge of Human Rights', *supra* n. 101, 213 (arguing that the process of custom should accommodate the contributions of non-state actors).

identification due to the 'notorious elusiveness of customary rules'.[105] Critics have targeted the absence of practice, a prerequisite for the second, 'essential element' of custom,[106] which is particularly evident in gross and systematic human rights violations perpetrated and tolerated by states all over the world.[107]

In terms of content also, custom does not provide precise answers,[108] and theories abound on custom as a source of human rights obligations[109] as illustrated by the case of the Universal Declaration of Human Rights (UDHR).[110] While '[t]he vast majority of States and authoritative writers would now recognize that the fundamental principles of human rights form part of customary or general international law, [although] they would not necessarily agree on the identity of the fundamental principles'.[111] The practical usefulness of custom as a means of addressing what has been termed here the accountability 'lacunae' is severely

---

105. Wolfke, 'Some Persistent Controversies Regarding Customary International Law', *supra* n. 103, 15.
106. G.J.H. van Hoof, *Rethinking the Sources of International Law* (Deventer: Kluwer Publishing, 1983), 106–113 (discussing 'usus'), 107–108 (in relation to human rights).
107. Michael Akehurst, 'Custom as a Source of International Law', *Yearbook of International Law* 47 (1974–75): 1, 53; Bruno Simma & Philip Alston, 'The Sources of Human Rights Law: Custom, *Jus Cogens*, and General Principles', *Australian Year Book of International Law* 12 (1992): 10.
108. *See, e.g.*, Martti Koskenniemi, 'The Pull of the Mainstream – Book Review of T. Meron, Human Rights and Humanitarian Norms as Customary Law', *Michigan Law Review* 88 (1990): 1946.
109. A seminal work in this area is Theodor Meron, *Human Rights and Humanitarian Norms as Customary Law* (Oxford: Clarendon Press, 1998). *See also* Anthony D'Amato, *International Law: Process and Prospect* (Dobbs Ferry, NY: Transnational Publishers, 1986), 123–147 (defending the thesis of treaty generation of customary law).
110. John Humphrey, 'The Universal Declaration of Human Rights: Its History, Impact and Juridical Character', in *Human Rights: Thirty Years After the Universal Declaration*, ed. B.G. Ramcharan (The Hague: Martinus Nijhoff, 1979), 37; Louis Sohn, 'The Human Rights Law of the Charter', *Texas International Law Journal* 12 (1977): 129, 133; Myres McDougall, Harold D. Laswell & Lung-chu Chen, *Human Rights and World Public Order* (New Haven: Yale University Press, 1980), 273–274; Kaladharan Nayar, 'Human Rights: The United Nations and United States Foreign Policy', *Harvard International Law Journal* 19 (1978): 817 (concluding that 'There is thus strong evidence suggesting that the principles embodied in the Universal Declaration of Human Rights have become customary international law or general principles of law recognized by nations.'). Similarly, in describing the 'internationalization of human rights' in the context of the Universal Declaration, Professor Louis Henkin writes: '[n]ow human rights everywhere are the responsibility of everyone'. Louis Henkin, 'The Universal Declaration at 50 and the Challenge of Global Markets', *Brooklyn Journal of International Law* 25 (April 1999): 21. Hurst Hannum, 'The Status of the Universal Declaration of Human Rights in National and International Law', *Georgia Journal of International and Comparative Law* 25 (1995–96): 289; Eibe Reidel, *The Charter of the United Nations – A Commentary*, ed. Bruno Simma (Oxford: Oxford University Press, 2002), 927; Louis Henkin (ed.), *The International Bill of Rights: The Covenant on Civil and Political Rights* (New York: Columbia University Press, 1981), Introduction.
111. Ian Brownlie, *Principles of Public International Law*, 5th edn (Oxford: Oxford University Press, 1998), 537.

constrained by the fact that the precise content of such principles remains unsettled and their substantive import in an operational context left unclear.[112]

'Given the fundamental importance of the human rights complement of a just world order the temptation to adapt or to re-interpret the concept of customary law in such a way as to ensure that it provides the "right" answer is strong, and at least to some irresistible [. . .].'[113] The same is true of custom as a means of addressing HRA in development because international lawyers 'cannot entirely dispel doubt as to whether custom really is an adequate means for embedding fundamental human rights obligations in general international law'.[114] This broader scepticism renders custom inadequate to ground human rights obligations in development or address HRA of IFIs,[115] or resolve decisively the question of what IFIs are bound by in terms of the content of customary international law obligations.[116]

General principles: Article 38(1)(c) of the ICJ statute identifies 'general principles of law recognized by civilized nations' as a separate source of law, but their status as a separate category remains controversial.[117] 'There are in fact no grounds for differentiating between general principles and customary rules, because the former as a rule, constitute precisely very abstract customary rules which have often already been codified in treaty law.'[118] These are distinguished only by their origin in municipal legal systems although there is acknowledgement that interaction is possible between customary international law and general principles. The controversy and disagreement surrounding them[119] reveals little to suggest

112. It is not contested here that at least some of the provisions of the Universal Declaration of Human Rights are binding as a matter of customary international law. On the UDHR more generally, *see, e.g.*, Hannum, 'The Status of the Universal Declaration of Human Rights in National and International Law', *supra* n. 110; B.G. Ramcharan, *The Concept and Present Status of International Protection of Human Rights: Forty Years After the Universal Declaration* (Dordrecht: Martinus Nijhoff, 1989). As Louis Henkin opines: 'Few claim that any state that violates any provision of the Declaration has violated international law. Almost all would agree that some violations of the Declaration are violations of international law.' Louis Henkin, *The Age of Rights* (New York: Columbia University Press, 1990), 19.
113. Simma & Alston, 'The Sources of Human Rights Law: Custom, *Jus Cogens*, and General Principles', *supra* n. 107, 82–108.
114. *Ibid.*, 17 (referring to the work of Oscar Schachter, 'International Law in Theory and Practice: General Course in Public International law', *Receuil des cours* 178 (1982): 333–342).
115. Bahram Ghazi, *The IMF, the World Bank group, and the Question of Human Rights* (London: Transnational Publishers, 2005), 129–212.
116. Schermers & Blokker, *supra* n. 97, 822 (on the notion that international organizations are bound by customary international law, and are under an obligation to observe customary international law in their operations discussed at pages 824 and 988).
117. Karol Wolfke, 'Controversies Regarding Customary International Law', *Netherlands Yearbook of International Law* (1993): 12 (citing Bela Vitanyi, 'Les positions doctrinales concernant le sens de la notion de "Principes généraux de droits reconnus par les nations civilisées"', *Revue Générale de Droit International Public* 86 (1982): 48).
118. Wolfke, 'Controversies Regarding Customary International Law', *supra* n. 117, 12.
119. There is even debate around whether general principles are a separate source of law. *See* Simma & Alston, 'The Sources of Human Rights Law: Custom, *Jus Cogens*, and General Principles', *supra* n. 107, 102; Richard Lillich, 'The Growing Importance of Customary International Human Rights Law', *Georgia Journal of International and Comparative Law* 25 (1995–96): 16–17.

that difficulties attaching to custom in respect of human rights obligations would be any less apparent in the context of general principles, so that their utility in the present context appears extremely limited.[120]

Obligations *erga omnes* and *jus cogens* norms (peremptory norms) belong to a special category of international law which may also generate international human rights obligations.[121] Like custom, these are attended by limitations that curtail their usefulness in addressing HRA in development.[122]

Obligations *erga omnes* were recognized by the ICJ in the *Barcelona Traction* case[123] in which the Court clarified that all states can be held to have a legal interest in protecting certain international obligations, due to the importance of the rights involved.[124] They are obligations of a state towards the international community as a whole. 'Such obligations derive [. . .] from the outlawing of acts of aggression, and of genocide, as also from the principles and rules concerning the basic rights of the human person, including protection from slavery and racial discrimination.'[125] Thus, if the norm creates an obligation *erga omnes*, this implies a legal interest by all states, not an obligation on other states to act. Thus, even assuming its applicability to IFIs, the legal construct underpinning such obligations renders *erga omnes* obligations a less than satisfactory way of grounding actionable human rights obligations in a way that would address HRA in development effectively.

Jus cogens norms are peremptory norms from which no derogation is permitted[126] including, it has been argued, derogation by specialized legal regimes.[127] They protect the overriding interests and values of the international

120. As Sigrun Skogly notes, 'The contents, or definitions, of "general principles of law" in Article 38 of the ICJ Statue have been the subject of major controversy in international law circles.' Skogly, 'The Human Rights Obligations of the World Bank and the IMF', *supra* n. 98, 87–88.
121. Simma & Alston, 'The Sources of Human Rights Law: Custom, *Jus Cogens*, and General Principles', *supra* n. 107; J.E.S. Fawcett, 'The International Protection of Human Rights', in *Political Theory and the Rights of Man*, ed. D.D. Raphael (Bloomington, IN: Indiana University Press, 1967); Christian Tomuschat & Jean Marc Thouvenin (eds), *The Fundamental Rules of the International Legal Order: Jus Cogens and Obligations Erga Omnes* (The Hague: Martinus Nijhoff, 2005); Michael Byers, *Custom, Power and the Power of Rules* (Cambridge: Cambridge University Press, 1999); Theodor Meron, 'On a Hierarchy of International Human Rights, Discussing the Hierarchical Terminology in International Human Rights', *American Journal of International Law* 80 (1986): 1.
122. Alexander Orakhelashvili, *Peremptory Norms in International Law* (Oxford: Oxford University Press, 2006).
123. *Barcelona Traction, Light and Power Co. Ltd Case* (1970) I.C.J. Reports 3, at 64.
124. Maurizio Ragazzi, *International Obligations Erga Omnes* (Oxford: Oxford University Press, 1997).
125. *Barcelona Traction, Light and Power Co. Ltd Case*, *supra* n. 123, 32.
126. *See, e.g.*, V. Nageswar Rao, '*Jus Cogens* and the Vienna Convention on the Law of Treaties', *International Journal of Innovation & Learning* 14 (1974): 362; Karol Wolfke, '*Jus Cogens* in International Law', *Polish Yearbook of International Law* 6 (1974): 145–162.
127. International Law Commission, *Fragmentation of International Law: Difficulties Arising from Diversification and Expansion of International Law: Report of the Study group of the International Law Commission*, U.N. Doc. A/CN.4/L.682 (13 Apr. 2006), 1–25, para. 154.

community of states.[128] Examples include the prohibition on unlawful use of force, performance of criminal acts under international law, and trade in slaves, piracy, and genocide.[129] Their content and relationship to natural law gives them an intuitive affinity to human rights.[130] However, despite the enumerated list being understood as non-exhaustive, the limited substantive reach of established *jus cogens* norms and the absence of agreement on whether other principles of customary international law may belong to this category confine its practical use in the development context. It is difficult to conceive of fact scenarios in the day-to-day operations of IFIs giving rise to instances where established *jus cogens* might apply, thus diminishing its potential function to ground HRA in development.

C. Charter-Based Human Rights Obligations

As a central framework of public international law, the UN Charter generates human rights obligations.[131] Human rights pervade the Charter like 'a golden thread',[132] emerging in its Charter's aims and purposes provision Article 1(3), and in Articles 13(1), 55, 56, 62(2), 68, and 76(c). The inclusion of human rights in the UN Charter's preamble is also persuasive.[133]

States that are members of the United Nations have obligations arising under Articles 55 and 56 of the UN Charter to take action individually and jointly to promote the respect for, and observance of human rights.[134] Referring to Article 55,

128. Lauri Hannikainen, *Peremptory Norms (Jus Cogens) in International Law: Historical Development, Criteria and Present Status* (Helsinski: Lakimieslliiton Kustannus, Finish Lawyers' Publishing Co., 1988).
129. *Yearbook of the International Law Commission*, vol. 2 (1966), 247–249.
130. Mark Janis, 'The Nature of *Jus Cogens*', *Connecticut Journal of International Law* 3 (1988): 359, 361.
131. Nigel White, 'The United Nations System, Conference, Contract or Constitutional Order?', *Singapore Journal of International & Comparative Law* 4 (2000): 291.
132. John Humphrey, *No Distant Millennium: The International Law of Human Rights* (Paris: UNESCO, 1989).
133. Vienna Convention on the Law of Treaties, 1155 U.N.T.S. 331, 8 I.L.M. 679 (1980), Art. 31 (establishing the status of the Preamble as part of the text of the Treaty for the purposes of interpretation).
134. UN Charter, *Article 55*:

> With a view to the creation of conditions of stability and well-being which are necessary for peaceful and friendly relations among nations based on respect for the principle of equal rights and self-determination of peoples, the United Nations shall promote:
>
> a. higher standards of living, full employment, and conditions of economic and social progress and development;
> b. solutions of international economic, social, health, and related problems; and international cultural and educational cooperation; and
> c. universal respect for, and observance of, human rights and fundamental freedoms for all without distinction as to race, sex, language, or religion.

Article 56: All Members pledge themselves to take joint and separate action in co-operation with the Organization for the achievement of the purposes set forth in Article 55. Charter of the

Eibe Riedel has written, '[t]here is wide consensus today that the article legally obligates not only the world Organization but also the [M]ember States to respect and protect human rights'.[135] Nothing prevents the application of such obligations in contexts outside the United Nations, whether states are acting alone, or jointly. These Charter provisions indicate that UN Member States have an obligation to act in conformity with human rights principles under Article 55(c) when they act in other contexts. In IFIs, this could imply some minimum obligation to take account of the human rights effects of their decisions to ensure the *respect* of human rights, and a duty to refrain from actions that might undermine the enjoyment or realization of human rights, or respect a principle of 'do no harm'. 'Even if the legal obligation is general in character, there can be no doubt that responsibility exists for any substantial infringement of the provisions and that Articles 55 and 56 impose the legal obligation on member States singly or jointly to stand up for respecting human rights.'[136]

The terms of Article 55 also contain a more active or programmatic component that may have a direct bearing on development institutions.[137] It contains affirmative obligations to promote and fulfil, requiring active steps on the part of states. Similarly, referring to the World Bank and the International Monetary Fund (IMF), the *Tilburg Guiding Principles on World Bank, IMF and Human Rights* provide:

> As members of the UN the [M]ember States of the two IFIs have legally committed themselves to uphold the purposes and principles of the UN Charter, including the promotion of respect for human rights. According to Article 103 of the UN Charter,[138] the obligations of States under the Charter, including obligations in the field of human rights would take precedence over other international obligations.[139]

United Nations (26 Jun. 1945), Arts 55–56, *available at* <www.un.org/en/documents/charter/index.shtml> (hereinafter UN Charter).

135. Reidel, *supra* n. 110, 920.
136. *Ibid.*, 923.
137. *Ibid.*, 920.
138. Article 103 of the UN Charter states, 'In the event of a conflict between the obligations of the Member of the Untied Nations under the present Charter and their obligations under any other international agreement, their obligations under the present Charter shall prevail.' UN Charter, *supra* n. 134, Art. 103.
139. Willem van Genugten, 'Tilburg Guiding Principles on World Bank, IMF and Human Rights', in *World Bank, IMF and Human Rights*, ed. Willem van Genugten, Paul Hunt & Susan Mathews (Nijmegen: Wolf Legal Publishers, 2003), para. 8, 247–255, *available at* <www1.umn.edu/humanrts/instree/Tilburgprinciples.html>. Also relevant are Principles:

> 26. In concluding agreements with their members, the IFIs shall respect the obligations of the members according to Article 103 of the UN Charter, including giving priority to respect for human rights. 27. When determining the policies, programmers and projects of the World Bank and the IMF, member States must comply with their obligations under international human rights law, including the duty to engage in international assistance and co-operation. Moreover, when member States decide upon policies, programs and projects that impact upon a State, they must take into account and respect the relevant

Indeed the primacy of obligations of Member States under the UN Charter, which include human rights, were explicitly noted by the former World Bank General Counsel Ibrahim Shihata. In discussing states' obligations under the UN Charter, Shihata concluded, 'Members' *obligations* under the UN Charter prevail over their other treaty obligations, including their obligations under the Bank's Articles of Agreement, by force of an explicit provision in the UN Charter (Article 103)'.[140]

IV. NATURE OF STATES' HUMAN RIGHTS OBLIGATIONS IN THE CONTEXT OF DEVELOPMENT: TACKLING ACCOUNTABILITY THROUGH TREATIES

Given the lack of emphasis on legal duties or obligations in development policy and discourse, and in light of the paucity of sources for direct human rights obligations on IFIs, it is submitted that a return to positive treaty law may be in order because it is still true that 'the primary responsibility under international human rights law is placed on the state'.[141]

International human rights treaties, as an articulated code of multilateral standard-setting conventions, constitute the principal source of international human rights obligations. They are the proper locus of legal accountability for human rights in the context of development, placing the primary, though not exclusive, responsibility for human rights in IFIs on states.[142] Human rights treaties are not without their limitations: '[i]n relying on international human rights law as a force indispensable to countering the negative effects of economic globalization, we are also confronted by its current limitations'.[143] However, one should work within those limitations rather than reinvent or deny them, and use

---

national and international human rights laws that apply to that State. Member States should not agree to measures that will impede their ability to comply with their national and international human rights obligations.

140. Ibrahim Shihata (ed.), 'Exclusion of Political Considerations in the Bank's Articles – Its Meaning and Scope in the Context of the Institution's Evolution', in *The World Bank in a Changing World Selected Essays and Lectures*, vol. II, ed. Ibrahim Shihata (Dordrecht: Martinus Nijhoff, 1991), 76.
141. Asbjorn Eide, 'Human Rights-Based Development in the Age of Globalization', in *Development as a Human Right: A Nobel Symposium Book*, ed. Bård A. Andreasson & Stephen Marks (Cambridge, MA: Harvard University Press, 2006), 242.
142. Eide's definition of the role of the state in this context is apposite: 'The role of the state under the human rights system is, therefore, on the one hand, to respect and to protect the individuals in their efforts to meet their own needs, and, on the other hand, to facilitate those efforts by appropriate policies and been a provider where the capabilities of the individual do not suffice to ensure an adequate standard of living in freedom.' Eide, 'Human Rights-Based Development in the Age of Globalization', *supra* n. 141, 220, 242.
143. Margot Salomon, Arne Tostensen & Wouter Vandenhole (eds), *Casting the Net Wider: Human Rights, Development and New Duty-Bearers* (Antwerp & Oxford: Intersentia, 2008), 11.

the unexplored potential of the international human rights law framework as it currently stands.[144]

The clearest way of tackling that accountability in development is through treaties,[145] which give substantive content and specificity to human rights obligations,[146] even if not perfectly or exhaustively. Even arguments in favour of human rights obligations of non-state actors tend to argue for ways in which these should 'complement the nation-states acting in their traditional role; they do not displace them'.[147] The current argument does not defend a Westphalian vision of sovereignty and international law, nor deny great transformation which such notions have undergone.[148] Nor does it dispute the existence of international human rights law obligations of non-state actors including IFIs under custom[149] or general principles of law,[150] but rather seeks to explore the latent and unexploited potential of the existing human rights obligation of traditional human rights duty-holders, which have been transformed but not eliminated or displaced.[151]

---

144. *See* International Law Commission (ILC), *Responsibility of International Organizations, available at* <http://untreaty.un.org/ilc/guide/9_11.htm> (reflecting emerging thinking on this issue and the progressive development and codification of international law).
145. Even the radical thrust of the Tilburg principles offer tacit support to the need for a binding and enforceable legal standard embodied in an instrument, and the insufficiency of non-treaty sources to address human rights accountability in this context. '28. For reasons of operationalization, general human rights obligations for the World Bank and the IMF should be specified in a practical and accessible instrument by which the two IFIs are to be guided in all their decisions and on the basis of which they can be held accountable'. Genugten, 'Tilburg Guiding Principles on World Bank, IMF and Human Rights', *supra* n. 139, 30.
146. As Steiner and Alston observe in relation to economic, social, and cultural rights, 'One of the greatest challenges however, is to identify effective approaches to implementation – i.e. to the means by which ESCR can be given effect and governments held to accountable to fulfill their obligations.' Alston, Steiner & Goodman, *International Human Rights in Context: Law, Politics, Morals*, 3rd edn, *supra* n. 5, 277.
147. Salomon, Tostensen & Vandenhole, *supra* n. 143, 3.
148. On the changing notion of state sovereignty in public international law, and its relationship to the evolution of human rights law, *see* Oscar Schachter, 'The Decline of the Nation-State and Its Implications for International Law', *Columbia Journal of Transnational Law* 36 (1997): 7; Louis Henkin, 'Human Rights and State "Sovereignty" ', *Georgia Journal of International & Comparative Law* 25 (1995/96): 31; August Reinisch, 'The Changing International Legal Framework for Dealing with Non-state Actors', *Non-State Actors and Human Rights*, ed. Philip Alston (Oxford: Oxford University Press, 2005), 37.
149. *See, e.g.*, Schermers & Blokker, *supra* n. 97, 1572–1591, 1578.
150. 'International organizations are subjects of international law and, as such, are bound by any obligations incumbent upon them under general rules of international law.' I.C.J., *Interpretation of the Agreement of 25 March 1951 between the WHO and Egypt*, Advisory Opinion 1980 I.C.J. Reports (20 December) at 90.
151. For a reaffirmation of the state as the central and primary repository of human rights obligations, *see Vienna Declaration and Programme of Action* confirmed the responsibility of states to protect and promote human rights. '1. The World Conference on Human Rights reaffirms the solemn commitment of all States to fulfill their obligations to promote universal respect for, and observance and protection of, all human rights and fundamental freedoms for all in accordance with the Charter of the United Nations, other instruments relating to human rights, and international law. The universal nature of these rights and freedoms is beyond question.

That 'international law is growing out of the idea that its subjects are only sovereign states'[152] does not relieve states of their duties, nor displace their responsibilities as primary duty-bearers for human rights under international law. The relative power of states and non-state actors in respect of human rights has obviously shifted, but fundamental differences in the nature of their responsibilities still exist, and the primacy of state responsibility under international human rights law remains intact.[153] Moreover, such a focus on state responsibility is not inconsistent with the contention that human rights in development require international cooperation or that specialized agencies, including the IFIs, have a role to play in upholding human rights and supporting their fulfilment in their operations and policies.

Human rights treaties prove 'a solid and compelling legal foundation'[154] for the consideration of human rights in development, entered into by donor and partner countries alike. Like obligations under any trade or environmental law agreement, the relevance and enforceability of these should be recognized in the context of development, and their terms upheld or at least not undermined. Connecting IFIs' consideration of human rights to treaties, also provides legitimacy, and protects against charges of political interference since such consideration would be delimited by states' consent in their voluntarily undertaken legal commitments.

The general Charter obligation to fulfil obligations in good faith under Article 2(2)[155] and the principle of *pacta sunt servanda* provide further support.

In this framework, enhancement of international cooperation in the field of human rights is essential for the full achievement of the purposes of the United Nations. Human rights and fundamental freedoms are the birthright of all human beings; their protection and promotion is the first responsibility of Governments'. 'Vienna Declaration and Programme of Action' (12 Jul. 1993), <www.unhchr.ch/huridocda/huridoca.nsf/(Symbol)/A.CONF.157.23.En>.

152. Christopher G. Weeramantry, 'Private International Law and Public International Law', *Revista di diritto internazionale private e processuale* 24 (1998): 313 (cited in Shyami Fernando Puvimanasinghe, *Foreign Investment, Human Rights and the Environment: A Perspective from South Asia on the Role of Public International Law for Development* (Leiden: Martinus Nijhoff, 2007), 65).
153. *See* Oscar Schachter's analysis of what he terms 'the resilience of the state system', concluding that '[i]t would be a mistake to consider that disparities in power render sovereignty insignificant'. Oscar Schachter, 'The Decline of the Nation-State and Its Implications for International Law', *Columbia Journal Transnational Law* 36 (1997): 23. Of course, a growing body of commentary exists downplaying these distinctions, and emphasizing power imbalances to argue for the existence of 'responsibility', *see, e.g.*, Judge Weeramantry describing the 'responsibility' of transnational corporations in the context of human rights, '[m]ultinationals are responsible actors in the field of international law no less than States, and the sooner this is realized, the better it will be for human rights across the globe'. Christopher Weeramantry, 'Human Rights and the Global Marketplace', *Brooklyn Journal of International Law* 15 (1989): 40–41, 49.
154. Simma & Alston, 'The Sources of Human Rights Law: Custom, *Jus Cogens*, and General Principles', *supra* n. 107, 3.
155. 'All Members, in order to ensure to all of them the rights and benefits resulting from membership, shall fulfill in good faith the obligations assumed by them in accordance with the present Charter.' UN Charter, *supra* n. 134, Art. 2(2).

Activities undertaken in the context of development and IFIs should not eviscerate the obligations voluntarily undertaken under human rights treaties. As the primary duty-bearers, states should ensure that actions in the development context at a minimum do not contradict or undermine the obligations to respect, protect, promote, and fulfil human rights.[156] As Sands and Klein note:[157]

> Members of international organizations may be responsible not for the consequences of the latter's illegal acts, but for their own participation in that act, or for their failure to ensure that the powers they have transferred to an organization have been exercised in conformity with their own international obligations.[158]

It appears therefore that the effective upholding of HRA under international law in the context of development must, at this stage, be indirect, and reliant on the 'instrumentality of the state'. This ensures the coherence and integrity of the notion of obligation, securing the essential contribution of human rights to development, and fosters convergence around duties in the human rights – development discourse. A more accurate appraisal of human rights obligations in the context of development underscores state duty and its ramifications for development and IFIs. '[M]embers of international organizations are under an obligation of due diligence, which compels them to make sure that the transfer of competences to the organization does not allow them to avoid their responsibilities under international law.'[159] This is consistent with emerging international principles:

> that states are to comply with their human rights obligations when pursuing international cooperation in other areas is emerging as an incontrovertible principle. To make this effective, they must ensure that their representatives have the knowledge, and instructions, to provide this assurance.[160]

'A major part of states' extraterritorial activities are undertaken through intergovernmental organizations, such as the Untied Nations and its specialized agencies. In their operations through these agencies, states are legally bound to carry out the mandate of the organization, and at the same [time] to do this within the general framework of international law.'[161] That framework constitutes a broader

156. What Sigrun Skogly has called 'the obligation to ensure that human rights are not compromised through the activities of those institutions'. Sigrun Skogly, *Beyond International Borders: States' Human Rights Obligations in International Cooperation* (Antwerp: Intersentia, 2006), 197.
157. *Matthews v. United Kingdom*, 18 Feb. 1999, Application 24833/94, para. 32.
158. Philippe Sands & Pierre Klein, *Bowett's Law of International Institutions*, 5th edn (London: Sweet & Maxwell, 2001), 525.
159. *Ibid.*, 524.
160. Margot Salomon, *Global Responsibility for Human Rights* (Oxford: Oxford University Press, 2007), 107 (citing to European Court of Human Rights jurisprudence including the case of *Waite and Kennedy v. Germany*, ECtHR App. No. 26083/94, Grand Chamber Judgment of 18 Feb. 1999, para. 67).
161. Skogly, *Beyond International Borders: States' Human Rights Obligations in International Cooperation*, *supra* n. 156, 195.

accountability framework, which includes human rights obligations, whether flowing from the UN Charter, from custom, or from human rights treaties. The fact that the obligations of such institutions are not settled under international law should not be taken to mean that their Member States do not have directly relevant obligations under human rights treaties or as members of the United Nations. 'States determine the policies of some global actors including the World Bank, the IMF and the World Trade Organization. When determining the polices of such global actors, a State must confirm to its international human rights duties and must be respectful of other States' international human rights obligations.'[162]

'International policy coherence'[163] is gaining prominence in a wide array of contexts.[164] 'Greater coherence among the various trends of international law and policy are necessary to allow for the exercise of human rights, which the international community has concluded, is first among the responsibilities of governments.'[165] In this context, coherence supports a focus on existing obligations, and applies that to 'the institutional structures under which old duty-bearers – i.e., states – act' to ensure that the actions of states in various institutional structures and processes not undermine human rights enjoyment.[166] It may demand coherence across policies governing different issues, as well as coherence in terms of their engagement with and participation in international organizations and processes.[167]

162. OHCHR (Paul Hunt, Manfred Nowak & Siddiq Osmani), 'Principles and Guidelines for a Human Rights approach to Poverty reduction strategies', HR/PUB/06/12, para. 95, *available at* <www2.ohchr.org/english/issues/poverty/guidelines.htm>.
163. *See* Salomon, *Global Responsibility for Human Rights*, *supra* n. 160, 106. *See also* her related discussion of incongruence and contradictory trends in international legal regimes and the need for international policy coherence. *Ibid.*, 156.
164. Development Co-operation Directorate (DCD-DAC), OECD Development Dimension Series on Policy Coherence (DACNews, September–October 2005), *available at* <www.oecd.org/document/54/0,2340,en_2649_33721_35320054_1_1_1_1,00.html>. This idea also has relevance to efforts in the UN human rights machinery to enhance coherence and harmonization between treaty bodies, *see, e.g.*, United Nations International Human Rights Instruments, 'Report of the Working group on Harmonization of Working Methods of Treaty Bodies', HRI/MC/2007/2 (Geneva, 9 Jan. 2007), *available at* <http://daccess-dds-ny.un.org/doc/UNDOC/GEN/G07/400/45/PDF/G0740045.pdf?OpenElement>; United Nations International Human Rights Instruments, 'Report on the working methods of the Human Rights Treaty Bodies relating to State Party reporting processes: Note by the Secretariat', HRI/MC/2007/4 (11 Jun. 2007), *available at* <www2.ohchr.org/english/bodies/icm-mc/docs/hri_mc_2007_4.doc>; United Nations International Human Rights Instruments, 'Report on the implementation of recommendations of the fifth inter-committee meeting and the eighteenth meeting of Chairpersons: Note by the Secretariat', HRI/MC/2007/6 (29 May 2007), *available at* <www2.ohchr.org/english/bodies/icm-mc/docs/hri_mc_2007_6.doc>.
165. Salomon, *Global Responsibility for Human Rights*, *supra* n. 160, 113.
166. For a discussion of policy coherence, *see* Piron & Watkins, *supra* n. 95, 29.
167. The definition provided by UK Department for International Development (DFID) captures these distinct dimensions, '[p]olicy coherence for development is achieved when policies across a range of issues (for example trade, migration, security) support, or at least do not undermine, the attainment of development objectives. There are two types of policy coherence of particular importance to DFID: coherence across UK government policies; and coherence within multilateral institutions such as the European Commission (EU)'. *See* DFID website, <www.dfid.gov.uk/>.

It may require that states act consistently in the boards of IFIs as they do in the United Nations, and at a minimum, 'do no harm'. In practical terms, this would involve identifying constructive approaches to determine the application of international human rights treaties to particular policies and operations of IFIs,[168] including through existing policies, tools, and assessments.[169]

Member States play a vital role in many intergovernmental organizations, as demonstrated by the fact that:

> States determine the policies of intergovernmental organization such as the World Bank, the International Monetary Fund, and the World Trade Organization. They bring to these prescribed cooperation engagements their existing external human rights obligations, compliance with which must be retained as they go about their mandated activities. The Member States of international organizations are compelled to ensure that the transfer of competences to the organization does not allow them to avoid their responsibilities under international human rights law.[170]

This need has become heightened, at least in part, by the expanding reach of impacts, and de facto overlap described in part 1. The potential influence of IFIs on the enjoyment of rights is such that the issue of human rights responsibility in those contexts cannot be ignored.[171] 'A state that has ratified a human rights treaty should not be allowed to argue that a legal norm it has bound itself to observe in that treaty must be excluded from a loan agreement on the grounds that human rights are too political and a matter of domestic jurisdiction.'[172]

The human rights responsibility of states in the context of IFIs can be understood in terms of the established tripartite structure of the duties to respect, protect, and fulfil.[173] Each implies obligations of conduct and result, requiring 'action

---

168. For an excellent examination of the concept of extraterritoriality of the human rights obligations of states in a variety of areas, including development cooperation, which argues for the extension of jurisdiction and therefore obligations 'to the extent not prohibited by international law', *see* Skogly, *Beyond International Borders: States' Human Rights Obligations in International Cooperation*, *supra* n. 156.
169. On the obligations of World Bank donor members under the ICESCR with respect to the right to health, *see* Rachel Hammonds & Gorik Ooms, 'World Bank Policies and the Obligations of Its Members to Respect, Protect and Fulfill the Right to Health', *Health and Human Rights* 8, no. 1 (2004): 27.
170. Salomon, *Global Responsibility for Human Rights*, *supra* n. 160, 106.
171. 'Yet while philosophical and social approaches to responsibilities have come to terms with these developments, the legal discipline has so far demonstrated some serious difficulty in adapting to this new reality.' Salomon, Tostensen & Vandenhole, *Casting the Net Wider: Human Rights, Development and New Duty-Bearers*, *supra* n. 143, 12.
172. Thomas Buergenthal, 'The World Bank and Human Rights', in *The World Bank, International Financial Institutions and the Development of International Law*, ed. Edith Brown Weiss, Andrés Rigo Sureda & Laurence Boisson de Chazournes (Washington, DC: American Society of International Law, 1999), 100.
173. Hammonds & Ooms, *supra* n. 169, 48.

reasonably calculated to realize the enjoyment of particular rights', that 'states achieve specific targets to satisfy a detailed substantive standard'.[174]

The obligation to respect requires states to refrain from actions that interfere with the enjoyment of economic, social, and cultural rights.[175] This is a 'negative duty' that could be conceived of as a due diligence requirement, or a principle of 'do no harm'. In relation to IFIs, and in substantive terms, the duty would require states to *refrain* from proposing or supporting policies or activities that might impact negatively on the level of enjoyment of rights of people in developing countries.

The obligation to protect is a more 'active' and potentially expansive one, which goes beyond the direct remit of a state's actions. It requires states to prevent violations of rights by third parties or to protect against violations of rights 'in the private domain'.[176] In the context of IFIs, this would require that states, through their oversight of development policies and activities, prevent potentially harmful actions on the part of third parties in their jurisdiction or under their effective control.[177] One could conceive of a host of fact scenarios in which it might apply,

---

174. *Maastricht Guidelines on Violations of Economic, Social and Cultural Rights* (Maastricht, 22–26 Jan. 1997), para. 7, *available at* <www1.umn.edu/humanrts/instree/Maastrichtguidelines_.html> (hereinafter *Maastricht Guidelines*).
175. *Ibid.*, para. 6.
176. *Ibid.*, para. 6. *See generally*, Andrew Clapham, *Human Rights in the Private Sphere* (Oxford: Clarendon Press, 1993); Siobhán McInerney, 'The European Convention on Human Rights and Fundamental Freedoms and the Evolution of Fundamental Rights in the "Private Domain" ', in *Renegotiating Westphalia: Essays and Commentary on the European and Conceptual Foundations of Modern International Law*, ed. Christopher Harding & C.L. Lim (The Hague: Kluwer, 1999), 277–320.
177. The ICESCR, like the ICCPR, can only impose obligations on states. Thus, any responsibility for any recognized harm or violation to rights under the Covenant perpetrated by a non-state actor falls to the states on the basis of omission and failing in the duty to protect. Discussion of the positive obligations of states under the ICCPR. In General Comment No. 31, the HRC stated:

> The article 2, paragraph 1, obligations are binding on States [Parties] and do not, as such, have direct horizontal effect as a matter of international law. The Covenant cannot be viewed as a substitute for domestic criminal or civil law. However the positive obligations on States Parties to ensure Covenant rights will only be fully discharged if individuals are protected by the State, not just against violations of Covenant rights by its agents, but also against acts committed by private persons or entities that would impair the enjoyment of Covenant rights in so far as they are amenable to application between private persons or entities. There may be circumstances in which a failure to ensure Covenant rights as required by article 2 would give rise to violations by States Parties of those rights, as a result of States Parties' permitting or failing to take appropriate measures or to exercise due diligence to prevent, punish, investigate or redress the harm caused by such acts by private persons or entities. States are reminded of the interrelationship between the positive obligations imposed under article 2 and the need to provide effective remedies in the event of breach under article 2, paragraph 3. The Covenant itself envisages in some articles certain areas where there are positive obligations on States Parties to address the activities of private persons or entities.

from procurement, to contractors and financial intermediaries. Such an obligation has particular relevance for development activities involving the private sector.[178] This obligation could cover the roles of both donor and partner countries in the identification, design, implementation, supervision of projects, and, depending on the source of financing, the implementing modalities or the operations in question.

The duty to fulfil is also an 'active' one,[179] but refers more directly to acts that the state may take to ensure the enjoyment and realization of rights through its established legal and regulatory channels. In the domestic context, this affirmative duty 'requires States to take appropriate legislative, administrative, budgetary, judicial and other measures toward the full realization of such rights'.[180] In the context of IFIs, this would require the state to take action to prevent any violations of the rights it is bound to protect under the International Covenant on Economic, Social, and Cultural Rights (ICESCR),[181] at least in the remit of its influence; and

---

UN ICCPR, Human Rights Committee, 'General Comment No. 31 [80] Nature of the General Legal Obligation Imposed on States Parties to the Covenant', CCPR/C/21/Rev.1/Add.13 (26 May 2004), *available at* <www.unhchr.ch/tbs/doc.nsf/0/58f5d4646e861359c1256ff600533f5f?Opendocument>.

178. *See, e.g.*, 'Business and Human Rights: Mapping International Standards of Responsibility and Accountability for Corporate Acts', Report of the Special Representative of the Secretary General on the issue of human rights and transnational corporations and other business enterprises, A/HRC/4/035 9 (February 2007), 5–7. For an argument in favour of direct responsibilities of TCN, *see* David Kinley & Junko Tadaki, 'From Talk to Walk: The Emergence of Human Rights Responsibilities for Corporations at International Law', *Virginia Journal of International Law* 44, no. 4 (2004): 931. Shyami Fernando Puvimanasinghe, *Foreign Investment, Human Rights and the Environment: A Perspective from South Asia on the Role of Public International Law for Development* (Leiden: Martinus Nijhoff, 2007), 59–95. On the related area of human rights issues in the context of privatized infrastructure projects, *see* Michael Likosky, *Law, Infrastructure, and Human Rights* (Cambridge: Cambridge University Press, 2006). Matt Shinn (on behalf of the Business & Human Rights Seminar, Ltd), *The 2005 Business and Human Rights Seminar Report: Exploring Responsibility and Complicity* (London: 8 Dec. 2005), <www.bhrseminar.org/BusinessHumanRightsSeminarReport2005.pdf>.

179. As is the less prominent duty to promote, which relates more to disseminating information about rights, than to facilitate their exercise.

180. *Maastricht Guidelines*, *supra* n. 174, para. 6. On the US Alien Tort Claims Act, *see* Ralph Steinhardt, 'Corporate Responsibility and the International Law of Human Rights: The New Lex Mercatoria', in *Non-state Actors and Human Rights*, ed. Philip Alston (Oxford: Oxford University Press, 2005); Mark Gibney & R. David Emerick, 'The Extraterritorial Application of United States Law and the Protection of Human Rights: Holding Multination Corporations to Domestic and International Standards', *Temple International and Comparative Law Journal* 10 (1996); Steven Ratner, 'Corporations and Human Rights: A Theory of Legal Responsibility', *Yale Law Journal* 111 (2001): 443; Daniel Aguirre, 'Multinational Corporations and the Realization of Economic, Social and Cultural Rights', *California Western International Law Journal* 35 (2004): 53, 60. For a recent overview of US jurisprudence under the Alien Tort Claims Act, *see* Frank Olah, 'MNC Liability for International Human Rights Violations under the Alien Tort Claims Act: A Review and Analysis of the Fundamental Jurisprudence and a Look at Aiding and Abetting Liability under the Act', *Quinnipiac Law Review* 25 (2007): 751.

181. Weeramantry, 'Human Rights and the Global Marketplace', *supra* n. 153, 48–49 (discussing 'Positive Action by States' in respect of the obligation of states under international law to take positive action in the furtherance of human rights with respect to corporations operating within their territory).

act to ensure the fulfilment of human rights, through its voting on a governing body, policy-making, financing, and the multitude of ways in which states influence organizations of which they are members. At the level of projects, programmes, or strategies, this might require donors and borrowers to take steps to integrate relevant human rights considerations and actively promote the human rights dimension of development activities; it might include encouraging or pursuing alignment with a country's human rights priorities and obligations, and promoting awareness of the human rights dimensions of policies or programs. More generally, it would impose on all Member States an obligation to be vigilant in promoting policy coherence in respect of human rights in various fora related to international development.

V. STATE PARTIES' OBLIGATIONS UNDER HUMAN RIGHTS TREATIES AS RELEVANT TO IFIs: THE EXAMPLE OF THE ICESCR

A. Human Rights Treaties

'In the development of this new human rights law, international treaties certainly play the most obvious role and give rise to the least jurisprudential difficulties.'[182] Today nine core human rights instruments adopted by the United Nations[183]

182. Simma & Alston, 'The Sources of Human Rights Law: Custom, *Jus Cogens*, and General Principles', *supra* n. 107, 28.

183. The 'nine core treaties' sponsored by the United Nations include: the International Covenant on Civil and Political Rights (ICCPR), UN Doc. A/6316 (1966), 999 U.N.T.S. 171 (entry into force 23 Mar. 1976), *available at* <www1.umn.edu/humanrts/instree/b3ccpr.htm>; the International Covenant on Economic, Social, and Cultural Rights (ICESCR), *infra* n. 187; the International Convention on the Elimination of All Forms of Racial Discrimination (CERD), G.A. Res. 2106(XX) (21 Dec. 1965, entry into force 4 Jan. 1969), *available at* <www2.ohchr.org/english/law/cerd.htm>; the Convention on the Elimination of All Forms of Discrimination against Women (CEDAW), G.A. Res. 1999 1577 (23 Jan. 1987, entry into force 26 Apr. 1995), *available at* <www.humanrights.ch/home/en/Switzerland/UN-Conventions/Woman/idart_4791-content.html>; the Convention against Torture and Other Cruel, Inhuman or Degrading Treatment or Punishment (CAT), G.A. Res. 39/36 (10 Dec. 1984, entry into force 26 Jun. 1987), *available at* <http://untreaty.un.org/cod/avl/ha/catcidtp/catcidtp.html>; the Convention on the Rights of the Child (CRC), G.A. Res. 44/25 (20 Nov. 1989, entry into force 2 Sep. 1990), *available at* <www2.ohchr.org/english/law/crc.htm>; the International Convention on the Protection of the Rights of All Migrant Workers and Members of Their Families (MWC), G.A. Res. 45/158 (18 Dec. 1990), *available at* <www2.ohchr.org/english/bodies/cmw/cmw.htm>; the Convention on the Rights of Persons with Disabilities (CRPD), A/61/611 (6 Dec. 2006), *available at* <www.un.org/disabilities/convention/about.shtml>; the International Convention for the Protection of All Persons From Enforced Disappearances, <www2.ohchr.org/english/law/disappearance-convention.htm>. For a comprehensive collection of the sources of human rights law, including regional and specialized sources, as well as treaty and non-treaty sources, *see* Ian Brownlie & Guy Goodwin-Gill, *Basic Documents on Human Rights*, 5th edn (Oxford: Oxford University Press, 2006).

comprise the international human rights treaty framework.[184] At its heart lies the 'international bill of rights' comprising the UDHR and the two covenants: '[t]he Covenants, which came into force in 1976 have legal force as treaties for the Parties to them and constitute a detailed codification of human rights'.[185] The four core labour standards, embodied in the eight International Labour Organization (ILO) sponsored treaties, some of which predate the UN treaties, may also be considered a part of that global framework.[186]

While civil and political rights may play equally important roles in different aspects of development, the following analysis focuses on economic, social, and cultural rights, to illustrate the core arguments related to obligations and accountability for development. The ICESCR[187] provides a vivid example as a widely ratified treaty,[188] and a cornerstone of the international bill of rights that also provides explicitly for a role for specialized agencies of the United Nations. Despite being endowed with the same formal legal status as civil and political rights, economic, social, and cultural rights have sometimes been relegated to a more tenuous position in the international legal order, with scepticism sometimes expressed about the feasibility of fulfilling such rights[189] and the particular formulation used in the Covenant.[190] 'Much of the literature on ESCR focuses on the

184. Johannes Morsink, *The Universal Declaration of Human Rights: Origins, Drafting, and Intent* (Philadelphia: University of Pennsylvania Press, 1999).
185. Brownlie, *Principles of Public International Law*, 5th edn, *supra* n. 111, 539 (under the heading 'The Substantive Rights: the International Covenants, 1966').
186. The four core labour standards have their source in eight ILO conventions: Convention 29: Forced Labour Convention (1930); Convention 87: Freedom of Association and Protection of the Right to Organise Convention (1948); Convention 98: Right to Organise and Collective Bargaining Convention (1949); Convention 100: Equal Remuneration Convention (1951); Convention 105: Abolition of Forced Labour Convention (1957); Convention 111: Discrimination (Employment and Occupation) Convention (1958); Convention 138: Minimum Age Convention (1973); and Convention 182: Worst Forms of Child Labour Convention (1999).
187. International Covenant on Economic, Social and Cultural Rights (ICESCR), 993 U.N.T.S. 3; 6 I.L.M. 368 (1967) (hereinafter ICESCR), *available at* <www2.ohchr.org/english/law/cescr.htm>. It was adopted unanimously by the UN General Assembly on 16 Dec. 1966 and came into force on 3 Jan. 1976. For more on the history of the ICESCR, *see* Mashood A. Baderin & Robert McCoquodale, 'The International Covenant on Economic, Social and Cultural Rights: Forty Years of Development', in *Economic, Social and Cultural Rights in Action*, ed. Mashood A. Baderin & Robert McCoquodale (Oxford: Oxford University Press, 2007), Ch. 1, 3–24.
188. ICESCR Ratification Status, <http://treaties.un.org/Pages/ViewDetails.aspx?src=TREATY&mtdsg_no=IV-3&chapter=4&lang=en> (status as of 23 Feb. 2010, where currently there are sixty-nine signatories and 160 parties that have ratified the ICESCR).
189. In particular, the obligations that flow from Art. 2(1): 'Each State Party to the present Covenant undertakes to take steps, individually and through international assistance and co-operation, especially economic and technical, to the maximum of its available resources, with a view to achieving progressively the full realization of the rights recognized in the present Covenant by all appropriate means, including particularly the adoption of legislative measures.' ICESCR, *supra* n. 187, Art. 2(1).
190. 'The language has been subject to conflicting critiques. On the one hand, it is often suggested that nature of the obligation under the ICESCR is so onerous that virtually no government will be able to comply. Developing countries, in particular, are seen to be confronting an

feasibility of recognizing them as legal, or even constitutional rights, and of making them justiciable.'[191] This recalls the additional challenges faced in attempts to integrate human rights into development and underscores the need for greater reliance to be placed on 'human rights law-making by way of treaties and the legal characteristics of such treaties', which appear 'more or less uncontroversial'.[192]

B. State Parties' Obligations under the ICESCR as Relevant to IFIs

Building on the foregoing discussion of policy coherence and the emphasis on states parties' obligations under treaties, this section explores the obligations of states under the ICESCR. The fact that only states can become party to the covenants[193] and that 'as a rule conventions are addressed to the [M]ember [S]tates of the organization'[194] indicate that the Covenant only generates obligations for states.[195]

---

impossible challenge. On the other hand, it is argued that the relative open-endedness of the concept of progressive realization, particularly in light of the qualification about availability of resources, renders the obligation devoid of meaningful content.' Alston, Steiner & Goodman, *International Human Rights in Context: Law, Politics, Morals*, 3rd edn, *supra* n. 5, 275.

191. *Ibid.*, 283.
192. Simma & Alston, 'The Sources of Human Rights Law: Custom, *Jus Cogens*, and General Principles', *supra* n. 107, 4.
193. On the question of organizations becoming party to treaties, such as the EC joining the UN Disability Convention on the Rights of Persons with Disabilities and Option Protocol, G.A. Res. A/RES/61/106 (13 Dec. 2006); *see* Tawhida Ahmed & Israel de Jesús Butler, 'The European Union and Human Rights: An International Law Perspective', *European Journal of International Law* 17, no. 4 (2006): 771–801; *see also Opinion on the Accession of the European Communities to the ECHR*, ECJ Opinion 2/94 (28 Mar. 1996); Olivier De Schutter, 'Anchoring the European Union to the European Social Charter: The Case for Accession', in *Social Rights in Europe*, ed. Gráinne de Búrca & Bruno de Witte (Oxford: Oxford University Press, 2005), 111. *See generally* Treaty of the European Union on Accession of the European Union to the European Convention on Human Rights, Art. 6(2); Protocol to Treaty of Lisbon amending the Treaty on European Union and the Treaty establishing the European Community, Official Journal C306 (Lisbon, 17 Dec. 2007), *available at* <http://eur-lex.europa.eu/en/treaties/dat/12007L/htm/12007L.html>; Charter of Fundamental Rights of the European Union, 2000/C 364/01 (18 Dec. 2000), *available at* <www.europarl.europa.eu/charter/pdf/text_en.pdf>.
194. Schermers & Blokker, *supra* n. 97, 1298.
195. ICESCR, *supra* n. 187, Art. 26:

    1. The present Covenant is open for signature by any State Member of the United Nations or member of any of its specialized agencies, by any State Party to the Statute of the International Court of Justice, and by any other State which has been invited by the General Assembly of the United Nations to become a party to the present Covenant.
    2. The present Covenant is subject to ratification. Instruments of ratification shall be deposited with the Secretary-General of the United Nations.
    3. The present Covenant shall be open to accession by any State referred to in paragraph 1 of this article[.]

Article 2(1) of the ICESCR requires states parties 'to take steps, individually and through international assistance and cooperation, especially economic and technical'. Article 2(1) has been relied upon to argue that 'the drafter included language in several articles that specifically indicates that obligations may go beyond the national borders of a ratifying state'.[196] The *travaux préparatoires* indicate that 'there was a general consensus that the inclusion of international cooperation in the Covenant would be necessary to implement economic and social rights, and that it would be necessary in order to get developing counties to ratify the Covenant'.[197] Skogly notes that the meaning of that cooperation was clear: the representative from Egypt confirmed '[b]y international cooperation he meant the co-operation achieved through international bodies such as the United Nations, the International Monetary Fund, the Technical Assistance Board, etc.'.[198]

The interpretations of the Human Rights Committee (HRC) (which supervises the implementation of the International Covenant on Civil and Political Rights (ICCPR)) on the nature of general obligations under the ICCPR are pertinent to the understanding of obligations under the ICESCR:

> The obligations of the Covenant in general and Article 2 in particular are binding on every State Party as a whole. All branches of government (executive, legislative and judicial) and other public or governmental authorities, at whatever level – national, regional or local – are in a position to engage the responsibility of the State.[199]

Obligations under Article 2 are those of states only and the provisions of the Covenant do not have horizontal applicability. This was confirmed by the HRC in relation to Article 2(1) of the ICCPR.[200] This does not, however, preclude the possibility that a state may be found responsible for violations committed by third parties, and indeed, both the HRC and the Committee on Social and Cultural Rights (CESCR) have confirmed the existence of affirmative obligations generated by the covenants.

The work of the CESCR remains the authoritative source of interpretation on the nature of ICESCR obligations.[201] *General Comment No. 3* on the nature of

---

196. Skogly, *Beyond International Borders: States' Human Rights Obligations in International Cooperation*, *supra* n. 156, 83.
197. *Ibid.*, 85.
198. E/CN.4/SR.236, 22, reproduced in Skogly, *Beyond International Borders: States' Human Rights Obligations in International Cooperation*, *supra* n. 156, 85.
199. HRC, General Comment No. 3, *Nature of the General Legal Obligation Imposed on States Parties to the Covenant*, para. 4 (hereinafter General Comment No. 3).
200. *Ibid.*, para. 8.
201. *See* Matthew Craven, *The International Covenant on Economic, Social, and Cultural Rights: A Perspective on Its Development* (Oxford: Oxford University Press, 1995), 89–92. *See also* Matthew Craven, 'The UN Committee on Economic, Social and Cultural Rights', in *Economic, Social and Cultural Rights: A Textbook*, ed. Asbjørn Eide, Catarina Krause & Allan Rosas (Dordrecht: Martinus Njihoff, 2001), 455.

states parties' obligations, which focuses on the meaning of Article 2, provides: 'Article 2 is of particular importance to a full understanding of the Covenant and must be seen as having a dynamic relationship with all of the other provisions of the Covenant. Those obligations include [...] obligations of conduct and obligations of result.'[202] Another provision of particular relevance to the current context is 'the undertaking in Article 2(1) "to take steps"', which in itself is not qualified or limited by other considerations.[203] The HRC confirmed the 'means' under Article 2(1) to be 'all appropriate means, including particularly the adoption of legislative measures'.[204] These 'appropriate means' may include action in international fora and actions related to international development cooperation.

This general comment has relevance to ICESCR obligations as they relate to development and to states' actions in IFIs. As paragraph 12 states:

> Even in times of severe resources constraints whether caused by a process of adjustment, of economic recession, or by other factors, the vulnerable members of society can and indeed must be protected by the adoption of relatively low-cost targeted programmes. In support of this approach the Committee takes note of [*inter alia*] the analysis prepared by the World Bank in the World Development Report 1990.[205]

In respect of Article 2, the committee confirms the obligation on states in relation to international cooperation, potentially extends obligations beyond a State's own interest or citizens. Finally, the committee highlights that in Article 2(1), the undertaking given by all states parties is 'to take steps, individually and through international assistance and cooperation, especially economic and technical'.[206] Moreover, the committee observes that the phrase 'to the maximum of its available resources' was intended by the drafters of the Covenant to refer to both the resources existing within states and those available from the international community through international cooperation and assistance. The essential role of such cooperation in facilitating the full realization of the relevant rights is further underlined by the specific provisions contained in Articles 11, 15, 22, and 23.[207]

In respect of adverse impacts of debt burdens and adjustment measures, the committee notes that efforts to protect the most basic economic, social, and cultural rights becomes more, rather than less, urgent. Although without addressing the specific policy and practical dimensions of this point, or the problems of causation and attribution it presents, the committee holds that '[s]tates parties to the

202. General Comment No. 3, *supra* n. 199, para. 1.
203. *Ibid.*, para. 2.
204. *Ibid.*, para. 3.
205. *Ibid.*, para. 12.
206. *Ibid.*, para. 13.
207. With respect to Art. 22 the committee has already drawn attention, in General Comment No. 2, *supra* n. 31, to some of the opportunities and responsibilities that exist in relation to international cooperation. Art. 23 also specifically identifies 'the furnishing of technical assistance as well as other activities, as being among the means of international action for the achievement of the rights recognized'.

Covenant, as well as the relevant United Nations agencies, should thus make a particular effort to ensure that such protection is, to the maximum extent possible, built into programs and policies designed to promote adjustment'.[208]

C. Limburg Principles

In 1986, the Limburg Principles on the Implementation of the International Covenant on Economic, Social and Cultural Rights established a framework of general guidance on the content and parameters of the Covenant.[209] The principles confirm the breadth of the states parties' obligations in their scope of applicability.[210] Principle 11 reads 'states parties are accountable to both the international community and to their own people for their compliance with obligations under the Covenant', and Principle 72 enumerates specific examples of violations, which include both acts and omissions.

Several principles bear directly on state parties' obligations as they relate to IFIs. The principles' treatment of *Relations between the Committee (on Economic, Social and Cultural Rights) and Specialized Agencies*, alludes to the potential for a stronger, cooperative relationship and constructive work modalities.[211] Principle 94 indicates that the proper supervision of the implementation of the Covenant relies on dialogue being developed between the specialized agencies and the committee on matters of common interest. The specific areas enumerated were the developing indicators for assessing compliance, drafting guidelines for the submission of reports, arranging for the submission of reports by specialized agencies under Article 18, consideration of relevant procedures adopted by the specialized agencies, and the participation of their representatives in meetings of committee.[212]

208. *Ibid.*, para. 9.
209. Ten years after the ICESCR and ICCPR entered into force in 1976, a group of experts in international law was convened in 1986 by the International Commission of Jurists, the Maastricht Centre for Human Rights of the University of Limburg (the Netherlands) and the Urban Morgan Institute for Human Rights, College of Law, University of Cincinnati (Ohio, USA) to discuss the nature and scope of the obligations of States Parties to the ICESCR. The result of that meeting was the Limburg Principles, which later became an official United Nations Document. Limburg Principles, UN Doc. E/CN.4/1987/17 (1987), Annex, *available at* <http://web.abo.fi/instut/imr/ESC-files/Kap1/The%20Limburg%20principles%20on%20the%20Implementation%20of%20the%20ICESCR.doc>.
210. *Ibid.*, 'Nature and Scope of the States Parties', obligation 6 (stating: 'The achievement of economic, social, and cultural rights may be realized in a variety of political settings. There is no single road to their full realization.').
211. *Ibid.*, Principle 92 (highlighting that: 'The establishment of the Committee should be seen as an opportunity to develop a positive and mutually beneficial relationship between the Committee and the specialized agencies and other international organs, and Principle 93 goes on to suggest that new arrangements might be considered which could enhance the contribution of the specialized agencies to the work of the Committee.').
212. This is consistent with Genugten, 'Tilburg Guiding Principles on World Bank, IMF and Human Rights', *supra* n. 139, 37.

D. Maastricht Guidelines on Violations of Economic, Social, and Cultural Rights, Maastricht, 22–26 January 1997

Ten years after the Limburg Principles, a group of experts convened to consider the nature and scope of violations of economic, social, and cultural rights, and to formulate appropriate responses and remedies. Their work culminated in the Maastricht Guidelines on Violations of Economic, Social and Cultural Rights, which were presented as a reflection of the evolution of international law since the 1986 Limburg Principles.

The Guidelines confirm that 'as a matter of international law, the state remains ultimately responsible for guaranteeing the realization of these rights'.[213] They note the global trend to reduce the role of the state and rely on the market to resolve problems of human welfare,[214] complicating the challenge of addressing economic, social, and cultural rights violations, 'it is more urgent than ever to take these rights seriously and therefore to deal with accountability of Governments for failure to meet their obligations in this area'.[215]

Of critical relevance to the question of states' obligations relevant to IFIs is the Maastricht Guidelines' treatment of 'Violations through acts of *Commission*'. Paragraph 14, provides as follows: '(a) Violations of economic, social and cultural rights can occur through the direct action of States or other entities insufficiently regulated by States'.[216]

This confirms that the primary obligations for human rights rest with states, vitiating the notion of unanchored human rights obligations under international law. The concerted focus on the responsibility of states to address a variety of forms of HRA is immediately evident: the state is responsible also for harms resulting from entities it legally or effectively controls. Examples of such violations include:

> (c) The active support for measures adopted by third parties which are inconsistent with economic, social and cultural rights . . . (g) The reduction or diversion of specific public expenditure when such a reduction or diversion results in the non-enjoyment of such rights and is not accompanied by adequate measure to ensure minimum subsistence rights for everyone.[217]

Of even greater relevance to the present discussion is the Guidelines treatment of 'Violations through acts of *Omission*.' Guideline 15 provides, '[v]iolations of economic, social, cultural rights can also occur through the omission or failure of States to take necessary measures stemming from legal obligations'.[218] The nature and extent of those 'necessary steps' under the Covenant is informed

213. *Maastricht Guidelines*, *supra* n. 174, para. 2.
214. *Ibid.*
215. *Ibid.*
216. *Ibid.*, para. 14.
217. *Ibid.*, para. 14.
218. *Ibid.*, para. 15.

by the general comments discussed above, which have direct ramifications for the responsibilities of states under the Covenant. The violations enumerated in Guideline 15 include:

> (a) The failure to take appropriate steps as required under the Covenant; . . . (d) the failure to regulate activities of individuals or groups so as to prevent them from violating economic, social and cultural rights; . . . [and especially,] (j) The failure of a State to take into account its international legal obligations in the field of economic, social and cultural rights when entering into bilateral or multilateral agreements with other States, international organizations or multilateral corporation.[219]

This last instance of potential violations through omissions may be one of the greatest significance for IFIs, illustrating how the obligations of states under human rights treaties, and the Covenant in particular, may be of direct import to operations within IFIs, including development activities with partners in the private sector.[220]

The principles address acts by international organizations under '*III. Responsibility for violations*'. Guideline 19 provides:

> The obligations of States to protect economic, social and cultural rights extend also to their participation in international organizations, where they act collectively. It is particularly important for States to use their influence to ensure that violations do not result from the programmes and policies of the organizations of which they are members. It is crucial for the elimination of violations of economic, social and cultural rights for international organizations, including international financial institutions, to correct their policies and practices so that they do not result in deprivation of economic, social and cultural rights. Member States of such organizations, individually or through the governing bodies, as well as the secretariat and non-governmental organizations, should encourage and generalize the trend of several such organizations to revise their policies and programmes to take into account issues of economic, social and cultural rights, especially when these policies and programmes are implemented in countries that lack the resources to resist the pressure brought by international institutions on their decision-making affecting economic, social and cultural rights.[221]

---

219. *Maastricht Guidelines*, *supra* n. 174, para. 15.
220. *See, e.g.*, *Doe v. UNOCAL* where the litigation related to alleged corporate complicity in human rights abuses in Myanmar. The decision of the 9th Circuit overturned the District Court dismissal of the plaintiff's claim under the Alien Tort Claims Act and the Racketeer Influenced and Corrupt Organizations Act, as well as state law. The case was settled in 2005 with compensation to the plaintiffs for human rights abuses by the defendants. *Doe v. Unocal Corp.*, 395 F.3d 932 (9th Cir. 2002).
221. *Maastricht Guidelines*, *supra* n. 174, para. 19.

E. TILBURG GUIDING PRINCIPLES ON WORLD BANK, IMF, AND HUMAN RIGHTS

Following from the Limburg Principles and the Maastricht Guidelines, a set of principles emerged in 2002 targeting the World Bank and IMF.[222] These purported to:

> relate to human rights obligations for international financial institutions (like the World Bank and the International Monetary Fund), link these legal obligations in the field of human rights to the economic and political realities the organizations are confronted with, and discuss the possible redress of adverse human rights impacts of the activities of the financial institutions.[223]

Even these principles, which represent a most ambitious attempt to promote the direct human rights responsibility of IFIs, are unequivocal about state responsibility. '[T]he primary responsibilities and obligations in the field of domestic human rights enjoyment, however, remain with the State: States cannot "delegate" human rights obligations ....'[224] The remainder of the principle is somewhat incongruous, as the principles proclaim the international legal obligations of international institutions to take full responsibility for human rights respect in situations where the institutions' own projects, policies, or programmes negatively impact or undermine the enjoyment of rights. However, nowhere is the statement anchored in positive legal obligations, nor is any evidentiary link established to impute the specific negative impact to the actions of IFIs.[225]

The formulation of Guiding Principle 7 supports the general thesis of this chapter:

> The World Bank and the IMF are governed by their member States. When representatives of member States determine the policies of the two IFIs, they are bound by their States international obligations, including those arising from international human rights law. This includes an obligation on those States in a position to assist, to provide international assistance and co-operation.[226]

---

222. *See generally* Genugten, 'Tilburg Guiding Principles on World Bank, IMF and Human Rights', *supra* n. 139.
223. *Ibid.*, Abstract.
224. *Ibid.*, 5.
225. *Ibid.*, 5. Principle 5 states:

> The responsibility for implementing human rights is universal and concerns all – state and non-state – actors whose activities may affect people's lives. The primary responsibilities and obligations in the field of domestic human rights enjoyment, however, remain with the State: States cannot 'delegate' human rights obligations to, for instance, international institutions and relieve themselves of these obligations. As international legal persons, the World Bank and the IMF have international legal obligations to take full responsibility for human rights respect in situations where the institutions' own projects, policies or programmes negatively impact or undermine the enjoyment of human rights.

226. *Ibid.*, 7.

Principle 7 might therefore have been given greater prominence and benefited from a clearer link to the treaty obligations of states.

Principle 11 speaks directly to international policy coherence. It states:

> Practice often shows that one part of government does not necessarily know what another part is doing, even if both parts are working in the same field. One segment of the government might even be resistant to what another governmental agency is doing. Often, governments do not ensure that all relevant departments are familiar with international human rights norms that bear upon policy-making processes. This is a problem in all States in the world, albeit in varying degrees.[227]

In this, the principles effectively connect political reality with human rights obligations.

VI. THE POTENTIAL ROLE OF IFIs UNDER THE ICESCR

A. Introduction: No Obligation, But a Role?

Having established the distinct strands of the obligations of states under treaties through the example of the ICESCR, this discussion explores the potential role of IFIs. The link to states' obligations remains essential, but does not preclude, and may even support, their fulfilment through IFIs. The role of IFIs under the ICESCR is thus properly conceived as distinct but connected to[228] the obligations of states parties; the two are complementary and could be mutually reinforcing. General Comment No. 2 confirms the potential role of the specialized agencies, such as the World Bank and IMF, without any obligation under the Covenant. 'Despite the importance of seeking to integrate human rights concerns into development activities, it is true that proposals for such integration can too easily remain at the level of generality.'[229] The committee lists specific measures that could contribute to that integration, although most are directed to UN organs, rather than to the states that govern these which have direct obligations under the Covenant. More expansive proposals exist suggesting that IFIs should collect information on the legal commitments and compliance of their borrower states 'to ensure that they only fund projects, policies and stabilization and adjustment programs that promote compliance with validly assumed international obligations'.[230] In respect of the

227. *See generally* Genugten, 'Tilburg Guiding Principles on World Bank, IMF and Human Rights', *supra* n. 139. 11.

228. For an overview of this area, albeit conceiving of it in terms of 'binding effect of economic and social rights on the World Bank and the IMF', *see* Sia Spiliopoulou Akermark, 'International Development Financial Institutions: The World Bank and the International Monetary Fund', in *Economic, Social and Cultural Rights: A Textbook*, ed. Asbjørn Eide, Catarina Krause & Allen Rosas (Dordrecht: Martinus Njihoff, 2001), 515, 526–530.

229. General Comment No. 2, *supra* n. 31, para. 8.

230. Bradlow & Grossman, 'Limited Mandates and Intertwined Problems: A New Challenge for the World Bank and the IMF', *supra* n. 16, 439.

ICESCR, such a proposal could require that states parties – both borrowers and donors – ensure that development projects and programmes are consistent with their obligations under the Covenant.

B. IBRD Articles of Agreement

It is well known that neither the Articles of Agreement of the International Bank for Reconstruction and Development (IBRD) nor those of the International Development Association (IDA) make any provision for human rights. Until recently, their interpretation by successive General Counsel have limited any potential import of human rights to the Bank's core operations, policies and mandate, confining their relevance to a few carefully circumscribed instances.[231] The Bank's role vis-à-vis human rights was viewed as tangential or 'coincidental', through activities that overlap with human rights, or even more indirectly through promoting economic development. This interpretation relied on a view of the limited and specialized nature of the Bank's mandate[232] and the political prohibitions of the Bank's Articles of Agreement,[233] most particularly Article IV, section 10, which prohibits political activity.[234] This was supported by a formalistic interpretation of the term 'political' and a restrictive reading of the position of human rights within the international legal framework.[235] In this, it ran counter to current thinking on sovereignty and human rights:[236] 'today, it is widely recognized that human rights protection no longer belongs to matters which

231. Discussing the potential relevance of individual political rights, Ibrahim Shihata noted (i) participation of affected people and consultation with local communities and NGOs in EAs which depends on a reasonable measure of free expression and assembly; (ii) 'to the extent that direct and obvious economic effects of political events and factors can be taken into account by the Bank, an extensive violation of political rights which takes pervasive proportions could impose itself as an issue in the Bank's decision. This would be the case if the violation had significant economic effects, or if it led to the breach of international obligations relevant to the Bank, such as those created under binding decisions of the UN Security Council'. Ibrahim Shihata, 'Political Activity Prohibited', in *The World Bank Legal Papers*, ed. Ibrahim F.I. Shihata (The Hague: Martinus Nijhoff, 2000), 235.
232. *See, e.g.*, exchange between former General Counsel Ibrahim Shihata & Professor Günther Handl, 'Correspondence', *American Journal of International Law* 93 (1999): 625.
233. Kneller, *supra* n. 26, 361.
234. John D. Ciorciari, 'The Lawful Scope of Human Rights Criteria in World Bank Credit Decisions: An Interpretative Analysis of the IBRD and IDA Articles of Agreement', *Cornell International Law Journal* 33 (2000): 331.
235. Shihata, 'Political Activity Prohibited', *supra* n. 231, 233–236.
236. Another way in which the remit of relevant human rights considerations was curtailed was by reliance on the distinction between economic, social, and cultural rights on the one hand, and civil and political on the other, emphasizing the relevance of the former rather than the latter for the World Bank, and tacitly downplaying the interconnectedness and interdependence of each 'category' of rights and the inevitable political content of both. Shihata, 'Human Rights and International Financial Institutions', *supra* n. 65, 553–554.

according to Article 2(7) "are essentially within the domestic jurisdiction of any State" '.[237]

More recent writings evidence greater flexibility in approach, which could support the definition of a supportive role for the World Bank relative to the ICESCR, based on the obligations of states. 'While the World Bank is not an enforcer of human rights, it may play a facilitative role in helping its members realize their human rights obligations.'[238] There is an emerging recognition of human rights as the subject of binding legal obligations, specifically acknowledging a role for the Bank. In 2006, then-General Counsel Roberto Dañino, wrote:

> The Bank has fulfilled and will continue to fulfill an important role in assisting its Members to progressively realize their human rights commitments . . . Our role is a collaborative one in the implementation of our member countries' human rights obligations. It is also a complementary one to that of our UN partners entrusted with the job of respecting, protecting, promoting and fulfilling human rights globally.[239]

The next General Counsel, Ana Palacio, concurred on the importance of human rights treaties:

> in certain cases and under certain circumstances, human rights generate actionable legal obligations. Such obligations arise from international treaties, or from rights enshrined in national laws. Here the World Banks' role is to support its Members to fulfill those obligations where they relate to Bank projects and policies.[240]

In a similar spirit, she confirmed, '[t]he World Bank's role is a facilitative one, in helping our members realize their human rights obligations, [. . .] in areas that fall within its mandate, and where development activities and human rights are interrelated'.[241]

These views of the Bank's Articles of Agreement endorse an auxiliary role with respect to human rights obligations under treaties such as the ICESCR.[242] Such a role would therefore be supportive of members who are parties to such treaties, including in their actions within the Bank; it could also involve cooperation with bodies charged directly with monitoring the implementation of human

---

237. Reidel, *supra* n. 110, 923 (quoting Brownlie, *Principles of Public International Law*, 5th edn, *supra* n. 111, 574.
238. World Bank, Human Rights, Frequently Asked Questions, <http://web.worldbank.org/WBSITE/EXTERNAL/EXTSITETOOLS/0,,contentMDK:20749693~pagePK:98400~piPK:98424~theSitePK:95474,00.html#3>.
239. Dañino, 'The Legal Aspects of the World Bank's Work on Human Rights: Some Preliminary Thoughts', *supra* n. 73, 30, 32.
240. Palacio, *supra* n. 77, 36.
241. *Ibid.*
242. Dañino, 'The Legal Aspects of the World Bank's Work on Human Rights: Some Preliminary Thoughts', *supra* n. 73, 32; Palacio, *supra* n. 77, 37.

rights obligations, but would preclude any supervisory, enforcement or compliance role for the Bank. The Bank's Articles of Agreement provide for cooperation, anticipating a constructive relationship between the Bank and other international organizations.[243] 'From an external perspective, this approach requires us to strengthen collaboration with our partners in the broader UN family and with other international actors who have a comparative advantage in this area.'[244]

C. 1947 Agreement between the IBRD and United Nations

While more often cited in support of the World Bank's institutional independence from the United Nations, the terms of the 1947 Agreement between the United Nations and the International Bank for Reconstruction and Development[245] are permissive, if not supportive, of potential cooperation between the Bank and other international actors, providing explicitly for reciprocal representation.[246] Under Article IV, the Bank and United Nations are required to 'consult together and exchange views on matters of mutual interest'.[247] Article IV, section 2 requires that 'any formal recommendations by either organization be considered as soon as possible by the appropriate organ of the other'.[248] Under Article VI:

> The Bank takes note of the obligation assumed under Paragraph 2 of Article 48 of the United Nations Charter, by such of its members as are also Members of the UN, to carry out the decisions of the Security Council through their action in the appropriate specialized agencies of which they are members, and will, in the conduct of its activities, have due regard for decisions of the Security Council under Articles 41 and 42.[249]

243. IBRD Articles of Agreement, *supra* n. 71, Art. V(8). Art. V, s. 8. 'Relationship to Other International Organizations' states:

    (a) The Bank, within the terms of this Agreement, shall cooperate with any general international organization and with public international organizations having specialized responsibilities in related fields. Any arrangements for such cooperation which would involve a modification of any provision of this Agreement may be effected only after amendment to this Agreement under Article VIII.

    (b) In making decisions on applications for loans or guarantees relating to matters directly within the competence of any international organization of the types specified in the preceding paragraph and participated in primarily by members of the Bank, the Bank shall give consideration to the views and recommendations of such organization.

244. Palacio, *supra* n. 77, 37.
245. Agreement between the United Nations and the International Bank for Reconstruction and Development, 16 U.N.T.S. 346 (1947) (entered into force on 15 Nov. 1947).
246. *Ibid.*, Art. II(1). Other matters provided for under the Agreement include: the proposal of agenda items (Art. III) and the exchange of information (Art. V).
247. *Ibid.*, Art. IV.
248. *Ibid.*, Art. IV(2).
249. *Ibid.*, Art. VI.

Thus, while the Agreement confirms the potentially broad scope for cooperation, the extent of the Bank's direct obligations is confined to 'paying due regard'.[250]

D. Role of Specialized Agencies under the ICESCR

There is likewise scope for a potential role for IFIs in implementing the rights under the ICESCR.[251] This section does not make a prescriptive argument that IFIs such as the World Bank should adopt such a role, but rather points to the legal frameworks that indicate that they could without displacing the primary legal obligations of states in this context.

The ICESCR makes provision for the role of specialized agencies of the United Nations, which includes the World Bank. Article 22 provides:

> The Economic and Social Council may bring to the attention of other organs of the United Nations, their subsidiary organs and specialized agencies concerned with furnishing technical assistance any matters arising out of the reports referred to in this part of the present Covenant which may assist such bodies in deciding, each within its field of competence, on the advisability of international measures likely to contribute to the effective progressive implementation of the present Covenant.[252]

This provision is enabling only and does not mandate or prescribe a role for IFIs, much less establish obligations for them. It empowers, but does not oblige, specialized agencies to take action in the implementation of obligations under the Covenant, and other provisions affirm the independence of the specialized agencies and the separateness of their responsibilities.[253] In describing the limited involvement of specialized agencies in the inter-agency consultation in 1976, Matthew Craven observed, '[a]lthough the provisions of the Covenant certainly do not limit the participation to these specialized agencies, there is no correlative power of the Committee to demand cooperation'.[254]

---

250. In support of the arguments in the previous section, one may ask whether, apart from the potential relevance of the direct responsibilities of the Bank in the last part of this provision, the obligation on members may provide a precedent and example to argue for analogies of the obligations on states that are parties to the ICESCR.
251. For arguments for and against such a role generally, Moris, *supra* n. 30, 173–200.
252. ICESCR, *supra* n. 187, Art. 22.
253. *Ibid.*, Art. 24 (stating: 'Nothing in the present Covenant shall be interpreted as impairing the provisions of the Charter of the United Nations and of the constitutions of the specialized agencies which define the respective responsibilities of the various organs of the United Nations and of the specialized agencies in regard to the matters dealt with in the present Covenant.').
254. Craven, *The International Covenant on Economic, Social, and Cultural Rights: A Perspective on Its Development*, *supra* n. 201, 78. It is pertinent to the present discussion that the formulation cites these international organizations as examples of the cooperation, not as repositories for direct obligations under the Covenant.

There is nevertheless unexplored potential in the constructive role that IFIs may play in relation to the implementation of the Covenant, though it remains contingent on the recognition by states of their obligations both within and outside IFIs. Craven also pointed out that:

> The Covenant makes specific reference to the possibility of the specialized agencies reporting to ECOSOC in the supervisory process. Indeed, that all but two articles of Part IV of the Covenant refer in some manner to the specialized agencies, emphasizes the important role envisaged for them during the drafting of the Covenant.[255]

Despite the obvious textual support for the participation of specialized agencies in the consideration of state reports,[256] it was certain states' deliberate efforts to minimize that role and limit the interaction between specialized agencies and the working group[257] that resulted in a subsequent narrowing of that role.[258] This is compounded by questions surrounding the entitlement of specialized agencies to comment specifically upon the reports of states parties.[259]

The interest in obtaining IFIs' input in the committee's work is well-documented.[260] The committee has requested the World Bank to provide it with country-specific information relating to the implementation of economic, social, and cultural rights, particularly in relation to statistical indicators in the committee's supervisory functions.[261] Noting the importance of economic, social, and

---

255. *Ibid.*, 76.
256. *See also* ECOSCO Resolution, 1988 (LX) (11 May 1976), in UN Doc. E/C.12/1989/4 (1988) (it expressly authorizes representatives of the agencies to take part in the proceedings of the Working Group).
257. The working group referred to here is the institutional predecessor to the current committee on Economic Social and Cultural Rights. *See* Craven, *The International Covenant on Economic, Social, and Cultural Rights: A Perspective on Its Development*, *supra* n. 201, 35–42.
258. *Ibid.*, 76.
259. *Ibid.*, 77 (citing B.G. Ramcharan, 'Implementing the International Covenants on Human Rights', in *Human Rights: Thirty Years After the Universal Declaration*, ed. B.G. Ramcharan (The Hague: M. Nijhoff, 1978), 159).
260. For a brief but incisive discussion of this need and of the absence of a breakthrough in the Committee using the relevant information of the specialized agencies and 'the need for both the Committee and specialized agencies to attach to the human rights monitoring process the importance it clearly warrants', *see* Philip Alston, 'The Economic Rights Committee', in *The United Nations and Human Rights: A Critical Appraisal*, ed. Philip Alston (Oxford: Clarendon Press, 1992), 500.
261. *See* Craven, *The International Covenant on Economic, Social, and Cultural Rights: A Perspective on Its Development*, *supra* n. 201, 78. *See also* General Comment No. 2 on Art. 22: 'Recommendations in accordance with article 22 may be made to any "organs of the United Nations, their subsidiary organs and specialized agencies concerned with furnishing technical assistance." The Committee considers that this provision should be interpreted so as to include virtually all United Nations organs and agencies involved in any aspect of international development cooperation.' General Comment No. 2, *supra* n. 31, para. 2. The list of enumerated organs and agencies to which such recommendations could be addressed includes the World Bank and IMF.

cultural rights in the work of the IFIs,[262] the committee has also noted that 'its own endeavors would be assisted and the relevant agencies would also be better informed, if they were to take greater interest in the work of the Committee'.[263]

Despite the potential for such coordination to address aspects of the HRA deficit in development, there are ways in which it might, from the Bank's perspective, test the boundaries of permissible political activity. Logistical questions also arise about the practical terms of such collaboration, how costly it might be, and how responsibilities between the agencies might be apportioned.

An excellent analysis has been made on the potential for such cooperation on 'supervision'[264] with respect to the right to food.[265] The approach charts the synergies between the Bank's position on world food problems and the right to food, arguing for greater cooperation between the Bank and the Committee on Economic, Social and Cultural Rights. The operative obligations remain those of states, whether under the Charter as members of the UN or under the ICESCR as states parties. It characterizes the Bank's role as one of positive support not enforcement and notes:

> [T]he previous position of the World Bank vis-à-vis human rights was taken in response to pressures on the World Bank to withhold loans from certain countries because of human rights violations. The present situation is quite the contrary: now the World Bank is being asked to engage in certain activities in order to further the implementation of human rights, *in casu*, the right to food.[266]

VII. CONCLUSIONS

Human rights are relevant to development. This is a statement of fact, but also of law. While a great deal has been written charting the relationship of human rights and development, the critical dimension of obligations has been neglected. This has resulted in the mischaracterization of development practice as 'human rights', and the transposition of human rights principles either incompletely or inaccurately. Human rights obligations warrant greater attention precisely because the accountability they bring defines their 'value-added' for development.

262. Report of the Committee's Fourth Session, UN Doc. E/1990/23, Annex III. UN ESCOR Supp. (no. 3) (1990).
263. General Comment No. 2, *supra* n. 31, para. 4.
264. Although the term 'supervision' may be somewhat misleading because the role is conceived more as a facilitative function in regard to the 'already existing rules of international law relating to the right to food'.
265. Van Hoof & Tahzib, 'Supervision with respect to the Right to Food and the Role of the World Bank', *supra* n. 19, 317.
266. *Ibid.*, 334.

This chapter has offered some perspectives on the nature and locus of human rights obligations in development, arguing that the eagerness to assign direct obligations to IFIs, particularly from non-treaty sources, has set the debate back because of the limitations attending those sources, deflecting attention from the relevant established obligations of states under human rights treaties. The example of the ICESCR illustrates the positive potential of treaty obligations to address HRA in development, both directly (through how states act in IFIs) and indirectly (through the supportive roles that IFIs may play in supporting the fulfilment of states' obligations).

It is hoped that this contribution has elucidated the potential in the existing treaty frameworks and the positive obligations of states, to encourage state actors within and outside IFIs to fulfil their obligations under international human rights law in order to uphold HRA in development.

Chapter 9

Indigenous Peoples and International Financial Institutions

Fergus MacKay

We have learnt that in order . . . to enable indigenous peoples to pursue their own self-determined development, we must first actively listen to them. We need to listen to what poverty means for indigenous peoples, how it affects their well-being – or indeed their ill-being. We know that poverty is more than low income. It is about historical processes of dispossession and discrimination. It is about lack of respect for indigenous peoples' political, cultural and economic rights. It is about decisions on territories and on the use and misuse of natural resources being imposed, without the participation of those whose livelihoods are at stake, and without their *free, prior and informed consent*.

If we collectively fail to listen to what indigenous peoples can tell us about poverty and about their solutions to overcome it, as primary stakeholders of development initiatives in their territories, then any action we take will be meaningless, or possibly even counterproductive.[1]

1. Gunilla Olsson, 'Statement of the International Fund for Agricultural Development, IFAD', statement presented on behalf of the IFAD President at the 7th Session of the UN Permanent Forum on Indigenous Issues (New York, 21 Apr. 2008), 2–3 (emphasis in the original), *available at* <www.ifad.org/english/indigenous/pub/statement_gunilla.pdf>.

Daniel D. Bradlow and David B. Hunter, *International Financial Institutions and International Law*, pp. 287–320.

I. INTRODUCTION

The statement above was made in April 2008 on behalf of the International Fund for Agricultural Development (IFAD) not, unfortunately, on behalf of all international financial institutions (IFIs). Indeed, with few exceptions, indigenous peoples maintain that the IFIs have persistently failed to listen to and, more importantly, respect their perspectives, and they have registered serious complaints about how IFI activities affect their rights and well-being. It is no coincidence that the World Bank Group's (WBG) first formal policy on indigenous peoples – the 1982 *Operational Manual Statement 2.34 Tribal People in Bank-Financed Projects* (OMS 2.34) – was adopted in response to 'internal and external condemnation of the disastrous experiences of indigenous groups in Bank-financed projects in the Amazon region'.[2] These experiences are not confined to the past as abuses have been identified in recent WBG performance evaluations[3] and in reports by non-governmental organizations (NGOs) and UN human rights bodies.[4] WBG studies also have recognized that indigenous peoples 'have often been on the losing end of the development process'.[5]

OMS 2.34 was preceded by a study entitled *Economic Development and Tribal Peoples: Human Ecologic Considerations*, which sought to provide guidelines for WBG operations.[6] The study argued that the WBG should avoid 'unnecessary or avoidable encroachment onto territories used or occupied by tribal groups'; rule out involvement with projects not agreed to by tribal peoples; require guarantees from borrowers that they would implement safeguard measures; and

---

2. Benedict Kingsbury, 'Operational Policies of International Institutions as Part of the Law-Making Process: The World Bank and Indigenous Peoples', in *The Reality of International Law: Essays in Honour of Ian Brownlie*, ed. Guy S. Goodwin-Gill & Stefan Talmon (Oxford: Clarendon Press, 1999), 324.
3. *See, e.g.*, 'Implementation of Operational Directive 4.20 on Indigenous Peoples: An Evaluation of Results', OED Report No. 25754 (Washington, DC: World Bank, 10 Apr. 2003); 'Implementation of Operational Directive 4.20 on Indigenous Peoples: An Independent Desk Review', Country Evaluation and Regional Relations (OEDCR), OED Report No. 25332 (Washington, DC: World Bank, 10 Jan. 2003).
4. *See, e.g.*, 'Report of the Special Rapporteur on the situation of human rights and fundamental freedoms of indigenous people, Mr. Rodolfo Stavenhagen, submitted pursuant to Commission resolution 2001/57', UN Doc. E/CN.4/2002/97 (2002), para. 56 (observing that '... resources are being extracted and/or developed by other interests (oil, mining, logging, fisheries, etc.) with little or no benefits for the indigenous communities that occupy the land. Whereas the World Bank has developed operational directives concerning its own activities in relation to these issues ... and some national legislation specifically protects the interests of indigenous communities in this respect, in numerous instances the rights and needs of indigenous peoples are disregarded, making this one of the major human rights problems faced by them in recent decades'). *See also* Korinna Horta, 'Rhetoric and Reality: Human Rights and the World Bank', *Harvard Human Rights Journal* 15 (2002): 227.
5. *The World Bank Participation Source Book* (Washington, DC: World Bank, 1996), 251.
6. Robert Goodland, *Economic Development and Tribal Peoples: Human Ecologic Considerations* (Washington, DC: World Bank, 1982).

advocate respect for indigenous peoples' right to self-determination.[7] Although OMS 2.34 did not incorporate these recommendations, this study is noteworthy because, as discussed below, its key recommendations presciently track the main demands indigenous peoples make today. Sustained criticism of WBG projects by indigenous peoples, NGOs, and others[8] led to the replacement of OMS 2.34 by the 1991 Operational Directive 4.20 on Indigenous Peoples (OD 4.20).[9] However, criticism continued, particularly in relation to inconsistent compliance with the policy,[10] and OD 4.20 was revised and replaced in May 2005 by Operational Directive 4.10 on Indigenous Peoples (OP 4.10).[11]

OD 4.20 and OP 4.10 both failed to incorporate the key recommendations of the 1982 *Economic Development and Tribal Peoples* study. Further, indigenous peoples have largely rejected both policies because they are incompatible with their rights and, therefore, ineffective as safeguards. This view is supported, at least with respect to OD 4.20, by an internal WBG evaluation, which found that only 38% of a sample of WBG projects that satisfactorily applied that policy actually mitigated adverse impacts and ensured benefits for indigenous peoples.[12] OP 4.10 is currently undergoing its first review, which is scheduled to be completed by the end of 2010.

The adoption of OP 4.10 in 2005 marked the beginning of a wholesale re-evaluation and revision by the IFIs of their 'safeguard' policy instruments pertaining to indigenous peoples, a process that is still ongoing. The International Finance Corporation (IFC), the private sector arm of the WBG, and the Inter-American Development Bank (IDB) adopted new policies in 2006; and the European Bank for Reconstruction and Development (EBRD) did so in May 2008. The Asian Development Bank (ADB) commenced its policy revision in 2006 and concluded in 2009. Additionally, the UN Food and Agriculture Organisation (FAO), IFAD, the UN Development Programme (UNDP), the UN Development Group, the European Commission, and a series of bilateral donors have all either adopted

7. *Ibid.*, 3, 27.
8. *See generally* Andrew Gray, 'Development Policy, Development Protest: The World Bank, Indigenous Peoples and NGOs', in *The Struggle for Accountability: The World Bank, NGOs, and Grassroots Movements*, ed. Jonathan A. Fox & L. David Brown (Cambridge, MA: MIT Press, 1998), 267 (describing the Bank projects and policies affecting indigenous peoples and criticism thereof).
9. *See* Shelton Davis, 'The World Bank and Operational Directive 4.20: The World Bank and Indigenous People', in *Indigenous Peoples and International Organisations*, ed. Lydia van de Fliert (Nottingham, UK: Spokesman, 1994), 75 (discussing the revision process and the contours of the new policy, OD 4.20).
10. *See* Thomas Griffiths & Marcus Colchester, 'Report on a Workshop on "Indigenous Peoples, Forests and the World Bank: Policies and Practice" ' (Washington, DC, 2000), 9–10, *available at* <www.wrm.org.uy/actors/WB/IPreport.html> (noting substantial failures to comply with the policy).
11. *See* Fergus MacKay, 'The Draft World Bank Operational Policy 4.10 on Indigenous Peoples: Progress or More of the Same?', *Arizona Journal of International & Comparative Law* 22, no. 1 (2005): 65 (discussing the draft policy and its revision process).
12. 'Implementation of Operational Directive 4.20 on Indigenous Peoples: An Evaluation of Results', *supra* n. 3.

new policies on indigenous peoples during this period or are in the process of doing so. The African Development Bank (AfDB) is conspicuously absent, having never adopted a policy on indigenous peoples despite the recognition by human rights bodies[13] and by other IFIs[14] that such peoples exist in Africa.

Indigenous peoples have proactively sought to influence IFI operational policies, and by extension the conduct of IFI projects, while also being acutely aware that these policies do not extend to structural adjustment programmes and most technical assistance projects. The latter, particularly where focused on liberalizing the extractive industries sector,[15] have had profound and mostly negative impacts on indigenous peoples.[16] Indigenous representatives explain that in many cases they continue to experience severe negative impacts and human rights abuses in relation to IFI projects and, therefore, a strong and effective safeguard regime grounded in, and consistent with, international human rights law is needed.

Indigenous peoples' engagement with the IFIs is based on a consistent set of demands that draws primarily on human rights standards. Their main demands are that IFI policies guarantee the right to free, prior, and informed consent (FPIC), that they respect indigenous peoples' right to own and control their traditional territories, that they prohibit involuntary resettlement, and that they respect indigenous peoples' right to self-determination.[17] The United Nations Permanent Forum on

13. *See* African Commission on Human and People's Rights (ACHPR) & IWIGIA, 'Report of the African Commission's Working Group of Experts on Indigenous Populations/Communities' (Copenhagen: ACHPR 28th Session, 2005) (note it was submitted in accordance with 'Resolution on the Rights of Indigenous Populations/Communities in Africa').
14. *See* Inspection Panel, 'Investigation Report, Democratic Republic of Congo, Transitional Support for Economic Recovery Grant (TSERO) (IDA Grant No. H 1920-DRC) and Emergency Economic and Social Reunification Support Project (EESRSP) (Credit No. 3824-DRC and Grant No. H 064-DRC)' (31 Aug. 2007), *available at* <http://siteresources.worldbank.org/EXTINSPECTIONPANEL/Resources/FINALINVREPwhole.pdf> (finding violations of OP 4.10 in Bank-financed project).
15. Between 1990 and 2003, for instance, the WBG funded and otherwise supported revision of mineral, hydrocarbon, and other related laws in over one hundred countries. *See* 'Striking a Better Balance-The World Bank Group and Extractive Industries: The Final Report of the Extractive Industries Review', vol. I (December 2003), 8. For a detailed overview of WBG structural and sectoral lending related to extractive industries, *see* Heike Mainhardt-Gibbs, *The World Bank Extractive Industries Review: The Role of Structural Reform Programs towards Sustainable Development Outcomes* (November 2003), *available at* <www.panda.org/who_we_are/wwf_offices/tanzania/news/?10082/The-World-Bank-Extractive-Industries-Review-The-Role-of-Structural-Reform-Programs-towards-Sustainable-Development-Outcomes>.
16. *See* Fergus MacKay, 'Making Molehills out of Mountains: Indigenous Peoples, the World Bank Group and the Extractive Industries Review', *Balayi: Culture, Law and Colonialism Journal, Special Issue: International Trade Law and Indigenous Peoples* 8 (2006): 31.
17. *See* 'World Bank Round Table Discussion of Indigenous Representatives and the World Bank on the Revision of the World Bank's Indigenous Peoples Policy: Summary Report', report of the meeting held at World Bank Headquarters (Washington, DC, 17–18 Oct. 2002), *available at* <www.forestpeoples.org/documents/ifi_igo/wb_ip_round_table_summary_oct_02_eng.pdf>. *See also* 'Statement by Indigenous Peoples Participating in the 19th Session of the UN Working Group on Indigenous Populations, about concerns regarding the revision of the World Bank's

Indigenous Issues (PFII), the body responsible for overall coordination of UN system activities relating to indigenous peoples, has echoed these demands, recommending in 2003 that the IFIs:

> Continue to address issues currently outstanding, including Bank implementation of international customary laws and standards, in particular human rights instruments, full recognition of customary land and resource rights of indigenous peoples, recognition of the right of free, prior informed consent of indigenous peoples regarding development projects that affect them, and prohibition of the involuntary resettlement of indigenous peoples.[18]

These issues were again discussed by the PFII at its 2006 session under the theme of 'Redefining the Millennium Development Goals'. In her background paper, the Chair of the PFII explains that a rights-based approach to the Millennium Development Goals (MDGs) is essential, and that for indigenous peoples it is difficult to talk about development without also addressing rights to lands and resources, identity and culture, and self-determination.[19] She further highlights the importance of moving beyond mitigation measures to concerted support for indigenous peoples' own development choices if pursuit of the MDGs is to benefit, rather than prejudice, indigenous peoples.[20] These same conclusions were also emphasized in two recent UN expert meetings, the first on the MDGs, Indigenous Participation and Good Governance,[21] and the second on Indigenous Peoples and Indicators of Well-Being.[22]

In addition to highlighting rights issues, indigenous peoples also point to the IFIs' internal evaluations that demonstrate that IFIs repeatedly fail to adhere to their policy prescriptions. A 1987 internal WBG implementation review of OMS 2.34, for example, found that only two out of thirty-three WBG projects

---

Indigenous Peoples Policy' (July 2001), *available at* <www.forestpeoples.org/documents/ifi_igo/wb_4_10_ip_statemnt_jul01_eng.shtml> (criticizing that draft OP 4.10 'fails to incorporate many of the key recommendations made by indigenous peoples during previous consultations on the Bank's "approach paper" on the revision process; uses language that confuses consultation with effective participation; lacks binding provisions that seek to guarantee indigenous land and resource security; fails to recognize the right to free, informed prior consent; does not prohibit the involuntary resettlement of indigenous peoples; is not consistent with existing and emerging international standards on human rights and sustainable development; [and] does not advance international standards for dealing with indigenous peoples in development').

18. 'Report of the Permanent Forum on Indigenous Issues on its Second Session'. UN Doc. E/2003/43; E/C.19/2003/22 (12–23 May 2003), para. 33.
19. Victoria Tauli-Corpuz, 'Indigenous Peoples and the Millennium Development Goals', submitted to the 4th Session of the UN Permanent Forum on Indigenous Issues (New York, 16–27 May 2005), 1.
20. *Ibid.*
21. 'Report of the International Expert Meeting on the Millennium Development Goals, Indigenous Participation and Good Governance', UN Doc. E/C.19/2006/7 (16 Mar. 2006).
22. 'Report of the Meeting on Indigenous Peoples and Indicators of Well-Being', UN Doc. E/C.19/2006/CRP.3 (20 Apr. 2006).

substantially complied with the policy.[23] Similarly, a 2003 review of OD 4.20, found that it was only fully or partially applied in 50% of projects affecting indigenous peoples, and of those, only 14% had the required 'Indigenous Peoples Development Plan'.[24] For this reason, indigenous peoples' representatives argue that compliance, enforcement, and grievance mechanisms must be built into policies and incorporated into project instruments and loan agreements if safeguards are to be meaningful and effective. In this vein, the World Bank's Extractive Industries Review recommended (without result) that there be tri-partite (IFI-government-indigenous peoples) covenants included in loan agreements so that indigenous peoples will have standing to challenge violations of their rights directly with the WBG and the relevant government.[25]

When talking about rights in relation to the IFIs today, indigenous peoples often refer to the United Nations Declaration on the Rights of Indigenous Peoples (UNDRIP), adopted by the UN General Assembly in September 2007.[26] The UNDRIP sets out in forty-six articles the views of the vast majority of the international community with regard to the rights of indigenous peoples, rights that are declared to be 'the minimum standards for the survival, dignity and well-being of the indigenous peoples of the world'.[27] It affirms that indigenous peoples hold the right to self-determination – and hence the right to freely pursue their own economic, social, and cultural development – and elaborates on components of that right such as the right to own and control traditional lands, territories, and resources, and the right to participate in and consent to decision-making that may affect them. This right to consent extends to the adoption of legislative or

23. Office of Environmental and Scientific Affairs, World Bank, *Tribal Peoples and Economic Development: A Five Year Implementation Review of OMS 2.34 (1982–1986) and a Tribal Peoples' Action Plan* (Washington, DC: World Bank, 1987).
24. 'Implementation of Operational Directive 4.20 on Indigenous Peoples: An independent desk review', *supra* n. 3. This study also found that participation by indigenous peoples in decision-making in WBG projects affecting them was 'low' and that just 20% of projects had included clear benchmarks to measure impacts on indigenous communities. For a discussion of institutional constraints in relation to safeguard policy compliance, *see* Natalie Bridgeman, 'World Bank Reform in the "Post Policy" Era', *Georgetown International Environmental Law Review* 13 (2001): 1013.
25. 'Striking a Better Balance – The World Bank Group and Extractive Industries: The Final Report of the Extractive Industries Review', *supra* n. 15, 50 (stating that it is 'necessary to include covenants in project agreements that provide for multiparty negotiated and enforceable agreements that govern various project activities, should indigenous peoples and local communities consent to the project').
26. 'United Nations Declaration on the Rights of Indigenous Peoples', UN G.A. Res. 61/295 (13 Sep. 2007), *available at* <www.ohchr.org/english/issues/indigenous/declaration.htm> and <www.un.org/esa/socdev/unpfii/en/drip.html> (hereinafter UNDRIP). The UNDRIP was approved by a vote of 147 to 4 with 11 abstentions. The four countries who voted against it were Australia, Canada, New Zealand, and the United States of America. Australia and New Zealand have since reversed their positions.
27. *Ibid.*, Art. 43.

administrative measures that may affect indigenous peoples as well as to activities defined as development initiatives by the state.[28]

While it is technically a non-binding statement of principle, the UNDRIP, in many respects, restates existing international law norms pertaining to indigenous peoples' rights, both as set forth in international human rights instruments and associated jurisprudence, and in customary international law.[29] The UN Committee on the Elimination of Racial Discrimination (CERD), for instance, holds that states should use the UNDRIP 'as a guide to interpret [their] obligations under the Convention [on the Elimination of All Forms of Racial Discrimination] relating to indigenous peoples'.[30]

Articles 41 and 42 of the UNDRIP directly address UN bodies and specialized agencies, and intergovernmental organizations more generally, which is understood to include the IFIs. Article 41 calls on these entities to contribute to the 'full realization of the provisions of this Declaration through the mobilization, inter alia, of financial cooperation and technical assistance'; and to establish '[w]ays and means of ensuring participation of indigenous peoples on issues affecting them ... '.[31] Article 42 adds that these entities, 'including the Permanent Forum on Indigenous Issues ... shall promote respect for and full application of the provisions of this Declaration and follow up the effectiveness of this Declaration'.[32]

The PFII, which has an oversight and coordination mandate in relation to UN agencies including some of the IFIs,[33] comprehends Article 42 to entail an extension of its mandate in relation to the UNDRIP.[34] An important 2008 PFII report proposes that the PFII establish a standing committee to promote and oversee the

28. *Ibid.*, Arts 19, 32(2).
29. *See* S. James Anaya & Siegfried Weissner, 'The UN Declaration on the Rights of Indigenous Peoples: Toward Empowerment', *Jurist: Legal News and Research* (3 Oct. 2007), *available at* <http://jurist.law.pitt.edu/forumy/2007/10/un-declaration-on-rights-of-indigenous.php> (explaining that the UNDRIP in large part restates existing customary international law). *See also* Siegfried Wiessner, 'The Rights and Status of Indigenous Peoples: A Global Comparative and International Legal Analysis', *Harvard Human Rights Journal* 12 (1999): 57 (noting the development and crystallization of customary norms protecting indigenous peoples' rights).
30. 'Concluding Observations of the Committee on the Elimination of Racial Discrimination: United States, 02/2008'. UN Doc. CERD/C/USA/CO/6 (February 2008), para. 29 (advanced unedited version).
31. UNDRIP, *supra* n. 26, Art. 41.
32. *Ibid.*, Art. 42.
33. The PFII is an advisory body to the Economic and Social Council, with six mandated areas: economic and social development; culture; environment; education; health; and human rights. According to its mandate, the PFII will, among others: 'Provide expert advice and recommendations on indigenous issues to the Economic and Social Council and to programmes, funds and agencies of the United Nations, through the Economic and Social Council; [and] Raise awareness and promote the integration and coordination of activities related to indigenous issues within the United Nations system.' UNPFII, About Us/Mandate, <www.un.org/esa/socdev/unpfii/en/about_us.html>.
34. Members of the Permanent Forum on Indigenous Issues, 'Structures, procedures and mechanisms that currently exist or that might be established to effectively address the human rights situation of indigenous peoples', UN Doc. E/C.19/2008/2 (19 Dec. 2007), para. 35 (explaining

implementation of the UNDRIP.[35] As the majority of the IFIs report annually to the PFII, and some are even members of the PFII's Inter-Agency Support Group, it can be expected that these bodies will also be questioned in the future about their efforts to apply and ensure the effectiveness of the standards set forth in the UNDRIP.[36] Further, IFI responsibilities in relation to the UNDRIP also may come to the attention of the Human Rights Council's Expert Mechanism on the Rights of Indigenous Peoples.[37]

From 14 to 17 March 2008, a workshop was held with indigenous peoples, UN bodies, and some IFIs to discuss how the latter could promote the UNDRIP in their policies, programmatic activities, and projects, or otherwise.[38] Many responded positively to the need to ensure that UNDRIP is a key reference point or more, and some indicated that they have already taken steps towards this end. IFAD, for instance, states that its forthcoming policy on indigenous peoples will be based on the UNDRIP.[39] The World Bank's representative explained that its legal department had conducted a review of OP 4.10 in relation to UNDRIP and concluded that its policy is inconsistent on only two points:[40] rights to lands, territories, and resources, and the right to consent.[41] However, this is a highly debatable conclusion, if only on the basis of the inter-dependent nature of all human rights.[42]

---

that UNDRIP Art. 42 'constitutes a new function for the Forum under its overall human rights mandate').

35. *Ibid.*, paras 37–39.
36. IFI members of the IASG include: the World Bank Group, the Inter-American Development Bank, and IFAD.
37. *See* Human Rights Council, 'Expert Mechanism on the Rights of Indigenous Peoples', Res. 6/36 (14 Dec. 2007). The mandate of this body is 'to provide the Council with thematic expertise on the rights of indigenous peoples in the manner and form requested by the Council'. This will be done mainly in the form of studies and research-based advice.
38. *See* 'Consultation Workshop and Dialogue on Indigenous Peoples' Self-determined Development or Development with Identity, Tivoli, Italy, 14–17 March 2008', UN Doc. E/C.19/2008/CRP.11 (18 Apr. 2008) (adopted by the Permanent Forum on Indigenous Issues, 7th session, 21 Apr.–2 May 2008).
39. Olsson, 'Statement of the International Fund for Agricultural Development, IFAD', *supra* n. 1.
40. *See also* General Counsel, World Bank, 'Legal Note on Indigenous Peoples' (8 Apr. 2005), para. 30 (submitted to the board of executive directors in connection with its consideration of the Indigenous Peoples Policy on 10 May 2005 and concluding that draft OP 4.10 'is consistent with the emerging international principles and practices'), *available at*, <http://siteresources.worldbank.org/INTINDPEOPLE/Publications/20571167/Legal%20Note.pdf>.
41. 'Consultation Workshop and Dialogue on Indigenous Peoples' Self-determined Development or Development with Identity, Tivoli, Italy, 14–17 March 2008', *supra* n. 38, para. 99.
42. In her December 2001 Presidential Fellow's Lecture at the World Bank, former UN High Commissioner for Human Rights Mary Robinson explains this inter-dependency argument. She states that 'economic improvements cannot be envisaged without protection of land and resource rights. Rights over land need to include recognition of the spiritual relation indigenous peoples have with their ancestral territories. And the economic base that land provides needs to be accompanied by a recognition of indigenous peoples' own political and legal institutions, cultural traditions and social organizations. Land and culture, development, spiritual values and knowledge are as one. To fail to recognize one is to fail on all'. Mary Robinson, 'Bridging the Gap between Human Rights and Development: From Normative Principles to Operational

With this background in mind, the remainder of this chapter focuses on whether IFI policies on indigenous peoples incorporate human rights norms, explicitly or implicitly. This question can be answered either by locating provisions in these policies that explicitly refer to or directly incorporate human rights norms, or through a comparative analysis of the various provisions in relation to human rights norms when there is no explicit reference or incorporation. Thus, section II looks at the extent to which the new IFI policies explicitly acknowledge the applicability or relevance of 'human rights' or specific rights norms to the conduct of their activities as they relate to indigenous peoples. It concludes that although some IFI policies incorporate explicit references to human rights or specific human rights norms, the effect, with two important exceptions, is little more than oratory.[43]

Section III analyses the extent to which the various policy instruments incorporate and guarantee indigenous peoples' right to give or withhold FPIC. FPIC is important because it lies at the heart of indigenous peoples' demands, relating as it does to the exercise and enjoyment of the right to self-determination, particularly territorial rights and freedom from involuntary resettlement.[44] Generally speaking, this analysis reveals that while the content of some human rights norms is reflected to varying degrees in the IFI policies, these policies nevertheless fall short in some important respects, namely in the absence of clear affirmations of FPIC in all but one instance. Also, deficiencies are especially apparent when one considers rights to effective remedies for violations of the policies or harm otherwise caused in project activities.

II. IFI POLICIES ON INDIGENOUS PEOPLES AND HUMAN RIGHTS

The IFIs have generally maintained – in some cases, insisted – that their constituent instruments define a role for them that does not obligate them, legally or otherwise, to account for human rights issues.[45] Indigenous peoples counter that IFIs cannot

Relevance', lecture given at the Presidential Fellow's Lecture at the World Bank (Washington, DC, December 2001), 3.

43. *See* Siobhán McInerney-Lankford, 'Human Rights and Development: A Comment on Challenges and Opportunities from a Legal Perspective', *Journal of Human Rights Practice* 1 (2009): 59 (stating that '[e]ven policies that make reference to human rights instruments tend to do so in a preambular way, or as framing propositions to identify the general sources of human rights rather than as positive binding legal obligations under international law'.). For further discussion, *see also* Siobhán McInerney-Lankford, 'International Financial Institutions and Human Rights: Select Perspectives on Legal Obligations', Ch. 8 herein.
44. *See generally* S. James Anaya, 'Indigenous Peoples' Participatory Rights in Relation to Decisions about Natural Resource Extraction. The More Fundamental Issue of What Rights Indigenous Peoples Have in Lands and Resources', *Arizona Journal of International and Comparative Law* 22 (2005): 8.
45. *See, e.g.*, Ibrahim Shihata, 'Democracy and Development', *International & Comparative Law Quarterly* 46 (1997): 635; Ibrahim Shihata, 'Human Rights, Development, and International

simply exempt themselves from compliance with generally applicable rules of the international legal system, including those pertaining to human rights. They also observe that the international community has repeatedly affirmed that respect for human rights is a fundamental part of sustainable development.[46] Therefore, while the IFIs should not become human rights enforcement agencies, they do need to ensure that their operating policies are consistent with human rights norms, including through the provision of effective remedies in relation to their own acts and omissions.

Indigenous peoples' views are informed and supported by a growing number of legal scholars who have concluded that IFIs do indeed have legal obligations with regard to human rights.[47] A number of UN expert studies have also looked at this issue and reached the same conclusion.[48] For example, the report on 'Globalization and its full impact on human rights' concludes, in relation to the WBG,

---

Financial Institutions', *American University Journal of International Law & Policy* 8 (1992); Siobhán McInerney-Lankford, 'International Financial Institutions and Human Rights: Select Perspectives on Legal Obligations', Ch. 8 herein.

46. *See, e.g.*, 'Report of the World Summit for Social Development', UN Doc. A/CONF.166/9 (1995), para. 26 (stating that sustainable and equitable development must include economic development, environmental protection, transparent and accountable governance, and universal respect for, and observance of, all human rights). *See also* Organisation for Economic Co-operation and Development (OECD), Development Assistance Committee, *On Common Ground: Converging Views on Development and Development Co-operation at the Turn of the Century* (February 2000) (surveying basic international principles of development and sustainable development and stating that, 'to achieve sustainable development, it is necessary to address economic and financial issues on the one hand, with structural, social and human issues, on the other, in a balanced way, thereby integrating the following key elements: . . . good governance and public management, democratic accountability, the protection of human rights and the rule of law').
47. *See inter alia* C.F. Amerasinghe, *Principles of the Institutional Law of International Organizations* (Cambridge: Cambridge University Press, 1996); Henry G. Schermers & Niels M. Blokker, *International Institutional Law: Unity within Diversity*, 3rd rev. edn (The Hague: Kluwer Law International, 1995); Sigrun Skogly, *The Human Rights Obligations of the World Bank and International Monetary Fund* (London: Cavendish Publishing, 2001), 84–87; Mac Darrow, *Between Light and Shadow: The World Bank, The International Monetary Fund and International Human Rights Law* (Oxford: Hart Publishing, 2003). In support of the position that IFIs have a legal obligation, *Bowett's Law of International Institutions* states that it 'has been suggested, for example, that the World Bank is not subject to general international norms for the protection of fundamental human rights. In our view that conclusion is without merit, on legal or policy grounds. . . . ' Philippe Sands & Pierre Klein (eds), *Bowett's Law of International Institutions*, 5th edn (London: Sweet & Maxwell, 2001), 458–459.
48. *See* 'Human rights as the primary objective of international trade, investment and finance policy and practice: Working paper submitted by J. Oloka-Onyango and Deepika Udagama, in accordance with Sub-Commission resolution 1998/12', UN Doc. E/CN.4/Sub.2/1999/11 (1999); 'Globalisation and its impact on the full enjoyment of human rights. Preliminary report submitted by Joseph Oloka-Onyango and Deepika Udagama, in accordance with Sub-Commission resolution 1999/8', UN Doc. E/CN.4/sub.2/2000/13 (2000); Fantu Cheru, 'The Highly Indebted Poor Countries (HIPC) Initiative: A Human Rights Assessment of the Poverty Reduction Strategy Papers (PRSP)', UN Doc. E/CN.4/2001/56 (2001) (Cheru is an independent expert on the effects of structural adjustment policies and foreign debt on the full enjoyment of all human rights, particularly economic, social, and cultural rights).

that, '[n]o entity that claims international legal personality can claim exemption from [the human rights] regime.... If such a claim were to be considered legitimate, it would seriously erode the international rule of law'.[49]

The relationship of the IFIs to international law, and particularly the nature and extent of any obligations that the IFIs may have under international human rights law, is discussed in detail elsewhere and will not be covered further here.[50] Instead, the remainder of this section will look at whether IFI policies on indigenous peoples explicitly refer to or incorporate 'human rights' or specific human rights norms. As discussed below, five of these policies do contain such explicit references: the World Bank, the IFC, and the ADB in their general objectives; the now-revoked 1998 ADB policy also has an extensive section on international human rights instruments pertaining to indigenous peoples; the EBRD policy references the UNDRIP; and the IDB directly incorporates the substantive provisions of human rights instruments and associated jurisprudence into its policy and the associated project approval process. What, though, is the effect of these references?

A. The World Bank Group

The World Bank's OP 4.10 and the IFC's Performance Standard 7 on Indigenous Peoples (PS7) both assert that a general objective of the policies is to ensure that the development process fosters 'full respect for the dignity [and] human rights' of indigenous peoples.[51] This objective can be read in two ways: first, that the policies on their face ensure that the development process fully respects indigenous peoples' rights; or, second, as a forward looking statement requiring that interpretation and implementation of the policies should be consistent with indigenous peoples' rights. However, and irrespective of which may be the correct interpretation, in meetings with indigenous peoples' representatives, World Bank legal staff have explained that this language is merely 'preambular' and should not be read as part of the mandatory requirements set forth in OP 4.10.[52]

---

49. 'Globalization and its full impact on human rights: Final report submitted by Joseph Oloka-Onyango and Deepika Udagama, in accordance with Sub-Commission decision 2000/105', UN Doc. E/CN.4/Sub.2/2003/14 (2003), para. 37.
50. *See* Siobhán McInerney-Lankford, 'International Financial Institutions and Human Rights: Select Perspectives on Legal Obligations', Ch. 8 herein. *See also* Daniel D. Bradlow, 'International Law and the Operations of the International Financial Institutions', Ch. 1 herein; David B. Hunter, 'International Law and Public Participation in Policy-Making at the International Financial Institutions', Ch. 7 herein; Celine Tan, 'Regulation and Resource Dependency: The Legal and Political Aspects of Structural Adjustment Programmes', Ch. 6 herein.
51. World Bank, 'Operational Policy 4.10 on Indigenous Peoples' (Washington, DC: World Bank, 10 May 2005), para. 1 (hereinafter OP 4.10); International Finance Corporation (IFC), 'Performance Standard 7 on Indigenous Peoples' (Washington, DC: International Finance Corporation, 30 Apr. 2006), objectives, *available at* <www.ifc.org/ifcext/sustainability.nsf/AttachmentsByTitle/pol_PerformanceStandards2006_PS7/$FILE/PS_7_IndigenousPeoples.pdf>.
52. Author's notes of the legal roundtable held by the World Bank's legal department and indigenous peoples' representatives (New York, 5 May 2005).

The IFC policy explains how it understands PS7's general objective to foster respect for indigenous peoples' rights. This explanation is set forth in the non-binding Guidance Notes issued with PS7 and, as with OP 4.10, should not be read as part of the mandatory requirements. It is nonetheless symbolically significant in as much as it represents an important statement by an IFI on human rights issues in the private sector context. Guidance Note 1 to PS7 provides:

> IFC recognizes that the rights of Indigenous Peoples are being addressed under both national and international law. Under international law, key UN human rights conventions . . . form the core of international instruments that provide the rights framework for the world's indigenous peoples. In addition, some countries have passed legislation or ratified other international or regional conventions for the protection of Indigenous Peoples. . . . While such legal instruments establish responsibilities of states, it is increasingly expected that private sector companies conduct their affairs in a way that would uphold these rights and not interfere with states' obligations under these instruments. It is in recognition of this emerging business environment that IFC expects that private sector projects financed by IFC foster full respect for the dignity, human rights, aspirations, cultures and customary livelihoods of Indigenous Peoples.[53]

What this language may mean in practice remains to be seen, particularly as it is non-binding and the IFC has yet to monitor whether corporations uphold indigenous peoples' rights and avoid interferences with states' obligations in IFC-funded projects. Together with the International Business Leaders Forum and the UN Global Compact, the IFC has developed a Human Rights Impact Assessment (HRIA) tool, which could be used to identify human rights risks and impacts in project design and implementation.[54] HRIA tools are an important part of ensuring that IFI operations respect human rights, but, to be effective, they must adequately reflect the specific rights of indigenous peoples and be developed and implemented with indigenous peoples' informed and effective participation.

The IFC-developed HRIA tool, which is currently being 'road-tested',[55] was not developed with indigenous participation (neither was PS7, at least not formally), and it is also not ideal on substantive grounds. For example, while the

53. International Finance Corporation, 'Guidance Note 7: Indigenous Peoples' (31 Jul. 2007), *available at* <www.ifc.org/ifcext/sustainability.nsf/AttachmentsByTitle/pol_GuidanceNote2007_7/$FILE/2007+Updated+Guidance+Note_7.pdf>.

54. International Finance Corporation, International Business Leaders Forum and the Global Compact, 'Guide to Human Rights Impact Assessment and Management: Road-Testing Draft' (June 2007), *available at* <www.iblf.org/resources/general.jsp?id=123946> (hereinafter 'Guide to Human Rights Impact Assessment and Management: Road-Testing Draft').

55. *See ibid.*; IFC, 'IFC Leads Development of a Guide to Human Rights Impact Assessment and Management (HRIA)', <www.ifc.org/ifcext/sustainability.nsf/Content/OurStories_Social Responsibility_HumanRights> (explaining that the HRIA tool is being 'road-tested with companies from various sectors to help them implement its methodology and the recommendations effectively and comprehensively' and once this is done the guide will be revised and likely published in 2010).

HRIA tool does recognize that indigenous peoples have a set of specific collective rights in addition to the individual rights of their members, it then falls into the common trap of discussing these rights almost exclusively in the context of the 1989 International Labour Organisation Convention No. 169 on Indigenous and Tribal Peoples.[56] Ratified by only twenty states, this instrument is seen by many indigenous peoples as substantially inadequate, particularly when viewed in light of contemporary international jurisprudence and the UNDRIP.[57] Also, in the HRIA tool, FPIC is not included as a 'key right' of indigenous peoples. Instead, FPIC is listed as a 'key emerging issue', even though the HRIA tool observes that this right is 'high on the agenda of international human rights'.[58] As discussed in the following section, FPIC is certainly a 'key right', and the IFIs and their borrowers or private sector clients face a number of serious risks if they ignore it.

B. Asian Development Bank (ADB)

The 1998 ADB policy on indigenous peoples stated that the 'international community has shown increasing concern for the protection of the rights of indigenous peoples', and contained a large section outlining some of the requirements contained in relevant international conventions and declarations.[59] Respect for indigenous peoples' rights is also highlighted in the objectives section of the policy, which provided that '[i]nitiatives should be conceived, planned, and implemented, to the maximum extent possible, with the informed consent of affected communities, and include respect for indigenous peoples' dignity, human rights, and cultural uniqueness'.[60] These statements, however, are not operationalized by inclusion in the mandatory sections of the policy. The policy was also adamant that implementation will take place 'within the context of country-level legal frameworks', rather than with reference to international human rights norms where

56. 'Guide to Human Rights Impact Assessment and Management: Road-Testing Draft', *supra* n. 54, 77–78.
57. For a compilation of contemporary treaty body jurisprudence concerning indigenous peoples, *see* Fergus MacKay (ed.), 'Indigenous Peoples and United Nations Treaty Bodies: A Compilation of United Nations Treaty Body Jurisprudence 1993–2004' (September 2005), *available at*, <www.forestpeoples.org/documents/law_hr/un_jurisprudence_comp_sept05_eng.pdf>; Fergus MacKay (ed.), *Indigenous Peoples and United Nations Treaty Bodies: A Compilation of United Nations Treaty Body Jurisprudence 2005–2006* (Moreton-in-Marsh: Forest Peoples Programme, 2006); Fergus MacKay (ed.), *Indigenous Peoples and United Nations Treaty Bodies: A Compilation of United Nations Treaty Body Jurisprudence 2007–2008*, vol. III, *available at* <www.forestpeoples.org/documents/law_hr/un_jurisprudence_comp_vol3_07_08_eng.pdf>.
58. 'Guide to Human Rights Impact Assessment and Management: Road-Testing Draft', *supra* n. 54, 78.
59. Asian Development Bank, 'The Bank's Policy on Indigenous Peoples' (Manila, April 1998), para. 22, *available at* <www.adb.org/Documents/Policies/Indigenous_Peoples/ADB-1998-Policy-on-IP.pdf>.
60. *Ibid.*, para. 32.

national laws may be inconsistent.[61] Consequently, as indigenous peoples from the Asia-Pacific region have explained on many occasions, ADB-funded operations often do not respect their rights and certainly do not seek their informed consent.[62]

The 1998 ADB policy underwent a revision process and was replaced by a new safeguard policy in 2009.[63] The revision process started with the 2007 'consultation draft', which was the subject of (often contentious) consultation meetings with indigenous peoples and others. The draft does not contain the prior language about international conventions and declarations, but it does state that its aims include safeguarding 'Indigenous Peoples' rights to maintain, sustain and preserve their cultural identities, practices and habitats, and ensure that projects affecting them will take into consideration necessary measures to protect these rights.'[64] The policy will also be triggered if 'a project impacts directly or indirectly on the dignity, human rights, livelihood systems, or culture of Indigenous Peoples, or affects the territories, natural or cultural resources that Indigenous Peoples own, use, occupy, or claim as their ancestral domain or asset'.[65] Following consultation, the ADB issued a second draft of the Safeguard Policy in October 2008, which was also subject to a comment period.[66] The penultimate draft, from June 2009, mentions the UNDRIP and explains that this 'non-binding declaration' was supported by many countries in Asia and the Pacific.[67] However, as with the 1998 policy, this language and that found in the 2007 consultation draft are not adequately operationalized in the mandatory requirements. Moreover, the mandatory requirements themselves appear to contravene indigenous peoples' rights. For example, the new policy has basically adopted the World Bank's language pertaining to indigenous lands and territories, language that the World Bank itself acknowledges is

61. Asian Development Bank, 'The Bank's Policy on Indigenous Peoples' (Manila, April 1998), para. 22, available at <www.adb.org/Documents/Policies/Indigenous_Peoples/ADB-1998-Policy-on-IP.pdf>. para. 62 (*see also* para. 22, stating, in relation to human rights laws, that 'the Bank must respect the will of governments, including legislation and policy that exists and the power of eminent domain that governments possess').
62. *See* Devasish Roy, 'The Asian Development Bank's Indigenous Peoples' Policy and Its Impact on Indigenous Peoples of Asia', in *Indigenous Peoples and the Human Rights-Based Approach to Development: Engaging in Dialogue*, ed. Chandra Roy (Bangkok: United Nations Development Programme, 2006).
63. Asian Development Bank's Safeguard Policy Update Timeline, <www.adb.org/Safeguards/timeline.asp> (providing a link to various consultations and drafts of the policy).
64. Asian Development Bank, 'Consultation Draft-ADB Safeguard Policy Statement' (October 2007), para. 2, *available at* <www.adb.org/Documents/Policies/Safeguards/Consultation-Draft.pdf>.
65. *Ibid.*, para. 7.
66. Asian Development Bank, 'Safeguard Policy Statement (Second Draft)' (October 2008), *available at* <www.adb.org/Documents/Policies/Safeguards/2nd-Draft-SPS.pdf>.
67. Asian Development Bank, 'Safeguard Policy Statement' (Manila, June 2009), Appendix 3, para. 1, *available at* <www.adb.org/Documents/Policies/Safeguards/Safeguard-Policy-Statement-June2009.pdf> (also stating that 'The Asian Development Bank (ADB) recognizes the rights of indigenous peoples to direct the course of their own development'). Para. 2 explains that 'the set of policy requirements will safeguard Indigenous Peoples' rights to maintain, sustain, and preserve their cultural identities, practices and habitats and to ensure that projects affecting them will take the necessary measures to protect these rights'.

inconsistent with UNDRIP.[68] Despite these potential problems, the ADB Board approved the new Safeguard Policy Statement on 20 July 2009.[69]

C. European Bank for Reconstruction and Development (EBRD)

The EBRD's 2008 Performance Requirement 7 on Indigenous Peoples (PR7), which applies to private sector financing, contains largely the same language as the World Bank and IFC policies concerning fostering respect for indigenous peoples' rights in its objectives.[70] This policy is substantially based on the IFC's PS7 and replaces the EBRD's 2003 policy on indigenous peoples. According to the EBRD, the reasons for the revision include advances in environmental and social issues since 2003, such as an increased focus on the impacts of financial intermediaries on human rights, and the need to better address social issues, including indigenous peoples' concerns, which are implicit in the 'sustainable development component of our mandate'.[71] In this same vein, the EBRD's 2008 Environmental and Social Policy provides that the EBRD 'will not knowingly finance projects that would contravene obligations under international treaties and agreements related to environmental protection, human rights and sustainable development as identified through project appraisal'.[72]

While the UNDRIP is not a treaty for the purposes of the Environmental and Social Policy, PR7 importantly contains an explicit reference to it, stating that:

> this PR recognises the principle, outlined in the UN Declaration on the Rights of Indigenous Peoples, that the prior informed consent of affected Indigenous Peoples is required for the project-related activities identified in paragraphs 31–37 below, given the specific vulnerability of Indigenous Peoples to the adverse impacts of such projects.[73]

As discussed below, FPIC is operationalized in relation to the referenced paragraphs in the EBRD policy and therefore this statement is not merely rhetorical.

---

68. *See ibid.*, para. 45; World Bank, OP 4.10, *supra* n. 51, para. 17 (both requiring measures to regularize indigenous land rights only in two limited circumstances (land titling projects and involuntary takings), and also providing for the possibility of granting individual titles to collectively held indigenous lands).
69. Asian Development Bank, 'Safeguard Policy Statement', *supra* n. 67.
70. European Bank for Reconstruction and Development (EBRD), 'Environmental and Social Policy' (London, 12 May 2008), 57–58, *available at* <http://www.ebrd.com/downloads/research/policies/2008policy.pdf>.
71. EBRD, 'Environmental Policy, Discussion Paper' (London, 2007), <http://www.ebrd.com/downloads/research/policies/issues.pdf>, 2–3.
72. EBRD, 'Environmental and Social Policy', *supra* n. 70, para. 9.
73. *Ibid.*, 57.

D. Inter-American Development Bank (IDB)

The IDB's 2006 Operational Policy 7-65 on Indigenous Peoples (OP 7-65) goes far beyond the other IFI policies.[74] It requires special safeguards for indigenous peoples in projects that directly or indirectly affect their traditional lands, territories, and resources, and specifies that 'one of those safeguards is respect for the rights recognized in accordance with the applicable legal norms'.[75] The definition of 'applicable legal norms' includes ratified international treaties 'as well as the corresponding international jurisprudence of the Inter-American Court of Human Rights or similar bodies whose jurisdiction has been accepted by the relevant country'.[76]

Apart from explicitly incorporating human rights norms into the IDB's operating requirements, OP 7-65 provides indigenous peoples with strong grounds to insist that proponents of IDB projects that affect indigenous peoples assess, document, and respect their rights. Importantly, in addition to the norms and jurisprudence developed in the UN system, the Inter-American Commission and Court of Human Rights have developed, and can be expected to continue to develop, substantial jurisprudence on the rights of indigenous peoples, some of which is discussed below. This jurisprudence sets out concrete rules that states must abide by when conceiving and implementing IFI-funded or other activities.

E. Conclusions on Current IFI Policies Regarding Human Rights

In principle at least, explicit incorporation of human rights standards into IDB operating requirements goes far toward adequately addressing indigenous peoples' demand that IFI-funded activities respect their rights. The EBRD's reference to international treaty obligations and the UNDRIP is also important and goes beyond the largely rhetorical statements made by the ADB, IFC, and the World Bank. However, many indigenous leaders would also point out that the 'the proof of the pudding is in the eating', and the IDB, and all other IFIs, need to demonstrate a stronger commitment to ensure that their policies are complied with (by their own staff and by borrowers or clients), if indigenous peoples' rights are to be respected in fact.

Finally, it is not strictly necessary that IFI policies explicitly refer to 'human rights' or to specific norms – they can and should, for instance, translate these norms into operational policy language suited to the IFIs' activities. It is nonetheless important that the IFIs explicitly acknowledge that indigenous peoples and others are rights-holders and that their rights and respect for their rights are a valid,

74. Inter-American Development Bank (IDB), 'Operational Policy 7-65 on Indigenous Peoples' (22 Feb. 2006 (adopted)), <www.iadb.org/sds/ind/site_401_e.htm>.
75. *Ibid.*, 8.
76. *Ibid.*, 5.

if not indispensable, part of the development process, and the most obvious place to address this is in their operating policies. The following section looks at whether the IFIs have incorporated FPIC into the operational language contained in their policies.

III. IFI POLICIES AND THE RIGHT TO FREE, PRIOR, AND INFORMED CONSENT (FPIC)

FPIC has been highlighted by indigenous peoples as a fundamental element of the exercise of their right to self-determination; as stated before the UN General Assembly in 2007, '"Free, prior and informed consent" is what we demand as part of self-determination and non-discrimination from governments, multinationals and the private sector.'[77] FPIC means the consensus or consent of indigenous peoples determined in accordance with their customary laws and practices.[78] In some cases, indigenous peoples may choose to express their consent through procedures and institutions that are not formally or entirely based on customary law and practice, such as statutory councils or tribal governments. Regardless of the nature of the process, the affected indigenous people(s) retain the right to refuse consent or to withhold consent until certain conditions are met. Consent must be obtained without coercion, prior to the approval of permits and commencement of activities, and after the project proponent's full disclosure of the intent and scope of the activity in a language and process understood and accepted by the affected indigenous peoples.

The UNDRIP explicitly affirms FPIC in three provisions. Article 10 provides in part that 'No relocation shall take place without the free, prior and informed consent of the indigenous peoples concerned and after agreement on just and fair compensation . . . .'[79] Article 19 provides that 'States shall consult and cooperate in good faith with the indigenous peoples concerned through their own representative

---

77. Les Malezer, 'Statement by the Chairman, Global Indigenous Caucus' (13 Sep. 2007), <www.treatycouncil.org/PDFs/STATEMENT%20BY%20THE%20IPS%20CAUCUS%20CHAIRMAN%2091307.pdf>.
78. *See* 'Preliminary working paper on the principle of free, prior and informed consent of indigenous peoples in relation to development affecting their lands and natural resources that would serve as a framework for the drafting of a legal commentary by the Working Group on this concept submitted by Antoanella-Iulia Motoc and the Tebtebba Foundation' UN Doc. E/CN.4/Sub.2/AC.4/2004/4 (8 Jul. 2004); United Nations, Economic and Social Council, Commission on Human Rights, 'Legal commentary on the concept of free, prior and informed consent. Expanded working paper submitted by Mrs. Antoanella-Iulia Motoc and the Tebtebba Foundation offering guidelines to govern the practice of implementation of the principle of free, prior and informed consent of indigenous peoples in relation to development affecting their lands and natural resources', UN Doc. E/CN.4/Sub.2/AC.4/2005/2 (21 Jun. 2005); 'Report of the International Workshop on Methodologies regarding Free, Prior and Informed Consent and Indigenous Peoples' given at the United Nations Permanent Forum on Indigenous Issues (New York, 17–19 Jan. 2005), UN Doc. E/C.19/2005/3.
79. UNDRIP, *supra* n. 26, Art. X.

institutions in order to obtain their free, prior and informed consent before adopting and implementing legislative or administrative measures that may affect them.'[80] Last, but not least, Article 32(2) provides that:

> States shall consult and cooperate in good faith with the indigenous peoples concerned through their own representative institutions in order to obtain their free and informed consent prior to the approval of any project affecting their lands or territories and other resources, particularly in connection with the development, utilization or exploitation of mineral, water or other resources.[81]

In most respects, these UNDRIP provisions restate the jurisprudence of the CERD, the UN expert body that oversees the convention of the same name (it has 173 state parties as of June 2009). CERD emphasizes indigenous peoples' right, effectuated through their own freely identified representatives or institutions,[82] to give their informed consent, in general[83] and in connection with specific activities, including: mining;[84] oil and gas operations; logging;[85] the establishment of protected areas;[86] dams;[87]

---

80. UNDRIP, *supra* n. 26, Art. 19.
81. *Ibid.*, Art. 32(2).
82. *See, e.g.*, 'Letter to the Permanent Mission of the Philippines, Urgent Action and Early Warning Procedure' (24 Aug. 2007), 2, *available at* <www.ohchr.org/english/bodies/cerd/docs/philippines_letter.pdf> (expressing concern about alleged manipulation of the right to consent related to a government agency's 'creation of a body with no status in indigenous structure and not deemed representative' by the affected people).
83. *See, e.g.*, 'General Recommendation XXIII on Indigenous Peoples', adopted by the Committee on the Elimination of Racial Discrimination at its 51st session (18 Aug. 1997), para. 4(d) (explaining that 'no decisions directly relating to their rights and interests are taken without their informed consent'); 'Australia', CERD/C/AUS/CO/14 (14 Apr. 2005), para. 11 (recommending that Australia 'take decisions directly relating to the rights and interests of indigenous peoples with their informed consent, as stated in its general recommendation XXIII').
84. *See, e.g.*, 'Guyana', CERD/C/GUY/CO/14 (4 Apr. 2006), para. 19 (recommending that Guyana 'seek the informed consent of concerned indigenous communities prior to authorizing any mining or similar operations which may threaten the environment in areas inhabited by these communities'); 'Guatemala', CERD/C/GTM/CO/11 (15 May 2006), para. 19; 'Suriname', Decision 1(67), CERD/C/DEC/SUR/4 (18 Aug. 2005), para. 3.
85. *See, e.g.*, 'Cambodia', CERD/C/304/Add.54 (31 Mar. 1998), paras 13, 19 (observing that the 'rights of indigenous peoples have been disregarded in many government decisions, in particular those relating to citizenship, logging concessions and concessions for industrial plantations' and recommending that Cambodia 'ensure that no decisions directly relating to the rights and interests of indigenous peoples are taken without their informed consent').
86. *See, e.g.*, 'Botswana', UN Doc. A/57/18 (23 Aug. 2002), paras 292–314 (para. 304 concerning the Central Kalahari Game Reserve); 'Botswana', CERD/C/BWA/CO/16 (4 Apr. 2006), para. 12 (hereinafter 'Botswana 2'). *But see*, 'Democratic Republic of Congo', CERD/C/COD/CO/15 (17 Aug. 2007), para. 14 (recommending, without mention of informed consent, that the state merely 'take the interests of the Pygmies and environmental conservation needs into account in matters of land use').
87. *See, e.g.*, 'India', CERD/C/IND/CO/19 (5 May 2007), para. 19 (stating that India 'should seek the prior informed consent of communities affected by the construction of dams in the Northeast or similar projects on their traditional lands in any decision-making processes related to such projects and provide adequate compensation and alternative land and housing to those communities').

agro-industrial plantations;[88] resettlement;[89] compulsory takings;[90] and other decisions affecting the status of land rights.[91] For example, in 2003, CERD stated with regard to exploitation of subsoil resources in indigenous territories:

> that merely consulting these communities prior to exploiting the resources falls short of meeting the requirements set out in the Committee's general recommendation XXIII on the rights of indigenous peoples. The Committee therefore recommends that the prior informed consent of these communities be sought and that the equitable sharing of benefits derived from such exploitation be ensured.[92]

FPIC, in principle, is also required, pursuant to the right to self-determination as set forth in common Article 1 of the International Covenants on Human Rights, as a logical corollary of indigenous peoples' right to *freely* determine their political status; *freely* pursue their economic, social, and cultural development; and *freely* dispose of their natural wealth and resources. In this respect, the Human Rights Committee has 'stress[ed] the obligation of the State party to seek the informed consent of indigenous peoples before adopting decisions affecting them'.[93] In its case law under the Optional Protocol I, the Committee has held that, that 'participation in the decision-making process must be effective, which requires not mere consultation but the free, prior and informed consent of the members of the community'.[94] Similarly, the Committee on Economic, Social, and Cultural Rights has

---

88. *See, e.g.*, 'Indonesia', CERD/C/IDN/CO/3 (15 Aug. 2007), para. 17 (recommending that Indonesia 'ensure that meaningful consultations are undertaken with the concerned communities, with a view to obtaining their consent and participation in the Plan'); 'Cambodia', *supra* n. 85, paras 13, 19.
89. *See, e.g.*, 'India', *supra* n. 87, para. 20 (stating that the 'State party should also ensure that tribal communities are not evicted from their lands without seeking their prior informed consent and provision of adequate alternative land and compensation'); 'Botswana 2', *supra* n. 86, para. 12 (recommending that the state 'study all possible alternatives to relocation; and (d) seek the prior free and informed consent of the persons and groups concerned'). *See also*, 'Laos', CERD/C/LAO/CO/15 (18 Apr. 2005), para. 18.
90. 'Guyana', *supra* n. 84, para. 17 (recommending that Guyana 'confine the taking of indigenous property to cases where this is strictly necessary, following consultation with the communities concerned, with a view to securing their informed consent').
91. 'Australia', *supra* n. 83, para. 11 (recommending 'that the State party refrain from adopting measures that withdraw existing guarantees of indigenous rights and that it make every effort to seek the informed consent of indigenous peoples before adopting decisions relating to their rights to land'); 'United States of America', A/56/18 (14 Aug. 2001), paras 380–407 (para. 400 concerning 'plans for expanding mining and nuclear waste storage on Western Shoshone ancestral land, placing their land up for auction for private sale, and other actions affecting the rights of indigenous peoples').
92. 'Ecuador', CERD/C/62/CO/2 (21 Mar. 2003), para. 16.
93. 'Concluding Observations of the Human Rights Committee: Canada', UN Doc. CCPR/C/CAN/CO/5 (20 Apr. 2006), para. 22.
94. *Ángela Poma Poma v. Peru*, Communication No. 1457/2006. UN Doc. CCPR/C/95/D/1457/2006 (24 Apr. 2009), para. 7.6 (in relation to 'the admissibility of measures which substantially compromise or interfere with the culturally significant economic activities of a minority or indigenous community . . . ').

noted 'with regret that the traditional lands of indigenous peoples have been reduced or occupied, without their consent, by timber, mining and oil companies, at the expense of the exercise of their culture and the equilibrium of the ecosystem'.[95] Its corresponding recommendation 'urges the State party to consult and seek the consent of the indigenous peoples concerned . . . '.[96]

In line with the UN human rights treaty bodies, the Inter-American Commission on Human Rights (IACHR) has consistently held that FPIC is required in relation to activities that affect indigenous peoples' traditional territories. As a general principle, it has observed that Inter-American human rights law requires 'special measures to ensure recognition of the particular and collective interest that indigenous people have in the occupation and use of their traditional lands and resources and their right not to be deprived of this interest except with fully informed consent, under conditions of equality, and with fair compensation'.[97]

Similarly, in the *Awas Tingni* case, the IACHR held that Nicaragua was responsible for violations of the right to property by granting a logging concession 'on the Awas Tingni lands, without the consent of the Awas Tingni Community'.[98] In the *Maya Indigenous Communities* case, it stated that the obligation to obtain indigenous peoples' consent is 'applicable to decisions by the State that will have an impact upon indigenous lands and their communities, such as the granting of concessions to exploit the natural resources of indigenous territories'.[99] In its March 2006 decision in *Twelve Saramaka Clans*, the IACHR stated unambiguously that 'in light of the way international human rights legislation has evolved with respect to the rights of indigenous peoples that the indigenous people's consent to natural resource exploitation activities on their traditional territories is always required by law'.[100] Also, as early as 1984, the IACHR found that the 'preponderant doctrine' holds that the principle of consent is of general application to cases involving relocation of indigenous peoples.[101]

95. 'Concluding Observations of the Committee on Economic, Social and Cultural Rights: Colombia', E/C.12/Add. 1/74 (30 Nov. 2001), para. 12.
96. *Ibid.*, para. 33. *See also*, 'Concluding Observations of the Committee on Economic, Social and Cultural Rights: Ecuador', UN Doc. E/C.12/1/Add.100 (7 Jun. 2004), para. 35.
97. 'Report N° 75/02, Mary and Carrie Dann (United States)', OEA/Ser.L/V/II.116, Doc. 46 (27 Dec. 2002), para. 131.
98. 'Report No. 27/98 (Nicaragua)', para. 142, *cited in*, *The Mayagna (Sumo) Awas Tingni Community Case*, Judgment on the Preliminary Objections of 1 Feb. 2000, Series C, No. 66.
99. 'Report No. 40/04, Maya Indigenous Communities of the Toledo District, Case 12.053 (Belize)' (12 Oct. 2004), para. 142 (footnotes omitted).
100. 'Report No. 09/06, Admissibility and Merits, Case 12.338, Twelve Saramaka Clans (LOS), (Suriname)' (2 Mar. 2006), para. 214, *available at* <www.forestpeoples.org/documents/s_c_america/suriname_iachr_12_saramaka_clans_mar06_eng.pdf>.
101. 'Report on the Situation of Human Rights of a Segment of the Nicaraguan Population of Miskito Origin', OEA/Ser.L/V/II.62, Doc. 26 (1984), 120.

A. SARAMAKA PEOPLE V. SURINAME

The Inter-American Court of Human Rights (the Court) has also developed jurisprudence on FPIC. Judgments of the Court are binding on respondent states and may be executed in domestic courts.[102] In 2007, the Court decided *Saramaka People v. Suriname*, which is the leading case on FPIC with an effect on relations and relevance to IFIs. In *Saramaka People v. Suriname*, the Court held that indigenous and tribal peoples hold the right to self-determination, by virtue of which they may 'freely pursue their economic, social and cultural development' and 'freely dispose of their natural wealth and resources'.[103] The Court ruled that this right cannot be restricted when interpreting the property rights guaranteed under Article 21 of the American Convention on Human Rights. As a consequence, indigenous peoples have the right 'to freely determine and enjoy their own social, cultural and economic development',[104] which in turn requires that recognition of their territorial rights must include recognition of 'their right to manage, distribute, and effectively control such territory, in accordance with their customary laws and traditional collective land tenure system'.[105]

Having ruled that the Saramaka people have protected property rights with regard to their traditionally owned territory and the traditionally-used natural resources within and under that territory,[106] the Court examines whether the state may restrict those rights pursuant to Article 21(1) of the American Convention, which provides that the 'law may subordinate use and enjoyment [of property] to the interest of society'.[107] On the basis of this provision, the Court has previously held that a state may restrict the use and enjoyment of the right to property only 'where the restrictions are: a) previously established by law; b) necessary; c) proportional; and d) with the aim of achieving a legitimate objective in a democratic society'.[108]

The same criteria apply to restrictions of indigenous peoples' property rights. However, in the case of indigenous peoples, the Court holds that 'another crucial factor to be considered is whether the restriction amounts to a denial of their traditions and customs in a way that endangers the very survival of the group and

102. Article 68 of the American Convention on Human Rights provides that '1. The States Parties to the Convention undertake to comply with the judgment of the Court in any case to which they are parties. 2. That part of a judgment that stipulates compensatory damages may be executed in the country concerned in accordance with domestic procedure governing the execution of judgments against the state'. American Convention on Human Rights, O.A.S. Treaty Series No. 36, 1144 U.N.T.S. 123 (18 Jul. 1978), Art. 68, *available at* <www1.umn.edu/humanrts/oasinstr/zoas3con.htm>.

103. *Saramaka People v. Suriname. Preliminary Objections, Merits, Reparations and Costs.* Judgment of 28 Nov. 2007, Series C No. 172, para. 93 (hereinafter *Saramaka People v. Suriname*).

104. *Ibid.*, para. 95.

105. *Ibid.*, para. 194.

106. *Ibid.*, para. 122.

107. *Ibid.*, paras 124–140.

108. *Ibid.*, para. 129.

of its members'.[109] Discussing the granting of logging and mining concessions, the Court explains that for the state to guarantee that such restrictions do not amount to 'a denial of [the Saramaka people's] survival as a tribal people', the state must comply with three safeguards:

> 1) it must ensure their effective participation with regard to any development or investment project within their territory. A 'development or investment' is defined by the Court as 'any proposed activity that may affect the integrity of the lands and natural resources within the territory of the Saramaka people, particularly any proposal to grant logging or mining concessions';[110]
>
> 2) the Saramaka people must receive a reasonable benefit from the project; and
>
> 3) independent environmental and social impact assessments must be undertaken.[111]

In its concluding remarks, the Court adds a fourth element: a duty to implement 'adequate safeguards and mechanisms in order to ensure that these activities do not significantly affect the traditional Saramaka lands and natural resources'.[112] This last requirement is highly important, though the Court did not explain what constitutes a 'significant effect' in this context.[113] According to the Court, these 'safeguards are intended to preserve, protect and guarantee the special relationship that the members of the Saramaka community have with their territory, which in turn ensures their survival as a tribal people'.[114] In August 2008, the Court interpreted its judgment in *Saramaka People* at Suriname's request and explained that the language 'survival as a tribal people':

> must be understood as the ability of the Saramaka to 'preserve, protect and guarantee the special relationship that they have with their territory', so that 'they may continue living their traditional way of life, and that their distinct cultural identity, social structure, economic system, customs, beliefs and

109. *Saramaka People v. Suriname. Preliminary Objections, Merits, Reparations and Costs.* Judgment of 28 Nov. 2007, Series C No. 172, para. 93 (hereinafter *Saramaka People v. Suriname*), para. 128 (also stating that 'under Article 21 of the Convention, the State may restrict the Saramakas' right to use and enjoy their traditionally owned lands and natural resources only when such restriction complies with the aforementioned requirements and, additionally, when it does not deny their survival as a tribal people').
110. *Ibid.*, para. 129, n. 127.
111. *Ibid.*, para. 129.
112. *Ibid.*, para. 158.
113. *Ibid.*, para. 154 (In finding a violation, one of the criteria identified by the Court was that Suriname 'failed to put in place adequate safeguards and mechanisms in order to ensure that these logging concessions would not cause major damage to Saramaka territory and communities').
114. *Ibid.*, para. 129 (The term 'survival' should not be read restrictively so as to exclude, for instance, indigenous and tribal peoples' right to continue to benefit from their traditional economy and to be secure in their means of subsistence. In this respect, *see* para. 130 and the jurisprudence cited in the attendant footnotes).

> traditions are respected, guaranteed and protected'. That is, the term survival in this context signifies much more than physical survival.[115]

The majority of the Court's analysis concerns the effective participation requirement. The Court explains that effective participation includes a duty to actively consult with affected communities, 'according to their customs and traditions', in relation to any proposed development or investment. In its August 2008 interpretation judgment, the Court adds that, 'By declaring that the consultation must take place "in conformity with their customs and tradition", the Court recognized that it is the Saramaka people, not the State, who must decide which person or group of persons will represent the Saramaka people in each consultation process ordered by the Tribunal.'[116] The same would also apply to obtaining FPIC given that the language is identical. It continues that:

> the Saramaka people must inform the State which person or group of persons will represent them in each . . . consultation process. The State must then consult with those Saramaka representatives to comply with the Court's orders. Once such consultation has taken place, the Saramaka people will inform the State of the decisions taken, as well as their basis.[117]

The Court further explains that the duty to consult includes:

- a duty on the State and those authorized by it to accept and disseminate information;
- constant communication between the parties;
- consultations undertaken in good faith, through culturally-appropriate procedures and with the objective of reaching an agreement;
- consultation with indigenous peoples, 'in accordance with their own traditions, at the early stages of a development or investment plan, not only when the need arises to obtain approval from the community. . . . Early notice provides time for internal discussion within communities and for proper feedback to the State';
- that the state must ensure that indigenous peoples are aware of possible risks, including environmental and health risks, so that the proposed project is accepted voluntarily and with full knowledge; and
- finally, that consultation should take account of indigenous peoples' traditional methods of decision-making.[118]

Some developments or investments, however, require a higher degree of participation than that described above. For these projects, the state has a duty not only to

---

115. *Saramaka People v. Suriname. Interpretation of the Judgment on Preliminary Objections, Merits, Reparations and Costs*, Judgment of 12 Aug. 2008. Series C No. 185, para. 37, *available at*, <www.corteidh.or.cr/docs/casos/articulos/seriec_185_ing.pdf> (hereinafter 'Interpretation Judgment').
116. *Ibid.*, para. 18.
117. *Ibid.*, para. 19.
118. *Saramaka People v. Suriname*, *supra* n. 103, para. 133.

consult with indigenous peoples, 'but also to obtain their free, prior, and informed consent, according to their customs and tradition'.[119] The developments or investments requiring FPIC are characterized as 'large-scale' projects that may have a major or significant impact within indigenous peoples' territories.[120] The Court observes that this is consistent with the jurisprudence of other international human rights bodies, which require FPIC in connection with projects that may have 'a significant impact on the right of use and enjoyment of ancestral territories'.[121] The Court ultimately ordered Suriname to adopt legislative or other mechanisms 'to recognize and ensure the right of the Saramaka people to be effectively consulted, in accordance with their traditions and customs, or when necessary, the right to give or withhold their free, informed and prior consent, with regards to development or investment projects that may affect their territory'.[122]

In its 2008 interpretation, the Court explains again that FPIC is required in certain circumstances, stating that:

> depending upon the level of impact of the proposed activity, the State may additionally be required to obtain consent from the Saramaka people. The tribunal has emphasized that when large-scale development or investment projects could affect the integrity of the Saramaka people's lands and natural resources, the State has a duty not only to consult with the Saramakas, but also to obtain their free, prior, and informed consent in accordance with their customs and traditions.[123]

Last but not least, the Court ordered that until the regularization of Saramaka territory has been completed, Suriname must abstain from acts that might 'affect the existence, value, use or enjoyment of the territory to which the members of the Saramaka people are entitled, unless the State obtains the free, informed and prior consent of the Saramaka people'.[124] The Court reiterated this order in its 2008 interpretation and explained that it was also applicable in relation to 'any other

119. *Saramaka People v. Suriname, supra* n. 103, paras 134, 137 (explaining that consent is required for 'major development or investment plans that may have a profound impact on the property rights of the members of the Saramaka people to a large part of their territory'). The Court has also required indigenous peoples' consent in relation to delimitation, demarcation, and titling of traditional lands in the *Moiwana Village* case. *Moiwana Community v. Suriname. Preliminary Objections, Merits, Reparations and Costs.* Judgment of 15 Jun. 2005. Series C No. 124, para. 210 (hereinafter *Moiwana Village* Case). In *Yakye Axa*, when traditional lands cannot be returned to indigenous peoples, the Court required that indigenous peoples' consent be obtained with regard to the provision of compensation or alternative lands and 'in accordance with their own consultation processes, values, uses and customary law'. *Yakye Axa Indigenous Community v. Paraguay*, 17 Jun. 2005. Series C No. 125, para. 151. *See also Sawhoyamaxa Indigenous Community v. Paraguay*, 29 Mar. 2006. Series C No. 146, para. 135.
120. *Saramaka People v. Suriname, supra* n. 103, para. 137.
121. *Ibid.*, para. 136.
122. *Ibid.*, paras 131, 214(8) (the Court cited Art. 32(2) of the UNDRIP to support its ruling).
123. 'Interpretation Judgment', *supra* n. 115, para. 17.
124. *Saramaka People v. Suriname, supra* n. 103, paras 194(a), 214(5).

indigenous or tribal territory as well'.[125] Similar orders were made in the *Moiwana Village* and *Awas Tingni* cases,[126] and have also been made in the Court's provisional measures jurisprudence.[127] The prohibition on affecting the existence, value, use or enjoyment of indigenous peoples' property rights until such time as demarcation and titling have been completed is a stricter standard than the 'large-scale project with major or significant impact' test applied by the Court with respect to restrictions on regularized indigenous property rights. Accordingly, it may be concluded that, to be valid, any restriction on indigenous peoples' property rights presupposes that those rights are first legally recognized and secured. When these rights have yet to be so secured states, acting with or without IFI support, are enjoined from any action that can affect such rights, at least unless they obtain FPIC.

The African Commission on Human and Peoples' Rights heavily relied on *Saramaka People* in its 2010 decision in the case of the *Centre for Minority Rights Development (Kenya) and Minority Rights Group International on behalf of Endorois Welfare Council v. Kenya*. In addition to demonstrating that indigenous peoples' rights are actionable in African human rights institutions, the decision states that '[i]n terms of consultation, the threshold is especially stringent in favour of indigenous peoples, as it also requires that *consent* be accorded';[128] and, 'the African Commission is of the view that any development or investment projects that would have a major impact within the Endorois territory, the State has a duty not only to consult with the community, but also to obtain their free, prior, and informed consent, according to their customs and traditions'.[129]

The Court and the African Commission are the first human rights bodies to make a distinction between situations where FPIC is required and those in which a lower standard of participation is required. CERD, for instance, makes no such distinction, requiring that 'no decisions directly relating to [indigenous peoples'] rights and interests are taken without their informed consent'.[130] As we shall see below, such distinctions are also employed by IFIs in their policies on indigenous peoples, although only explicitly in connection with FPIC in one instance. Similarly, the extent to which IFI policies on indigenous peoples apply is largely determined by the significance of impacts identified during screening and/or environmental and social impact assessments and, in some policies, different criteria are applied to 'high-risk' projects.

---

125. 'Interpretation Judgment', *supra* n. 115, paras 54–55.
126. *Moiwana Village* Case, *supra* n. 119, para. 211; *Mayagna (Sumo) Awas Tingni Community Case*, 31 Aug. 2001. Series C No 79, para. 164.
127. *Mayagna (Sumo) Indigenous Community Case*, Provisional Measures of 6 Sep. 2002; *Sarayaku Indigenous Community Case*, Provisional Measures of 17 May 2005.
128. *Centre for Minority Rights Development (Kenya) and Minority Rights Group International on Behalf of Endorois Welfare Council v. Kenya* (February 2010), para. 226, *available at* <www.minorityrights.org/9587/press-releases/landmark-decision-rules-kenyas-removal-of-indigenous-people-from-ancestral-land-illegal.html>.
129. *Ibid.*, para. 291.
130. 'General Recommendation XXIII on Indigenous Peoples' (18 Aug. 1997), para. 4(d).

B. Evaluation of IFI Policies against the FPIC Standard

How do the IFI policies measure up against the FPIC standard? Looking at the ADB, World Bank, IFC, EBRD, and the IDB, we see that only the EBRD explicitly acknowledges and requires that FPIC be obtained, and then only for 'high-risk projects'. The IDB and IFC both require some form of 'agreement' for some, but not all projects. The World Bank and ADB require 'free, prior and informed consultation leading to broad community support', a standard that the World Bank concedes is not equivalent to FPIC. While not discussed further herein, it should be noted that major donor institutions such as the UNDP, IFAD, the European Commission, and a number of large bilateral donors also require FPIC in their extant or draft policies on indigenous peoples.[131]

The IFC's PS7 includes the objective of fostering 'good faith negotiation with and informed participation of Indigenous Peoples when projects are to be located on traditional or customary lands under use by the Indigenous Peoples'.[132] PS7 consequently requires IFC clients to enter into and successfully conclude good faith negotiations with indigenous peoples, but only for 'high-risk' projects (see below). All IFC projects not falling into the high-risk category only require: consultation, impact assessment, benefit sharing, mitigation and avoidance measures, and compensation for adverse impacts, and, when there will be 'adverse impacts', verified 'broad community support' for the project.[133] The existence of this 'broad community support' is to be verified exclusively by the IFC.

According to the IFC, '[b]road community support is a collection of expressions by the affected communities, through individuals and/or their recognized representatives, in support of the project. There may be broad community support even if some individuals or groups object to the project'.[134] The IFC's 2007 Environment and Social Review Procedure (ESRP), an internal staff manual setting out operating procedures, including compliance with PS7, provides some additional information about broad community support.[135] Generally, the ESRP requires that staff determine the existence of broad community support by assessing two issues: (1) has the client conducted free, prior, and informed consultation, and enabled the informed participation of affected communities; and (2) what is the

131. The United Nations Development Programme's official policy on indigenous peoples provides that the 'UNDP promotes and supports the right of indigenous peoples to free, prior informed consent with regard to development planning and programming that may affect them'. UNDP, 'UNDP and Indigenous Peoples: A Policy of Engagement' (2001), paras 26–30. *See also* European Union, Council of Ministers Resolution, 'Indigenous Peoples within the framework of the development cooperation of the Community and Member States' (1998) (providing that 'indigenous peoples have the right to choose their own development paths, which includes the right to object to projects, in particular in their traditional areas').
132. IFC, 'Performance Standard 7 on Indigenous Peoples', *supra* n. 51.
133. *Ibid.*, para. 9.
134. IFC, 'Guidance Note 7: Indigenous Peoples', *supra* n. 53, Guidance Note 19.
135. International Finance Corporation, 'IFC Environment & Social Review Procedure', Version 2.0 (31 Jul. 2007), 3.

level of support and dissent related to the project among the project-affected communities?[136]

On the second point, the ESRP explains that this will be assessed based on 'an accumulation of "material considerations" ', which includes formal and informal expressions of support or objection to the project.[137] The material considerations include minutes of meetings of elected local government, village councils, or council of elders; written agreements; client records, photographs, media reports, personal letters, or third-party accounts regarding support for, or opposition to, the project; and, somewhat bizarrely given voting behaviour, the results of local and community elections 'won on popular mandates, with explicit reference in the manifesto and campaigning messages of the winning parties to a particular opinion about the project'.[138] If nothing else, this convoluted assessment provides the IFC with considerable latitude when verifying if broad community support is present.

As noted above, PS7 requires that IFC clients will enter into and successfully conclude good faith negotiations with indigenous peoples for 'high-risk' projects. The 'high-risk' category is defined broadly by the IFC as projects:

- that may be on, or commercially develop natural resources within, indigenous peoples' 'traditional or customary lands under use, and adverse impacts can be expected on the livelihoods, or cultural, ceremonial, or spiritual use that define the identity and community of the Indigenous Peoples';[139]
- involving physical relocation;[140]
- involving 'economic displacement' due to land acquisition or compulsory takings for project purposes;[141] and

136. *Ibid.*, 33–34.
137. *Ibid.*, 38.
138. *Ibid.*, 38–39.
139. IFC, 'Performance Standard 7 on Indigenous Peoples', *supra* n. 51, para. 13. 'Guidance Note 23' explains that 'Customary use of land and resources refers to patterns of long-standing community land and resource use in accordance with Indigenous Peoples' customary laws, values, customs, and traditions, including seasonal or cyclical use, rather than formal legal title to land and resources issued by the State.' IFC, 'Guidance Note 7: Indigenous Peoples', *supra* n. 53. 'Cultural, ceremonial and spiritual uses are an integral part of Indigenous Peoples' relationships to their lands and resources, are embedded within their unique knowledge and belief systems, and are key to their cultural integrity. Such uses may be intermittent, may take place in areas distant from population centers, and may not be site specific. Any potential adverse impacts on such use must be documented and addressed within the context of these belief systems.'
140. IFC, 'Performance Standard 7 on Indigenous Peoples', *supra* n. 51, para. 14; IFC, 'Performance Standard 5' (30 Apr. 2006), para. 19, *available at* <www.ifc.org/ifcext/sustainability.nsf/AttachmentsByTitle/pol_PerformanceStandards2006_PS5/$FILE/PS_5_LandAcqInvolResettlement.pdf>.
141. IFC, 'Performance Standard 5', *supra* n. 140, para. 21 (according to PS5, para. 1, 'economic displacement' includes 'loss of assets or access to assets that leads to loss of income sources or means of livelihood . . . as a result of project-related land acquisition').

– containing commercial use of cultural resources, or traditional knowledge, innovations, and practices.[142]

While there is no definition of the term 'good faith negotiation', the (non-binding) Guidance Notes explain that, at a minimum, it involves:

> (i) willingness to engage in a process and availability to meet at reasonable times and frequency; (ii) provision of information necessary for informed negotiation; (iii) exploration of key issues of importance; (iv) mutual[ly] acceptable procedures for the negotiation; (v) willingness to change initial position and modify offers where possible; and (vi) provision for sufficient time for decision making.[143]

A 'successful outcome' of the good faith negotiations is similarly not defined in PS7. However, it would be perverse to interpret the successful outcome of a negotiation to be anything other than some form of agreement. This is reflected in the Guidance Notes, which provide that documentation indicating a successful outcome includes 'a memorandum of understanding, a letter of intent, a joint statement of principles, and written agreements'.[144] Therefore, while the IFC's standards do not use the term FPIC or some variant thereof, in the case of broadly defined 'high-risk projects', indigenous peoples' agreement or consent is nonetheless a prerequisite for financing from the IFC. This standard has also been accepted by the so-called 'Equator Principles' banks in relation to any project requiring financing over USD 10 million.[145] These large commercial banks cumulatively financed USD 125 billion of direct foreign investment in 2005, around 80% of global private sector project finance.

The EBRD policy employs the same scheme as the IFC's PS7, including the distinction between 'high risk' or, as the EBRD calls them, 'special requirement' projects and other projects, which are defined in the same way as PS7. However, in the EBRD policy, the client is explicitly required to 'obtain the prior consent' of indigenous peoples in addition to good faith negotiation for high-risk projects.[146] EBRD defines 'consent' as 'the process whereby the affected community of indigenous peoples, arrive at a decision, in accordance with their cultural traditions, customs and practices, as to whether to become involved in the proposed project'.[147]

For all projects that may affect indigenous peoples, the IDB's OP 7-65 requires: participatory impact assessments; consultation and informed participation; benefit

142. IFC, 'Performance Standard 7 on Indigenous Peoples', *supra* n. 51, para. 15.
143. IFC, 'Guidance Note 7: Indigenous Peoples', *supra* n. 53, Guidance Note 25.
144. *Ibid.*
145. *See* 'Equator Principles', <www.equator-principles.com>.
146. EBRD, 'Environmental and Social Policy', *supra* n. 70, 55 (referring to PR7, para. 31). *See also ibid.*, 56 (referring to PR 7, para. 33, which provides that '[t]he client will enter into good faith negotiation with the affected communities of Indigenous Peoples, and document their informed participation and consent as a result of the negotiation'.)
147. *Ibid.*, 55 (referencing, PR7, para. 31).

sharing; mitigation and avoidance measures; and compensation for adverse impacts. For projects with 'significant potential adverse impacts that carry a high degree of risk to the physical, cultural or territorial integrity of the affected indigenous peoples, the Bank will further require and verify that the project proponent demonstrates that it has, through a good faith negotiation process obtained agreements regarding the operation and the measures to address the adverse impacts . . . '.[148] These agreements must be submitted to the IDB's Board as part of its consideration of the approval of the project. Indigenous peoples' 'consent' is explicitly required by the IDB in relation to resettlement.[149] Further, as noted above, Inter-American and other human rights jurisprudence with regard to FPIC is incorporated by reference into OP 7-65's substantive and procedural requirements.

The World Bank and ADB policies require participatory impact assessment, benefit sharing, mitigation and avoidance measures, and compensation for all projects that may adversely affect indigenous peoples. They additionally require 'a process of free, prior, and informed consultation[150] with the affected indigenous peoples' communities at each stage of the project, and particularly during project preparation in order to fully identify their views and to ascertain their broad community support to the project . . . '.[151] These IFIs 'will provide project financing only where free, prior, and informed consultation results in broad community support to the project by the affected Indigenous Peoples'.[152] The term 'broad community support' is not defined and the only indication of how to interpret it is found in Bank Procedures 4.10, a document that complements OP 4.10 and contains procedural instructions for World Bank staff. This instrument states that Bank staff shall 'verify that the borrower has gained the broad support from representatives of major sections of the community required under the policy'.[153]

As noted above, World Bank lawyers have concluded that OP 4.10 does not incorporate FPIC and is therefore inconsistent with the UNDRIP on this point. In fact, the World Bank's Board of Executive Directors rejected FPIC in relation to the recommendations of both the World Commission on Dams and the Extractive

148. Inter-American Development Bank (IDB), 'Operational Policy 7–65 on Indigenous Peoples' (22 Feb. 2006), s. IV.B.4.4.a.iii (the Borrower must provide, 'no later than by the date of consideration of the operation by the Board', evidence of the agreements reached with the affected people. *See also* ss V.5.3.c and IV.B.4.4.e).
149. Inter-American Development Bank, 'Operational Policy 7–10 on Involuntary Resettlement' (1998), s. IV, para. 4.
150. World Bank, OP 4.10, *supra* n. 51, para. 1, n. 4 (defining 'free, prior and informed consultation' as 'a culturally-appropriate and collective decision-making process subsequent to meaningful and good faith consultation and informed participation regarding the preparation and implementation of the project. It does not constitute a veto right for individuals or groups').
151. *Ibid.*, para. 6.
152. *Ibid.*, para. 1.
153. 'Bank Procedures 4.10 on Indigenous Peoples' (July 2005), para. 7, *available at* <http://wbln0018.worldbank.org/Institutional/Manuals/OpManual.nsf/0/DBB957522502 7E678525703100541C7D?OpenDocument>.

Industries Review and, instead, decided that the standard to be adopted and applied would be 'free, prior, and informed consultation resulting in broad community support'.[154] Some of the executive directors cited a legal opinion on FPIC written by the WBG's General Counsel to justify their opposition.[155] This opinion maintains that recognition of FPIC by the WBG would contravene the Bank's Articles of Agreement because it would give 'the equivalent of a veto right to parties other than those specified in the countries' legal framework. This would be inconsistent with the Bank Group's governance structure, which establishes the critical role of member governments in Bank Group financing'.[156]

The logic employed here is obscure given that the WBG's Member States are all represented on its Board of Executive Directors, which has ultimate authority to interpret the Articles of Agreement.[157] This authority would nevertheless be subject to the rules of international law relating to the interpretation of treaties. Also, as with any other policy statement adopted by the WBG, the member governments would be involved in determining the conditions of WBG financing through their participation in the Board, which typically reaches decisions by consensus. Moreover, the WBG has long required safeguard measures in policies that may not be included in national laws, for example, OD 4.20's requirement of informed participation. Similarly, OP 4.10's (elusive and opaque) 'broad community support' requirement is certainly not a common principle of national

154. *See* World Bank Group Management Response, 'Striking a Better Balance – The World Bank Group and Extractive Industries: The Final Report of the Extractive Industries Review' (17 Sep. 2004), 7, 9.
155. *See* Paulo Gomes & Louis Kasekende, 'The World Bank Group and Extractive Industries: The Final Report of the Extractive Industries Review', EDS2004-0625 (unpublished World Bank doc.) (2 Aug. 2004), 2 (joint African statement); Otaviano Canuto, 'The World Bank Group and Extractive Industries: The Final Report of the Extractive Industries Review', EDS2004-0617 (unpublished World Bank doc.) (2 Aug. 2004), 2–3.
156. Senior Vice President & General Counsel, World Bank, General Counsel IFC, Vice President & General Counsel MIGA, 'Legal Note on Free, Prior and Informed Consultation', unpublished World Bank doc. (2 Aug. 2004), para. 3 (footnote omitted). The omitted citation states that the 'primary role of member governments in Bank Group operations is reflected, for instance, in the requirement for Bank lending to or with the guarantee of the member (IBRD Article III, Section 4) and in the specific prohibition on IDA financing or IFC financing if the member objects (IDA, Article V, Section 1(c); IFC Article III, Section 3(jj))'.
157. International Bank for Reconstruction and Development, 'Articles of Agreement', 2 U.N.T.S. 13 (27 Dec. 1945), Art. 9 (describing the process of review for any question of interpretation of the provisions of the Agreement). *See also* John Head, 'For Richer or for Poorer: Assessing the Criticisms Directed at Multilateral Development Banks', *University of Kansas Law Review* 52 (2004): 271 (stating that 'the charters place with the MDBs' own governing bodies the complete authority to decide questions of charter interpretation or application'). For the views of two former General Counsels, *see* Shihata, 'Human Rights, Development, and International Financial Institutions', *supra* n. 45, 29–30; Ko-Young Tung, 'Shaping Globalization: The Role of Human Rights – Comment on the Grotius Lecture by Mary Robinson', *American University International Law Review* 19 (2003): 34, 41–42 (stating on page 34 that '[i]t should be noted that while the General Counsel's opinions carry enormous weight, the ultimate authority in interpreting the Articles of Agreement rests with the Bank's Executive Directors, of whom there are twenty-four representing the 184 member countries').

legislation, and the World Bank states that it will not finance projects without such support.

The 2009 ADB policy on indigenous peoples takes avoidance of FPIC to new heights. It provides that indigenous peoples' 'consent' will be obtained for projects that involve:

> (i) commercial development of the cultural resources or knowledge; (ii) physical displacement; and (iii) commercial development of natural resources within customary lands provided that this may impact the livelihoods or the cultural, ceremonial, or spiritual uses that define the identity or community of indigenous peoples.[158]

In contrast to the IFC and others, note that the ADB does not include 'economic displacement' in the list of project activities requiring consent or agreement.

The ADB policy then explains that 'the consent of indigenous peoples' communities refers to a collective expression, by the affected indigenous peoples' communities, through individuals and/or their recognized representatives, of broad community support for the proposed project activities'.[159] The ADB will review the borrower/client's documentation to 'assure itself' of the existence of broad community support and will not finance the project if it does not exist.[160] In other words, consent means broad community support, given that the requirements are no different than those in OP 4.10. Thus, ADB continues to verify and support OP 4.10.

IV. CONCLUDING REMARKS

A discrete body of human rights norms in international law adheres to indigenous peoples as self-determining collectivities.[161] These rights are recognized and guaranteed by a number of universal and regional human rights instruments, both those specifically addressing indigenous peoples and those of general application. Many of these rights have been codified in the UNDRIP, which is the primary reference point for comprehending the nature and scope of indigenous peoples' rights. Moreover, because the UNDRIP in many respects restates existing rules of international law, it should not be discounted as merely an aspirational or 'soft law' instrument. The UNDRIP also calls on the IFIs to promote 'respect for and full

158. Asian Development Bank, 'Safeguard Policy Statement' (Manila, June 2009), Appendix 3, 60 (para. 30) (hereinafter 'ADB Safeguard Policy Statement').
159. *Ibid.*, para. 31.
160. *Ibid.*, 20, para. 55.
161. *See* S. James Anaya, *Indigenous Peoples in International Law*, 2nd edn (Oxford & New York: Oxford University Press, 2004); Patrick Thornberry, *Indigenous Peoples and Human Rights* (Manchester: Manchester University Press, 2002); Alexandra Xanthaki, *Indigenous Rights and United Nations Standards: Self-determination, Culture and Land* (Cambridge: Cambridge University Press, 2007).

application' of its provisions as well as to 'follow up the effectiveness of this Declaration'.[162]

The UNDRIP and other international norms recognize that indigenous peoples have the right to freely determine and pursue their own development choices through their own institutions and within the framework of autonomy and self-government regimes. Indigenous peoples refer to this as 'self-determined development', meaning development that is based on, but not limited by, indigenous custom and tradition.[163] These rights are intended to be exercised within existing states rather than through the creation of new entities. Therefore, in addition to rights that define the nature and extent of autonomy and self-government regimes, a set of rights defines relationships between indigenous peoples and states. FPIC is a governing principle and right in these relationships, and stipulates that consent is the basis for the vast majority of indigenous-state interactions.

Indigenous peoples insist that the IFIs must respect their rights, both in terms of their policies and their activities. As the IFIs primarily fund activities implemented by states or invest in private sector operations authorized by those states, this includes respecting FPIC and the relationship that it, in principle, establishes between indigenous peoples, the state, and private sector entities. While there are discernable improvements in recent years, the response of the IFIs remains mixed; only the IDB and EBRD have convincingly addressed their role in relation to human rights law. Even in their case, it remains to be seen exactly how they will understand and implement their new-found appreciation for human rights, or what lessons may be drawn from their experience. This failure to account for human rights norms stands in stark contrast to the manner in which the IFIs have regarded international environmental law, including through policy-based conditions relating to compliance with international environmental instruments.[164] It also

---

162. UNDRIP, *supra* n. 26, Art. 42.
163. *See* Victoria Tauli-Corpuz, 'IFAD's Work in Support of Indigenous and Tribal Peoples: Challenges and Ways Forward' presented at the IFAD/UNPFII side event 'Integrating Indigenous Peoples Perspectives on Development to Reach the MDG' (Rome, Italy, 17 Feb. 2005), 5, *available at* <www.un.org/esa/socdev/unpfii/documents/workshop_IPPMDG_ifad_indigenous_en.pdf> (discussing lessons learned from IFAD projects 'and how these projects or aspects of these reinforced or integrated indigenous and tribal peoples' perspectives on self-determined development').
164. World Bank, 'OP 4.01 Environmental Assessment' (1999), para. 3; World Bank, 'OP 4.36 Forestry' (2002), para. 6 (two existing World Bank policies that prohibit the Bank from financing activities that contravene a Member State's obligations under ratified environmental treaties). *See also* Ibrahim Shihata, 'Implementation, Enforcement and Compliance with International Environmental Agreements – Practical Suggestions in Light of the World Bank's Experience', *Georgetown International Environmental Law Review* 9 (1996); Mohammed Abdelwahah Bekhechi, 'Some Observations Regarding Environmental Covenants and Conditionalities in World Bank Lending Activities', in *Max Planck Yearbook on United Nations Law*, ed. J.A. Frowstein & Rüdiger Wolfrum, vol. 3 (London: Kluwer Law International, 1999); McInerney-Lankford, 'Human Rights and Development: A Comment on Challenges and Opportunities from a Legal Perspective', *supra* n. 43, 67 (stating that '[t]he lack of emphasis on the legal dimension of human rights in development may be contrasted with the prominence of international treaty obligations pertaining to well integrated issues like trade

contrasts with generally accepted understandings about the role of human rights as a fundamental condition for achieving sustainable development.

This is not to say that IFI policies are entirely inconsistent with indigenous peoples' rights; they are not, but at the same time significant deficiencies at a minimum raise serious questions about their ultimate effectiveness as safeguards. The World Bank's Extractive Industries Review raised this issue and concluded that, '[t]o be legitimate and effective, a Safeguard Policy must be seen by the intended beneficiaries to provide adequate safeguards and must be consistent with their internationally guaranteed rights. This is presently not the case [with OP 4.10]'.[165]

One major discrepancy is the manner in which the IFIs have addressed FPIC. Only one of the IFIs reviewed here, the EBRD, has explicitly adopted FPIC into its policy on indigenous peoples. The IFC and the IDB both require some form of agreement with indigenous peoples for high-risk projects, which include a large percentage of the projects that may affect indigenous peoples. However, there is little extant evidence from actual projects to verify if this is the case in practice or whether the IFC and the IDB are employing restrictive or inconsistent interpretations. Moreover, obtaining agreements through negotiation is not necessarily the same as obtaining FPIC.

While good faith negotiation resulting in some form of agreement could be tantamount to FPIC in practice, the latter is an iterative process that demands full respect for indigenous peoples' culture and traditions, particularly as related to decision-making processes and reaching consensus. Traditional decision-making processes are frequently diffused and extended. Formal meetings are generally only a small part of the process, and such meetings are not normally the locus for decision-making. For FPIC to be validly obtained there must be a demonstrable understanding of the project, its risks and potential benefits, among most of the affected community members. FPIC is thus in part about attempting to bridge a cultural divide between indigenous peoples and states, IFIs, and the private sector, and about fostering meaningful and mutually beneficial relationships in addition to serving a protective function. FPIC is not checking boxes in an administrative process or obtaining a signed piece of paper, it is much more than that. It is, as IFAD acknowledges in the quote that begins this chapter, about actively listening to indigenous peoples and, more so, actively respecting their perspectives, values, and decisions.

The World Bank and the ADB have adopted a standard that is elusive conceptually, and purposely is not equivalent to FPIC. This 'broad community support' standard is simply not amenable to coherent and consistent application in practice and is likely to foment serious community divisions and conflicts. The rules pertaining to existence and verification of broad community support

---

and environment which are explicitly provided for in the policies and guidance of several development institutions').

165. 'Striking a Better Balance – The World Bank Group and Extractive Industries: The Final Report of the Extractive Industries Review', *supra* n. 15, 41.

provides the IFIs with a degree of discretion that would likely be judged arbitrary by many domestic and international tribunals. Broad community support is also the standard that the IFC and EBRD apply to non-high-risk projects. The ADB is now seeking to define FPIC as broad community support, thus undermining its effective application in the region of the world that is home to the majority of indigenous peoples.

Though some IFIs are seeking to change the definition of FPIC, courts have the ability, and at present one has shown the willingness, to ensure that IFIs secure FPIC before implementing projects. In the Americas at present, IFI and state decisions may be subject to review in cases brought before the Inter-American Court of Human Rights, including on the grounds of failing to secure FPIC in the case of large-scale projects that could affect the integrity of indigenous and tribal peoples' territories. The Court has the authority to order states to refrain from violative activities and to compensate indigenous peoples for material and immaterial damages. In the future, this may be the case in the human rights courts of the African and European systems, and perhaps in the Asia-Pacific region should the newly established Association of Southeast Asian Nations' (ASEAN) human rights body transcend its relatively conservative rules of operation. Failure to respect indigenous peoples' rights may therefore translate into legal, commercial, and other risks to IFI investments in addition to reputational risks, especially in private sector operations. Indigenous peoples will continue to insist that respect for their rights is not simply a discretionary option for the IFIs or a function of risk, but rather an obligation that is incumbent on all subjects of international law.

Chapter 10

Worker Rights and the International Financial Institutions

Jerome I. Levinson

The question of worker rights and the International Financial Institutions (IFIs)[1] – must be understood in the context of the overall economic philosophy of the IFIs and the conditions that they attach to their financing for their member countries. From their inception, the 'conditionality' attached to IFI financing has been a contentious issue between the institutions and their borrowing Member States. But the issue of worker rights and the degree to which it should be a part of that conditionality did not emerge as a central focus of the institutions until the 1990s. That focus was part of a larger evolution that led the IFIs into a much deeper intrusion into areas that had been previously thought to be a domestic policy concern for their Member States.

I. THE BEGINNING

The central problem for the architects of the post-war system was how to construct a multilateral trade and investment regime that would avoid the vices of the inter-war

1. This chapter focuses primarily on the examples of the International Monetary Fund (IMF), the International Bank for Reconstruction and Development (the World Bank), and the Inter-American Development Bank (IDB).

Daniel D. Bradlow and David B. Hunter, *International Financial Institutions and International Law*, pp. 321–342.

period: the tendency of countries to engage in competitive devaluation of their currencies for the purpose of boosting exports and limiting imports, and exporting unemployment to their trading partners, a process that became known as 'beggar thy neighbour'.

Such a system also had to accommodate the political realities of the post-war era, namely: the collapse of colonial regimes in Asia, Africa, and the Middle East, as well as the emergence of a more assertive group of countries in the Latin American region. The industrialized countries could no longer dominate with an imperial reach spanning the continents, but they still controlled the sources of capital necessary for economic development. Countries in Latin America in the inter-war period defaulted on bonds they had marketed in international markets. Thus, in the immediate aftermath of World War II, these countries were ineligible to borrow in commercial capital markets. The states that emerged from colonial rule with uncertain credit and economic management were equally dubious credit risks.

The reconstruction of Europe and Japan presented formidable challenges that required financing and terms on a scale that private capital markets appeared unable or unwilling to provide. For geopolitical reasons, the United States ultimately provided the financing through a bilateral programme, the Marshall Plan.[2] The need for public, multilateral sources of financing for the development needs of the lesser developed countries in Asia, Africa, and Latin America appeared to be equally compelling.

Even before World War II ended, planning to confront these issues had begun. That planning culminated in a 1944 conference at Bretton Woods, a New Hampshire resort hotel. The Bretton Woods conference gave birth to the two multilateral financial institutions that have played such a critical role in international finance in the succeeding sixty years: the International Monetary Fund (IMF)[3] and the World Bank.[4] The ambitious proposal by the British delegation, headed by the

---

2. European Recovery Act ('Marshall Plan'), PL 472, Ch. 169 (3 Apr. 1948) (for images of the first and last pages *see* the National Archives, <www.archives.gov/exhibits/featured_documents/marshall_plan>; *see also* General George Marshall, speech delivered at Harvard University (Cambridge, MA, 5 Jun. 1947), *available at* <www.fordham.edu/halsall/mod/1947marshallplan1.html> (this speech by General George Marshall laid out the basis for the Marshall Plan); *see generally* Library of Congress, 'For European Recovery: The Fiftieth Anniversary of the Marshall Plan', <www.loc.gov/exhibits/marshall> (providing links to information about the Marshall Plan).
3. Articles of Agreement Establishing the International Monetary Fund, 2 U.N.T.S. 39 (established 22 Jul. 1944, amended 11 Nov. 1992), *available at* <www.imf.org/external/pubs/ft/aa/index.htm> (hereinafter IMF Agreement).
4. World Bank Articles of Agreement, <http://web.worldbank.org/WBSITE/EXTERNAL/EXTABOUTUS/0,,contentMDK:20040600~menuPK:34625~pagePK:34542~piPK:36600~theSitePK:29708,00.html> (provides links to the Articles of Agreement of the different entities of the World Bank Group); International Bank for Reconstruction and Development Articles of Agreement, 2 U.N.T.S. 13 (established July 1944, amended 16 Feb. 1989), *available at* <http://siteresources.worldbank.org/EXTABOUTUS/Resources/ibrd-articlesofagreement.pdf> (hereinafter IBRD Articles of Agreement).

distinguished economist John Maynard Keynes, which would have created a world central bank to finance an expanding level of international trade and investment, was rejected. Instead, a more limited arrangement sponsored by the United States delegation was adopted: countries could only change the par value of their currencies after securing IMF approval. To avoid domestic political pressures to adopt restrictive measures such as tariffs, quotas, or currency devaluation if they confronted a drastic imbalance in their external accounts, the plan provided that countries could ask the IMF for short-term financing to ease the economic adjustment needed to bring their external accounts into balance. The financing would be conditional, based on the IMF's judgment that the proposed economic measures – usually fiscal austerity, monetary restraint, and realistic exchange rates – were likely to redress the external imbalance.

Louis Rasmiskey, the former Governor of the Bank of Canada, observed that with the Bretton Woods Agreement, the 'world community took control of the international monetary system'.[5] But this financial assistance to IMF Member Countries to ease problems in the external accounts was conceived as a temporary measure; it was never intended to place the IMF in the position of being a permanent monitor of a country's economic policies.

In post-war Western Europe and Japan, the primary task was reconstructing railways, factories, ports, and electric-power facilities destroyed during the war. The newly de-colonized countries and those in Latin America needed to establish and improve that same infrastructure to augment their production and delivery of goods and services. Financing these complements to productive capacity was beyond the mandate of the IMF. The commercial banking system, still marked by the memory of debt defaults in the inter-war period, particularly by countries in the Western Hemisphere outside of the United States and Canada, was unwilling to extend long-term credits for development. The Bretton Woods meeting established the World Bank to provide such financing. After a few initial loans for European reconstruction, the World Bank concentrated its efforts on funding for the other borrowing members of the Bank.

By informal agreement among the major shareholders, the president of the World Bank would be a US national, and the managing director of the IMF, a European. Unlike the IMF, the World Bank proposed to raise funds for on-lending to its borrowing member countries by issuing its own bonds to be marketed by private investment banks in the financial markets. In order to establish its financial bona-fides, the initial president of the World Bank, and his immediate successors, were drawn from Wall Street. In February 1947, the Truman Administration persuaded John J. McCloy to assume the presidency of the World Bank. McCloy was closely associated with the Chase Manhattan Bank, and had been the former High Commissioner for the Occupation in Germany and Deputy Secretary of the War Department during World War II.

5. Robert Solomon, *The International Monetary System, 1945–1981* (New York: Harper & Row, 1982), 11.

In a 1948 speech to Latin American leaders in Bogota, Columbia, McCloy defined the Bank's mission as one of blazing 'the trail for private international investments'.[6] In contrast to the early reconstruction loans for commodity imports for European recovery, the World Bank limited its lending for specific projects to its borrowing Member Countries in Latin America, Africa, and Asia. Such lending disbursed funds at a slower rate than commodity import loans and were more closely supervised by Bank staff. The Bank conditioned its loan programme to individual countries on reaching an agreement with the government on an overall economic policy framework acceptable to the World Bank. Early, the principle was established that Bank lending should be linked to an acceptable macroeconomic policy as well as to project criteria establishing the economic worth of the project to be financed.

Summarizing its experience in dealing with its borrowing Member Countries, the Bank's tenth anniversary report observed:

> [The Bank] could not expect that the projects it helped to finance however well planned and carried out, could function efficiently in isolation from the economy of the borrowing member country as a whole. The Bank carried on a dialogue with the borrowing country authorities on a whole range of questions: it has consistently urged attempts to settle defaulted external debt, to put economic and fiscal policies on a sound footing and direct public investment in such a way as to promote, rather then to obstruct or displace, the flow of private capital.[7]

A. Other Priorities: Latin America

This policy dialogue collided with the political and economic realities of many of the Bank's borrowing Member Countries. In Latin American countries, notably, Brazil, Mexico, and Argentina, the war years led to an expansion of domestic industry to substitute for goods previously imported. In the case of capital intensive industries such as the steel industry, that import substitution initiative was beyond the capital mobilization capacity of the domestic private sector. In order to maintain support for the allied cause in these countries, the US Export-Import Bank loaned money for construction of local steel and other heavy industry plants. With the availability of limited local private capital, the state invested in these industries as well.

The success in constructing a domestic capital goods industry during war time was cited as an example of successful import substitution industrialization which could be duplicated in the post-war era. The import substitution industrialization strategy was given an intellectual justification by the United Nations Economic

6. Kai Bird, *The Chairman, the Making of the American Establishment* (New York: Simon & Schuster, 1992), 279.
7. World Bank, 'Tenth Anniversary Report' (Washington, DC, 1955), 34.

Commission on Latin America (ECLA), headed by the distinguished Argentine economist, Raul Prebisch.[8] He stressed that Latin American commodity producers confronted permanent unfavourable terms of trade in the international economy, namely, that the prices of industrial goods imports tended to increase in real terms, adjusted for inflation, more than their exports. The way out of this conundrum for the Latin American countries was industrialization and the fastest way to accomplish this objective was through import substitution industrialization.[9] The World Bank emphasis on the role of private capital, domestic and foreign, and export-led economic growth, conflicted with the Latin American war-time experience and the ECLA analysis.

In 1954, at a meeting at Quitandinha, Brazil, Latin American leaders made the case for a separate financing institution for development in the hemisphere that would be more responsive to their concerns than the World Bank. The meeting was attended by many of the individuals who would rise to prominence in the following decade as presidents (Carlos Lleras Restrepo, Columbia, and Eduardo Frei, Chile), ministers of economy (Roberto Campos, Brazil), and finance ministers (Antonio Ortiz Mena, Mexico).[10]

The initiative for a lending institution separate from the World Bank to finance Latin American development was reiterated by Juscelino Kubitschek, then-President of Brazil. In 1957, he launched a hemisphere-wide initiative for development, Operation Pan-American,[11] which the United States rejected. Then-Secretary of State John Foster Dulles emphasized the Communist threat to the hemisphere as a reason for rejecting the initiative.

The Cuban Revolution in 1959 and a preceding mission to Latin America by Milton Eisenhower, the brother of President Dwight Eisenhower, in contrast, spotlighted the great inequities in Latin American societies as the major cause of social and political unrest. In order to address these issues and respond to the Latin American demand for an institution more attuned to Latin American development needs, first the Eisenhower administration, and then the succeeding Kennedy administration, agreed to the long-standing Latin American ambition for a financing institution specifically for Latin America. That initiative became the Inter-American Development Bank (IDB).[12]

---

8. 'Raúl Prebisch: Latin America's Keynes', *The Economist*, 5 Mar. 2009, *available at* <www.economist.com/books/displaystory.cfm?story_id=13226316>.
9. *See* James M. Cypher & James L. Dietz, *The Process of Economic Development*, 2nd edn (London & New York: Routledge, 1997), 162–164 (discussing Prebisch's book *The Economic Development of Latin America* and the development of 'import substitution industrialization' and advocacy of its use in Latin America).
10. *See* Jerome Levinson & Juan DeOnis, *The Alliance that Lost Its Way: A Critical Report on the Alliance for Progress* (Chicago, IL: Quadrangle Press, 1970).
11. 'THE AMERICAS: Operation Pan American', *Time*, 30 Jun. 1958 (reporting about President Juscelino Kubitschek's announcement of his development plan, 'Operation Pan American'), *available at* <www.time.com/time/magazine/article/0,9171,891915,00.html>.
12. *See* Levinson & DeOnis, *supra* n. 10.

The IDB became a key component of the Alliance for Progress programme launched in 1961 by President Kennedy.[13] That programme sought to place the United States on the side of social reform in the hemisphere and respond to the desire for a more tolerant attitude towards industrialization initiatives, involving state participation in the financing of enterprises. Like the World Bank, however, the IDB remained primarily a project financing institution. Unlike the World Bank, it did not require approval of overall economic management policies as a precondition for financing.

The IFIs did not address labor market abuses, such as the use of the coercive power of the state to deny workers the rights of free expression and to bargain collectively; nor did they intervene to influence the collective bargaining regime prevailing in a particular country. Conditions attaching to the financing provided by the development banks, the World Bank and regional development banks, like the IDB, related to the specific projects being financed. The IMF primarily concerned itself with the policies most directly influencing the balance of payments, namely, fiscal, monetary, exchange, and interest rate policies.

B. The International Labour Organization

The International Labour Organization (ILO) arose out of the 1919 post-World War I Versailles peace conference. The 1917 Bolshevik revolution in Russia:

> helped to work a miraculous change of attitude among the Western ruling classes. The workers, even in the victorious democracies, were restless. Who knew how far they would go down the path to revolution?... The day the League of Nations commission was appointed, another was set up on international labor... the International Labour Organization came into existence with a minimum of fuss and held its first conference before the end of 1919.[14]

The ILO had neither the resources of the IFIs, nor the ability to impose financial or trade sanctions on offending Member States. In revealing abuses of worker rights, the ILO relied on the sunshine effect, by which it highlighted labor market abuses to shame the country and offending companies to redress worker grievances. Relations between the ILO and the IFIs were minimal to non-existent.

---

13. *See generally* President John F. Kennedy, 'On the Alliance for Progress', address given at a White House Reception for Latin American Diplomats and Members of Congress (Washington, DC, 13 Mar. 1961), *available at* <www.fordham.edu/halsall/mod/1961kennedy-afp1.html> (address outlining his Alliance for Progress).
14. Margaret MacMillan, *Paris 1919* (New York: Random House, 2001), 95.

II. THE DEBT CRISIS OF THE 1980s

In the aftermath of the 1973 Arab oil embargo of the United States and the Netherlands resulting from their resupply of Israel with weapons during the Yom Kippur war between Israel and Egypt and Syria, the price of crude oil increased by 400% between October 1973 and January 1974. Several oil producers, particularly in the Persian Gulf, could not spend their oil riches. The then-US Secretary of the Treasury, William Simon, promoted the petro-dollar recycling strategy, which encouraged the oil producing states with huge financial surpluses to deposit them with the subsidiaries of multinational banks, primarily in London. These banks would then on-lend the funds, in large part, to oil importing countries. This lending primarily went to the more developed countries or newly industrializing countries (NICs).[15]

The lending took the form of syndicated commercial bank loans by the bank subsidiaries that had been receiving the deposits of the surplus oil producing states. This form of lending was based upon a variable interest rate periodically revised in accordance with market conditions. Consequently, it was vulnerable to changes in economic policy in the industrialized countries.

With the 1979 appointment of Paul Volcker to head the US Federal Reserve Bank, the US government adopted a radical change in economic strategy. In order to bring inflation under control in the United States, interest rates were raised, which caused the United States economy to enter into a deep recession. The immediate consequences for the borrowing countries were a commensurate rise in the interest payments due on their outstanding syndicated bank loans and a decline in their major export market demand for their goods. Much of the borrowed money had not been used for productive purposes. The result was the Latin American debt crisis of the 1980s.

In 1982, the finance minister of Mexico, Jesus Silva Herzog, informed US Secretary of the Treasury Donald Regan, that Mexico could not meet its debts service obligations to the private commercial banks from which Mexico had borrowed billions of dollars.[16] Fearful that the Mexican default indicated a more generalized problem with syndicated bank lending, private commercial bank financing for the NICs dried up.

During the 1970s, following the oil price increase of 1973–1974, the US Treasury had sought to diminish the influence of the IFIs. It had encouraged the major borrowing countries of the IFIs to rely on private markets for resources to finance their development. Upon the Mexican default, the US Treasury shifted course and enlisted the Bretton Woods institutions to oversee a programme of private bank debt repayment as a means of restoring the credit-worthiness of the debtor countries and enabling them to return to voluntary borrowing from the commercial banking sector.

---

15. Karin Lissakers, *Banks, Borrowers and the Establishment* (New York: Basic Books, 1991).
16. *Institutional Investor*, International Edition (1987): 71 (providing an oral history of the debt crisis).

Whereas in the post-1974 years the influence of these institutions had receded, the debt crisis of the 1980s propelled them back into prominence. An IMF seal of approval of economic policy was a pre-condition for lending from both private and public sources. The IMF conditioned its approval of financing for a debtor country on an economic programme that included repaying part of the debt to the private banks and maintaining current interest payments. Almost invariably, such a programme involved severe economic austerity measures, including reducing investments for infrastructure, health, and education.

III. A CHANGE IN STRATEGY: 1985

In 1985, Alan Garcia, then President of Peru, announced that Peru would limit its debt service payments to external creditors to not more than 15% of export earnings. Fearing that this measure indicated a growing 'debt fatigue' among the debtor countries and that other such countries might emulate Peru, Secretary of the Treasury James A. Baker III set forth a change in United States government strategy.

Instead of the austerity strategy for borrowing countries, Secretary Baker, in an October 1985 speech to the annual meeting of the IMF and the World Bank in Seoul, South Korea, announced that the United States would support a strategy focused upon renewed economic growth.[17] The private banks would provide net new lending to the debtor countries of USD 20 billion over three years, which amounted to more than what was needed to maintain current debt service payments, amortization, and interest. To complement the private bank financing, the IFIs would also increase their lending commitments and disbursements to the debtor countries.

The programme was linked to a commitment on the part of the borrowing counties to adopt structural reforms, including reducing the role of the state in the direct production of goods and services; reliance upon domestic and foreign private investment as the primary motor for development; and greater reliance upon private markets in the allocation of resources. The IFIs would supervise the reform programme and condition their lending on the debtor country adopting a programme of structural reforms satisfactory to them and in line with the Baker speech.[18] The proposed development strategy outlined by Secretary Baker was a return to the strategy advocated in the 1950s by US Government officials and the successive presidents of the World Bank who were drawn from Wall Street.

---

17. James A. Baker III, 'Statement Before the Joint Annual Meeting of the International Monetary Fund and the World Ban' (Seoul, South Korea, 8 Oct. 1985) (hereinafter Baker Plan). *See also* James M. Boughton, *Silent Revolution: The International Monetary Fund, 1979–1989* (Washington, DC: International Monetary Fund, 2001), 417–429, *available at* <www.imf.org/external/pubs/ft/history/2001/ch10.pdf> (discussing the Baker Plan, its development, reactions to it, its implementation, and its effects).
18. Baker Plan, *supra* n. 17.

Almost no aspect of economic policy-making was exempt from IMF and World Bank scrutiny. The IMF summarized the expanded scope of the institution's intrusion into economic policy-making in its borrowing Member Countries:

> Over the years, both the policy content and the breadth of issues have expanded. Increased emphasis has been placed on the appropriateness of a country's exchange rate policies, the medium-term implications of its economic policies, its structural reform efforts, and the stance of its trade policies . . . social, industrial, labor market and environmental issues have increasingly been taken into account if these have significant implications for macroeconomic policies and performance.[19]

No longer having access to direct financing from the private financial markets, the debtor countries were in a poor position to reject the IFI conditions for lending. Further, a new generation of economists had assumed policy-making roles in much of Latin America. Largely educated in United States graduate schools of economics, this younger cadre embraced the Treasury and IFI critique of past policies, and the desirability of a development strategy based upon market allocation of resources and reliance upon foreign and domestic private investment.

In 1990, John Williamson, a conservative Washington-based economist, summarized the consensus evolving among policy-makers in the southern hemisphere, the IFIs, and the Washington complex of US government agencies and private think tanks. The document was intended to demonstrate that the prior conflicts between the Latin American countries and the IFIs over development strategy were largely a thing of the past. Williamson set out ten criteria, all of them dealing with economic efficiency, macroeconomic policy, and measures designed to encourage foreign direct investment (FDI). Using these criteria, Williamson showed that instead of disagreement between borrowing Member Countries and 'Washington' over strategy, there was now a general consensus.[20]

Neither in Williamson's paper, nor in Baker's 1985 Seoul speech, was there any mention of equity considerations: distribution of income, poverty, or human resource investment in such areas as health and education. As Williamson justified it: 'I deliberately excluded from [my] list of [the ten areas] anything which was primarily redistributive . . . because I felt the Washington of the 1980s to be a city that was essentially contemptuous of equity concerns.'[21]

The Washington Consensus and Baker strategies did not yield the expected results. The USD 20 billion in net new resources from the private banks that Baker envisioned in 1985 did not materialize. Additionally, the 1970s type of syndicated bank lending to the NICs did not resume. Economic growth did not achieve the anticipated goals and the private sector proved unable to provide the stimulus for

19. International Monetary Fund, 'IMF Survey' (September 1995), 97.
20. John Williamson, *The Progress of Policy Reform in Latin America* (Washington, DC: Institute for International Economics, 1990).
21. Robin Broad & John Cavanaugh, 'The Death of the Washington Consensus?', *World Policy Journal*, XVI, no. 3 (Fall 1999).

investment, job creation, and economic growth. Further, in an effort to be internationally competitive, companies limited employment creation. This opening of the economy to imports often led to the devastation of small business enterprises producing for the local market, which was, traditionally, an important source of employment creation in Latin American economies.

IV. RISING UNEMPLOYMENT AND INCOME INEQUALITY

Even where there was economic growth and an increase in social spending, the IDB observed:

> [income] inequality has swept away many of the benefits of economic growth for large sectors of society. A prime example of this phenomenon is Mexico. Between 1996 and 1998, GDP per capita increased 9.7 percent in real terms, which is a spectacular gain as judged by the country's macroeconomic performance of the previous 16 years. However, poverty barely declined... In fact, the incomes of the poorest 30 percent of the population actually declined. The huge increase in mean income was due entirely to income gains among the richest 30 percent – particularly the richest 10 percent – of the population.[22]

Mexico was not an isolated case. Other countries that embraced the Washington Consensus strategy increasingly found themselves facing rising levels of unemployment and income inequality. In Latin America, these tendencies were super imposed on levels of income inequality that were already the highest in the world. Alarmed by these trends, the Bretton Woods institutions identified the culprit to be labor market rigidities, namely the strong protection for workers in the organized sector of the economy in hiring and firing, and the collective bargaining regimes that were in place. These protective measures, according to the World Bank, increased the cost of labor, made it more difficult to reduce staff in adverse economic conditions, and discouraged firms from hiring more employees.

Robert Holzmann, then-Director of Social Protection in the World Bank, set forth the prevailing view within the IFIs:

> the second one has to do with the economics of, in particular, the freedom of association, because while there are studies out – and we agree with them that trade union movements may have a strong and good role in economic development – there are studies out that also show that this depends. So the freedom by itself does not guarantee that the positive effects are achieved.[23]

22. Inter-American Development Bank Research Department, 'Is Growth Enough?', vol. 14 (2001).
23. Robert Holzmann, 'A Role for Labor Standards in the New International Economy', given at a seminar at the International Monetary Fund Annual Meeting (Washington, DC: September 1999).

The IFIs tended to believe that core labor standards like freedom of association and the right to bargain collectively were not rights; their utility depends upon whether the particular arrangements promote economic efficiency.

The 2000–2001 World Bank 'World Development Report: Attacking Poverty' was more explicit:

> Implementation of the standards on freedom of association and collective bargaining also raise complex issues for economic development . . . empirical evidence on the economic benefits is generally quite mixed and suggests that both costs and benefits are complex and context specific. Particularly important are the rules that govern collective bargaining and resolution of labor disputes. Some form of collective bargaining rules may be better at producing efficient and equitable outcomes than others.[24]

With respect to continental Europe, the IMF observed:

> [t]he most important reason for continental Europe's lack of economic dynamism and persistent unemployment is the slow pace of structural reform . . . . There is wide agreement on the root causes of this 'excess' structural unemployment problem: the adverse and (unintended consequences) of elaborate job and income protection arrangements that raise the cost of labor . . . discourage job creation and favor substitution of capital for labor . . . . A common problem has been the failure to implement sufficiently comprehensive labor market reforms because of strong opposition of insiders – those who have jobs and feel they benefit, rather than suffer from existing labor (and product) market institutions and regulations.[25]

This view was not limited to an analysis of the causes of European unemployment, but also reflected the development approach of the Bretton Woods institutions. They saw structural rigidities in the labor market as the principal cause of persistently high unemployment among developing countries, and argued for labor market flexibility measures, a euphemism for making it easier for firms to fire workers without large severance payments; and for diluting collective bargaining arrangements, which had the effect of weakening union bargaining power.[26]

The prevailing view among the Bretton Woods institutions was summarized by Joseph Stiglitz, former Chief Economist at the World Bank:

> I am just completing three years as Chief Economist of the World Bank. During that time, labor market issues did arise, but all too frequently from a narrow economics focus, and even then, looked at even more narrowly

24. World Bank, *World Development Report 2000–2001: Attacking Poverty* (New York: Oxford University Press, 2001), 74, *available at* <http://siteresources.worldbank.org/INTPOVERTY/Resources/WDR/English-Full-Text-Report/toc.pdf>.
25. International Monetary Fund, *World Economic Outlook* (Washington, DC: IMF, 1997), 12, *available at* <www.imf.org/external/pubs/ft/weo/weo1097/weocon97.htm>.
26. World Bank, *World Development Report: Workers in an Integrating World* (New York: Oxford University Press, 1995).

> through the lens of neo-classical economics. Wage rigidities – often the fruits of hard fought bargaining – were thought to be part of the problem facing many countries, contributing to their high unemployment; a standard message was to increase labor market flexibility – the not so subtle text was to lower wages and lay off unneeded workers. In East Asia, it was reckless lending by international banks and other financial institutions combined with reckless borrowing by domestic financial institutions – combined with fickle investor expectations – which may have precipitated the crises; but the cost – in terms of soaring unemployment and plummeting wages – were borne by workers.[27]

The IFIs' view that labor market rigidities were the causes of persistent high unemployment in Europe and in developing countries was not universally shared. The ILO articulated a contrary analysis:

> The case for labour market deregulation rests crucially on the claim that labour market regulations in developing countries mandate excessively high benefits and are highly distortionary. Yet there has been very little direct empirical evidence to support this claim. Countries throughout the developing world tend to provide very much standardized levels of employment security and maternity protection levels. In other words, employers face very similar levels of costs in terms of the notice period for dismissal, severance pay, period of maternity leave, and maternity cash benefits. This does not therefore seem to be a major factor that influences the relative international competitiveness of developing countries.[28]

Stiglitz outlined an alternative strategy that extolled the benefits, 'the high road', of core worker rights in assuring labor market stability: a more equitable distribution of income and worker participation in the peaceful transformation of developing economies.[29] This broader definition of development as transformation and of the unions as playing a positive role in accomplishing this objective, as well as the ILO concept of worker rights, conflicted with the World Bank and IMF's emphasis on the adverse economic efficiency consequences of freedom of association and collective bargaining agreements.

In 1998, the ILO International Labour Conference approved a Declaration on Fundamental Principles and Rights at Work (ILO Declaration), which focused on four internationally recognized core principles: freedom of association and the 'effective recognition of the right to collective bargaining'; freedom from forced labor; the effective abolition of child labor; and non-discrimination in

27. Joseph Stiglitz, 'Democratic Development as the Fruits of Labor', keynote address given at the Industrial Relations Research Association (Boston, MA, January 2000); *see also* Toke Aidt & Zafiris Tzannatos, 'The Cost and Benefits of Collective Bargaining', The World Bank SP Discussion Paper, No. 0120 (September 2001).
28. International Labour Organization, *World Employment Report 1996/97: National Policies in a Global Context* (Geneva: International Labor Office, 1997), 85.
29. *See* Stiglitz, *supra* n. 27.

employment.[30] Within this context, no single collective bargaining regime was preferred so long as unions were freely chosen by the membership and not subject to government direction.[31]

Critics alleged that core worker rights were a disguised form of protectionism and reflected cultural preferences rather than international 'rights'.[32] In the 1998 deliberations over the ILO Declaration, the African Vice Chairperson of the Workers Group replied to such criticism:

> The workers' group is quite clear that to ask to belong to a trade union and for it to bargain on your behalf is not protectionism; . . . to wish to eradicate discrimination in the workplace is not protectionism; to call for an end to slavery or forced labor is not protectionism; but to deny those rights to workers in the name of comparative advantaged – that is truly protectionism.[33]

Not once however, has the World Bank or the IMF denied financing to a country on the grounds that the government used the coercive power of the state to deny workers the rights of free association and collective bargaining. Such intervention by the IFIs was considered 'political' and therefore contravened by the charter provisions that prohibited decisions on financing to be made on anything other than economic criteria.[34] In contrast, conditions attaching to financing that required 'labor market flexibility measures' advanced economic efficiency and, consequently, economic development. In the IFIs' views, therefore, such conditions did not contravene the 'political' provisions of the World Bank charter.

Although the IMF has no comparable 'political' prohibition in its governing charter, it followed the same philosophy as the World Bank in espousing labor market flexibility measures and declining to intervene to deny financing to countries that were egregious abusers of workers' rights. Within the IMF, critics have noted that the IMF emphasis upon labor market flexibility had the effect of weakening core worker rights.[35]

30. *See* International Labour Organization, 'Declaration on Fundamental Principles and Rights at Work' (Geneva, June 1998), *available at* <www.ilo.org/declaration/thedeclaration/textdeclaration/lang--en/index.htm>; *see also* ILO Declaration, Programme for the Promotion of the ILO Declaration on Fundamental Principles and Rights at Work, 'The Four Fundamental Principles and Rights at Work', *available at* <www.ilo.org/declaration/principles/freedomofassociation/lang--en/index.htm> (providing a description of each of the four core principles).
31. Kimberly Ann Elliott, 'The ILO and Enforcement of Core Labor Standards', *Institute for International Economics: International Economics Policy Briefs* 00-6 (July 2000).
32. Jagdish Bhagwati, 'Labour Standards, Social Clause and WTO', seminar at the Department of Labor (1993); Gary Hufbauer & Theodore Moran, 'Why a "Grand Deal" on Labour Could End Trade Talks', *Financial Times*, 13 Mar. 1997, Asia edition.
33. United Nations Association of the United States, 'Worker Rights in the Global Economy', A Briefing Book of the UNA-USA Global Policy Project; *see also* International Labour Organization, 'Report of the Committee on the Declaration of Principles', prepared as part of the 86th Session (Geneva, June 1998), *available at* <www.ilo.org/public/english/standards/relm/ilc/ilc86/com-decd.htm>.
34. IBRD Articles of Agreement, *supra* n. 4, Art. IV(10).
35. Hector Torres, 'Reforming the International Monetary Fund – Why Its Legitimacy Is at Stake', *Journal of International Economic Law* 10 (2007): 443–460.

During the 1997–1998 East Asia financial crisis, the IMF demonstrated a degree of flexibility in interpreting the limits of its intervention to address labor market abuses. The IMF intervened with the government of South Korea to soften measures intended by the government to weaken worker collective bargaining rights; and in Indonesia, the IMF intervened to obtain the release of an imprisoned, ill labor union leader.[36] More recently, as the IMF has limited the degree of its intervention in the economic policy-making of Member Countries, it has de-emphasized its role in setting conditions related to the functioning of labor markets. The limits of that intervention were graphically illustrated in Argentina in the mid-1990s.

A. Argentina

Of all the countries in South America, Argentina, during Carlos Saul Menem's administration in the 1990s, most enthusiastically embraced the Washington Consensus policies. In 1989, faced with a raging inflation that had caused the resignation of President Raul Alfonsin prior to the formal close of his term of office, the Menem government adopted a policy of linking the Argentine peso to the dollar. This meant that the Argentine government guaranteed that each peso could be exchanged in a one-to-one relationship with the dollar.[37] Argentine economic policy, fiscal and monetary policy, then was limited by the amount of dollar holdings of the Central Bank. The constraints imposed by the convertibility plan, as it was known in Argentina, limited the ability of the Argentine government to employ counter-cyclical economic measures, such as higher fiscal expenditures, in the face of weak economic growth. This strategy also encouraged foreign borrowing in order to enlarge the size of government dollar reserve holdings.

These limitations were compounded by the adoption of the Washington Consensus measures: privatization of state-owned enterprises, opening the economy to imports, and reducing the role of the state in the direct production of goods and services. In Argentina, this economic strategy was associated with a stubbornly high rate of unemployment. Privatized state enterprises reduced employment as part of cost-savings programmes; and cost-cutting measures were accentuated by the need to be internationally competitive and the opening of the economy to imports.

According to the IMF, labor market rigidity caused the continued high unemployment. The IMF observed:

> Flexible labor markets are an essential condition for the smooth functioning of a fixed exchange rate regime and yet Argentina's labor market continues to be

36. Stanley Fischer, testimony before the Congressional Advisory Commission on International Financial Institutions (1999) (Fischer was the Deputy Managing Director of the International Monetary Fund).
37. Domingo Cavallo & Joaquin Cottani, 'Argentina's Convertibility Plan and the IMF', *The American Economic Review* 87, no. 2 (May 1997): 17–18 (explaining the development of the Convertibility Plan that linked the peso to the dollar one-to-one).

> characterized by a centralized bargaining process, high dismissal costs and a host of payroll taxes and contributions .... There is evidence that double-digit unemployment rates has been due not only to transitional factors pertaining to economic liberalization and industrial restructuring, but also the high cost of labor relative to capital resulting from high payroll taxes ... as well as from the stringent constraints to hiring and firing perpetuated by the existing legislation.[38]

The issue came to a head in 1996. Since the late 1940s, Argentina has had a strong union movement closely linked to the Justicialista political party, which was popularly known as the Peronista party, named after the Argentina 'strong man' Juan Peron. Peron brought the 'shirtless' ones (los descamisados), who were the factory workers, particularly those in the meat packing plants, into the mainstream of Argentine society by empowering their unions. The unions not only negotiated salaries and working conditions for their members, but also administered 'obras sociales', which were health plans for both members and non-members of unions, and this service enhanced member loyalty to their unions.

Menem, a Peronista himself, in endorsing the Washington Consensus policies of relying upon domestic and foreign private enterprise as the motor of the economy and embracing a diminished role for the state, appeared to be abandoning Peronista priorities: a reliance upon the state for economic leadership and a suspicion of Argentine and foreign private enterprise. Menem accepted the IMF and World Bank analysis of labor market rigidity as the primary cause of continuing high unemployment and the consequent policy prescription of labor market flexibility measures, weak centralized collective bargaining, and significant reduction of severance payments for dismissed workers. In so doing, he set up a confrontation with the unions.[39]

That confrontation was further accentuated by the World Bank's demands that the unions be prevented from administering the obras sociales. Bank technicians presented this recommendation to union leaders as an administrative efficiency measure, but it was not so interpreted by those leaders. Instead, they saw it as a part of a larger strategic objective of weakening union loyalty and thereby diminishing union influence in economic policy.

Still, Menem retained the loyalty of an older group of union leaders, who formed a part of his 'kitchen' cabinet. This group urged caution in confronting the Menem government over the proposed labor market flexibility measures. A younger group of union leaders were convinced that if they did not take a stand against the labor flexibility measures recommended by the government, it would mean a loss of power and prestige for the unions in Argentine society and among their members from which they would never recover.

---

38. International Monetary Fund, *World Economic Report* (Washington, DC: International Monetary Fund, 1999), 53.
39. The following account of what transpired is based on the author's conversations with union leaders in 1996 while he was on a speaking tour in Argentina sponsored by the AFL-CIO and CGT.

The issue was decided in the Confederación General del Trabajo de la República Argentina (CGT), the Argentine Confederation of Labour, which is the umbrella group of the Argentine labor movement. Those arguing for a more aggressive stance against the government prevailed. A general strike was called for August 1996. However, given the divisions among the union leadership, and that the middle and upper classes generally distrusted Argentine union leaders, the call for a general strike appeared to be highly problematic. Contrary to the forebodings of union leaders, the strike was highly successful. Unease over the government's economic policies and the labor market flexibility initiatives had engendered more opposition on the factory floor than government officials and political commentators had anticipated. Unlike previous strikes during the Menem Administration, this strike also enjoyed broad support among Argentina's middle class. As one commentator noted, '[a] 24 hour general strike brought Argentina to near standstill yesterday as police clashed with marchers protesting against an economic policy they blame for recession and record unemployment'.[40]

Encouraged by the success of the August stoppage, in late September 1996, the CGT called for another general strike. Following that strike, one commentator noted:

> In the largest demonstration against the economic policies of President Carlos Saul Menem since he took office seven years ago, striking labor unions and a disgruntled public brought Argentina to a near standstill today .... The unions are particularly upset over a recent government proposal to overhaul decades-old labor laws. The plan, which officials say will create new jobs and increase productivity, will also reduce traditionally high severance pay and make it easier for companies to hire and fire workers.[41]

What was also notable about the September general strike was not only the broad support evident in Argentina, but also that labor union leaders from neighbouring countries, including Brazil, Bolivia, and Uruguay, came to Buenos Aires to march in solidarity with the Argentine CGT. This showed the growing opposition in the region to the Washington Consensus economic policies dominant during the 1990s. That opposition culminated in elections in Argentina in 2001, in which the government party was defeated, and the Radical Party, led by Fernando De la Rua, returned to power.[42]

Determined to maintain the Convertibility Plan at any cost, the De la Rua government imposed economic austerity measures. Unconvinced that the plan was feasible, the IMF refused further financing. In December 2001, broad-based demonstrations in the streets of Buenos Aires and other major cities, and the prospect of continued social and political unrest, led to the resignation of President

40. David Haskel, 'Largest Strike yet for Workers in Argentina', *Houston Chronicle*, 9 Aug. 1996.
41. Calvin Sims, 'Argentina Stops for a Day as Millions Strike', *The New York Times*, 28 Sep. 1996.
42. In Latin America, 'Radical' generally denotes a political party with its base of support in the lower middle class with a high tolerance for state intervention in the economy.

De la Rua.[43] The Argentine Congress selected Eduardo Duhalde, the Mayor of Buenos Aires, and a leader of the Peronista party who had opposed the Menem government economic policies, to serve out the presidential term of De la Rua.[44]

The Duhalde government rejected the economic policy advice of the IMF. Several days after taking office, President Duhalde abandoned the policy that linked the peso to the US dollar at a one-to-one ratio.[45] Argentina defaulted on billions of dollars of foreign debt. Following that default, the successor-elected government of Nelson Kirchner, also a Peronista leader, but from the far southern province of Patagonia, continued to reject advice from the IMF. The Kirchner government declined to offer its external creditors a generous debt deal, and instead, insisted upon a drastic reduction in the nominal amount of Argentina's bond indebtedness as a part of any debt renegotiation deal with the creditors.[46]

On 3 March 2005, President Kirchner announced that 76% of Argentina's external creditors had accepted a draconian reduction in the external debt. The creditors would receive at most thirty cents repayment on each dollar of indebtedness, or, put another way, a 70% reduction in the nominal value of the bonds. Approximately USD 20 billion of external indebtedness, representing creditors who refused to participate in the deal, remained outstanding.[47]

Fuelled in large part by Chinese and Indian purchases of Argentine agricultural commodities, the Argentine government achieved economic growth rates of 8% per annum in real terms, in 2005 and subsequent years. Argentina repaid its outstanding financing from the IMF with money borrowed from Venezuela. Without recourse to the international financial markets, but with historically strong trade surpluses, Argentina had, in effect, declared its independence from the economic and debt policy guidance of the IMF.

B. The Aftermath of the Argentinean Experience

The labor market flexibility initiatives of the Menem years were shelved. In the other Southern Cone countries, Chile, Brazil, Uruguay, and Bolivia, successive elections brought to power governments of the centre-left. These governments

43. Rupert Cornwell, 'Argentine President Resigns After Second Day of Rioting', *The Independent*, 21 Dec. 2001, *available at* <www.independent.co.uk/news/world/americas/argentine-president-resigns--after-second-day-of-rioting-620872.html>; U.N. Wire, 'President Resigns As Chaos Reigns, Debt Default Possible', 21 Dec. 2001, <www.unwire.org/unwire/20011221/22754_story.asp>.
44. BBC News, 'Argentina's New President Sworn In', 2 Jan. 2002, *available at* <http://news.bbc.co.uk/2/hi/americas/1738175.stm>.
45. Larry Rohter, 'Argentina Unlinks Peso from Dollar, Bracing for Devaluation and Even Harder Times', *The New York Times*, 7 Jan. 2002, s. A, 6, *available at* <www.nytimes.com/2002/01/07/world/argentina-unlinks-peso-from-dollar-bracing-for-devaluation-and-even-harder-times.html>.
46. Paul Blustein, 'Argentina Didn't Fall on Its Own', *Washington Post*, 3 Aug. 2003, s. A1.
47. Larry Rohter, 'Argentina Announces Deal on Its Debt Default', *The New York Times*, 4 Mar. 2005, s. C3.

represented a broad spectrum of economic policy initiatives from the radical Venezuelan attempt to restructure the economy along 'socialist' lines to the more market-friendly policies of the government of Luiz Inacio 'Lula' da Silva in Brazil. Whatever their differences in overall economic policy-making, it seems clear that, for these governments, labor market flexibility measures intended to weaken the role of unions in collective bargaining would not be a part of the policy mix.

The World Bank Group, including the International Finance Corporation (IFC) and the International Development Association (IDA), has made adherence to core labor standards a requirement in all IFC financing and infrastructure financing by the World Bank and the IDA.[48] The World Bank's 2006–2007 publication *Doing Business*, however, promotes the view that:

> labor standards have no beneficial impact but should be seen as possible impediments to investment because they increase the cost of doing business. The publication grades and ranks countries according to whether they have various kinds of worker protection rules – ranging from limitations on hours of work, to minimum wages and requirements of advance notice of dismissal – and encourages countries to improve their ranking by eliminating these regulations.[49]

After Congressional hearings highly critical of the *Doing Business* report labor market comments, the World Bank has minimized its reliance on that report.[50] These conflicting approaches within the World Bank accurately reflect the Bank's continued ambivalence concerning core labor standards.

V. UNITED STATES POLICY

That ambivalence has also characterized United States policy with respect to core worker rights in the international economy. Congress has set forth a clear position with respect to trade policy. Legislation concerning a generalized system of preferences for poorer countries, including the Caribbean Basin Initiative,[51] the Andean Trade Preference Act,[52] the Overseas Private Investment Corporation,[53]

48. Global Unions, 'Statement by Global Unions to the 2007 Annual Meetings of the IMF and World Bank' (Washington, DC, 20–22 Oct. 2007).
49. *Ibid.*
50. 'The Fight Against Global Poverty and Inequality: The World Bank's Approach to Core Labor Standards and Employment Creation', Hearing before the Committee on Financial Services, United States House of Representatives, 110th Congress, First Session (3 Oct. 2007).
51. The Caribbean Basin Initiative was launched by the Caribbean Basin Economic Recovery Act (CBERA), 19 U.S.C. 2701 et seq. (5 Aug. 1983, amended 20 Aug. 1990). *See also* US Department of Commerce International Trade Administration, 'Guide to the Caribbean Basin Initiative' (Washington, DC: International Trade Administration, November 2000), *available at* <www.sice.oas.org/TPD/USA_CBI/Studies/USITCcbi2000_e.pdf>.
52. Andean Trade Preference Act (ATPA), 19 U.S.C. 3201 et seq. (4 Dec. 1991).
53. Overseas Private Investment Corporation (OPIC), <www.opic.gov> (established in 1971).

and the Omnibus Trade Act of 1974, as amended,[54] all contain language conditioning the awarding of benefits of the various measures to an individual country upon its adherence to internationally recognized worker rights.[55] Most of the legislation antedates the 1998 ILO core worker rights standard, hence, the difference in language, 'internationally recognized worker rights' rather than the 'ILO core worker rights', but the intent of the various legislative provisions is clear: countries should not benefit from the trade preferences accorded by the legislation if they deny workers basic rights, particularly freedom of association and the right to bargain collectively.

After a decade of often bitter dispute, there has emerged a consensus in Congress over linking core worker rights to international trade agreements. In 1997, President Clinton was denied fast-track authority to negotiate trade agreements.[56] Fast-track authority refers to a congressional procedure by which the executive branch could negotiate a trade agreement and be assured of an up or down vote in Congress without amendments and within defined time limits. The 1997 initiative failed over disagreements as to whether worker rights and environmental conditions should attach to the granting of such authority to the Executive.

By 2002, a consensus had emerged in Congress and with then-President George W. Bush. The President was granted fast-track authority (renamed Trade Promotion Authority (TPA)), and worker rights and environmental conditions were elevated to the same plane of importance as negotiating objectives as commercial considerations.[57] Labor and environmental provisions were to be incorporated in the main body of the agreement; and dispute settlement provisions concerning labor and the environment were to be 'equivalent' to those governing commercial disputes. Each country was to ensure effective enforcement of its own labor and environmental laws.[58]

---

54. Trade Act of 1974, 19 U.S.C. 2101 et seq. (3 Jan. 1975).
55. AFL-CIO Task Force on Trade, *Worker Rights in U.S. International Trade and Investment Law* (May 1996).
56. *See* John F. Harris, 'Clinton Offers Assurances on Free Trade: President Tells Mexico, Other Latin Nations Not to be Discouraged', *Washington Post*, 15 Nov. 1997, s. A, 21; David E. Sanger, 'The Trade Bill: The Impact; A Handicap, but Clinton Still Has Trade Levarage', *The New York Times*, 11 Nov. 1997, s. A, 6, *available at* <www.nytimes.com/1997/11/11/world/the-trade-bill-the-impact-a-handicap-but-clinton-still-has-trade-leverage.html?pagewanted=1>; *see also* Lenore Sek, 'IB10084: Fast-Track Authority for Trade Agreements (Trade Promotion Authority): Background and Developments in the 107th Congress', <http://fpc.state.gov/documents/organization/16806.pdf> (providing background information on fast-track authority and linking to H.R. 2621, which was not passed and therefore denied President Clinton of fast-track authority).
57. To Extend the Andean Trade Preference Act, to grant additional trade benefits under that Act, and for other purposes, P.L. 107–210 (6 Aug. 2002) (for information about it, including the fact that the Trade Act of 2002 gave the President fast-track authority, *see* <www.opencongress.org/wiki/Trade_Act_of_2002>); *see* Trade Act of 2002, H.R. 3009 (passed by House, 27 Jul. 2002; passed by Senate, 1 Aug. 2002), *available at* <http://thomas.loc.gov/cgi-bin/bdquery/z?d107:H.R.3009:>.
58. Committee on Ways and Means, United States House of Representatives, 'Trade Promotion Authority: Summary of Bipartisan Conference Report' (27 Apr. 2002).

In a subsequent agreement involving Peru, the criteria was changed to core worker rights rather than enforcement of one's own laws thereby avoiding the situation in which the laws themselves failed to accord core worker rights.[59] While the dispute settlement provisions were identical to those governing commercial disputes rather than 'equivalent', thus eliminating possible disputes over the meaning of 'equivalent'.

This evolving consensus was only partially due to the change in control of the US Congress in 2006 from Republican to Democratic leadership. The seeds of change could be seen in 1998, when, in the midst of the East Asian financial crisis, the Clinton Administration sought an increase in the United States quota subscription in the IMF.[60] A Republican-controlled Congress accepted amendments offered by Congressman Barney Frank (D-Mass) to the proposed legislation that directed the Secretary of the Treasury to direct the United States Executive Director (USED) of the IMF to use the 'voice and vote' of the United States in the institution to promote core worker rights in the IMF financing programmes with Member Countries.[61] The legislation further instructed the USED to ensure that labor market flexibility measures sought by the IMF as a part of such programmes did not undermine core worker rights. However, there is no recorded instance in the executive board where the USED voted against a programme of financing in a country where the government used the coercive power of the state to deny core worker rights.

Both in the trade regime and the financing programmes of the IFIs, the United States has sought to promote policies that open the economies of Member Countries to FDI, but it has imposed no commensurate obligations on companies or governments to respect core worker rights. In China, the Clinton Administration negotiated favourable terms to enable United States companies to operate within China, and did so as a pre-condition for China's admission to the World Trade Organization (WTO).

In 2006, the Chinese government had become concerned over the growing income inequality accompanying the wild west capitalist model of development it had adopted. In order to mitigate this growing income inequality, the government proposed modest changes in the labor laws that would effectively strengthen the hand of workers and their unions in collective bargaining negotiations with

59. United States-Peru Trade Promotion Agreement, Art. 17 (12 Apr. 2006), <www.ustr.gov/trade-agreements/free-trade-agreements/peru-tpa/final-text> (for the text of Art. 17, *see* <www.ustr.gov/sites/default/files/uploads/agreements/fta/peru/asset_upload_file73_9496.pdf>).

60. BBC News, 'Clinton Urges Global reform', 5 Oct. 1998, <http://news.bbc.co.uk/2/hi/special_report/1998/10/98/imf/185193.stm> (noting that President Clinton urged the US Congress to approve increased funds for the IMF).

61. Encouragement of Fair Labor Practices, 22 U.S.C. 262p-4 (20 Aug. 1996), *available at* <www.law.cornell.edu/uscode/html/uscode22/usc_sec_22_00000262---p004p.html>; *see also* International Monetary Fund Reform and Authorization Act of 1998, H.R. 3114 (27 Jan. 1998), *available at* <http://thomas.loc.gov/cgi-bin/query/z?c105:H.R.3114.IH:>. *See generally* Dick Nanto, 'The Asian Financial Crisis', CRS Report for Congress (6 Feb. 1998), *available at* <www.fas.org/man/crs/crs-asia2.htm> (explaining the IMF funding at the Sanders-Frank Amendment).

employers. These changes were opposed by the United States Chamber of Commerce, which represented the United States business community in China, and by the European equivalent organization. They warned that such changes, however modest, would discourage FDI.[62] Yet, there was little reaction in the United States: no editorial comment in the major media, television coverage, or statements by administration officials. This lack of reaction shows the continued US ambivalence towards protecting workers' rights abroad, especially when outrage may hinder business.

VI. THE WORLD TRADE ORGANIZATION AND WORKERS' RIGHTS

The ambivalence within the World Bank with respect to core worker rights is mirrored in international trade and investment policy. Although in the United States the majority view is in favour of linking worker rights to trade agreements, as can be seen in TPA, at the global level, no consensus exists on such linkage. The first WTO Ministerial Declaration relegated the subject to consultation with the ILO; and the Ministers even declined to form a working group to discuss the issue.[63] The Doha WTO communique included one sentence referring to the ILO as the proper forum for dealing with worker rights.[64] This refusal within the WTO to begin a dialogue relating core worker rights to the international trade regime embodied by the WTO contrasts with the Ministers' willingness to form a working group to discuss possible linkage of environmental considerations to trade agreements.

The WTO Doha round of negotiations is at an impasse, largely over agricultural policy. If by some miracle, differences over the agriculture issue could be overcome, the contrast between the emerging consensus in the United States on core worker rights and international trade, and the impasse in the WTO over this issue could emerge as a further stumbling block to any agreement. That discrepancy between the evolving consensus in the United States on the desirability of linking core worker rights to international trade and investment agreements and development finance is in conflict with the view of some important borrowing countries of the IFIs who oppose such linkage and who are also members of the WTO. Thus, core worker rights as it relates to FDI may prove to be the next topic of debate in the WTO Doha round.

---

62. Geoff Dyer, 'China's Labour Debate Spurs War of Words for US Interests', *Financial Times*, 3 May 2007, P7; Zana Z. Bugaighis, 'What Impact Will the Revised Trade Union Law of China Have on Foreign Business', *Pacific Rim Law & Policy* 16 (March 2007): 405.
63. World Trade Organization, 'First Ministerial Declaration' (Singapore, December 1996).
64. World Trade Organization, 'Ministerial Declaration, Fourth Session' (Doha, November 2001).

VII. CONCLUSION

The issue of core worker rights cannot be separated from the larger question of the shape of the international trade, investment, and development finance regime. The emergence of China and India as major commodities consumers, and in the case of China, as a source of investment capital for commodity producers, has reduced the reliance of member countries upon the IFIs for investment capital. Countries such as Argentina and Brazil are earning the largest trade surpluses in their history. In Africa, countries with commodities in demand by China are recipients of investment capital from China without the conditionality that attaches to IFI financing. Therefore, they have little need to borrow from the IFIs. Even in the midst of the financial crisis which erupted in the fall of 2008, it is notable that no major Latin American country has recurred to the IMF for financing. IMF financing has, for the most part, been concentrated in Eastern European countries and Africa.

Indeed, both Brazil and Argentina, among others, have repaid the debt from the previous financing they received from the IMF. The ability of the IMF and World Bank to impose intrusive conditions to their financing, like labor market flexibility measures, is severely constrained. At the same time their ability, if they were so inclined to address labor market abuses, is now also non-existent.

The impasse in the Doha negotiations may also reflect a more fundamental rethinking of the role of the WTO. The stalemate over core worker rights in the trade and investment regime, and the ambivalence of the World Bank on this issue, are a surrogate for the more fundamental issue of whether the existing structure of international institutions, constructed in the aftermath of World War II – the IMF, World Bank, and the WTO (as it has evolved from the General Agreement on Tariffs and Trade (GATT)) – which have essentially governed that regime, are any longer viable. And, if not, what if any substitute set of institutions or arrangements is to take its place.[65]

An enhanced role for the IMF in the aftermath of the financial crisis that erupted in the Fall of 2008, is unlikely to change the IMF approach to core worker rights. Indeed the IMF is beginning to limit the conditions it attaches to its financing to those issues most directly related to achieving external balance equilibrium, and those conditions are unlikely to include labor market reforms. Nor is the emergence of the Group of 20 (G-20) nations as a forum for the discussion of international economic and financial issues likely to tackle the impasse over worker rights existent in the WTO. That group now includes, among others Brazil, China, India, and Russia, all of whom are opposed to linking core worker rights to international trade and development financing. There is then a fundamental disagreement within the traditional and new international fora over the role of core worker rights in the globalized economy.

65. George P. Schultz, William E. Simon & Walter H. Wriston, 'Who Needs the IMF?', *The Wall Street Journal*, 3 Feb. 1998, Op-Ed; Mervyn King, 'Reform of the International Monetary Fund', speech given by the Governor of the Bank of England at the Indian Council for Research on International Economic Relations (New Delhi, India, 20 Feb. 2006), *available at* <www.bankofengland.co.uk/publications/speeches/2006/speech267.pdf>.

Chapter 11

International Environmental Law, the World Bank, and International Financial Institutions

Charles E. Di Leva

I. INTRODUCTION

This chapter addresses the treatment of international environmental law at international financial institutions (IFIs), particularly the World Bank.[1] While the World Bank and the major IFIs take similar approaches towards international

1. This chapter was prepared in the author's individual capacity and does not represent the views of the World Bank, or any of its affiliated organizations, or any of its officers or staff. The author would like to express his gratitude for the research and contributions of his colleagues, Sachiko Morita, Counsel, and Ms May Agcaoili. The IFIs discussed here are those multilateral financial institutions in which governments are the owners and are represented by their appointed representatives on the boards for the institutions. The discussion has not included government-owned bilateral agencies, though some of them maintain very similar policies and procedures as do the IFIs. While governments are the owners of the institutions, each of the IFIs transacts with both public- and private-sector entities either on its own or through an affiliated entity. Regardless of whether the funds are directed toward public or private enterprises, the activities of most IFIs are generally geared to be implemented only in developing countries.

Daniel D. Bradlow and David B. Hunter, *International Financial Institutions and International Law*, pp. 343–385.

environmental law, the field is not easily defined. Illustrative of the definitional challenge is the following description:

> When attempting to determine the boundaries of international environmental law, one finds that no clear definition can be applied. Like many other branches of international law, international environmental law is interdisciplinary, intersecting and overlapping with numerous other areas of research, including economics, political science, ecology, human rights and navigation/admiralty.[2]

Thus, the sheer breadth of international environmental law makes it difficult to define its boundaries. As Professors Birnie and Boyle in their treatise on the subject note: 'A number of preliminary problems arise in any attempt to define "international environmental law".'[3] They use the term broadly as a 'convenient way to encompass the entire corpus of international law, public and private, relevant to international environmental issues or problems'.[4] Other definitions of international environmental law abound in the literature,[5] but for the purposes of this chapter, Professor Philippe Sands offers a particularly helpful definition of IEL: 'International environmental law comprises those substantive, procedural and institutional rules of international law which have as their primary objective the protection of the environment.'[6] This definition is apt here because international environmental law should have environment firmly within its ambit, and international law should include the policies and procedures of international organizations such as the World Bank that make up their internal body of law.

The environmental policies and procedures of the World Bank can therefore be seen to be part of international environmental law, especially when noting that the World Bank has been a United Nations specialized agency since 1947.[7] This

---

2. Anne Burnett, 'International Environmental Law', in *American Society of International Law Guide to Electronic Resources for International Law*, ed. Kelly Vinopal (1997), *available at* <www.asil.org/resource/env1.htm>.
3. Patricia W. Birnie & Alan E. Boyle, *International Law and the Environment*, 2nd edn (Oxford University Press, 2002).
4. *Ibid.*
5. *See, e.g.*, Alexandre Kiss & Dinah Shelton, *Guide to International Environmental Law* (Leiden, Netherlands & Boston, MA: Martinus Nijhoff Publishers, 2007).
6. Philippe Sands, *Principles of International Environmental Law*, 2nd edn (Cambridge & New York: Cambridge University Press, 2003), 15.
7. In 1947, in accordance with the United Nations ability to enter into agreements pursuant to Art. 63 of the United Nations Charter, the World Bank (then referred to solely as the International Bank for Reconstruction and Development) entered into an agreement with the United Nations that defined the terms on which the United Nations and the Bank were brought into a relationship. It was approved by the World Bank Board of Governors of the Bank on 16 Sep. 1947 and by the General Assembly of the United Nations on 15 Nov. 1947. *See* Agreement between the United Nations and International Bank for Reconstruction and Development, 16 U.N.T.S. 346 (1947) (hereinafter UN-World Bank Relationship Agreement); *see also* United Nations, *Official Records of the General Assembly, Second Session* (A/519), 28. *See also* Agreement between the United Nations and the International Bank for Reconstruction and Development (acting for and on behalf of the International Finance Corporation) on Relationship Between the United

view of international environmental law is also supported by Birnie and Boyle who noted that:

> [m]uch of international environmental law is the product of an essentially legislative process involving the interplay of international organizations, conference diplomacy, codification and progressive development, and international courts, and a relatively subtle interplay of treaties, non-binding declarations or resolutions, and customary international law.[8]

Even more specifically, Birney and Boyle note that 'international institutions, including the UN and its specialized and regional agencies and programmes, have played a leading role in setting law-making agendas and providing negotiating forums and expertise'.[9]

To bring additional clarity to the definition of international environmental law, Sands notes that 'the term "environment" encompasses both the features and the products of the natural world and those of human civilization'.[10] Thus, the view of Sands, as well as Birnie and Boyle, seems to comport with the approach used in the World Bank to include forests and natural habitats, as well as physical cultural resources as part of Bank environmental policies.

While support for the environment has long been a significant aspect of the World Bank's work, this became especially true following the United Nations Conference on Environment and Development (the 'Rio Conference').[11] Particularly since then, the Bank has used a range of instruments to directly and indirectly support the objectives set forth in a wide range of the international environmental law instruments cited above, especially those that were prominent at the Rio Conference.[12] These instruments include the environmental and social policies that the Bank uses when carrying out its activities, a range of environmentally supportive projects and financial instruments, and the Bank's research programme and sector specific strategies. In addition, the World Bank has several hundred environmental professionals on staff, has been the only IFI with a dedicated environmental law unit (though others are considering creating the same and have lawyers working on these same issues), and is one of the three original Implementing Agencies of the Global Environment Facility (GEF).[13] These factors contribute

---

Nations and the International Finance Corporation, 265 U.N.T.S. 314 (1957), *available at* <http://untreaty.un.org/unts/1_60000/8/32/00015584.pdf> (hereinafter UN-IFC Relationship Agreement).

8. Birnie & Boyle, *supra* n. 3.
9. *Ibid.*, 10.
10. *Ibid.*
11. UN Conference on Environment and Development (The Earth Summit) (1992), <www.un.org/geninfo/bp/enviro.html>.
12. Independent Evaluation Group (IEG)-World Bank, *Environmental Sustainability: An Evaluation of World Bank Group Support* (Washington, DC: The International Bank for Reconstruction and Development, 2008), *available at* <http://siteresources.worldbank.org/EXTENVIRONMENT/Resources/environ_eval.pdf>.
13. *See* Global Environment Facility, 'Instrument for the Establishment of the Restructured Global Environment Facility' (March 2008 (revision of original October 1994 publication)), *available at* <http://www.thegef.org/gef/sites/thegef.org/files/publication/GEF_Instrument_March08.pdf>.

to the Bank being the 'largest multilateral source of environment-related financing'.[14] This chapter reviews IFIs' environment-related policies, projects, and programmes to provide a sense of the range of efforts IFIs take in support of international environmental law.

After a brief overview of the institutional setting, this chapter will focus on the policies of the World Bank and selected IFIs, and, in particular, how these policies support the broadly accepted international environmental law principles set forth in the Rio Declaration. The chapter will then review a sampling of projects, programmes, and financial instruments that are developed specifically to support international environmental law.

II. BACKGROUND: THE MATURING OF ENVIRONMENT WITHIN THE WORLD BANK AND OTHER IFIs

When marking his first hundred days as president of the World Bank, Robert Zoellick stressed the importance of the Bank's role in addressing the global environment and stated that '[i]t is the vision of the World Bank Group to contribute to an inclusive and sustainable globalization – to overcome poverty, enhance growth with care for the environment, and create individual opportunity and hope'.[15] Similar concern for the environment has been expressed by previous heads of the World Bank,[16] as well as the heads of other multilateral financial institutions. For example, in 2008, the Asian Development Bank (ADB) published its long-term strategic framework for 2008–2020, in which President Haruhiko Kuroda declared that, '[u]nder Strategy 2020, [the ADB] will redirect [its] focus onto the region's three critical strategic agendas: inclusive economic growth, environmentally sustainable growth, and regional integration'.[17]

Despite this commitment to environment at the highest level of the IFIs, there continues to be ample discussion and criticism of how and whether the World Bank and other IFIs have fully supported the goals of international environmental law.[18]

---

14. IEG-World Bank, *Environmental Sustainability: An Evaluation of World Bank Group Support*, *supra* n. 12, xvi.
15. The World Bank, 'Zoellick: Globalization Must Benefit the World's Poor', Press Release No. 2008/090/EXC (10 Oct. 2007), *available at* <http://web.worldbank.org/WBSITE/EXTERNAL/NEWS/0,,contentMDK:21504682~pagePK:64257043~piPK:437376~theSitePK:4607,00.html>.
16. *See* Charles Di Leva, 'International Environmental Law and Development', *Georgetown International Environmental Law Review* 10 (1998): 501, 504 (referring to remarks of former President James D. Wolfensohn), and 540 (to remarks of former President Barber Conable).
17. Asian Development Bank, *Strategy 2020: The Long-Term Strategic Framework of the Asian Development Bank 2008–2020* (Philippines: Asian Development Bank, April 2008), *available at* <www.adb.org/documents/Policies/Strategy2020/default.asp?p=strtg>.
18. In the 1980s, there was extensive criticism of the Bank and its role in large hydroelectric facilities, foremost the Sardar Sarovar projects in India. The engagement was chronicled in the Morse-Berger report. Bradford Morse & Thomas Berger, *Sardar Sarovar: Report of the Independent Review* (Ottawa: Resource Futures International, 1992). The report found evidence

At the same time, the international community has realized the importance in encouraging the World Bank and other IFIs to become fully engaged in the objectives of sustainable development. One outcome of this effort is that the World Bank became one of the GEF implementing agencies and its trustee. The GEF was established to provide grant and concessional financing to achieve the objectives of the major environmental treaties adopted at Rio. In addition, the Rio Conference identified IFIs as key actors in Agenda 21, the global blueprint to achieve sustainable development.[19]

With time, as the World Bank began to improve its environmental record, environmental groups shifted some of their criticism away from the World Bank and began concentrating on the growing role of IFI private-sector operations, as well as export credit agencies and commercial banks. For example, Citigroup was a major target of their campaigns in the time leading up to the World Summit on Sustainable Development in Johannesburg in 2002.[20] Today, however, some of the focus of criticism seems to have turned back to the World Bank and the public sector IFIs, because of the concern that they have increased their focus on infrastructure, including providing a certain, though historically declining, level of fossil fuel-based energy in developing countries.[21]

Despite this history of criticism, IFIs have provided significant financial assistance for the environment. The World Bank's financial commitment to the environment and natural resource management has been tracked since 1990, though because environment is cross-cutting and of such breadth, such measurements are

---

that the Bank had failed to comply with environmental and social policies and that these failures had major adverse impacts on local communities. The Morse-Berger report was joined by criticism of the Bank from environmental NGOs as well. *See, e.g.*, Bruce Rich, *Mortgaging the Earth: The World Bank, Environmental Impoverishment, and the Crisis of Development* (Boston: Beacon Press, 1994).

19. *See* Di Leva, 'International Environmental Law and Development', *supra* n. 16, 504, fn. 12 (referring to United Nations Conference on Environment and Development, Agenda 21: Programme of Action for Sustainable Development, UN Doc. A/CONF.151/26 (vol. 1) (12 Aug. 1992)).
20. *See* criticism of Citigroup by environmental groups, 'CEH plays leadership role at the UN World Summit on Sustainable Development' (2002), *available at* <www.wssd-and-civil-society.org/docs/CEH_01.pdf>. In response, Citigroup worked with the Rainforest Action Network to develop and later put in place a new environmental policy for their operations including a policy on illegal logging. Rainforest Action Network, 'Citigroup Adopts a Comprehensive Environmental Policy' (2003), *available at* <www.mongabay.com/external/citigroup_ran.htm>.
21. *See, e.g.*, Christopher Swann, 'World Bank Criticized for Helping Fossil Fuel Plants', *International Herald Tribune*, 11 Aug. 2008, *available at* <www.iht.com/articles/2008/08/11/business/energy.php> (focusing on a plant financed by IFC to be constructed in India). A project proposed for World Bank financing came under criticism as well. *See* David Wheeler, *Crossroads at Mmamabula: Will the World Bank Choose the Clean Energy Path? – Working Paper No. 140* (Center for Global Development, 2008), *available at* <www.cgdev.org/content/publications/detail/15401/>. It is important to note that some of this increase in the Bank's engagement in large-scale infrastructure is due to the global recession and the resulting inability to obtain private sector finance in a wide range of developing countries.

not always easy to measure. From 1990 until 2007, the World Bank provided over USD 400 billion in lending, of which USD 50 billion was reportedly for environment-related activities, though this amount might be overstated depending on how the sums are calculated.[22] A recent report by the World Bank's Independent Evaluation Group (IEG)[23] stated as follows: '[t]he Bank's thematic coding process . . . appears to overstate actual commitment for ENRM: the Bank tends to overstate the amount dedicated to environmental improvement in many of the largest investment projects'.[24]

Regardless of the exact amounts, the total sums provided for the environment are certainly increasing and have been noteworthy, especially given that the IFIs' founders did not so much as refer to the environment when they created IFIs. The charter for the World Bank (i.e., the International Bank for Reconstruction and Development) focused on economic development. The charter states that:

> The Bank shall make arrangements to ensure that the proceeds of any loan are used only for the purposes for which the loan was granted, with due attention to considerations of economy and efficiency and without regard to political or other non-economic influences or considerations.[25]

Indeed, the charters of most IFIs state that 'only economic considerations' can play a role in the decisions of the IFIs.

Similarly, the Charter of the ADB states as follows:

> The purpose of the Bank shall be to foster economic growth and co-operation in the region of Asia and the Far East (hereinafter referred to as the 'region') and to contribute to the acceleration of the process of economic development of the developing member countries in the region, collectively and individually.[26]

Similar prescriptions exist at the Inter-American Development Bank (IDB) and the African Development Bank (AfDB),[27] although the AfDB refers to '*sustainable* economic development'.[28]

---

22. IEG-World Bank, *Environmental Sustainability: An Evaluation of World Bank Group Support*, *supra* n. 12, 22.
23. *Ibid.* (The IEG reports directly to the President of the World Bank.).
24. *Ibid.*, 22.
25. International Bank for Reconstruction and Development (IBRD), Articles of Agreement (signed 27 Dec. 1945, *as amended* effective 16 Feb. 1989), III(5), *available at* <http://web.worldbank.org/WBSITE/EXTERNAL/EXTABOUTUS/ORGANIZATION/BODEXT/0,,contentMDK:20049557~isCURL:Y~menuPK:64020045~pagePK:64020054~piPK:64020408~theSitePK:278036,00.html> (hereinafter IBRD Articles of Agreement).
26. Agreement Establishing the Asian Development Bank (22 Aug. 1966), Art. 1 ('Purpose'), *available at* <www.adb.org/Documents/Reports/Charter/default.asp> (hereinafter ADB Charter).
27. Agreement Establishing the Inter-American Development Bank (8 Apr. 1959), Art. 5(f) ('Only economic considerations shall be relevant to their decisions, and these considerations shall be weighed impartially in order to achieve the purpose and functions stated in Article 1'), *available at* <www.iadb.org/leg/Documents/Pdf/Convenio-Eng.Pdf> (hereinafter IDB Charter).
28. Agreement Establishing the African Development Bank (10 Sep. 1964), Art. 1 ('Purpose'), *available at* <www.afdb.org/fileadmin/uploads/afdb/Documents/Legal-Documents/30718627-

The European Bank for Reconstruction and Development (EBRD) is the only major IFI to refer to environment in its articles of incorporation.[29] Among IFIs, the EBRD charter was the last to be enacted, and the only one that specifically requires it 'to promote in the full range of its activities environmentally sound and sustainable development'.[30]

The frequent absence of reference to environment is not for lack of opportunity to include it in the charters of these institutions. Most of these charters have been amended several times in recent years. Indeed, although the European Investment Bank lends more on an annual basis than does the World Bank, its charter, revised in 2007, also does not refer specifically to 'environment'.[31]

While the original design of the IFIs did not focus on the environment, all of them now have environmental professionals on staff, and possess at least one substantive unit or department that focuses on compliance with environmental policies.[32] Additionally, all of these institutions have developed loan and grant products that fund projects that include an exclusive focus on environment, such as environmental remediation or biodiversity protection. They have also made some degree of effort to mainstream environmental considerations into all the operations of their institutions. In essence, then, despite the lack of explicit reference to the environment in their charters, most of the IFIs are now institutions whose principal goal is to address sustainable development.[33]

The expanding attention to environmental matters has spilled over to the private-sector arms of the IFIs as well, and indeed, the International Finance Corporation (IFC), the private-sector arm of the World Bank Group, serves as a global model for bringing environmental and social corporate responsibility into commercial banks and commercial operations. This emerging trend is best seen through the launch and application of the Equator Principles,[34] the code of environmental and social principles that guides most of the world's foreign direct

---

EN-AGREEMENT-ESTABLISHING-THE-AFRICAN-DEVELOPMENT-BANK-6TH-EDITION.PDF> (hereinafter AfDB Charter).

29. *See* Agreement Establishing the European Bank for Reconstruction and Development (29 May 1990), Art. 2(1)(vii), *available at* <www.ebrd.com/pubs/insti/basics.htm> (hereinafter EBRD Charter).
30. *Ibid.*, Art. 2(1)(vii). The Agreement even requires annual reporting on the environmental impact of its activities. *See ibid.*, Art. 35(2).
31. Statute of the European Investment Bank (version dated 1 Jan. 2007), *available at* <http://europa.eu/legislation_summaries/institutional_affairs/institutions_bodies_and_agencies/o10009_en.htm>. *See* Treaty on European Union (29 Jul. 1992), *available at* <http://eur-lex.europa.eu/en/treaties/dat/11992M/htm/11992M.html>.
32. *See, e.g.*, The World Bank and the Environment, <http://web.worldbank.org/WBSITE/EXTERNAL/TOPICS/ENVIRONMENT/0,,menuPK:176751~pagePK:149018~piPK:149093~theSitePK:244381,00.html> (providing details about the World Bank and its environment related programmes).
33. Provisions relating to the European Investment Bank (EIB) in the Treaty establishing the European Community, Art. 177 of that treaty refers to the obligation of the EIB to provide annual reports on the environment.
34. *See* The Equator Principles, <www.equator-principles.com/index.shtml>.

investment in developing countries. These principles emanate from the environmental and social performance standards of the IFC. In turn, those IFC standards were adopted for the private sector principally from the World Bank's environmental and social safeguard policies.[35]

Despite the IFIs' increased commitment to the environment, more can be done to ensure that they provide all they can to support environmentally sound sustainable development. As an example, the World Bank Group's Independent Evaluation Group reported that the Bank still needs to improve its performance with regard to the environment in four areas: (1) increase its attention to environmental sustainability, work more effectively with governments and private partners to help them get better results, and strengthen internal cooperation; (2) have a group-wide new environment strategy focusing on the most underperforming regions, sectors, and countries;[36] (3) improve its monitoring and evaluation systems concerning environmental results, and better understand the environmental impacts of their operations; and (4) increase its support for public-private partnerships and take measures that can help improve the private-sector's potential for technology transfer, especially related to clean energy and sustainable supply chains, while continuing efforts related to improving environmental governance at the country level.[37]

The section below will provide a background on the role and relationship of the World Bank policies to help achieve the objectives of international environmental law. Following this section, the chapter will provide examples of some of the efforts taking place to address the types of concerns noted above. It will provide these examples by highlighting some of the new environmentally focused financial instruments and projects in which the Bank and its IFI partners are now engaged.

III. ENVIRONMENTAL POLICIES AND THEIR ROLE AND RELATIONSHIP WITH INTERNATIONAL ENVIRONMENTAL LAW

A. BACKGROUND TO WORLD BANK ENVIRONMENT-RELATED POLICIES

The environment-related policies of the World Bank and IFIs are not only elements of international environmental law; they also play a major role in supporting the

35. For a discussion of how environmental and social policies are transferred from one IFI to another, *see* David Hunter, 'Civil Society Networks and the Development of Environmental Standards at International Financial Institutions', *Chicago Journal of International Law* 8 (2008): 437.
36. The World Bank Group has launched its efforts to develop a new environment strategy, with a target completion date of December 2010. World Bank Group's Environment Strategy 2010, <http://web.worldbank.org/WBSITE/EXTERNAL/TOPICS/ENVIRONMENT/0,,contentMDK:22276657~pagePK:210058~piPK:210062~theSitePK:244381,00.html> (laying out the process for consultations and development of the policy).
37. IEG-World Bank, *Environmental Sustainability: An Evaluation of World Bank Group Support*, *supra* n. 12, 87–91.

implementation and progressive development of the field. This support occurs because the IFIs' environmental and social policies set forth the means and manner under which IFI funds can be disbursed, as well as the management tools to be used to enhance and protect the environment. As noted above, a generally similar set of policies can be found in place for almost all IFIs.

While there have been various iterations of environment-related policies in the World Bank since its inception, it is only during the last decade that the Bank has operated under a relatively unified set of ten environmental and social policies.[38] Despite their breadth of coverage, these ten policies do not include an umbrella policy toward the environment.[39] Nor since 2004 have they applied to loans that are provided for development policy support.[40]

The Bank's environmental and social policies provide the cornerstone for its efforts at sustainable poverty reduction.[41] These policies are also a considerable part of how the Bank supports the objectives of sustainable development, as that term is defined,[42] and as it is represented in the various principles of the 1992 Rio Declaration on Environment and Development.[43] Although the Rio Declaration is not a binding legal instrument, it is widely regarded as reflecting a political consensus surrounding the foundational principles of sustainable development, some of which reflect emerging principles of customary international environmental law.

Some of the key IFI safeguard policies support the principles and objectives of international environmental law as set forth in the Rio Declaration. These policies, and their relationship to the Rio Declaration, are provided below, divided into both procedural and substantive elements.

---

38. These are policies on environmental assessment, natural habitats, forest, pest management, physical cultural resources, involuntary resettlement, indigenous peoples, safety of dams, international waterways, and disputed areas. The discussion in this article of these and any other World Bank or IFI operational policies and procedures is not meant to be comprehensive. For more detail on these ten safeguard policies, *see* The World Bank, Safeguard Policies, <http://web.worldbank.org/WBSITE/EXTERNAL/PROJECTS/EXTPOLICIES/EXTSAFEPOL/0,,menuPK:584441~pagePK:64168427~piPK:64168435~theSitePK:584435,00.html>.
39. *See* Di Leva, 'International Environmental Law and Development', *supra* n. 16, 519–521, for a brief history of the development of World Bank environmental policies.
40. *See* World Bank Operational Policy (OP) 8.60 – Development Policy Lending (August 2004). That policy sets out a requirement for environmental and social review of potential impacts due to policy lending, but does not require an environmental impact assessment with its attendant requirements related to multiple public consultations and participation. *See* discussion below at s. III(A)(1)(a) and (b).
41. *See* IEG-World Bank, *Environmental Sustainability: An Evaluation of World Bank Group Support*, *supra* n. 12.
42. The classic definition of the term as coined by the Brundtland Commission is '[s]ustainable development is development that meets the needs of the present without compromising the ability of future generations to meet their own needs'. *See Report of the World Commission on Environment and Development: Our Common Future*, Annex to UN General Assembly document A/42/427 (2 Aug. 1987), Ch. 2, *available at* <www.un-documents.net/wced-ocf.htm>.
43. *See* Di Leva, 'International Environmental Law and Development', *supra* n. 16. *See also* Ibrahim Shihata, *The World Bank in a Changing World* (Boston: M. Nijhoff Publishers, 1995) (providing an extensive treatment of the World Bank and the environment).

1. Rio Principles Related to Procedural Rights and World Bank Environmental Procedures

a. Environmental Assessment (EA)

Both the World Bank policy on environmental assessment and the Rio Declaration highlight the importance of using the EA as a tool to address projects that can have a significant adverse impact on the environment.[44] The Bank policy sets out the procedures under which the Bank and its borrowers must ensure the assessment of the potential environmental impacts of investment projects to be financed by the Bank, as well as how such impacts must be avoided or mitigated. In carrying out this assessment, the Bank's policy makes clear that the environment should be broadly defined, by 'tak[ing] into account the natural environment (air, water, land); human health and safety; social aspects (involuntary resettlement, indigenous peoples, and cultural property); and transboundary and global environmental aspects'.[45] Indeed, all IFIs have a policy that requires environmental assessment of their projects that could have an adverse impact on the environment. The degree and scope of the EA may vary depending upon the potential of the impact, but the application is universal.[46]

b. Access to Information/Public Participation

Because the environmental assessment policy applies near the time a project is first formally identified, it provides IFIs with an opportunity to fulfil certain transparency and participation goals set forth in the Rio Declaration – especially those noted in Principle 10 that include public consultation, participation, and sharing of information.[47] In this context, the World Bank's environmental assessment policy requires a number of measures to ensure that consultation with affected people takes place in a manner that is 'meaningful'.[48]

---

44. Rio Declaration on Environment and Development, U.N. Doc.A/CONF.151/26; 31 I.L.M. 874 (1992), Principle 17.
45. The World Bank, OP 4.01 – Environmental Assessment (January 1999), para. 3, *available at* <http://siteresources.worldbank.org/INTFORESTS/Resources/OP401.pdf>.
46. Di Leva, 'International Environmental Law and Development', *supra* n. 16, for discussion on how IFIs have harmonized their approach toward environmental assessment.
47. Also noteworthy in this context is the entry into force of the Aarhus Convention in 2001. The objective of the Convention is as follows: 'In order to contribute to the protection of the right of every person of present and future generations to live in an environment adequate to his or her health and well-being, each Party shall guarantee the rights of access to information, public participation in decision-making, and access to justice in environmental matters in accordance with the provisions of this Convention.' United Nations Economic Commission for Europe, Convention on Access to Information, Public Participation in Decision-making and Access to Justice in Environmental Matters, UN Doc. ECE/CEP/43 (Aarhus, Denmark, 25 Jun. 1998), art. I, *available at* <www.unece.org/env/pp/documents/cep43e.pdf> (hereinafter 'Aarhus Convention').
48. The World Bank, OP 4.01, *supra* n. 45, para. 15.

One such measure is to ensure that information sharing takes place in a timely and comprehensive manner. Thus, both the World Bank EA and information disclosure policies require that key documents be made available in relevant languages for the affected community, and in advance of key decision-making benchmarks.[49] Moreover, for projects with significant adverse impacts, the affected community has at least two opportunities for consultation on the environmental assessment documentation before a project has been finally appraised by the institution.[50]

In addition, the Bank Policy on Disclosure of Information[51] facilitates the implementation of that policy by establishing sites for access to information at Bank offices in all countries in which it operates, as well as at the Bank headquarters' 'Infoshop'. Project documents are also accessible anywhere in the world via the internet. The World Bank has continued to add to the list of documentation required to be made available to the public, though certain documents that would normally be considered of privileged or deliberative nature, such as project supervision reports, are still considered confidential.[52] In addition, despite the added costs for project preparation and implementation, the Bank has strengthened its provision of translated documents in a wide range of languages, included making efforts where appropriate to provide oral translation for unwritten languages of indigenous peoples.

c. *Notification for Projects with Transboundary Impacts*

In addition to concerns of the affected local community, the Bank's environment-related policies also address the Rio Declaration's principles urging dialogue with potentially affected neighbouring states and ensuring the actions of one state do not harm another.[53] These goals have a long history in international environmental law, and are reflected in many international treaties and regional agreements, including in international jurisprudence.[54] They are also reflected in several of

49. *Ibid.*; The World Bank, The World Bank Policy on Disclosure of Information (June 2002), paras 40–42, *available at* <http://siteresources.worldbank.org/OPSMANUAL/Resources/DisclosurePolicy.pdf> (hereinafter World Bank Disclosure Policy). The Bank will have a new policy on disclosure of information beginning July 2010 having launched a process to revise its policy to shift from using a positive list of included items, to an approach in which all items will be assumed as eligible for disclosure, but for certain selected items. *See* The World Bank, Disclosure Policy Review and Global Consultations, <http://web.worldbank.org/WBSITE/EXTERNAL/PROJECTANDOPERATIONS/EXTINFODISCLOSURE/0,,menuPK:64864911~pagePK:4749265~piPK:4749256~theSitePK:5033734,00.html>.
50. The World Bank, OP 4.01, *supra* n. 45, para. 14.
51. *See* The World Bank Disclosure Policy, *supra* n. 49.
52. There is a commitment under the new policy, to be issued in July 2010, to make portions of these reports available to the public. *See ibid.*
53. Rio Declaration on Environment and Development, *supra* n. 44, Principle 19.
54. *See, e.g.*, Convention on Environmental Impact Assessment in a Transboundary Context, 1989 U.N.T.S. 309 (25 Feb. 1991), *available at* <www.unece.org/env/eia/> (hereinafter Espoo Convention); Trail Smelter Arbitration (1938/1941) 3 R.I.A.A. 1905.

the Rio Principles, and in turn, are evident in several Bank policies, especially those on environmental assessment, international waterways, and disputed areas.

EA policy requires that the assessment include 'transboundary and global environmental aspects'.[55] Information contained in this assessment would be available to other states, at a minimum, through the circulation of an environmental assessment report to the World Bank Board of Executive Directors, and through making the full environmental assessment available through the Bank's Infoshop.[56]

In fact, the concept of transboundary notification predates the Bank's EA policy. The World Bank has been fostering this form of notification since the 1950s when it became involved in financing hydroelectric works on international rivers.[57] In its most recent incarnation, the Bank policy on International Waterways requires notification to both upstream and downstream riparian states for a range of works that take place on international waterways. For fifteen years, Bank practice for such notification has also included notification for projects that affect transboundary groundwater.[58]

The World Bank Policy on Disputed Areas[59] has a similar theme to the policy on International Waterways in that it seeks to ensure that before international finance is committed for activities within one sovereign state, there is review of possible conflicting territorial claims. Where conflicting claims may exist, Bank staff detail the nature of the dispute in documents that are submitted to the Bank's board. According to the policy, the Bank may only support a project in disputed areas under certain circumstances.[60]

Project documents must describe the nature of the dispute and indicate that Bank staff are satisfied that either: (i) the other claimants to the disputed area have no objection to the project; or (ii) the special circumstances of the case warrant the

---

55. *See* The World Bank, OP 4.01, *supra* n. 45, para. 3.
56. *Ibid*., para. 17.
57. *See* Salman M.A. Salman & Laurence Boisson de Chazournes (eds), *International Watercourses: Enhancing Cooperation and Managing Conflict – Proceedings of a World Bank Seminar* (Washington, DC: World Bank, 1998); Salman M.A. Salman, *The World Bank Policy for Projects on International Waterways: An Historical and Legal Analysis* (Washington, DC: World Bank, 2009).
58. *See* The World Bank, OP 7.50 – International Waterways (June 2001), *available at* <http://web.worldbank.org/WBSITE/EXTERNAL/PROJECTS/EXTPOLICIES/EXTOPMANUAL/0,,contentMDK:20064667~menuPK:4564185~pagePK:64709096~piPK:64709108~theSitePK:502184,00.html>. For more extensive discussion of this policy, *see* Charles Di Leva, 'Access to Information, Public Participation and Conflict Resolution at the World Bank', in *International Freshwater Resources*, ed. Carl Bruch (New York: United Nations University Press, 2005). *See also* Di Leva, 'International Environmental Law and Development', *supra* n. 16, 530 (for discussion on relation of OP 7.50 and the Convention on Law of Non-navigational Uses of International Watercourses).
59. The World Bank, OP 7.60 – Projects in Disputed Areas (June 2001), para. 2, *available at* <http://web.worldbank.org/WBSITE/EXTERNAL/PROJECTS/EXTPOLICIES/EXTOPMANUAL/0,,contentMDK:20064615~menuPK:4564185~pagePK:64709096~piPK:64709108~theSitePK:502184,00.html>.
60. *Ibid.*

Bank's support of the project notwithstanding any objection or lack of approval by the other claimants. In all cases that require the application of the policy, OP 7.60 mandates that project documentation bears a disclaimer stating that, by supporting the project, the Bank does not intend to make any judgment on the legal or other status of the territories concerned, or to prejudice the final determination of the parties' claims.[61]

d. Access to Justice

Rio Principle 10 also stresses the importance of judicial access, so that affected people can have redress and remedies, when they are harmed.[62] To this extent, World Bank policies note the importance of providing means to address grievances, specifically in the context of projects involving involuntary resettlement or indigenous peoples.[63] For example, the policy on indigenous peoples requires as follows:

> (h) Accessible procedures appropriate to the project to address grievances by the affected Indigenous Peoples' communities arising from project implementation. When designing the grievance procedures, the borrower takes into account the availability of judicial recourse and customary dispute settlement mechanisms among the Indigenous Peoples.[64]

In addition to the importance of access to grievance mechanisms set out in these policies, the Bank has developed an extensive portfolio of projects to assist countries in addressing legal and judicial reform. These projects have been instituted in all regions of the Bank, and have had extensive focus in recent activities linked to the United Nations and the World Bank-supported Commission on Legal Empowerment of the Poor.[65]

In addition to efforts to support judicial access outside the institution, in 1993 the World Bank set up an accountability mechanism to provide affected people

61. *See ibid.*
62. As mentioned above, the concept of 'access to justice' is also one of the pillars of the Aarhus Convention. *See* Aarhus Convention, *supra* n. 47.
63. *See* The World Bank, OP 4.10 – Indigenous Peoples (July 2005), Annex B, para. 2(h), *available at* <http://web.worldbank.org/WBSITE/EXTERNAL/PROJECTS/EXTPOLICIES/EXTOPMANUAL/0,,contentMDK:20553653~menuPK:4564185~pagePK:64709096~piPK:64709108~theSitePK:502184,00.html>; The World Bank, OP 4.12 – Involuntary Resettlement (December 2001), para. 7, *available at* <http://web.worldbank.org/WBSITE/EXTERNAL/PROJECTS/EXTPOLICIES/EXTOPMANUAL/0,,contentMDK:20064610~pagePK:64141683~piPK:64141620~theSitePK:502184,00.html>; The World Bank, OP 4.12: Annex A – Involuntary Resettlement Instruments (December 2001), paras 7, 15(d), 24, *available at* <http://web.worldbank.org/WBSITE/EXTERNAL/PROJECTS/EXTPOLICIES/EXTOPMANUAL/0,,contentMDK:20066696~menuPK:4564185~pagePK:64709096~piPK:64709108~theSitePK:502184,00.html>.
64. The World Bank, OP 4.10, *supra* n. 63, Annex A, para. 2(j).
65. *See* United Nations Development Programme, Initiative on Legal Empowerment of the Poor, <www.undp.org/legalempowerment/>.

with a means to register claims stating that they have been harmed or may face harm due to Bank-financed activities. The World Bank Inspection Panel was established to allow members of the public to file complaints if the Bank is alleged to have failed to comply with Bank operational policies or procedures.[66] It has since spawned a number of similar mechanisms in other multilateral development banks and IFIs, as noted in other chapters in this book.[67]

The Panel carries out independent investigations and reports directly to the Bank's Board of Executive Directors. Since its establishment, the Panel has received more than sixty investigation requests.[68] The Panel's mandate allows it to address non-compliance with any of the Bank's operational policies and procedures other than those related to procurement; however, much of the Panel's attention has focused on the environmental and social safeguard policies. In many of the Panel's investigations, the Panel has focused on the fact that the environmental and social design features of Bank projects and the manner in which the projects are then carried out must ensure the meaningful consultation of affected peoples. They have stressed the benefits of public consultation and participation; and that such consultation and access to local knowledge can help improve project design, reduce adverse impacts, potentially reduce project costs, and result in fewer conflicts and delays through participatory consensus building because it can help ensure that compensation is fair.

2. Substantive 'Environmental' Principles

a. Precautionary Principle and Polluter Pays Principle

Two Rio principles stand out as core substantive elements related to the environment: the principle of precaution[69] and that the polluter should pay for the cost of pollution.[70]

---

66. International Bank for Reconstruction and Development, International Development Association, 'The World Bank Inspection Panel', Resolution No. IBRD 93-10, Resolution No. IDA 93-6 (22 Sep. 1993).
67. *See, e.g.*, Eisuke Suzuki, 'Responsibility of International Financial Institutions under International Law', Ch. 3 herein; B.S. Chimni, 'International Financial Institutions and International Law: A Third World Perspective', Ch. 2 herein.
68. For Inspection Panel cases, *see* The World Bank, The Inspection Panel – Requests for Inspection, <http://web.worldbank.org/WBSITE/EXTERNAL/EXTINSPECTIONPANEL/0,,contentMDK:21692308~menuPK:64129250~pagePK:64129751~piPK:64128378~theSitePK:380794,00.html> (providing links to the requests for inspection).
69. Rio Declaration on Environment and Development, *supra* n. 44, Principle 15 (stating that 'In order to protect the environment, the precautionary approach shall be widely applied by States according to their capabilities. Where there are threats of serious or irreversible damage, lack of full scientific certainty shall not be used as a reason for postponing cost-effective measures to prevent environmental degradation.').
70. *Ibid.*, Principle 16 (stating that 'National authorities should endeavour to promote the internalization of environmental costs and the use of economic instruments, taking into account the approach that the polluter should, in principle, bear the cost of pollution, with due regard to the public interest and without distorting international trade and investment.').

While not expressly incorporating the precautionary principle, the World Bank's EA policy supports the principle, or the approach of precaution, in several ways. First, it specifically requires that the Bank project 'favor[s] preventive measures over mitigatory or compensatory measures, whenever feasible'.[71] Second, when carrying out an EA for any project with potential for significant adverse impact, the policy requires that the assessment examine the 'without project' alternative.[72] Third, the policy requires that the EA be carried out by independent experts, to ensure it is handled with objectivity, including by an independent panel of experts for projects that are 'highly risky'.[73]

While these provisions are not verbatim recitations of the precautionary principle, at a minimum they help ensure that the project design and implementation take a conservative approach toward carrying out activities where damage can occur, by at least trying to avoid or prevent it. In addition, for projects that affect natural habitats, the Bank policy states that it 'expects borrowers to apply a precautionary approach to natural resource management to ensure opportunities for environmentally sustainable development'.[74] The Natural Habitats policy adds that the Bank will not finance projects that, 'in the Bank's opinion, involve the significant conversion or degradation of critical natural habitats'.[75]

Bank policies do not expressly refer to the polluter pays principle, but the environmental policies are geared to support it, which can be seen through several examples in operation. For one, the EA policy makes clear that environmental management and mitigation measures are the responsibility of the borrower.[76] To that extent, the cost for those measures to address and protect against those impacts will be paid for out of the project budget.

Another example of this approach is the incorporation in both World Bank and IFC policies of the World Bank Group's Pollution Prevention and Abatement Handbook,[77] and the Environmental, Health, and Safety Guidelines contained within the framework of the Handbook.[78] The first two parts of the Handbook contain reference materials for a broad approach toward pollution. The third part, known as the 'Environmental Health and Safety Guidelines', contains specific emission guidelines for over sixty types of industries. The World Bank requires that these guidelines be applied for any projects it finances within these industries, unless there is technical justification provided within the environmental assessment for a deviation from the guidelines. Thus, as part of environmental

71. The World Bank, OP 4.01, *supra* n. 45, para. 2.
72. *Ibid.*, para. 8(a).
73. *Ibid.*, para. 6.
74. The World Bank, OP 4.04 – Natural Habitats (June 2001), para. 1, *available at* <http://web.worldbank.org/WBSITE/EXTERNAL/PROJECTS/EXTPOLICIES/EXTOPMANUAL/0,,contentMDK:20064757~menuPK:64701637~pagePK:64709096~piPK:64709108~theSitePK:502184,00.html>.
75. *Ibid.*, para. 4.
76. The World Bank, OP 4.01, *supra* n. 45, para. 4.
77. *Ibid.*, para. 6.
78. International Finance Corporation, <www.ifc.org> (hereinafter IFC).

assessment, potential pollution from a proposed project must be assessed, and measures put in place to finance the prevention or minimization of those impacts.

To help implement the precautionary principle and the polluter pays principle, governments need sound environmental legislation. In this context, the Rio Declaration proclaims that 'States shall enact effective environmental legislation', though such '[s]tandards applied by some countries may be inappropriate and of unwarranted social and economic cost to other countries, in particular developing countries'.[79] Through numerous means, the World Bank has facilitated the development and enforcement in developing countries of modern, effective environmental legislation. This progress has occurred through, for example, grants and credits that can be used to help implement environmental laws.[80] An important basis for this facilitation is the fact that the Bank's EA policy requires review of the government's applicable legal and institutional framework.[81] In a number of instances, through this EA process, Bank staff identified with Bank borrowers the need for sound environmental legislation. In addition, Bank legal publications have been well-received primers for development of environmental legislation, such as in laws related to sustainable forest management, fisheries, water, and environmental impact assessment.[82]

b. *Addressing Transboundary Movement of Harmful Substances*

The World Bank and many of its collaborating institutions have supported the design and implementation of projects that seek to prevent transboundary movement of harmful substances, as well as to try and remediate contaminated sites to reduce exposure to local communities, and to minimize the possibility of dangerous waste transport.[83] These activities have taken place at both the regional and local level. In addition, these activities have been instituted to support international environmental agreements, as well as national and local laws.[84]

c. *Providing Substantive Benefits to Indigenous Peoples*

The importance of engaging indigenous people in development decisions that affect them was enshrined in the Rio Declaration, and recently underscored in the

---

79. Rio Declaration on Environment and Development, *supra* n. 44, Principle 11.
80. *See, e.g.*, International Development Association and Global Environment Facility Trust Fund, 'West Africa Regional Fisheries Program (WARFP)', Project Appraisal Document (18 Sep. 2009), *available at* <www-wds.worldbank.org/external/default/WDSContentServer/WDSP/IB/2009/10/22/000350881_20091022113524/Rendered/PDF/489650PAD0342008B01PUBLIC1.pdf> (helping support enforcement of fisheries legislation).
81. The World Bank, OP 4.01, *supra* n. 45, para. 3 & Annex B, para. 2(b).
82. *See, e.g.*, Lawrence Christy, Charles Di Leva, Jonathan Lindsay & Patrice Talla Takoukam, *Forest Law and Sustainable Development: Addressing Contemporary Challenges Through Legal Reform* (Washington, DC: World Bank, 2007).
83. *See* Rio Declaration on Environment and Development, *supra* n. 44, Principle 14.
84. Di Leva, 'International Environmental Law and Development', *supra* n. 16, 523.

United Nations Declaration on the Rights of Indigenous Peoples (UNDRIP).[85] The UNDRIP affirms the principle of free, prior, and informed consent of Indigenous Peoples. The UNDRIP, as with Rio Principle 22, notes 'the vital role' Indigenous Peoples have regarding environmental management.[86] Consistent with the spirit of these instruments, the World Bank policy on Indigenous Peoples ensures that the Bank does not undertake project activities that affect indigenous peoples unless they have been able to benefit from free, prior, and informed consultation, and unless the indigenous community has given its broad community support to the project.[87]

Some contend that the Bank policy does not meet the requirements of international law because it does not provide indigenous peoples with a veto right over projects that take place within their territories.[88] They contend that such a veto right has become customary law. However, a comprehensive study by the Environmental Law Institute related to prior informed consent in the context of mining operations concluded that there is no universally accepted definition of the term 'consent'.[89] The study noted:

> Many states do not in fact require companies to obtain community consent in practice, even if they may profess to do so. Moreover, even where States have required companies to obtain community consent, they have diverged in their interpretation of what this right actually involves. The right to community consent has ranged from simply providing information to communities regarding the impacts of a proposed mine, to actually according communities the right to veto a proposed mining project. Therefore, the lack of consistent State practice makes it more difficult to establish the existence of a customary right to community consent.[90]

As the principle of free prior informed consent has been strengthened with the adoption of the UNDRIP, the Bank has continued to work with Indigenous Peoples

85. United Nations Declaration on the Rights of Indigenous Peoples, A/RES/61/295 (13 Sep. 2007), *available at* <www.un.org/esa/socdev/unpfii/en/declaration.html> (hereinafter UNDRIP).
86. *Ibid.*, 2.
87. *See* The World Bank, OP 4.10, *supra* n. 63, para. 11. 'The Bank reviews the process and the outcome of the consultation carried out by the borrower to satisfy itself that the affected Indigenous Peoples' communities have provided their broad support to the project. The Bank pays particular attention to the social assessment and to the record and outcome of the free, prior, and informed consultation with the affected Indigenous Peoples' communities as a basis for ascertaining whether there is such support. *The Bank does not proceed further with project processing if it is unable to ascertain that such support exists.*' (Emphasis added by author.)
88. *See* Fergus Mackay, 'Indigenous Peoples and International Financial Institutions', Ch. 9 herein, for a different view of Bank policy and actions on indigenous people. *See, e.g.*, Bank Information Center, Indigenous Peoples and the World Bank, <www.bicusa.org/en/Issue.Concerns.24.aspx>.
89. *See* Susan Bass, *Prior Informed Consent and Mining, Promoting Sustainable Development of Local Communities* (Washington, DC: Environmental Law Institute, 2004), 41.
90. *Ibid.*

groups to help ensure that the process by which the Bank addresses issues that affect them is harmonious with the principle of free prior informed consent. This is evident in the application of the OP 4.10, as well as in developing operational guidelines for activities that affect indigenous peoples. Thus, the Forest Investment Program (FIP) administered by the World Bank as part of the Climate Investment Funds (CIFs), recently developed guidelines in collaboration with Indigenous leaders for processing FIP projects. These guidelines as well make it clear that the consultation process and any project activity must have their community support before a project goes forward.[91] Among other requirements, the guidelines state:

> 6. A consensus reflecting broad community support for the investment strategy, program or project should emerge from the consultations before the strategy, program or project moves forward.
>
> 7. In the case of indigenous peoples, such consensus should include support from the community as expressed by their leader(s). In addition, for both indigenous peoples and local communities, the strategy, program or project should not proceed without acquiring broad community support, as set forth in these FIP guidelines.
>
> 8. Conclusions and recommendations arising from the consultation should be integrated in the design and implementation of the investment strategy, program or project.[92]

By following the detailed approach for engaging indigenous peoples set out in the Bank policy, there can be longer lasting local benefits. These benefits include building local capacity for participatory processes (including monitoring and evaluation); helping improve government transparency and accountability; enhancing the likelihood for project sustainability by increasing a sense of government and local ownership; and buy-in and reaching the traditionally excluded.

d. Developing Effective Environmental Legislation

Rio Principle 11 notes the importance of states enacting effective environmental legislation, including within it 'standards, management objectives and priorities' that 'should reflect the environmental and developmental context to which they apply'.[93] The World Bank environmental and social policies consistently seek to ensure that there is full analysis of the legal context in which the project will

91. *See* Climate Investment Funds, 'Design Document for the Forest Investment Program, A Targeted Program Under the SCF Trust Fund' (7 Jul. 2009), Annex III, *available* at <www.climateinvestmentfunds.org/cif/sites/climateinvestmentfunds.org/files/FIP_Final_Design_Document_July_7.pdf> (laying out 'Guidelines for Consultations to be carried out in accordance with subparagraph 16(d) of the Design Document for the Forest Investment Program').
92. *Ibid.*
93. Rio Declaration on Environment and Development, *supra* n. 44, Principle 11.

operate, and when necessary, strengthening takes place to help make effective legislation a reality.[94]

Effective national legislation is often a *sine qua non* for the ratification and implementation of the many environmental treaties found in international environmental law. In this connection, OP 4.01 also supports the requirements that the Bank does not finance any activities that contravene the borrower's obligations under applicable environmental treaties. Thus, a project EA must identify the relevant international environmental treaty that is implicated by the proposed project and help the Bank ensure that the project does not violate it. Among other things, many of these treaties expressly require that states do not cause harm to the environment of other states.[95]

More recently, the Bank has been moving forward with an approach referred to as 'Use of Borrower Systems' that represents an effort to put in place incentives for borrowers to strengthen their domestic environmental and social systems. One way is to eliminate the need for dual environmental and social analyses in appropriate cases. Thus, for example, if a domestic environmental impact assessment law is equivalent to the Bank's policy, and where the domestic review system is acceptable, it might be unnecessary, perhaps redundant, to also have an environmental assessment prepared specifically to meet OP 4.01. The potential time and cost savings by using the borrower's own system can also provide an incentive to create lasting improvements to a developing country's systems. For these reasons, with endorsement from the World Bank Board of Executive Directors in 2005, the Bank adopted a pilot programme for using a borrower's environmental and social laws or systems.[96] There has been some concern that this would weaken the Bank's policies.[97] However, the use of the borrower's system can only take place after the system has been tested for equivalence with the Bank's policy and reviewed by the Bank Legal Department Environmental and International Law Unit (LEGEN).[98] If the project uses the borrower's system, any gaps identified between the objectives and operational principles set out in the Bank's policy and the borrower's system must be filled by use of conditions included in the loan agreement. Further, the method for putting in place the systems must be determined to be acceptable based on a review by the Bank.[99]

---

94. *See, e.g.*, The World Bank OP 4.01, *supra* n. 45, para. 3.
95. *See, e.g.*, Convention on Biological Diversity (CBD), 1760 U.N.T.S. 79 (1992), Arts 3, 14.1(c-e).
96. The World Bank, OP/BP 4.00 – Piloting the Use of Borrower Systems to Address Environmental and Social Safeguard Issues in Bank-Supported Projects (March 2005), *available at* <http://web.worldbank.org/WBSITE/EXTERNAL/PROJECTS/EXTPOLICIES/EXTSAFEPOL/0,,contentMDK:20931764~menuPK:2575517~pagePK:64168445~piPK:64168309~theSitePK:584435,00.html>. While the country's system would be evaluated for most Bank-Supported pilot projects under OP 4.00, the term 'borrower' is used to ensure that if a non-state entity is responsible to implement a project, the Bank can require assessment of the equivalence and acceptability of the non-state entity's system.
97. *See, e.g.*, Center for International Environmental Law, 'The Use of Country Systems in World Bank Lending: A Summary of Lessons from the Pilot Projects and Recommendations for a Better Approach' (April 2008), *available at* <www.ciel.org/Ifi/WB_CountrySystems_Apr08.html> (a review by Center for International Environmental Law).
98. The World Bank, OP/BP 4.00, *supra* n. 96, para. 1.
99. *Ibid.*, paras 2, 3.

The Bank considers the Use of Borrower Systems approach to be responsive to the development community's landmark Paris Declaration on Aid Effectiveness.[100] Additionally, the Bank has noted that the implementation of this programme would not alter the role of Bank accountability mechanisms such as the World Bank Inspection Panel. To date, the implementation of this pilot programme has met with some success, though not at a pace and scale as some had expected.[101] Additional efforts remain underway, and more reporting will be presented to the board and made available to the public to assess the Use of Borrower Systems approach. Its success will provide sound data on the effectiveness of environment-related legislation.

e. *Seeking to Remove the Gender Gap*

The World Bank policy on gender[102] is not considered a safeguard policy because it does not expressly state that it applies to investment projects. This distinction from the suite of safeguard policies does not preclude (though does not require) the considerations set forth in the gender policy from being included as part of project design, for example, as part of EA or related social assessment, even though the policy is not specifically mentioned in the relevant environmental assessment policy. The Bank gender policy seeks to:

> assist member countries to reduce poverty and enhance economic growth, human well-being, and development effectiveness by addressing the gender disparities and inequalities that are barriers to development, and by assisting member countries in formulating and implementing their gender and development goals.[103]

In this manner, the Bank strongly supports the Rio Declaration principle that the full participation of women is key to sustainable development.[104]

100. *See* OECD, 'The Paris Declaration on Aid Effectiveness' (2 Mar. 2005), 1, 7, *available at* <www.oecd.org/dataoecd/11/41/34428351.pdf>. Pursuant to this declaration, among other matters, aid agencies agreed that they would help in '[d]efining measures and standards of performance and accountability of partner country systems in public financial management, procurement, fiduciary safeguards and environmental assessments, in line with broadly accepted good practices and their quick and widespread application'.
101. The World Bank, Vice President & Corporate Secretary, 'First Year Review of Implementation of Incremental Scaled-Up Program to Pilot Use of Country Systems to Address Environmental and Social Safeguard Issues in Bank-Supported Projects' (14 Jul. 2009), *available at* <http://siteresources.worldbank.org/PROJECTS/Resources/40940-1097257794915/1stYear_Review-ScaledUpPilotUseCountrySystemsJuly09.pdf>.
102. The World Bank, OP 4.20 – Gender and Development (March 2003), *available at* <http://web.worldbank.org/WBSITE/EXTERNAL/PROJECTS/EXTPOLICIES/EXTOPMANUAL/0,,contentMDK:20064559~pagePK:64141683~piPK:64141620~theSitePK:502184,00.html>.
103. *Ibid.*, para. 1.
104. *See* Rio Declaration on Environment and Development, *supra* n. 44, Principle 20.

B. Environmental Safeguard Policies among the IFIs

As noted previously, the World Bank has been joined by other IFIs in its efforts to develop environmental policies that support international environmental law. These shared efforts reflect that the IFIs have common stakeholders, and many of these stakeholders have made longstanding efforts to achieve policy harmonization among IFIs. While harmonization efforts have often focused on financial management and procurement issues, environment has also been an important part of the focus. The Paris Declaration on Aid Effectiveness contains the following provisions concerning harmonization on the environment:

> 40. Donors have achieved considerable progress in harmonisation around environmental impact assessment (EIA) including relevant health and social issues at the project level. This progress needs to be deepened, including on addressing implications of global environmental issues such as climate change, desertification and loss of biodiversity.
>
> 41. Donors and partner countries jointly commit to: [s]trengthen the application of EIAs and deepen common procedures for projects, including consultations with stakeholders; and develop and apply common approaches for 'strategic environmental assessment' at the sector and national levels. [and] Continue to develop the specialised technical and policy capacity necessary for environmental analysis and for enforcement of legislation.[105]

Indeed, even prior to this Declaration, IFIs collaborated in pursuing this agenda through a Multilateral Financial Institution Working Group on the Environment. This group began collaboration in the early 1990s and operated prior to the Declaration to finalize a common set of principles for Environmental Impact Assessment.[106]

The IFI environmental policy agenda did not slow after the Paris Declaration. In recent years, many of these institutions reviewed and updated their safeguard policies to reflect some of the advancement and changes in the international environmental regime. Below is a short summary, highlighting some of the key or unique aspects of recently adopted or proposed environmental and social policies.

1. Inter-American Development Bank (IDB)

The IDB's Environment and Safeguards Compliance Policy (2006) implements and reinforces IDB's Environment Strategy (2003).[107] The Environment and

105. 'The Paris Declaration on Aid Effectiveness', *supra* n. 100, paras 40–41.
106. *See* The Multilateral Financial Institutions Working Group on Environment, *A Common Framework for Environmental Impact Assessment (EIA: A Good Practice Note)* (28 Feb. 2005), *available at* <www.aidharmonization.org/download/255377/EAcommonframework-apr05.pdf>.

Safeguards Compliance Policy provides that the 'Bank will only finance operations and activities that comply with the directives of this policy' and 'environmental laws and regulations of the country where the operation is being implemented, including national obligations established under ratified Multilateral Environmental Agreements'.[108] The policy also states that all Bank-financed operations are screened and classified according to their potential environmental impacts so that 'the appropriate environmental assessment or due diligence requirements' can be carried out.[109] As part of the environmental assessment process, transboundary issues associated with the operation are also considered. In an IDB directive on pollution prevention and abatement, the policy includes a provision on greenhouse gas emission reduction: 'the Bank encourages the reduction and control of greenhouse gas emissions in a manner appropriate to the nature and scale of operations'.[110] The policy also encourages the use of in-country systems, by stating that 'the Bank will consider the use of the borrowing member countries' existing system of safeguards for identifying and managing environmental and social impacts'.[111]

IDB's Independent Investigation Mechanism (IIM), established in 1994, affords people whose lives are affected by Bank projects a means to ensure that the Bank complies with its own operational policies during the preparation and implementation of its projects.[112] In 2010, the IDB adopted a revised Independent Consultation and Compliance Review Mechanism (ICIM),[113] which was developed as part of the Bank's effort to increase transparency, accountability, and effectiveness, and it goes into effect in mid-2010, replacing the IIM.[114]

107. *See generally* Inter-American Development Bank, 'Environment and Safeguards Compliance Policy' (19 Jan. 2006), *available at* <http://idbdocs.iadb.org/wsdocs/getDocument.aspx?DOCNUM=665902> (hereinafter IDB Environment and Safeguards Compliance Policy); Inter-American Development Bank, 'Environment Strategy' (August 2003), *available at* <http://idbdocs.iadb.org/wsdocs/getdocument.aspx?docnum=1448830>.
108. IDB Environment and Safeguards Compliance Policy, *supra* n. 107, 4.14–4.15.
109. *Ibid.*, 4.17 (part of Directive B.3 Screening and Classification). Directives B.5 and B.6 spell out in detail the requirements for environmental assessment, including public consultations.
110. *Ibid.*, 4.28. In addition to this policy addressing climate change, IDB has taken steps to ensure that its own practice is climate-friendly. In 2006, it became the first multilateral development bank to measure and manage its carbon footprint when it piloted a carbon neutral concept. Since 2007, the IDB has been neutralizing unavoidable emissions from its headquarters through a series of investments in offset projects in Latin America and the Caribbean.
111. *Ibid.*, 4.33 (as part of B.16 In-Country Systems).
112. Inter-American Development Bank, Independent Investigation Mechanism, <www.iadb.org/aboutus/iii/independent_invest/independent_invest.cfm>.
113. Inter-American Development Bank, 'Policy Establishing the Independent Consultation and Compliance Mechanism' (17 Feb. 2010), *available at* <http://idbdocs.iadb.org/wsdocs/getdocument.aspx?docnum=35074768> (hereinafter IDB ICIM).
114. Inter-American Development Bank, 'IDB Boosts Access, Accountability with New Policy for Communities to Voice Concerns', press release (17 Feb. 2010), *available at* <www.iadb.org/

2. European Bank for Reconstruction and Development (EBRD)

The EBRD approved new Environmental and Social Policy and Performance Requirements on 12 May 2008. The new EBRD Policy is much more detailed and prescriptive than the 2003 Policy, and it has ten Performance Requirements (PR): Environmental and Social Appraisal and Management; Labour and Working Conditions; Pollution Prevention and Abatement; Community Health, Safety, and Security; Involuntary Resettlement and Displacement; Biodiversity Conservation and Sustainable Natural Resource Management; Indigenous Peoples; Cultural Heritage; Financial Intermediaries; and Information Disclosure and Stakeholder Engagement.[115] Another noteworthy aspect of the 2008 Policy is that it addresses some of the 'newer' environmental issues, including climate change,[116] invasive alien species,[117] and genetically modified organisms.[118]

EBRD's requirement for an environmental assessment is similar to that of other development banks: 'through appraisal activities such as risk assessment, auditing, or environmental and social impact assessment, the client will consider in an integrated manner the potential environmental and social issues and impacts associated with the proposed project', and that these issues and impacts will be appraised in the context of the 'project's area of influence'.[119] With respect to pollution prevention, EBRD Performance Requirement 3 requires that:

> during the design, construction, operation and decommissioning of the project (the project lifecycle), the client will consider technical characteristics of the installation concerned, its geographical location and local/ambient environmental conditions and apply pollution prevention and control technologies and practices (techniques) that are best suited to avoid or, where avoidance is not feasible, minimize or reduce adverse impacts on human health and the

---

news-releases/2010-02/english/idb-boosts-access-accountability-with-new-policy-for-communities-to-voice-concer-6531.html>.

115. European Bank for Reconstruction and Development, 'Environmental and Social Policy' (May 2008), *available at* <http://www.ebrd.com/downloads/research/policies/2008policy.pdf> (hereinafter EBRD Environmental and Social Policy).
116. PR 3: Pollution Prevention and Abatement provides that, 'the client will promote the reduction of project-related greenhouse gas emissions in a manner appropriate to the nature and scale of project operations and impacts'. *Ibid.*, 28 (para. 17 of PR 3).
117. PR 6: Biodiversity Conservation and Sustainable Management of Living Natural Resources prohibits clients from 'intentionally introduc[ing] alien or non-native species into areas where they are not normally found unless this is carried out in accordance with the regulatory framework governing such introduction. Under no circumstances must species known to be invasive be introduced into new environments'. *Ibid.*, 47 (para. 16 of PR 6).
118. PR 6 states that, 'no GMOs should be used or released to the environment without approval being given by the competent authorities, or where the relevant local authority has declared itself as GMO free . . . the Bank will also take these elements into account during its own due diligence'. *Ibid.*, 48 (para. 17 of PR 6).
119. *Ibid.*, 15 (para. 5 of PR 1: Environmental and Social Appraisal and Management).

> environment while remaining technically and financially feasible and cost-effective.[120]

This policy is important in that it takes into consideration the full lifecycle of a project.

Similar to the World Bank's Inspection Panel, EBRD has established the Independent Recourse Mechanism (IRM) to assess and review complaints about Bank-financed projects. The IRM gives local groups that may be directly and adversely affected by a Bank project a means of raising complaints or grievances with the Bank independently from banking operations. The IRM has two functions: a compliance review function, which assesses whether the Bank has complied with its policies; and a problem-solving function, which aims to restore a dialogue between the parties, typically the members of the affected group and the project sponsor.[121]

3. Asian Development Bank (ADB)

With the adoption of its new Safeguard Policy Statement in July 2009, the ADB has just completed the revision process of its Safeguard Policy, which started in 2005. As a result of the Safeguard Policy Update (SPU), the ADB's Safeguard Policy is now comprised of the following:

> 1) A safeguard policy statement (SPS) that describes common objectives of ADB's safeguards, lays out policy principles, and outlines the delivery process for ADB's safeguard policy.[122]
>
> 2) A set of specific safeguard requirements that borrowers/clients are expected to meet when addressing social and environmental impacts and risks (there are four safeguard requirements: environment, indigenous peoples, involuntary resettlement, and special requirements for different finance modalities).
>
> 3) A consolidated *Operations Manual* section that specifies ADB's internal review procedures for due diligence and for supervision throughout the project cycle.[123]

All three safeguard policies involve a structured process of impact assessment, planning, and mitigation to address the adverse effects of projects throughout the

---

120. *Ibid.*, 27 (para. 10 of PR 3: Pollution Prevention and Abatement).
121. *See* European Bank for Reconstruction and Development, Independent Recourse Mechanism, <www.ebrd.com/about/integrity/irm/index.htm>.
122. *See* Asian Development Bank, 'Safeguard Policy Statement' (July 2009), *available at* <www.adb.org/Documents/Policies/Safeguards/Safeguard-Policy-Statement-June2009.pdf>.
123. *See* Asian Development Bank, 'Operations Manual: Bank Policies (BP)', OM s. F1/BP (20 Jan. 2010), *available at* <www.adb.org/Documents/Manuals/Operations/OMF01-20Jan10.pdf>.

project cycle.[124] Specifically, the safeguard policies require that (i) impacts are identified and assessed early in the project cycle; (ii) plans to avoid, minimize, mitigate, or compensate for the potential adverse impacts are developed and implemented; and (iii) affected people are informed and consulted during project preparation and implementation.[125]

In 2003, ADB revised its accountability mechanism, which has two separate but related functions: (1) consultation to assist people who are adversely affected by ADB-assisted projects in finding solutions to their concerns and grievances; and (2) compliance review by the Compliance Review Panel if there are alleged violations of ADB's operational policies and procedures, including safeguard policies.[126]

4. African Development Bank (AfDB)

In 2004, the AfDB adopted a new Bank Group Policy on the Environment,[127] along with two related guidelines, one on the Strategic Impact Assessment Guidelines (SIA, 2003)[128] and another one on the Integrated Environmental and Social Impact Assessment Guidelines (IESIA).[129] The Policy states that for Category 1 projects, which are 'likely to induce important adverse environmental and/or social impacts that are irreversible, or to significantly affect environmental or social components considered sensitive by the Bank or the borrowing country', the Bank requires a 'full Environmental and Social Impact Assessment, including the preparation of an Environmental and Social management Plan'.[130] With respect to 'global public goods', the policy provides that the Bank will 'promote the role of private sector in financing initiatives to combat climate change, particularly in the use of permit trading as a major mechanism to implement the Kyoto Protocol'.[131] The policy

124. *See generally* Asian Development Bank, Environment: Important Information on ADB Safeguards, <www.adb.org/Environment/safeguard-policy.asp> (providing links to the new Safeguard Policy Statement, Operations Manual, and other safeguards and policies).
125. Asian Development Bank, Safeguard Policy Statement, *supra* n. 122, para. 15.
126. *See* Asian Development Bank, 'Review of the Inspection Function: Establishment of a New ADB Accountability Mechanism' (May 2003), *available at* <www.adb.org/Documents/Policies/ADB_Accountability_Mechanism/ADB_accountability_mechanism.pdf>.
127. *See* African Development Bank, 'African Bank Group's Policy on the Environment' (February 2004), *available at* <www.afdb.org/fileadmin/uploads/afdb/Documents/Policy-Documents/10000027-EN-BANK-GROUP-POLICY-ON-THE-ENVIRONMENT.PDF> (hereinafter AfDB Policy on the Environment).
128. *See* African Development Bank, 'Bank Group Guidelines for Strategic Impact Assessment' (2003), <www.afdb.org/en/topics-sectors/sectors/environment/> (discussing the SIA along with other environment policies).
129. African Development Bank, 'Integrated Environmental and Social Impact Assessment Guidelines' (October 2003), *available at* <www.afdb.org/fileadmin/uploads/afdb/Documents/Policy-Documents/Integrated%20Environmental%20and%20Social%20Impact%20Assesment%20Guidelines.pdf> (hereinafter AfDB IESIA).
130. AfDB Policy on the Environment, *supra* n. 127, para. 6.6.
131. *Ibid.*, para. 5.3.5. The Bank Group's Boards of Directors also approved the Climate Risk Management and Adaptation Strategy (CRMA) in April 2009. The Strategy supports three

also includes a specific section on mining, where it provides that the Bank will 'support environmental control measures to reduce the adverse effects from industrial, mining and energy resource and utilization projects'.[132]

In 2006, the AfDB established an Independent Review Mechanism (IRM) to provide individuals who are adversely affected by a project financed by the Bank Group with the possibility to lodge their complaints in case they suffer harm due to the violation of the Bank's applicable policies and procedures in that project.[133]

5. International Finance Corporation (IFC)

The IFC is the private-sector arm of the World Bank Group. In February 2006, the IFC adopted a new IFC environmental and social policy framework, consisting of: the 'Policy on Social and Environmental Sustainability' (Sustainability Policy), which defines IFC's responsibility for supporting project performance in partnership with clients;[134] and the 'Performance Standards', which define clients' roles and responsibilities for managing their projects and the requirements for receiving and retaining IFC support.[135] There are eight Performance Standards (PS): (1) Social and Environmental Assessment and Management System; (2) Labor and Working Conditions; (3) Pollution Prevention and Abatement; (4) Community Health, Safety, and Security; (5) Land Acquisition and Involuntary Resettlement; (6) Biodiversity and Sustainable Natural Resource Management; (7) Indigenous Peoples; and (8) Cultural Heritage.[136] The IFC is currently reviewing its Environmental and Social Standards and plans to complete this revision in 2011.[137]

---

main areas of intervention: (1) climate proofing investments; (2) policy, legal, and regulatory reforms; and (3) knowledge generation and capacity building. For more details, *see* 'Bank Group Climate Risk Management and Adaptation Strategy' (2009), *available at* <www.afdb.org/fileadmin/uploads/afdb/Documents/Policy-Documents/Climate%20Risk%20Management%20and%20Adaptation%20Strategy%20_CRMA_%20%282%29.pdf>.

132. AfDB Policy on the Environment, *supra* n. 127, para. 5.3.8.
133. *See* African Development Bank, Independent Review Mechanism, <www.afdb.org/en/about-us/structure/independent-review-mechanism/>.
134. *See generally* IFC, 'International Finance Corporation's Policy on Social and Environmental Sustainability' (30 Apr. 2006), *available at* <www.ifc.org/ifcext/sustainability.nsf/AttachmentsByTitle/pol_SocEnvSustainability2006/$FILE/SustainabilityPolicy.pdf> (hereinafter IFC Sustainability Policy).
135. *See generally* IFC, 'International Finance Corporation's Performance Standards on Social & Environmental Sustainability' (30 Apr. 2006), *available at* <www.ifc.org/ifcext/sustainability.nsf/AttachmentsByTitle/pol_PerformanceStandards2006_full/$FILE/IFC+Performance+ Standards.pdf> (hereinafter IFC Performance Standards).
136. *See ibid.*
137. IFC, Review and Update of IFC Sustainability Framework, <www.ifc.org/policyreview>.

The Sustainability Policy provides that 'when a project is proposed for financing, IFC conducts a social and environmental review of the project as part of its overall due diligence'.[138] The review includes three key components:

> i) the social and environmental risks and impacts of the project as assessed by the client; ii) the commitment and capacity of the client to manage these expected impacts, including the client's social and environmental management system; and iii) the role of third parties in the project's compliance with the Performance Standards.[139]

If a project has 'significant adverse impacts on affected communities', the IFC assures itself that there is 'broad community support for the project within the affected communities'.[140] The Sustainability Policy further provides that the 'IFC does not finance new business activity that cannot be expected to meet the Performance Standards over a reasonable period of time'.[141] The IFC also has a list of activities that it does not finance.[142]

The IFC can take substantial credit for the adoption of the IFC Performance Standards by the 'Equator Banks' as the Equator Principles. In March 2008, more than sixty of the world's leading commercial banks agreed to revise the Equator Principles by incorporating the IFC Performance Standards. According to the Equator Principles' website,[143] these commercial banks provide an amount of finances that represents over 80% of the world's foreign direct investment in developing countries. Despite this achievement, the World Bank Group IEG noted that more information is needed before the effect of this adoption on environmental and social impacts will be well understood. The IEG encouraged greater transparency in support of this understanding.

The IFC's efforts to enhance transparency and accountability are reflected in the creation of the Office of the Compliance Advisor/Ombudsman (CAO), whose central role is to provide an accessible and effective mechanism for handling complaints from individuals who are affected (or are likely to be affected) as a result of the social and environmental impacts of IFC-sponsored projects.[144] The environmental community has on occasion chided the Equator Banks for not having a similar office to help gauge the effectiveness of and compliance with the principles.

---

138. IFC Sustainability Policy, *supra* n. 134, para. 13 (describing the IFC's 'Overall Approach').
139. *Ibid.*, para. 15.
140. *Ibid.*
141. *Ibid.*, para. 17.
142. Examples of these activities include: production or trade in any product or activity deemed illegal under host country laws or regulations or international convention and agreements; production or trade in weapons and munitions; production or trade in alcoholic beverages; and production or trade in tobacco.
143. The Equator Principles, <www.equator-principles.com/index.shtml>.
144. *See generally* IFC, Compliance Advisor/Ombudsman, <www.cao-ombudsman.org/>.

IV. SUPPORTING INTERNATIONAL ENVIRONMENTAL LAW THROUGH PARTNERSHIPS FOR SUSTAINABLE DEVELOPMENT

Sound policies alone do not determine whether the actions of IFIs support the objectives of international environmental law. These policies must be implemented and applied to programmes and projects whose design and operation will also be environmentally and socially sound. Further, even if these objectives are achieved, successful partnerships among the public and private sector and civil society will be required for sustainable development to take hold across the broad range of developing countries.

President Zoellick of the World Bank has noted this relation between international policies and agreements and sustainable development, stating: '[i]t is the purpose of the [World] Bank Group to advance ideas about international projects and agreements on trade, finance, health, poverty, education, and climate change so that they can benefit all, especially the poor seeking new opportunities'.[145] He further noted that: '[i]t is the purpose of the World Bank Group to assist countries to help themselves by catalyzing the capital and policies through a mix of ideas and experience, development of private market opportunities, and support for good governance and anti-corruption – spurred by our financial resources'.[146]

As the earlier reference to President Zoellick's remarks pointed out,[147] his views underscore that the World Bank Group can only achieve the objectives set forth in international environmental law through successful partnerships, while using its own resources and expertise as catalysts for sustainable development. Both President Zoellick and prior World Bank presidents have noted that it is not realistic to expect the Bank to devote all its resources to the environment, despite the call from British Prime Minister Gordon Brown for it to become an environment bank.[148] The tensions between the old-fashioned views of environment as anti-development and the views of the pro-growth movements for development are still too real to achieve that objective. Moreover, it is not realistic to expect that Bank funds on their own can achieve sustainable development unless larger sums of finance are geared in the same direction.

Nevertheless, as noted in section II above, funding for environment in the World Bank is on the rise, as are key new partnerships to tackle the challenges of sustainable development. In this connection, the Global Monitoring Report 2008 noted that environment-related lending in the World Bank had grown over the last five years, and amounted to USD 10.2 billion.[149] During the same time, lending

145. The World Bank, 'Zoellick: Globalization Must Benefit the World's Poor', *supra* n. 15.
146. *Ibid.*
147. *See ibid.*
148. *See* House of Commons International Development Committee, *DFID and the World Bank: Sixth Report of Session 2007-08*, vol. I (London: The Stationary Office Limited, 2008), *available at* <www.publications.parliament.uk/pa/cm200708/cmselect/cmintdev/67/67.pdf>.
149. The World Bank and International Monetary Fund (IMF), *Global Monitoring Report 2008: MDGs and the Environment: Agenda for Inclusive and Sustainable Development*

was approximately USD 100 billion.[150] The IEG confirmed that the number of environment projects reached an all-time high in 2007 and the number of key environmental partnerships was also on the rise.[151] Despite a recent decline in the number of GEF projects administered through the World Bank, during this period the Bank also provided several billion dollars in grants in its role as Implementing Agency of the GEF,[152] as well as being a key partner and contributor to a range of other global public good grant-making facilities, such as the Critical Ecosystem Partnership Fund and the Consultative Group on International Agricultural Research. These partnerships are financially supported by grants from the World Bank's Development Grant Facility.

While these amounts have been significant in support of international environmental law, the global community still faces a critical need to increase amounts of funding for the environment, and improve the ability to mainstream environment into the overall operations of IFIs. Chief among these reasons is the fact that according to leading scientific reports, such as those of the Fourth Assessment of the Intergovernmental Panel on Climate Change[153] and the Millennium Ecosystem Assessment,[154] many of the world's environmental systems are considered to be under severe threat that, in many cases, is potentially irreversible. Thus, despite the many multilateral environmental agreements and other instruments that constitute international environmental law, these instruments have not generated the action and the funding to reverse threats to key ecosystems.

Indeed, leading economic reports have recently detailed the sums that are needed to tackle the most pervasive environmental challenge of the day: climate change. The Stern Review on the Economics of Climate Change[155] is the most well-known of these, but a series of others are delineated in the World Bank's Strategic Framework for Climate Change and Development.[156] As these reports make clear, at a minimum, the developing world will need an average of

---

(Washington, DC: The International Bank for Reconstruction and Development, 2008), 176, *available at* <http://siteresources.worldbank.org/INTGLOMONREP2008/Resources/4737994-1207342962709/8944_Web_PDF.pdf> (hereinafter *Global Monitoring Report 2008*).

150. *Ibid.*
151. IEG-World Bank, *Environmental Sustainability: An Evaluation of World Bank Group Support*, *supra* n. 12, 24.
152. However, the amount of GEF funding provided through the Bank fell off in fiscal years 2006 and 2007. *See ibid.*, 23.
153. *See* Intergovernmental Panel on Climate Change (IPCC), *Fourth Assessment Report – Climate Change 2007: Synthesis Report* (2008), *available at* <www.ipcc.ch/pdf/assessment-report/ar4/syr/ar4_syr.pdf>.
154. *See* Millennium Ecosystem Assessment, <www.millenniumassessment.org/en/Index.aspx> (providing links to both full and synthesis Millennium Assessment Reports).
155. Nicholas Stern, *Stern Review Report on the Economics of Climate Change* (Cambridge: Cambridge University Press, 2006), *available at* <www.hm-treasury.gov.uk/independent_reviews/stern_review_economics_climate_change/sternreview_index.cfm>.
156. The World Bank, *Development and Climate Change – A Strategic Framework for the World Bank Group*, Consultation Draft (21 Aug. 2008), *available at* <http://siteresources.worldbank.org/EXTCC/Resources/407863-1219339233881/DevelopmentandClimateChange.pdf>.

USD 30 billion per annum additional to current resources to provide clean energy to help achieve mitigation from global warming gases and seek to stabilize the global CO_2 concentration at 450 parts per million.[157] In addition, the developing world will need between USD 4 and USD 37 billion per year to help them successfully adapt to climate change.[158] The bulk of these sums will have to come through the private sector given the current sums available through existing public mechanisms. For mitigation, those mechanisms provide roughly USD 7 billion per year through the United Nations Framework Convention on Climate Change (UNFCCC) Clean Development Mechanism (CDM), and USD 250 million per year through the GEF. For adaptation, roughly USD 100 million per year is now available even if the newly launched Adaptation Fund begins operation.[159] Thus, there are massive shortfalls in the funds necessary to address mitigation and adaptation.

Another critical funding factor is that the decisions today concerning how to spend these sums on infrastructure may put greenhouse gas emitting facilities in place that affect the planet for many years to come – so the need to make correct decisions about the environment has great urgency. Unfortunately, in many countries, often those with the most wealth in terms of extractive resources, the decision-makers have failed to take into account the impact of development on the environment. As noted by the Global Monitoring Report 2008:

> Concerns about environmental sustainability arise because, unlike labor and produced capital, the environment is often an unpriced input into production. This is true for much natural capital. Fisheries and forests in many countries are open access natural resources, as is groundwater. Lack of property rights to these resources prevents them from being used sustainably. Without appropriate institutions, an open-access fishery will be overharvested and habitat for biodiversity will be destroyed. Users of these resources will impose externalities on others. The same is true for air and water as receptors of pollution. In the absence of appropriate institutions, a power plant will impose external costs on households in the form of local air pollutants (such as particulate matter) and also on the earth's climate in the form of carbon dioxide emissions.[160]

In light of these factors, how can IFIs best ensure principles of sustainability guide these expenditures and associated infrastructure investments? In the same vein, how can the Bank fulfil the recommendations laid out by the World Bank's Independent Evaluation Group?[161]

157. *Ibid.*, Annex 5, 87.
158. *Ibid.*
159. *Ibid.*, Annex A5.
160. *Global Monitoring Report 2008*, *supra* n. 149, 180.
161. IEG-World Bank, *Environmental Sustainability: An Evaluation of World Bank Group Support*, *supra* n. 12.

A. Increasing of Financial Support for Multilateral Environmental Agreements and for Global Public Goods

The World Bank played perhaps the most extensive role of any international institution in setting up the GEF, the world's largest grant funding source dedicated to global environmental concerns.[162] The GEF was founded on a partnership among three implementing agencies: the World Bank, the United Nations Environment Program, and the United Nations Development Program. The World Bank also serves as the Trustee for the GEF. The GEF was established with a functionally independent secretariat headed by a chief executive officer and chairperson and operated with full-time professional staff. It is governed by a council that meets twice per year to approve GEF funded projects, and by an assembly that meets every three to four years.

To ensure a continued flow of funds, the GEF is replenished every four years.[163] Over time, the sums available have increased, and an aggressive campaign is underway now for its upcoming replenishment (in late 2010). In August 2006, the Fourth Replenishment generated pledges of USD 3.13 billion. In addition to enhanced financing, opportunities to carry out GEF projects have increased for other IFIs and UN agencies, as well as some non-governmental organizations.[164]

The governments set up the GEF mostly to provide grants for global environmental benefits:

> GEF shall operate, on the basis of collaboration and partnership among the Implementing Agencies, as a mechanism for international cooperation for the purpose of providing new and additional grant and concessional funding to meet the agreed incremental costs of measures to achieve agreed global environmental benefits in the following focal areas:
>
> (a) biological diversity;
> (b) climate change;
> (c) international waters;
> (d) land degradation, primarily desertification and deforestation;
> (e) ozone layer depletion; and
> (f) persistent organic pollutants.[165]

In support of the above stated aims, the GEF is expressly identified in several treaties as the financial mechanism for a number of environmental treaties.

---

162. *See generally* Global Environment Facility (GEF), <www.gefweb.org/> (providing information about the GEF, its programmes, policies, projects, etc.).
163. GEF Replenishment, <www.gefweb.org/Replenishment/replenishment.html>.
164. *See* 'Council Decisions concerning Expanded Opportunities for Executing Agencies', GEF/R.3/CRP.1 (14 May 2002), *available at* <www.gefweb.org/Replenishment/Reple_Documents/R.3.CRP.1.pdf>.
165. *See* Global Environment Facility, 'Instrument for the Establishment of the Restructured Global Environment Facility' (Washington, DC: Global Environment Facility, 2004), para. 2, *available at* <www.gefweb.org/GEF_Instrument3.pdf>.

Additionally, it supports a number of other environmental treaties in which it is not directly mentioned as the primary financial mechanism.

Despite its mission to tackle a wide range of global concerns, the GEF approves projects in amounts averaging only about USD 1 billion per year. On its own, it is not funded sufficiently to enable achievement of all the objectives of the focal areas on which it concentrates. Achieving environmental sustainability throughout the developing world requires tens of billions of dollars. It is therefore clear that sound environmental decision-making needs to be mainstreamed into the operations of IFIs and development finance to maximize financial support for international environmental law-related objectives. In this light, the international environmental community is closely watching the ongoing GEF replenishment discussions. The GEF has set a replenishment target as high as USD 10 billion, though more recent discussions seem to have lowered that amount to a range between USD 4.5 and USD 6.5 billion.

1. Climate Change

The World Bank Group's recent Strategic Framework on Climate Change and Development[166] makes clear that a range of financial instruments will be required to provide the funds needed to address climate change mitigation and adaptation, and to catalyse the private sector to support these objectives. Thus, funding for the clean energy of tomorrow will come from a range of sources, and the UNFCCC estimates that as much as 80% will have to come from private-sector funding.[167] Especially at the current stage, and in the absence of a global carbon regulatory framework, important funding will come from innovative financing instruments such as the World Bank's Carbon Finance operations, as well as through the recently launched CIFs.

These financial instruments are necessary to address problems related to climate change because the UNFCCC made clear that developing countries would not be expected to bear the burden of all costs for mitigation and adaptation.[168] The Convention also stated that it expected that a range of different sources of funds would be used, and that the burden would not be on the GEF alone.[169] In this manner, the UNFCCC also noted that the social and economic development of

166. *See* The World Bank, 'Development and Climate Change: The World Bank Group at Work' (Washington, DC: The World Bank Group, 2009), *available at* <http://siteresources.worldbank.org/EXTCC/Resources/WBGatWork.pdf>.

167. UNFCCC, 'Dialogue on long-term cooperative action to address climate change by enhancing implementation of the Convention', Dialogue working paper 8 (Vienna, 27–31 Aug. 2007), *available at* <http://unfccc.int/files/cooperation_and_support/financial_mechanism/>. financial_mechanism_gef/application/pdf/dialogue_working_paper_8.pdf>.

168. United Nations Framework Convention on Climate Change, 1771 U.N.T.S. 107 (1992), Art. 3 (hereinafter UNFCCC).

169. *Ibid.*, Art. 11.5. ('The developed country Parties may also provide and developing country Parties avail themselves of, financial resources related to the implementation of the Convention through bilateral, regional and other multilateral channels.')

developing countries should not be relegated to a lesser status as a result of climate change goals, but that financial assistance should be provided to achieve both. Thus, the UNFCCC stated the following:

> The extent to which developing country Parties will effectively implement their commitments under the Convention will depend on the effective implementation by developed country Parties of their commitments under the Convention related to financial resources and transfer of technology and will take fully into account that economic and social development and poverty eradication are the first and overriding priorities of the developing country Parties.[170]

Against this background, the World Bank began developing the legal and financial instruments that could serve these various objectives. The Bank's legal department largely drafted the instruments that enabled the launch of the GEF, including the resolution that was approved by the World Bank Board of Executive Directors that was necessary for the GEF to get underway as a financial mechanism for the UNFCCC. The Bank legal department also drafted various grant agreements that are necessary to transfer funds to GEF recipients, including agreements to transfer funds to non-governmental organizations.

In addition, the Bank began developing instruments that could seek to tap into market incentives offered by the 'flexibility mechanisms' of the UNFCCC Kyoto Protocol.[171] In 1999, after years of working at the pilot project stage on jointly implemented projects, the World Bank formally established its carbon finance business with the launch of the Prototype Carbon Fund (PCF).[172] This fund serves as a partnership of public- and private-sector participants who have pooled their resources to support project-based greenhouse gas emission reductions in developing countries. The PCF has supported more than USD 100 million in projects.

With the entry into force of the Kyoto Protocol in February 2005,[173] World Bank carbon funds continued to grow. Over time, nine additional funds were created, and today, the World Bank is managing over USD 2 billion in funds set aside for carbon finance. The majority of these funds are for emission reduction projects that have been registered for approval by the Kyoto Protocol Clean Development Mechanism. Thus, these funds generate emission reduction units that can be credited against fund participant's quantified emission reduction obligations under the first commitment period of the Kyoto Protocol. The funds provide a small, but important percentage of the roughly USD 106 billion total that have been provided through the Clean Development Mechanism since 2002.[174]

170. *Ibid.*, Art. 4(7).
171. Kyoto Protocol to the United Nations Framework Convention on Climate Change, FCCC/CP/1997/L.7/Add.1 (1997), Arts 6, 12, 17 (hereinafter Kyoto Protocol).
172. The World Bank Carbon Finance website, <http://carbonfinance.org/>.
173. The Kyoto Protocol entered into force on 16 Feb. 2005, <http://unfccc.int/meetings/kyoto_eif/items/3363.php>.
174. *See* The World Bank, 'State and Trends of the Carbon Market 2009' (Washington, DC, May 2009), 41, *available at* <http://wbcarbonfinance.org/docs/State_____Trends_of_the_

More recently, the future of climate finance was a key element of discussions during the Fifteenth Meeting of the Parties to the UNFCCC in Copenhagen, Denmark (COP-15) and coincidental Fifth Meeting of the Parties to the Kyoto Protocol to the UNFCCC (CMP-5). It was envisaged in the months leading up to COP-15 that under the Bali Action Plan, adopted at the Thirteenth Meeting of the UNFCCC Conference of Parties (COP) in Bali, Indonesia, governments would complete international negotiations on the next stage of the Kyoto Protocol and on Long-term Cooperative Action (LCA) under the UNFCCC.[175] Had Copenhagen fully succeeded in fulfilling the Bali Action Plan, it could have launched a global regulatory framework to address climate change and put in place a strong carbon market that would have put a rising price on carbon and provided significant sums needed for mitigation and adaptation efforts. However, parties at Copenhagen failed to reach a legally binding agreement. Instead, all but five parties at COP-15 agreed to 'take note' of a non-legally binding 'Copenhagen Accord' that pledged to continue efforts to take measures to reduce carbon emissions, but did not set binding emission targets, nor a date for peak emissions.[176] Indeed, the final version of the Copenhagen Accord omitted earlier language that called for the Accord to mature into a legally binding agreement within six to twelve months.

The Copenhagen Accord states that by 31 January 2010, all UNFCCC Annex I Parties will submit in writing to the UNFCCC their quantified economy wide reduction targets.[177] By the same date, Non-Annex I parties will also submit in writing to the UNFCCC the mitigation actions that they pledge to implement. In addition, while these pledges are not legally binding, the Accord does present for the first time a form of monitoring, reporting, and verification for these actions by both Annex I and non-Annex I parties, though the text addressing these actions differs between the two.[178]

The lack of a successful conclusion to the Copenhagen negotiations does not necessarily mean the World Bank and IFIs will have less work to do concerning mitigation or adaptation to climate change. Indeed, the Copenhagen Accord called for the establishment of a Copenhagen Green Climate Fund to help address climate

---

Carbon_Market_2009-FINAL_26_May09.pdf> (noting that 'The CDM has potentially benefited about US$106 billion (€75 billion) of overall 2002–08 investment in projects that reduce GHG emissions . . . '. The report was written for the Bank by Karan Capoor & Philippe Ambrosi).

175. *See* UNFCCC, 'Bali Action Plan', Decision CP.13 (Advance Unedited Version) (Bali, 2007), *available at* <http://unfccc.int/files/meetings/cop_13/application/pdf/cp_bali_action.pdf>.

176. UNFCCC, 'Copenhagen Accord', Decision-/CP.15 (Advance unedited version) (Copenhagen, Denmark, 19 Dec. 2009), <http://unfccc.int/files/meetings/cop_15/application/pdf/cop15_cph_auv.pdf> (hereinafter Copenhagen Accord).

177. On 29 Jan. 2010, the United States announced that in keeping with its pledge in Copenhagen, it would reduce greenhouse gas emissions by 17% from 2005 levels by 2020. Juliet Eilperin, 'U.S. Pledges 17 percent Emissions Reduction by 2020', *Washington Post*, 29 Jan. 2010, *available at* <www.washingtonpost.com/wp-dyn/content/article/2010/01/28/AR2010012803632.html>.

178. Copenhagen Accord, *supra* n. 176, paras 4, 5.

mitigation and adaptation needs. The Accord did not preclude a role for IFIs in relation to that Fund. The Accord states as follows:

> The collective commitment by developed countries is to provide new and additional resources, including forestry and investments through international institutions, approaching USD 30 billion for the period 2010–2012 with balanced allocation between adaptation and mitigation. Funding for adaptation will be prioritized for the most vulnerable developing countries, such as the least developed countries, small island developing States and Africa. In the context of meaningful mitigation actions and transparency on implementation, developed countries commit to a goal of mobilizing jointly USD 100 billion dollars a year by 2020 to address the needs of developing countries. This funding will come from a wide variety of sources, public and private, bilateral and multilateral, including alternative sources of finance. New multilateral funding for adaptation will be delivered through effective and efficient fund arrangements, with a governance structure providing for equal representation of developed and developing countries. A significant portion of such funding should flow through the Copenhagen Green Climate Fund.[179]

Efforts to mobilize such funding are underway, as witnessed in the first meeting of the UN High-Level Advisory Group on climate change finance, in London on 31 March 2010.[180] Moreover, as many as eighty-one nations, both developed and developing have responded to the Copenhagen Accord's 31 January 2010 deadline, submitting their[181] pledges to the UNFCCC Secretariat. These pledges include historic firsts from many developing countries, such as Brazil, China, India, and South Africa that have noted in their submissions their intended nationally appropriate mitigation action.[182] While these pledges are not legally binding, they may form the basis for binding commitments or part of a legally binding future agreement.

In part, because COP-15 failed to produce a global climate regulatory framework, it seems fortuitous that shortly after the Bali COP, the World Bank joined with a wide range of donors and other international organizations to develop and launch the CIFs that can continue to provide at least interim climate related funding.[183] The CIFs were approved by the World Bank Board of Executive

179. *Ibid.*, para. 8.
180. *See* Ben Norman (WWF), 'High Level UN Finance Group meets to set new direction' (1 Apr. 2010), <http://blogs.panda.org/climate/2010/04/01/high-level-un-climate-finance-group-meets-to-set-direction/>.
181. Copenhagen Accord, Information provided by Parties to the Convention relating to the Copenhagen Accord, <http://unfccc.int/home/items/5262.php>.
182. For nationally appropriate mitigation actions of developing countries, *see* Appendix II – Nationally appropriate mitigation actions of developing country Parties, <http://unfccc.int/home/items/5265.php>.
183. 'Building Partnerships for Climate Action: CIF – Climate Investment Funds' (1 Nov. 2008 to 31 Oct. 2009), *available at* <www.climateinvestmentfunds.org/cif/sites/climateinvestmentfunds.org/files/annual_report_published_version_113009.pdf>.

Directors in July 2008.[184] The funds' documents expressly state that the funds are not meant to pre-empt any aspect of the UNFCCC negotiations or outcome, and as such, have included a 'sunset clause' so that they can close once an international financial framework has become effective.

As an initial launch, the CIFs were targeted to be established with USD 5 billion and by October 2009 thirteen countries had pledged USD 6.9 billion. The CIFs combine grants with highly concessional funding and risk reduction instruments to address mitigation and adaptation needs for developing countries. The CIFs are established through two funds: a Climate Technology Fund (CTF)[185] and the Strategic Climate Fund (SCF).[186] The CTF will provide funds to focus on low carbon technologies and the SCF is to be 'broader and more flexible and serve as an overarching fund for various programmes to test innovative approaches to climate change'.[187] The SCF also includes within it a Pilot Program for Climate Resilience (PPCR) that can address the needs of developing countries to adapt to climate change. More than USD 600 million has been pledged for this effort. A novel governance structure was established for PPCR activities that includes representation of the Kyoto Protocol Adaptation Fund Board and six eligible recipient countries along with six contributor countries.

The CIFs also include a FIP that can help developing countries address emissions caused by deforestation and degradation, consistent with the Copenhagen decision to support efforts known as 'REDD Plus', which addresses emissions from deforestation and forest degradation, as well as conservation and sustainable forest management.[188]

The FIP can support the Forest Carbon Partnership Facility (FCPF).[189] The FCPF was launched at the Bali COP with pledges by a number of government donors and The Nature Conservancy. The fund now has over USD 140 million. It has a governance structure similar to the FIP in that it includes developing countries and indigenous peoples in the decision-making arrangements. The goal of the FCPF is to work with tropical and subtropical developing countries

184. The World Bank, 'World Bank Board Approves Climate Investment Funds', Press Release No. 2009/001/SDN (1 Jul. 2008), *available at* <http://web.worldbank.org/WBSITE/EXTERNAL/TOPICS/ENVIRONMENT/EXTCC/0,,contentMDK:21713769~menuPK:4860081~pagePK:210058~piPK:210062~theSitePK:4>.
185. The World Bank, *The Clean Technology Fund* (9 Jun. 2008), *available at* <http://siteresources.worldbank.org/INTCC/Resources/Clean_Technology_Fund_paper_June_9_final.pdf>.
186. The World Bank, *Strategic Climate Fund* (3 Jun. 2008), *available at* <http://siteresources.worldbank.org/INTCC/Resources/Strategic_Climate_Fund_final.pdf#Strategic_Climate_Fund>.
187. *Ibid.*
188. 'Methodological guidance for activities relating to reducing emissions from deforestation and forest degradation and the role of conservation, sustainable management of forests and enhancement of forest carbon stocks in developing countries', Draft decision – CP/25 (advance unedited version) (2009), *available at* <http://unfccc.int/files/na/application/pdf/cop15_ddc_auv.pdf>.
189. The World Bank, Forest Carbon Partnership Facility, <www.forestcarbonpartnership.org/fcp/>.

'to reduce emissions from deforestation and forest degradation [REDD] and to tap into any future system of positive incentives for REDD'.[190] In addition, the FCPF has a goal to help reduce the rate of deforestation and forest degradation by 'providing an incentive per ton of carbon dioxide of emissions reduced through specific Emission Reductions Programs targeting the drivers of deforestation and forest degradation'.[191]

Efforts such as the FCPF need to succeed to help address the fact that up to 20% of global greenhouse gas emissions come from land and forest conversion. Just as the Bank has been a leader in promoting incentives for protecting ecosystem services for carbon sequestration and biodiversity, the FCPF affords opportunities to protect forests for carbon sequestration and for their many other benefits.

In addition to the FCPF, the World Bank announced during the Copenhagen COP that it also was launching the Carbon Partnership Fund (CPF).[192] The CPF will focus on programmatic funding for projects that will deliver carbon emission reductions over much longer periods of time than the five-year period that is common in many of the current carbon funds. In doing so, it will be willing to make riskier investments, but at the same time aim to achieve emission reductions over a much greater scale than was previously possible.

While a robust financial carbon market has developed for mitigation projects such as those to be covered in the CPF, there is little market incentive provided by any climate treaty instrument to provide funds to help countries adapt to climate change. For a number of reasons linked to development outcomes, such as increasing evidence demonstrating the link between climate change and adverse impacts on the poor from severe weather, the Bank has focused on adaptation efforts. The recent replenishment of the International Development Association (IDA) was accompanied by a paper on IDA and Climate Change.[193] It notes the importance of IDA's concessional flows to address adaptation. Dedicated amounts from this replenishment of the IDA will be identified to fund adaptation. Additionally, as mentioned above, adaptation efforts can draw upon the PPCR.

In addition to concessional flows from IDA, risk management funding through insurance as a tool to help adapt to climate change is also being developed in the World Bank Group. The Caribbean Catastrophe Risk Insurance Facility (CCRIF) launched in June 2007 is the first regional catastrophe insurance facility in the world.[194] It provides sixteen participating governments from the Caribbean

---

190. *Ibid.*
191. *Ibid.*
192. *See* The World Bank, 'World Bank Launches New Carbon Facility for Greenhouse Gas Emission Reductions at COP 15: Carbon Partnership Facility to develop programmatic approaches', press release (Copenhagen, Denmark, 11 Dec. 2009), <http://beta.worldbank.org/climatechange/sites/default/files/CPFLaunchPressRelease12-11.pdf>.
193. *See* International Development Association, 'IDA and Climate Change: Making Climate Action Work for Development' (IDA: Sustainable Development Network (SDN), October 2007), *available at* <http://siteresources.worldbank.org/IDA/Resources/Seminar%20PDFs/73449-1172525976405/3492866-1175095887430/IDAClimateChange.pdf>.
194. Caribbean Catastrophe Risk Insurance Facility (CCRIF), <www.ccrif.org/>.

region[195] with immediate liquidity in the aftermath of a natural disaster. By pooling their risks together, participant countries save approximately 40% over individual premiums. From 1 June to 31 December 2007, five earthquakes and two hurricanes were reported by the CCRIF participants.

The World Bank Group is also investing in renewable energy and energy efficiency.[196] During the past five years, the WBG approved 366 renewable energy and energy efficiency projects in ninety countries. There were ninety-nine projects in forty-eight countries last year alone. Moreover, in 2009, the WBG financing of renewable energy and energy efficiency projects and programmes in developing countries increased 24% to reach USD 3.3 billion, the highest ever. The lending for new renewables (solar, wind, geothermal, biomass, and hydro below 10 MW) and energy efficiency reached USD 3.1 billion. Below is a portfolio of energy lending at the World Bank Group.

Sectoral Breakdown of WBG Energy Lending, FY03–FY08[197]

(in USD millions)

Project Type	FY03	FY04	FY05	FY06	FY07	FY08
EE	177	92	217	425	262	1,192
Large Hydro (larger than 10MWs)	23	83	538	250	751	1,007
New RE	206	138	246	344	421	473
Upstream Oil, Gas and Coal	333	496	578	1,074	627	981
Other Energy (including energy policy support projects)	954	386	278	248	374	903
Thermal Generation	461	255	100	511	360	957
Transmission and Distribution	216	248	906	1,801	809	2,031
WBG Energy (USD million)	2,370	1,699	2,864	4,653	3,603	7,545

195. These countries are Anguilla, Antigua & Barbuda, Bahamas, Barbados, Belize, Bermuda, Cayman Islands, Dominica, Grenada, Haiti, Jamaica, St Kitts & Nevis, St Lucia, St Vincent & the Grenadines, Trinidad & Tobago, and the Turks and Caicos Islands.

196. World Bank Group, 'Beyond Bonn: The World Bank Group Reaches Record High Investments for New Renewable Energy and Energy Efficiency, Lends US 3.1 billion in FY 2009' (October 2009), *available at* <http://siteresources.worldbank.org/INTENERGY/Resources/2009REEE4PageFinal.pdf?resourceurlname=2009REEE4PageFinal.pdf>.

197. The World Bank, Energy Portfolio, <http://web.worldbank.org/WBSITE/EXTERNAL/TOPICS/EXTENERGY2/0,,contentMDK:21651596~menuPK:4140787~pagePK:210058~piPK:210062~theSitePK:4114200,00.html>.

Project Type	FY03	FY04	FY05	FY06	FY07	FY08
Total Low Carbon (include RE, EE, power plant rehabilitation, district heating, biomass waste fuelled energy, gas flaring reduction, high efficiency coal fired plants, thermal plants)	406	350	1,237	1,660	1,440	3,003
Total Access (includes projects aimed at increasing access to electricity services)	794	537	1,136	1,018	1,239	2,321

2. Biodiversity

The focus on climate change has perhaps made it more difficult to tap into some of the traditional sources of finance needed to protect globally valuable biodiversity.[198] This imbalance in funding was not fully anticipated at the time the two conventions were adopted in 1992. Nevertheless, the World Bank has been one of the largest sources of funding for biodiversity, both terrestrial and marine. Much of this support has come through the Bank's role as an implementing agency for the GEF.

These grant resources have been crucial to biodiversity because the developing country parties to the Convention on Biological Diversity (CBD), as with the UNFCCC, insisted that support for the environment should not come at the expense of development. Thus, the CBD repeated verbatim the UNFCCC caveat that 'social development and poverty eradication are the first and overriding priorities of developing country parties'.[199]

Largely with the aforementioned GEF grant resources, and with loans leveraged through GEF grants, the Bank has supported more than five hundred biodiversity projects in over one hundred countries. Between 1988 and 2004, the WBG committed over USD 2.5 billion in loans and GEF resources and leveraged another USD 2.2 billion in co-financing, resulting in a total biodiversity investment

198. For the linkage of biodiversity and climate change work at the World Bank, *see* The World Bank, 'Biodiversity, Climate Change, and Adaptation: Nature-Based Solutions from the World Bank Portfolio' (Washington, DC: The World Bank, 2008), *available at* <http://siteresources.worldbank.org/INTBIODIVERSITY/Resources/Biodiversity_10-1-08_final.pdf>.

199. Convention on Biological Diversity, *supra* n. 95, Art. 20(4).

portfolio of USD 4.7 billion.[200] Much of this financial support has gone to the establishment or maintenance of protected areas. In fact, since its inception, the GEF has committed more than USD 1.5 billion for new and existing protected areas, targeting more than 1,500 protected areas covering a land area of three hundred million hectares, some 17% of all land protected globally.[201]

In addition to the GEF as a means to support globally important biodiversity, the World Bank has also been a partner in the Critical Ecosystem Partnership Fund (CEPF).[202] This fund is housed at the Washington-based non-governmental organization, Conservation International. The fund focuses on hotspots of global biodiversity. The Bank and the GEF have contributed both financially and administratively to the CEPF.

3. Global Agriculture

With the global impact of rising fossil fuel prices driving up the cost of food and farming, the World Bank has launched support for the poor to help them have better access to food and farming. The Global Food Crisis Response Program[203] was approved by the Bank Board in May 2008 and is allowed to be implemented under fast track decision-making to facilitate rapid disbursement to the poor. This programme will have funding of over USD 1 billion available to assist the poorest countries in addressing this global crisis. This approach is relatively new and underscores how the Bank is seeking to find flexible ways to operate and deliver needed protection faster than in years past. The Bank is also working at revitalizing its long relationship in support of the Consultative Group on International Agriculture and Research (CGIAR)[204] and the fifteen global centres in developing countries that have played a critical role in providing agricultural innovations and research for developing countries.

4. Chemicals and Hazardous Substances

The World Bank has also been an active participant in the global efforts to address concerns about hazardous substances. This has been manifest in extensive and

200. The World Bank, *Ensuring the Future: The World Bank and Biodiversity, 1988–2004* (October 2004), 4, *available at* <www-wds.worldbank.org/external/default/WDSContentServer/WDSP/IB/2005/07/15/000160016_20050715155744/Rendered/PDF/32937a10Ensuring1the1Future.pdf>.
201. The World Bank, UNDP & GEF, *Reducing Threats to Protected Areas: Lessons from the Field* (Washington, DC: The World Bank, 2007), 3, *available at* <http://siteresources.worldbank.org/INTBIODIVERSITY/Resources/ReducingThreats-web.pdf>.
202. Critical Ecosystem Partnership Fund, <www.cepf.net/Pages/default.aspx>.
203. Christopher Delgado, 'The Global Food Crisis Response Program (GFRP) at the World Bank', presentation given at the Food & Energy Price Briefing (9 Jul. 2008), *available at* <http://siteresources.worldbank.org/SOCIALPROTECTION/Resources/280558-1138289492561/2158434-1215439855252/Delgado_GFRP.pdf>.
204. Consultative Group on International Agriculture and Research (CGIAR), <www.cgiar.org/>.

highly successful efforts to eliminate ozone depleting substances (ODS)[205] through operations that fulfil the objectives of the Montreal Protocol. By the end of 2006, the World Bank reported that, at the twentieth anniversary of the Montreal Protocol, it had financed USD 800 million dollars to purchase and destroy nearly 260,000 tons of potential ODS.[206] This included more than 900 investment and non-investment activities in some twenty-five developing countries.

The Africa Stockpiles project has similar aims, but destroys a different set of hazardous chemicals – obsolete stockpiles of persistent organic pollutants (POPs).[207] This project has financial support from the GEF, given that it directly addresses a focal area of the GEF, and the objectives of the Stockholm Convention on POPs. Not only does the project support identification of these stocks and their destruction, it is also putting in place measures to prevent the development of unneeded stockpiles in the future. It operates across all of Africa, and is one of the largest projects of the GEF and several of its partners, including the Bank.

5. Implementing International Environmental Law at the Regional and National Level

While global issues like climate change, biodiversity, agriculture, and transboundary hazardous wastes attract significant funding as well as global grant support, some of the traditional 'nuts and bolts' of development lending have received less support, though the impacts on environment can be just as significant. This issue has resurfaced within the World Bank in large part because lending for critical infrastructure has failed to materialize for many developing countries. The private-sector resources have been concentrated in a smaller range of developing countries, and there remains within a much broader range of developing countries, particularly the least developed ones, a demand for the lending and guarantee instruments of the World Bank and other IFIs. With the recent release of the Sustainable Infrastructure Action Plan,[208] the World Bank has laid out the principles under which it will provide infrastructure finance going forward.

A project that, at least at this stage, appears to represent the fulfilment of these principles is the Nam Theun 2 hydroelectric project in the People's Republic of Laos.[209] Begun in the early 1990s, this project took close to fifteen years to come to

205. The World Bank, Montreal Protocol: Themes and Strategies, <http://web.worldbank.org/WBSITE/EXTERNAL/TOPICS/ENVIRONMENT/EXTTMP/0,,contentMDK:20502662~menuPK:1246986~pagePK:148956~piPK:216618~theSitePK:408230,00.html>.
206. *See* The World Bank, *The 20th Anniversary of Montreal Protocol: Preserving the Ozone Layer* (September 2007), *available at* <http://siteresources.worldbank.org/INTMP/214578-1110890369636/21474014/WBMPPolicy.pdf>.
207. Africa Stockpiles Programme, <www.africastockpiles.net/>.
208. The World Bank, 'Questions and Answers on the Sustainable Infrastructure Plan' (July 2008), <http://siteresources.worldbank.org/INTSDNETWORK/Resources/SIAP-Q-A-July08.pdf>.
209. The World Bank, Nam Thuen 2 Hydroelectric Project in Lao People's Democratic Republic (Lao PDR): Project Overview and Description (September 2009), <http://web.worldbank.org/WBSITE/EXTERNAL/COUNTRIES/EASTASIAPACIFICEXT/LAOPRDEXTN/0,,contentMDK:21109109~pagePK:141137~piPK:141127~theSitePK:293684,00.html>.

fruition. Yet, today it offers one potential model for how to carry out sensitive infrastructure lending. Prior to presenting the project for board approval, consultation took place with each affected village. Plans for resettlement and livelihood restoration were developed with input from the villages and from independent experts. In addition, independent experts were engaged to determine the potential impact on natural habitat and to design mitigation measures that included the legal creation of national protected areas to compensate for areas that would be affected by the facility. Protection of the forests around the Nam Theun 2 Dam has been founded on a thirty-one year conservation fund[210] to manage the watershed. At 4,000km^2, the protected area is the largest in mainland Southeast Asia (almost four times the size of Hong Kong, and nine times the size of the reservoir). Rehabilitation of upland watersheds and wetlands contributes to regulating water flow, regulating floods and sedimentation, reducing vulnerability, and improving water quality for downstream communities.[211] The facility should soon begin exporting close to 1,000 MW to Thailand, while retaining close to 100 MW for domestic use.

Efforts to address the environmental effects of mining and of hazardous substances have also taken place at regional and national levels. As but one example, the World Bank, in partnership with regional organizations and the AfDB, launched the West Africa Mineral Sector Strategic Assessment to help understand and address the environmental and social impacts and issues related to mining operations in West Africa.[212] This review will include a comparative analysis of current environmental and social legislation and of its gaps in West Africa. Another effort to address the environmental impacts from mining operations will assist the Republic of Argentina to address uranium mill tailings left over from years of mining to support the nuclear power industry.[213] In some cases, these tailings are in close proximity to communities. The assistance will directly support Argentina's compliance with the Joint Convention on the Safety of Radioactive Waste Management.[214]

---

210. USD 1 million is allocated annually for thirty-one years.
211. Kathy MacKinnon (World Bank Environment Department), 'Biodiversity and Adaptation – Challenges and Opportunities', in *Environment Matters at the World Bank: Climate Change and Adaptation* (Washington, DC: The World Bank, 2007), 22–23, *available at* <http://web.worldbank.org/WBSITE/EXTERNAL/TOPICS/ENVIRONMENT/EXTENVMAT/0,,contentMDK:21652257~pagePK:64168445~piPK:64168309~theSitePK:3011351,00.html>.
212. For background, *see* West Africa Regional Mining Forum (11–12 Feb. 2008), <http://web.worldbank.org/WBSITE/EXTERNAL/TOPICS/EXTOGMC/0,,contentMDK:21661184~menuPK:336936~pagePK:148956~piPK:216618~theSitePK:336930,00.html>.
213. *See* World Bank, 'Argentina Mining Environmental Restoration Project', Project No. 100462 (approval date 31 Jul. 2008), <http://web.worldbank.org/external/projects/main?Projectid=P110462&theSitePK=40941&piPK=73230&pagePK=64283627&menuPK=228424>; *see also* http://siteresources.worldbank.org/INTMP/214578-1110890369636/21474014/WBMPPolicy.pdf.
214. International Atomic Energy Agency, 'Joint Convention on the Safety of Spent Fuel Management and on the Safety of Radioactive Waste Management', INFCIRC/546 (18 Jun. 2001 (entry into force)), *available at* <www.iaea.org/Publications/Documents/Conventions/jointconv.html>.

V. CONCLUSION

Critics of the World Bank and other IFIs in the environmental community have often stated that these institutions have acted ambiguously or against international environmental law objectives. These critics may point to certain findings in the reports of the World Bank Inspection Panel or its Independent Evaluation Group for support. Moreover, they may also express the concern that just when the Bank's environmental and social policies have begun to mature, there appears to be an effort to move away from the safeguards per se, and use borrower systems in their place.[215] In some cases, they have accused the Bank of seeking to dilute the safeguards through the adoption of borrower systems, despite the fact that there is an extensive and public process to determine whether the borrower system is equivalent to the Bank's safeguards, and whether the country has institutions at an acceptable level to implement its systems.

While these views are important, the environmental community should also acknowledge that the Bank and its developing country counterparts operate under acute pressure to improve the economic growth of the many millions living in poverty. Well-meaning voices from wealthy countries have claimed that the Bank should not finance developing countries to pursue the same energy path to growth as developed countries, though it may result in delay for universal access to electricity, and use of more expensive, and perhaps less dependable technology. Many in developing countries see as hypocritical those who advocate against IFI financing of fossil fuels, especially if such advocates live with ample power for schools, homes, and hospitals, and when most electricity in the richest countries will be largely fossil fuel-based for a significant time to come.

The historical and continuing discrepancy in living conditions between developed and developing countries is a key reason why the Copenhagen Accord made clear that developing countries will not cede their right to pursue economic development.[216] Indeed, developing countries remain wary of the environmental agenda, seeing it as a way for some to seek to slow the economic growth that they contend is their right. Nevertheless, many developing countries have taken bold climate action as part of a sustainable development platform.[217] They know that they stand to suffer the most from climate change impacts. Time will soon tell how well the nearly universal political commitments voiced in Copenhagen will translate into the aspirations of international environmental law for concrete action.

215. Bank Information Center and Center for International Environmental Law, 'Country Systems Approach to Environmental and Social Safeguards: Concerns and Challenges' (2 Dec. 2004), *available at* <www.bicusa.org/en/Article.1775.aspx>.
216. Copenhagen Accord, *supra* n. 176, para. 2.
217. *See* Barbara Finamore, 'China Records Its Climate Actions By Copenhagen Accord Deadline' (4 Feb. 2010), <www.greenlaw.org.cn/enblog/?p=2267>.

Conclusion: The Future of International Law and International Financial Institutions

Daniel D. Bradlow and David B. Hunter

The starting point for this book was our concern about an anomaly in the legal position of the international financial institutions (IFIs) that appeared to enable them to operate without being subjected to any effective legal control. We found this lack of legal accountability particularly troubling because of the profound, and sometimes irreversible, impact that IFI operations can have in many of those Member States that actually use their financial services.

The source of this anomaly seemed to lie in two gaps in the applicable legal regime. The first relates to the applicability of international law to the IFIs. The IFIs as international organizations are clearly subjects of international law. This would seem to indicate that their rights, responsibilities, and obligations can be defined by applicable international law and that they can be held accountable for their compliance with applicable international legal principles. However, holding the IFIs accountable under international law is difficult. Although their status as subjects of international law is clear, their substantive rights and responsibilities are not. The IFIs contend that many international legal obligations found in customary law are not applicable to them and that they are not bound by treaties to which they are not signatories. When the IFIs do recognize specific international law principles as being applicable to them, they claim the discretion to decide how

Daniel D. Bradlow and David B. Hunter, *International Financial Institutions and International Law*, pp. 387–397.

to operationalize these principles. The IFIs' position is not without some force, but it leaves uncertain the applicability of broad areas of international law, including human rights, the environment, and labour, and allows the IFIs almost unfettered discretion in deciding whether they are required to comply with particular international legal principles. Their ability to decide for themselves both with which international legal principles they will comply and how they should implement those obligations they accept is further enhanced by the fact that no obvious international forum exists in which to test the IFIs' exercise of discretion with respect to their international legal responsibilities. The result is that de facto international law imposes few constraints on IFI operations.

The IFIs' privileged exceptionalism under international law is compounded by the second source of the accountability gap – IFI claims to extensive immunity under domestic legal regimes. Intriguingly, the scope of IFI immunity under municipal law has expanded even as the scope of sovereign immunity has contracted. This follows from the fact that the range of their activities and the depth of their penetration into domestic policy-making has grown even as their immunity, unlike that of states, has remained constant. As the contributors to this book demonstrate, this immunity was never intended to be absolute and has been waived when the IFIs have deemed it necessary. Nevertheless, given their expanding responsibilities and scope of operations, the extent of IFI immunity from either domestic suit or some other comparable forum is becoming more problematic and a serious impediment to the full legal accountability of the IFIs. While the IFIs do have a legitimate need for some immunity, absent good justification this should not be broader than what is necessary to carry out their mandates in a way that is consistent with all their legal obligations. Such limited immunity would remove the absolute barrier that prevents all affected stakeholders from having their claims, that the IFIs should be accountable for the harm their operations cause, adjudicated in some appropriate forum, but would allow the IFIs to retain their functional immunity.

The net effect of these two gaps is that the IFIs are able to claim the power to decide for themselves what law is applicable to them, and then to act on their view of the applicable law. If, as Phillip Allott puts it: 'Law constrains or it is a travesty to call it law',[1] then IFIs are essentially lawless institutions.

Interestingly, international lawyers have not explored or rigorously analysed the anomalous accountability gap identified above. We embarked on this book project with the goal of seeking to fill this gap in the literature and to test our contention about the apparently lawless situation of the IFIs. As one would expect, the contributors to this volume have shown that the issue is more complex than we initially postulated, but also that the rights, responsibilities, powers, and obligations of IFIs are not at all settled and are in need of greater elaboration. Nevertheless, a number of conclusions can be drawn from the contributions to this volume.

First, it is clear that the IFIs, like all inter-governmental organizations, are subjects of international law. As such, their status, powers, and responsibilities are

1. Philip Allott, *Eunomia: New Order for a New World* (New York: Oxford University Press Inc. 1990), Preface, xlvii.

defined by the treaties that create them – in the case of the IFIs, their Articles of Agreement. In addition, they are governed by any other international agreements to which they are signatories, for example headquarters agreements, relationship agreements, and, in the case of the multilateral development banks (MDBs), their loan agreements. Further, they are bound by applicable customary international law and by any applicable general principles of law accepted by all nations. As the contributions to this book demonstrate, there are both customary international law and general principles of law applicable to the conduct of IFIs even if they are difficult to operationalize.

Moreover, the conduct of the IFIs is constrained by those clearly defined and universally accepted international legal obligations of their Member States. As several contributors to this book recognize, it would be incongruous for the international legal system to allow Member States to create an institution that can violate legal norms that the Member States themselves cannot violate. Few would argue, for example, that Member States, feeling constrained by their obligations under international human rights law, could legally create an institution with the power to violate those same human rights. Such a situation should result in the Member States being held responsible under international law. However, this should not necessarily absolve the IFI itself from responsibility for its own actions. In fact, given the growing discretion, power, and reach of the IFIs in carrying out their expanding mission, a failure to hold the IFIs responsible for their own actions can result in the institutions, and their officers and agents, being able to act with impunity. This suggests that the IFIs have their own international legal obligations that are independent of their Member States, and that, to comply with good governance, we need to define more carefully how their responsibilities are similar to, and different from, the state's responsibilities.

Second, the international legal principles applicable to IFIs are not neutral,[2] they are heavily influenced by the interests and objectives of the IFIs' key Member States and by the role that those Member States want the IFIs to play in international economic governance. This is significant because, historically, the richest Member States – the United States, the Member States of the European Union, and Japan – have dominated the decision making governance structures of the IFIs, and so are able to direct decisions on issues related to how, and to what extent, international law should apply to the IFIs. However, these Member States are not directly affected by the IFIs' operational decisions. In addition, because they often seek to use the IFIs to advance their own agendas, it is not in their interest for the IFIs to be constrained by international law, except perhaps in areas relating directly to raising capital or ensuring enforcement of loan agreements. Nevertheless, their decisions have direct and important impacts within those Member States that actually use the financial services of the IFIs. This situation, in which there is a split between those Member States that have real decision-making power in the IFIs and those that are most directly affected by IFI decisions, means

2. *See, e.g.*, B.S. Chimni, 'International Financial Institutions and International Law: A Third World Perspective', Ch. 2 herein.

that the key decision-makers have power without responsibility. Not surprisingly, therefore, the actual decision-making process in the IFIs has distorted the evolution of international law with respect to the rights and responsibilities of the IFIs. It also suggests that relying on other means to hold the IFIs accountable under international law for their decisions and actions might both benefit affected people and mitigate the adverse consequences of the current power imbalance between those who have the most influence in the IFIs and those who actually use their services.

This conclusion is particularly pertinent at the present time when power in global economic governance seems to be shifting. The rise of new powers – for example the BRIC countries (Brazil, Russia, India, and China) – is beginning to affect the ability of the hitherto dominant powers to control the IFIs, and therefore their ability to control the IFIs' decisions on international legal issues. Given that these changes in international governance relations are still fluid and their eventual resolution difficult to predict, their impact on the IFIs' views of their international legal obligations is difficult to discern. However, there is no reason to assume that the rising powers, should they eventually gain greater say over the affairs of the IFIs, will prove any less willing to use the IFIs for their own purposes, including in regard to international law, than the current powers.

Third, and not surprisingly, the current accountability gap surrounding IFIs does not affect all stakeholders equally. Member States have both legal and political options for holding IFIs to account. Notwithstanding the significant imbalance among Member States in legal and political power within IFIs, all Member States, at least in theory, can use their 'voice and vote' in the governance structures of the IFIs, and may be able to petition international tribunals, if need be, to hold the institutions accountable. Those non-state actors who have contractual relationships with the IFIs, for example, bondholders and borrowers, also have some protections. Bondholders are able to enforce their contractual rights in national courts because the IFIs waive their immunity in their financial contracts, while borrowers of the MDBs are able to enforce their rights through the dispute settlement procedures established in the MDBs' loan or credit agreements.[3] Additionally, the IFIs' employees have access to internal administrative tribunals in each of the organizations.

There is, however, one important group for whom the combination of limited application of international legal principles and extensive immunity from the application of national law results in the IFIs operating essentially in a lawless vacuum – non-state actors who are not in a contractual relationship with the IFIs, but who are nonetheless directly affected by their actions. Until the relatively recent creation of independent accountability mechanisms at the MDBs,[4] such

3. The situation with the IMF is more complex because it claims that most of its financial transactions with its Member States are non-contractual in nature. However, the Member States do have some recourse, at least in principle, because they are able to raise their concerns through the governance structure of the IMF.
4. The World Bank established its Inspection Panel in 1993. Then in 1994, the Inter-American Development Bank established the Independent Investigation Mechanism, which was replaced

affected people had no opportunities to hold the IFIs accountable regardless of the extent of the harm they may have suffered because of these MDB operations. These people are among those who are expected to benefit from international law relating, for example, to human rights and the environment.

It is important to note that the independent accountability mechanisms at the MDBs have created a limited means of accountability for these stakeholders. These mechanisms are not empowered to offer non-state stakeholders compensation for any harm they have suffered, or to order the IFIs to change their operations or conduct. Some of the existing mechanisms have also had to undergo significant revisions because they were not sufficiently independent or effective to provide claimants with meaningful recourse. In addition, the International Monetary Fund (IMF) does not yet have such an independent accountability mechanism, and, consequently, its non-state stakeholders have no direct means of holding the IMF accountable.

The people affected by IFI operations and the civil society groups that represent them are increasingly arguing that the IFIs' anomalous international legal situation undermines their rights as recognized and protected under international law. Their voices have joined the debate formerly monopolized by the Member States and the IFIs, thus building pressure on the IFIs to reconsider their position vis-à-vis both the applicability of international law to their operations and the extent of their immunity. Traditional boundaries are starting to crumble, and, as reflected in many contributions to this volume, different strategies have emerged for dealing with the international legal anomaly associated with the IFIs.

One way to resolve the accountability gap is to strengthen and clarify the applicability of international law rules to IFIs as subjects of international law. This would necessarily help clarify the responsibilities of the IFIs under international law. This issue was discussed in the International Law Association study on accountability of international organizations and is partly the goal of the International Law Commission's (ILC's) ongoing exploration of the responsibility of international organizations under international law.[5] These efforts may eventually contribute to an understanding of the powers, rights, and responsibilities of international organizations. However, they are unlikely, for several reasons, to be sufficient in the near term to deal with the situation of the IFIs. First, these processes are notoriously cumbersome and slow to react to the changing nature of

by the Independent Consultation and Investigation Mechanism in 2010. The European Bank for Reconstruction and Development's Independent Recourse Mechanism (IRM) was established in 2003, and in 2009, the Board approved the establishment of the Project Complaint Mechanism to replace the IRM. The African Development Bank's Independent Review Mechanism was approved in 2004 and its operating rules and procedures were established in 2006. The Asian Development Bank approved a new Accountability Mechanism in 2003.

5. For more information on the work of the International Law Commission as it relates to its ongoing work involving the responsibility of international organizations, *see* International Law Commission, Responsibility of International Organizations, <www.un.org/law/ilc/> (follow the link for 'Responsibility of international organizations' under the Current Programme of Work heading).

international society. In addition, it often takes considerable time for their findings and recommendations to become legally binding. Second, the ILC process has stumbled by relying too heavily on state responsibility as an analogue for the responsibility of international organizations.[6] Although the analogy has value, over-reliance on it tends to underplay the differences between states, which are geographically defined and have general powers and responsibilities, and international organizations, which can operate across regions and national borders, but have particular structures and limited powers and mandates defined by their founding treaties. Third, most discussion of the responsibility of international organizations focuses on those institutions involved with peace and security. Much less ILC attention has been focused on IFIs whose specialized monetary, financial, and development mandates, as pointed out by several contributors to this volume, raise a number of specific issues of responsibility under international law that may not be as relevant to organizations dealing with international peace and security.

Many of the chapters in this book explore the general approaches that can be taken to clarify the international legal obligations of the IFIs. Mackay, for example, argues that principles of international law protecting the rights and interests of indigenous peoples, including their rights of free, prior, and informed consent, should be reflected in the internal policies of the IFIs.[7] Similarly, the core labour standards promoted by the International Labour Organization (ILO) or clear prohibitions found in international environmental law should 'constrain' at least some activities of IFIs. In recent years, the MDBs have begun responding to these approaches. For example, in some cases, they have strengthened their internal operational policies in ways that make their internal law more consistent with their international legal obligations.

Clarifying the international law obligations of IFIs will also help build coherence between the IFIs' development objectives, their operations, and their international legal obligations. This, in turn, will contribute to resolving the general challenge of fragmentation in international law – there is no logical reason why the situation of a person whose economic or social rights have been adversely affected by the acts of a state or a transnational corporation should be given more attention and protection than a similarly situated person whose rights have been adversely affected by the operations of an IFI. As explained by McInerney-Lankford, an expanded approach to human rights at the IFIs holds the promise of improving policy coherence between the twin goals of development and human rights.[8] Similar benefits are likely to follow from the International Finance Corporation's

6. *See* José E. Alvarez, 'International Organizations: Accountability or Responsibility?', luncheon address given at the Canadian Council of International Law, 35th Annual Conference on Responsibility of Individuals, States and Organizations (Ottawa, Canada, 27 Oct. 2006), *available at* <www.asil.org/aboutasil/documents/CCILspeech061102.pdf>.
7. Fergus Mackay, 'Indigenous Peoples and International Financial Institutions', Ch. 9 herein.
8. *See* Siobhán McInerney-Lankford, 'International Financial Institutions and Human Rights: Select Perspectives on Legal Obligations', Ch. 8 herein.

(IFC's) incorporation of labour standards into its performance standards;[9] the European Bank for Reconstruction and Development's (EBRD's) clear endorsement of free, prior, and informed consent for indigenous peoples;[10] and the World Bank's prohibition against funding projects that are inconsistent with a country's international environmental treaty obligations.[11]

Thus far, however, the IFIs' efforts at incorporating international law norms into their internal laws has been somewhat ad hoc responding to areas where civil society has been able to organize significant pressure on them. Thus, the IFIs have never clearly stated that their policies will comply with all applicable international law. Instead they have only made commitments in rather specialized and limited contexts, for example in the environmental area. Such actions tend to reinforce the view that they alone will determine what law applies to them and how it should apply. Recent developments with respect to IFI policies relating to human rights, including labour rights and the rights of indigenous peoples, suggest that the IFIs are recognizing that their position on their international legal obligations is problematic. They also raise hopes that the IFIs may move more decisively in the future to define their human rights and related responsibilities.

One necessary consequence of the IFIs acknowledging their international legal obligations will be a re-invigoration of efforts to strengthen the mechanisms for reviewing IFI compliance, particularly given their continued immunity from national courts. As noted above, all of the MDBs have created internal accountability mechanisms, albeit exhibiting different degrees of independence and effectiveness. As pointed out by several authors in this volume, strengthening the existing internal accountability mechanisms (e.g., the World Bank Inspection Panel or similar institutions) is one way to improve IFI accountability. Suzuki, for example, suggests expanding the function of existing administrative tribunals that currently issue binding decisions with respect to complaints from IFI employees to incorporate other categories of complaints.[12] He argues that these tribunals should also issue binding decisions on appeals that third-party complainants

9. *See* IFC, *International Finance Corporation's Performance Standards on Social & Environmental Sustainability*, 'Performance Standard 2: Labor and Working Conditions' (30 Apr. 2006), 7–10, *available at* <www.ifc.org/ifcext/sustainability.nsf/AttachmentsByTitle/pol_PerformanceStandards2006_full/$FILE/IFC+Performance+Standards.pdf>.
10. *See* European Bank for Reconstruction and Development, *Environment and Social Policy*, 'PR 7: Indigenous Peoples' (May 2008), 50–57, *available at* <www.ebrd.com/about/policies/enviro/policy/2008policy.pdf>.
11. *See* World Bank, 'OP 4.01: Environmental Assessment' (January 1999), *available at* <http://web.worldbank.org/WBSITE/EXTERNAL/PROJECTS/EXTPOLICIES/EXTOPMANUAL/0,,contentMDK:20064724~menuPK:64701637~pagePK:64709096~piPK:64709108~theSitePK:502184,00.html>; *see also* Charles E. Di Leva, 'International Environmental Law, The World Bank, and International Financial Institutions', Ch. 11 herein.
12. *See* Eisuke Suzuki, 'Responsibility of International Financial Institutions under International Law', Ch. 3 herein.

submit to existing accountability mechanisms.[13] Chimni also calls for strengthening the legal basis and effect of the existing accountability mechanisms.[14]

These efforts to close the accountability gap at the international level should complement (and not be a substitute for) efforts to close the gap from the bottom-up – i.e., by reviewing the scope and extent of IFI immunity in national courts. In this respect, as implied by Reinisch and Wurm, and as recommended by Herz, the role of domestic courts should be expanded to accommodate the accountability of IFIs to non-state actors. As these chapters explain, the IFIs' claim to absolute immunity has not gone unchallenged, even if the IFIs have thus far prevailed in most cases. As these chapters show, the trend is against absolute immunity for international organizations, just as it is for states. Some courts, before agreeing to dismiss a case on grounds of an international organization's immunity, are inquiring into whether an adequate alternate forum exists. In their chapter, Reinisch and Wurm embrace recent national jurisprudence that suggests equity and fairness should defeat the IFIs' need for immunity, at least when third parties who are wronged by an IFI's activities have no other legal recourse.[15] Herz agrees and argues further that the purposes and scope of the IFIs' functional immunity should be narrowed over time to allow such third parties to bring actions in national courts.[16]

Of course, defining the international responsibility of the IFIs or extending national jurisdiction over their actions does not obviate the need for states to fulfil their own obligations under international law in their relations with IFIs. As McInerney-Lankford argues, some portion of the international legal responsibility gap surrounding IFIs can be filled indirectly by ensuring that states fulfil their own international obligations when they participate in IFI activities – either as donors or borrowers. State responsibility for their own behaviour in the governance and operations of IFIs is also an area that could benefit from further elaboration and development. Addressing the issue of international legal responsibility from the perspective of both the state and the IFIs should help ensure that neither states nor IFIs are complicit in international law violations committed by the other.

An important issue in regard to this discussion, which is addressed in the chapters by Bradlow and by Hunter,[17] is the recognition that the IFIs are not just passive recipients of rights and obligations under international law. Through their internal operational policies and directives and their decisions and actions they are often forced to deal with questions that raise unsettled international legal issues. Their efforts to resolve or address these matters necessarily results in them

13. *Ibid.*
14. *See* B.S. Chimni, 'International Financial Institutions and International Law: A Third World Perspective', Ch. 2 herein.
15. *See* August Reinisch & Jakob Wurm, 'International Financial Institutions before National Courts', Ch. 4 herein.
16. *See* Steven Herz, 'Rethinking International Financial Institution Immunity', Ch. 5 herein.
17. *See* Daniel D. Bradlow, 'International Law and the Operations of International Financial Institutions', Ch. 1 herein; David B. Hunter, 'International Law and Public Participation in Policy-Making at the International Financial Institutions', Ch. 7 herein.

becoming actively engaged in the creation of the international law applicable to these issues. Examples of topics in which the IFIs are helping to shape the applicable international legal principles are the rights of indigenous people; international human rights law and development; the relationship between international organizations, states, and non-state actors; and the environment. The relevant substantive international legal principles relating to these topics and their application to the IFIs are discussed in a number of chapters in this book – for example, Mackay, McInerney-Lankford, and Di Leva.[18] In all these cases, the IFIs' policies and actions are both shaped by and help shape the relevant international legal principles. While the IFIs' actions and decisions may not set binding international legal principles in these areas, they do constitute informative and persuasive examples that other international legal subjects use in formulating their own decisions and positions on these issues. In this way, they are contributing to the accretion of precedents that inform the creation of international customary law and the principles incorporated into international agreements. In some cases, the IFIs' policies and actions create expectations about the type of treatment that stakeholders can expect in certain circumstances, thereby helping to create applicable soft international law that can affect the expectations of these same categories of stakeholders in their dealings with other economic actors. An example is the way in which the IFC's performance standards are influencing the expectations relating to, and the conduct of, transnational banks.

The decisions of the independent accountability mechanisms are of particular interest in this regard. Although not adjudicatory bodies, findings by the Inspection Panel and the other accountability mechanisms necessarily depend on interpretations of the institutions' operational policies. As pointed out by both McInerney-Lankford and Di Leva, the MDBs' operating policies often implicitly reflect norms of international law. In some cases, the Inspection Panel has also explicitly referenced relevant international legal principles, norms, and standards in making these interpretations.[19] In this way, the accountability mechanisms' findings, and

---

18. *See respectively*, Fergus Mackay, 'Indigenous Peoples and International Financial Institutions', Ch. 9 herein; Siobhán McInerney-Lankford, 'International Financial Institutions and Human Rights: Select Perspectives on Legal Obligations', Ch. 8 herein; Charles E. Di Leva, 'International Environmental Law, the World Bank, and International Financial Institutions', Ch. 11 herein.
19. For a general discussion of the World Bank Inspection Panel reports and international law, *see* Andria Naudé Fourie, *The World Bank Inspection Panel and Quasi-Judicial Oversight: In Search of the 'Judicial Spirit' in Public International Law* (Utrecht: Eleven International Publishing, 2009). For a detailed discussion of the World Bank Inspection Panel reports regarding human rights violations resulting from projects in Chad and Honduras, *see* Steven Herz & Anne Perrault, 'Bringing Human Rights Claims to the World Bank Inspection Panel' (October 2009), *available at* <www.accountabilityproject.org/downloads/Inspection%20Panel%20and%20Human%20Rights%20Oct09.pdf>. Herz and Perrault discuss the *Honduras: Land Administration Project* (2007) claim, which marked the first time the Inspection Panel addressed a claim based on international human rights law. The Panel recognized that its mandate only related to questions of compliance with the Bank's operating policies, but found that these policies mandated the Bank comply with provisions relating to human rights that are in the

the sometimes legalistic responses of management, are creating a dialogue that can contribute to the progressive development of the international law applicable in the context of IFI operations.[20]

The evolving role that the IFIs play in the creation of international law highlights the relevance to international law of not only the substance of their internal operating rules, but also their internal rule-making procedures, as has been discussed in some detail in the chapter by Hunter.[21] While the substance of their rules is shaped by and helps shape international law in some areas, their internal rule-making procedures are in many ways path-breaking and establishing important precedents in international administrative law. The IFIs have led the way in creating rule-making procedures that are relatively transparent and participatory. The result is operating rules and procedures that have created expectations and facilitated more communication between IFIs and the stakeholders who are most affected by their operations. Hopefully, other international organizations will learn from their examples. In addition, these procedures are deserving of more study so that we better understand their role in international law creation, particularly in creating law that can constrain the IFIs in the future.

The role of IFIs in the progressive development of international law is not limited to their internal operational policies and procedures, however, as they are also both deliberately and coincidentally shaping state practice in the context of development. As suggested by both McInerney-Lankford and Di Leva, the World Bank, in particular, sees itself as a significant player in helping countries meet their international obligations.[22] What these authors say about human rights and environmental law, respectively, can also be true more generally of international law. For example, the IFIs view strengthening the rule of law as a critical step in maintaining a climate conducive for development. In this context, it is important that the IFIs make sure that their advice is consistent with their own practices.

---

international agreements applicable to the project. Herz & Perrault, *supra* n. 19, 4. Similarly, the Inspection Panel in Chad, the *Chad: Petroleum Development and Pipeline Project* (2002), determined that the Bank had to consider international human rights principles when they 'impede the implementation of the Project in a manner compatible with the Bank's policies' and not just when they have a 'significant direct economic effect on the project'. *Ibid.*, 5–6. Further the Inspection Panel here found that the Bank neglected to consider the Democratic Republic of Congo's (DRC) obligations under the Convention for the Protection of the World Cultural and Natural Heritage (World Heritage Convention) and the Convention on International Trade in Endangered Species of Wild Fauna and Flora (CITES), in *Democratic Republic of Congo: Transitional Support for Economic Recovery Credit and Emergency Economic and Social Reunification Support Project* (2007), *available at* <http://siteresources.worldbank.org/EXTINSPECTIONPANEL/Resources/FINALINVREPwhole.pdf>. Thus, the Inspection Panel has routinely referred to international law when determining whether the Bank has complied with its operational policies.

20. Herz & Perrault, *supra* n. 19.
21. *See* David B. Hunter, 'International Law and Public Participation in Policy-Making at the International Financial Institutions', Ch. 7 herein.
22. *See* Siobhán McInerney-Lankford, 'International Financial Institutions and Human Rights: Select Perspectives on Legal Obligations', Ch. 8 herein; Charles E. Di Leva, 'International Environmental Law, The World Bank, and International Financial Institutions', Ch. 11 herein.

This means that they need to ensure that their operations within a country lead by example and comply with applicable international and domestic laws.

A rising number of voices (including many in this volume) are calling for increased exploration of the responsibility of IFIs under international law. The IFIs themselves should become even more active participants in this debate. In this regard, the IFIs, as well as international legal scholars and activists should systematically review the wide range of international law fields that are relevant to the mission of the IFIs in order to identify applicable international legal principles and to determine how they can most effectively be implemented in the work and policies of the IFIs. They should also engage in debates about how the IFIs can be accountable for their compliance with all their international responsibilities.

This book reveals both the complexity and the potential value of such a dialogue over the relationship of international law and IFIs. It is our hope that the book will stimulate the IFIs and all the stakeholders in their operations to actively participate in this dialogue.

Index

A

E

F

G

H

I

K

M

V

W

www.ingramcontent.com/pod-product-compliance
Lightning Source LLC
Chambersburg PA
CBHW071236230926
51849CB00001B/128
9789041128812